by Virginius Dabney

VIRGINIA: THE NEW DOMINION
DRY MESSIAH: THE LIFE OF BISHOP CANNON
BELOW THE POTOMAC
LIBERALISM IN THE SOUTH

VIRGINIA
The New Dominion

Virginius Dabney

VIRGINIA
The New Dominion

UNIVERSITY PRESS OF VIRGINIA
CHARLOTTESVILLE

THE UNIVERSITY PRESS OF VIRGINIA
Copyright © 1971 by Virginius Dabney.
All rights assigned to the Rector and Visitors
of the University of Virginia

Fourth paperback printing 1996

PHOTO CREDITS

Library of Congress Cataloging in Publication Data

Dabney, Virginius, 1901-
    Virginia, the new dominion.

    Reprint. Originally published: 1st ed. Garden City, N.Y.: Doubleday,
1971.
    Includes index.
    1. Virginia—History. I. Title.
F226.D32 1983   975.5   83-18232
ISBN O-8139-1015-3 (pbk.)

Printed in the United States of America

TO MY MOTHER
IN LOVE AND GRATITUDE

CONTENTS

ILLUSTRATIONS

MAPS

FOREWORD

THE TASK of compressing the history of Virginia into a single volume
is a difficult one. The Virginia story is not only longer than that
of any other state, but it is also probably the most diversified of them
all. Whole shelves of books have been written about the early
settlements, about the colonial era that followed, and the Civil War,
to name only three examples.

The least-written-about period, and the one that is least understood,
is that which followed the Civil War. Next would probably come the
nineteenth century for the four or five decades preceding the war,
and then the early years of the twentieth century. We are getting
a much better understanding of the period from 1865 to date as a
result of graduate studies undertaken at the University of Virginia
under Dr. Edward Younger of the History Department. Scores of
M.A. and Ph.D. theses and dissertations have been written under
Dr. Younger's knowledgeable direction, and they have shed light
upon many heretofore obscure happenings and trends. Several have
been published as books.

I have sought in the present work to bring together the salient
facts concerning Virginia's history and to describe the events and
personalities, both good and bad, that make up the long and exciting
Virginia story.

I have also attempted to give new emphasis to certain elements
in the population which previously have been largely bypassed or
accorded too little notice. Our Negro citizens are among those who
have not received their due. Their achievements have too often
been ignored, and they have suffered from a one-sided presentation

of the facts. On the latter point, the widespread impression prevails that Nat Turner's slave insurrection in 1831 was the first and only thing of the kind in Virginia history. The much more dangerous and greatly ramified plot of the slave Gabriel, in 1800, is almost ignored. If Gabriel's attempted insurrection, involving thousands of slaves in the Richmond area, had been successful, it would have made Nat Turner's horrible, but more limited massacre, seem almost negligible by comparison. As a matter of fact, another large-scale insurrection was thwarted in Norfolk in 1802, only two years after the failure of Gabriel's intended uprising.

Quite a few blacks were rewarded by the Virginia General Assembly for gallantry in the American Revolution, but this is unknown to most Virginians, as is the high opinion expressed by General Robert E. Lee concerning the fighting qualities of black soldiers.

As for General Lee himself, episodes are mentioned in this book which tend to accentuate his more human traits, and there is less emphasis on those characteristics that often have made him resemble a marble statue, godlike and unapproachable. The same is true of George Washington, whose deep and apparently unrequited love for Sally Fairfax, at the time he married Martha Custis, is documented. In attempting to humanize these supremely great men, I have sought to make them more understandable than the revered but remote figures we have heretofore known.

So much emphasis has been laid in most histories on the English settlers and their descendants that I have tried to give due recognition to the Scotch-Irish, the Germans and the French Huguenots, each of whom made lasting contributions to the development of Virginia.

And since the historians have concentrated so heavily on the Williamsburg-Jamestown-Yorktown triangle and the Richmond area, I have, without in the least ignoring those sections, given particular attention to the region around Hampton Roads and to the Shenandoah Valley and the southwest.

Owing to space limitations, the author of a one-volume work who seeks to cover nearly four centuries of history inevitably must omit many things. Events and personalities that would be included in a longer chronicle have to be left out. Every reader of the present work will doubtless regret that some individual or happening is not mentioned or given more extended treatment. To all such, my apologies.

I have called this book *Virginia: The New Dominion* in recognition of the new era into which the commonwealth has moved.

A Virginia Rip Van Winkle who went to sleep in, say 1950, and awakened in 1970 might have difficulty realizing that he was in the same state.

Race relations in the commonwealth have been transformed, and many of the manifest injustices from which black citizens suffered have been ended, albeit not without certain traumatic effects, accompanied by swings of the pendulum that have gone too far in the opposite direction. But the changes in the past two decades have greatly transcended the area of race relations. Politically, Virginia is in a new and different age, with a Republican governor and six Republican congressmen out of ten. The long-dominant Byrd machine has disappeared. In addition, the population of this once rural state is exploding, especially in the "urban corridor," and the leisurely commonwealth we once knew, revolving mainly around the country courthouses, has vanished. Industry is coming into Virginia on an unprecedented scale, and tourists are flooding in. New ideas also are permeating the state, and there is a greater receptivity to them.

All this and more is to be seen in the Virginia that is emerging in the late twentieth century. It is not the commonwealth that George Washington and Thomas Jefferson knew, nor yet that of Woodrow Wilson and Carter Glass. It retains many of the qualities that endeared it to those notable men, but it also is imbued with characteristics nowhere evident in the Virginia of their time. Some Virginians are nostalgic at this hour for the *Old* Dominion, and all of us must cherish and revere its virtues. But let us today salute the *New* Dominion, with its challenge and its promise.

I am indebted to many friends for invaluable help in the preparation of this book. John M. Jennings, director, and William M. E. Rachal, editor of publications for the Virginia Historical Society, have given me the benefit of their immense knowledge, have read the entire manuscript and have provided much helpful criticism. Others who have read all or part of the work, and to whom I am greatly indebted, are Prof. Edward Younger of the University of Virginia; Prof. Robert D. Meade of Randolph-Macon Woman's College; Clifford Dowdey, who also made available to me the first draft of his recently published *The Virginia Dynasties*; J. Ambler Johnston, Mary Wells Ashworth, Judge and Mrs. Ralph T. Catterall, William J. Van Schreeven, J. Harvie Wilkinson, Jr., J. Harvie Wilkinson III, Lewis F. Powell, Jr., James Latimer and Prof. James T. Moore.

Others whom I wish particularly to thank are the staff of the Virginia State Library, notably Milton C. Russell, John W. Dudley, Mrs. Katherine M. Smith, State Librarian Randolph W. Church and State Archivist Louis H. Manarin, together with the always accommodating ladies at the front desk; the staff of the Richmond City Library, especially Miss Gertrude Dyson and Miss Betty Winston, and their pleasant and efficient colleagues; the uniformly helpful Reference Department of Richmond Newspapers, Inc., particularly Miss Mary Morris Watt, chief librarian, and Earl Jones, who performed many favors for me; the Alderman Library at the University of Virginia, notably Librarian Ray W. Frantz, Jr., Edmund Berkeley, Jr., Lauren C. Stayton, Miss Helena C. Koiner and Mrs. Harriet Claiborne; and the staffs of the University of North Carolina Library and the Duke University Library, who were always co-operative. Other individuals to whom I am grateful for assistance of many kinds are, Dr. Louis B. Wright, Prof. Richard L. Morton, Parke Rouse, Jr., Prof. Joseph C. Robert, Leslie Cheek, Jr., William R. Gaines, Robert B. Mayo, Dr. Robert F. Williams, the Reverend Patrick H. Carmichael, Dr. Edward K. Graham, Harold Baumes, Dr. Mack W. Shanholtz, Dr. Allen Peters, French Skinner, Edwin Cox, FitzGerald Bemiss, Elbert W. Cox, Prof. J. Maurice Duke, Dr. Russell V. Bowers, A. S. Rachal, Jr., Ben H. Bolen, John M. Goodwin, Prof. Alvin L. Hall, Prof. James W. Ely, Jr., Staige D. Blackford, Jr., Richard S. Gillis, Phil Flournoy, William S. Meacham, T. Edward Temple, H. I. Willett and F. D. Cossitt.

Grants were made to me by the Guggenheim Foundation and the National Endowment for the Humanities which were of inestimable assistance. My esteemed former secretary for many years, Mrs. Edward S. McCarthy, aided me enormously by copying my slovenly manuscript in a professional manner. Miss Sally Arteseros, my editor at Doubleday, provided me with incisive counsel, valuable guidance and complete co-operation. And last but far from least, my wife, Douglas, has not only read the entire manuscript with a critical eye, such as only a wife of forty-seven years can provide, but she has been patient, as always, with my peccadilloes, long-suffering with my rigorous work schedule and understanding of my various perplexities and problems.

VIRGINIUS DABNEY

Richmond, Virginia
January 9, 1971

VIRGINIA
The New Dominion

ONE

Into the Storm

A COMET flashed across the somber winter sky as the three tiny ships prepared to sail down the Thames en route to the distant land of Virginia. This startling celestial phenomenon (later called Halley's Comet) was deemed to be an ill omen, for, in the words of a contemporary poet, a comet was said to bring:

> Wind, Famine, Plague and Death to Kings,
> War, Earthquake, Floods and Direful Change.

Approximately 105 men, not counting the crews of the three ships, were in the company which was about to sail. The flagship, the *Susan Constant*, 100 tons, was commanded by Captain Christopher Newport; the *Godspeed*, 40 tons, by Captain Bartholomew Gosnold, and the *Discovery*, 20 tons, by Captain John Ratcliffe. It was December 1606.

Included were some fifty-nine gaudily-appareled "gentlemen," mostly younger sons, few of whom appeared to have the least intention of doing any serious work in Virginia or anywhere else.[1] Fortunately there were others of a more practical turn of mind, including artisans of various kinds. Among these were bricklayers, carpenters, a mason, a blacksmith, a barber and a tailor. Also included were a surgeon, a clergyman, some soldiers, a sailor and several small boys. Hardly any of these individuals had the training or experience to fit them for the rigors, privations and terrors of the Virginia wilderness.

Fate seemed to intervene at once as the three vessels sailed down the Thames into the English Channel. Storms and high winds kept them from moving out into the ocean, and they were tossed about for six weeks off the English coast, waiting for the weather to moderate. All on board occupied incredibly cramped quarters, with a minimum of sanitary arrangements, and most were seasick. If many decided in the face of these truly epoch-making ordeals and discouragements that they wanted to forget Virginia and return to their English homes, the feeling would be understandable. But the Reverend Robert Hunt, the only clergyman on the expedition, would not hear of it. Although almost fatally ill, and "making wild vomits into the black night," he not only refused to abandon ship, but exhorted all others to stand fast. Hunt's fortitude was admirable, but as we shall see, his unwillingness to abandon the enterprise when ill may have had lethal consequences later for many settlers.

Finally, about mid-February the expedition got under way. It had consumed six weeks' rations which would be sorely needed the following summer and fall at Jamestown.

The southern route—approximately that followed by Columbus on his second voyage more than a century before—and the one normally preferred in those times, was chosen. It went via the Canaries and the West Indies.

After taking on fresh water in the Canaries (then known as the Fortunate Isles), the settlers made a number of stops in the Indies. Among the islands visited were Martinique, Dominica, Guadeloupe, Nevis, the Virgin Islands and Mona. The weary voyagers seized the opportunity to refresh themselves and feast upon the game, wild fowl, turtles, fish and eggs which they found in abundance. On Guadeloupe there was a spring so hot that Captain Newport "caused a piece of pork to be put in it, which boiled it in the space of half an hour." On Mona occurred the only fatality of the voyage. In the course of a six-mile march into the interior over rough terrain, Edward Brookes, gentleman, died. In the words of Captain George Percy, later president of the council and deputy governor of Jamestown, "his fat melted within him by the great heat and drought of the country."

But while all but Brookes survived the ocean crossing, there was much bickering and dissension on board the ships. Captain John Smith, the ablest, bravest and most charismatic, but most mercurial of the settlers, evidently had some sort of role in these disturbances. Its precise nature remains a mystery.

At all events, Smith was arrested for "mutiny." He wrote long afterward that "a pair of gallowes was made; but Captain Smith, for whom they were intended, could not be persuaded to use them." Smith was kept under at least nominal arrest for a reported thirteen weeks and was not released until about June 20, more than a month after the landing at Jamestown.

Following their rather leisurely journeyings through the West Indies, the three ships "disembogued" on April 20 and headed northward in the direction of Virginia. But having been plagued almost interminably by winter storms off the English coast, they now found themselves violently assailed by the thunder, lightning and wind of a spring tempest. The commanders feared that the vessels would be scattered or sunk. But they rode out the gale, and at "about foure a clocke in the morning" on April 26 they sighted the low-lying Virginia shoreline.

It must have been a brave and welcome sight for the weary and storm-tossed travelers. Newport, Gosnold, Percy and other leaders went ashore with about twenty men. The landing was on the south side of the entrance to Chesapeake Bay. They would soon erect a cross there and name the spot "Cape Henry" in honor of the Prince of Wales, and the point of land opposite, "Cape Charles," in honor of the Duke of York.

The men were enchanted with the sights, smells and sounds of springtime in Virginia—"faire meddowes and goodly tall trees, with such Fresh Waters running through the woods as I [Percy] was almost ravished at the first sight thereof."

Wild flowers brightened the dim corridors of the forest, and white dogwood blooms flashed among the green leaves. Roses and honeysuckle shed their fragrance and hummingbirds flitted in the sunshine among the blossoms, while violets carpeted the earth, mockingbirds trilled, and sea birds wheeled in the sky.[2]

Several days were spent in exploring the vicinity in a shallop, and the men regaled themselves with "fine and beautiful strawberries, four times bigger and better than ours in England." They also found "good store of mussels and oysters," many containing pearls.

And now these Englishmen were to have their first encounter with the Indians, the opening engagement in a long, continued series of bloody affrays lasting for some two centuries. The natives, who had lived upon their ancient fields and hunting grounds for many generations—indeed, the original Paleo-Indians are believed to have arrived in the area at least ten thousand years ago—are not to be blamed for resenting violently the coming of these heavily armed intruders. They fought back with all their courage and cunning, pouncing like panthers from dark places or rushing upon the foe with demoniacal yells. However, they were quite friendly at times, and, indeed, saved the Jamestown colony from starvation on more than one occasion.

When, on that spring day in 1607, the Indians first saw the strange "pale faces" coming ashore from Chesapeake Bay, they reacted predictably. As the English were returning to their ships at dusk, the natives came "creeping upon all fours . . . like bears, with their bows in their mouths, charged us very desperately in the faces, hurt Captain Gabriel Archer in both his hands, and a sailor in two places of the body very dangerous." However, when "they felt the sharpness of our shot, they retired into the woods with a great noise." The encounter occurred on the shore of the present Lynnhaven Bay.[3]

The voyagers had brought with them from London a sealed box, containing instructions from King James's Council. They opened it that night. It contained, among other things, the names of the seven councilors who were to be in charge of the colony in Virginia. These were Edward Maria Wingfield, Christopher Newport, Bartholomew Gosnold, John Ratcliffe, John Martin, John Smith and George Kendall. Wingfield was elected president by the group. Gabriel Archer served as secretary.

These men had been brought together haphazardly with little advance planning. Wingfield had served in the army but he was physically below par and was not a good executive. Captain Newport was an experienced and respected naval officer who had had his right arm "strooken" off in a fight with the Spaniards. Gosnold was a seasoned mariner and was admired for his personal qualities and his ability as a leader. Martin had sailed with Drake, and his sojourn in Jamestown was long, controversial and vigorous. Ratcliffe was hardly a notable figure. Little is known about Kendall's background.

The truly exceptional man in this group was Captain John Smith. Only an inch or two above five feet in height, but powerfully built and utterly fearless, Smith, then only twenty-seven years of age, was a natural leader. As a soldier of fortune in eastern Europe, he had conquered three Turks in succession in hand-to-hand combat and had cut off their heads. A coat of arms with three Turks' heads was accordingly granted him by Prince Zsigmond Bathory of Transylvania. And although Smith was born a yeoman, the prince, usurping a prerogative that was not his, named him "an English gentleman." Smith boasted excessively at times, and made unfair charges against the other councilors, but it was he who pulled the reeling and starving colony through some of its worst crises.[4] He was still under arrest when the opening of the box revealed that he had been named one of the councilors. It was not until some five weeks later that he was permitted to go entirely free and to assume his councilmanic duties.

After the landings in Chesapeake Bay, the settlers spent a couple of weeks exploring the lower James. They were cordially received by various Indian werowances or chiefs during this period. Percy was particularly impressed with a tribe on the south side of the James whose members he described as "goodly men as I have seen, of savages or Christians."

After examining various sites, they chose on May 13 a permanent location where the ships could be moored to the trees in six fathoms of water. This site, some sixty miles upstream from the Chesapeake Bay capes, was defensible against Indians and Spaniards, since it was a virtual island, linked to the mainland by a narrow isthmus.

A trumpeter sounded appropriate flourishes as the men disembarked the following morning, bringing with them their few personal belongings and the ships' stores. Spirits were high, for few grasped the deadly implications of the low-lying site with its brackish water and adjacent marshes. Nor did the settlers appear to realize that a critical shortage of food impended. Much of the supply had been consumed on the overlong voyage, and a substantial portion of the remainder had been damaged or spoiled in the ships' holds.

It was May 14 (May 24 by our modern calendar). Before autumn turned the leaves on the island to gold and crimson, more than half of those who had come ashore with such light hearts would be in their graves.

Why had these men crossed thousands of miles of ocean, with the attendant hardships and dangers, only to be faced with even more terrible hazards, as they confronted the vast and silent forest and its many unknown perils? Typhoid fever, beriberi, scurvy, dysentery, starvation and Indians were soon to emerge as deadly enemies in the "Virginia slaughterhouse."

The explanation for their venturing thus into the unknown lies chiefly in the fact that it was the Age of Elizabeth, an age characterized by a dynamism which carried English explorers and privateers to the far corners of the earth.

England's chief rival, Spain, was moving aggressively in various directions, especially in the Western Hemisphere. Governor Menendez de Aviles of Florida made two attempts to establish colonies near Chesapeake Bay, which the admiring Spaniards called "The Bay of the Mother of God." The first attempt, in 1566, was a complete failure, but a Jesuit mission returned in 1570. Sailing up the James, apparently to the mouth of what is now College Creek, the expedition crossed the peninsula near the site of present-day Williamsburg and reached the York. There the fathers built a chapel and hut, but eight of the nine missionaries were killed by Indians. The ninth, a boy, escaped.

No other efforts were made to establish Spanish settlements in that region.

As early as 1578 Elizabeth had granted to Sir Humphrey Gilbert, half brother to Sir Walter Raleigh, letters patent to plant a colony in America. Gilbert's efforts were unsuccessful, and when he was drowned in a storm on the second attempt, Raleigh was permitted to organize several expeditions.

The first of these, under Philip Amadas and Arthur Barlow, reached the coast of what is now North Carolina in 1584. The entire region, of continental dimensions, was named "Virginia" in honor of England's "Virgin Queen."

Spain was then the greatest and most acquisitive power in Europe, and Philip and Elizabeth were moving steadily toward a decisive confrontation. It came in 1588, when the Spanish sent an armada of fighting galleons, armed not only with cannon and cutlasses but with the racks and thumbscrews of the Inquisition,[5] against the outnumbered and outgunned English fleet. English courage and resourcefulness, combined with a storm which scattered the mighty armada, inflicted a shattering defeat upon Spain. England's victory gave sharp impetus to Elizabeth's colonization plans.

The year before the defeat of the armada, Raleigh had sent another expedition to the North Carolina coast, under the command of John White, the artist. Among the settlers, as a significant innovation, were women and children, destined to make permanent homes in "Virginia."

They selected Roanoke Island, and after they had become reasonably well established there, White went back to England for additional supplies. Circumstances prevented his return for four years. When he did so, in 1591, the entire colony had vanished. The word "Croatoan" on a post seemed to indicate that the colonists had gone to Croatan Island, but no trace of them was ever found. Among the members of the "Lost Colony" who were never heard from again was the infant, Virginia Dare, the first child born in America of English parents. The Croatan Indians of southeastern North Carolina, known today as Lumbees, believe that the blood of these lost colonists flows in their veins.

Queen Elizabeth died in 1603, after a magnificent reign of nearly forty-five years. Her death set back the colonization movement temporarily, but the impetus she had given it carried over into the reign of James I. James was far from being as courageous and vibrant as Elizabeth, but he had some redeeming features. He had a certain fondness for literature and the drama. A lover of peace, he moved, almost as soon as he took the throne, to put an end to hostilities with Spain. A treaty was signed, but this did not prevent intensive espionage and other hostile acts by the Spanish in the ensuing years.

Soon after the signing of the peace treaty, plans were set in motion by a group of prominent and well-to-do Englishmen to establish a colony in Virginia. Upon their petition, a London Company and a Plymouth Company were chartered. Under this charter of 1606, the colonists were to "have and enjoy all the liberties, franchises and immunities . . . to all intents and purposes as if they had been abiding and born within this our realm of England."

Why were these men anxious to invest in such an enterprise? There were several reasons. They hoped to make substantial profits. Reports that vast natural resources, including gold, precious stones and other treasures, were to be had in those distant lands fired the imagination of many inhabitants of Shakespeare's "scepter'd isle." A play, *Eastward Ho!*, which was popular on the London boards in 1605, and went through four editions in three months, contained the following concerning Virginia:

"I tell thee golde is more plentifull there than copper is with us . . . Why man all their dripping pans and their chamber pottes are pure golde; . . . and as for rubies and diamonds, they goe forth on holy dayes and gather 'hem by the seashore to hang on their children's coates and sticke in their cappes."

Some who saw or read this play may well have been skeptical concerning the above, but a widespread belief prevailed that Virginia contained much natural wealth and that money was to be made through the establishment of a colony there.

However, this was by no means the sole motive. On the home front, the country's forests were being denuded, and timber and other forest products were vitally necessary, not only to shipbuilding and smelting but to the important woolen industry. In addition, population shifts, with migration to the cities, caused unemployment and gave the impression that the country was overpopulated. The conclusion was reached that some of these problems could be solved through emigration.

The investors in the Virginia enterprise hoped that even though tangible financial dividends might be long delayed, the impact of a thriving colony on England's overall industrial posture would be strongly felt, and the country's economic independence and world prestige would be promoted.

The need for checkmating Spanish plans for expansion also loomed large in the thinking of the sponsors. Seizure of strategic areas in America was deemed to be a salient factor in meeting this objective, along with the much-desired discovery of a new route to the South Sea.

Last, but not least, was the religious motive. Clergymen rang the changes from English pulpits on the need for founding a colony in order that they might bring to the heathen Indians the blessings of Protestant Christianity. They were careful to point out that this noble objective could be worthily combined with the acceptance of sizable dividends from overseas investments. In the words of the Reverend Richard Hakluyt, whose writings had done much to promote the sending of English colonizers into far places: "Wee forgotte, that Godliness is great riches, and that if we first seeke the kingdome of God, al other thinges will be given unto us."

Fervent anti-Catholic zeal was exhibited by various members of the cloth, some of whom viewed objectors to the Virginia venture with much suspicion. One expressed a widespread view when he declared that such antagonistic attitudes were "hatched in some popish egge."

Not only leading clergymen but poets of great renown hymned the glories of Virginia. Edmund Spenser in his *Faerie Queen* referred to "fruitfullest Virginia," while Michael Drayton, the poet laureate, termed Virginia "earth's only Paradise."

Strange wonders also were proclaimed. A Londoner, William Cope, who specialized in collecting curious phenomena, announced that there were in Virginia some little flies "which glow at night instead of lights, since there is often no day there for more than a month."[6]

It remained for the first group of settlers, weary from their long voyage across a stormy ocean but exultant over their safe arrival in the face of tremendous obstacles, to learn the truth about Virginia.

TWO

Starvation, Disease and Indians

THERE WERE no shirkers on that first day at Jamestown, as the settlers began "in the name of God to raise a Fortresse."

"Now falleth every man to worke," Captain John Smith wrote, "the Councell contrive a Fort, the rest cut downe trees to make place to pitch their tents; some provide clapbord to relade the ships, some make gardens, some nets."

This was an auspicious beginning. Unfortunately, there was a grievous lack of leadership and planning. Wheat was sown promptly, and it came up with remarkable speed, but there was not nearly enough. Neither were the plantings of vegetables and fruits sufficient to meet minimum needs. And the early enthusiasm soon wore off, with the result that many began shirking.

One of the best reasons was that a communal plan, based on principles similar to today's communism, had been prescribed for the settlers before they left England. Under it, property and produce were owned jointly. The results were devastating. Ralph Hamor, colonial secretary, described them vividly after the system had been abandoned:

"When our people were fed out of the common store, and laboured jointly together, glad was he who could slip from his labour, or slumber over his taske, he cared not how . . . neither cared they for the increase, presuming that howsoever the harvest prospered the generall store must maintaine them, so that wee reaped not so much Corne from the labours of thirtie as now three or foure doe provide for themselves."

Heedless of the foregoing, the Pilgrims tried a similar communal experiment at Plymouth in the early 1620s. They abandoned it for exactly the same reasons.[1]

A week after the landing at Jamestown, Captain Newport led an expedition of twenty-one men up the "king's river" to the falls, the site of present day Richmond. Various friendly Indian tribes were encountered en route. When the party arrived at the falls, they erected a cross on one of the islets, "with a great shoute." On it were inscribed the words "Jacobus Rex, 1607," with Newport's name below, signifying that the English claimed the region.

All went well in the explorers' relations with the redskins until the settlers returned to Jamestown. There they found that the unpredictable natives had attacked the fort, killing a boy, mortally wounding another settler, and inflicting lesser wounds on about eleven more. It was the beginning of a period in which the Indians harassed the colonists almost continually. Any who strayed carelessly outside the palisades of the fort were picked off by bowmen lurking in the nearby tall grass.

But worse, by far, than this were the frightful inroads made by starvation and disease. By mid-July this had reached epidemic proportions, and it grew more deadly as the days passed.

It was during this period that Captain Smith, on a journey of exploration up the Chickahominy River, was captured by Indians. After "some six weeks fatting amongst those Salvage Courtiers," he was taken before the mighty Emperor Powhatan, who ordered his men to beat out Smith's brains with clubs. As the sentence was about to be executed, Pocahontas, Powhatan's "dearest daughter," then twelve or thirteen years old, rushed forward, took Smith's head in her arms, and saved him. The story of this rescue was long felt to be one of Smith's more picturesque fictions, but most historians now believe it to be substantially correct. Smith also credited the young girl with seeing that he was "safely conducted to Jamestowne."

On the expedition with Smith when he was captured was George Cassen, who had become separated from the others earlier and was seized by the Indians. They tied him to a tree and proceeded to saw off his fingers and toes one by one, using mussel shells and sharp reeds. Not satisfied with inflicting these excruciating tortures, they flayed Cassen alive. Beginning with his scalp and moving downward, they ripped the skin from his quivering frame, after which they set

him and the tree on fire, and danced about the dying man with
fiendish yells.[2]

Such horrors were enough to make the stoutest spirit quail, but
the ghastly sufferings of the starving and ill men at Jamestown were
comparable. The food supply was vanishing and the percentage of
sickness and death was climbing steadily. George Percy's vivid and
moving prose tells the dreadful story:

"Our men were destroyed with cruel diseases as swellings, fluxes,
burning fevers, and by warres, and some departed suddenly, but for
the most part they died of meere famine. There were never Englishmen
left in a foreign country in such miserie. . . . We watched every three
nights, lying on the bare cold ground . . . and warded all the next
day, which brought our men to be most feeble wretches. Our food
was but a small can of barley, sod in water, to five men a day, our
drink cold water taken out of the river, which was at a flood
verie salt, at low tide full of slime and filth . . . our men night
and day groaning in every corner of the fort most pitiful to hear . . .
some departing out of the world, many times three or four in a night;
in the morning their bodies trailed out of their cabins like dogges
to be buried."

The Reverend Robert Hunt, the beloved parson who was so ill
for six weeks off the English coast the previous winter, may well have
been the innocent cause of the typhoid fever epidemic which wrought
such havoc at Jamestown. A modern student has reached the conclusion that Hunt's illness was very likely typhoid, and that he
probably served as a "carrier" after the colony was established. This
finding is based, in part, on the theory that Hunt tended the "common
kettle" from which for months the colonists were fed.[3] Dr. Wyndham
B. Blanton, the leading authority, feels that typhoid probably killed
more of the early Jamestown settlers than all other diseases combined.
Hence if Hunt was a "typhoid Mary," the catastrophic results are
obvious. There must have been something special about the staggering
mortality at Jamestown, for practically no deaths had occurred on
similarly low-lying Roanoke Island during its first year. Parson Hunt
could well have made the tragic difference.

He himself died during the winter of 1607–08, when calamity
was piled on calamity for the colonists. First there was a fire which
destroyed the common storehouse, the church and all but three
dwellings, with most of the settlers' food, clothing and ammunition.

Then came the Great Frost, one of the coldest winters on record, both in this country and Europe.

By great good fortune, the Indians at that time were friendly, and they brought food, as they had done at a critical period in the early fall. They even instructed the starving and freezing men in the best methods of setting fish traps. Unfortunately, additional colonists had arrived from England just before the fire, as part of Captain Newport's First Supply. Many of these soon fell ill. This was the fate of nearly all newcomers to Virginia during those years. It was not until they had undergone a period of "seasoning" that they became relatively immune. In addition to requiring medical treatment, these just-arrived settlers consumed a goodly share of the colony's scanty rations.

Spanish spies added to the complications. They were operating in the most unexpected places, and George Kendall, member of the council, is believed to have been in the pay of Spain. Certain it is that he was tried and convicted of being involved in some sort of plot against the colony. He was shot.[4]

There were further strong dissensions and disagreements in the council. Smith falsely accused several councilors of various types of malfeasance, and they retorted in kind. Misappropriation of supplies was one of the allegations against President Wingfield, and he responded that Smith and others had plotted against him. This constant bickering did much to lessen the effectiveness of the loosely functioning government and to compound the already tremendous problems confronting the colony.

Newport traveled back and forth four times in the early years. When he brought his Second Supply (October 1608), Newport introduced a new and exciting factor. He included two women, the first in the colony—Mrs. Thomas Forrest, wife of a settler, and Ann Burras, her maid. The latter was soon married to John Laydon, a carpenter. Stephen Vincent Benét celebrated the nuptials in verse:

—And the first white wedding held on Virginia ground
Will marry no courtly dame to a cavalier.
But Ann Burras, lady's maid, to John Laydon, laborer,
After some six weeks' courtship—a Fall wedding
When the leaves were turning and the wild air sweet,
And we know no more than that but it sticks in the mind,

For they were serving-maid and laboring man
And yet, while they lived (and they had not long to live),
They were half of the first families in Virginia.[5]

It was the first wedding in the Anglo-American colonies. The Laydons' first child, born the following year, was named Virginia.

Captain John Smith was busying himself much of the time in exploring, map making and trading with the Indians for large quantities of food. On one of his expeditions he was spearing fish with his sword near the mouth of the Rappahannock River, and he speared a stingray. The fish struck him so viciously with its barbed and poisonous tail that his life was despaired of. Smith's grave was accordingly dug, at his direction. But Dr. Walter Russell, who was one of the party, probed the wound and applied a "precious oil," which so relieved the captain's distress that he "eate the fish for his supper." The place where this occurred is called Stingray Point to commemorate the event.

Soon afterward (September 1608), Smith was made president of the council, a post which he held for about ten months. His dynamic drive and capacity for leadership were felt immediately, and malingering colonists were soon aware that more work would be required of them. His general concept is said to have been expressed in the dictum, "He that will not worke shall not eate."

During that winter, Pocahontas saved Captain Smith for the second time. Her father, Powhatan, determined to capture Smith again by pretending friendship. Powhatan's warriors were to pounce on him while he was dining as Powhatan's guest, on venison, turkey and bread. Pocahontas learned of the plot and stole through the woods at night to Smith's camp and gave the warning, risking death at the hands of her father, as Smith said, in doing so. Smith escaped.

Newport's above-mentioned Second Supply included a message from the London Company concerning the need for making "ship-stores, such as pitch, tar and turpentine, also soapashes, deal and wainscot." There were "skillful workmen from forraine parts" on board, including eight Dutchmen and Poles. The latter were brought in to establish a glassworks.

Under Smith's no-nonsense directives, the foregoing products were fashioned and made ready for shipment to England, although only in small quantities. The company in London was to be disappointed for many years because production in Virginia failed to reach expectations, except in the case of tobacco. Some products, such as gold and silver, were never discovered at all.

Smith saw to it that a well "of excellent sweete water" was dug in the fort. He also accomplished the construction of about twenty houses, together with a blockhouse for defense on the narrow isthmus linking Jamestown to the mainland. Hogs and chickens were raised in substantial quantities, and the hogs became so numerous that they were removed to Hog Island in the river below Jamestown.[6]

However, things were never simple in the colony during this period. For example, just as matters appeared to be reasonably well in hand, the vital corn supply was found to have been virtually destroyed. Either it had rotted or rats had escaped from the ships and eaten it. This was another crisis, and Smith ordered most of the colonists to leave Jamestown and go wherever food was obtainable. Thanks to this and other decisions made by Smith, only a few died during that winter.

The colonists suffered frequently for the bare necessities, despite the astounding abundance in primeval Virginia of birds, game, fish and other varieties of seafood, whose individual dimensions were often as amazing as their numbers. Innumerable sturgeon from three to twelve feet long, shad sometimes three feet in length, crabs measuring one foot from tip to tip, oysters thirteen inches in diameter (perhaps including the shell), large flocks of forty-pound wild turkeys, enormous flights of wild pigeons which took three or four hours to pass a given point, and huge bullfrogs with voices like the bellowing of an ox were all described by eyewitnesses, some of them many times. The forests teemed with deer.[7]

A gigantic frog, encountered by Robert Beverley, was said by him to have been "of so prodigious a Magnitude that when I extended its Leggs, I found the distance betwixt them to be seventeen Inches and a half." He added: "I am confident six French-Men might have made a comfortable meal of its Carcase." This was written nearly a hundred years after the original settlement at Jamestown, but witnesses testified in the early seventeenth century to the existence of similarly impressive amphibians.

Chesapeake Bay and the four great rivers emptying into it, plus the Atlantic shore, offered almost unrivaled opportunities, not only for obtaining food but also for the construction of harbors and docks.

Inland Virginia, furthermore, was almost one vast forest. Oak and walnut trees of colossal size predominated, but there were also the chestnut and the ash, together with cedars, cypresses, pines and other varieties. Wild grapes grew in profusion, with vines often as large as a man's thigh where they issued from the ground. They climbed to the tops of the tallest trees and were laden with fruit.

Thus it will be seen that Virginia offered a wealth of forest products, as well as an abundance of food. The problem was to organize and administer the Jamestown colony in such a manner as to capitalize on these natural resources. By 1609 it had become apparent to the Virginia Company in London that the colony was being wretchedly managed, and that a different form of government was essential. A squabbling council with a constantly changing president was seen to be a gravely defective administrative device.

Consequently a new charter was drawn up. Sir Edwin Sandys, a leading member of the company since 1606, was its apparent author. This Charter of 1609 provided for "one *able* and *absolute* governor," appointed for life, subject to the council and the company in England. He was to be called Lord Governor and Captain General of Virginia, and he would choose his own deputy to govern in his stead when he was absent from the colony (as happened the majority of the time). The new charter also extended the boundaries of the colony to include a tremendous area two hundred miles north and two hundred miles south of Point Comfort and extending "west and northwest" from sea to sea. Sir Thomas Smith was named by King James to serve as the first "treasurer" or head of the company, with extraordinary powers. Sir Thomas, the leading figure among the company's organizers, was a man of wide experience and marked executive ability. He was for many years governor of the East India Company.

The new charter was overdue, for despite President John Smith's best efforts, the Jamestown colony was in dire straits. Five hundred more settlers were accordingly sent from England, including women and children. Thus it was hoped to put the enterprise on a solid foundation.

This Third Supply, nine shiploads in all, left England in May 1609. When the expedition reached the tropics, disease took a heavy toll of passengers and crew. Yellow fever appears to have broken out on several ships, and thirty-two persons died. Their bodies were thrown overboard.

Then in July a tropical hurricane which roared over the sea for four days and nights put the entire fleet in grave peril. The *Catch*, a pinnace, went down with all hands, and the *Sea Venture*, the flagship, commanded by Captain Newport and with several other high officials on board, was wrecked on the coral reefs of Bermuda.

Shakespeare almost certainly derived some of his inspiration for *The Tempest* from the brilliant account of this storm written by William Strachey in his *True Reportory*. Strachey, the first officially appointed secretary of the colony, was on the flagship. He gives vivid word pictures of the thundering hurricane, the towering waves, the shrieking winds laced with lightning, and the "mighty leak" which threatened to sink the vessel. Silvester Jourdain, another passenger, wrote that at one point hope was abandoned, and an exhausted group, finding "comfortable waters" on board, "fetched them and drunk one to the other . . . until their more joyful and happy meeting in a more blessed world."

The awe and terror of those on the vessel was increased by the electrical phenomenon known as "St. Elmo's fire," regarded in that era as a supernatural manifestation. Strachey said it was "an apparition of a little round light, like a faint Starre, trembling and streaming along with a sparkeling blaze, halfe the height upon the Maine Mast, and shooting sometimes from Shroud to Shroud." It remained with the ship for several hours.

By sheer luck, the *Sea Venture* was wedged between two rocks off one of the Bermuda Islands, and all on board were able to wade ashore. The other seven surviving ships managed to get to Jamestown in August.

On one of the new arrivals was Captain Ratcliffe. Captain Percy sent him with fifty men to Emperor Powhatan to trade for food. Ratcliffe allowed himself to be trapped by that "subtele owlde foxe," with the result that most of his men were killed. Ratcliffe himself was put to the torture before being slain. He was tied naked to a tree before a fire, while Indian women scraped the flesh from his body with sharp shells and threw the bloody gobbets into the flames.

The several hundred settlers who had finally made it to Jamestown after the devastating summer hurricane were half sick and badly shaken by the experience. In addition, what was left of their supplies of food had been severely damaged by sea water. Furthermore, it was late in the season, with no opportunity for planting. Here was

another instance where supposed reinforcements for the colony turned
out to be liabilities.

The best hope that the five hundred settlers now at Jamestown
would be able to survive the approaching winter lay in the leadership
of Captain John Smith. But at this critical juncture, Smith sustained
a painful and almost fatal injury. He was asleep in his boat, returning
from the falls of the James, when someone "accidentally fired his
powder." It "tore the flesh from his bodie and thighes 9 to 10 inches
square . . . To quench the tormenting fire, frying him in his cloathes,
he leaped over board in the deepe river, where ere they could recover
him, he was neere drownd."

Smith was so sorely injured that he felt it necessary to return to
England. He left in early October 1609 and never came back. His
going was a severe loss to the colony. He had been unsparing and
often unfair in his criticisms of the other leaders, and they had been
similarly critical of him. He was inordinately boastful and conceited.
Yet the council in England expressed "greate confidence and trust . . .
in his care and diligence," and it was he, more than any man,
who pulled Jamestown through the worst crises of its earliest years.

The colony appeared to be in reasonably good condition when
Smith sailed for England. "Ten weeks' provision in the store," plus
several hundred swine, a similar number of hens and chickens, as
well as goats would seem to have been fairly adequate. Yet the
winter of 1609–10 brought the greatest disaster of all. It is known
to history as the "Starving Time."

The settlers had depended on the Indians in former crises to
bring them food, but now the redskins were implacably hostile. They
placed Jamestown under siege, and killed all who ventured forth. The
colonists were accordingly unable to reach their principal stocks of
pigs and chickens, or to use the nets which they had stored up for
fishing. Percy, who had succeeded Smith, did his best to cope with
the desperate situation, but even Smith might have found the difficulties insuperable.[8]

Percy left a moving account of Jamestown's ghastly ordeal—how the
settlers began to feel the "sharpe pricke of hunger which no man can
trewly describe butt he wch hath Tasted the bitternesse thereof." Some
robbed the public store, and Percy had them executed. The famished
settlers were reduced to eating "dogges, Catts, Ratts and myce," as
well as "Serpents and Snakes," boots and shoes, to satisfy "crewell

hunger." Some went so far as to "Digge up dead corpses out of graves to eate them." Percy added that "many of our men this Starveing Tyme did Runn Away unto the Salvages, whome we never heard of after."

These tragic events were being closely watched by the Spaniards. The Spanish ambassador in London, informed by his spies in Virginia that Jamestown was tottering, had been urging King Philip to wipe out the colony. Had this happened, or if the colony had been abandoned by the English, the consequences for America and the world would have been incalculable. Virginia, instead of being the first of Britain's globe-girdling dominions, might well have become an important Spanish possession, added to the already large Spanish domain in this hemisphere.

That almost happened. For the "Starving Time," one of the most terrible periods in American history, very nearly caused Jamestown to be abandoned.

Of the approximately five hundred men, women and children who were there in late 1609, only sixty were alive with the coming of spring. These breathing skeletons had barely been able to survive famine, disease and massacre, and the colony was on the verge of total collapse. Suddenly, on May 23, two ships hove into view off Jamestown. They were the *Patience* and the *Deliverance*, built in the Bermudas by Captain Newport, Sir Thomas Gates, Virginia's new governor, and the others who had been shipwrecked in the *Sea Venture* the preceding summer.

Jamestown's sixty "anatomies," crying out "Wee are starved!" greeted the new arrivals with such enthusiasm as they could muster. Wreckage and desolation were everywhere. Some of the homes had been torn down and used for firewood, since those who lived in them had died or been slain, and it was suicidal to go outside the fort and search for fuel in the forest, where the Indians lurked. Much of the palisade was gone and the gates were open and off their hinges. The Indians could undoubtedly have killed the hollow-eyed survivors, but for some reason had not done so.[9]

Governor Gates told the anguished settlers that he had brought only enough provisions to feed them for sixteen days. It was accordingly decided that the colony would have to be abandoned. Some wanted to set fire to Jamestown, but this was prevented.

On June 7, the colonists filed out of their crumbling settlement and went on board their flotilla of four small ships. They dropped down-

stream to Mulberry Island. While they were lying there, a boat
approached. In charge was Captain Edward Brewster, with word that
Lord De la Warr, the newly appointed governor and captain general,
had arrived from England with a relief expedition of three hundred
men, including "many gentlemen of quality." Anchored off Fort
Algernon, his lordship had received the "heavie newes" that the settlers
were giving up the colony and had sent Brewster to prevent it. De la
Warr's orders to return to Jamestown were obeyed. The weak and
emaciated settlers went back, and were soon joined there by the
governor and his formidable reinforcements.

When his lordship arrived at the south gate of the "Pallizado," he
"caused his company in arms to stand in order, and to make a Guard."
Whereupon he fell on his knees, and "before us all made a long and
silent prayer, and after, marched up into the Towne." He then "passed
into the Chappell," where a sermon was delivered by the Reverend
Richard Buck, who had arrived from Bermuda shortly before with Sir
Thomas Gates.

We note here a renewed emphasis upon religion at Jamestown.
The Reverend Robert Hunt had held Holy Communion as one of
his first acts, following the arrival of the original settlers in 1607, and
had conducted services twice daily. But after his death, there had been
no minister until the coming of the Reverend Mr. Buck. Some attributed the series of disasters involving the town to the lack of a resident
clergyman. Lord De la Warr arranged for two sermons every Sunday,
accompanied by a rather elaborate ceremonial, and one on Thursday,
plus prayers twice daily.

The governor had found Jamestown to be "a verie noysome and
unholsome place." A broad operation involving both cleaning and
reconstruction was accordingly instituted. The palisades were repaired
and efforts made to acquire more adequate stocks of food. Yet appalling mortality among the settlers from the "summer sickness" reduced their number by more than half in a few months.

Bitter warfare with the Indians also was resumed. It was claimed that
the Indian women were especially cruel in inflicting tortures on the
whites. This may account for the barbarous manner in which the
queen of the Paspaheghs and her children were murdered by the
settlers. George Percy describes the horrible episode in his *Trewe
Relacyon* as follows:

"A Councell beinge called itt was Agreed upon to putt the Children

to deathe w'h was effected by Throweinge them overboard and shote-
inge owtt their Braynes in the water yett for all this Crewellty the
Sowldiers were nott well-pleased."

Since the soldiers were "nott well-pleased," it was actually suggested
that the queen be burned to death. Percy says he prevented this, but
he allowed the men to take her ashore and kill her in cold blood.

Not long afterward, the queen of the Appomattuck invited some
of the English to a feast, during which the natives "slew divers" and
"mortally wounded all the rest." Seething with anger, the English
burned this queen's town at what is now Bermuda Hundred and killed
some of her principal warriors.[10]

Lord De la Warr was continually plagued by illness, like so many
others who had not undergone the "seasoning." He finally had to
leave Virginia early in 1611 and return to England. He retained the
title of governor until his death in 1618. De la Warr named Captain
George Percy as his deputy, pending the arrival of "the Marshall, Sir
Thomas Dale." Dale, in turn, would be succeeded by Sir Thomas
Gates, who would later be replaced by Dale. During this period, Percy,
Gates and Dale had such titles as deputy governor and lieutenant governor. As with many of their successors, especially in the eighteenth
century, they were the chief administrative officers in the colony, while
the governor remained in England.

Two months after the departure of De la Warr, Dale arrived with a
substantial "supply," which included people and livestock, as well as
food. In the late summer, Gates brought in another sizable fleet, with
a score of women, as well as large consignments of cattle and provisions. Dale and Gates were able administrators and, like other leaders
at Jamestown, had served with the armed forces in the Low Countries.

The two co-operated in putting the colony on a sounder basis.
Numerous artisans had been brought over, and such types were obviously far more useful than non-working "gentlemen" and persons who
had got into trouble of one sort or another in England. Reports that the
early Virginia settlers were mostly "convicts" are untrue, of course, but
the percentage of ne'er-do-wells and other such characters was too high.
It should be borne in mind that many "convicts" in that era had
committed thoroughly trivial offenses by modern standards. There were,
for example nearly three hundred "crimes" in England calling for the
death penalty.[11]

The well-nigh incredible mortality in the miasmic atmosphere of

Jamestown had given concern to the company in London as well as to
the leaders in Virginia. Dale recognized the need for a more elevated
site, and accordingly explored upriver. There, in 1611, he chose "a
convenient, strong, healthie and sweet seate" on Farrar's Island at the
point where it then joined the mainland, at a sharp bend in the stream
near Dutch Gap. It was named Henrico, for Henry, Prince of Wales.
(The town was never known as Henricopolis in the seventeenth or even
in the eighteenth century, despite widespread belief to the contrary.)

Ralph Hamor, colonial secretary, described it as including "two fair
rowes of howses," and "three large . . . store howses," the whole being
strongly impaled for protection from attack. In addition, there were
blockhouses "to observe and watch least the Indians at any time should
swim over the back river." There was also a hospital, the first in English
America, with "fourscore lodgings" and "keepers to attend the sick"
"for their comfort and recoverie." A "faire and handsome church" was
likewise constructed.

This settlement was completed in four months, under the rigid
discipline introduced by Marshal Dale. He was conscious of the lamen-
table manner in which many settlers had failed to do their duty, and
of how, with their sloth, worthlessness and thievery, they had jeopardized the colony. So the most Draconian penalties were imposed, such
as shootings, burnings at the stake, hangings and breakings on the
wheel. It was drastic, even for that era, but it got results.

These punishments were applied under the code known as *Lawes
Divine, Morall and Martiall*. Since Dale was stern and puritanical in
the manner of the New England Puritans, his rule bore little re-
semblance to the sybaritic hedonism of the supposedly pleasure-loving
"Cavaliers." Other Virginia governors or their deputies in that era
were strict and far from rollicking, but Dale surpassed them all. Under
his rule, swearing brought a whipping for the first offense, a bodkin
thrust through the tongue for the second, and death for the third.
Death also was decreed for impious or malicious speaking against the
Blessed Trinity or any Person of the Godhead or against the "Knowne"
Articles of the Christian faith. There was a possible death penalty for
violations of most regulations of all kinds. Enforcement was sometimes lax, but many harsh punishments were imposed. However, these
may well have been essential to the colony's survival.[12]

It was also Marshal Dale who saw the absolute necessity for
abandoning the disastrous plan under which, for five or six years, all

land had been held and worked in common, with rations distributed from a central storehouse. Dale recognized the value of private initiative by assigning small plots of land to worthy settlers. They were told that they could grow crops for their own benefit. The results were electric, and production increased almost immediately. The discredited system based on communal ownership was never permitted to return.

THREE

Tobacco, Pocahontas, The First Assembly and the First Negroes

ELIMINATION of the communal ownership of property and produce at Jamestown was followed by the intensive development of a profitable tobacco culture. The combination was almost enough to guarantee the survival of the colony.

The "joviall weed," the "bewitching vegetable," the "precious stink," the "deceavable weed" and the "chopping herbe of hell," as tobacco was variously known, served as the basis for the colony's economic viability.

John Rolfe is the man who developed in Virginia a type of tobacco for which there was a great demand in Europe. An English gentleman whose fame rests also on the fact that he became the husband of Pocahontas, Rolfe grasped the possibilities in the development of a milder type of leaf than the native variety. The latter, deemed soothing by the Indians, was described by English colonials as "poore, weake and of a byting tast."

Rolfe was not dismayed by King James's famous *Counterblaste to Tobacco*, issued in 1604. The "esteemed weed" had been introduced into England about a half century before, and was touted as a remedy for many diseases, including "the pox," but His Majesty was not amused. Said King James of the smoker: "All his members shall become feeble, his spirits dull, and in the end, as a drowsie, lazie bellygod he shall evanish in a Lethargie." In fact James went on, smoking was "A custome Lothsome to the eye, hateful to the Nose, harmfull to the braine, daungerous to the Lungs, and in the black, stinking fume thereof, neerest resembling the horrible Stigian smoke of the pit that is bottomelesse." Despite this royal blast, Sir Walter Raleigh and many others puffed on their pipes contentedly.

And Rolfe proceeded to plant some sweet-smoking West Indian tobacco seed which he had somehow acquired. He thus began a form of agriculture which would serve not only as the foundation of Virginia's economy throughout the colonial era but also as the basis for its plantation system, and would later become a vital element in the state's industrial development. Rolfe's first plantings were made in 1612, and expansion of the crop was steady. By 1618 the yield was 20,000 pounds, and before 1630, annual exports from Virginia had reached 500,000 pounds. The settlers at one point were planting the leaf in the streets of Jamestown. Virginia tobacco was here to stay.

The Virginia Company's stockholders felt the need, in 1612, for another revision of the charter. The first revision, three years before, had provided the machinery for a much more effective operation, but other changes were desired. Control was placed under the entire group of stockholders, and provision was made for expanding their number substantially.

One or more annual lotteries were authorized to raise funds for the colony. The initial lottery was held in London, and a tailor won first prize—"four thousand crownes in fayre plate, which was sent to his house in a very stately manner." Throughout this particular lottery "there was alwaies present divers worshipfull knights and esquires accompainied by sundry grave and discreet citizens."

At about this time, the Virginia Company was granted a seal. It bore the arms of England, France, Scotland and Ireland, with the motto *En Dat Virginia Quintam*—"Virginia Gives a Fifth Crown."

Pocahontas who, as a girl of twelve or thirteen, had twice saved Captain John Smith, had not been to Jamestown since his departure some four years before. Now sixteen or seventeen, and on the threshold of mature womanhood, this romantic and alluring figure, in some respects the most romantic in Virginia history, emerged once more to play a highly important role in the life of the colony. Her father had sought to seize and slay her idol, Captain John Smith, and now Captain

Samuel Argall, lately arrived from England, was plotting to seize Powhatan's daughter as a hostage, in order to win concessions from the werowance.

Argall learned in 1613 that Pocahontas was visiting among the Potomac Indians, when he was on a trading expedition to that tribe. He bribed one of the native chieftains with a copper kettle to connive at her capture. With the aid of this brave, Pocahontas was enticed on board Argall's ship, and taken as a hostage to Jamestown. She was sent thence to the newly established town of Henrico, and placed in the custody of Marshal Dale. It was there that she was instructed in the Christian religion and baptized—apparently in the church at Henrico[1]— with the Christian name "Rebecca." (Her Indian name was actually "Matoaka"; "Pocahontas" was a nickname which meant "playful one.")

John Rolfe, then deeply involved on his Varina plantation with the development of his new and milder variety of tobacco, was now to become still more deeply involved, but in a different fashion. He fell in love with the attractive Indian princess during the months when she was being transformed from an "unbeleeving creature," as Rolfe put it, into the first Indian to be converted to Christianity by the English. Pocahontas returned his affection.

Rolfe, an earnestly religious man, wrote a long and pious communication to Governor Dale, confessing to his consuming passion, and asking permission to marry Pocahontas—

"To whom my hartie and best thoughts are, and have a long time bin so intangled, and inthralled in so intricate a laborinth, that I was even awearied to unwinde my selfe thereout."

Dale was quick to see the great political value of a union between the daughter of Powhatan and one of the leading planters, and he agreed at once. Powhatan also gave his consent. The wedding was held in the church at Jamestown, on April 5, 1614, with Parson Buck officiating. It signalized the beginning of eight years of almost uninterrupted peace with the Indians.

Rolfe estimated that there were 351 English colonists living in Virginia in 1616, including 65 women and children. In that year there were also 144 cattle, 6 horses, 216 goats, "hoggs, wild and tame, not to be numbered. Poultry, great plenty." Alexander Brown, one of the most reliable writers on the period, estimated that 1650 people had come to Virginia in the first nine years, of whom approximately 1000 had died on the way over or in the colony, and about 300 had gone back.

Richard L. Morton, whose *Colonial Virginia* is the most authoritative work on the era with which it deals, sums up the situation as it existed in 1616:

"The Virginians, few but well 'seasoned,' had reason to be encouraged. Sinced De la Warr, Gates and Dale had arrived in 1610, order had been restored; the colony had greatly extended its area of settlement; starvation no longer threatened; a staple crop had developed; the English were at peace with the Indians; and French and Spanish invasions had been averted. The colony had passed through the experimental 'seasoning' period, but there was bitter suffering ahead."

In 1616 Rolfe and his wife, and their infant son, Thomas, sailed to England, accompanied by about a dozen Indians who were supposedly to be educated in the mother country. Also on board the vessel were Sir Thomas Dale, whose stay in Virginia was thus terminated; Don Diego de Molina, a notorious Spanish spy who had been held at Jamestown, and Francis Lymbry, an Englishman who had also been spying for Spain. The ever-efficient Dale allowed Lymbry to glimpse his native land as the ship approached the English coast and then had him hanged from the yardarm.

The ship's hold contained a few of the scanty commodities produced in Virginia—pitch, potash, sturgeon and caviar, plus sassafras, which last was widely used in the treatment of various ailments. Also on board was "exceedinge good tobacco," then coming into production in the colony.

Rolfe and Pocahontas and their infant son remained in England for some ten months. Pocahontas, known there as "Lady Rebecca" and honored as a princess, was something of a sensation in London society. Though almost totally unaccustomed to British ways, this young woman, who had spent most of her life in the Virginia wilderness, conducted herself with poise and dignity. She was presented at court, where ladies leaving her presence often curtsied and backed out of the room. The Lord Bishop of London "entertained her with festivall state and pompe," according to the Reverend Samuel Purchas, who was present. Purchas added that she "did not onely accustome her selfe to civilitie, but still carried her selfe as the Daughter of a King, and was accordingly respected, not onely by the [London] Company, which allowed provision for her selfe and sonne, but of divers particular persons of Honor, in their hopeful zeale by her to advance Christianitie." Captain

John Smith quoted friends as observing that many English ladies of
the highest rank "were worse favored, proportioned and behaved
than she."

Smith had renewed his acquaintance with her, after a lapse of seven
years. He says he greeted her "with a modest salutation," but she said
nothing and "turned about, obscured her face as not seeming well
contented." Smith came back two or three hours later, and her attitude
was more cordial. She revealed that she had long understood that Smith
was dead. They chatted of old times, and she said she would call him
"father," since Smith, she asserted, had called Powhatan "father."

Pocahontas apparently was charmed by life in England, and she
prepared, "sorely against her will," to return to Virginia in March 1617.
She was taken sick as the ship sailed from London, and on reaching
Gravesend, a short distance downstream, was too ill to continue. She
died—perhaps of smallpox, which was widely prevalent at the time—
and was buried in or near St. George's Church, Gravesend. An entry
in the vestry book says she was "buried in the chancel," but her name
and that of her husband are both erroneously inscribed, and there is
reason to believe that burial may have been in the churchyard.

Thus ended the brief life of the Indian girl who saved John Smith
on two occasions, and whose marriage to John Rolfe brought almost
complete peace between the Indians and the settlers in Virginia from
1614 to 1622.

Her infant son, Thomas, was left in England by his father, who
feared that the hazardous sea voyage might endanger the boy's life.
John Rolfe never saw his son again, and was probably killed in the
great Indian massacre of 1622. Thomas Rolfe came to Virginia years
afterward as a young man and married Jane Poythress. Many leading
Virginia families proudly trace their descent from this union, and
hence from Princess Pocahontas, without whom the colony would have
been in serious danger of collapse.

Pocahontas lived for but a score of years, and her bones lie beside
the Thames, far from the wigwams and forests of her native land. But
the vision of this Indian girl, compassionate and unspoiled, yet proud
and regal, haunts us across the centuries. She left her mark indelibly
upon the history of her time.

The year 1619 was one of the most notable in American annals. The
first representative assembly in the new world convened in that year

at Jamestown. A few weeks later the first Negroes were brought to Virginia.

When the General Assembly met in July and August, 1619, in the little church beside the river, it marked the first step in the building of this country's democratic institutions. Antedating the Mayflower Compact by more than a year, this first Virginia General Assembly was a milestone in the history of liberal government.

The progressive influence of Sir Edwin Sandys, who has been termed the father of democratic institutions in Virginia, was an important factor in bringing these things to pass. A son of the Archbishop of York, and educated at Oxford, he was also a leader in the House of Commons. His aggressive espousal of popular rights and his advocacy of the abolition of feudal tenures had antagonized powerful members of the nobility. He also had taken issue with King James on certain matters, a fact which did not endear him to that royal personage.

Sir Edwin was the prime mover in achieving the reorganization of the London Company in 1618, with a view to providing a more effective operation in Virginia. He received essential support from able Sir Thomas Smith, whom he soon replaced as head of the company, and from John and Nicholas Ferrar. The result was "The Greate Charter," which laid the groundwork for a much less authoritarian form of governance for the colony. This meant abandonment of the rigorous *Lawes Divine, Morall and Martiall,* and their replacement with a legislative, administrative and judicial system much more closely in accord with that prevailing in England.

Members of the newly created House of Burgesses were to be elected by the "inhabitants" of the colony, or the "freemen," and this term was interpreted to include a new class of citizens known as "indentured servants." Various plans designed to tempt emigrants to Virginia had been tried by the London Company. Finally, not long before the Assembly met, the company offered to give such emigrants half of whatever they could produce from their own labors. When this brought negligible results, the planters began importing white servants whose passage they paid, and who agreed, in return, to work for a given number of years—usually four or five—after which they gained their freedom. This plan was enacted into law by the Assembly of 1619. Thus it formalized the indentured-servant system, and helped to create an element in the Virginia population which was to become more and more important.

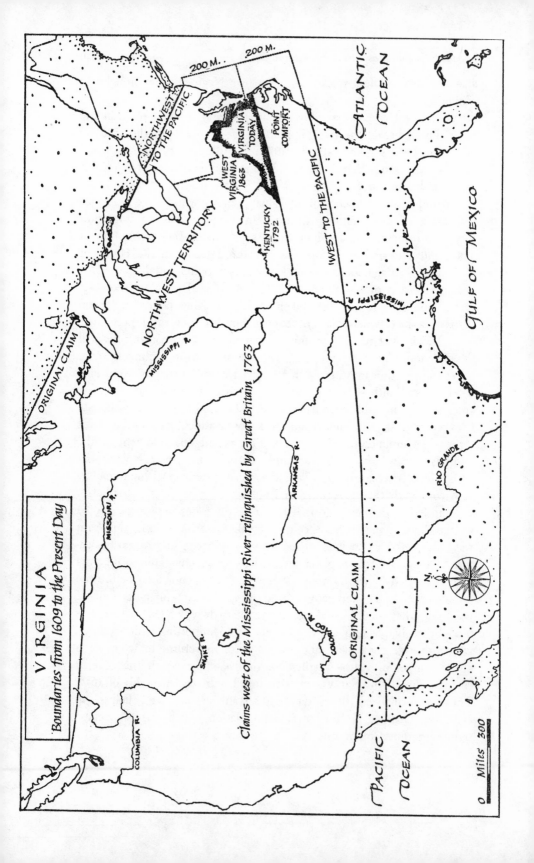

VIRGINIA
Boundaries from 1609 to the Present Day

ORIGINAL CLAIM

NORTHWEST
TO THE PACIFIC

200 M.   200 M.

WEST
VIRGINIA
1863

VIRGINIA
TODAY

POINT
COMFORT

KENTUCKY
1792

WEST to THE PACIFIC

ATLANTIC
OCEAN

NORTHWEST TERRITORY

MISSISSIPPI R.

MISSOURI R.

Claims west of the Mississippi River relinquished by Great Britain 1763

ARKANSAS R.

MISSISSIPPI R.

GULF OF MEXICO

SNAKE R.

COLUMBIA R.

COLORADO R.

ORIGINAL CLAIM

RIO GRANDE

PACIFIC
OCEAN

N

0   Miles   300

The number of indentured servants was sharply increased by the "headright system." Under it, each person who was willing to pay for his own passage and settle in Virginia was offered fifty acres of land, and fifty more for each member of his family and each servant brought over. This plan, with certain modifications, remained in effect throughout most of the century.

When the Assembly convened in the summer heat, Jamestown was in a reasonably good state of repair, thanks to the vigorous program of rehabilitation carried out by Deputy Governor Samuel Argall. He had found the town in grievous condition when he took over from Deputy Governor George Yeardley, and had begun "repayring and making straight what he found decayed and crooked." When, in the spring of 1619, Yeardley again became the colony's chief executive, things were in much better case than they had been two years before.

The mighty Emperor Powhatan had died in 1618. A man of immense dignity and a great leader among his people, he was succeeded by his unimpressive brother, Opitchapam, who, like Powhatan, proclaimed his friendship for the English. Opitchapam was to be replaced ere long by the devious and shifty Opechancanough.

Although Indian relations presented no particularly urgent problems at that moment, the first legislative assembly in the new world addressed itself to these matters at considerable length.

Its members conducted their deliberations in the knowledge that the common law of England was applicable in Virginia—a fact emphasized once more in "The Greate Charter." It is interesting to note that the members of this first Assembly were elected under a franchise more liberal than that prevailing in England.[2]

Virginia had been divided into four "plantations"—James City, the City of Henrico, Charles City and Kecoughtan or Elizabeth City. These "cities" included adjacent areas along the rivers and bays. Some settlements were known as "hundreds," a term used in England to denote an area inhabited by about a hundred families, or able to provide a hundred fighting men. Representatives of the plantations met in the choir of the church, with Governor Yeardley presiding.

About thirty persons were present. The plantations sent twenty-two elected burgesses, and the governor's council of six members, chosen by the company, sat with them. John Pory, one of the councilors who had recently arrived and been named secretary of the colony, was appointed Speaker. Since he had served for six years in the English

Parliament, the choice was an excellent one. A clerk and a sergeant at arms also were on hand. Parson Buck asked divine blessings upon the Assembly's labors. The oath of supremacy was administered to each burgess, "none staggering at it." (The term "burgess" was used by the Virginia Assembly since that was the term used in England to denote a representative in Parliament of a borough.)

A half-dozen revisions of the "Greate Charter" were enacted by the Assembly. These involved mainly the distribution of land. There were also instructions to the settlers to plant mulberry trees, grapes and hemp, and laws fixing the price of tobacco. Stern enactments against gambling, drunkenness and immorality were passed, and other penalties were imposed for idleness and "excesse in apparell." Everyone was required to attend divine service twice on Sunday. All arms-bearing citizens were directed to bring with them to church "their pieces, swords, powder and shot." Here was evidence that the burgesses were far from assuming that the Indians would remain friendly forever.

But the lawmakers endeavored to promote cordial relations with the redskins. One bit of legislation provided that "no injury or oppression be wrought by the English against the Indians." There was also legislation requiring each town, city, borough and plantation to educate some Indian children "in true religion and civile course of life." The statute stipulated further that "the most towardly boyes in witt and graces of nature" should be "fitted for the Colledge intended for them." This college was to be built in the immediate future at Henrico City, and ten thousand acres of land had been set aside for the purpose.

The humid heat of low-lying Jamestown caused several of the burgesses to become ill, and one, Walter Shelley of Smith's Hundred, died. The ceremonial velvets and silks, and elaborate felt hats, in which they were dressed were murderously unsuited to the summer climate of Tidewater Virginia. The Assemblymen asked that they be pardoned for adjourning so abruptly, but six days of suffering in such clothing in so hot and sodden an atmosphere left them hardly any alternative. After sweating through six days of this, from July 30 to August 4, they went their separate ways, to reconvene the following March. The first legislative assembly on American soil, and in the history of the British Empire, had ended.

Only two or three weeks later there was another event of great significance. About twenty Negroes were brought in, the first of that race to enter Virginia, although a few Negroes had accompanied Spanish explorers. The vessel carrying the blacks to Virginia was owned or controlled by the Earl of Warwick. It was erroneously described by John Rolfe as a "Dutch man-of-war."[3]

Its human cargo consisted not of slaves but of indentured servants. However, the flow of Africans to America had begun, and there would be no stopping it for more than two hundred years. A system of chattel slavery, made inevitable by the mounting traffic in Negroes, and the dependence of the tobacco plantations upon such traffic, was to be the catastrophic result. The Civil War and its tragic aftermath, with consequences which endure to this very hour, lay two and a half centuries in the future. But its seeds were planted at Jamestown in 1619.

The flow of blacks into the colony was negligible at first. Only two Negroes were brought in during the next four years, and it would be several decades before Virginia law formally recognized slavery. But the disastrous trend was under way.

The year 1619 was also notable for the arrival in Virginia of ninety "younge, handsome and honestly educated maydes," sent over by the company for the benefit of such settlers as felt the need of matrimony. Each yeoman who married a maid was required to reimburse the company in tobacco for his wife's passage from England. After arrival of the ninety, a series of other shipments of young women was sent out to Virginia for the solace of lonely bachelors and for the greater stability of the colony. The overall result, in the words of Colonel William Byrd II, was that in early Virginia a spinster was so rare as to be "as ominous as a Blazing star."

Substantial shipments of able-bodied men and their families also were a feature of the year 1619. A total of 1261 persons arrrived in eight vessels, approximately doubling the Virginia population. Included were a hundred boys and girls from London who were sent as apprentices. Many of these were orphans or waifs who were largely destitute, and the motive for transporting them was a humanitarian one. Less welcome were the convicts whom King James insisted be sent to Virginia. They were apparently not numerous, and some were simply shipped to Virginia instead of being confined in jail for debt.

The company was diligent in dispatching men from the European Continent who were believed to be expert in certain industrial and agricultural disciplines. In addition to the Dutchmen and Poles mentioned earlier as glassmakers, Frenchmen were brought in for the promotion of vineyards and silk, Poles for producing pitch and tar, and Italians for grape growing and glassmaking. The Italian glass blowers were among the continentals who did not endear themselves to the English. "A more damned crew hell never vomited," George Sandys, brother of Sir Edwin, exclaimed in a letter from Jamestown. These artisans and agriculturists were never able to produce in accord with the company's expectations.

The indentured servants who were arriving in such large numbers were often persons in good standing in England, even "gentlemen." Some of them quickly worked their way up to positions of responsibility. Seven men listed as servants in Virginia in 1624 were members of the House of Burgesses five years later. Many others were from the "lower orders" and remained so. Perhaps 75 per cent of all immigrants who came in the first fifty years arrived as indentured servants.[4]

The leaders in Virginia during the early years of the century were of good English stock, but none was from the upper reaches of the English aristocracy. No earls or dukes were among them, and they were predominantly from the merchant class. They were men of conspicuous ability, industry and courage, and it was by virtue of these qualities that they rose to dominant positions. But to call many of them Cavaliers, as is sometimes done, is to transgress the eternal verities.

FOUR

A Massacre and a Martinet

RELATIONS between the colonists and the Indians had been almost entirely peaceful since the marriage of John Rolfe and Pocahontas in 1614, and they were apparently becoming even more so as the year 1622 dawned. Some of the English remained suspicious, but Governor Francis Wyatt "solemnly ratified" a peace treaty with the Indians upon taking office late in 1621. The prevailing view was that the natives could be trusted. The settlers showed their trust by lending them their boats, lodging them in their homes, and going about unarmed.

Chief Opechancanough pretended to utmost friendship for the English, and protested that "the sky should fall" before he would perform a hostile act. He was in frequent contact with George Thorpe, a former member of the British Parliament and a deeply religious man, who had sold his estate in England and emigrated to Virginia to convert the heathen. Thorpe was instrumental in having a house built for Opechancanough. The werowance reacted with delight, especially over the novelty of the locks on the doors, "admiring the strangenesse of that Engine, the Lock and Key." He was said to have tested its operation "a hundred times a day."

But ere long, the chieftain was plotting to massacre the English. The latter were thrown off guard by last-minute gestures of friendship.

And then, like a bolt from the heavens, the blow fell at exactly eight o'clock on Good Friday morning, March 22, 1622. With amazing co-ordination and diabolical ferocity the Indians suddenly attacked the settlers for a distance of a hundred and forty miles on both sides of the James, from Hampton Roads to the falls. With tomahawk, club, and scalping knife they slaughtered men, women and children wherever they could be found—as they sat at breakfast, walked about their farms, hoed their crops or fed their cattle, or as they lay in their beds. Many bodies were mangled, and portions were carried off by the rampaging redskins. More than 350 persons of all ages and both sexes perished.

Jamestown and the immediate vicinity escaped through a timely warning given by Chanco, an Indian youth who had been converted to Christianity. Chanco was living with Richard Pace at "Pace's Paines" across the river from Jamestown. He was told by his brother to murder Pace at eight o'clock the next morning as part of the colony-wide plot. But Pace had "used him as a sonne," and Chanco was not only unwilling to carry out the directive, but he rose in the night and revealed the plot to Pace. The latter rowed three miles across the river before dawn and alerted Jamestown. It was put in a posture of defense, and couriers were sent to warn persons in the adjacent area.

Thus the principal settlement in Virginia escaped destruction. However, the devastation wrought elsewhere up and down the James was tremendous. The worst carnage was at Martin's Hundred, only seven miles from Jamestown, where a warning could not be given in time, and seventy-six were slain. At Edward Bennett's plantation across the river, fifty-two were killed, and at Falling Creek, far upstream where iron works had been established, the works were wrecked and twenty-seven persons were stabbed, shot, clubbed or tomahawked to death. Berkeley Hundred, settled in 1619, and the scene of the first regularly scheduled annual Thanksgiving service on American soil, was virtually wiped out.[1]

At Henrico Town, where a college primarily for the benefit of the Indians was under construction, twenty-two whites were killed, some of the completed or partially completed buildings were burned, and the enterprise was brought to a standstill. The destruction was not total, for sixty persons were living there slightly more than a year later.[2] Yet the college could never be revived. Furthermore, a plan for the erection of a free school in Charles City for the education of white children had to be abandoned.

There were notable examples of bravery on the part of persons who were attacked on isolated plantations. In a number of instances they were able to drive off the Indians. Conspicuous among these was "Mrs. Proctor, a proper, civil, modest gentlewoman," who not only

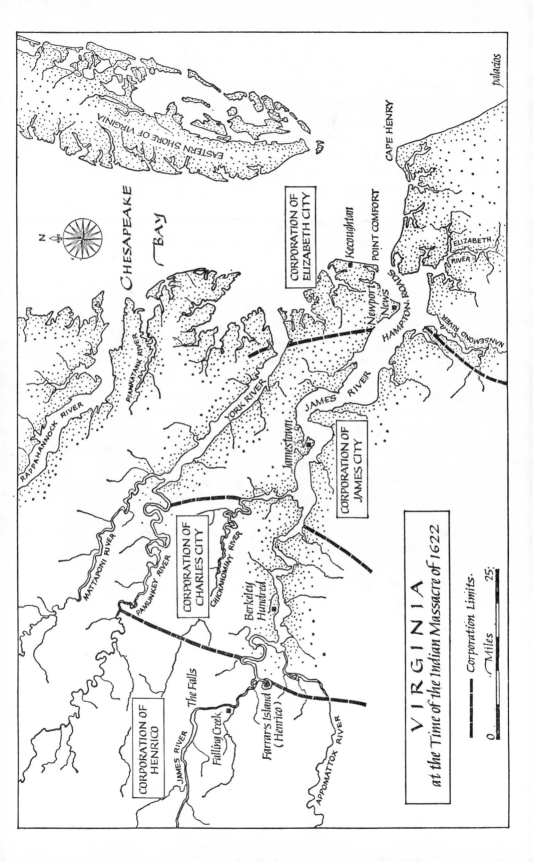

VIRGINIA
at the Time of the Indian Massacre of 1622

━━━ *Corporation Limits.*

Miles

0   25.

CHESAPEAKE *Bay*

EASTERN SHORE OF VIRGINIA

N

CORPORATION OF ELIZABETH CITY

Kecoughtan

POINT COMFORT

Newport News

HAMPTON ROADS

CAPE HENRY

ELIZABETH RIVER

NANSEMOND RIVER

JAMES RIVER

CORPORATION OF JAMES CITY

Jamestown

YORK RIVER

PIANKATANK RIVER

RAPPAHANNOCK RIVER

MATTAPONI RIVER

PAMUNKEY RIVER

CHICKAHOMINY RIVER

CORPORATION OF CHARLES CITY

Berkeley Hundred

CORPORATION OF HENRICO

The Falls

JAMES RIVER

Falling Creek

Farrar's Island (*Henrico*)

APPOMATTOX RIVER

Palacios

fought off her assailants and defended her family but insisted on remaining at her homestead. Indeed, her insistence was such that she disregarded orders from Jamestown to bring her family to a central and more easily defended place. It was not until the authorities threatened to burn her house that she consented to leave it.

Most of the surviving settlers were only too happy to obey the directives from Jamestown, and to come together in areas which could be readily defended.

It is noteworthy that the Indians did not harm any of the score of Negroes in Virginia. However, they not only killed hundreds of whites, including several councilors; they also burned numerous houses and drove off large numbers of cattle. It was the planting season, but settlers ordered from their farms and plantations found it impossible to put in crops. The massacre was a shattering blow to the colony.

The English, quite understandably, reacted in a fury of revenge. Expeditions against the Indians were organized and carried out ruthlessly. Gone were plans for peaceful relations. Not only were the redskins slain wherever found, but their villages and crops were destroyed. When the elusive natives could not be overtaken, the colonist concentrated on burning their villages and corn.

Agreement appeared rather general with the extraordinary sentiments expressed in a work published contemporaneously in England, entitled *Good Speed in Virginia*. The author declared that "the savages have no particular propertie in any part or parcell of that countrey, but only a generall residencie there, as wild beasts have in the forests."

George Sandys, treasurer of the colony, led the first expedition against the Indians. He termed them "swift as Roebucks" and added, "like the violent lightning they are gone as soon as perceived." (Sandys was not only a competent colonial leader; he was also one of the leading poets of his era. At the time of the Indian uprising, he was engaged in translating Ovid's *Metamorphoses* into English verse, an achievement which enlisted the admiration of John Dryden. Sandys also translated the First Book of Virgil's *Aeneid*. Alexander Pope praised his poetical talents.)

The settlers carried out their raids against the Indians despite the fact that their own ranks were grievously depleted by illness and hunger, as well as by the loss of nearly one-third of their number in the massacre. Disease was still taking a heavy toll, and the toll became far heavier during the winter of 1622–23, when no fewer than five hundred died from an outbreak of "pestilent fever" and other maladies. The virulence of disease among the colonists was greatly augmented by the near starvation resulting from the meagre plantings in the previous spring and the driving away of the cattle by the Indians. One distraught settler wrote his family in England that he had often eaten more at home in a day than he was able to consume that winter in a week.

Disease was brought to the colony in what were called "pestered" ships. These vessels often were germ-laden and wholly unsanitary; in one instance a ship lost 130 of its 180 passengers and crew on the way to Virginia. On arrival, it doubtless spread the lethal malady to the mainland.

Another problem was attacked by Governor Wyatt in 1624. He suggested that colonists bring over "a proportion of mault . . . to make themselves beer, that the sudden drinking of water cause not too great alteration in their bodyes."

On the other hand, an English brewer named Dupper was said to have provided the colonists with beer which was actually fatal to many. A letter from Jamestown at this time declared that "the country will be pleased to hear that revenge has been taken of Dupper for his stinking beer, which has been the death of two hundred persons."

The ghastly mortality figures for the entire period from 1607 through 1624 are almost incredible. In February 1625, only 1095 settlers were alive in Virginia of the 7549 who had come to the colony. In other words, not one in six had survived.[3] The death rate was less staggering thereafter, but for many years Virginia was a hazardous place in which to live. The wonder is that the colony avoided total collapse. That it did so is a tribute to the fortitude, endurance and courage of the men and women who carried on despite these truly epochal ordeals.

The colonists also had to cope with the hostility of King James. He did not believe in popular government, and he made clear his lack of sympathy for the establishment of a legislative assembly in Virginia.

James determined in 1624 to dissolve the Virginia Company and to make Virginia a royal colony. This was achieved through an order from the Court of King's Bench. Sir Francis Wyatt was reappointed governor, and was directed to govern with the aid of a newly named council. No provision was made for a General Assembly.

And then, early in 1625, King James died. His successor, Charles I, approved his father's action in making Virginia a royal colony, but he was more favorably disposed toward the colony's adventure in popular government. Yet he dillydallied for a decade and a half before granting authority to the Virginians for the permanent establishment of their lawmaking body. During several of these years, the Assembly met only spasmodically and for brief periods, and then, in 1629, it began holding annual sessions without specific authorization. Finally, in 1639 the royal imprimatur was placed upon Virginia's House of Burgesses and council as the continuing legislative arm of the colonial government. Thus, in the words of Charles M. Andrews, the eminent New England historian and authority on the colonial era:

"The principle was finally laid down that a royal colony should be, in part at least, a self-administering community, with a governor and council appointed in England and a representative assembly chosen by the freemen or freeholders in the colony . . . a factor of vast consequence in the development of American political practices."

The Assembly and council were soon to demonstrate exceptional intrepidity in the face of serious provocations from a governor who was a notorious martinet with a largely uncontrolled temper.

This was Governor John Harvey, who succeeded Dr. John Pott as chief executive of the colony. Pott was a convivial soul, and a somewhat mysterious character, who is said, among other things, to have poisoned a number of Indians in the course of the running fight between the colonists and the natives. Pott got into a controversy with Harvey when the latter took over the government—the first of numerous controversies in which Harvey became embroiled. If Pott had not been the only physician in the colony, it would have gone quite hard with him, but his indispensability caused the governor and the king to forego the imposition of heavy penalties.

In the spring of 1635, Harvey had a head-on clash with the council. There had been rumblings of popular discontent against him for several years. Some of this concerned the decision to award Maryland the ownership of Kent Island in Chesapeake Bay, despite the claims of Virginia. (Maryland had been settled the preceding year. Other colonies in existence in 1635 were Massachusetts, settled in 1620; New York, 1621; New Hampshire, 1623; Maine, 1624; and Connecticut, 1635.) Harvey had been instructed by the Crown to further Maryland's cause, and he had done so. The ruling in favor of Maryland was vigorously disapproved throughout Virginia.

The revolt against him reached a climax following certain events in York County. Speeches were delivered there in sharp criticism of the governor, and he flew into one of his rages. He had a number of the leaders arrested, and when they demanded to know the charges against them, Harvey retorted that they would have an answer "at the gallows."

The governor summoned the council, and demanded that the offenders in York County be tried under martial law. The council insisted on the customary legal procedures. Whereupon His Excellency engaged in a vehement dispute with that arm of the government, during which he punched Councilor Menefie and exclaimed: "I arrest you on suspicion of treason to His Majesty!" "And wee the like to you, Sir!" retorted Councilor Samuel Mathews, as he and Councilor John Utie seized the governor. Dr. Pott signaled through a window, and forty musketeers surrounded the house. Finally, both sides cooled off a bit, and the councilors agreed to Harvey's demand that they put their grievances in writing.

The result of all this was that the governor departed in alarm for England—the so-called "thrusting out of Sir John Harvey." On his arrival there, the charges against him were aired. He admitted that he had assumed authority over the council, but denied that he had exceeded his prerogatives in this or in other respects. He succeeded in convincing the authorities in England of his innocence, and was given a new commission as governor in 1636. He returned to Virginia early in the following year.

Governor Harvey's clashes with the council were due, in part, to the fact that the councilors were themselves determined and not always reasonable men. The councilors, furthermore, were anxious that the Crown issue "confirmation of theire lands and priviledges," which one recent observer terms "the true motive for the mutiny."[4]

Richard L. Morton points out that Harvey had some genuine achievements to his credit, such as developing local (county) government, diversifying crops, and erecting a palisade about four miles long from the James to the York as a protection against Indians. This barrier fenced off a huge area at the lower end of the peninsula in which cattle and hogs could be confined, and where they would be largely immune from Indian raids.

Harvey's accomplishments were often overlooked as he brawled with the council—knocking out Councilor Richard Stephens' teeth "with a cudgel," and otherwise conducting himself in an unseemly manner. The council, for its part, is to be credited with putting up a courageous fight against the governor's arbitrary exercise of authority. The members admitted that they were anxious to retain their "lands and priviledges." Yet they were also zealous in the protection of the ancient liberties for which Englishmen have died over the centuries.

The Virginia frontier was being pushed forward into the wilderness during these years. Roads of a rudimentary character were threading the forest clearings and traversing the river valleys. Relatively comfortable houses were being built beside the shimmering James and York, which were beautifully clear streams in that day, and along Chesapeake Bay. By 1635 the population of the colony was just under five thousand.

County government, as previously noted, was inaugurated during this period, under the somewhat lurid ministrations of Governor Harvey. The General Assembly of 1634 divided the colony into eight shires or counties, similar to those in England. They were Henrico, Charles City, James City, Warwick River (later Warwick), Charles River (York), Warrosquoake (Isle of Wight), Elizabeth City and Accomack.

County courts were created. County commissioners, later known as justices of the peace, were appointed by the governor and council, along with sheriffs, constables, clerks and coroners. A jury trial was available to any defendant. Convictions could be appealed to the General Court, on which sat the governor and council, or to the General Assembly (consisting of the burgesses and the council). Justices of the peace not only tried cases but performed various other duties, such as fixing rates on ferries, regulating the price of liquor and laying out parishes. They received no pay—only expenses, but the office, like that of sheriff, carried great prestige. Both posts were usually held by recognized leaders.

Members of the House of Burgesses were the only colonial officials who were elected by popular vote during the entire colonial era. All freemen were eligible to cast ballots in these elections from 1619 to 1670, with the exception of the year 1655, when the franchise was restricted to freeholders (owners of real estate). The following year it was restored to all freemen. Voting requirements were tightened in 1670, and the franchise was limited to freeholders and householders.

During Bacon's Rebellion (1676) the law was changed again to give the vote to freemen, but then Bacon's Laws were repealed, and only freeholders were made eligible for the franchise. This restriction remained in effect until long after the American Revolution.

Since the Church of England was the official state church—in colonial Virginia, as in the mother country—there was much interlocking of the political and ecclesiastical structures. The leading families dominated in both areas, and there was frequent overlapping. For several decades in the mid-seventeenth century the powerful vestries in the Episcopal churches were self-perpetuating, thus giving these families an even firmer grip on positions of leadership. The importance of the churches was accentuated by the fact that in a completely rural colony, with Jamestown the only place that qualified even as a small village, the churches provided one of the few centers of social life, with their services, weddings and funerals. Other meeting places for the people were at the race tracks, at the general muster of the militia, and on county court day.

Discipline for members of the Established Church was maintained through laws covering misbehavior. For example, one Henry Coleman was excommunicated for forty days "for using scornful speeches and putting on his hat in church." Thomas Tindall was sentenced "to be pillory'd for two hours for giving my Lord Baltimore the lye and threatening to knock him down."

Difficulties evidently were being experienced at that early date with some of the Episcopal clergy. A statute was passed providing that "Mynisters shall not give themselves to excesse in drinking, or ryott, spending their tyme idellye by day and night, playing at dice, cards of any other unlawful game."

The minister of each parish was chosen by the vestry. The vestrymen were also responsible for preferring charges against any cleric who became unduly bibulous or excessively addicted to such extracurricular activities as horse racing or cockfighting.

Morals of the laity were supposedly scrutinized by two churchwardens, chosen by the vestry. The churchwardens were charged with the duty of preventing "ungodly disorders," including "skandalous offenses such as suspicions of whoredoms, dishonest company keeping with women and such like . . . or other enormous sinnes."

FIVE

Governor Berkeley's Golden Years

IN THE YEAR 1642, there came upon the Virginia scene a major figure of the colonial era, Sir William Berkeley. Then thirty-four years of age, a talented playwright and magnetic personality, a member of an ancient family, who had served in the King's Privy Chamber, Sir William was to dominate the colony for more than a quarter of a century.

He succeeded the able Sir Francis Wyatt, who had been brought back into the governorship for some eighteen months, following the departure of Governor Harvey, who was finally ousted by His Majesty's Privy Council.

Governor Berkeley exhibited statesmanship of a high order during the early years of his administration. He quickly made it clear that he would not indulge in reprisals against the leaders who had risked their necks by grappling with the choleric Harvey. Not only so, but he ingratiated himself with all classes by demonstrating an unselfish attitude with respect to his own personal fortunes, and an active concern for the well-being of the poor yeomen as well as for the better-circumstanced members of society.

Berkeley encouraged crop diversification and set a good example himself by planting flax, cotton and rice. He experimented with silkworm culture, and managed to produce in the colony three hundred pounds of silk, which he presented to King Charles.

But only two years after he took office a near-disaster struck. The Indians suddenly swooped down with tomahawk, gun and scalping knife, and killed even more men, women and children than they had in 1622. In excess of five hundred were butchered in this holocaust, which occurred on Holy Thursday, April 18, 1644. Once again in the devious brain of Opechancanough a plot had been hatched. He was now an aged and feeble man who was carried about on a litter, and whose eyelids had to be raised by his attendants, in order for him to see. But he was mentally keen and grimly determined to kill every Englishman in Virginia.

Fortunately, Jamestown and the other well-fortified settlements were too strong to be overwhelmed by the redskins and too alert to be taken by stealth. Frontier settlements near the heads of the rivers and below the James were more vulnerable, and they felt the full brunt of the attack, but the colony was too well-populated in 1644 to be wiped out.

Governor Berkeley, a man without fear, took the field at once against the Indians. He led several expeditions, and many of the natives were slain, their villages burned and their corn crops destroyed. Opechancanough was captured and taken to Jamestown. Berkeley planned to carry him to England and exhibit him to the king. However, a common soldier "basely shot him thro' the Back," in revenge for the dreadful suffering he had brought upon the colony. The Indians sued for peace shortly thereafter.

The second, and last, great massacre in the colony's history seriously disrupted various plans and programs, including one for the exploration of the interior. Four men, Walter Austin, Rice Hoe, Joseph Johnson and Walter Chiles had petitioned the General Assembly in 1641 for permission to "undertake the discovery of a new river or unknowne land bearing west southerly" from the Appomattox River. Two years later, after the coming of Governor Berkeley, the Assembly granted them any profits they might make for the next fourteen years, the Crown retaining the "royal fifth" from any mines that might be discovered.

The massacre seems to have prevented the four men from pursuing their plan. However, a precedent had been set, and similar trade monopolies were established for others in subsequent legislation.

The Indian uprising did contribute indirectly to the launching of the exploratory career of Abraham Wood, one of the extraordinary men of seventeenth-century Virginia. The Assembly provided in 1645 for several forts for protection, and Captain Wood was put in command of Fort Henry, on the site of the present City of Petersburg. It was garrisoned with forty-five men.

Wood had come over from England as a boy, and been apprenticed to Captain Samuel Mathews, one of the great planters of that era. After completing his apprenticeship, young Wood advanced rapidly. At the time of his death in 1680 he had served for about two dozen years on the council, and had risen to the rank of major general of militia. He spent some thirty years at Fort Henry, which became one of the principal colonial trading posts. From Fort Henry, at the confluence of the Appomattox and James, expeditions of traders and explorers sallied forth into the back country for hundreds of miles.

Abraham Wood's contribution to the opening up of the frontier areas was exceptional, and one authority declares that "the history of westward expansion during the period is almost a biography of this remarkable man." Wood discovered and named the New River in 1654. He also sent out the expedition in 1671, under Captain Thomas Batts, which crossed the Allegheny Mountains through the gap formed by the New River a few miles north of the present City of Radford. Some anonymous and mysterious whites had preceded him, as was evidenced by letters and other "scratchments" cut into the bark of trees, but the Batts expedition was the first to leave a written record of a crossing of the Allegheny divide.

Governor Berkeley was active in furthering these excursions into the back country. He not only encouraged Abraham Wood; he also supported John Lederer, a German who spent a couple of years in Virginia and made several attempts to cross the Blue Ridge. In 1669, he reached the top of the range, apparently somewhere in Madison County, from which point he viewed the Alleghenies rising mistily beyond the Valley of Virginia. Another expedition the following year produced similar results. Unlike Governor Spotswood's jaunty "Knights of the Golden Horseshoe," who crossed the mountains nearly half a century later, Lederer never got beyond the summit of the Blue Ridge.

The mid-seventeenth century not only marked the launching of significant exploration; it was also the period when several notable emigrants, representing families which were later to assume positions of conspicuous leadership, came to Virginia. Among these were the first Carters, Lees, Randolphs and Byrds. John Carter, Richard Lee and Henry Randolph arrived in the colony in the 1640s, after civil war broke out in England. The first William Byrd arrived somewhat later. All were apparently from substantial and cultured English backgrounds. All rose quickly to posts of political and social importance.

These were among the foremost of approximately one hundred families whose members intermarried frequently over the years, and dominated the public life of colonial and revolutionary Virginia for some two centuries. Others who were conspicuously influential were the Harrisons, Pages, Wormeleys, Burwells, Masons, Beverleys, Grymseses, Carys, Nelsons, Diggeses, Ludwells and Fitzhughs. As an example of how a single marriage involving such families could affect the life of the colony, the commonwealth and the nation, consider the direct descendants of William Randolph of "Turkey Island" and Mary Isham of "Bermuda Hundred," who were wed in the middle 1670s. The list includes Thomas Jefferson, John Marshall, and Robert E. Lee, not to mention "Light-Horse Harry" Lee, Edmund Randolph, Peyton Randolph and John Randolph of Roanoke.

The first Byrd—William I—reached Virginia about 1670. He had been preceded in the 1630s by his grandfather, Thomas Stegg, a prominent merchant and ship captain engaged in the Virginia trade. Stegg's daughter, Grace, married John Byrd, a London goldsmith. Stegg was drowned in 1651, and the following year his grandson, William Byrd, was born. As the boy grew older, he went to live in Virginia with his uncle, Thomas Stegg, Jr., who made Byrd his heir. Thus Byrd inherited Stegg's estate at the latter's death. Byrd married the daughter of a Cavalier officer, Mary Horsmanden, which gave him added prestige.

William Byrd was a man of unusual practical ability and business acumen. He set himself up promptly as an Indian trader at "the falls," on the site of present-day Richmond—at that time on the outer edge of civilization. For more than a third of a century he sent traders into the wilderness, over aboriginal trails, as much as five hundred miles to the country of the Cherokees and Catawbas in what are now North and South Carolina. Byrd traded the natives such commodities as rum, guns, ammunition, cloth, kettles and hatchets in return for deerskins, beaver skins, furs, rare herbs and what he hoped were valuable minerals. At times Byrd and his associate traders had as many as a hundred horses in a single pack train. Byrd also dealt extensively in tobacco, indentured servants and Negro slaves. The African slave traffic was then rising in volume.

When he and other frontier traders operated over the wilderness trails to far-flung settlements, they not only had to guard against Indian attacks; they also passed through forests wherein roamed bears, panthers and wolves. The timber wolves—like the panthers long since extinct in Virginia—were fierce, and they sometimes hunted in packs, attacking horses, cows, sheep and swine. Wolves were numerous all over the colony, and they preyed on livestock to such an extent that bounties were offered for their pelts. These bounties were paid over a period of at least two hundred years.[1]

Conditions at the falls of the James, at Fort Henry and other such outposts were decidedly primitive, but at Jamestown and on the plantations of lower Tidewater a better scale of living prevailed. While modern conveniences were, of course, non-existent, and sanitary arrangements left much to be desired, frame or brick houses, of modest dimensions and no architectural distinction,[2] were the habitations of the more prosperous citizens. The vast majority, the yeomen or small farmers—about whom too little has been written—lived in one- or two-room frame dwellings.

Governor Berkeley's brick manor house at Green Spring, some three miles from Jamestown, was the most famous residence in seventeenth-century Virginia. It contained "eight or nine ground floor rooms, two of which were basements," and various outbuildings. Nothing is known of its external appearance.

Hospitality, even to strangers, was widespread in Virginia during the century and was offered by all classes. This is testified to by Robert Beverley, for example, who wrote that a traveler needed no other recommendation than that he was a "human creature." Upon arriving at a "gentleman's seat," if the master happened to be absent, the wayfarer "was certain to find that the servants had received orders to set before strangers the very best that the plantation had to offer." Beverley added that "even the poor planters, who have but one bed, will very often sit up or lie upon a form or couch all night to make room for a weary traveler." The General Assembly actually passed a law in 1663 providing that if an innkeeper failed to advise a guest in advance that a charge would be made, there could be none, irrespective of the length of the stay.[3]

Inns and taverns were not only stopping places for travelers; they were also places where guests, whether of high or low degree, diverted themselves. Tenpins was one of the most popular forms of amusement in these caravanserais, and gambling games involving cards and dice were others.

Most popular of all divertissements in seventeenth-century Virginia was horse racing. It too was surrounded by a great deal of betting.

But the cleavage between the classes was made glaringly evident in 1673 when a famous episode occurred in York County. One James Bullock, a tailor, entered his horse in a race against Mathew Slader, a "gentleman," and wagered two thousand pounds of tobacco on the outcome. Poor Bullock was arrested and fined a hundred pounds of tobacco for his virtually unprecedented presumption. Horse racing, the county justices ruled, was a "sport for gentlemen alone," in which no laboring man could legally participate.

And yet there were numerous instances during this period in which men of humble beginnings quickly rose to places of influence—in the House of Burgesses and elsewhere. In fact, the development of a strong and vigorous middle class was one of the striking phenomena of the colony's first half-century. These small, independent farmers constituted a great source of strength.

It is important also to note that despite such episodes as that involving the tailor who didn't "know his place," there was, in general, a much greater social acceptance of members of the crafts and trades, both in England and America in that era than there was later. As for the merchants, they enjoyed an even more complete acceptance; many of the ranking planters were descended from them, and themselves performed mercantile functions. In not a few instances, however, these planters traced their pedigrees back to England's landed proprietors.

In view of the fate of the York County tailor who got out of line, one seems justified in interpreting the prevailing attitude in Virginia to mean that so long as a man remained a practitioner of such a trade or craft as tailoring, he was expected to show proper deference to his betters. When he had worked his way up and become a significant owner of land, he was entitled to exercise the privileges and prerogatives of the gentry.

These prerogatives included, among other things, the wearing of clothes which today seem exceptionally garish, especially for males. The men of that day were arrayed in such items as collars of rich lace, embroidered doublets (sometimes made of "camlet," a combination of camel's hair and silk); incredible garments known as

"petticoat trousers," hose lined with a type of crinoline called "bombast," scarves edged with gold lace, steeple hats of beaver or wide-
brimmed hats of felt, often with a feather in the brim; shoes with
silver buckles, and swords with gilt belts. Occasionally the gallant
exhibited a lovelock or tress over one ear, curled and tied with a
ribbon, a keepsake for the object of his affections. And in one instance
a particularly foppish gentleman boasted of "an Eare-Ring with a
diamond in itt."

The ladies also wore spectacular raiment, which is not too surprising. It included the amazing farthingale, an enormous hoop skirt.
There were, of course, silk and flowered gowns, bodices of green
satin or blue linen, petticoats trimmed with silver lace, calico hoods
and scarves, crimson taffeta mantles, laced and "gallooned" shoes,
richly decorated fans, bonnets trimmed in silver lace and heaven
knows what else, and a variety of lavish diamond and pearl jewelry
set in silver or gold.

So much for the gaudily-bedight gentry of the seventeenth century
and their ladies. As for their diet, once the fatal food shortage of
the early years was surmounted, they could usually count on setting
a table fit for an epicure. Every gentleman was a huntsman, so that
the vast herds of wild deer supplied venison in virtually unlimited
quantities. Ducks, geese, turkeys and quail were similarly ready to
hand, as well as oysters and fish. Cows, chickens, sheep and hogs
were raised by almost everyone. Many varieties of vegetables and
fruits were grown, the forests provided chestnuts and walnuts, and
the bees honey. Homemade beer was the most popular drink, but
apple and peach brandy were widely distilled. European wines were
in the cellars of leading planters, and such vintages were likewise
available in the inns, even those frequented by the less prosperous
farmers. And such farmers, in normal times, were also in no danger
of starvation, if they were willing to work, as nearly all of them
were.

The privileges and prerogatives of the gentry in the political sphere
were extremely far-reaching. The same official often exercised so many
functions that he frequently supervised his own operations, a situation
in some ways nothing short of comical.

Louis B. Wright, whose writings on the colonial era are among
the most engaging and perceptive that we have, says concerning the
members of the Council of State: "Their power was so great and

their offices and duties so multifarious that a recital of them sounds like a burlesque of government in a Gilbert and Sullivan opera." He quotes Philip Alexander Bruce with respect to the overlapping of various offices and the temptations to which their occupants were subjected:

"The members of the Council appropriated to themselves all those higher offices . . . which were attended with the largest salaries, or presented the most numerous chances of money-getting. They deliberately disregarded the fact that the concentration of these offices in so few hands brought about serious damage to the public interests whenever the Councilor was required by his incumbency of two separate positions to perform two sets of duties really in conflict with each other; a Councilor, for instance, was called upon to pass upon the correctness of his own accounts as collector; . . . as a farmer of the quitrents he practically owed the success of his bid to himself as a Councilor; as an escheator, who was a ministerial officer, he took and returned the inquisitions of escheats to himself as a judicial officer, and as such passed upon points of law coming up in his own inquisitions."

Thomas J. Wertenbaker, another colonial historian of notable distinction, puts matters more bluntly. He writes:

"In their political capacity the leading men of the colony were frequently guilty of inexcusable and open fraud. Again and again they made use of their great influence and power to appropriate public funds to their private use, to escape the payment of taxes, and to obtain under false pretenses vast tracts of land."

As an example, Wertenbaker cites the case of Colonel Philip Ludwell, who had brought to the colony 40 immigrants, which at 50 acres per immigrant entitled him to 2000 acres. Ludwell "changed the record with his own hand by adding one cipher each to the 40 and 2000, respectively." This enabled him to get "ten times as much land as he was entitled to."

Wertenbaker declares, however, that such thieveries were far less prevalent in Virginia during the late eighteenth century and throughout the nineteenth century. "A high sense of honor," he writes, "became eventually one of the most pronounced characteristics of the Virginians."

SIX

Requiem for a Rebel

THE OUTBREAK of Civil War in England in 1642 provoked a violent reaction from Sir William Berkeley. The young governor had just taken office in Virginia, and he was completely loyal to the Crown. He not only expressed himself in strong language; he was instrumental in obtaining from the General Assembly a vigorous condemnation of the English Puritans, led by Oliver Cromwell.

Berkeley encouraged Cavalier sympathizers to come to Virginia for refuge, and they did so in substantial numbers. Among them were the first Lees, Carters, Randolphs and Masons. While a goodly number of the immigrants who arrived at that time were representatives of the landed gentry in England, few were from the ranking nobility. In the sense that most Englishmen who came to Virginia during this period sided with the Cavaliers in the Civil War, they were entitled to be called "Cavaliers."

The beheading of King Charles in 1649 roused Governor Berkeley to fury. Later in that year the General Assembly, meeting at Jamestown, proclaimed Prince Charles king, and declared that anyone who disagreed was guilty of high treason. In the face of this defiant gesture, the English Parliament, dominated by Cromwell, was conciliatory. It sent four moderate commissioners to Virginia, with instructions to seek an agreement from the colony to submit peaceably to the Commonwealth Government. The agreement was achieved. Berkeley gave up the governorship in 1652, but continued to live at Green Spring. Richard Bennett, Edward Digges and Samuel Mathews, Jr., were elected, successively, as governor by the General Assembly, and served until the Restoration. When Charles II ascended the throne in 1660, Berkeley was re-elected governor by the Assembly. He was also appointed by the Crown.

In the following year, 1661, a fateful decision was made by the Virginia General Assembly. It legalized Negro slavery. The legislature of Massachusetts had taken similar action in 1641 and that of Connecticut in 1650. Many New Englanders were to make fortunes in the African slave trade.

The number of slaves in Virginia had risen to two thousand by 1671, according to Governor Berkeley, who said the overall population of the colony was forty thousand. White indentured servants totaled about six thousand. Berkeley added that "not above two or three ships of Negroes in seven years" had come to Virginia. But the trend was under way.

The planters would almost certainly have preferred to work their estates with white tenants, as in England.[1] However, their tobacco plantations, which constituted the economic lifeblood of the colony, could be much more readily operated with slave labor; in fact, it became virtually impossible to work the large plantations profitably on any other basis. The cost of maintaining an adequate force of white indentured servants was prohibitively high, for they "struck out" on their own as soon as they had completed their terms, and other laborers had to be found. Slave ships were bringing Negroes in from Africa in larger and larger numbers, despite the barbarities involved, and these slaves would furnish cheap labor as long as they lived and were able to work. The temptation was too great for the planters. It was an age when slave systems were not regarded with the revulsion felt against such systems today by all civilized peoples.

Slavery was, of course, an institution of long and recognized standing in Africa.[2] Many of the Negroes brought to America by force had been chattels in their native habitat. It would be difficult to imagine a more brutal system than that which prevailed widely in Africa. Princes, tribal chiefs or other potentates in Guinea or neighboring countries regularly sold Negroes on the coast to Dutch, British or New England traders whose slave ships anchored there. African leaders either seized the blacks, often far inland, or they sold to the traders Negroes who were enslaved already. Consider the following from *The Negro in Our History* by two leading black scholars, Carter G. Woodson and Charles H. Wesley:

"The slaves thus purchased [by foreign traders] had been driven to the coast in coffles, sometimes for distances of more than one thousand miles. They had to cross a country which had practically no facilities for transportation except those with which nature had endowed it. And it was necessary to go most of the way walking, and as the means of subsistence were not always to be secured, many of the captives dropped dead from thirst and famine. Those who succeeded in surviving . . . were presented for sale on arrival, only to face other horrors of the 'middle passage.'"

Those horrors were, indeed, almost beyond imagining, but the Negroes who were alive when a slave ship docked on our shores faced further ordeals. The "seasoning" that had laid whites low by the thousands in Virginia in earlier years was even more fatal to the blacks. As explained by Dr. Wyndham B. Blanton, "disease played a part . . . but far harder for him [the Negro] to bear was the change of diet, the difference in climate and clothes, and the hard work." Blanton adds that probably "far more than half of the Negroes caught in Africa" died in the first three years in Virginia.

However, in referring to "hard work," Dr. Blanton does not mean to say that slaves were often subjected to inhuman treatment by the planters. On the contrary, he points out that "even if there had been no law to protect sick slaves from cruel masters, economic motives made it very necessary to keep Negroes in good health."[3] The blacks were simply not accustomed to the type of work that they were called on to do on the plantations, mainly in the tobacco fields.

It is around those fields that the entire plantation economy revolved, with far-reaching implications for the business, political, social and religious life of the Old Dominion. The significance of the "joviall weed" in the development not only of Virginia but of the nation is strikingly set forth by Joseph C. Robert in his The Story of Tobacco in America:

"The staple guaranteed the permanence of the Virginia settlement; created the pattern of the Southern plantation; encouraged the introduction of Negro slavery, then softened the institution; begot an immortal group of colonial leaders; strained the bonds between mother country and Chesapeake colonies; burdened the diplomacy of the post-Revolutionary period; promoted the Louisiana Purchase; and, after the Civil War, helped create the New South."

Not only Virginia but England came to depend on the revenue

derived from tobacco, and this sealed the fate of all efforts in the colony to produce other raw or finished materials in quantity. The infant industries for turning out iron and glass products never prospered, and such commodities as pitch, tar, turpentine, potash and silk were produced only in minuscule lots. The scale of wages for the type of skilled labor which worked in these industries was much higher than that prevailing in competing countries of northern Europe. But the basic reason why none of these efforts succeeded was that tobacco pre-empted the center of the stage, and everything else was subordinated to it.

The result was that Virginia developed a one-crop economy. When tobacco prices were high, there was prosperity; when they were low, there was genuine suffering among the smaller planters and much hardship and dissatisfaction among the larger ones.

In the two decades following the restoration of Charles II in 1660, tobacco was in a severe depression. This was due, in large measure, to the passage by an English Parliament unappreciative of Virginia's loyalty to the Crown, of the Navigation Acts, which seriously restricted Virginia's foreign market for the leaf. The results were devastating to the planters. Governor Berkeley protested loudly but to no avail. Limitations such as the Navigation Acts imposed, requiring that all Virginia and Maryland tobacco be shipped to England, rather than to the continent, and that it pay a special duty to the king, remained in effect, with slight variations, throughout the colonial era.

Tobacco, unfortunately, exhausted the soil, adding to the problems of the growers. Only three or four crops could be raised on a given piece of land, after which other fields had to be cleared. This put a premium on the possession of extensive tracts, and tended to favor the large-scale operators, with their numerous slaves. The result was a greater and greater concentration of the tobacco plantations in a few hands.

To the woes of the planters caused by the Navigation Acts must be added several others. Storms, rains, hurricanes, hail—with stones "as bigg as Turkey Eggs"—and floods of great magnitude, wrecked countless homes and farms in 1667, played havoc with tobacco and grain crops, and killed many cattle and hogs. From ten to fifteen thousand houses were blown down, according to estimates, and at least two-thirds of the crops were destroyed. On top of all else, England declared war on Holland, and the Dutch seized several ships loaded with Virginia leaf.

A few years later, in 1673, war broke out again between England and Holland, and the Dutch captured eleven Virginia tobacco ships destined for Europe. On top of all else, a virulent plague among the colony's cattle wiped out some fifty thousand animals—more than half of the entire number that had survived the hurricanes, storms and floods of 1667. As a result of all this, many Virginians were living in poverty and rags.

Governor Berkeley was not to blame for these calamities, and he exerted himself to prevent or ameliorate them. However, he was by then a different type of person from the youthful governor who had won all hearts three decades before. He had changed, with advancing years, into a much less appealing individual. As he grew older, Sir William used the great power which was concentrated already in his office to browbeat and punish those who disagreed with him.

He had never married, but in 1670, at age sixty-four, he ended his long bachelorhood and was wed to Frances Culpeper, aged thirty-six, the attractive widow of Captain Samuel Stephens of Warwick County. Criticism of the aging governor continued; indeed, his marriage seemed, if anything, to increase it. In the words of one of his subjects, "Old Governor Barkly [had been] altered by marrying a young wyff from his wonted public good."

It was in 1671 that Berkeley made the statement for which he is best known, and which has damaged colonial Virginia in the eyes of the world. Replying to a questionnaire sent him by the Lords Commissioners of Foreign Plantations, he declared: "I thank God there are no free schools nor printing, and I hope we shall not have these hundred years; for learning has brought disobedience, and heresy and sects into the world, and printing has divulged them, and libels against the best government. God keep us from both!"

This notorious declaration was as remarkable for its arrogance as for its inaccuracy. While there was, indeed, no printing press in Virginia at that time—few existed anywhere else in the American colonies—it was preposterous to say that there were "no free schools." While the exclusively rural nature of the colony made it impossible to operate a free school system comparable to that established, for example, in much more thickly settled New England, several free schools were operating in Virginia at the time of Berkeley's assertion.

(The township system in New England contrasted with the plantation system in the South, and in the Middle Colonies the people tended to live on small farms or in small towns.)

The two best-known free schools in Virginia were in Elizabeth City County—endowed in 1635 and 1649, respectively, by Benjamin Syms and Thomas Eaton. These small schools for the benefit of poor children continued in operation until 1805, when they were consolidated into Hampton Academy. Furthermore, Robert Beverley referred in his *History and Present State of Virginia* (1705) to the "large tracts of land, houses and other things granted to free schools for the education of children in many parts of the country," namely Virginia. The records show that Beverley's statement was justified. It should be noted, however, that these were "charity schools," i.e., supported by the contributions of an individual or individuals, and not by public taxation.[4]

The ruling class of large planters relied on tutors for the instruction of their own children, and some sent them to England to complete their education—although the number thus sent abroad for schooling was much larger in the eighteenth century. But the well-to-do planters were not oblivious to the needs of the less fortunate children. It will be recalled that plans for a free school in Charles City and a college in Henrico were thwarted by the Indian massacre of 1622. In 1661 the General Assembly passed an act creating a free school and a college, but for one reason or another there were no tangible results. The college finally became a reality in 1693, with the establishment of the College of William and Mary.

The leading seventeenth-century planters were often notable for their cultural interests, and some assembled libraries of several hundred volumes. The percentage of their books dealing with religious subjects was surprising, considering the reputation of these gentry, often deserved, for high living and worldly diversions. For example, Colonel Ralph Wormeley, in most respects as far removed from New England's Jonathan Edwards as one can get, nevertheless had at least eighty books in his library which were concerned with morality and the after-life. An even larger percentage was to be found in the library of Colonel John Carter. Thus it will be seen that there was a greater philosophical affinity between the Virginians and the New Englanders at this period than is sometimes realized, although Michael Wigglesworth's lugubrious lamentation, *The Day of Doom*, which had all

Boston shuddering for generations, was never a favorite in the Old
Dominion.

The situation in Virginia in the middle 1670s was ominous of things
to come. As previously noted, the disastrous effects of England's
Navigation Acts on the tobacco growers, plus the havoc wrought by
storms and floods and the seizures of tobacco ships by the Dutch,
had combined to create widespread suffering and discontent. On top
of all else, war with the Indians broke out.

This war was one of the bloodiest and most terrible in the colony's
history. It was triggered in 1675 by the killing of a Stafford County
man and his son by the Doegs, an Indian tribe, but spasmodic conflicts
with the redskins had been occurring for a decade and a half.

The Indian war widened in 1676 and included atrocities on both
sides. The whites were guilty of treachery and bad faith in slaying
five werowances or "great men" of the Susquehannock tribe. The
latter responded by murdering men, women and children in the
frontier settlements. Savage tortures were inflicted on many captives
by the Indians.

By the time the General Assembly met in March, nearly three
hundred whites had been killed. Governor Berkeley at first prepared
to send a force against them, but then concluded that the immediate
danger was past, and abandoned the plan. Instead, it was decided on
the governor's recommendation to build forts at strategic points, a
defensive approach to the Indian threat which turned out to be
largely valueless. The terror-stricken dwellers on the frontier saw that
forts would be ineffective, since the redskins soon found out where
"these mouse traps were sett." Berkeley's popularity was declining
already, partly because he had a "Long Parliament" of his own,
similar to that of Charles I in England. He had refused for fourteen
years to order new elections of the burgesses. His failure to provide
adequate protection against Indian attacks accelerated the mounting
criticism. Over two hundred more settlers were slain in the spring by
the Indians, bringing the total for the period of January–May, 1676,
to around five hundred, a figure comparable to that for the great
one-day massacre of 1644, and well in excess of that for the massacre
of 1622. The Indians were now well-supplied with firearms, which
helps to explain the heavy toll in white lives.[5]

In fear and apprehension, a group of citizens from Charles City
County requested Governor Berkeley to grant them permission to "goe

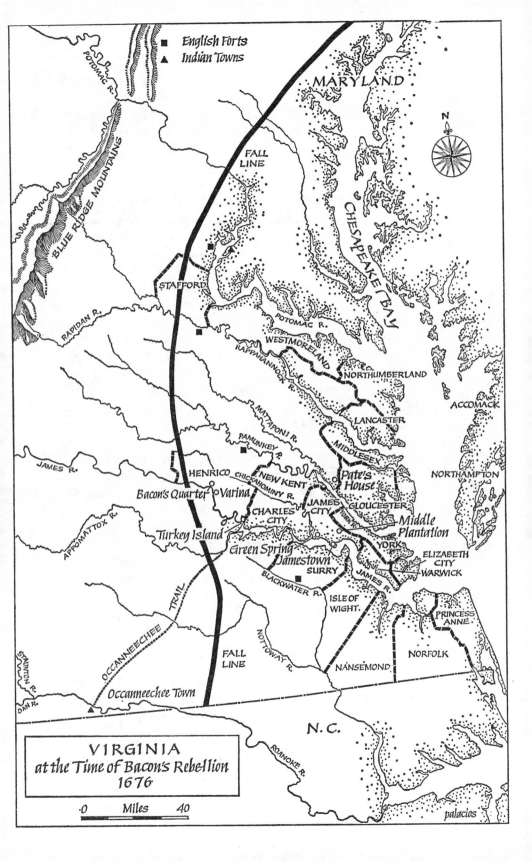

English Forts ■
Indian Towns ▲

MARYLAND

POTOMAC R.

BLUE RIDGE MOUNTAINS

FALL LINE

CHESAPEAKE BAY

N

RAPIDAN R.

STAFFORD

POTOMAC R.

WESTMORELAND

RAPPAHANNOCK R.

NORTHUMBERLAND

ACCOMACK

MATAPONI R.

LANCASTER

PAMUNKEY R.

MIDDLESEX

JAMES R.

HENRICO   CHICKAHOMINY R.

NORTHAMPTON

Bacon's Quarter   Varina

NEW KENT

Pate's House

APPOMATTOX R.

CHARLES CITY

JAMES CITY

GLOUCESTER

Turkey Island

Green Spring

YORK

Middle Plantation

Jamestown

ELIZABETH CITY

SURRY

WARWICK

OCCANNEECHEE TRAIL

BLACKWATER R.

JAMES R.

ISLE OF WIGHT.

PRINCESS ANNE

STAUNTON R.

FALL LINE

NOTTOWAY R.

NANSEMOND

NORFOLK

DAN R.

Occanneechee Town

ROANOKE R.

N. C.

VIRGINIA
at the Time of Bacon's Rebellion
1676

0   Miles   40

palacios

out against the Indians." The governor refused. Thus the stage was set for the emergence of a strong leader to take matters into his own hands and to organize an expedition against the redskins, permission or no permission. That leader was ready to take the field, despite the grave risks involved. He was twenty-eight-year-old Nathaniel Bacon, Jr.

Born in England at Friston Hall, Suffolk, and related to the renowned Francis Bacon, this young man evidently possessed remarkable capacity. Of gentle blood, he was an M.A. of Cambridge University and had traveled widely in Europe. He had married Elizabeth Duke in a runaway wedding, contrary to her father's not altogether comprehensible objections, and they had come to Virginia separately in 1674. Young Bacon not only was related to Governor Berkeley by marriage; he was also a cousin of an older Nathaniel Bacon who had achieved prominence in the colony and was a councilor. The governor welcomed the younger Bacon with the words, "Gentlemen of your quality come very rarely into this country, and therefore when they do come are used by me with all respect." Berkeley appointed him to the council, an extraordinary accolade for one of his age, especially since he had been in the colony for only a few months. Bacon's prominent connections unquestionably were decisive in bringing this about.

No portrait of Bacon survives, and the descriptions of his appearance and manner are fragmentary or partisan. He is described as black-haired, slender and of medium height, of a pensive and melancholy disposition, but "bold, active, of an inviting aspect, and powerful elocution." A hostile critic termed him in "every way qualified to lead a giddy and unthinking multitude." Governor Berkeley said that "God damn my blood!" was his "usual oath," and perhaps it was. On the other hand, while Bacon undoubtedly had his very real faults, it seems certain that he had good reason for strong dissatisfaction with Berkeley's conduct, and with the manner in which the governor had established a virtual dictatorship in Virginia. Certainly, too, Berkeley's lack of an effective policy for fighting the Indians left much to be desired.

When the citizens of Charles City expressed alarm for their safety, they turned to Bacon. He agreed to lead them against the murderous natives, whether or not he got a commission to do so from the governor. The rugged frontiersmen drank "damnation to their soules to be true to him." They found him to be a "master and owner of those inducements which constitute a compleate man (as to intrince-calls), wisdom to apprehend and discretion to chuse."[6]

Without authorization from Berkeley, Bacon led an expedition against the Occaneechees, a tribe whose fortified village was on an island in Roanoke River near the present town of Clarksville. This tribe claimed to be friendly, but as Bacon was parleying with their leaders for food, a shot killed one of his men. Instantly he stormed the village, set it on fire, and slaughtered more than a hundred Indians, including the chief and many women and children.

This bloody and highly controversial episode, which took place in May 1676, has never been fully explained. Berkeley charged Bacon with treason and rebellion for going against the Indians without authorization, suspended him from the council, and claimed that he had attacked the Occaneechees "to the dishonour of the English nation." Bacon, by contrast, declared that "we cannot in our hearts find one single spot of rebellion or treason."

But no matter what charges the governor made, the people strongly approved of Bacon's leadership in fighting the redskins who had butchered many of their relatives and friends, often after the most frightful tortures. He and his men were acclaimed on their return, and Bacon was unanimously elected to the House of Burgesses from Henrico County.

A general election had at last been called by Berkeley, after fourteen years. In one respect, at least, the election boomeranged on His Excellency, for the Henricoans now idolized the "traitor" Bacon as their long-sought protector and champion.

Berkeley succeeded in capturing Bacon and bringing him to Jamestown. Hundreds of the latter's following promptly poured into the capital with a view to rescuing their leader.

The governor summoned the burgesses to the Council chamber, and brought in Bacon. Turning to him, Berkeley exclaimed: "Now I behold the greatest rebell that ever was in Virginia!" and added: "Sir, doe you continue to be a gentleman and may I take your word? If soe, you are at liberty upon your owne parrol."

Bacon kneeled, thanked the governor, and handed him a written admission of guilt and a request for a pardon. Nathaniel Bacon, the elder, had advised him to go to these lengths, in the hope of bringing about a reconciliation between Berkeley and the people of Virginia, who had grown increasingly hostile toward the governor.

Berkeley thereupon not only forgave Bacon, but added that he forgave his followers also. A few days later he reinstated Bacon to the council and promised him the long-sought commission to fight the Indians.

Some strange things were happening in these June days. Although Bacon's supporters constituted by now a great majority of the Assembly, that body proceeded to express official praise of Governor Berkeley, accompanied by a request to King Charles that he be retained as the colony's chief magistrate. This despite the fact that Berkeley was seventy years old, and his physical and mental powers were declining. Only about a week before he himself had formally requested that the Crown name "a more vigorous Governor."

The explanation for the Assembly's action seems to be that the members were aware of the old gentleman's vindictive propensities. His outbursts of temper, accompanied by such epithets as "Dog!" "Rogue!" and "A pox take you!", were becoming more and more frequent. Having witnessed Bacon's almost groveling submission, his followers elected to take no chances.

Despite evidences of apparently improved relations between the two factions, Bacon concluded that the governor was plotting against him, and might even have him killed. Bacon escaped in the night from Jamestown, barely eluding Berkeley's men, who were searching for him.

Bacon's promised commission had not been forthcoming, and he felt therefore that he was no longer obligated to honor his oath of allegiance to the governor. Accordingly, at the head of about a hundred well-armed men—some put the number much higher—he returned to Jamestown on June 23, 1676, and lined up his forces outside the statehouse. The Assembly was in session. Bacon demanded his commission—with "fyer and sword" as the alternative.

Governor Berkeley came fuming out of the building to confront him, and denounced him as a rebel and traitor. Exclaiming, "Here, shoot me, foregod, fair mark, shoot!", the infuriated Berkeley drew his sword and taunted Bacon to fight him. The latter replied that he had no intention to "hurt a haire of your Honor's head, and for your sword your Honor may please putt it up." But Bacon added ominously: "I came for a commission against the heathen who dayly and inhumanely murder us and spill our brethrens blood, and noe care is taken to prevent it.

"God damne my blood, I came for a commission, and a commission I will have before I goe!"

Bacon ordered his men to point their cocked guns at the windows of the statehouse, from which many Assemblymen were peering. Again demanding the commission, and accompanying the demand with "new coined oathes," he showed that he would not be put off. A commission was not only signed for him, but others were granted to several of his officers.

And that was by no means all, for the Baconians—a number of leading planters among them—obtained other far-reaching concessions. These included a pardon for all their "treasonable" actions, together with a letter to the king approving and praising those actions. In addition, important statutes, known thereafter as "Bacon's Laws," were passed in the final three days of the session.

These laws did much to loosen, at least temporarily, the viselike grip which a small clique of officeholders from a handful of families had on the colony. Government in colonial Virginia had always been oligarchic rather than democratic, but under Berkeley this situation had been intensified.

The newly enacted legislation liberalized the franchise by once more giving the ballot to all freemen. It also permitted the citizens to choose representatives who would exercise equal authority with the justices of the peace in laying taxes and making local ordinances. Much overlapping in the holding of two offices by the same individual was abolished. The powerful vestries which had long been self-perpetuating were to be elected popularly every three years. Penalties were prescribed for public officials who charged excessive fees. Exemptions for members of the council from taxation were ended.

These were the last days of June, and the hot summer sun beat down upon a colony which apparently had barely managed to avoid civil war. Bacon and his men left Jamestown with the commissions they had sought, and also with a series of enactments which loosened the hold of the central oligarchy. But the Baconians had hardly begun to move against the Indians when Governor Berkeley suddenly denounced them as traitors and rebels, and made it known that he was raising an army to subdue them.

Bacon, evidently a masterful orator, roused his 1300 men to instant

action. Berkeley, for his part, soon found that the militia of Gloucester
and Middlesex, whose aid he sought, were completely unwilling to go
against Bacon. The militiamen walked from the field, leaving Berkeley
and his entourage frustrated and bewildered. Shortly thereafter, on
learning that Bacon's forces were approaching, Sir William fled across
Chesapeake Bay to Accomack. He was joined there by a number of
his adherents.

Bacon's men were now in possession of the mainland, but they
were in deadly confrontation with an aroused governor. A conflict
with the king also appeared to be in the offing, which greatly disturbed
some of Bacon's supporters. Warfare with the Indians was relegated
to a secondary position.

Bacon established headquarters at Middle Plantation (now Williamsburg), and ordered some of the leading planters who were opposing him to be brought before him. Plantations of some of those
who had joined Berkeley on the Eastern Shore had been looted by
his rebels.

What was termed a "convention" was held by the Baconians, and
a Declaration of Principles was issued on August 3. The intention
was to put their rebellion in perspective and to elucidate their objectives. In this document, Berkeley was excoriated for launching a
civil war against loyal subjects of the king who were merely trying
to save the colonists from being murdered by the Indians. The surrender of the governor and his principal supporters, nineteen in
number, was demanded within four days. Else they would be seized
as traitors and their estates confiscated. This do-or-die manifesto was
signed "Nathaniel Bacon, General by Consent of the People."

Bacon also managed to exact from all those in attendance at the
convention, including some of the leaders in Berkeley's government, a
pledge not to aid the governor in any way. He sought, furthermore,
to obtain a commitment from them to fight any forces sent against
them from England, until the king could be advised of the true
situation in Virginia. There were violent objections to this commitment, but Bacon locked the doors, and by threats and persuasion,
over a period of some twelve hours, managed to get the signatures.
Many were swayed to his side by news which arrived during the
session: Berkeley had absconded with all the arms and ammunition
from York Fort, leaving the people thereabouts at the mercy of the
Indians. Several in the neighborhood had just been murdered by the

redskins, but when the terrified survivors fled to the fort, they found it defenseless, thanks to Sir William.

The oath of loyalty to Bacon was circulated widely through the colony by his followers, and prominent Berkeleyites who refused to subscribe were taken into custody. This was civil war, and Bacon and his men were using desperate measures.

They decided to pursue Governor Berkeley to the Eastern Shore and to capture him, if possible. Bacon's men commandeered two ships and headed across Chesapeake Bay, adding other vessels en route. Bacon, meanwhile, went in pursuit of the Pamunkey Indians in the Dragon Swamp. He achieved a victory against them and gathered considerable plunder. But on his return he received the shocking news that Berkeley had outmaneuvered the rebels, and had captured all their ships, the only ones Bacon had, together with the leaders of the expedition and the 250 soldiers on board. Berkeley sailed back to Jamestown, in full control of the Chesapeake and the mouths of the coastal rivers. He fortified and garrisoned the capital.

Bacon headed for Green Spring, Berkeley's plantation. Arriving September 13, five days after the governor had returned to nearby Jamestown, the rebel prepared to lay siege to the latter place. Many recruits had joined him, for he was still a popular idol, especially so, since he had once more successfully attacked the Indians.

Bacon realized that his forces were greatly outnumbered by Berkeley's army defending Jamestown. The tired rebels, furthermore, had been marching back and forth in one of the hottest and wettest summers on record, sleeping in the rain, wading through swamps and undergoing other similar ordeals. Yet Bacon did not hesitate to go on the offensive against the entrenched governor.

Bacon addressed his men, telling them of the dangers they faced. He was obviously effective in inspiring them, but one quotation that has come down to us is something less than inspirational. It follows: "Come on, my hearts of gold! He that dyes in the field lyes in the bedd of honour!" Let us hope that the seventeenth-century scribe who attributed such fustian to Nathaniel Bacon was drawing on his imagination.

At all events, the rebel forces set to work immediately in preparation for the assault on the colonial capital. Fortifications commanding the narrow neck of land joining Jamestown to the mainland were constructed. At this juncture, Bacon resorted to an unchivalrous expedient to protect his men from being fired on. Wives of leading Berkeley supporters were kidnaped on nearby plantations by Bacon's mounted raiders and put in front of the rebel trenches. One wife was sent to inform Governor Berkeley and the husbands immediately concerned. The stratagem worked, but it reflected no credit on those responsible. After the trenches were completed, the wives were removed from the front, and the fighting began.

Berkeley ordered his men to attack, but the governor's lack of popular support soon became evident. The attackers fled headlong when Bacon's soldiers stood firm and fired volley after volley. In the words of a chronicler, the governor's halfhearted troops, "(like scholers goeing to schoole), went out with hevie harts, but returned hom with light heeles." It was a debacle for Berkeley.

He saw that the sympathies of the soldiers who were supposedly loyal to him were actually with his enemies. At the end of only five days, he took ship and fled to the Eastern Shore again. Bacon entered Jamestown.

However, a new threat loomed. Colonel Giles Brent, a Berkeley adherent, was reported to be assembling a thousand men in northern Virginia to march against Bacon. The latter feared that if he moved to meet Brent, Berkeley would return to Jamestown and reorganize there for an attack on his rear. He accordingly determined to burn the town. It consisted of a dozen brick residences, plus a few frame structures, the statehouse and the church. All these buildings were set afire, after the colony's official records had been removed to a place of safety.

The destruction of Jamestown turned out to be unnecessary. For when Colonel Brent's army heard that Jamestown had fallen to Bacon, it melted away. The threat from that quarter was ended. Yet Governor Berkeley, with complete control of the bay and the principal rivers, plus the constant support of the British Crown, remained an extremely formidable adversary. In fact, he was apparently unbeatable, over the long pull.

Yet Bacon planned to continue the fight, and was formulating his strategy when illness laid him low. He had been under constant strain since the arduous expedition in the spring which took him hundreds of miles through the wilderness against the Occaneechees. Then came the marches and countermarches against Berkeley's forces, as well as the Pamunkeys, across trackless terrain and in abominable weather combining stifling heat with almost uninterrupted rain and enervating humidity. All this lowered his resistance. In the soggy trenches before Jamestown he is believed to have contracted the dysentery which carried him off a few weeks later. Death came on October 26 at the home of Major Thomas Pate on Portopotank Creek in Gloucester County, a short distance from West Point. Bacon was buried secretly, lest perchance Governor Berkeley seek to inflict indignities upon his corpse.

Bacon's death deprived the rebellion of its magnetic leader, and rendered hopeless any effective opposition to Berkeley. Joseph Ingram, who was chosen to succeed Bacon, was not of the same mold, although his selection seemed popular with the men when it was announced, and they cried "as loud as they could bellow, God save our new Generall!" But Ingram permitted his dwindling forces to become divided and to be attacked separately. That was the beginning of the end.

The vengeful old governor hunted down various leaders of the rebel faction and hanged them. Among these was Captain Thomas Hansford, who pleaded unavailingly to be shot rather than hanged, protesting to the end that he had merely fought the Indians and was no disloyal subject of the king. William Drummond, who had been governor of North Carolina, was captured in the Chickahominy Swamp. Governor Berkeley bowed low when Drummond was brought before him, saying: "Mr. Drummond, you are very welcome! I am more glad to see you than any man in Virginia. Mr. Drummond, you shall be hanged in half an hour!" Major Thomas Cheeseman also was captured. His wife begged on her knees to be hanged in his stead, saying that she had been primarily responsible for his actions against the governor. Berkeley spurned her request and called her a "whore." Major Cheeseman escaped the noose by dying in prison.

In all, about twenty-three persons were executed. Many are familiar with the remark attributed to King Charles II: "That old fool has hanged more men in that naked country than I did for the murder of my father."

Nathaniel Bacon, who led this rebellion, was no saint, despite the tablet at Gloucester Courthouse which thus describes him. He had his irreconcilable enemies and severe critics, and some of the criticism was justified. But he gave courageous leadership to Virginians who were outraged by Indian atrocities and suffering under tyrannical rule. Thanks to Bacon, the Indian threat was effectively countered, and some of the worst injustices of Berkeley's regime were ameliorated. While Bacon's Laws were repealed a few months after his death, some of them were then partially re-enacted. The revolt also had the salutary effect of warning the British Crown against future excesses. True, full-fledged revolution erupted a century later, so the warning seems not to have been fully taken to heart.

In addition to its impact on political and social conditions in the colony and on its relations with the Indians, Bacon's Rebellion was the subject of what Jay B. Hubbell, Louis Untermeyer and others have called the first notable poem written in America. This is "Bacon's Epitaph, Made By His Man." Dr. Hubbell has demonstrated that the author almost certainly was John Cotton, a Virginia planter who lived at the time of the rebellion.[7]

Nathaniel Bacon's body rests in an unknown grave, perhaps beneath the waters of the River York, near whose banks he died. Nowhere is his case more movingly presented than in the poem mentioned above. It opens with the following lines:

> Death why so cruel! What no other way
> To manifest thy spleen, but thus to slay
> Our hopes of safety; liberty, our all
> Which, through thy tyranny, with him must fall
> To its late chaos?

And the poem's central theme is in this quatrain:

> While none shall dare his obsequies to sing
> In deserved measure, until time shall bring
> Truth crowned with freedom, and from danger free,
> To sound his praises to posterity.

SEVEN

The Capital, the Commissary and Spotswood

THE COLLAPSE of Bacon's Rebellion was far from bringing peace to distraught Virginia. The overwhelming mass of the people, together with some of the principal planters, had been supporters of Bacon, and they were by no means reconciled to the turn of events. As for bitter old Governor Berkeley, he was grimly determined to continue the hangings.

Three commissioners, plus a regiment of a thousand men, had been dispatched from England to Virginia in the autumn of 1676, before the rebellion had fallen apart. They arrived in midwinter, 1677, when resistance to the governor had ended. They brought word to Berkeley that the king was granting his request to be relieved as governor, because of his infirmities, and that Colonel Herbert Jeffreys, one of the commissioners, was to succeed him, with the title of lieutenant governor.

His Majesty likewise made it known that he was pardoning all who had taken part in the revolt, with the single exception of Nathaniel Bacon. (Word of the latter's death had not reached the king when his proclamation was prepared.)

Berkeley proceeded to defy the royal pronouncement of clemency by announcing that eighteen persons, whom he did not name, were being excluded from its benefits. The widespread unease caused by this gubernatorial ukase can well be imagined. His Excellency made it plain, moreover, that although he had been ordered by the king to return to England, he would do so when it was convenient, and not before.

The Assembly was now subservient to Berkeley, and it joined him in his contumacious refusal to obey the royal commands. The legislators prescribed further hangings, as well as imprisonments, banishments and fines.

This left Lieutenant Governor Jeffreys in nominal control, but the Assembly and council were still dominated by the Berkeleyan faction. Jeffreys, furthermore, was ill. He struggled with the difficult situation for about eighteen months and then died. The colony was still divided and unhappy.

To the disruptions and animosities aroused by Bacon's Rebellion and its aftermath must be added the continued low price of tobacco. All classes of colonists were suffering severely. Overproduction and low prices caused wholesale plant-cutting in several counties, to such an extent that the activity took on the dimensions of a widespread revolt or riot. So grave was the official view of this slashing of the tobacco plants that it was termed "treason," and two of the leaders were hanged. Tobacco, it must be remembered, was a prime revenue producer for the Crown.

Finally, in 1682, the long depression in the tobacco market came to an end. It had lasted for a quarter of a century. The upturn in the fortunes of the planters would continue for about two decades, and during that time the colonists were to move farther and farther away from the rebellion and its divisive aftereffects.

Much has been written concerning Virginia's large landed proprietors, luxuriating on their baronial estates in the seventeenth and eighteenth centuries. While they constituted the ruling group in the colony, too little has been said of the vastly more numerous group who held a few hundred acres each. There were thousands of them and they were in many ways the backbone of the colony.

These owners of medium-sized farms, who often lived in modest clapboard houses with dormer windows, were especially strong and prosperous in the latter years of the seventeenth and the early years of the eighteenth century. The Virginia rent roll for 1704, which included everything except the Northern Neck, showed that their holdings averaged roughly from three hundred to five hundred acres. There were few, if any, slaves on these plantations in those years and few indentured servants. This group of sturdy tobacco growers had to depend mainly on themselves and their families for the long, arduous and involved process of raising and curing the leaf. Many tobacco fields adjoined swamps and bogs, and the death rate of tobacco farmers was dismayingly high. But so long as these farmers were able to operate on this self-reliant basis—rigorous though it was—they could maintain a decent standard of living.

Yet the condition was a temporary one. The competing slave economy of the large planters was still in its infancy, since only about six thousand slaves had been brought into the colony by 1700. However, the flow of Africans became a torrent in the succeeding decades, and the great plantation owners were able to grow and market tobacco much more cheaply. In addition, they increased their landholdings to the maximum degree possible, and instituted a system of mass production. This put more and more pressure on the small growers, who found such competition increasingly severe. By the middle of the eighteenth century, the result was greatly reduced incomes for these agriculturalists. Many were impoverished, and a class of "poor whites," living in squalor, sprang up.

Wertenbaker rightly terms the "undermining of the yeoman class by the importation of slaves one of the great crimes of history." And he adds: "The wrong done the Negro himself has been universally condemned; the wrong done the white man has attracted less attention. It effectively deprived him of his American birthright—the high return for his labor. It transformed Virginia and the South from a land of hard-working, self-respecting yeomen to a land of slaves and slaveholders."

With the death of Colonel Herbert Jeffreys as lieutenant governor, Sir Henry Chicheley, a royalist refugee, was named deputy governor. He was to serve until the coming of Thomas Lord Culpeper, who had been appointed governor, but who did not actually arrive from England until three years later, in 1680.

Culpeper was a gentleman whose acquisitive instincts were highly developed. Charles II had appealed to those instincts in 1673 when he once more showed his lack of gratitude for Virginia's loyalty during the Commonwealth period by granting to Culpeper and Henry Bennet, Earl of Arlington, the whole of Virginia, except the Northern Neck, for a period of thirty-one years! This incredible performance was protested by the Assembly, which sent agents to England. Culpeper and Arlington finally agreed to give up their claims, while retaining the income from land taxes or fees derived from quitrents or escheats. In 1681, Culpeper bought out Arlington's share. Three years later he traded his entire interest for a twenty-year annuity, paid by taxes collected in Virginia.

Culpeper was succeeded as governor by Francis Lord Howard of Effingham, who may have been somewhat less rapacious than Culpeper, but who was even more overbearing. His constant and unremitting efforts to hamper and bully the House of Burgesses were the most notorious features of his administration. Howard's imperious attitude was admirably exemplified in his reference to "the publique . . . a name certainely most odious under a Royal government and that which doth in name, so in consequence, but little differ from that destestable one (republick)." The burgesses showed impressive courage in fighting against the arbitrary edicts of this worshiper at the shrine of autocracy.

When James II succeeded Charles II, on the latter's death, the woes of the burgesses were in no degree lessened. Then came the Glorious Revolution of 1688, and the accession of King William and Queen Mary. Parliament passed the Act of Toleration and adopted the Bill of Rights, and the newly crowned monarchs exhibited a genuine concern for the well-being of the Virginia people. This was in refreshing contrast to the situation which had previously prevailed.

Lord Howard of Effingham returned to England and retained the title of governor. Captain Francis Nicholson was sent over as lieutenant governor. Despite Nicholson's highly erratic behavior on several subsequent occasions, he was an able man who achieved importantly for the colony. He was the first of several competent chief executives whose abilities and attitudes contrasted with those of Culpeper and Howard.

The arrival of Francis Nicholson in the "Old Dominion"—a term then coming into fairly widespread use and reflecting the fact that Virginia was England's oldest dominion—synchronized with the upturn in the colony's fortunes. Various omens were favorable at that period. The settlements were spreading into the interior, as far as the fall line, and Indian warfare was becoming less virulent. Many of those who were taking positions of influence in Virginia were the sons of the original settlers. The rights of the House of Burgesses and of the average citizen, in the main, survived the frontal attacks and backstage maneuvers of Charles II and James II and their agents on this side of the ocean.

There was scientific progress on a modest scale. The first of two John Claytons who were to make significant contributions to various scientific disciplines was the Reverend John Clayton, an Anglican clergyman, who spent two years at Jamestown in the 1680s and was a pioneering observer of soils, climate and medicine. A contemporary, John Banister, who sojourned for about a decade and a half in the colony, was eminent as a botanist. A later John Clayton, related to the first, and still more accomplished, came to the colony in 1705. Some decades later he published *Flora Virginica*, a work regarded highly by both Thomas Jefferson and Benjamin Franklin. More important than any of these was John Mitchell, a practicing physician in Middlesex County in the 1730s and 1740s, and perhaps a native Virginian. His contributions to botany, zoology, medicine and map making were exceptional.

Virginia was a beneficiary at this period of the revocation in 1685 by Louis XIV of the Edict of Nantes. Hundreds of thousands of Huguenots fled from France, since their Protestant religion was no longer tolerated there. Virginia gave asylum to an estimated eight or nine hundred. From the outset they were excellent citizens, whose ability, industy and other fine qualities were at once appreciated here.

Their major settlement in Virginia was at Manakin Town, twenty miles west of Richmond, across the James River from the present Manakin. This fertile site had been occupied by the Monacan Indians, but was abandoned by them. Some five hundred Huguenots settled on the deserted tract near Manakin Town about the year 1700. Among those settlers were members of such families as Michaux, Battle, Jordan, Moncure, Munford, Latané, Marye, Taliaferro, Flournoy, Norman, Barrow, Gerow, Lacy, Lewis, Dashiell, Larus and Duvall. Other Huguenots, including the Fontaines and Maurys, came independently and bought land. All intermarried with the English and for many years have taken leading roles in Virginia affairs.

Manakin Town was significant because of the large number of Huguenots who established themselves there, and also by virtue of the fact that it was the westernmost important settlement in the valley of the James. The movement past the fall line of the rivers into the Piedmont was just beginning in 1700. Three decades later the great migration down from Pennsylvania into what is now the Shenandoah

Valley would get under way, and the transmontane region would be opened up.

Various large planters made strenuous efforts in the late seventeenth and early eighteenth centuries to bring Huguenots from Europe and to place them on their plantations as tenants. One of these planters was William Fitzhugh, who sought to develop 21,000 acres of his Stafford County estate by this means.

A Huguenot named Durand who visited the Fitzhugh plantation, "Bedford," reported on the sumptuous manner in which the proprietor lived and entertained. Durand was one of twenty sportive horsemen who descended upon "Bedford" at Christmastime, 1686. He wrote later:

"We were all supplied with beds, though we had indeed to double up. Colonel Fitzhugh showed us the largest hospitality. He had a store of good wine and other things to drink, and a frolic ensued. He called in three fiddlers, a clown, a tight rope dancer and an acrobatic tumbler . . . It was very cold but no one thought of going near the fire, because they never put less than the trunk of a tree upon it, and so the entire room was kept warm."

It was during these years that efforts to establish a college at Middle Plantation (Williamsburg) were coming to a head. The central figure in these endeavors was the Reverend James Blair, a Scotsman who had come to the colony a few years before and been named rector at Varina. In 1689, he was appointed commissary or deputy of the Bishop of London. (There was no Anglican bishop in Virginia or in America during colonial times.)

Commissary Blair was to be a power in ecclesiastical, political and educational circles for two generations, a sort of *éminence grise* on the Virginia scene. Able and farseeing, yet arbitrary and domineering, he was largely responsible for the removal of no fewer than three governors with whom he was at odds.

Blair's efforts to establish a college in Virginia bore fruit on a visit to London. However, he encountered a slightly sordid reaction from Sir Edward Seymour, one of the Lords of the Treasury. When that worthy was told by Blair that the projected institution in Virginia would prepare students for the ministry, and thus save the souls of erring Virginians, Seymour is said to have retorted: "Souls! Damn your souls. Make Tobacco!"

The college of William and Mary received its royal charter in 1693. Blair, who deserves to be called the founder of the institution, was also named its first president, for life. Since he was, furthermore, a member of the governor's council almost continuously for half a century, and its president during part of that time, and he married into the influential Harrison family, Commissary Blair was the most powerful man in Virginia over a long period.

One of the first manifestations of his political puissance is seen in his successful effort to terminate the gubernatorial career of Governor Edmund Andros. Sir Edmund had been sent to Virginia when Lord Howard of Effingham resigned. Lieutenant Governor Nicholson, who had been discharging the latter's executive functions, was accordingly transferred to Maryland, after a two-year incumbency in Virginia.

Andros, meanwhile, rendered acceptable service. However, he ran afoul of Commissary Blair, especially in connection with the college, then under construction. Blair's criticisms of Andros to officials in England were so numerous and all-embracing that King William ended by recalling Sir Edmund. Colonel Francis Nicholson was brought back as governor.

Nicholson also would clash later with the redoubtable commissary. For the present, however, their relations were amicable, and Nicholson was influential in securing the removal of the capital of the colony from Jamestown to Williamsburg. Jamestown had never recovered from its burning in Bacon's Rebellion, and the statehouse, which had been rebuilt, had burned again in 1698. Only three or four "good, inhabited houses" remained. Advocates of making Middle Plantation the capital found the situation propitious. The college was especially active in urging the change.

The decision to move the capital was made by the General Assembly in 1699, and the name of Middle Plantation was changed to Williamsburg. Far more healthful than miasmic Jamestown, it was to remain the colonial capital until the American Revolution. For eighty years Williamsburg was the place where the great Virginians of the pre-revolutionary and revolutionary eras gathered, passed laws, discussed public affairs and diverted themselves. Few cities in America can point to a more scintillating galaxy of men than those who trod the streets of this little town. From Alexander Spotswood, William Byrd II and "King" Carter on through Patrick Henry, Thomas Jefferson, George Washington and a host of others, the list is almost endless.

Governor Nicholson had given useful leadership in several directions, but his career was irreparably marred by his violent rages and his irrational conduct on various occasions. His behavior in suing for the hand of Miss Lucy Burwell illustrates the point. Nicholson, a bachelor, wrote Major Lewis Burwell, Lucy's father, of his impassioned desire to "address" her, saying that "Madam Lucy . . . by her beauty, many extraordinary vertues and rare accomplishments &c hath charmed me to a degree beyond expression &c." Nicholson then proceeded to threaten all rivals, real or imagined. When he met the Reverend Stephen Fovace on the road, coming from the Burwell home, where Fovace had called on the ill Major Burwell, Governor Nicholson flew into a jealous fury. Armed with a pistol and sword, he became insulting and so menacing that the poor clergyman fled in terror, and soon thereafter escaped on a ship to England. Having disposed of this non-existent rival, Nicholson declared that if anybody else married Lucy he would slay not only the bridegroom but also the clergyman performing the rite and the justice of the peace who signed the license.

Despite his bizarre behavior, Governor Nicholson had genuine accomplishments to his credit—especially in strengthening Virginia's defenses, giving economic stability to the colony, laying out the town of Williamsburg and warring on pirates. Among his supporters were most of the Virginia clergy, for he was a religious man and zealous in defending their interests. But one clergyman, more influential than all the rest, was determined to unhorse him. This was Commissary Blair, who went to England and poured out charges against the governor. Nicholson was recalled soon afterward by Queen Anne.

Alexander Spotswood's term as Virginia's chief executive began in 1710 and lasted for twelve years. It was one of the most notable in the entire colonial era. He was a military man, a former soldier in Marlborough's armies, and a veteran of Blenheim and Oudenarde. As a thirty-four-year-old lieutenant colonel and an aristocrat, he exhibited in Virginia the imperious attitudes of his class. The "vulgar people" and the "meaner sort," as he termed them, held no appeal for him. He was born into a stratum of society which felt itself destined to rule, and he intended to do so. He would achieve significantly for the colony, but in the process would encounter strong resistance at various times from both the council and burgesses.

Lieutenant Governor Spotswood took office after a four-year period during which Edmund Jenings, president of the council, served as acting governor. Prior to that time, Edward Nott had held office for only one year, for he died in Williamsburg almost exactly twelve months after his arrival there.

Under Lieutenant Governor Spotswood's vigorous and purposeful direction, Williamsburg burgeoned impressively. The Governor's Palace and Bruton Parish Church were built, along with the Powder Horn. The main college building, said to have been from plans by Sir Christopher Wren, had been destroyed by fire in 1705, but was being reconstructed when Spotswood arrived in Virginia, and his designs were used extensively. The Capitol was standing already at the other end of Duke of Gloucester Street. That thoroughfare was no longer an unglamorous horse path.

Thus the little capital was ready for the transaction of public and private business. At Publick Times—that is, when the General Court or the General Assembly was in session—the population doubled almost overnight.

Bewigged councilmen, burgesses, planters and merchants poured in by carriage or on horseback over the dusty roads, or came by boat to the nearby James and York River landings. Gentlemen who had town houses occupied them, with guests, while those less fortunate crowded the taverns to the eaves, sometimes sleeping three or four in a bed.

There were auctions, horse races and fairs. Plays were offered, after 1717, at the first theater built in English continental America. Spirited dice and card games went forward at the inns. Candlelight flickered on polished mahogany at the Governor's Palace, minuets were danced and toasts were drunk in mellow Madeira.

But even at that early date, the shadow of slave insurrections hung over the colony. In his first address to the General Assembly, Spotswood mentioned the dangerously rapid increase in the number of Negroes, and alluded to "all those who long to shake off the fetters of slavery." (By 1715 the slave population would reach approximately 23,000, compared with 72,500 whites.) An insurrection in James City, Surry and Isle of Wight counties had occurred shortly before Spotswood's arrival, and the two leaders had been executed. Their heads were cut off and their bodies quartered, and the gruesome fragments were exhibited at various places as a warning. One head was displayed at Williamsburg.[1]

The Assembly of 1710–11 sought to curb the importation of slaves by levying an almost prohibitive tax on all Negroes brought into the colony, but British merchants and slave traders put such pressure on the British Government that the action was disallowed after eight years.[2] As early as 1672, the Virginia Assembly had passed special legislation designed to control runaway slaves, and in 1680 an "Act for Preventing Negroes Insurrections" had been approved. The latter statute declared that "the frequent meeting of considerable numbers of Negroe slaves under pretence of feasts and burialls is judged of dangerous consequence . . ."[3]

Spotswood's desire to pursue a more enlightened and humane policy toward the Indians also was thwarted by the British. The Indian Act of 1714, which he sponsored, called for the formation of the Virginia Indian Company, designed to improve relations between white and red men in Virginia, and to educate and Christianize the natives. The act provided that all trading with the Indians south of the James be carried on in an open market at Christanna, an outpost constructed on the Meherrin River under Spotswood's direct supervision. An excellent schoolhouse for the Indians was erected there, and seventy young Indians were enrolled, with an Englishman, Charles Griffin, as instructor. All this came to naught in 1717 when the king in council repealed the Indian Act of 1714. The burgesses, who had been in a prolonged controversy with Spotswood, and who, in any event, favored slaughtering Indians instead of educating them, refused to continue the outpost at Christanna.

Another minority group with whom Spotswood was concerned was a small contingent of German-Swiss immigrants who came at his invitation to work at the iron mines. Iron ore had been discovered above the falls of the Rappahannock, and the settlers were brought over in 1714 and established at a place which he named Germanna. It was situated "on the south bank of the Rapidan . . . about twelve miles above its confluence with the Rappahannock." The Europeans removed to the present Fauquier County in 1717, and Spotswood brought over some seventy German indentured servants. Within a few years he was selling backs, frames and andirons for fireplaces in Williamsburg, and shipping pig iron to England.

Spotswood sought to regulate land transactions and the improper practices that had grown up in the colony for the acquisition of enormous tracts, and avoiding land taxes. His efforts were undermined by the council, with its interlocking families, many of whom were

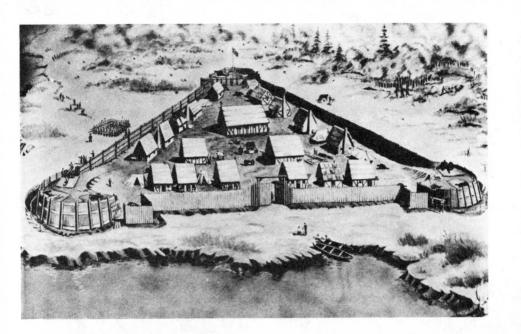

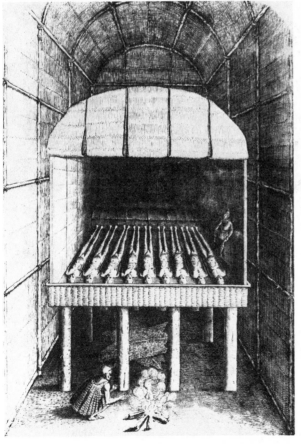

(1) *Above*, James Fort, the triangular palisade where the first settlers at Jamestown tried for several years to defend themselves against Indians, famine and disease. The church, storehouse and guardhouse are surrounded by fifteen dwellings. Cannon are posted at the three corners.

(2) *Left*, burial place of Indian chiefs in seventeenth-century Virginia. A drawing by the French artist, B. Picart.

(3) and (4) The "Adam and Eve of Virginia"—William Randolph of Turkey Island and Mary Isham of Bermuda Hundred, who were married in the mid-1670s and had the following direct descendants: Thomas Jefferson, John Marshall, "Light-Horse Harry" Lee, Robert E. Lee, Peyton Randolph, Edmund Randolph and John Randolph of Roanoke.

Sir WILLIAM BERKELEY Brother
to IOHN the first Lord BERKELEY of
STRATTON.

(5) Sir William Berkeley, the dashing Cavalier who was popular and beloved for years as leader of the colony, but who later became arrogant and crotchety. He was the storm center in Bacon's Rebellion, in which Jamestown was burned and the colony was torn apart.

opposed to restrictions on land-grabbing. As Spotswood grew older, he himself obtained huge tracts of land.

He was greatly interested in exploring and opening up the West, not only for the benefits which this might bring to the colony, but also as a means of checkmating the French, who were pushing into the area. His policies designed to facilitate the purchase of small farms there were forward-looking.

As an initial step toward obtaining access to the western regions, Spotswood led a party of convivial gentlemen and others across the Blue Ridge Mountains in August and September 1716—a group known to later generations as the Knights of the Golden Horseshoe.

This expedition included sixty-three men, seventy-four horses, miscellaneous dogs, and a vast quantity of alcoholic beverages. It set out from Chelsea, the home of Augustine Moore on the Mattaponi River, continued to Germanna, and went thence along the Rapidan, and up to the crest of the Blue Ridge. The explorers were beset by rattlesnakes and hornets, as well as occasional attacks of measles and other minor disabilities. For the most part, however, the horsemen and their retainers enjoyed themselves. They shot bear and deer, and dined on bear steaks and venison around campfires, washing down the viands with potent drinkables of many varieties.

The precise route followed is uncertain. For many years it was assumed that the party crossed the mountains at Swift Run Gap, and passed down into the valley, striking the Shenandoah River near the present Elkton. Of late, doubts have arisen as to the correctness of this thesis. It is argued that various circumstances point to the likelihood that the route went past Big Meadows through Milam Gap, some thirteen miles north of Swift Run, and reached the Shenandoah at a point about fourteen miles downstream from Elkton near the present village of Alma.[4]

At all events, the lively journal of John Fontaine, a member of the company, tells us that on reaching the summit of the range, they "drank King George's health, and the Royal family's, at the very top of the . . . mountains." They then descended into the valley, camped overnight beside the river, fished and hunted. After taking possession of the region in the name of Britain's king, Fontaine records that:

"We had a good dinner, and after we got the men together, and loaded all their arms, and we drank the King's health in champagne and fired a volley, and all the rest of the Royal Family and fired a volley—the Princess' health in Burgundy, and fired a volley, and all the rest of the Royal Family in claret and fired a volley. We drank the Governor's health, and fired another volley. We had several sorts of liquors, viz., Virginia red wine and white, Irish usquebaugh, brandy, shrub, two sorts of rum, champagne, canary, cherry, punch, water, cider, &c."

Following these exploits, the expedition turned homeward. The "Knights" were on the road for four weeks and covered 438 miles. Governor Spotswood gave each of his companions on the journey a golden horseshoe as a memento of the picturesque excursion.

As a military man, Spotswood was especially concerned over the serious depredations of pirates and privateers off the Virginia coast. Governor Nicholson had made war on these plunderers, including Captain Kidd, who was notable, among other things for the gold toothpick which he wielded. Now the pirates were again to the fore, with the notorious Edward Teach, alias Blackbeard, as the principal threat. Spotswood organized an expedition against this formidable buccaneer, a swarthy monster whose heavy beard was twisted at the ends into small pigtails, and tied with ribbons. Brought to bay in Ocracoke Inlet off the North Carolina coast, Blackbeard was killed in a bloody hand-to-hand fight between his crew and that of the Virginia vessel sent to capture him. The pirate's head was cut off and tied to the bowsprit, and the Virginians sailed up the James in triumph, taking with them fifteen members of Blackbeard's gang, including a number of Negroes. All were lodged in the Williamsburg gaol and, after trial, thirteen were hanged. That was the end of Blackbeard's picaroons, but other pirates continued their brigandage in and around Chesapeake Bay and off the coast. So did Spanish and French privateers.

An accumulation of grievances, real or imagined, against Spotswood finally led to his removal as lieutenant governor. He had crossed swords at various times with the doughty Commissary Blair, especially with respect to matters affecting the clergy. He had also had long and acrimonious disagreements with the burgesses and the council, particularly the latter. Opposition from Blair is considered to have been the principal cause of his undoing—in which respect he was a fellow sufferer with Governors Andros and Nicholson.

Alexander Spotswood passed most of the rest of his life in Virginia.

He served for the final eight years as deputy postmaster of all the colonies. In 1738 he announced that by dint of improvements in the service, a post rider would be able to leave from just below Fredericksburg on Wednesday and reach Annapolis on Friday.

Spotswood's iron mines, with their temporary and also limited prosperity, were among the few enterprises of the kind in colonial Virginia. The Old Dominion's rural economy and emphasis on tobacco culture almost precluded widespread development of arts or crafts, certainly of the finer kind. Shortly before the Revolution a few crude iron products such as axes and hoes were made at Providence Forge, in New Kent County. At about the same period, Isaac Zane, Jr., developed an ironworks near Winchester which turned out kettles, pots, pestles and mortars. There were also gristmills for grinding grain, especially on the Northern Neck. In the frontier regions beyond the mountains other gristmills were in operation, and tanners, shoemakers and blacksmiths were active. But such things as china, silverware, jewelry, clothing or household ornaments were not made anywhere in Virginia or in the other southern colonies. A quite small amount of fine furniture was made in Virginia and South Carolina. A French traveler described the situation tersely when he said:

"From England, the Virginians take every article of Convenience or ornament which they use, their own manufactures not being worth mentioning."

EIGHT

Gooch, Carter, Byrd
and the Clergy

VIRGINIA's colonial civilization was now entering the period during which it reached its highest degree of development. The foundations were being laid for the emergence of the men who furnished such peerless leadership to the nation in the American Revolution.

Well over a century had passed since the first beachhead was established at Jamestown. Virginians were permanently settled on their farms and plantations, and seasoned lawmakers, administrators and jurists were coming to the fore. Such impressive mansions as Westover, Shirley, Brandon, Sabine Hall and Mount Airy were rising beside the tidal rivers. Lieutenant Governor Spotswood's Palace at Williamsburg, setting a new architectural standard for residences in the colony, had provided the pattern for these stately homes.

William Gooch, the able and amiable man who took office as lieutenant governor in 1727, was to extend the boundaries of the colony and to cross new frontiers into the Shenandoah Valley and the southwest. Gooch succeeded Hugh Drysdale, an excellent executive who died after four years in office.

For about twelve months prior to the coming of Gooch, Robert ("King") Carter of Corotoman, president of the council, was acting governor. Carter had been growing steadily in prominence and had held virtually every office of importance in the colony. The list of posts to which he had been elected or appointed (only burgesses were popularly elected), included member of the House of Burgesses and Speaker of that House, member of the council for thirty-three years and its president for six, treasurer of the colony, rector of the College of William and Mary, colonel and commander-in-chief of Lancaster and Northumberland counties, naval officer of the Rappahannock River, vestryman for many years, and agent of the Fairfax family for the Northern Neck. While this list is somewhat longer than that for most of the influential planters of that era, several other leaders were almost equally involved with public matters.

However, public office represented by no means all of their responsibilities. Robert Carter, for example, had to administer the complex affairs of his two-score subsidiary plantations, in addition to those of Corotoman, and to supervise their manifold farming, marketing and manufacturing operations. There were hundreds of slaves to be cared for, a vast tobacco crop to be harvested, shipped and sold. These matters required Carter's personal attention, despite the fact that he employed numerous overseers. Anyone who imagines that these Virginia planters reclined under the magnolias and left to others the responsibility for directing plantation affairs, has no conception of the realities. These men were hard-working and dynamic—widely recognized for their qualities of leadership. They could never have succeeded as they did without constant attention to the business in hand, whether that business was attending a meeting of the council, supervising the manufacture of clothing for their slaves, or arranging to have their children educated in England or Scotland.

Robert Carter of Corotoman (on the Rappahannock) was in many ways typical of the small group of well-to-do planters who dominated Virginia in the first third of the eighteenth century. His operations were the most extensive of all, for when he died, he owned 300,000 acres and a thousand slaves. The sobriquet "King" was said by some to have been bestowed because of his haughty mien, but all conceded that he was in many ways a superior representative of his class.

That class was aware of the obligations inherent in the possession of wealth and privilege. Its members were at times excessively grasping, especially where land—the indispensable badge of the gentleman— was concerned. On the other hand, they recognized that being born into a select class carried with it definite obligations for public service, many of which obligations they discharged without any financial compensation whatever. The training they received in holding public office and in managing their extensive private affairs combined to produce one of the greatest groups of leaders any generation in history has known.

Since Virginia's colonial civilization revolved about tobacco—it was "founded upon smoak," in the words of one contemporary—the growers both large and small were almost completely dependent upon the tobacco market for their well-being. Governor Gooch devoted constant attention to the passage and enforcement of statutes designed to regulate the shipment and sale of the leaf to Great Britain.

The Virginia planters operated with a system of credit extended by British merchants, and many of them were in debt to those merchants throughout most of their lives. Thomas Jefferson's famous statement that Virginia planters were "a species of property annexed to certain mercantile houses in London" contained only a slight measure of exaggeration. The merchants usually allowed the planters to keep open accounts. This encouraged extravagance on the part of the latter, who ordered goods of all kinds for their plantations, and charged them against anticipated receipts from the tobacco crop. The system kept them on the merchants' books to such an extent that at the time of the Revolution their total indebtedness to those merchants was estimated at two million pounds sterling. The merchants, for their part, were often annoyed at being treated like glorified errand boys by the planters, who sent them long lists of supplies and special articles to be purchased. The merchants assuaged their annoyance by charging a stiff commission for these services.

The dependence of Virginia upon tobacco carried with it an apparently inexorable involvement with slavery. The General Assembly made repeated efforts to slow down the slave traffic by placing special taxes on importations of Africans. Governor Gooch approved these levies, but the British merchants who were making huge profits from the mounting shipments managed, in one way or another, to obtain repeal of the taxes, or to have them disallowed by the king.

Gooch, a military veteran who, like Spotswood, had trained under Marlborough, was anxious to prevent any further slave revolts. One of these was seriously threatened in 1730, three years after he took office. A number of Negroes assembled in Norfolk and Princess Anne counties while the whites were at church. The blacks planned a bold stroke for liberty, but they were discovered. Many were arrested and several were executed. There were other evidences of restlessness among the slave population, and runaways were numerous.[1]

Gooch wrote the Bishop of London that some masters treated their Negroes "no better than their cattle," but he added that "the greater number, having kind masters, live much better than our poor laboring men in England." William Byrd II expressed the view of many of the colonists when he said he wished Virginia would exclude the chattels entirely, on the ground that slavery was harmful to both the slaveowner and the slave.

The small group of free Negroes in the colony was forbidden to vote or to serve on juries. These restrictions were defended by Gooch, who suspected free Negroes, without proof, of having had a part in a recent attempted insurrection. He also spoke of their "insolence," and of the prevailing tendency of the free Negro to consider himself "as good a man as the best of his neighbors." These freemen were to suffer from many disabilities until the Civil War.[2]

One result of the spread of slavery over a wider and wider area of the tobacco economy was to give increasing political power to the smaller plantation owners. These had now entered the slaveholding aristocracy, and were competing for prestige with the group of great landowners, who had dominated the scene in the seventeenth century. Whereas the council had previously been the legislative branch which wielded by far the greater power, the House of Burgesses now replaced it as the center of political potency.[3]

Gooch's talents as a manager of men and a student of human nature were severely tested during the first sixteen years of his twenty-two-year incumbency by his relations with Commissary Blair. The latter still sat upon the battlements in Argus-eyed scrutiny of all that went on.

The two men came into contact immediately upon Gooch's arrival in the colony. Only a short time later, Gooch was describing Blair in a letter as "a very vile old fellow, but he does not know that I am sensible of it." He added that "there is no perplexing device within his reach that he does not throw in my way." Since Gooch was acutely aware of the manner in which Blair had achieved the liquidation of three previous colonial executives he was determined not to suffer the same fate. It is impressive evidence of his tact, ingenuity and resourcefulness that he managed somehow not to run hopelessly afoul of the commissary. Upon the latter's death in 1743 at age eighty-seven, Gooch was still in complete control of his gubernatorial prerogatives and office. In Blair's behalf, it should be said that he rendered services of permanent value to the colony. Despite his meddlesomeness, and the bitter enmities which he aroused, he was a man of force, capacity and constructive achievement.

Another highly significant figure in colonial Virginia whose career ended during the administration of Governor Gooch was William Byrd II. One of the most erudite and literate men of his time, he read six languages and gathered a library of over 3600 volumes at Westover, the largest in the colonies, with the single exception of Cotton Mather's in Boston.

Distinctly cosmopolitan in outlook, Byrd spent some thirty of his seventy years in Europe. After getting the conventional classical education in England, he pursued legal studies at London's Middle Temple, and was called to the bar. At age twenty-two he was elected to the Royal Society, a rare honor. He returned to Virginia, but went back to London several times for extended stays on official missions for the colony. Despite the fact that he passed so much of his life abroad, Byrd was in many ways a typical member of the ruling group of Virginia planters. He served on the council for more than a third of a century, and briefly as its president.

His writings are among the most delightful in American literature. Witty, sprightly and allusive, they set a new high for the colonial era. Byrd wrote an account of the expedition on which he was sent by Governor Gooch in 1728 to adjudicate the boundary line between Virginia and North Carolina. His *History of the Dividing Line* and the subsequently published *A Journey to the Land of Eden* and *A Journey to the Mines,* tell in urbane prose of interesting and often amusing adventures on Byrd's excursions into the wilderness.

A few samples of Byrd's writings give the flavor:

"We hardly allowed ourselves leisure to eat, which in truth we had the less stomach to, by reason of the dinner was served up by the landlord, whose nose stood on such ticklish terms that it was in danger of falling into the dish."

"Our chaplain, for his part, did his office, and rubbed us up with a seasonable sermon. This was quite a new thing to our brethren of North Carolina, who live in a climate where no clergyman can breathe, any more than spiders in Ireland."

"The worst of it was, we had unluckily outrode the baggage, and for that reason were obliged to lodge very sociably in the same apartment with the family, where, reckoning women and children, we mustered all no less than nine persons, who all pigged lovingly together."

"My landlady received us with a grim sort of welcome, which I did not expect, since I brought her husband back in good health, though perhaps that might be the reason."

It was on Byrd's *Journey to the Land of Eden*, in 1733, that he tells of having "laid the foundations of two large cities," Richmond and Petersburg.

In addition to the above-mentioned books, Byrd kept a diary in cipher for many years. Less readable than his other works, it nevertheless provides an invaluable insight into his day-to-day occupations and interests, both in Virginia and in England. His *London Diary*, 1717–1721 is particularly revealing concerning the amorous propensities of the widower Byrd in the British capital. Virginians were startled to read, upon this volume's appearance in 1958, of Byrd's unorthodox extracurricular activities. He frankly set forth that he had spent a good part of his time in London's bagnios, and in seducing matrons or their serving maids, and picking up wenches on the street. These last he sometimes took into his coach or into the shrubbery of St. James's Park. Byrd was a religious man, and he usually said his prayers after these lapses.

He was also a brilliant man—one of the major ornaments of the eighteenth century in Virginia. His *London Diary* does no credit to his morals, but the colony owed him much. His elegant mansion on the James, representing the best in the architecture of his times; his catholic taste in many directions, his literary flair and his achievements as a linguist and bibliophile, to say nothing of his long service in public office, all placed our colonial civilization, as well as future generations, greatly in his debt.

As a loyal member of the Anglican communion, Byrd donated the site for Westover Church about a quarter of a mile from his mansion, and it was there that he and his family worshiped.

Byrd's own transgressions of the moral code—which seem to have occurred mainly during his sojourns in England—might be attributed by some to the reputedly unclerical behavior and bad example set by the colonial clergy in America. Much has been written of their supposed penchant for divertissements not altogether in accord with the accepted canons (although sexual lapses were seldom charged against them). Are these strictures justified?

It must be remembered that the clergy were a part of the upper strata of colonial society in Virginia. True, until the early eighteenth century, the Anglican clergy in England were considered unworthy to marry into the families of the English nobility, or even those of the gentry.[4] But the situation was otherwise in Virginia. The Anglican parsons moved easily among the social élite of the colony, and they participated in the latter's sports and other diversions.

Undoubtedly there was a fondness on the part of the clergy for card playing and horse racing, and few were total abstainers. On the contrary, they were often connoisseurs of Burgundy or Bordeaux, and when the opportunity arose, they sometimes consumed these vintages to excess. Their behavior must be judged, of course, in the context of what was considered proper in that age. Under the standards of the seventeenth and eighteenth centuries in both England and Virginia, such diversions, when moderately pursued, were deemed acceptable. There were, of course, examples of drunkenness and other gross misbehavior on the part of Anglican clergymen. A number were tried and unfrocked. But Edward L. Goodwin, in his *Colonial Church in Virginia*, lists 645 clergymen of that era, only seventeen of whom were dismissed for drunkenness or other derelictions. (There were black sheep among the dissenting clergy, too, some of whom were revoltingly unclerical.)

Richard L. Morton concludes that "the Virginia clergymen of the Established Church of the colonial period have received very unfair treatment at the hands of later historians—even from some of their own denomination." He adds that "this was because these historians measured and recorded these men's lives by the puritanical, evangelical yardstick of the 'New Lights.'"[5]

The analysis appears to be a just one. The Anglican parsons attended horse races, rode to hounds, danced, and pleasured themselves around the flowing bowl, and were no strangers to the card table and perhaps the cockfight. Yet, since these forms of merrymaking and relaxation, when temperately indulged in, were considered acceptable by the upper strata of colonial society, we should judge the Virginia Anglicans on that basis. It is hardly fair to condemn them because a small minority behaved in an unseemly, even a swinish manner.

The standards of conduct which Lieutenant Governor Gooch had set for the colony were approximately those which prevailed in England.

There was gaiety among the upper classes. Gooch himself boasted that "the gentlemen and ladies here are well bred, not an ill dancer in my government." The Reverend Hugh Jones, whose *The Present State of Virginia* had appeared in 1724, wrote concerning the Williamsburgers: "They live in the same neat manner, dress after the same modes, and behave themselves exactly as the gentry in London; most families of any note having a coach, chariot, berlin or chaise."

Unusual amusements were offered on special field days, set apart for the purpose. At the end of the seventeenth century one such fete, in Surry County, included the offering of prizes "to be shott for, wrasttled, played at backswords & run for by Horse and foot . . . by the better sort of Virginians onely, who are Batchelors."

Some years later, in 1737, a Hanover gentleman, described as of Scottish birth but nonetheless generous, "provided handsome entertainment for gentlemen and ladies" on St. Andrew's Day. The *Virginia Gazette*, which had appeared in Williamsburg for the first time the year before, set forth the details, in part, as follows:

A hat worth twenty shillings to be "cudgelled for." A violin to be played by twenty fiddlers, and given to the best performer. Twelve boys twelve years of age to run twelve yards for a hat worth twelve shillings. A "Quire of Ballads" to be sung for, all contestants to have "liquor to clear their windpipes." A pair of silver buckles to be wrestled for by a number of "brisk young men," plus "many other whimsical and comical diversions too tedious to mention."

Governor Gooch approved of these amusing interludes, and his perspicacity was evidenced in various other ways, as when he proclaimed to all and sundry that Virginia had "the best Pork in the world." He reinforced this dictum by sending the Bishop of London "Virginia Hamms" at regular intervals.

A notable event of the Gooch administration was the establishment of the first printing press in Virginia. This took place at Williamsburg in 1728, with William Parks as the proprietor. In contrast to Governor Berkeley, Lieutenant Governor Gooch rejoiced that there was now a press in the colony. Publication of the *Virginia Gazette* followed eight years thereafter.

Gooch had not been in the best of health since 1740, when he led a Virginia regiment in the unsuccessful British attack on the Spanish city of Cartagena on the northern coast of South America.

A 24-pound cannon ball passed between his ankles, inflicting a wound from which he never recovered.

By 1749 his health was such that he begged to be relieved, and his request was granted. His farewell address to the General Assembly, after twenty-two years in office, reflected the mutual affection which existed between him and his constituents. Lieutenant Governor Gooch was one of a succession of colonial administrators in Virginia who were conspicuously competent. He was also one of the most popular and beloved of them all.

NINE

Pioneers Beyond the Mountains

ALEXANDER SPOTSWOOD had blazed a trail in 1716 across the mountains into the Shenandoah Valley, with its sparkling rivers and limestone caverns, and William Gooch was now to accelerate the movement of settlers into both the Valley and the southwest. It was important to populate these regions as soon as possible, in order to strengthen the colony. The Indians—whose lovely word "Shenandoah" means "Daughter of the Stars"—were still a serious threat there. The greater the number of white settlers, the better the chance of coping successfully with the red men.

An ultimate clash with the French also seemed probable. The latter were ambitious to obtain the maximum amount of territory in North America, and they were established already in the Illinois country and along the Gulf coast. The Virginia leaders hastened the movement of settlers into the regions beyond the Blue Ridge and the Alleghenies, in order to pre-empt those large and strategic areas. The bloody French and Indian War was a couple of decades in the future.

The James, the Rappahannock and the Roanoke rivers were crucially important to the settlers as they pushed westward in their buckskins. The Potomac, to a lesser degree, served a similar purpose. The fall line had been crossed by westward-moving migrants in the early eighteenth century, after which they traveled steadily upstream along these rivers and their tributaries.

Simultaneously, a flood of Scotch-Irish and Germans who had fled from persecution in Europe, poured down from Pennsylvania into the lush valley of the Shenandoah. This mass migration began in

the early 1730s and resulted in peopling the region with thousands of
hard-working, sturdy farmers. With them came smaller numbers of
Mennonites and Quakers. These diverse ethnic and religious groups
brought to the colony an admirable infusion of literate immigrants,
deeply religious for the most part, but critical of the Established
Church, and profoundly dedicated to ideals of freedom. They would
be an element of immense importance to the colony and the state
throughout all future years.

As the colonials of English background moved westward from
Tidewater, and newcomers of other national origins arrived from
Pennsylvania, their first requirement was land. Large landholders in
eastern Virginia were in a position to aid them. These speculators
were anxious to make a profit, and, as we have seen, their methods
were sometimes far from admirable. But in numerous instances, large
tracts were acquired by honorable means, or means considered legitimate in that era, and portions were sold at reasonable prices
to settlers in need of acreage. This process was facilitated by Spotswood
and accelerated by Gooch. It resulted in greatly hastening the settlement of the Valley and the southwest, for it provided an almost
essential service to the immigrants. They had neither the time nor
the money for a trip to Williamsburg in order to comply with
patent requirements or other legal formalities. The enterprising speculators, some of whom moved permanently into such frontier areas as
Spotsylvania and Goochland—then much larger counties than they
are today—could do the needful on the spot.

As examples of the type of conspicuous leaders from Tidewater
who became active in land speculation, two may be mentioned.
Capable Thomas Lee, president of the council and builder of Stratford, was the organizer of the Ohio Company whose founders, like
Lee, were mainly from that nursery of great men, the Northern
Neck. Dr. Thomas Walker, a native of King and Queen County and
a leading physician and botanist, as well as a notable explorer, was
the dominant factor in the equally important Loyal Company. Walker
had moved to Castle Hill, in Albemarle County, and most of his
associates in the company were from that area. These two men, and
their companies, were exceptional in the contributions they made
to the opening up and settling of Virginia's western areas. The
versatile Dr. Walker was personally active for many years as an explorer,

and his wide-ranging expeditions went through Cumberland Gap and into Kentucky.

A significant element in the promotion of the western settlements was the controversy over the Fairfax Proprietary, involving vast tracts of land extending from the Northern Neck beyond the Alleghenies. The huge grant by Charles II to Lord Culpeper in the late seventeenth century has been referred to in Chapter Ten. The grant was passed on to Culpeper's daughter, who married the fifth Lord Fairfax, and to their son, the sixth lord. Under the terms, quitrents or taxes on these lands went to Fairfax instead of to the colony.

Robert ("King") Carter was named agent for the Fairfax claims. He entered an official objection in 1729 to the execution of certain grants made the previous year for lands in the Shenandoah Valley, on the ground that this area was within the bounds of the Fairfax Proprietary. The British Board of Trade was asked to adjudicate the dispute, and a survey was recommended. Thomas Lord Fairfax came to Virginia, and commissioners were appointed to resolve the differences. Their verdict, rendered in 1746, was in favor of Fairfax, whose title to the quitrents from no fewer than six million acres was confirmed. Grants previously made by the Virginia government in the area under contention were, however, validated. With these exceptions, Fairfax was awarded the quitrents from the entire Northern Neck, plus a belt of territory extending northwestward across much of northern Virginia, and over the mountains into several fringe counties of what is now West Virginia. This arrangement remained in effect until the Revolution.

As Gooch's administration drew to its close, western lands were being patented on a huge scale. This made it desirable that an authentic map of the colony be prepared. The Board of Trade accordingly chose for the task Joshua Fry, a former William and Mary professor, "eminent for his skill in the mathematicks," and Peter Jefferson, father of Thomas Jefferson, a powerful and rugged frontiersman, but also a man of intellectual breadth and curiosity. During this excellent map's preparation, Fry and Jefferson are said to have been forced at times to defend themselves from wild beasts, to sleep in trees and to eat raw flesh.

The Shenandoah Valley, into which so many settlers were pouring, provided good pasturage in the eighteenth century. It was one huge prairie, unbroken except by clumps of great trees here and there.

The mountains on both sides were heavily wooded, but much of the valley floor was covered with luxuriant grass, often five or six feet high, which attracted herds of buffalo. Since the Indians depended on the buffalo for both hides and meat, they kept the valley attractive to the bison, as well as to deer and other game, by burning it over at regular intervals.

When the first Scotch-Irish and Germans arrived on the scene, traveling in wagons or on horseback, the Valley was no longer the home of any Indian tribe. However, it was traversed with some regularity by Indians for hunting or warring parties, using the ancient buffalo trail or Warrior's Path, which much later became the Valley Turnpike. These Indians were friendly for some years, but they became murderously hostile.

The white settlers who built their log cabins in that frontier region were fearless men and women who did not flinch before the terrors of the wilderness. Sometimes they gathered in forts for greater protection, but often they were alone with their children, and entirely dependent upon their own quick wits and accurate marksmanship.

Every backwoodsman had his rifle, but in the early decades the settlers had to content themselves with the most primitive food, clothing, household furnishings and kitchen utensils. They killed game for much of their sustenance, and raised a few vegetables. The crudest linsey, made of flax and wool, or wild nettles and buffalo hair, was woven into garments for all members of the family. Knives and forks were frequently unobtainable. When no table knife was at hand with which to cut up the bear steak or buffalo meat, the men used the scalping knives which they carried at all times.

During those years in the mid-eighteenth century, no merchant of any kind was to be found in the entire Valley. Nor were there any mills for grinding grain, tanners for making leather, shops for making or repairing utensils, or carpenters, tailors, cabinet workers, weavers or shoemakers. All these services had to be performed by the individual settlers. There was, furthermore, no money. The men and women of the Valley swapped furs and pelts for the crude articles brought to them on horseback across the Blue Ridge.[1]

To the danger of Indian assault was added that of being attacked by wild animals. Bears were everywhere, wolves were fierce, and panthers were not only vicious but they were sometimes of prodigious dimensions. One well-known huntsman slew a panther which he said "measured upwards of fourteen feet from the end of his nose to the end of his tail." Another mighty hunter in the area was ready to believe this, saying that he himself killed a panther "of enormous size."[2]

The restless pioneers were pushing beyond the basin of the Shenandoah into the rugged regions of the southwest—into the southern reaches of the Great Valley, whose green meadows and laurel-flecked uplands extend for hundreds of miles, with the mist-shrouded peaks of the Blue Ridge and the Alleghenies brooding over all. The Great Valley stretches from below the Virginia-Tennessee line along the North and South forks of the Holston River and the Clinch, past Great Lick, the present city of Roanoke, to the sources of the Shenandoah and along that stream's entire length to where, at Harpers Ferry, it surges breathtakingly, between crags, into the Potomac.

Adam Harman (Heinrich Adam Hermann), a pioneer German who settled in the Shenandoah Valley in 1736, led the first group of settlers to the New River about 1743.[3] He and his descendants were influential thereafter in the affairs of southwest Virginia.

Under the leadership of Colonel James Patton, a doughty Indian fighter associated with Dr. Thomas Walker in the Loyal Company, a steady flow of settlers, mostly Scotch-Irish, moved into the southwestern region traversed by the New and Holston rivers. In the basin where the town of Saltville now stands there was a salty lake frequented by thousands of deer, elk and buffalo. From the lake the pioneers were able to obtain vital supplies of salt, and game was plentiful in the area.

A settlement in this trans-Allegheny region was made in 1750 by Colonel Patton at Draper's Meadow, on the site of the present Virginia Polytechnic Institute and State University. Five years later, Indians swooped down in a surprise attack, killing Patton and others who were living there. Women and children were among the wounded and slain. Mary Draper Ingalls was carried off into captivity, but later escaped and made her way back to her husband. Leading southwest Virginia families are descended from this couple.

In a later massacre, in Abb's Valley, Tazewell County, every adult was killed by Indians. A young girl, Mary Moore, was carried off. She managed to make her way back years later, and was married to the Reverend Samuel Brown, a Presbyterian pastor. The Browns had eleven children, five of whom entered the Presbyterian ministry.

They have numerous descendants today, especially in the Shenandoah Valley.

As the frontiersmen pushed out into the unexplored regions of Virginia and Kentucky, they crossed the eastern continental divide somewhere in the present Blacksburg-Cambria-Radford area. On one side of this watershed the streams flow into the Atlantic and on the other into the Mississippi.

The coming of the Scotch-Irish to Virginia in great numbers brought into sharp focus the issue of religious freedom. They were nearly all Presbyterians, and there arose at once the question of their relationship to the Established Church.

Urbane Lieutenant Governor Gooch stated that Presbyterian clergymen would not suffer "interruption," so long as they "conform themselves to the rules prescribed by the Act of Toleration in England by taking the oaths [of loyalty to the Crown and the Protestant religion] enjoined thereby, and registering the places of their meeting, and behave themselves peaceably towards the government." This seemed a reasonable position. However the Presbyterians would soon be split into factions, as would become apparent when a vigorous presbytery was planted in Piedmont Virginia's Hanover County.

The founder of that presbytery was Samuel Davies, "the greatest pulpit orator of his generation," still in his twenties, but a conspicuous leader in a denomination noted for its able and educated ministry. Davies conformed to the regulations by presenting his credentials, taking the oaths and registering as a dissenting minister. But other members of the Hanover presbytery, under the leadership of two so-called New-Side or New-Light ministers, William Robinson and John Roan, ignored these legal requirements. "So," in the words of the noted church historian, G. MacLaren Brydon, "they came into the colony breaking the very law which served as a protection to all recognized dissenting denominations." Not only so, but certain New-Side preachers "attacked with the utmost vigor of vituperation the clergy and worship of the Anglican Church and the Old-Side Presbyterians."

Davies belonged to the former group, but he was shocked by their abusive tactics. He also disliked their pulpit technique and the physical gyrations which accompanied much of their preaching. Davies, furthermore, preached patriotism as a part of the Christian religion. When the French and Indian War broke out in 1754, he was a tower of strength in recruiting the tough-thewed Scotch-Irish frontiersmen. His eloquent exhortations to them to defend their country were helpful to the government in Williamsburg and induced a more sympathetic attitude there and throughout the colony toward religious dissenters.

The influence wielded by such a clergyman as Davies in the eighteenth century is illustrated in a statement of William Henry Foote in his authoritative work on Presbyterianism in Virginia. Speaking of certain members of that faith in Henrico, he declares: "The nearest of his [Davies'] churches was about fifty miles distant. They went on horseback, often fording James River and sometimes taking a child or two on horseback with them . . . Who rides fifty miles to church now [1850] and carries a child or two on horseback?"

The Scotch-Irish were spreading into other areas. John Caldwell, grandfather of John C. Calhoun, led a group of settlers from the Shenandoah Valley into the Staunton-Roanoke basin of Southside Virginia. They settled along Cub Creek near the Little Roanoke, and on nearby Buffalo Creek. Churches were built in what are now Campbell, Charlotte and Prince Edward counties. Hampden-Sydney College was to be one ultimate result.

A noteworthy religious phenomenon of the mid-eighteenth century was the Great Awakening, which was sweeping the colonies from North to South. Its effects were being strongly felt in Virginia. George Whitefield, the fiery British evangelist, had preached in Williamsburg's Bruton Parish Church as early as 1739, with great effect. He was a member of the Anglican Church, but was considered a New-Light. The Reverend Patrick Henry, uncle of the more famous Patrick, let Whitefield occupy his Anglican pulpit in Hanover. The clergyman declared that if he had refused permission, Whitefield "would have preached in the church yard . . . and then the whole congregation would have gone over to him."

The Germans who came to Virginia in the early eighteenth century were members of either the Lutheran or the German Reformed church. Small groups had arrived in response to Spotswood's appeals, and settled at Germanna on the Rapidan. About two decades later they came down from Pennsylvania in much larger numbers into the Shenandoah Valley, with a smaller group of Mennonites, and established themselves mainly in the Valley's northern end, with its rich limestone soils, in the vicinity of Strasburg and Woodstock.

The Scotch-Irish were predominantly in the Valley's southern end, in the lower portion of what is now Rockingham County, and in Augusta and Rockbridge counties, including Staunton and Lexington. Such leading families as the Lewises, McDowells, Paxtons, Wallaces, Stuarts, Alexanders, Moores, Robertsons, Grahams, Johnstons and Buchanans settled here.[4]

When the German Reformed members moved from Germanna to the present Fauquier County, they had their own church and school-house. Although many German settlers, mostly Lutherans, arrived in the Shenandoah from the North in the 1730s, they had no resident pastors until about forty years later. In the meantime they appear to have worshiped in private homes or schoolhouses. Small numbers of Dunkers and United Brethren came in the latter part of the eighteenth century.

The Shenandoah Valley Germans not only provided a significantly stable element of knowledgeable farmers, but their record in the American Revolution was a notable one. It will be referred to here-after, along with the even more impressive record of the Scotch-Irish in both the Indian wars and the Revolution.

Adam Miller (or Mueller), a German pioneer, was the first of all the settlers in the Valley when he established his frontier home there about 1727. He was soon followed by Joist Hite and Jacob Stover.

Jacob Stover may have been the great-great-great-grandfather of President Dwight D. Eisenhower, whose mother, Ida Stover, was born in the Fort Defiance area of Augusta County in 1862. But Klaus Wust, author of The Virginia Germans, believes that the President's ancestors were Stoevers. Both the Stoevers and the Stovers —Germans or German-Swiss—were among the first of all the settlers in the Valley. The Reverend John Casper Stoever, Jr., "the first German clergyman to officiate in the Shenandoah Valley," according to Wust, was holding Lutheran services there as early as 1734. Either he or one of the various other early Stoevers or Stovers—one of whom, Peter Stover, founded the town of Strasburg—was evidently the forebear of President Eisenhower's mother.[5]

Among other German families who settled early in the Valley and have made important contributions in various fields of endeavor were the Bowmans, Henkels, Ruffners, Riddlebergers, Rousses, Brocks, Harmans, Maucks, Conrads, Neffs, Zirkles, Koiners, Rhoadses, Rosen-bergers, Keezells, Holtzclaws, Obenshains and Deyerles.

Abraham Lincoln had no German blood, but his father Thomas Lincoln, was born in the Valley in 1778, about four miles west of Lacey Spring, Rockingham County. Thomas' father took him as a four-year-old to Kentucky. When he grew up, Thomas Lincoln married Nancy Hanks, who became the mother of Abraham Lincoln in 1809.

Also in the Valley of Virginia was a small colony of Quakers, located north and west of the present city of Winchester. Quakers had been in Virginia since the mid-seventeenth century, and had been persecuted for their religious non-conformity and their refusal to bear arms. They had not been hanged, as happened several times in Boston, but they had been fined, whipped and imprisoned.[6]

Although the Anglican Church was the Established Church of the colony, it scarcely existed west of the mountains throughout the seventeenth and during the first decades of the eighteenth century. The Anglicans were, of course, completely dominant in the Tidewater and Piedmont, but prior to 1738 they had not erected a single chapel beyond the Blue Ridge. Nor did any Episcopal bishop cross the Allegheny mountains for another hundred years.[7]

It was official policy at Williamsburg to invite members of dissenting faiths into the transmontane region. The colonial government realized, among other things, that the fighting Scotch-Irish, in particular, would be extremely useful on the frontier as bulwarks against the Indians and the French. When enough Anglicans finally crossed the mountains to establish small congregations, they were so few in number in the early days that vestrymen had to be chosen, in part, from among the dissenters. A full complement of vestrymen was essential in each parish, in view of the important duties, both religious and secular, performed by the vestries.

TEN

French, Indians and Washington

THE NEXT administration, that of Robert Dinwiddie, was especially memorable for the outbreak of the French and Indian War, which occurred in 1752 soon after he took office. In that war, fought in the wilderness over a vast area, and with global repercussions, a young man named George Washington was to demonstrate some of the qualities that have enshrined him among the great men of the world.

Dinwiddie, a Scot, became lieutenant governor in 1751, after an interlude in which Thomas Lee and Lewis Burwell, presidents of the council, served successively as acting chief executives. Dinwiddie had lived in Virginia, and had enjoyed considerable administrative and business experience.

The situation in the Ohio Valley was increasingly alarming, as the Indians grew more belligerent and the French sought to capitalize on this in their contest with Great Britain for control of all North America.

An Indian tribe, the Miamis or Twightwees, who were friendly to the British, had built a settlement on the upper Great Miami River. This settlement, called Pickawillany, fell to Indian allies of the French a few months after Dinwiddie's arrival in Williamsburg. As one historian puts it, the fall of this outpost beyond the Ohio—with the slaying of its inhabitants, accompanied by cannibalism[1]—was the beginning of the war which was to decide whether France or Britain would control the North American continent.

As these portentous events were occurring, Dinwiddie became embroiled in a bitter contest with the burgesses over his imposition of a fee for the patenting of each tract of land in the colony. Since thousands of these patents either had been actually applied for when Dinwiddie took office or were pending, a substantial sum of money was involved. More important, the burgesses rightly discerned that a principle was at stake, namely, the constitutional right of the executive to collect such a fee without their consent.

The fee in question was a Spanish gold pistole. Many of these were coined in Scotland, strange as that seems, and they were readily available in Virginia. The pistole was worth something over sixteen shillings sterling. While this may not appear to be a large amount, its payment would have imposed a heavy burden on the bulk of the colonists, especially those seeking to establish themselves in frontier regions. A pistole in that era would buy "a good cow and calf," according to one estimate.

The acrimonious controversy between the governor and the burgesses, involving some of the same principles which arose more than a decade later in connection with the Stamp Act, ended with Dinwiddie's abandonment of his plan.

Receipts from the pistole fee would have gone to Dinwiddie personally, which laid him open to the charge of venality. Whatever his motives, and he appears to have been an honest man, he was rash in proposing the fee and naïve in imagining that its imposition, without approval of the burgesses, would be acceptable. Fortunately for the colony, his relations with the legislative branch were reasonably good thereafter.

Events meanwhile were moving to a climax on the wild frontier, where British, French and Indians were maneuvering, with an empire at stake. Governor Dinwiddie was alert to the situation, and he cast about for a dependable emissary whom he could send to the French, demanding that they relinquish huge areas to which they laid claim. He entrusted this arduous and dangerous mission, with its far-reaching military and diplomatic overtones to George Washington, aged twenty-one.

This tall and powerfully built youth was already a major in the Virginia militia, but his limited experience on the frontier as a surveyor, and in Tidewater with military drills and musters, made his selection a risky one. It was, however, a great opportunity for a man of Washington's ambition and patriotism. He accepted the offer at once.

With half a dozen men, including a guide and an interpreter, he set out in the autumn of 1753 on an expedition that would take him 450 miles from Williamsburg, much of it through deep snows, pathless wastes and frozen bogs, to Fort Le Boeuf near Lake Erie in what is now northwestern Pennsylvania. Cold, torrential rains followed by near blizzards and marrow-piercing cold, plus the perils of Indian attack, tested Washington's mettle to the utmost. The French at Fort Le Boeuf, not too surprisingly, rejected Dinwiddie's demand as soon as Washington presented it.

On the return trip in late December, he and his veteran guide, Christopher Gist, fell into the ice-filled Allegheny River, and barely got out alive. After these and other well-nigh incredible hardships, Washington reached Williamsburg in mid-January and reported to Dinwiddie. He had not obtained the desired relinquishment of the Ohio lands by the French, but he had shown that he was brave, resourceful and indomitable.

He had also gathered incontrovertible evidence that the French were determined to hold the disputed frontier areas. Governor Dinwiddie accordingly moved at once to thwart them. He promoted Washington to lieutenant colonel and directed him to raise a force and march to the "forks of the Ohio," later the site of Pittsburgh.

After many difficulties and frustrations, Washington set out with a small contingent. At Great Meadows he encountered a force of Frenchmen, and in a fifteen-minute engagement killed ten of them, while losing one of his colonials. "I heard the bullets whistle," Washington wrote his brother, "and, believe me, there is something charming in the sound."

It was not only Washington's own baptism of fire, but with the killing of French soldiers by his men, the conflict acquired a new and ominous dimension. He prepared at once to complete Fort Necessity, the small fortified outpost at Great Meadows.

A short time later, he was surrounded there, and attacked by a much larger force of French and Indians. As a result, he had to capitulate, after suffering heavy losses. He was by no means solely to blame for this serious reverse, but his inexperience had led him to make several blunders.

He and Dinwiddie saw that reinforcements from Great Britain must be had, if the war on the frontier was to be prosecuted to a successful conclusion. But Dinwiddie was dissatisfied with Washington's performance at Fort Necessity, and apparently planned to demote him from colonel to captain. This would have made the young Virginian subordinate to officers whom he had previously commanded. He resigned from the army.

A few months later, General Edward Braddock arrived from Britain with two inferior regiments of regulars. He offered Washington a position as aide on his staff, and the offer was accepted. Washington was in the thick of the disastrous battle on the Monongahela River in which Braddock was mortally wounded. Washington distinguished himself in that action. He got four bullet holes in his coat and had two horses shot from under him. But with Braddock dead, his appointment as aide became void, and he returned to Mount Vernon.

Governor Dinwiddie promptly showed renewed confidence in Washington by naming him commander-in-chief of all the Virginia forces, with the rank of colonel. He was twenty-three. In this position, despite huge problems involving food, clothing, weapons and pay, he managed to protect the frontier more effectively than was done in the other colonies.

With the fall of Fort Duquesne to the British and the colonials in late 1758, an event in which Washington played a leading role, the Virginia colonel felt that he could retire from the service. The capture of this French stronghold on the site of the present Pittsburgh had long been a special objective, and its attainment caused a general relaxation in Virginia.

Washington, then twenty-six, had been elected, in his absence, to the House of Burgesses from Frederick County, with his friends putting on the successful campaign. They made expenditures in his behalf for liquors of various types. This offering of alcoholic refreshments to the voters, customary in that era, was described by one observer as "swilling the electors with bumbo," and by another as plying them with "strong grogg and scorched piggs."

Washington had won the hand of Martha Custis, widow of Daniel Parke Custis, and they were married in early 1759. During the next decade and a half, during which they lived at Mount Vernon, and he experimented with improved farming methods and attended to his legislative duties at Williamsburg, they were apparently exceptionally happy.

This despite the fact that, at the time of his marriage, Washington was obviously in love with Sally Cary Fairfax, the flirtatious, lissome

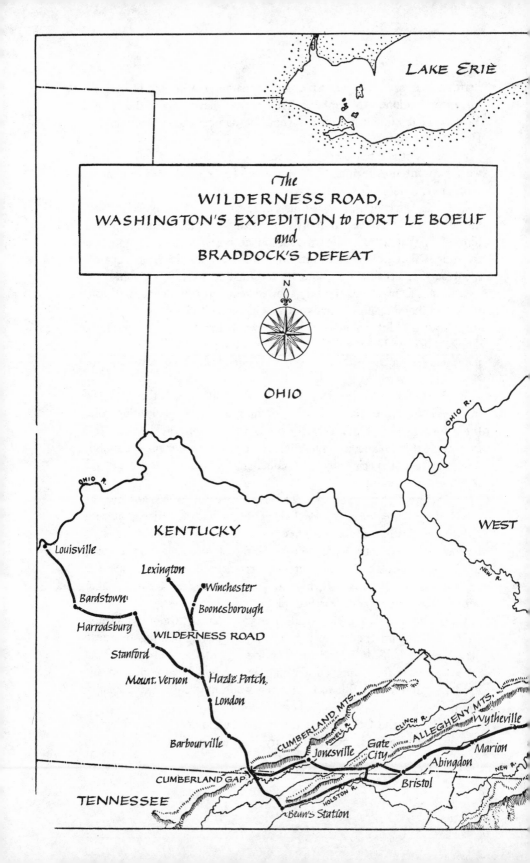

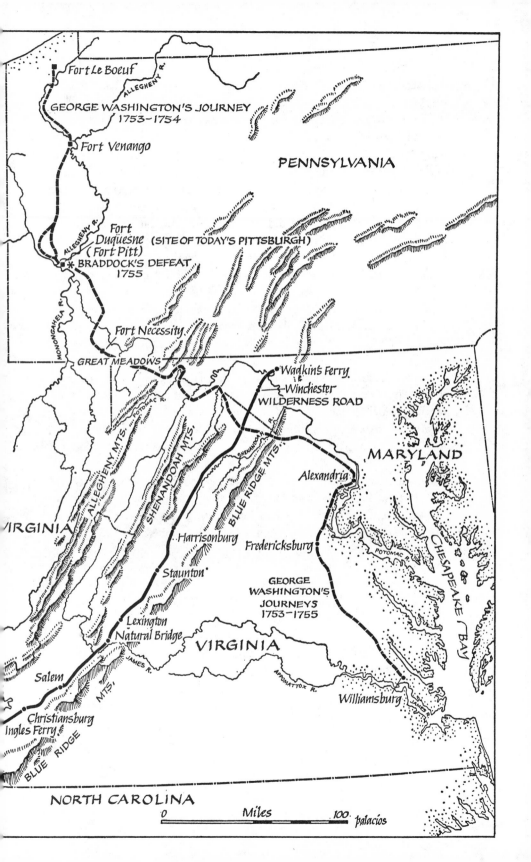

and alluring wife of his friend and neighbor, George William Fairfax of Belvoir.

Letters written by George to Sally were found after Sally's death, carefully tied in a bundle. The first, dated September 12, 1758, said, in part: "The world has no business to know the object of my Love, declared in this manner to you." George was engaged to Martha at the time, and he was to marry her in four months; yet he wrote in these terms. He said, further, "One thing above all things in this world I wish to know." He did not spell this out, but he was clearly seeking to learn if Sally loved him. Her discreet reply did not give him the answer. She had teased and flirted with him, but apparently nothing more. For example, when he returned to Mount Vernon after Braddock's defeat she sent word to him that she would walk to Mount Vernon from Belvoir unless he came to see her immediately.

The Fairfaxes went to England in 1773 and never returned. Washington did not forget Sally. In 1798, the year before he died, he wrote a long letter to the woman he had loved long before the Revolution, and who was now a widow. Although Martha was still living, Washington referred in his letter to "those happy moments, the happiest of my life, which I have enjoyed in your company." Washington's deep emotional involvement with Sally Fairfax tends to make him seem less the "cast iron man on a horse" so often depicted, and more the human being.[2]

He was fond of boat racing, horse racing, hunting, fishing, cards and the theater. Yet such diversions must have been somewhat solemnly pursued, for Douglas S. Freeman tells us that "no surviving record of his youth credits him with a laugh, even with a smile."

Washington's relations with Governor Dinwiddie ended on an unfortunate note. Their final exchange of correspondence showed that each was suffering from wounded feelings and was unhappy over the position taken by the other in connection with certain military matters.

Dinwiddie closed out his term in early 1758, and left for England. He was succeeded temporarily by John Blair, president of the council, pending the arrival of Francis Fauquier as lieutenant governor.

Fauquier was to be described in later years by Thomas Jefferson as the ablest governor who had ever served in Williamsburg. He was extraordinarily versatile, sophisticated and well-educated. The son of a Huguenot physician who had taken refuge in England, Fauquier served in the mint, which was directed by Sir Isaac Newton. Dumas

Malone, Jefferson's biographer, terms Fauquier "the 'compleat gentleman.'" Jefferson, as a student at the College of William and Mary, was invited to dine on various occasions with the governor, in company with two of his greatly venerated teachers at the college, George Wythe and William Small. The young student was also a participant in amateur musicals at the Governor's Palace, in which the talented Fauquier took part.

Fauquier's only serious fault seems to have been an excessive fondness for gambling. The vice was widely prevalent in Tidewater Virginia at the time, and it was unfortunate that the chief executive set an example which tended to make matters even worse. On the other hand, as a classicist, a man knowledgeable in the sciences, and a musician, not to say an exceptionally informed student of finance and a polished man of the world, Francis Fauquier made a lasting impression on the colony.

Dress worn by Tidewater and Piedmont Virginians in that pre-revolutionary era was no longer what it had been half a century before. Gentlemanly wigs were not so stylish as of yore and were giving way to powdered hair, worn in a braided pigtail and queue, tied with a black bow or placed in a black silk bag. Knee breeches were still *de rigueur*, but the cocked hat was now the style.

The ladies were gaudily garbed, in the fashions of the period, emphasizing the latest importations from London. Their dress, quite naturally, had gone through many transmutations. The farthingale had given way to the hooped skirt. Toward the close of Queen Anne's reign the hair had risen in "mountains of puffs, curls, and powder ornamented with tufts and feathers, flowers or ribbons known as egrets." Later, in 1774, Philip Fithian, the Presbyterian divinity student who served as tutor for the children of Robert Carter of Nomini Hall, wrote in his diary that seventeen-year-old Jenny Washington had her "light brown hair craped up with two rolls at each side." This type of "ornate topknot" was then the vogue.

The observant divinity student found Miss Betsey Lee "pinched up rather too near in a long pair of new-fashioned stays," and he deplored the fact that "the late importations of stays, said to be most fashionable in London, are produced upwards so high that we can have scarce any view of the Ladies Snowy Bosoms."

An insight into class distinctions prevailing among eighteenth-century Virginians is seen in the comment of William Byrd II concerning the marriage of a friend's daughter to her uncle's overseer. "Had she run away with a gentleman or a pretty fellow," Byrd wrote, "there might have been some excuse for her, though he were of inferior fortune; but to stoop to a dirty plebeian is the lowest prostitution."

And then there was that different kind of wedding reported by the *Virginia Gazette* in 1771. It carried a dispatch from Henrico County, telling of the marriage of handsome, twenty-three-year-old William Carter to "Madam Sarah Ellyson," an eighty-five-year-old widow, described as "a sprightly old Tit with three thousand pounds fortune."

With the retirement of Colonel Washington from the service, following the fall of Fort Duquesne, Governor Fauquier entrusted the command of the Virginia forces to Colonel William Byrd III.

Fauquier and the General Assembly became concerned, meanwhile, over the depredations of the Cherokee Indians in the Carolinas. The General Assembly directed the executive to raise seven hundred men, add them to the three hundred already on the Virginia frontier, and march to the relief of Fort Loudoun, situated deep in Cherokee territory. This proved an impossible assignment, and Fort Loudoun fell, with the massacre of part of the garrison. After other unsuccessful attempts by Virginia troops to reach and attack the Cherokees, a peace with these Indians was arranged by the governor of South Carolina in 1761, and was concurred in by Governor Fauquier.

The Virginia regiment raised for the Cherokee war was disbanded. However, Britain and Spain entered into hostilities shortly thereafter, and Spain held American territory which adjoined certain Cherokee lands. Hence another regiment had to be put together to meet the new threat. It remained on the frontier until after the Peace of Paris was signed in 1763.

The Peace of Paris ended the Seven Years' War between Britain and France, of which this country's French and Indian War was a part. Fighting had raged in Canada for several years, but with the fall of Quebec to the British in 1759, following the famous battle on the Heights of Abraham, and the fall of Montreal in 1760, the whole of Canada passed from French control.

The French and Indian War is sometimes termed "Virginia's war," Alf J. Mapp points out in his book, *The Virginia Experiment*. He quotes Voltaire's declaration apropos of the fall of Fort Necessity: "Such was the complication of political interests that a cannon shot fired in America could give the signal that set Europe in a blaze." Mapp also points to the statement of Louis Koontz in *The Virginia Frontier, 1754–1763* concerning Governor Dinwiddie's role, i.e., that the war "was begun in his [Dinwiddie's] attempt to protect Virginia territory . . . the first hostile forces sent out were Virginians; and the first blood was shed by Virginians."

ELEVEN

A Young Man Named Patrick Henry

In 1763, just after the Seven Years' War ended, there emerged upon the Virginia scene an as yet unknown orator whose "torrents of sublime eloquence," in Jefferson's phrase, were to electrify the colonies. It was in the so-called Parson's Cause, that Patrick Henry, a twenty-seven-year-old Hanover lawyer, was catapulted to public notice. His victory in that case launched him upon the career which made him one of the great figures of the American Revolution.

The Parson's Cause grew out of an argument between the clergy of the Established Church and the government over the clergy's compensation. At the end of the seventeenth century, legislation had been passed fixing the parsons' annual salary at 16,000 pounds of tobacco. Tobacco in that era was the equivalent of currency, and exchangeable for goods. Then in 1755, when the tobacco harvest was small, a law was passed to permit payment of the salaries in money at the rate of sixteen shillings and eight pence per 100 pounds, which came to two pence per pound. Hence the act was called the Two Penny Act. This rate of compensation was not pleasing to the parsons, since when the market went up to three or four pence, they would not receive the benefit. Their pay, furthermore, had always tended to be modest. The Reverend Patrick Henry was among those who signed a letter of protest to the authorities in Great Britain. His nephew and namesake would become famous through his eloquent advocacy of the opposite view.

The Two Penny Act of 1755 was to lapse after only ten months, but the clergy saw, with concern, that it represented a departure from previous practice. Their intuition was correct, for when prospects for the size of the tobacco crop became dim again in 1758, another such act was passed.

This caused the clergy to send one of their number to England in protest—a step which was certain to arouse much resentment in Virginia, since the ministers were going "over the head" of the government in Williamsburg. It also raised sharply the question whether in the case of so local an issue the will of the Assembly should not be paramount.

The Reverend James Maury of Louisa County was one of several clergymen who sued for the additional salary. He sought the difference between two pence per pound, as prescribed in the act, and what the tobacco actually brought in 1758, an amount in excess of £250 for the allotted 16,000 pounds. His attorney was Peter Lyons, the leading lawyer in that part of the colony, while John Lewis, also prominent in the profession, represented the defendants, the tax collectors for the parish.

The case, tried in Hanover County, took a significant turn when Lyons filed a demurrer, claiming that the Two Penny Act had been invalid since its enactment. Colonel John Henry, the presiding judge, upheld this contention. All that remained, therefore, was for a jury to fix the amount of the damages.

Lewis dropped out of the case, perhaps feeling that the main issue had been decided. Whereupon the tax collectors retained Patrick Henry, the son of Judge Henry, to represent them.

This was Patrick's great opportunity, and he seized it. Although he had little time to prepare his argument, he showed in court that he was a veritable genius at developing a theme on short notice in a manner to transfix and almost to mesmerize an audience.

The deeply learned Colonel Richard Bland, who had a large share in the authorship of both Two Penny Acts, also had written pamphlets critical of the clergy. These furnished Henry with ammunition for his argument before the jury at Hanover Courthouse.

Henry not only attacked the ministers, a number of whom were present, but he also assailed the British King, who had disallowed the Two Penny Act of 1758. His assault on the clergy was particularly sharp, even demagogic. He is quoted as having said that "these rapacious harpies would, were their power equal to their will, snatch from the hearth of their honest parishioner his last hoe-cake, from the widow and her orphaned children their last milch-cow, the last bed, nay the last blanket, from the lying-in woman." While the colonial clergy had their faults, this language was altogether extreme and unjustified. The Reverend Mr. Maury wrote later that Henry apologized to him after the court adjourned, saying that he had said these things "to render himself popular."

Henry also proclaimed to the jury that "a king by annulling or disallowing laws of this salutary nature [the Two Penny Act] from being the father of his people degenerates into a tyrant and forfeits all rights to his subject's obedience."

At this point there were murmurs of "treason, treason" in the courtroom.

After speaking for nearly an hour, Henry closed by conceding that since the court had ruled the Two Penny Act void, the jury would have to find for Mr. Maury, but it need not be for more than a farthing. The jury was out for only five minutes and gave Maury one penny damages.

It was a stunning victory for the youthful lawyer, and, as one historian puts it, he "leaped with one bound into the center of the Virginia political ring." Henry had discovered in the words of another writer, that the way to achieve political preferment and fame was to "strive with terrific oratorical power after he had assured himself that he was in the wake, not the van, of an inarticulate public opinion."

Henry was seized by the courthouse crowd and carried on their shoulders around the courtyard. He had become a popular hero overnight, and would soon be elected to the House of Burgesses.

The principal importance of the Parson's Cause lay in the fact that it was the vehicle which propelled Patrick Henry to prominence and put him in a position to exercise his astounding oratorical powers in a wider theater. The Parson's Cause had little lasting effect upon the fortunes of the Church or the clergy in Virginia, or upon the cause of religious liberty. But Henry discovered in the courtroom, as the case was tried, that he possessed a degree of eloquence rare in any age. The consequences of that discovery were to be international in their repercussions.

Great Britain under George III was bumbling toward the crisis which was to result in the loss of her thirteen North American colonies. Heedless of the heavy financial burden which those colonies had borne in the successful prosecution of the French and Indian War, Parliament proceeded to impose on them a stamp tax. The colonies were not consulted.

This tax was to be paid on nearly all legal documents, on newspapers, pamphlets, advertisements, playing cards, dice, almanacs, calendars, land grants and many appointments to public office.

When news of the Stamp Act's passage reached Virginia in 1765, the House of Burgesses, then in session, was at first passive in its attitude. However, Patrick Henry had been elected a member from Louisa County shortly before—he had moved there from Hanover— and nine days after he took his seat in the House he introduced resolutions against the Stamp Act which were to shake not only the burgesses but the thirteen colonies, as well.

In the account which Henry wrote many years later, he said he "determined to venture, & alone, unadvised & unassisted," to lead the attack on the obnoxious legislation passed by the British Parliament. This appears to be a considerable exaggeration. All credit to Henry for what he undoubtedly did, which was to serve as the spearhead of the assault on the Stamp Act, and to do so with blazing eloquence. But it strains one's credulity to believe that he was "alone, unadvised and unassisted." Carl Bridenbaugh declares in refutation that Henry "had been designated one of the leaders of the western members, who were posted to stay until the end of the session." This last was crucial, since many of the conservative members from Tidewater had left for their homes. "Henry knew this," writes Bridenbaugh. "He did not stand alone or unmanaged." Among those with whom he co-operated closely were John Fleming of Cumberland and George Johnston of Fairfax.

By the time Henry introduced his resolutions against the Stamp Act, attendance in the House was "the thinest ever known." This made it more likely that the less numerous and more liberal members from the upcountry, who had remained, would be able to obtain passage of the highly controversial paper.

The crucially important fifth resolution read as follows:

"Therefore, that the General Assembly of this Colony have the *only and sole exclusive* Right & Power to lay Taxes and Impositions upon the Inhabitants of this Colony and that every Attempt to vest such Power in any Persons whatsoever other than the General Assembly

Aforesaid has a manifest tendency to destroy British as well as American Freedom."

The five resolutions were proposed by Henry and seconded by Johnston. The first four were not particularly controversial, and Henry's discussion of them appears not to have been especially noteworthy. But when he reached the fifth, he rose to heights which probably surpassed those he had reached at Hanover Courthouse eighteen months before.

As with most of his other famous orations, this one was not taken down verbatim, and it has been necessary to reconstruct his words from the recollections of those who heard him.

"Tarquin and Caesar had each his Brutus, Charles the First his Cromwell, and George the Third . . . ," shouted the twenty-nine-year-old Henry, as he paused for dramatic effect.

"Treason!" came the cry from Speaker John Robinson, and "Treason!" was echoed around the chamber.

But the unruffled member from Louisa finished his sentence:

". . . may profit by their example. If *this* be treason, make the most of it."

The fifth resolution passed by only 20 to 19, and it seems certain that its passage was due to the overwhelming effect of Henry's words.

"By God, I would have given one hundred guineas for a single vote," Peyton Randolph exclaimed after the result had been announced.

Some have questioned the correctness of the quotations that have come down to us from Henry's address, but Robert D. Meade, Henry's definitive biographer, concluded after an exhaustive study, that they are substantially accurate. Certainly there is impressive evidence from various directions of the immense impact of Henry's words. Thomas Jefferson, then a tall, ruddy-haired, seventeen-year-old college student, stood in the door while Henry was speaking. He never forgot the impression Henry's eloquence made upon him. Jefferson was in some respects no admirer of Henry, but he referred long afterward to the "splendid display of Henry's talents" and added, "He appeared to me to speak as Homer wrote." On another occasion he called Henry "the greatest orator that ever lived."

The gentleman from Louisa left Williamsburg the day after the vote on his resolutions, wearing the frontier dress in which he had appeared before the burgesses. As soon as he was gone, the House voted to rescind the fifth resolution. However, copies of all five resolutions somehow got into the press of the other colonies, as though all had passed. So the final defeat of the most far-reaching of the five was not too significant, insofar as the ultimate effect was concerned.

The colonies had been aroused against Great Britain, and although the clash of arms was a decade away, tension was rising and colonial discontent was growing. At Leedstown, Westmoreland County, in February 1766, more than a hundred of the Northern Neck's foremost citizens adopted resolutions drafted by Richard Henry Lee denouncing the act and any "abandon'd wretch" who paid the iniquitous tax.

On the economic front, many of Virginia's leading planters had run into extremely difficult times, and some were actually bankrupt. Taxes were heavy and the supply of specie in the colony was severely limited. The law required that treasury notes be burned or retired when they were received in payment of taxes. As the supply of this paper shrank, the position of the planters who had been unable to pay their taxes and other debts became increasingly critical.

The treasurer of the colony and Speaker of the House was John Robinson of King and Queen County, a man greatly admired and beloved in the colony, and the most powerful individual in Virginia, except possibly the governor, during the last twenty-five years of his life. He also has been termed "probably the most powerful native politician in eighteenth-century colonial Virginia."[1]

Robinson was on intimate terms with virtually all the leaders of the colony. Many of them were facing ruin in the early 1760s, for they were heavily in debt and without the means of getting the money to discharge those debts. Robinson was charged with the duty of burning the paper currency issued during the French and Indian War as soon as he received it in payment of taxes. As David J. Mays writes, in his masterful biography of Edmund Pendleton: "He could burn the paper money and bankrupt his friends, or ignore the law and make the paper available to those in desperate need. He chose to save his friends."

So Robinson took more than £100,000 illegally from the treasury of Virginia and lent it to these friends, among whom were many of the leading men in the colony.

These facts remained unknown until Robinson died in 1766. He was one of the colony's wealthiest men, and Edmund Pendleton, a highly regarded leader in the House of Burgesses from Caroline County, was chosen administrator of his estate, along with Peter Lyons and Peter Randolph. Pendleton, who did most of the work, soon discovered what a huge sum Robinson had taken from the colonial treasury and lent to his intimates. The Speaker and treasurer apparently had gambled on a return of prosperity and an end of the money panic, which would have made possible repayment of at least a large part of the sums borrowed. But Robinson's death intervened, the magnitude of the scandal became apparent, Robinson's fine reputation was destroyed, and his large estate went toward the payment of these debts.

The list of borrowers, with the amounts owed, did not become public until nearly two centuries after Robinson's passing. The court records were unearthed in Richmond by David Mays, and listed in his Pendleton biography. William Byrd III, an inveterate plunger and gambler—who was a Tory at the outset of the Revolution, but later modified his position,[2] and finally killed himself in 1777—turned up as the largest borrower of all. He owed £14,921. Other large borrowers, with the amounts, included Bernard Moore of Chelsea, £8500; Lewis Burwell, £6274; Benjamin Grymes, £5406; Archibald Cary, £3975; Carter Braxton, £3848; Charles Carter, Jr., £3834, and so on down the list.

While the foregoing names and amounts were not revealed at the time, the fact that the treasury was found to be short by more than £100,000, as a result of loans made by Robinson to his friends, caused the burgesses to separate the offices of Speaker and treasurer. The former post went to Peyton Randolph and the latter to Robert Carter Nicholas. This separation remained in effect throughout the remaining years of the colonial era.

TWELVE

Stamps, Tea and Long Knives

VIRGINIA had been foremost among the colonies in opposing the Stamp Act. This was the first of numerous examples of the Old Dominion's leadership in the prerevolutionary era. As Professor Edward Channing of Harvard wrote, "Virginia led, as she constantly did in the constitutional opposition of the next few years."

However, it was Massachusetts which issued a call for a Stamp Act Congress of all the colonies to meet in New York and protest the passage of the act. Nine colonies sent representatives, but Virginia didn't, since the burgesses were not in session, and hence could not name delegates.

Yet when Colonel George Mercer arrived in Williamsburg from England, bearing the first of the stamps, he ran into a grim crowd composed mainly of "gentlemen of property in the colony." They demanded that he resign as His Majesty's stamp distributor. He demurred and was protected by Governor Fauquier from possible manhandling. There were angry mutterings, and Mercer found next day that his position was impossible. He stated that he would distribute no stamps until he had received additional "orders from England," and furthermore that he would do nothing contrary to the wishes of the General Assembly.

This was merely one example of the feeling against the Stamp Act which erupted not only in Virginia but throughout the colonies. The stamps were burned in some places, and stamp distributors were mobbed or hanged in effigy. Britain's Parliament saw the light and repealed the act the following year.

But in 1767, Parliament was still seeking revenue from the colonies, and it adopted the Townshend Acts. They imposed customs duties at American ports on importations of paint, glass, paper and tea. Certain colonial pamphleteers had argued that duties could be constitutionally levied by Parliament on English manufactures entering this country, whereas, they said, an internal tax like that levied under the Stamp Act was beyond the powers of Britain's legislative body. So the colonies had almost invited the duties prescribed in the Townshend Acts.

Yet the Americans were soon to provide counterarguments, based mainly on a series of articles by John Dickinson of Pennsylvania. The core of the contention against the Stamp Act had been, "No representation, no taxation," but the position now shifted to the broader thesis, "No representation, no legislation." The Townshend Acts were opposed, although not as vehemently as the Stamp Act. The Virginia Assembly, following the example set by that of Massachusetts, sent formal protests to the king and Parliament.

Governor Fauquier had died, and John Blair, president of the council, was acting briefly as head of government, pending the arrival of the new chief executive, Norborne Berkeley, Baron de Botetourt. The latter had been named governor—not lieutenant governor, as so many of his predecessors had been with the actual holder of the title living in England. It was announced that governors thereafter would reside in the colony.

Botetourt was extremely popular from the first, thanks to his affability and his ingratiating ways. The fact that he was bankrupt when he arrived,[1] apparently did not diminish the admiration and affection in which he was held.

He was unable, however, to persuade the Virginians to accept the Townshend duties. When the burgesses reiterated that they, and not Parliament, had the right to levy taxes on the people of the colony, Botetourt ordered them adjourned. Whereupon they went to the nearby Raleigh Tavern, elected Peyton Randolph moderator, and proceeded to formulate a non-importation, non-consumption agreement. While the document was unofficial, since this was a rump session, it was significant that so weighty a group as the members of Virginia's House of Burgesses had promised not to import any goods taxed by Parliament for the purpose of raising revenue. True, the significance was lessened by the fact that there was no machinery for enforcement. But the other colonies fell into line, and announced that they too would not import the taxed merchandise.

Unfortunately, the non-importation agreements were imperfectly observed, although one patriotic Virginia lady, "a little incommoded with corns," chose to wear moccasins, rather than imported footwear. But in Virginia, Maryland and the Carolinas imports actually increased. Most of the Virginia and Maryland merchants were Scots "who had no sympathy with colonial liberties."

The death of Botetourt was an unhappy event of the year 1770. The popular governor is said to have succumbed, at least in part, because of his unhappiness over the conflict between the Virginians and the government in London concerning the obnoxious enactments by Parliament.

William Nelson, president of the council, served as acting governor, pending the arrival of John Murray, Earl of Dunmore, in 1771. Dunmore reached Williamsburg a few months after one of the worst floods in Virginia history. Almost unprecedented rains in May had caused the rivers to rise to what may have been record-breaking heights. The James, Rappahannock and Roanoke were all reported to have risen suddenly "forty feet perpendicular above the common level," and havoc was wrought along their valleys. Some human beings and uncounted animals were swept away in the raging flood, and 2,300,000 pounds of tobacco were destroyed or damaged along the James alone. The total financial loss to the colony as a whole was estimated at £2,000,000.[2]

Although the non-importation agreements resulting from the Townshend Acts were imperfectly observed, opposition to them was so widespread that they had been repealed in 1770, for everything except tea.

An attack in 1772 by Rhode Islanders on the British sloop *Gaspee*, which was engaged in the repression of smuggling, brought indignant orders from England that the guilty Americans be taken to London for trial. This conflicted with strong expressions by Virginia leaders that colonials were entitled to be tried by a jury of their peers from the area where the offense occurred.

So the Virginia House of Burgesses created a standing Committee of Correspondence for the colony as a whole, apparently at the suggestion of Richard Henry Lee. It was the first such colony-wide committee, although there had been local committees in Massachusetts.

The important and far-reaching resolution setting up the Virginia
committee, and asking the other colonies to follow suit, was introduced
by Dabney Carr, Jefferson's twenty-nine-year-old brother-in-law, husband of Martha Jefferson. Carr, whom Dumas Malone describes as
"the most serious forensic rival" of Patrick Henry who had yet
appeared, was soon to die tragically in Charlottesville of bilious
fever. Carr, to whom Jefferson was deeply devoted, was buried in the
graveyard at Monticello, under an oak tree where the two had often
sat, and near the spot where Jefferson himself was buried more than
half a century later.

Intercolonial Committees of Correspondence, so important in building a united front against British encroachments, were set up, in
accordance with the Virginia burgesses' resolution. William Lee wrote
from London that the effect there was immediate, and that the
committees had "struck a greater panic in the ministers than anything
that had taken place since the Stamp Act."

Tea was still dutiable, under British law, but it happened that tea
shipments were not made to Virginia ports. When the tea ships
arrived in Boston late in 1773, the "Boston Tea Party" was the result.
A mob disguised as Indians and Negroes threw 342 chests of the East
India Company's best into Boston harbor.

A true stalwart in organizing this party was Samuel Adams who,
Samuel Eliot Morison says, "alone among leaders of the American
Revolution was a genuine revolutionary, resembling in several respects
the communist agitators of our time." He and his scholarly and
intensely patriotic friend, James Otis, were implacably determined to
resist these British encroachments at all costs.

The Boston Tea Party was so greatly irritating to the British
Parliament that it passed a series of laws known in the colonies as the
Coercive and Intolerable Acts. Boston was virtually blockaded, until it
promised to pay for the tea which had been heaved into the harbor.
This it had no intention of doing, and the other colonies promptly
sent food and money for the relief of the embattled Bostonians.
Virginia's contribution was 8600 bushels of corn and wheat and
several hundred barrels of flour, together with funds. The burgesses
also adopted resolutions of sympathy and set aside June 7, 1774, as a
day of fasting and prayer.

But disturbed as Virginia was by the closing of the port of Boston,
her concern was even greater over another act passed by Parliament,

namely the Quebec Act. This measure provided for annexation to the province of Quebec of the territory northwest of the Ohio River. This enormous area was the very region which George Washington and others had been developing for years as a part of Virginia.

Governor Dunmore was angered by the action of the burgesses in denouncing the closing of the port of Boston as "a hostile invasion," and setting aside a day of prayer. He dissolved the Assembly. Once more the burgesses strolled over to the Raleigh Tavern a few blocks away, and after again electing Peyton Randolph to preside, proceeded to business. They resolved that "an attack made on one of our sister colonies, to compel admission to arbitrary taxes, is an attack made on all British America." They suggested moreover that a convention of all the colonies be called, and directed the Virginia Committee of Correspondence to communicate the proposal to the other twelve such committees. The latter agreed unanimously. The first Continental Congress, which met in Philadelphia on September 5, 1774, was the result.

Delegates named from Virginia by the First Virginia Convention, held in Williamsburg, were Peyton Randolph, Richard Henry Lee, George Washington, Edmund Pendleton, Patrick Henry, Richard Bland and Benjamin Harrison. It was generally conceded that no other delegation exceeded this one in ability or dedication, and that few were at all comparable.

Peyton Randolph was chosen first among Virginia's seven delegates; yet he is hardly known to the present generation, and might be termed "the forgotten Randolph." Consider the fact that he was elected unanimously to preside over the first Continental Congress, one of the most important assemblages in our history. He was also to preside over the even more important second Continental Congress. Randolph had been Speaker of the Virginia House of Burgesses for several terms in an era when that body contained more brilliantly talented personalities than at any time, before or since. He was president of every important revolutionary assemblage held in Virginia. Portly in stature, learned in the law, honorable, wise and judicious, "of attic pleasantry in conversation," he was the most popular leader in Virginia during the decade immediately preceding the Revolution. It is difficult to think of a man of his capacity and distinction who has suffered such almost complete oblivion.

Thomas Jefferson was not a delegate to Philadelphia, but he sent a paper he had prepared for the Virginia Convention, entitled *A Summary View of the Rights of British America*. It was intended as a guide for the Virginia delegates in Congress. In it he denied all parliamentary authority over the colonies. Although he did not advocate separation from Great Britain, he did propose that Britain relinquish any claims to the right of taxation. Jefferson showed little recognition of the seriousness of Britain's own problems or of the contributions she had made to the colonies. The *Summary View* was considered to be too radical by the Virginia Convention, but it was widely read and decidedly influential.

The delegates to the Congress were hard put to it to transact their business, while coping with the spectacular hospitality of the Philadelphians. John Adams wrote his wife, Abigail, concerning Pennsylvania Chief Justice Chew's four o'clock dinner: "Turtle and every other thing—Flummery, jellies, sweetmeats, of 20 sorts, trifles, whip'd syllabubbs, floating islands, fools, &c." There were thirty-two toasts at one of these affairs, enough to test the capacity of the stoutest patriot. Entertainment of this general type, although not always of such staggering magnitude, was the order of the day throughout the Congress. The delegates worked in the forenoon and early afternoon, after which they relaxed amid the Lucullan enticements of the City of Brotherly Love.

During their working sessions, the delegates adopted a Declaration of Rights and stated that Parliament had violated some of these rights during the past decade. In addition, the Congress adopted a non-importation, non-exportation and non-consumption agreement, virtually eliminating imports from Britain after December 1, 1774, and exports to Britain after September 10, 1775, if the Coercive Acts were not repealed by then. This agreement was called The Association.

Virginia's delegation was particularly disturbed over the proposal to ban all tobacco exports, a move potentially disastrous to the colony's economy. Yet it was agreed that such exports would stop after the date specified, unless Britain's Coercive Acts were wiped from the books.

One of the arguments advanced by Thomas Jefferson in his *Summary View* was that the British king had no right to dispose of western lands. Following the great Pontiac Conspiracy of the Indians in the northwest, the redskins had been brought to terms, but the British had set up a Proclamation Line in 1763, reserving all western territory between Quebec and Florida for the Indians. Whatever the rights and wrongs of this particular arrangement—and certainly the Indians were swindled out of their lands over and over again by both the British and the Americans—the announcement of the Proclamation Line was not gratefully received by Virginia's land-hungry frontiersmen. It was, in fact, ignored.

For example, in about the year 1770, John and Arthur Campbell moved from their home near Staunton to a broad tract near Wolf Hills, on the site of the present Abingdon. This tract on the Holston River was west of the royal Proclamation Line, a fact which did not disturb the Campbells. Other prominent families from the Staunton area, such as the Russells, Christians, Flemings, Looneys and Prestons moved into the same general region at about this time. These were educated men and women, mainly Scotch-Irish in background, with conspicuous talents for leadership.

Relations with the Indians in the area had been relatively peaceful for several years. Then in 1773 and 1774 several particularly brutal Indian murders of white settlers, including women and children, occurred. The whites struck back with what Samuel Kercheval, in his *History of the Valley*, terms "a hypocritical strategem, which reflects the deepest dishonor on the memory of those who were agents to it." This involved the wiping out of the entire family of the famous Cayuga Chief Logan, although Logan himself survived.

Relations with the Indians had become so tense, and there was so much violence along the frontier that Governor Dunmore ordered Colonel Andrew Lewis in 1774 to raise a thousand men from the Valley and southwest and march to the Ohio River for a confrontation with the redskins. Dunmore said he would raise an equal number from the colony's northern counties and join him. "Dunmore's War" had begun.

Andrew Lewis was the son of John Lewis, a Scotch-Irishman who had fled from Ireland to Augusta County after slaying his Irish landlord in self-defense. Andrew Lewis was a hard-fighting frontiersman, over six feet tall, strongly knit and an ideal leader for this type of warfare.

The men of the Valley and southwest whom he was to lead against the Shawnees, came for the most part from modest homes. The regions beyond the mountains did not lend themselves to tobacco growing—hemp was the principal crop there at the period—so that slaves were nothing like so necessary or so numerous as in Piedmont and Tidewater Virginia. Mansions such as the Lees' Stratford or Carter Burwell's Carter's Grove were non-existent. Up to a couple of dozen slaves were to be found on a few of the estates, such as those of the Breckinridges, Hites, Prestons, Zanes, Stephens and Flemings, but Isaac Zane's "mansion," at Marlboro, was only twenty by forty feet. The better homes had some silverware at this period just before the Revolution, "as well as an occasional piece of unusual furniture, such as a bookcase, a great chair or a bureau," Freeman H. Hart writes in his *The Valley of Virginia in the American Revolution*. More than half of the families had books, although sometimes there was merely a copy of the Bible. As for the less pretentious dwellings, Hart says:

"Not half the homes had kitchen utensils, only about a third had beds, and only one-family in six had chairs or tables. A few of these semi-frontiersmen evidenced a fondness for fine clothes, although buckskin and coarse cloth made up the usual attire."

It must be borne in mind that the first permanent settlers had arrived in the Valley as recently as the 1730s, and in the southwest in the 1740s. Most of them had brought with them only what they could carry in wagons or on horseback, and the great majority had been in the region for not more than one generation, if that.

Over eight hundred of these rugged frontiersmen who had staked out their claims in the wilderness and were ready to fight to protect them, met at Camp Union, on the site of today's Lewisburg, West Virginia, under command of Colonel Andrew Lewis and on call of Governor Dunmore. Known to the Shawnees as "the Long Knives," they marched in nineteen days 160 miles over mountains, through forests and across rivers to Point Pleasant at the confluence of the Ohio and Kanawha rivers. There were eleven companies from Augusta County, seven from Fincastle County, eight from Botetourt County and the rest scattered. Most of these men were to fight in the Revolution, seven became generals and six commanded regiments. They were equally eminent later in civil life, many serving as governors, senators, and congressmen. Literally dozens of counties, cities and towns bear their names.[3]

At Point Pleasant the hardy backwoodsmen with the deadly rifles met the Shawnee warriors under the great Chief Cornstalk. In an all day battle on October 10, 1774, the "Long Knives," led by the intrepid and resourceful Colonel Andrew Lewis, defeated the Shawnees, whose eloquent and majestic Chief Cornstalk exhorted them in stentorian tones throughout the sanguinary and desperately fought engagement. Both sides sustained heavy losses, but the Indians were driven across the Ohio.

It was one of the most decisive victories for the whites in the annals of Indian warfare, since the frontier was thereby stabilized for some three years, enabling the Americans to concentrate against the British instead of the Indians. The victory also had the effect not only of virtually eliminating the royal Proclamation Line of 1763 but also the Quebec Act of 1774, both of which were intended seriously to hamper Virginia's penetration of the western regions. In addition, the triumph of Andrew Lewis and his "Long Knives" paved the way for the epochal conquests in the Northwest a few years later by George Rogers Clark.

THIRTEEN

Richmond, Norfolk, Williamsburg and Philadelphia

GOVERNOR DUNMORE's exultation over the victory at Point Pleasant was tempered by his concern over the provocative actions of the colonials at the Continental Congress. He was anxious to call the Virginia General Assembly into session, but uneasy as to what might happen if he did so. The result was that he issued several calls but each time changed his mind. He finally fixed on May 1775, as the date for the session, but by then the defiant actions of the Virginia Convention in St. John's Church, Richmond, and the reverberating fusillades at Lexington and Concord had taken matters out of his hands.

The convention which met in St. John's in March 1775, did so at the behest of Peyton Randolph, who had been empowered to issue the call. Richmond was chosen over Williamsburg as being less amenable to pressure from Dunmore. As early as the previous November, Patrick Henry had confided to friends that he believed war with England was inevitable. While this opinion was by no means general at that time, the convention met in the little church overlooking the James in an atmosphere of tension, if not apprehension. Small as St. John's was—much smaller than it is today—it was the largest building in the sprawling little town.

The delegates, among whom were practically all the great Virginians of that revolutionary generation, including six of the seven future signers of the Declaration of Independence, tied their horses in or near the churchyard. Some had ridden for days, even a week, over primitive roads and trails.

Peyton Randolph was in the chair, by unanimous vote. He put the affairs of the recent Continental Congress first on the agenda. After two days of reports and discussions, the delegates approved the decisions reached at Philadelphia.

When one or two other matters had been attended to, Patrick Henry was recognized. He offered a resolution declaring that:

"A well regulated militia . . . is the natural strength and only security of a free government . . .

"Resolved, therefore, That this colony be immediately put into a posture of defense. . . ."

Similar resolutions calling for a trained militia had been passed in other colonies, so there was nothing inherently revolutionary in this proposal. Yet George Washington, Edmund Pendleton and other patriotic conservatives regarded the statement as unduly provocative and tantamount to a prophecy of war.

But Patrick Henry was not to be silenced. Rising in his pew, he began in a moderate tone, as was his wont. His carefully chosen words were those of a man reared on the near-frontier, yet by cultivated parents who stood well in the society of that day. His Scottish-born father was not only a judge and a former teacher but he had studied for four years at King's College, Aberdeen, and was knowledgeable in the classics. His mother, Sarah Winston, was of a good family. Patrick himself had read Virgil and Livy before he was fifteen, although like most of his contemporaries, he had apparently read relatively few books.[1]

So when the Revolution's greatest orator began his immortal deliverance, he was speaking from a background of reading and culture which many today are unaware that he possessed.

As he warmed to his subject, the strangely indefinable quality of his voice, so often mentioned by his contemporaries, seemed to hold his hearers enthralled. Finally he almost lifted them out of their seats with his blood-tingling climax:

"The war is actually begun! The next gale that sweeps from the North will bring to our ears the clash of resounding arms! Our brethren are already in the field! Why stand we here idle? . . . Is life so dear, or peace so sweet as to be purchased at the price of chains and slavery? Forbid it, Almighty God! I know not what course others may take, but as for me, give me liberty, or give me death!"

The "Tongue of the Revolution" had inspired his listeners with flaming words—words which were to reverberate throughout the colonies, beyond the seas and far down the centuries. Those who heard Patrick Henry on March 23, 1775, remembered the occasion all their lives. "Let me be buried at this spot!" exclaimed Edward Carrington, who was listening through a window. His wish was granted more than a third of a century later.

When the stunned convention had gathered its wits, Richard Henry Lee, whose aristocratic profile resembled that of an ancient Roman senator, rose to second Henry's resolution. Lee's was a more elegant mode of speech than Henry's, his diction more polished, his voice smoother and more mellifluous, but the impact of his words was less overwhelming. Lee's gestures were flawless, despite the fact that he kept his left hand wrapped in a black silk handkerchief to hide the loss of its fingers in a hunting accident.

Thomas Jefferson, whose talents as a speaker were modest, at best, also spoke in favor of Henry's resolution.

It passed by a small majority. Henry was named chairman of the committee to put the colony in a posture of defense, with Lee as vice-chairman.

These events caused Governor Dunmore to become gravely concerned. He ordered British sailors to seize the powder in the powder horn at Williamsburg, and they carried off a wagonload. Whereupon the militia turned out, intent on marching to the Palace and seizing the governor. They were restrained by cooler heads when His Lordship promised to return the powder.

There were rumblings in the countryside, and horsemen gathered at Fredericksburg, with a view to marching on the capital. They were barely restrained by Peyton Randolph. Patrick Henry then led a group of Hanover County militia toward Williamsburg. They were joined en route by others from New Kent and King William, determined either to obtain £330 in compensation for the embezzled powder or to bring the powder back by main force. Dunmore was thrown into such a state of perturbation, if not panic, by these tidings, that the £330 was produced before the militia reached Williamsburg. The governor thereupon pronounced Henry an outlaw.

News of the fighting at Lexington and Concord during the previous month had finally reached Virginia. "The Sword is now drawn," said the *Virginia Gazette*, "and God knows when it will be sheathed."

It was early May, and the second Continental Congress was convening in Philadelphia. The Virginia delegation was the same as at the first Congress—Randolph, Washington, Henry, Lee, Pendleton, Harrison and Bland. The "shot heard 'round the world," fired in Massachusetts shortly before, had greatly heightened the tension, and there was much more excitement than there had been at the first Congress. This was also a much harder-working group, with far less attention given to merrymaking and conviviality.

Peyton Randolph, as usual, had been chosen unanimously as president, but he deemed it necessary to return to Virginia on May 24 to preside over the House of Burgesses which had been called into special session. Jefferson replaced him in the Virginia delegation at Philadelphia. John Hancock of Massachusetts was named to preside over the Continental Congress in Randolph's stead. The portly, overweight Randolph, back in Philadelphia, that autumn, died of a stroke.

George Washington was elected unanimously by the Congress to command the Continental Army. John and Samuel Adams were chiefly responsible for his selection. The two New Englanders felt that the choice of a Virginian, as representing the largest and most populous colony, would tend to promote unity. They were also impressed with Washington's ability and character, although the austere Virginian was not described by anyone in the Congress as possessing "superlative military qualities." Washington, recognizing that his combat experience was limited to the command of a regiment in the French and Indian War some sixteen years before, was keenly aware of his deficiencies. But his sense of duty compelled him to accept. He insisted on serving without pay, and would take only his expenses.

His strong feeling of inadequacy and deep pessimism is seen in the remark he made, with tears in his eyes to Patrick Henry: "Remember, Mr. Henry what I now tell you: from the day that I enter upon the command of the American armies, I date my fall and the ruin of my reputation."

For the next five years, General Washington was to be engaged in leading the fight against the British in the northeast. The theater of operations would not move to Virginia again until 1779, and Washington himself would not be in command there until 1781.

But let us return to events in Virginia in May 1775. The burgesses learned soon after they had convened that Governor Dunmore had fled to the British man-of-war *Fowey*, anchored in York River. After transacting some necessary business, the burgesses invited his lordship to attend the usual legislative exercises in Williamsburg, but he insisted that they join him on board the *Fowey*. They refused. When the burgesses adjourned on June 20, 1775, they terminated the long service of that lawmaking agency which had begun in 1619. It would be superseded ere long by the legislative body which we know today.

Dunmore remained aboard the *Fowey*, and then departed for Norfolk, after the erudite Richard Bland had made the somewhat drastic suggestion that he be hanged. At Norfolk, Dunmore was less unwelcome than at Williamsburg, for as Thomas J. Wertenbaker writes in his history of that port, Norfolk "was a thing apart from the rest of Virginia." As the colony's chief seaport and largest city, with six thousand inhabitants, it was cosmopolitan in population and outlook. And while leading citizens there exhibited the same standards of culture and civilized living as other Virginians in Tidewater, the milieu was urban rather than rural. Since most of the port's business was done with Great Britain, through Scottish merchants living in the town, Tory sentiment was stronger.

With Dunmore in flight, the Virginia convention which met in July decided to put the colony on a war footing. Two regiments of troops were to be raised and the militia were to be revitalized. A Committee of Safety was created, with Edmund Pendleton as chairman.

This committee of safety was "the most powerful body that had ever exercised executive authority in Virginia," says David Mays in his biography of Pendleton. It could meet when and where it pleased, and "wield almost dictatorial power over both the sword and purse of the colony." It would discharge these functions until the next Virginia convention met.

Actual hostilities with the British got under way when Captain Squire of the British sloop of war *Otter* began raiding plantations along the Chesapeake. He appears to have carried off chickens as well as slaves. There was some spasmodic rifle fire from a point on shore near Hampton, and two Britons were killed.

At the same time, a virtual blockade was instituted against Norfolk by patriotic county committees, while Dunmore remained aboard his flotilla in the harbor.

Dunmore landed a small force and seized a printing press which had been issuing revolutionary material. This gave the people of Norfolk such concern that perhaps one-third of the population either left for the interior or sailed for Britain.

Dunmore and the forces controlled by the colonial Committee of Safety got into a minor skirmish near Kempsville, county seat of Princess Anne. The small British contingent of regulars won an easy victory over the disorganized colonials. In fact, Colonel Joseph Hutchings of the colonials was captured in a swamp by two Negro slaves who were fighting on the side of the British.[2] There were to be other such feats by Negro soldiers and sailors in the Revolution, some of which have been overlooked by historians.

The easy British victory at Kempsville caused certain Norfolkians to conclude that it would be the part of wisdom to swear allegiance to Great Britain. Revolutionary patriots in Isle of Wight retaliated by tarring and feathering several leading loyalists.

Dunmore thereupon thought to make a ten-strike by proclaiming freedom for all slaves and indentured servants who would join his forces. This was felt by the colonials to be tantamount to inciting a slave insurrection, and it infuriated and alarmed the revolutionary leaders.

The Committee of Safety, under Pendleton, decided to move against Dunmore with the Second Regiment, under command of Colonel William Woodford. Patrick Henry, colonel of the First Regiment, but without military experience, was thus passed over. Pendleton and Henry had been at odds on various issues, but the former's decision in favor of Woodford appears justified. Henry resigned his commission and returned to civil life, which may well have been in his own best interest.

Colonel Woodford was not only a veteran soldier, but he commanded a regiment of hardened fighters, many of whom wore hunting shirts with the legend "Liberty or Death!" and carried tomahawks and scalping knives. Dunmore, flushed with his easy victory at Kempsville, and unaware of the caliber of the opponents he now faced, decided to attack Woodford at Great Bridge, on the southern branch of the Elizabeth River near Norfolk. He assembled perhaps six hundred troops, including all his regulars, sixty Tories, a couple of hundred Negroes, now known as the Ethiopian Corps, and a few sailors.

The Americans were entrenched behind breastworks, and they waited until the attackers came within fifty yards. At that point their sharpshooters opened up and mowed down the assaulting force. The latter fell back in disorder. On arriving in Norfolk, they rowed out to their ships. Tory families in the town made haste to follow them, beyond reach of the enraged patriots.

Two Negroes rendered valiant service to the Americans in the Great Bridge engagement. William Flora, a free Negro from Portsmouth, was the last sentinel to leave his post as the enemy approached, and he withdrew "amidst a shower of musket balls," returning fire eight times.[3] A slave belonging to Thomas Marshall, father of the future Chief Justice, crossed into the British lines, according to Colonel Woodford, and duped the British into thinking that Great Bridge fort was lightly manned and its defenders' morale low.[4]

Despite his humiliating reverse, Dunmore once more assumed a threatening posture. He indicated that a general bombardment of Norfolk by his warships was imminent. Whereupon a large percentage of the population decided to leave at once, by whatever means were available, taking with them such possessions as they could. Shortly thereafter, on January 1, 1776, the four British vessels standing offshore opened up with all their guns. British sailors rowed ashore and set fire to warehouses and other buildings on the waterfront. American soldiers, many of whom regarded Norfolk as a nest of Tories, proceeded to help matters along by systematically putting the torch to much of the city, and looting on a wholesale scale. Over nine hundred houses, more than two-thirds of the entire community, were destroyed. The innocent suffered along with the guilty. It was midwinter and shelter was not only extremely scarce but food and water were equally so. Smallpox broke out, adding to the misery.

The American commanders decided in February to evacuate Norfolk, but the Virginia Convention was determined to leave nothing there which might be useful to the British. It ordered the remaining 416 houses burned. Nothing was left of the city but "complete desolation, charred timbers, blackened foundations, ashes." Citizens who were able to prove their allegiance to the Revolution were given compensation for their staggering losses, but the amounts were far from adequate. It would be several years before the community could recover from this disaster. Norfolk suffered perhaps more severely than any city in America during the Revolution.

Despite everything, there remained a stanch band of Norfolk patriots who carried on the fight for freedom. And in the late years of the eighteenth century the courage and fortitude of the Norfolkians again asserted themselves. Once the war was over, the city recovered rapidly, and resumed its place as a thriving seaport.

After the destruction of Norfolk, Dunmore was harassed by the eccentric Major General Charles Lee, who had been given temporary command of all Virginia forces. Lee's long green trousers, called "sherry-vallies," and the fact that he had a virtual herd of dogs which shared his bedroom, made him an object of considerable curiosity. He fired on Dunmore's ships from the shore. Shortly thereafter the governor, his noxious and germ-laden vessels crowded with runaway Tories and Negroes, sailed to Gwynn's Island, just off Gloucester County, and within range of its coastal batteries. Before long the redoubtable General Andrew Lewis, who had replaced Charles Lee in command of all Virginia forces on General Washington's recommendation—Lee having been transferred to Charleston, South Carolina—opened fire with a heavy cannonade against the British flotilla. Dunmore was unable to stand the punishment. He upped anchor and left Virginia forever. When the American forces landed on Gwynn's Island next day they viewed a shocking spectacle. The shore was strewn with corpses, and persons half-dead, victims either of the bombardment or of the smallpox and jail fever that had broken out on Dunmore's crowded and filthy ships.

The British governor's permanent departure in July 1776, ended until 1779 any serious threat of significant military activities against Virginia. But the colony was faced with many domestic wartime problems, and it had to put itself in a position to cope with possible attacks by land or sea.

The all-important final revolutionary Virginia Convention met in Williamsburg on May 6, 1776. It included the leading men of the colony, save only those who were attending the Continental Congress. Such figures as Edmund Pendleton, the president, Patrick Henry, Edmund Randolph, George Mason, Richard Bland, Archibald Cary and Robert Carter Nicholas were leaders in this notable assemblage.

Independence was the overriding theme. A North Carolina convention at Halifax, North Carolina, had adopted a resolution on April

12, instructing its delegation to the Continental Congress to vote for independence, if it should be proposed, but not directing the Carolinians to take the initiative in this regard.[5]

Many counties in Virginia and other colonies had passed vigorous resolutions in 1774 and 1775, in response to an appeal from the first Continental Congress that Committees of Safety be widely formed. One of the most courageous of these resolutions had been adopted on January 20, 1775, in the Virginia County of Fincastle, on the southwestern frontier. It declared that the free holders of Fincastle were deliberately and resolutely determined never to surrender their "inestimable privileges . . . to any power upon earth but at the expense of our lives."

The Virginia Convention of 1776 was not only determined to retain the "inestimable privileges" to which the Fincastle Resolutions referred, but also to move firmly and inexorably toward complete separation from Great Britain. Delegates arrived from all corners of the colony with that thought in mind. Some were clad in the elegant dress of Tidewater, while others wore the buckskin or homespun of the mountain regions. From every section came men with tall and rangy physiques. Hugh Blair Grigsby, the indefatigable chronicler of three major Virginia conventions, wrote:

"Washington . . . the Lewises, the Randolphs, George Mason, Pendleton, the Cabells, the Carringtons, Henry, Bland, the Lees, Jefferson, the Campbells, Blair, Tazewell were nearly all fully six feet . . . Madison was probably the only very small man in the Convention of 1776. Of a later date, Marshall and Monroe were tall . . . It was for a long time believed in England that the Virginians approached the gigantic."

Many of the Virginians of this "great generation"—the phrase is Dumas Malone's—were not only tall in stature but were endowed with creative and perceptive intellects. The plantation system of Tidewater and Piedmont, and the more rugged frontier civilization of the Valley and southwest had produced masterful and resourceful men, capable of coping with the approaching crisis. The positions of leadership they had held in their communities, the habits of command they had acquired, and the wide reading they had done in the works of ancient and modern writers on philosophy, government, law and politics enabled them to take "at the flood" this historic "tide in the affairs of men."

Henry Adams assessed the Virginians of that age in his *History of the United States,* as follows:

"Those whom Liancourt called 'men of the first class' were equal to any standard of excellence known to history. Their range was narrow, but within it they were supreme . . . Law and politics were the only objects of Virginia thought, but within these bounds the Virginians achieved triumphs. . . .

"Nowhere in America existed better human material than in the middle and lower classes of Virginia. As explorers, adventurers, fighters —wherever courage, activity and force were wanted—they had no equal; but they had never known discipline, and were beyond measure jealous of restraint."

The Convention of 1776, composed of such men as are here described by the New England historian, was ready to take the lead in forcing a permanent and irreparable breach with the British. There were both "radicals" and "conservatives" in the convention, but the difference between them was mainly one of method. They had one common objective—independence.

There was the question whether the colonies should proceed at once in an endeavor to force separation, or whether they should find out first whether they would have any European allies in such a hazardous enterprise. Patrick Henry, despite his belligerence of the year before, was one of those who stressed the importance of first ascertaining the intentions of France and Spain. Impatient General Charles Lee, on the other hand, denounced the hesitancy of Edmund Pendleton as comparable to that of "an old midwife drunk with bohea tea and gin."

However, it was Pendleton who produced a resolution that appealed to each school of thought in the convention and placed Virginia in the van of all the colonies. It was adopted May 15 without a dissenting voice, and it directed the delegates from Virginia at Philadelphia to "declare the United Colonies free and independent states, absolved from all allegiance to, or dependence upon, the Crown or Parliament of Great Britain." The resolution proposed, furthermore, "whatever measures may be thought proper and necessary by the Congress for forming foreign alliances, and a confederation of the colonies." There was great jubilation in Williamsburg, with firing of cannon, and the British flag was pulled down from the Capitol.

Preparation of a Declaration of Rights was called for in another resolution, and also "such a plan of government as will be most likely to maintain peace and order in this colony, and secure substantial and equal liberty to the people."

George Mason, the tall, dark-eyed master of Gunston Hall, one of the most erudite students of government in his time, was the natural choice to compose a Declaration of Rights. Endowed with brains, character and scholarly insights, Mason could seldom be persuaded to take public office. He even refused to serve in the Continental Congress, for he was not only a chronic sufferer from gout but contemptuous of most politicians and their methods. Yet he was passionately concerned for the preservation of civil liberties as a fundamental element in "republican government." He had written the Fairfax Resolves in 1774, termed "perhaps the most important pre-revolutionary document prepared in Virginia." It laid down "the fundamental principle of the people's being governed by no laws to which they have not given their consent by Representatives freely chosen of themselves." Mason's Declaration of Rights was the prototype upon which the Federal Bill of Rights and the similar bills adopted by all the states were modeled. The guarantees it contained of freedom of the press, trial by jury, religious toleration and free and regular elections, and its declaration that "all men are by nature equally free and independent, and have certain inherent natural rights" were beacon lights on the road to American liberty. True, there was the anomalous fact that Mason was a slaveholder, although like many leaders of his generation in Virginia, he was a bitter critic of slavery.

Dean Roscoe Pound of the Harvard Law School pronounced Mason's Declaration of Rights "the first and, indeed . . . the model of a long line of politico-legal documents that have become the staple of American constitutional law." Yet the name of George Mason, the author of this epoch-making document, is hardly known today beyond the borders of his native state.

When the Virginia Convention of 1776 proceeded to write a full-fledged constitution for the commonwealth, it turned once more to Mason, a man whom Jefferson described as "of the first order of greatness." Mason was also endowed with a caustic wit. When a political opponent toward the end of Mason's career said it was well known that his mind was failing, the master of Gunston Hall is reported to have replied: "Sir, when yours fails nobody will ever discover it."

The constitution drafted in large part by Mason exhibited a sensitivity on the part of Virginians to the dangers of executive tyranny. Having just launched a revolution against a tyrannical British king, they were in no mood to provide machinery whereby Virginia's own chief executive might seize despotic power. The new governor was to be chosen for a term of only one year by the General Assembly, and he was to have no right of veto over that body, which was composed of a House of Delegates and a Senate. The former branch, which included two representatives from each county elected annually, would be the legislative arm where all bills originated. Senators would be chosen for four-year terms from each of twenty-four districts. Patrick Henry was among those who felt that the governor was given entirely too little power. The new form of government would remain substantially unchanged for more than half a century. Under its terms, Virginia was officially designated a "commonwealth," which designation continues today. The other commonwealths are Kentucky, Massachusetts and Pennsylvania.

In formulating this constitution for an independent state, after adopting its own resolution for independence, Virginia once more led the way. It was the first of the thirteen colonies to establish its own code of organic law, after formally cutting its ties with Great Britain.

Virginia's resolution throwing down the gauntlet to the mother country had been taken to Philadelphia. It was like a time bomb ticking in the pocket of Richard Henry Lee, the "American Cicero," as he sat among the delegates. (Patrick Henry was widely known as the "American Demosthenes.")

Many of the delegates to the Continental Congress were unprepared for anything as drastic as the Virginia resolution. This was especially true of the middle colonies and South Carolina.

Yet Lee rose on June 7 and moved that the Congress declare "that these united colonies are, and of a right ought to be, free and independent states." He went on, in language virtually identical with that adopted in Williamsburg the month before, to declare that the colonies were absolved from all allegiance to the British Crown.

This went beyond anything that some of the delegates were prepared to undertake, and by a vote of seven colonies to five—Georgia not being represented—it was decided to postpone action until July 1. In the meantime, Congress appointed a committee to draft a Decla-

ration of Independence. Thomas Jefferson, aged thirty-three was instructed to do the drafting.

It was the first great opportunity of Jefferson's life. An authentic
genius whose catholicity of knowledge and brilliance of intellect are
well-nigh unparalleled in American history, he was ready despite his
relative youth to accept the challenge. He worked for seventeen days
in his rented room with his "writing box" or portable desk, and
produced the first draft. John Adams and Benjamin Franklin made a
few helpful suggestions, but the document was overwhelmingly Jefferson's.

Congress kept the paper "on the table" for a few days while it
debated the Virginia resolution for independence which Lee had presented. This was approved July 2. Then, for two more days the precise
wording of Jefferson's Declaration was carefully considered, and a few
alterations, some of them for the better were made. Jefferson was sorely
grieved by these alterations, but he refrained from trying to start a
revolution of his own. On July 4 the Declaration was adopted.

The Virginia signers were George Wythe, Thomas Jefferson, Richard
Henry Lee, Francis Lightfoot Lee, Carter Braxton, Thomas Nelson,
Jr., and Benjamin Harrison. However, along with nearly all the other
signers, they did not actually affix their signatures to the Declaration
until weeks later.

We need repeat here only a small part of the language of this
imperishable document, the best known and most revered of all
American state papers. One of its most quoted passages is, of course,
the following:

"We hold these truths to be self-evident, that all men are created
equal, that they are endowed by their Creator with certain unalien-
able rights, that among these are Life, Liberty and the Pursuit of
Happiness."

Samuel Eliot Morison adds this comment upon the foregoing
language from the pen of one of the greatest of all Virginians:

"These words are more revolutionary than anything written by
Robespierre, Marx or Lenin, more explosive than the atom, a continual
challenge to ourselves, as well as an inspiration to the oppressed of
all the world."

FOURTEEN

The Rocky Road
to Yorktown

WITH INDEPENDENCE from Britain officially proclaimed, Virginia set about the task of putting into effect its just-adopted state constitution and playing its crucial role in the Revolution which now had begun. The lives, the fortunes, and the sacred honor of its leaders, in the memorable words of Jefferson's Declaration, were in the balance. There could be no turning back.

Election of a governor was a primary need. Patrick Henry, who did not seek the office, was chosen over the elder Thomas Nelson, the last man to serve as president of His Majesty's Council. Henry was extremely popular and influential in every part of the state, and was to remain so throughout his life. He would serve three successive one-year terms as governor (three was the limit under the law), two more later on, and would decline a sixth. Several of his elections by the General Assembly were unanimous.

Governor Henry was acutely conscious of his lack of authority, under the constitution, and referred to himself as a "mere phantom." It should be emphasized, too, that despite his overall popularity, he had strong critics and enemies. Some of these preferred to have him in the governor's chair, where he was relatively powerless, to battling him in the legislature, where he was tremendously powerful. The governor was required to function with the "advice" of a council of eight members, chosen by the General Assembly. These councilors were in a position almost to make or break his administration.

One of the major concerns of this period was enforcement of the agreement not to trade with Great Britain. This pact, reached at the first Continental Congress and known as The Association, covered both imports and exports. County committees had been set up to check on the activities of citizens. The committees were elected by the freeholders, much as legislators were chosen.

Prominent planters were leaders in establishing these agencies and serving on them. Ostracism or exile were penalties imposed for violations of the boycott against trade with Britain. Special attention was paid to Scottish merchants, whose businesses suffered severely if they were found to be violating the agreement.

An example of how breakers of the covenant were handled is seen in the case of one John Pigg of Pittsylvania. He was summoned to explain his having committed the heinous sin of drinking tea. Pigg did not appear before the committee, and was pronounced "a traitor to his country and inimical to American liberty."

Merchants and planters who remained loyal to Britain departed, perhaps in the hundreds, for the mother country in 1775 and 1776. Many were men and women of substance who sincerely preferred to remain British subjects, and whose departure represented a real loss to the colony.

One of these was John Randolph, attorney general of Virginia and brother of Peyton Randolph. He resigned his office and went to England. Other prominent Tory sympathizers who remained in Virginia, usually without any punishment, included Ralph Wormeley, Richard Corbin, Thomas Lord Fairfax and John Grymes; William Byrd III, whose enthusiasm for the Tory cause lessened as the Revolution proceeded, the Reverend John Camm, president of the College of William and Mary, and Archibald Ritchie, father of Thomas Ritchie, the noted nineteenth-century editor.

Treatment of Tories, in general, was mild at the outset of the Revolution, and the council, which had principal jurisdiction in such matters, along with the various county committees, tended to be lenient. But by the end of 1776, when American arms had received serious reverses in the North, a more drastic policy was adopted.

Punishment for disaffection was increased by the General Assembly which met in October of that year. The penalty for "treason," i.e., levying war against the commonwealth, and aiding and comforting its enemies, was fixed at death, with confiscation of property. There were other severe punishments for lesser offenses. On the other hand, enforcement of these penalties was sometimes mild.

In the southwest, William Campbell, then county lieutenant for Washington County, was the leader in stamping out disaffection. In fact, several Tory outlaws were captured by Campbell and his men, and are said to have been unceremoniously hanged. Others suffered confiscation of property. Some of these men were not only Tories but highway robbers.

The lead mines in Montgomery County were vital to the American cause, and Tory efforts were directed to their seizure or destruction. Rough treatment, which apparently included hanging, was resorted to by Colonel Charles Lynch, superintendent of the mines.

The drafting of soldiers met with much resistance, nowhere more violently than in Northumberland County on the Northern Neck. A riot broke out at Northumberland Courthouse in 1780, and a number of persons were killed or wounded. These and other evidences of disloyalty to the American cause brought the enactment of tighter restrictions.

The lower Tidewater area should have been especially conscious of the need for resistance to Britain, since the first serious attacks on Virginia had occurred there in 1779. After raiding extensively along the shores of Chesapeake Bay, British naval units not only took Portsmouth but sent forces inland and seized Suffolk. Great quantities of stores were destroyed. The poorly prepared and inadequately trained Virginia militia offered little resistance. Disaffection increased in that area, especially along the vulnerable shores of Chesapeake Bay. In one of the raids, British ships carried off three hundred slaves, along with much other property. In fact, Thomas Jefferson estimated that in 1778 alone more than thirty thousand slaves ran away from their masters and joined the British, and that the latter took away one-fifth of the entire black population in a single revolutionary raid.

By 1779, the fortunes of the Americans were not prospering, and there was confiscation of hundreds of estates of British loyalists by the Virginia authorities. The owners were mostly Britons who had gone back to the mother country. H. J. Eckenrode says in his history of the Revolution in Virginia that "much corruption and injustice were practiced" and "many estates were wrongfully condemned and sold."

One group of Virginians who hoped to better their condition as a result of the political and social upheaval caused by the Revolution was the large element of poor farmers in the Tidewater and Piedmont. They had been inspired by Patrick Henry and Thomas Jefferson to believe that independence from Great Britain would improve their lot. They were often illiterate and eking out a miserable existence in squalid huts.

French philosophers, decades in advance of the French Revolution, had been disseminating ideas on behalf of equality, and their ideas had somehow percolated down to the hovels of these impoverished wretches in Virginia and the other colonies. Now that the American Revolution was actually under way, it seemed to afford them a heaven-sent opportunity for a better life. In fact, Jefferson, at the outset of the Revolution sponsored a program of reform in the General Assembly designed to ameliorate some of these evils. Of which, more anon.

However, on the faraway edges of the Virginia frontier, life was hard, at best, and the liberal stirrings inspired by Voltaire and Rousseau were not especially meaningful to men who were stalking bears and Indians. There, "on the Western waters," in the terminology of the day, settlers were beginning to arrive. A powerful twenty-three-year-old red-haired frontiersman named George Rogers Clark was one of them. A native of Albemarle County, he had gone to the Kentucky country which had voted for adherence to Virginia and was soon to become a county. Clark and another rugged backwoodsman, John Gabriel Jones, had been elected to represent Kentucky in the Virginia Assembly.

They set out for Williamsburg several hundred miles away. The men had to walk a good part of the distance, a horse having somehow been lost. Communications were so primitive that they were unaware that the Assembly had adjourned long before their arrival. However, having learned of this, Clark stopped off at Scotchtown in Hanover County to see Governor Henry. Powder for the defense of the Kentucky settlements was Clark's main objective, and Henry was sympathetic. This was the more true since a young man named Daniel Boone, a Pennsylvania native then living in North Carolina, had been sent to Kentucky by Judge Richard Henderson, a Virginian who had moved southward across the Carolina line. Boone went as agent for the Transylvania Company, organized by Henderson with a view to establishing a great colony in Kentucky.

Henry gave Clark a letter to the governor's council in Williamsburg recommending that the powder he desired be made available. The council was reluctant, but finally agreed to send twenty-five kegs to Pittsburgh for the use of Clark and his fellow frontiersmen.

Kentucky was only one of numerous Virginia counties that were being formed. In fact, more than thirty new ones were created between 1740 and 1776, the greater part of them between the fall line of the various rivers and the Blue Ridge.

Governor Henry would serve his first three one-year terms in Williamsburg. During those terms his health was none too good at several different periods. He made a creditable showing, nevertheless, often under difficult circumstances. The council and General Assembly were usually co-operative.

George Washington's fluctuating fortunes, and his enormous problems and frustrations as commander-in-chief of the Continental armies in the North, were of great concern to Henry. The latter was not only kept busy trying to send weapons and supplies to hard-pressed Washington, but he was also responsible for obtaining necessary arms and provisions for the defense of Virginia. Such a vital commodity as salt, for example, was in extremely short supply and had to be imported, since the southwestern Virginia salt mines had not yet been adequately developed.

Henry's marriage to youthful Dorothea Dandridge, a second cousin of Martha Washington—his first wife, Sarah Shelton had died—was an event of 1777. There were seventeen children of these two marriages, which led wits to remark that Patrick Henry rather than George Washington should be called "The Father of His Country."

A few months after Henry's marriage, Washington went into winter quarters at Valley Forge. The almost unbelievable hardships and sufferings which the Continental troops endured there during the winter of 1777-78 gave Washington's friend, the governor of Virginia, immense concern. Governor Henry was distraught over the plight of the entire force, and especially the Virginia units, starving and shivering in the Pennsylvania snows. There were frightful shortages of food, clothing, shoes and blankets, with hungry and almost naked men making bloody footprints in the snow, and often lacking not only doctors and medicines, but going without pay for long periods. Speculators and extortioners were getting rich, while the soldiers died.

At about the time when Washington and his men were beginning to suffer in the frozen hell that was Valley Forge, George Rogers Clark was back in Williamsburg from Kentucky on a highly important mis–

sion. He and his small band of sharpshooting frontiersmen had been enduring hardships and dangers of a different character from those of the Continentals under Washington, but much of the year 1777 in Kentucky had been one long horror of torture and murder. The Indians had been spurred on by the British to try to exterminate the American settlements. It was a fight to the death.

Clark persuaded Henry that with a small band of men, schooled in the ways of frontier warfare, he would be able to make a ten-strike in the northwest and thwart British objectives in that vast region. Utmost secrecy was deemed essential, so that only Thomas Jefferson, George Mason and George Wythe were told of the plan, lest it leak out and the element of surprise be lost. Clark was authorized to raise seven companies of fifty men each, and attack the British fort at Kaskaskia in the Illinois country. Spies had brought word that it was weakly held and could be taken. The governor and his three confidants agreed that they would try to get from the Assembly three hundred acres of land for each participant, if the hazardous expedition was successful.

Clark set out in the spring of 1778 from Redstone on the Monongahela River and moved slowly downstream. There had been recruiting difficulties, and he commanded only 178 men when he reached the present site of Louisville on the Ohio. It was a six days' march from there to Kaskaskia through a trackless wilderness, infested with Indians. There was no food on two of these days. But Kaskaskia was reached on July 4, and it fell quickly to Clark's men. A few weeks later, the British outposts at Cahokia and Vincennes also surrendered. Clark then showed diplomacy as well as military daring. He won to his side the French villagers in the region, as well as the Indians in the area.

Word of these triumphs finally reached Williamsburg, and the Assembly voted to make the huge Illinois country a county of Virginia.

But Lieutenant Governor Henry Hamilton, the British commander in Illinois, had no intention of conceding defeat. Clark had left Vincennes in the hands of a garrison consisting almost entirely of Frenchmen, and Hamilton returned to the assault with a large force of French and Indians. He recaptured it easily.

At this point, Clark performed one of the most memorable feats in the annals of war. It was midwinter, the rivers were high and much of the country was flooded. In the face of these apparently insuperable obstacles, Clark set out to recapture Vincennes 180 miles away. Much of the intervening terrain was under water, at times up to the shoulders of the men. For days they were virtually without food, all game having been driven off by the floods. As they neared Vincennes, many became exhausted and had to be rescued by their companions from drowning.

Clark was at all times in the van, encouraging and exhorting. Fortunately, the February weather was not severe, and there was not much ice on the swollen rivers, but they were extremely cold. The men were soaking wet, shaking with chills and fever, hungry and on the point of collapse.

The sudden emergence from this waterlogged wilderness of Clark's muddy, buckskin-clad warriors, with their flintlock rifles and tomahawks, took the Vincennes garrison so completely by surprise that the fort fell, after a brief struggle. It was one of the most heroic feats of arms ever performed, and it saved Illinois and Kentucky from falling to the British. When the treaty of peace was signed in 1783, Clark's conquests were the major factor in the award of the entire northwest to the Americans.

The man who was chiefly responsible for this master stroke had not only risked his life countless times, but also had spent much of his own money to finance the expedition. The state of Virginia owed him some $15,000 in payment for his military services and for sums he had advanced to obtain supplies for his men. Clark and his entire command went for years without pay, incredible as that must seem.

After peace was declared, a commission was sent from Richmond to Kentucky to make a settlement of these debts. The hodgepodge of documents kept by Clark and his officers while fighting in the wilderness, frequently drenched to the skin or under heavy attack, was not readily deciphered. However, the Virginia commission recommended that Clark be reimbursed for the $15,000 owed him. At this point the entire collection of thousands of vouchers disappeared. Payment was refused by Virginia until they could be produced, and they could not be found. They turned up in 1913 in the attic of the Capitol in Richmond and constitute today one of the treasured collections in the Virginia State Library's archives.

Clark was awarded certain tracts of land after the war, but these were seized by creditors. He was in straitened circumstances for many years. In 1812, when he was crippled and impoverished, the state of Virginia finally voted him an annual pension of $400. Twenty years after his death, it appropriated $30,000 to his estate.[1]

While such shabby treatment for a valiant military hero seems almost beyond belief, it should be said, in partial extenuation, that Virginia's finances during the Revolution were in extremely unsatisfactory condition. For example, in early 1780, thirty-three of the sixty-odd counties had failed, in whole, or in part, to meet their tax obligations to the commonwealth. Radical retrenchment was accordingly proposed. It included sharp reductions in naval ships, army commands and officers, but none in the number of privates.

This crisis arose soon after Thomas Jefferson succeeded Patrick Henry as governor in 1779. The matter of finances was a perpetual problem which plagued both the state and the national governments. There was no effective central authority in Philadelphia, and the Congress was almost powerless.

As the western areas of the state became more populous, there was an increasing demand that the capital be moved from Williamsburg to a more central location. In fact, the House of Burgesses approved such a move in 1752. A difficulty was that agreement could not be reached on which town should be chosen as the new seat of government. The council, furthermore, preferred to remain in Williamsburg. Finally, in 1779, it was voted to move the capital to Richmond, then an unimpressive village of a few hundred souls. One motive in the decision to abandon Williamsburg was the desire to get away from British depredations in lower Tidewater. The actual move to Richmond was made in 1780.

The problems which Jefferson inherited at the new seat of government were extremely serious. The currency was not only depreciating steadily, but the treasury was exhausted. The population was unable to carry the burden of taxes which had been imposed. Military and naval forces for the defense of Virginia were virtually non-existent. All effective army units had been sent out of the state, either to the North or the South to fight the British in those theaters. The Virginia militia, largely untrained and of limited use under any circumstances, had also been made available for the defense of other states. Few militiamen remained on Virginia soil.

Two military catastrophes in the South in 1780 added greatly to Governor Jefferson's burdens. The fall of Charleston, South Carolina, to the British involved the surrender of Virginia's best troops in the Continental service. They had been released by General Washington for duty in the Charleston campaign and were inside the city when it fell. A few months later came the disastrous defeat of the Americans at Camden, South Carolina. The latter action was especially shocking, since the Virginia militia were heavily involved and gave an extremely poor account of themselves. There were also grievous losses in materiel which Virginia could ill afford. Included were hundreds of wagons and many horses and tents, as well as quantities of small arms—since Virginia had been serving as the principal source of supply for the southern armies.

In contrast to the disasters at Charleston and Camden, frontiersmen from southwestern Virginia, mostly Scotch-Irish, were to fight with deadly effect a few months later at the Battle of King's Mountain, near the boundary between North and South Carolina. Under Colonels William Campbell and John Sevier, both Virginia natives, and Colonel Isaac Shelby, another hardened warrior, they crushed the forces of Colonel Patrick Ferguson, composed mainly of Tories from the Carolinas.

Redheaded and fiery Colonel Campbell, of the famous Scottish clan, marched at the head of 400 Washington County men to the scene, and Sevier, of French extraction, led 240 backwoodsmen across the Great Smokies from Tennessee. They joined with forces under Shelby, and the three groups combined, under Campbell's leadership, to assault the enemy. Ferguson challenged "all the rebels outside of hell" to dislodge him from the ridge known as King's Mountain. It took the rugged American pioneers and their veteran sharpshooters exactly one day— October 7, 1780. Ferguson was killed, along with many of his men, and more than 700 Tories surrendered.

It was a stunning blow to British General Cornwallis. Yet the overall picture for American arms was so bleak that Jefferson was still deeply discouraged and Washington had "almost ceased to hope."

Virginia's fragile naval forces were not even remotely capable of coping effectively with British naval might. Not only were the Chesapeake Bay and Hampton Roads areas vulnerable to raids, but so was the James River all the way to Richmond, as would soon become apparent.

It was with the Virginia naval units that Negroes made some of their principal contributions to the patriot cause. The Virginia historian Luther P. Jackson states that black sailors fought on the American ships *Liberty, Patriot, Tempest, Dragon, Diligence* and various other vessels. They did so under particularly difficult circumstances, in view of the overwhelming British superiority.

Consider the example set by the slave Caesar, who "behaved gallantly" while piloting the schooner *Patriot*. He was accordingly set free in 1789, the Virginia General Assembly voting to purchase him from his owner. Many years after his death, his daughter Nancy, was given 2667 acres of land in Ohio in recognition of her father's service to the American Revolution.[2]

John Hope Franklin, the historian, says that "of the 300,000 soldiers who served the cause of independence, approximately 5000 were Negroes," the majority of them from the North.

More free Negroes served in the regular military or naval forces from Virginia than from any other state outside New England, according to Benjamin Quarles in his *The Negro in the American Revolution*. Only free Negroes were allowed in the regular Virginia forces, but slaves performed valuable services, not only as spies but also in the essential lead mines. A number were given their freedom, in consequence, and some received pensions for life from the Virginia General Assembly. True, thousands of Virginia slaves went over to the British, not only in response to Dunmore's appeal but later, on the general theory that the British would give them freedom. But there were few examples of rebellion by Virginia slaves during these years.[3]

Quarles states that the typical black served as a private with the infantry—"a non-armsbearing infantryman, detailed for duty as an orderly or assigned to functions in support of combat operations." A frequent assignment was that of drummer.

Quarles estimates that at least 140 blacks served with the Virginia fleet—the number of whites was, of course much greater—and adds: "The *Dragon*, for example, had at one time or another ten Negroes, one of whom was John De Baptist from Spotsylvania, whose son and grandsons would serve, respectively, in the War of 1812 and the Civil War." Negroes were especially valuable as pilots. Two of these lost their lives and another, Aaron Weaver, received two dangerous wounds and was voted an annual pension of fifty dollars.[4] Other similar examples might be cited.

Espionage was a field of operation in which Virginia Negroes were useful. Reference has been made to the valuable work of a slave at the Battle of Great Bridge, but the most famous Negro spy was James, a slave attached to the entourage of General Lafayette who took the name "James Lafayette." He made a number of trips to Portsmouth, then held by the British, delivered letters to other American spies, and kept his eyes open for useful information. He was greeted warmly by General Lafayette on the latter's return trip to the United States in 1824. James Lafayette was not only given his freedom by the General Assembly but was voted a forty-dollar annual pension. Saul Mathews, another slave who did good work as a spy in the Portsmouth area, was also freed by the Assembly.[5]

With Portsmouth in the hands of the British, and the patriot navy completely outnumbered and outgunned, the way was open for Benedict Arnold to lead a raid into the interior. The notorious traitor had gone over to the enemy in 1780, and in late December of that year he sailed into Virginia waters. The Old Dominion had been denuded of defenders to such an extent, in order to aid the other colonies, that Arnold, with only sixteen hundred men, was able to brush past any remaining naval defenses and sail virtually at will up James River.

Both Washington and Jefferson were eager to bag Arnold, but the renegade landed at Westover and marched on Richmond. The newly designated capital of the state was largely defenseless, and the British destroyed the few public buildings as well as substantial quantities of military stores. Arnold then headed back toward Hampton Roads, putting further stores to the torch en route.

All this was humiliating to Governor Jefferson, who was severely criticized. He deserved criticism for having been taken so completely by surprise, but he was at all times without the authority he needed, and he was also without the means to put up an adequate defense. He had felt it necessary to discontinue the express riders from Hampton as a measure of economy.

Jefferson was praised by Washington for his dedicated efforts as governor and his loyal co-operation, in the face of great difficulties. Although without military experience himself, Jefferson grasped the essentials of the military situation. He was aware, for example, that unless he could obtain effective naval forces, Virginia would be wide open to other devastating raids from the sea and the bay.

Arnold went into winter quarters in Portsmouth, following his destructive foray up James River. He organized expeditions in lower Tidewater with the special purpose of destroying warehouses stored with Virginia tobacco. Tobacco exports made it possible for Virginia, to a greater extent than the other colonies, to buttress its tottering finances by collecting tariffs on imports of various kinds.

Washington was finally able to dispatch a force southward, under Lafayette, to aid in Virginia's defense. Since the British had been reinforced at Portsmouth, this assistance was particularly vital. Lafayette's New England troops were ragged and hungry, as were most of the other Continentals, but their arrival in Virginia lifted the spirits of the state's struggling defenders.

Lafayette reached Richmond just as the British were approaching the town on the south side of the river. The latter did not attempt to cross the James, and elected to join forces at Petersburg with Cornwallis, who had moved up from the Carolinas. Cornwallis had suffered a severe setback at the hands of General Nathanael Greene at the Battle of Cowpens. The Continental victory had been due in large measure to the daring and imaginative leadership of General Daniel Morgan of the Shenandoah Valley and his cavalrymen. Dashing "Light-Horse Harry" Lee of Virginia, another brilliant commander in the Revolution, had also given Cornwallis some extremely bad moments in the South, notably at Guilford Courthouse. It was at Guilford Courthouse, too, that gigantic Peter Francisco performed some of his legendary feats. He had come to Virginia as a young boy from either Portugal or Spain, and enlisted as a private in the Continental Army. Francisco is said to have killed eleven British soldiers with his huge sword at Guilford Courthouse, and to have bested nine British dragoons in a later engagement.

Cornwallis decided to invade Virginia, the largest of the colonies. Governor Jefferson and the General Assembly moved from Richmond to Charlottesville, in view of the danger of capture by the fast-moving and numerically superior enemy.

The British general thereupon plotted a bold coup. Hoping to seize the governor and the General Assembly, he detached Colonel Banastre Tarleton, known as "The Hunting Leopard," with 180 dragoons and 70 mounted infantrymen, for a quick dash on Charlottesville. The quarry he was seeking included the author of the Declaration of Independence, three additional signers, Patrick Henry and an assorted variety of other revolutionary leaders.

It was the night of June 3-4, 1781, and the fortunes of the Americans, North and South, were at a low ebb. As for Virginia, the

(6) Sally Cary Fairfax, beloved
of George Washington at the time
he married Martha Custis.
Sally Fairfax was the wife of
George Fairfax of Belvoir, adjoining
Mount Vernon. Washington's
letters to her were found in a castle
in England after her death.

(7) Andrew Lewis, the great
Indian fighter, who led his
"long knives" against the Shawnees
under Chief Cornstalk at the
Battle of Point Pleasant, and dealt
the redskins one of the most
decisive defeats in their history.

(8) Patrick Henry addressing the court at Hanover
Courthouse in the "Parson's Cause." The judge,
Colonel John Henry, Patrick's father, is wiping his eyes
with emotion, and several clerics are departing down
the steps, under the lash of Henry's denunciations.
A nineteenth-century painting attributed to George Cook.

(9) *Below,* bust of Thomas Jefferson made by Houdon from life when Jefferson was minister to France, now in the Boston Museum of Fine Arts.

(10) The famous Houdon statue of George Washington, made by the celebrated French sculptor from life. It stands in the rotunda of the Capitol at Richmond and is regarded as the most valuable piece of marble in the United States.

legislature had abandoned the capital and the state appeared to be largely helpless against the invader.

"The Hunting Leopard" would almost certainly have pounced upon his prey, but for the intuition, ingenuity and dash of a six-foot-four-inch member of the Virginia militia, Captain John Jouett, Jr. This powerfully constructed citizen of Charlottesville happened to be in the vicinity of Cuckoo Tavern, Louisa County, when he saw the British cavalrymen moving rapidly along the main road toward the temporary capital of Virginia. Instantly suspecting their object, Jouett leaped upon his horse. It was about 10 P.M. and the moon was almost full. The latter circumstance made it possible for him to gallop at high speed by a little-used route and over rough and at times dangerous terrain to Charlottesville, some forty miles away. It was a ride that overshadows Paul Revere's much more famous but far less difficult feat.

Dawn was breaking over the hills of Albemarle as "Jack" Jouett arrived at Monticello on his panting and sweating steed. Jouett warned Jefferson and then roused the legislators in the town in time for nearly all to escape. The assemblymen convened a few days later in Staunton, forty miles farther west.

Thomas Jefferson was so leisurely in his preparations for leaving Monticello that he was almost captured by Tarleton's raiders. In fact, the British were ascending one side of the mountain, and Charlottesville was swarming with them when he finally made his exit. Yet he was attacked inside and outside Virginia, largely for political reasons, for having made a "cowardly retreat." Nothing could be more absurd. Jefferson had made mistakes as governor, but no one could properly charge him with a lack of physical courage.[6]

He did not stand for a third term as governor, as he felt that the office should be held in such difficult times by a man with military experience. The Assembly, meeting in Staunton, accordingly chose Thomas Nelson, Jr., of Yorktown, who had served as a brigadier general and commander-in-chief of Virginia forces. Nelson was to sacrifice his large fortune in the patriot cause, and to turn his guns on his own mansion at Yorktown, then serving as headquarters for Cornwallis. A cannon ball is embedded in the brick wall today. Nelson died in poverty.

A bright light was shed in those dark days by Brigadier General J. P. G. Muhlenberg, most distinguished of all the Germans who had come down to the Shenandoah Valley from Pennsylvania in the eighteenth century. He was active and zealous in the defense of Virginia.

As a Lutheran clergyman, stationed at Woodstock before the outbreak of hostilities with Great Britain, Muhlenberg had been ardent in the revolutionary cause. He headed the Committee of Safety for his area, and worked especially among the Valley Germans on behalf of the struggle for independence. He was active in recruiting the German Regiment, composed mainly of Germans from the Valley and adjacent regions, and was named its colonel. When recruiting was complete, the tall, handsome pastor entered his pulpit wearing his sword and cockade. Next day he marched off at the head of his regiment to join the revolutionary forces.

The German Regiment gave an excellent account of itself at Brandywine and Germantown, and passed the gruesome winter of 1777–78 at Valley Forge. Then, after fighting at Monmouth, its numbers had become so reduced that it was merged with the Fourth Virginia.

Muhlenberg was promoted to brigadier general in March 1780, and put in charge of Virginia's defenses. When a British force landed at Portsmouth and threatened to move inland, Muhlenberg organized "a tolerably respectable array of several thousand men," sufficient to check the enemy. At the end of the year, Major General Von Steuben, the Prussian drillmaster who had served under Frederick the Great, superseded him as commander of the Virginia forces, but Muhlenberg remained next in line. After a difficult and disheartening series of Virginia campaigns during the spring and summer of 1781, Muhlenberg was to play a significant role in the decisive events of October.

In the spring of 1781, George Washington had written in his diary that "scarce any State in the Union has, at this hour, an eighth part of its quota in the field and little prospect that I can see of ever getting more than half." He added that "instead of having the prospect of a glorious offensive campaign before us, we have a bewildered and gloomy defensive one."

That was before he learned of the decision of Louis XVI of France to commit the greater part of his fleet to the support of the American Revolution, and to dispatch a strong naval force under a first-class fighting man, the Count de Grasse.

By midsummer the French warships were in position and ready to co-operate with the Americans, in besieging either New York or York-town. It was the one thing needed to give heart to the hard-pressed Continentals.

Cornwallis had concentrated his army at Yorktown and De Grasse decided that the greatest potentialities for success lay in that direction. Washington accordingly embarked at once upon an elaborate ruse to convince the British that he and De Grasse were about to attack New York. False intelligence was made available to British spies, and fake hardtack bakeries were constructed in New Jersey to deceive the enemy into thinking that this was to be the advance American base for the siege. Washington's Continentals linked up with a French army under Rochambeau, and the British were sure that the siege of New York had begun.

But the allied forces hurried past New York and headed south. They reached the head of Chesapeake Bay on September 5, just as De Grasse was entering the bay. The British Admiral Graves attacked De Grasse, but was driven off. Washington and Rochambeau arrived outside Yorktown with sixteen thousand men, and Cornwallis was in the trap. It was one of the most perfectly conceived and executed military triumphs of the eighteenth century.

This extraordinary achievement came when Virginia seemed to be nearing the end of its resources. The long conflict had brought wide-spread exhaustion and pessimism. While there was, in the words of historian Eckenrode, "no semblance of a Tory party" in Virginia, and many Tories were in jail, there was "doubt, dissatisfaction, and a dis-inclination to make sacrifices."

Despite all this, the leaders of the Continental Army and of the French forces had collaborated to outmaneuver Cornwallis and to bottle him up in Yorktown. Not only was he surrounded by both land and sea, but the combined American and French land armies were approximately twice as large as his.

Trenches were dug by the allies and cannon were brought up. There were mines and countermines. British redoubts were erected and were duly stormed and taken by the Americans. General Muhlenberg com-manded the American brigade which stormed one of these, with Colonel Alexander Hamilton leading the advance force.

Cornwallis was a good enough soldier to know when he was beaten. After a few weeks of this, he recognized the inevitable, and on October 17, he sent out a white flag. Terms of surrender were accordingly drawn up at the Moore house on nearby Temple farm. The formal surrender took place on October 19.

Cornwallis pleaded indisposition and named Brigadier Charles O'Hara to perform the unpleasant and humiliating office. Washington designated General Benjamin Lincoln to accept his surrender.

The American and French forces formed two lines under the bright October sun, while Washington, one of the great horsemen of the age, surveyed the scene, astride his fine charger.

The British regiments laid down their arms and marched back to camp between the ranks of the victorious French and Americans. The melancholy tunes played by the British bands reflected their dejection. Apparently the climactic air, which must have seemed appropriate to the almost incredible occasion, was "The World Turned Upside Down."

Strictly speaking, the war was not over, for it would be nearly a year and a half before peace would be formally declared. But for all practical purposes, American independence had been won. The mighty British empire had been humbled by a ragged, often half-starved aggregation of colonials.

This could never have happened, of course, without the aid of France. De Grasse, Lafayette, Rochambeau and the men and ships they brought with them were essential to victory.

Yet towering above all was the one man who furnished the indispensable leadership and the inflexible will to win—George Washington. George III was to pronounce him the greatest of living men, and John Richard Green, the renowned English historian, would write:

"No nobler figure ever stood in the forefront of a nation's life."

FIFTEEN

Religious Freedom Wins, Public Education Loses

THE PEACE TREATY was signed February 3, 1783, yet many details remained to be settled, in Virginia as elsewhere. Not until December of 1783 was General Washington able to say farewell to his officers—at a dinner in the Fraunces Tavern, New York City. The commander-in-chief and the veterans of many desperate battles shed tears unashamedly as they embraced.

Washington left New York on horseback for Annapolis, where Congress was sitting, to turn in his commission. The normally imperturable warrior was almost overcome, and his hands shook as he delivered his brief address. "The spectators all wept," one eyewitness wrote, "and there was hardly a member of Congress who did not drop tears." They were tears of joy, of course, evoked by the realization that seven years of struggle and sacrifice had finally brought independence.

Anxious to join Martha for Christmas, Washington again mounted his horse, and reached Mount Vernon in time to relax at the family hearth on Christmas Eve.

Meanwhile in Virginia the people were trying to bring matters back to something approaching normalcy. The state had not suffered great physical devastation, except in limited areas. However, much of the mercantile class had returned to Great Britain, a serious loss in a rural state, while the emigration of valuable citizens to Kentucky further depleted the commonwealth's resources.

Feeling against the Tories still ran high. The General Assembly was less bitter against them than were many of the Virginia people. American soldiers made depredations against the property of the Tories, especially in the Chesapeake Bay area, where there had been British raids and thieveries throughout the year 1782, since there was no Virginia navy to offer resistance. Outlaws of various kinds and runaway slaves had joined in the plundering.

British subjects remaining in the state during the closing months of the war were driven harshly into exile, and refugees who attempted to return from New York were forbidden to do so.

With the formal signing of the peace treaty early in 1783, many applications were made by refugees for permission to return to Virginia. Citizens were sometimes violent in their reactions, and objectionable returnees were decorated with tar and feathers, or otherwise victimized. These bellicosities occurred in the face of official directives to the contrary by local or state bodies.

The General Assembly in the fall of 1783 repealed the laws forbidding Tories to return to Virginia, the sole exceptions being those who had taken an active part on the British side in the war. There was considerable opposition to this demonstration of official leniency, however, and had it not been for Patrick Henry, the measure might not have passed. The once-fiery leader of the revolutionary patriots was the principal spokesman for the legislation. His magnanimous attitude and the eloquent manner of its expression evidently influenced many Assemblymen.

The Assembly of 1783 also passed legislation to enforce agreements made by masters that slaves who had served in the armed forces in their stead would be given freedom at the end of hostilities. In a good many instances, masters did not carry out these agreements, and they sought to re-enslave the black men who had served for them.

According to Benjamin Quarles, the historian:

"Governor Benjamin Harrison, like many other Virginians, was indignant at this violation of the 'common principles of justice and humanity,' and was determined to 'lay the matter before the Assembly, not doubting but they will pass an act giving to those unhappy creatures that liberty which they have been in some measure instrumental in securing for us.' Harrison quickly got what he wanted . . . the legislature decreed that each slave who had served as a substitute was henceforth fully and completely emancipated."

As for the thousands of Virginia blacks who had joined the British during the Revolution, in the hope of obtaining freedom, they suffered an uncertain fate. Great numbers died of smallpox, which was prevalent in the British camps and on board the British ships. In addition, "many Negroes were carried away without regard for their own wishes," writes Quarles, who adds that "this would be particularly true of slaves belonging to departing loyalists."

Congress had instructed General Washington to arrange for delivery of all Negroes who were then in the hands of the British or their adherents. The general held an interview with Sir Guy Carleton, British commander-in-chief, and reported, "I have discovered enough to convince me that the slaves which absconded from their masters will never be restored." Apparently few of them were.

Many of the revolutionary leaders in Virginia were strongly opposed both to slavery and the slave trade, although they were themselves slaveowners. The practical difficulties in the way of abolishing slavery were great, but it was less of a problem to prohibit the importation of chattels into the state by sea or land. Virginia had passed a law in 1778 banning that traffic and thus became the first community in the civilized modern world to do so, with the single exception of Delaware.[1]

Another advance for Virginia in the area of race relations had been its admittance of mentally afflicted free blacks to its Hospital for the Insane at Williamsburg, erected in 1773, the first mental hospital in America. The Old Dominion thus became the first colony or state to provide professional care for free black persons of unsound mind.[2] Slaves were not admitted to the Williamsburg hospital until 1841. A separate building for Negro patients was erected in 1850.

However, during the years immediately following the end of hostilities with Great Britain, the pressing issue in Virginia was not so much that of slavery or related aspects of the race problem; more than all else it was the issue of religious freedom. And as with so many other progressive movements in that era, the man who furnished the imaginative insights and served as the spearhead of the advance was Thomas Jefferson. The fight for religious freedom was reaching its successful climax in the year after peace was declared.

An important contribution had been made by the Virginia Convention of 1776, which adopted George Mason's pronouncement on behalf of religious "toleration," but James Madison wanted to go even further, and to declare for complete religious freedom. If he had succeeded, the subsequent enactment of Jefferson's far-famed statute would have been well-nigh superfluous.

Jefferson had decided at the outbreak of the Revolution that, in addition to his leadership in obtaining independence from Great Britain, he would launch an assault on the Established Church in Virginia and seek to introduce a system of universal education. He would also lay "the axe to the root of the pseudo-aristocracy" by introducing legislation to abolish the long-standing system of entails and primogeniture, under which the estates of the great planters could be kept largely intact from generation to generation.

An idea of the immense versatility of this youthful Virginian who thus was embarking on one of the most precedent-shattering crusades in American history may be gained from the words of Julian P. Boyd, editor of the multivolume edition of Jefferson's collected papers. Boyd wrote that at age thirty-three Jefferson could—". . . 'calculate an eclipse, survey an estate, tie an artery, plan an edifice, try a cause, break a horse, dance a minuet and play the violin,' to say nothing of being an informed parliamentarian, a collector of manuscript laws, an author of a revolutionary tract, a craftsman in metal, a creative pioneer in archaeology and an organizer of plans for improving the navigation of a river."

When Jefferson moved against the bulwarks of the aristocracy at the General Assembly's session of 1776, entails were speedily abolished. It was not until 1785, however, that primogeniture was outlawed. As a matter of fact, neither of these legal devices was particularly popular with the substantial planters at that time, and the rights which existed under these laws were often not exercised. Material wealth, chiefly land, was normally the passport to social and political preferment in the eighteenth century, but the acreage was frequently distributed among several sons, under the will of the planter, rather than to the eldest son. For example, in the 1750s, no fewer than seven Lees of the same generation were sitting together in the General Assembly, an illustration of the manner in which the Lee estates had been divided.

At the Assembly session of 1776 Jefferson also introduced a highly important bill providing for the appointment of a committee to report upon revision and codification of the laws of the state. He served on this committee, or Board of Revisors, for two years and had a major role in producing a greatly improved code of laws. Its criminal section was especially enlightened, as it eliminated many of the incredibly harsh penalties which were still in force in Great Britain. The Assembly eventually accepted most of these recommendations. They were well in advance of those prevailing for many years thereafter in most of the other states.

In the course of his work as a revisor, Jefferson framed two statutes of far-reaching importance—his Bill For the More General Diffusion of Knowledge and his Statute For Religious Freedom, separating church and state. The former, providing for a system of public education from elementary school through college, would not pass until almost the end of the century, and then only after being fatally weakened. The latter would be enacted by gradual stages, and would finally be placed on the statute books in a form satisfactory to its sponsor.

Jefferson's Statute for Religious Freedom was introduced in 1779 by John Harvie of Albemarle, when its author was serving his first term as governor. Jefferson said the struggle over this bill involved him in the severest political contest of his life. This despite his estimate that in 1776 two-thirds of the people of Virginia had become dissenters. However, the powerfully entrenched planters of the Tidewater and Piedmont were almost all members of the Established Church and most of them were strongly opposed to the bill.

Let us look back briefly at the events leading up to the introduction of the Statute for Religious Freedom. Reference was made in Chapter Nine to the fact that the issue of religious liberty had arisen sharply when the Presbyterians began moving into the Shenandoah Valley in large numbers several decades before the Revolution. At that time Samuel Davies was the most conspicuous and influential leader of these dissenters.

Davies demanded the right to establish as many preaching points as he desired, under Britain's Toleration Act of 1689. He was informed that since that act had never been adopted by the General Assembly of Virginia, it was not in effect in the colony. Colonel Richard Bland, whose scholarly treatises greatly influenced the revolutionary generation of Virginia leaders, had stressed that laws passed by the British were without force and effect until they had been re-enacted by the legislature of the Old Dominion.

In 1769 a bill was introduced in Virginia's lawmaking body "granting toleration to his majesty's subjects being Protestant dissenters." This legislation was the result not only of pressure from the Presbyterians but also from the Baptists, especially a group of independent members of that denomination terming themselves "Separate" Baptists. However, the bill was not approved.

The "Separate" Baptists, who had come from outside of Virginia, were more belligerent than the "Regular" Baptists who had been living quietly in the colony for many years and had been legally recognized as a dissenting denomination. The Regular Baptists were not numerous at that time, and when they first encountered the Separate Baptists in 1767 in Orange County, they refused to affiliate with the newcomers. The older group disagreed with the younger, not only on doctrinal grounds but also because it was out of sympathy with the crude behavior of the latter's ministers in the pulpit.

But the two groups of Baptists gradually became more friendly and co-operative, and their highly emotional appeal to the masses became steadily greater. The Separate Baptists managed an important coup when they won over Samuel Harris of Hanover, a former Anglican vestryman who had served in the House of Burgesses. Harris became a Baptist minister in 1760 and was a significant factor in the spectacular growth of the denomination from that year until the outbreak of the Revolution.

The Separate Baptists exceeded the extreme wing of the New-Light (or New-Side) Presbyterians in the violence of their attacks on the Established Church and in the sensationalism of their preaching. The Separate Baptists also refused to obey the law requiring every dissenting minister to secure a license in the county court and register the places at which he preached.

The Separate Baptists were entirely sincere in believing that theirs was the one true faith. They were also extremely courageous in stating their views, in the face of physical attacks, as well as jail sentences.

Their method of preaching found its inspiration, at least in part, in the pulpit technique of George Whitefield, who, as we have seen, came to this country from Great Britain as early as the 1730s, and gave marked impetus to the religious movement termed the "Great Awakening." In Virginia, which he visited frequently over the years, his unorthodox preaching methods encouraged some dissenting clergymen to excesses of emotional appeal which had almost unbelievable effects on those who heard them.

At revivals held by the Separate Baptists were noted such phenomena—described by Wesley M. Gewehr in his *The Great Awaken-*

ing in Virginia 1740–1790—as "muscular contortions known as the 'jerks,' excessive trembling, falling, rolling on the ground, crying and 'barking like dogs' . . ." Gewehr quotes Daniel Fristoe's description of a meeting of some two thousand Separate Baptists "where he saw 'multitudes, some roaring on the ground, some wringing their hands, some in exstacies [sic], some praying, some weeping; and others so outrageous [sic] cursing and swearing that it was thought that they were really possessed of the devil.'"

The Baptists became the leading denomination crusading for religious freedom in Tidewater and Piedmont Virginia on the eve of the Revolution, for the Presbyterians had transferred their efforts primarily to the Shenandoah Valley.

One can imagine the disdainful reactions of the staid and dignified Anglicans of central and eastern Virginia to the hysterical shrieks and contortions of the Separate Baptists and their fellows, as roaring and pulpit-pounding evangelists depicted for these "sinners" the terrors of hell.

But there was no gainsaying that the Baptists and the Presbyterians were making important inroads against the Established Church and arousing the Virginia masses as they had never been aroused before. Important Anglican conservatives decided that the way to meet this threat was to enforce the law against preaching by unlicensed dissenters, and in 1768 this process began. Between that year and the outbreak of the Revolution, about thirty-four Baptist ministers were arrested and thrown into jail, some of them several times. They often preached through the bars to those on the outside.

A number of Baptist clergymen also were attacked by mobs. Some were "plunged into mud until they were nearly drowned, out of ridicule of the Baptist rite of dipping."

The most prominent defender in the courts of these suffering clergymen was Patrick Henry. "The Baptists found in Patrick Henry an unwavering friend," wrote Robert B. Semple, the Baptist historian. "May his name descend to posterity with unsullied honor."

A potent factor in achieving the downfall of the Established Church was a petition filed with the legislature by the Hanover Presbytery in 1775. G. MacLaren Brydon writes that it "seems beyond doubt to have been the document which cleared the way for the statement declaring man's right to worship God in his own way as it appears in George Mason's Declaration of Rights." This same Hanover Presbytery was to

remain a strong influence on behalf of religious freedom until that
objective was achieved.

Virginia Methodists had their earliest conspicuous leader in Dever-
eaux Jarratt, and their first great revival in 1776. They were at that time
members of the Anglican communion, both in Great Britain and
America.

However, they were evangelical in their approach, and hence were
not happy with the sedate ritual of the Anglicans. The prolonged
Methodist revival contributed to the further weakening of the Establishment and accelerated the growth of dissent. The Methodists
split off as a separate denomination after the Revolution.

While hostilities with Great Britain were in progress, not only the
Methodists but also the Baptists and Presbyterians were militantly
on the side of the patriots. This tended to strengthen the cause of
disestablishment. That cause was strengthened further by the fact
that a majority of the Anglican clergy on the administrative and teaching staff of the College of William and Mary were pro-British. This last
was in contrast to the attitude of the other Anglican clergymen
throughout Virginia, most of whom were strongly on the side of the
Revolution.[3]

As early as 1776, legislation which weakened the Anglican Church
considerably was passed after what Jefferson described as "desperate
contests." It is noteworthy, however, that opposition on the part of
the Establishment was not so great as many have supposed. Brydon
points out that too little consideration has been given to the fact that
"out of nearly a hundred [Anglican] parishes in active existence in
1776 only two or three sent in petitions against disestablishment."

Under the legislation adopted at this time, dissenters were exempted
from all taxes toward support of the Established Church, and no
acts of Parliament which rendered criminal any opinion on matters
of religion were conceded to have any further validity.

Yet the Anglican vestries retained the right to levy taxes for relief
of the poor; the church edifices and glebes, purchased through general
taxation, were retained by the Established Church, and the question of
a general assessment for the support of all churches was left unsettled.
A quarter of a century would pass before all these matters were concluded, and disestablishment was complete.

The general assessment issue, involving taxation for the support
of all religion, soon was revived, and petitions in favor of this levy

were filed by various groups, and even by the Presbyterian clergy, though they later reversed their position. Patrick Henry, who became more conservative with the passing years, was the chief sponsor of the tax, although its effect would have been to rivet upon the commonwealth the union of church and state. But after prolonged discussion at several sessions of the Assembly, the tax was voted down decisively in 1785, thanks in large measure to the leadership of young James Madison. Jefferson was absent from the country as minister to France, and he entrusted the handling of this vitally important matter to his friend.

Madison, whose great ability and influence were coming to be recognized, also took charge of Jefferson's much-cherished Statute for Religious Freedom. It had been introduced in 1779, as noted above, but had never passed. However, opposition to the Established Church and its privileges had been mounting steadily. It reached such a crescendo by 1786 that the statute was approved by the lopsided vote of 74 to 20.

While this statute is one of the great charters of American freedom, the principles it expressed had, in large measure, been laid down in the immediately preceding years. Separation of church and state in Virginia had, in effect, been achieved through defeat of the assessment. yet the significance of the statute, expressing fundamental principles, was tremendous. The gist is in the following paragraph:

"Be it enacted by the General Assembly, That no man shall be compelled to frequent or support any religious worship, place, or ministry whatsoever, nor shall be enforced, restrained, molested or burthened in his body or goods, nor shall otherwise suffer on account of his religious opinions or belief; but that all men shall be free to profess, and by argument to maintain, their opinions in matters of religion, and that the same shall in no wise diminish, enlarge or affect their civil capacities."

Thomas Jefferson's successful sponsorship of this legislation was one of the three accomplishments of his life in which he took the greatest pride, and which, at his direction, were inscribed on his tomb. The others were "Author of the Declaration of Independence" and "Father of the University of Virginia."

Although Jefferson was assailed as an "atheist" in political campaigns, this was wholly unjustified. He seems to have approximated

Unitarianism in his religious beliefs, and, like Washington, Madison and Mason, to have tended toward deism.

James Madison, whose work in furthering Jefferson's plans in the General Assembly was so essential, was only in his middle twenties when he entered that body, and his middle thirties when he led the successful fight for the Statute for Religious Freedom. In the following year this immensely learned young man was to be the dominant figure in the convention which drafted and adopted the Constitution of the United States. One cannot fail to be impressed by the astonishing intellectual maturity of such men as Madison and Jefferson.

Madison was of small physical stature, and hence was much less striking in appearance than the tall and rangy Jefferson. Washington Irving described "Jeemy" Madison as "no bigger than half a piece of soap." Although he was a convincing debater, his voice was weak and virtually inaudible in any large chamber. His nose was frozen when he addressed a German audience in the snow outside a country church, and this slightly marred his appearance. He was a delightful storyteller, with a keen sense of humor, when relaxing with friends, but was grave and serious in most of his public utterances and private contacts.

Passage of the Statute for Religious Freedom left the Anglican Church in possession of its churches and glebe lands. Petitions in great numbers were accordingly filed with the legislature, asking that these properties be sold, and the proceeds used for the poor. Finally, in 1799 the Assembly repealed legislation passed in 1776 which had specifically reserved to the church all its property. In 1802 the Assembly directed the overseers of the poor to sell all glebe lands not then occupied, and to sell the remainder when the incumbent ministers died or resigned.

The Episcopal Church fought the sale of its properties in the courts, on constitutional grounds. Its position would have been upheld, and the act of 1802 declared unconstitutional, had not Edmund Pendleton, president of the Virginia Court of Appeals, died suddenly—with his opinion that the act was unconstitutional already written. Two of the other three justices agreed with him. But then Judge St. George Tucker was named to succeed Pendleton on the court, and Tucker took the opposite view. A two-to-two tie left the statute on the books, and sale of the glebes proceeded. This almost wrecked the Episcopal Church in Virginia, but it finally recovered.

While funds realized from these sales were supposed to go to the poor, in some counties the money went to support private academies, and in others it gravitated into the pockets of politicians.

If the Virginia General Assembly had caught the vision of Thomas Jefferson, as expressed a generation before in his Bill for the More General Diffusion of Knowledge, the funds realized from the sale of the properties of the Episcopal Church could have been used to implement that legislation. In that event, the system of public education which the Master of Monticello envisioned might have become a reality in the early years of the nineteenth century. But public schools were not to be established on a general scale in Virginia until after the Civil War, and Jefferson's comprehensive plan for educating the ablest white students from elementary school through college at public expense would never come to fruition.

Instead, the state, and most of the southern region, would rely on privately financed academies for precollege training. Virginia, of course, looked to the College of William and Mary for those who desired to pursue learning into the higher echelons, until Hampden-Sydney and Washington Academy, later Washington College, were established in 1776.

One of the most notable academies in Virginia prior to the Revolution was conducted by a Scotsman, Donald Robertson, in King and Queen County. Among his pupils was James Madison, who is said to have remarked in his old age: "All that I have been in life I owe largely to that man." George Rogers Clark, whose aunt became Robertson's second wife, was enrolled briefly, but hunting and fishing appear to have taken precedence with this youth over Latin declensions, and Robertson "bounced . . . Clark back to the home farm." Greater aptitude for learning was displayed by such other pupils as John Taylor "of Caroline" and Edmund Pendleton, "Jr.", nephews of Edmund Pendleton.

Similar institutions which furnished schooling at the preparatory level for many leaders in that era were Prince Edward Academy, later Hampden-Sydney; Liberty Hall Academy, later Washington College; and Norfolk Academy, Fredericksburg Academy, Winchester Academy, Petersburg Academy, Alexandria Academy and several others. Ebenezer School in Brunswick County, founded about 1790, is said to have been the first Methodist school in this country.

These academies were to multiply in Virginia during the antebellum era. Some were non-denominational while others were church-affiliated. They performed a vital function, but it can readily be seen that their scope was narrow, and that the great mass of the whites and all of the Negroes were untouched by them.

SIXTEEN

The Battle for the Constitution

THE AMERICAN REVOLUTION had been won despite the fact that until 1781 the patriot cause had hardly anything remotely resembling central governmental direction. Even the loosely constructed piece of legislative and administrative machinery known as the Articles of Confederation was not finally ratified until a few months before the surrender at Yorktown. Throughout the preceding five years, each colony had been free to contribute to the Revolution such men, money and supplies as it saw fit, and this situation was not changed by final ratification of the Articles.

Furthermore, in 1784, the year after peace was formally concluded, George Washington wrote Governor Benjamin Harrison that "unreasoning jealousy" of the states toward one another was threatening "our downfall as a nation." In fact, the government under the Articles of Confederation was, in the words of Charles A. and Mary R. Beard, "little more than a council of diplomatic agents engaged in promoting thirteen separate interests without authority to interfere with the economic concerns of any." All questions were decided by a vote of the states, and powerful Virginia had one vote, just as did little Rhode Island. Any amendment of the Articles required unanimous approval.

Squabbles over trade were among the most prolific causes of dissension. Duties were levied against imports into one colony, or state, from another. Virginia imposed generally moderate import duties on a number of commodities and products, such as salt, hemp, cordage, cheese, snuff and certain liquors. Virginia also placed export duties on tobacco.

The chaotic currency situation in Virginia and the other colonies or states was a constant source of trouble. Congress, under the Articles of Confederation, had no power to issue currency, and various states printed their own. Virginia accordingly authorized huge issues of treasury notes, without adequate taxation as security for their redemption. The inevitable result was that these tens of millions in notes became largely worthless. After Yorktown, there was almost wholesale repudiation, and patriotic Virginians who had relied on the good faith of the commonwealth and exchanged valuable property for the notes, were ruined. Virginia's policy of returning one dollar for every $1000 of notes surrendered was in contrast to that followed in some other states, where these obligations were honored much more fully—at forty for one in Maryland, for example, and completely in Connecticut.[1]

Virginia's post-Revolutionary role with respect to the Northwest Territory was a more admirable one. This enormous region north of the Ohio and east of the Mississippi, claimed by Virginia under the Charter of 1609, and also by virtue of its conquest in the Revolution by George Rogers Clark, was ceded voluntarily to the nation. Certain concessions were sought in return, but only a few were obtained.

Jefferson drafted the Territorial Ordinance of 1784, containing, among other provisions, the assurance that the states formed from this vast area should remain forever a part of the United States, and that slavery should not exist there after 1800. The prohibition against slavery failed of adoption "accidentally by a single vote."

This statesmanlike ordinance, forerunner of that adopted three years later, is often ranked second only to the Declaration of Independence among Jefferson's official papers.

The Ordinance of 1787 did prohibit slavery in the states formed from the Northwest Territory—thanks, at least in part, to Jefferson. These states were Ohio, Indiana, Illinois, Michigan and Wisconsin. When names for these great political subdivisions were being chosen, Jefferson's suggestions that they be called Chersonesus, Assensisipia and Pelisipia were mercifully ignored.

The movement for a stronger national government gathered strength in the years following the coming of peace. Irritations and complications of many kinds, involving such things as trade, currencies, tariffs, clearance regulations and legal-tender laws made the need for a more unified nation increasingly obvious. For example, when Virginians, or citizens of other states, embarked on their laborious journeys over the rough roads of that era, they were constantly worried lest currency that was good in one state be unacceptable in another or be subjected to a heavy discount.

The power of Congress to make a valid treaty of peace was brought sharply into question, owing to differences between the United States and Great Britain over the terms of the treaty acknowledging this country's independence. A Virginia law, similar to laws in other states, forbade British creditors to collect debts owed them or to recover other property. Many Virginians were heard to remark, "If we are now to pay the debts due to British merchants, what have we been fighting for all this while?" Yet the British made it clear in 1784 to James Monroe, who was on a northern tour, that they had no intention of returning the Negroes they had seized or who had come to them voluntarily, or fulfilling other terms of the peace treaty, until the obnoxious debt laws passed by the states had been repealed. Congress sent a formal request for their repeal, and Virginia was among those which refused. It was obvious that the states did not consider that the national government had the power to make a treaty that was binding upon them. Some Americans even considered the states to be "thirteen independent republics."

Such conditions were clearly intolerable, and a stronger Union became essential. Interestingly enough, the first step in that direction was taken by Virginia in a dispute with Maryland over their respective rights to oyster fisheries in the Potomac River. Aware that other interstate controversies were likewise in need of settlement, the Virginia Assembly, in 1786, suggested a conference of all the states at Annapolis "to take into consideration the trade of the United States."

Only five states sent representatives. This was so unsatisfactory that Alexander Hamilton and James Madison, two of the youngest delegates, led in advocating a convention for the following year. This was to "devise such further provisions as shall appear . . . necessary to render the constitution of the federal government adequate to the exigencies of the Union." Congress accordingly invited the thirteen states to send delegates to Philadelphia in May 1787, "for the sole and express purpose of revising the Articles of Confederation. . . ."

Virginia played the leading role at the Philadelphia convention, which was composed of one of the most talented groups of men ever assembled. George Washington, whose arrival in Philadelphia was heralded by the firing of an artillery salute and the ringing of chimes, was the unanimous choice for president. He had come with great reluctance, however, "too zealously attentive to his reputation and his popularity—too much the self-conscious national hero and too little the daring patriot," although the country was facing a peacetime crisis almost comparable to that which had confronted it in the War for Independence.[2] But having taken his seat as the presiding officer, Washington did the needful. He was no parliamentarian and no speaker, but his mere presence in the chair augured for the success of the enterprise.

Another Virginian, the immensely learned James Madison, was the foremost figure in the deliberations and the debates—so much so that he earned the sobriquet of "Father of the Constitution." Madison's notes on the proceedings—all formal sessions were held behind closed doors—are our most valuable source of information concerning what occurred at Philadelphia. The notes were published after Madison's death. His contributions to *The Federalist*, along with those of Alexander Hamilton, were also extremely valuable.

Virginia's other major participant in the Philadelphia convention was Edmund Randolph, then governor of the state. It was he who presented the "Virginia Plan," favorable to the large states. New Jersey countered with the "New Jersey Plan," favorable to the small states. The final result was a compromise between the two.

George Mason, another prominent Virginia delegate, delivered an impassioned speech against the slave trade, terming it an "infernal traffic," and declaring that "every master of slaves is born a petty tyrant." He urged the trade's immediate abolition, but the New England states joined with the Carolinas and Georgia in insisting upon its continuance until 1808.

Neither Thomas Jefferson nor Patrick Henry was at Philadelphia. Jefferson was still serving as minister to France, while Henry declined election as a delegate to the convention, saying that he "smellt a rat." Henry's opposition the following year to ratification by Virginia came close to succeeding and could have precipitated a national crisis.

The Virginia Convention of 1788 produced some of the ablest debates in this country's annals. It was held in Richmond's newly constructed Academy, a wooden building on the east side of Twelfth Street between Broad and Marshall. The hall was only a few blocks from the Swan Tavern on Broad, the town's leading hostelry. George Mason, Patrick Henry, James Madison and other delegates had rooms at the Swan, in easy strolling distance from the convention hall.

The convention lasted from June 2 to June 27, and the published debates filled 652 printed pages. Of these, 136 pages, or more than one-fifth, contain the words of Patrick Henry. It was the era when speeches often lasted for hours, even for an entire day. When Henry was speaking, no matter at what length, he seems to have held the attention of those who crowded the floor and the galleries. Since shorthand reporters were available for the first time in the history of Virginia conventions, the record is much more complete than for previous conclaves.

The widely respected Edmund Pendleton was named president of the convention without opposition. He had been crippled for life in a fall from his horse in 1777 and had to preside sitting in his chair, since he was unable to stand or walk without crutches. His once-powerful body had been twisted and wrenched by the painful injury to his hip, and his handsome face showed unmistakable signs of age and failing health. But his mind was keen, and he presided with dignity and ability.

Pendleton's presidency of the convention was an advantage for the advocates of ratification, since he was a stanch Federalist. When the convention went into the Committee of the Whole, he several times vacated the chair to George Wythe and took part in the debates. Since Pendleton was described by Jefferson as the ablest debater he had ever encountered, his importance to the cause of the Constitution may be imagined.

Allied with him were James Madison, Edmund Randolph, "Light-Horse Harry" Lee, John Marshall and Wythe, among others. This was a combination of erudition, prestige and forensic ability which the opposition could not equal.

The latter boasted of such men as Patrick Henry, George Mason, James Monroe and William Grayson. Henry, with his matchless oratory and great personal influence, was practically a host in himself, and Mason was a speaker and statesman of superlative gifts; yet they and their compatriots were unable to prevail.

They could not defeat ratification despite the fact that a majority of the people of Virginia were assumed, apparently correctly, to oppose adoption. The advocates of the Constitution in the convention were better organized, they had superior leadership and they outmaneuvered the opposition from the beginning.

The opponents of ratification faced other serious handicaps. Henry

and Mason were unable to co-ordinate their strategy. Henry wanted
to attack the Constitution as a whole, whereas Mason preferred to
analyze it clause by clause.

The "antis" ran into a further setback when widely admired Governor Edmund Randolph, on whom they had counted as an eloquent and
potent ally, since he had refused to sign the Constitution when he
was a delegate at Philadelphia, decided to support ratification at
Richmond. Randolph's change of position was a shattering blow,
and caused George Mason to refer to him bitterly in private conversation as "Benedict Arnold." If the popular governor had remained in the
camp of the opposition, they might well have won their fight.

The proponents enjoyed a priceless advantage in the support of
George Washington. He had declined to be a delegate to the Richmond convention, but by correspondence from Mount Vernon to
friends in Richmond he had made clear his earnest hope for ratification. No one could have been more aware of the need for a viable,
functioning central government than the man who had led the tattered,
hungry and often shoeless and payless Continental Army for seven
years, against what seemed hopeless odds, while the bickering colonies
refused to provide their quotas of men or material, and there was no
central authority which could compel them to do so.

The debates at Richmond were, for the most part, conducted with
the elaborate punctilio and courtesy characteristic of that era. There
were, however, moments when personalities were resorted to, notably
when Randolph referred on the floor, in an exchange with Henry, to
the fact that he had considered disclosing certain facts that "would
have made some men's hair stand on end." Randolph also made a
pointed reference to "the curious and the malicious," and both phrases
seemed directed at Henry. Although dueling was not prevalent in that
age, the possibility of an armed encounter between Henry and Randolph caused apprehension. Fortunately, Henry and his representative, Colonel William Cabell, called on Randolph that evening, and
the matter was amicably adjusted.

There was another rather tense moment during the convention when
young "Light-Horse Harry" Lee, a hero of the Revolution but still
in his early thirties, assailed Patrick Henry—twenty years his senior,
and seeming much older than that—in terms which caused many to
wonder at his temerity. Terming Henry "tremblingly fearful of the fate
of the commonwealth," Lee expressed astonishment that a man of

Henry's talents and reputation could envision such "horrors" and "apprehensions," instead of examining the question of ratification on its merits. On another occasion, young Lee was equally sharp in his phraseology, declaring in answer to one of Henry's sallies, "I hold his unsupported authority in contempt."

This latter exchange was in connection with the Kentucky question, which was charged with considerable dynamite. Kentucky, still a part of Virginia and divided into several counties, was vitally interested in keeping the Mississippi open to navigation, as an outlet for its goods. The long and arduous journeys over the mountains for hundreds of miles to Virginia ports were, quite naturally, not to the Kentuckians' liking. Opponents of ratification spread the word among them that adoption of the Constitution would mean the relinquishment to Spain of control of the Mississippi. This was not a fact, but the Kentuckians were alarmed, and for a time it appeared that their delegation in the convention would deliver a solidly negative vote.

As a counter to this and other arguments against ratification, the proponents relied heavily on James Madison. Despite his weak voice and small stature, and his strange habit while speaking, as Grigsby described it, of holding his hat in his hand and his notes in his hat, Madison's influence in the convention was tremendous. His great erudition concerning the history of governments and political institutions, and his unparalleled understanding of the Constitution and its meaning, as adopted at Philadelphia, were assets which the opposition could never match.

Madison's casual manner and lack of dynamism were in startling contrast to the impassioned deliverances of Patrick Henry, who became so emotionally involved while thundering his denunciations that he sometimes twirled his wig around on his head several times in rapid succession.

Aware that ratification might fail, the proponents shrewdly promised, as the final vote neared, that they would earnestly seek a series of amendments, notably a Bill of Rights. This tipped the scales in their favor.

Even so, the outcome was extremely close. The real test came when Wythe moved ratification and Henry offered an amendment which would have nullified the effect of Wythe's motion. As the votes of the individual counties were tallied, Henry's "antis" showed considerable strength at the outset. They were leading, 25 to 12 at one point.

Gradually the backers of the Constitution closed the gap, however, thanks in part to the fact that three Kentuckians violated their instructions and voted against Henry's motion. As the tally mounted, and with it the tension, the score was 69 to 69. But the counties at the bottom of the alphabet turned the tide, and Henry's motion was beaten, 88 to 80. Then came the vote on final approval of the Constitution. One man switched from anti to pro, and Virginia ratified, 89 to 79. Under terms of the ratification, the Old Dominion retained the right to secede.

New Hampshire had ratified the week before and thus had become the ninth state, as required by the Constitution. But if Virginia, the largest and most populous of all, whose territory bisected the country from the Atlantic to the Mississippi, had refused to go along, the future of the nation might well have been in doubt. Even with the Old Dominion's example before it, New York ratified in the following month by a margin of only three votes. The majority in highly important Massachusetts also had been small. South Carolina had ratified with written reservations, and North Carolina and Rhode Island were still standing aloof.

So the outcome in Virginia was of crucial importance. A switch of half a dozen votes there might have wrecked the Union, with incalculable consequences, not only for this country but for the world.

SEVENTEEN

Washington's Climactic Role

GEORGE WASHINGTON was the inevitable and unchallenged choice for President of the newly created federal union. He did not seek the office, and was reluctant to accept it. He was uncertain of his ability to discharge the duties that would devolve upon him, and after the prolonged strain of the Revolution, he was more than ready to relax at his beloved Mount Vernon.

But the unanimous call of his countrymen to be the first President of the United States, which he had done more than anyone to bring into being, was hardly less than a command to one of his temperament.

Washington was fifty-seven, and he now had cultivated occasional low-keyed flashes of humor—something absent from his make-up in earlier years—which would stand him in good stead as the difficulties loomed. He was also capable of enormous wrath, as had been evident at certain moments during the Revolution, and would once more become manifest, at times, as he faced the burdens and harassments of his new post.

Washington, unfortunately, has been almost completely dehumanized by his idolators, who have depicted him as a wholly faultless and godlike figure. The ironic words of Nathaniel Hawthorne are appropriate in this connection: "Did anybody ever see Washington nude? It is inconceivable . . . he was born with his clothes on, his hair powdered and made a stately bow on his first appearance into the world."

As Washington prepared to accept the presidency, he remarked that he felt somewhat like a culprit "going to the place of his execution." He even had to borrow three thousand dollars to clear up certain debts and pay his traveling expenses to his inauguration in New York, the new capital. He insisted, nonetheless, that he would accept no pay as President. He chose a cabinet which included two Virginians—Thomas Jefferson as Secretary of State, and Edmund Randolph as Attorney General.

In appreciation of Washington's heroic services in the Revolution, the Virginia General Assembly had voted in 1784 to erect a statue of him. The great French sculptor, Houdon, was brought over from Paris, and spent two weeks at Mount Vernon. The statue, when executed some years later, would be placed in the rotunda of the Capitol at Richmond upon the completion of that edifice. Considered an almost perfect likeness of the subject, exhibiting the resolute courage, quiet dignity and calm serenity of the commander-in-chief of the Continental Army, Houdon's Washington has been termed the most valuable single piece of sculpture in the United States.

Gilbert Stuart's portrait, the so-called Athenaeum Head, painted about a decade later when Washington was contending with serious dental problems, is also greatly admired. However, in the opinion of the historian Joseph C. Robert, he was wearing a "spring-hinged set" of dentures "of improper dimensions, plus some cotton wadding" which created "a sort of 'grandmotherly' appearance, faithfully caught by the painter."

As Washington struggled with the manifold problems which inevitably confronted him as he sought to organize the national government, there were strong stirrings in Kentucky, near the frontier where, in his younger days, he had rendered much valuable service. An insistent demand for separation from Virginia had arisen in that wild, unexplored region, settled by thousands of dauntless men and women who had traveled through Cumberland Gap along Daniel Boone's Wilderness Road. Kentuckians were nearly all emigrants from Virginia, but they had been arguing for about a decade that Richmond was too far away, that communication was too slow, and that their economic and other interests were too different from those of Virginia east of the Alleghenies.

The comfortable citizens of Richmond and lower Tidewater, no longer facing the threat of Indian massacre, were derisively termed "Salt Water Geniuses" by one irate Kentuckian. He accused them of believing that the rampaging natives could be bribed to behave themselves every time they "raised the Hatchet."

As early as 1780, nearly seven hundred Kentuckians had signed a memorial requesting Congress to establish Kentucky as a separate state. Several conventions were held in succeeding years, making similar requests. One of these, in 1785, formally petitioned the Virginia Assembly for separation. The Assembly agreed, on the not unreasonable condition that Kentucky assume a part of Virginia's debt. The legislature also insisted that Congress give its consent.

Confusion resulting from a new Indian war and other events on the frontier combined with many complications incident to the establishment of the new federal government, caused Congress to delay action until 1792. In that year, Kentucky entered the Union as a separate state.

President Washington was by then deeply involved in the duties of his office at the nation's capital, but he had been concerned for many years with the desirability of improving communications between the frontier regions of the west and Virginia's ports.

Following the close of the Revolution, he had hardly become well-settled at Mount Vernon when he embarked on horseback upon a 680-mile expedition into the region beyond the Alleghenies. Accompanied by his nephew, Bushrod Washington, Dr. James Craik and Craik's son, together with three servants, he set out September 1, 1784, and was back at Mount Vernon October 4, three weeks ahead of schedule.

The opening up of the western regions by the creation of links between the upper waters of the Ohio and certain Virginia rivers had been under consideration for some time, and this was one object of the journey. The other was to examine the status of Washington's western lands, since trespassers were occupying some of them, and others were even being offered for sale, without his knowledge or consent.

A few days after his return, Washington wrote Governor Harrison emphasizing some of his conclusions as to the development of east-west trade.

"Smooth the road and make easy the way for them [the western settlers] and see what an influx of articles will be poured upon us; how amazingly our exports will be increased by them, and how amply we shall be compensated for any trouble and expense we may encounter to effect it."

Analyzing the difficulties involved in diverting traffic from the Mississippi eastward, Washington went on to say that "the western settlers . . . stand as it were upon a pivot . . . the touch of a feather could turn them any way." He speculated that these settlers had "looked down the Mississippi . . . for no other reason than because they could glide gently down the stream; without considering, perhaps, the difficulties of the voyage back again."

Washington persuaded James Madison to introduce bills to promote navigation on the upper reaches of the Potomac and James rivers. The Potomac was regarded at that time as having more potential for developing the western regions than the James, but it was hoped that both could be linked by canals or otherwise with the "Western waters." The Shenandoah was an element in these projections, since it could carry the products of the Valley into the Potomac. A connection between the headwaters of the James and the Ohio by way of the Kanawha was under consideration.

The Potomac Company and the James River Company were created, with a view to furthering these projects. Stock in both was sold, with the states of Virginia and Maryland subscribing, along with private individuals and organizations. Washington was the driving force behind these efforts.

Suddenly, in 1785, he was embarrassed when the General Assembly of Virginia voted him personally fifty shares of stock in the Potomac Company and a hundred shares in the James River Company. The legislators expressed the hope that the public improvements anticipated as a result of his leadership would serve as "durable monuments of his glory."

But Washington had refused to accept any compensation beyond expenses for his long years of service in the Revolution, and he was to do the same during his two terms in the presidency. He accordingly wrote the General Assembly a letter of appreciation, asking its permission to use the stock for "objects of a public nature," a request which it readily granted.

He donated the shares in the James River Company, worth some $50,000, to Liberty Hall Academy at Lexington, which soon became Washington College. This gift constituted the original endowment of the college, which promptly took the name of its benefactor. It would become Washington and Lee University three-quarters of a century later.

Washington, whose deep concern for the cause of education is manifest, said he wanted his shares in the Potomac Company to be devoted to the creation of a national university in the District of

Columbia. His desire for such an institution which would, he thought, tend to promote national unity and understanding, was further evidence of his vision. He provided for the bequest in his will. However, the Potomac Company failed and the stock became worthless, so this particular project came to nothing.

Washington encouraged James Rumsey of Maryland in the latter's pioneering efforts to build a steamboat. The Virginia and Maryland legislatures gave Rumsey the exclusive right to construct and operate his mechanically propelled craft on the waters of those states. For a brief period he was superintendent of canal construction for the Potomac Company, of which Washington was president. By 1787 Rumsey was able to construct and operate a primitive type of steamboat on the Potomac at Shepherdstown. He went to London in the hope of getting financial aid, but just when completion of a new and improved model was in sight, Rumsey died.

His effort thus ended in failure, but he was part of the thrust which George Washington generated toward the opening of avenues of communication between the east and the west. The canals, turnpikes and railroads built in Virginia in subsequent years were to a considerable degree the outgrowth of Washington's imaginative planning.

As Robert McColley has written: "If Jefferson was possessed by dreams of freedom, education and rustic tranquility, Washington was equally, if less poetically, possessed with visions of roads, canals, factories and cities, all knitted together in a richly varied, self-supporting and powerful America."

Washington was also a leader in creating better relations between the various religious denominations. During the year 1790 he wrote letters stressing his desire for interdenominational amity to groups of Roman Catholics, Quakers and Jews. The most famous of these was to the Hebrew congregation at Newport, R.I., in which he declared: "It is now no more that toleration is spoken of, as if it was by indulgence of one class of people that another enjoyed the exercise of inherent natural rights. For happily the government of the United States, which gives to bigotry no sanction, to persecution no assistance, requires only that they who live under its protection should demean themselves as good citizens . . . May the children of the Stock of Abraham, who dwell in this land, continue to merit and enjoy the good will of the other inhabitants." Washington's admiration for his

Jewish fellow citizens was doubtless enhanced by the notably patriotic and unselfish assistance rendered him by Haym Salomon of Philadelphia during the Revolution. Salomon had made his entire fortune of over $600,000 available for the financing of Washington's struggling forces, and had left his own family virtually penniless at his death.[1]

The end of the Revolution found the cities of Richmond and Norfolk far from prepossessing, with narrow streets that were muddy or dusty, depending on the weather, and no buildings of any distinction.

The new state Capitol, modeled at Jefferson's suggestion after the Maison Carrée at Nîmes, France, was being slowly constructed in Richmond. The General Assembly would hold its first session there in 1788. Capitol Square surrounding it was a rough piece of terrain, riddled with gullies and permeated with the pungent aroma of horses, cows and goats.

Norfolk, after its destruction in the Revolution, was recovering. La Rochefoucauld-Liancourt described it in 1796 as "one of the ugliest, most irregular, dirtiest towns that I have ever seen." Tom Moore, the Irish poet, reported a few years later that the city "abounds in dogs, in Negroes and in democrats."

Yet Norfolk, like Richmond, was experiencing a substantial boom, now that the Revolution was over. Products from the interior were being shipped down the James to Richmond, and then on to Norfolk. Hampton Roads was carrying on a growing trade not only with ports on the Atlantic seaboard but also with the West Indies and Europe.

The outbreak of a European war in 1793, as a sequel to the French Revolution, created a special demand in the West Indies for shipments in American vessels, since Britain's merchant fleet was occupied elsewhere. This was Norfolk's opportunity, and cargoes of corn, lumber, tobacco and naval stores poured into the West Indian islands from the Virginia seaport.

Meanwhile there was a special kind of traffic in the opposite direction —from the Indies into Norfolk. Slave revolts in Haiti (Santo Domingo), beginning in 1791 and continuing for several years, accompanied by bloody massacres on the part of both the natives and the French, caused an exodus of terrified whites. In 1793, refugees streamed into Norfolk and other American ports, and appropriations for relief were voted by the legislatures of Virginia and other states, as well as by Congress. Some two or three thousand destitute French refugees seem to have come to Norfolk at this time. A goodly number remained and opened small shops, but the majority moved on.

The presence of this unusual number of French citizens in Norfolk when the French Revolution was at its height led to many arguments, and even physical encounters, over the merits or demerits of the cataclysm that was shaking France. Since France and Britain were also at war, the clashes between the French refugees and the Englishmen and Scotsmen resident in Norfolk were especially sharp.

The dreadful atrocities in Haiti aroused fears on the part of Virginians lest similar slave insurrections break out in the Old Dominion and the other slave states.

The excesses of the French Revolution were also alarming to many Americans, especially the Federalists, two of whose principal leaders were George Washington and Patrick Henry.

Henry, whose increasingly conservative views on public questions now paralleled those of Washington in many respects, declined to accept the posts of Secretary of State and Chief Justice during Washington's second term. Henry's health was failing. He had been trying, through a revived law practice, mostly with criminal cases, and through extensive land speculation, to support his large family. He seemed willing to defend almost any criminal who sought his services. He charged large fees and usually insisted on payment in cash. But now, less vigorous than formerly, he settled down on his newly acquired plantation, Red Hill, on the Staunton River in Charlotte County, to spend his remaining years. Some of the great figures of the revolutionary era with whom he had been closely associated had passed away, notably George Mason and Richard Henry Lee. They had died in 1792 and 1794, respectively, after years of ill health.

Washington prevailed on Henry, despite his enfeebled condition, to offer for the House of Delegates in 1799. Henry, still the most revered public man in Virginia, with the single exception of Washington himself, managed to open his campaign in March with a speech at Charlotte Courthouse. He was obviously ill, but showed flashes of his old fire. Another candidate was young John Randolph of Roanoke, on the threshold of what was to be a meteoric, if erratic, career. Both were elected by substantial majorities, but Henry was never able to take his seat. A fatal illness, perhaps a malignancy, was sapping his vitality. He grew steadily weaker, and on June 6, he died. He was buried in the garden at Red Hill.

Washington, too, had only a few months to live, although no one suspected it at the time. He had retired to Mount Vernon in 1797, at the close of his second presidential term, and was at last free of the heavy demands of public office and military command. An unending stream of visitors and relatives shared his hospitality.

Apparently in good health, and enjoying the personal supervision and development of his plantation, he looked forward at sixty-seven to the leisure which he had so abundantly earned. But on a snowy December day in 1799, things suddenly changed.

A five-hour ride in rain, snow and hail to his various farms was followed by dinner at Mount Vernon without a change of clothing. Next day he had a sore throat, and he stayed indoors until the late afternoon, when the snow stopped, and he went out on the lawn for an hour, to mark certain trees for removal.

Washington retired that night in good spirits, but at around 2 or 3 A.M. he had a severe chill. He awakened Martha and, scarcely able to speak, told her that he was ill. Next morning his breathing was labored and doctors were sent for. He was bled copiously at intervals, and Dr. James Craik, his friend of long standing, applied a blister of cantharides, or Spanish flies, to relieve the acutely painful inflammation of his throat, which appeared to be almost strangling him. Several times Washington seemed to be in danger of suffocation. He sensed that he was dying, and said several times calmly, "I find that I am going" or "I feel myself going." Blisters were produced on his feet and legs, and soft poultices of wheat bran were applied to his throat, in accord with the quaint medical practice of that era.

It was all to no avail. Washington died quietly that night, December 14. His last words were, " 'Tis well."

Although he had requested in his will that he be buried in the family vault at Mount Vernon "in a private manner, without parade and funeral oration," the many who announced that they were coming could not be denied. There was the firing of guns offshore in a final salute, followed by the long procession to the grave, to the accompaniment of a dirge and muffled drums.

After it was over, there was much criticism throughout the land of the physicians who, it was argued, could have saved Washington's life, with proper handling of his case. This criticism seems to have been largely unwarranted. Most medical authorities appear to be of the opinion today that Washington's life could not have been saved, and at least one says that "death was a foregone conclusion." One modern diagnosis is that he suffered from "inflammatory oedema of the larynx." It is now felt that although the bleeding certainly did no good, it was not excessive, by late eighteenth-century standards. However, some believe that the bleeding and the other treatment may have hastened his death.[2]

The passing of Washington was indeed the end of an era.

He was no paragon of all the virtues; he had his human frailties, which makes ordinary mortals better able to understand and appreciate him. He was, for example, extremely sensitive to criticism. Denounced by his enemies and in the partisan press "in such . . . indecent terms," as he put it, "as could scarcely be applied to a Nero, a notorious defaulter or even to a common pickpocket," he triumphed over his natural resentment and sense of outrage. He was acutely, even excessively, jealous of his reputation, and as a man of complete integrity he resented any aspersions upon it.

If one tries to sum up the significance of Washington's career in a single word, that word might well be "character." It was character that carried him, at age twenty-one, across hundreds of miles, through bitter cold, snow and sleet, and past Indian ambushes to Fort Le Boeuf, bringing the message from Governor Dinwiddie to the French. It was character that made him fight on in the Revolution when a large percentage of the American people were against the cause for which he stood, and all thirteen of the colonies failed dismally to support him with men, money, weapons and supplies. And it was character that enabled him to win the respect of the world and to give to the position of President of the United States the dignity and prestige which it achieved during his eight years in that office.

George Washington epitomized what subsequent generations have come to recognize as a great, a good, a brave and a patriotic American. Without him there would have been no victory in war, no stability in peace. He came as close as anyone in our history to being the indispensable man.

EIGHTEEN

Slavery in Virginia
and a Thwarted Revolt

THE YEAR 1800 opened with the nation grieving over the death of Washington. In Virginia the scene appeared peaceful, except for some skirmishing on the political front. Relations between the races seemed harmonious.

Yet within a few months an attempted slave revolt of monumental proportions, known as Gabriel's Insurrection, was to be organized in the vicinity of Richmond, with perhaps thousands of slaves involved, and tentacles stretching as far as Petersburg and Charlottesville, Hanover, Louisa and Caroline.

White Virginians, as noted in the preceding chapter, had been gravely alarmed by the bloody atrocities in Haiti, where slaves had revolted against the French. But they did not suspect the existence in the Old Dominion of this widely ramified plot engineered by a gigantic slave named Gabriel—a plot far more extensive than anything of the sort, before or since, in the history of Virginia.

It had been worked out over a period of months by Gabriel on a plantation in Henrico County owned by Thomas Prosser. Gabriel had as a confederate another slave of huge dimensions named Jack Bowler. The plot called—incredible as this seems—for the wholesale killing of the whites in and near Richmond, the seizure of the city, and the entire commonwealth, if possible. The precise plans and detailed ultimate objectives remained to some extent undefined, but there can be no doubt that this was a desperate design, and that its leaders were ready to risk their lives in what they apparently envisioned as a state-wide revolt of the blacks and a wholesale massacre of the whites. They hoped that the uprising would spread to other states.

Gabriel and Bowler were men of obvious ingenuity, intelligence and daring. They had collected powder and shot, had sharpened scythes, made clubs and fashioned spears. Gabriel had actually managed to enter the closed Capitol on Sundays and had inspected and tallied the weapons stored there. The arsenal in Richmond was also an important element in the plan.

The plot called, on the day of the uprising, for a large group of slaves to set fire to the lower end of the city, consisting mainly of wooden buildings. When masses of whites rushed to put out the flames, armed blacks would seize the arsenal, with the arms stored therein, as well as the Capitol and the other public buildings, and begin slaughtering the whites. Gabriel and his followers would then take over.

The extent to which large groups of slaves were willing to go along with this audacious scheme is evidence of the persuasive powers of Gabriel and Bowler, or of widespread yearning for freedom on the part of the slaves, or hatred of the whites, or all three factors combined. Certainly a cataclysm of extensive proportions was shaping up, to go into operation on the night of August 30. Governor James Monroe reported officially to the General Assembly later in the year that the scheme "embraced most of the slaves in the city and neighborhood, and . . . extended to several of the adjacent counties."

The plan was thwarted at the last moment. Slaves on the plantation of Mosby Sheppard near Richmond alerted their master to the plot, and he promptly got word to Governor Monroe. The governor called out all available militiamen, guards were thrown around the arsenal and the Capitol, and roads leading into Richmond were patrolled. Secondly, a thunderstorm of great magnitude flashed and roared out of the sky, with the result that Gabriel's "army," gathered at Brook Swamp about five miles northwest of the city, could not get to Richmond, as the bridge over the swamp had been washed away by the flood. In fact, the whole area was rendered almost impassable by torrents of rain, raging streams and fathomless mud.

The plot had accordingly been set at naught, but Richmond and Virginia had had a narrow escape. Governor Monroe promptly offered rewards for the capture of Gabriel and Bowler, and began rounding up as many of the conspirators as possible. Bowler was taken early, but Gabriel eluded his pursuers for several weeks. Slaves alerted constables at Norfolk to Gabriel's impending arrival there, just as other slaves faithful to their masters had given advance warning of the initial uprising. Gabriel was seized when the ship on which he was concealed docked at Norfolk.

It is clear from the foregoing warnings given by slaves that some, doubtless a great many, of the blacks were totally out of sympathy with the plot. On the other hand, the dimensions of the conspiracy were truly staggering.[1]

Gabriel refused steadfastly to answer any questions after his arrest, or at his trial. He was hanged along with Bowler and some thirty-five others. Several of the executions were in Caroline County, which affords some indication of the extent of the area over which slaves had become actively involved.

On the other hand, scores of those tried were freed—evidence that despite widespread fear, and even hysteria, among the whites, mass executions of the innocent along with the guilty were not resorted to. A restraining factor was the law requiring the state to compensate any master whose slave was executed.

As a precaution against future uprisings, a permanent guard was stationed at the Capitol. It would be noted by travelers in their journals at periodic intervals until the Civil War.

Gabriel's Insurrection had been crushed, but the effects lingered on. It had a powerful impact on the minds of the whites in Virginia, and perhaps elsewhere, and coupled with the increasingly gruesome events in Santo Domingo caused a strong reaction against liberalization of the laws covering chattel servitude. The erroneous impression prevails that this anti-liberal trend in Virginia did not set in until the Nat Turner Insurrection of 1831 and William Lloyd Garrison's almost simultaneous founding of his wildly abusive journal, *The Liberator*.

Nearly all the great Virginians of the Revolutionary era, such as Washington, Jefferson, Madison, Mason and Henry, had been in favor of emancipation, provided—and this is important—the blacks, both slave and free, were removed from the state. Unfortunately, there were immense practical difficulties in the way. There was not only the question of how to compensate the owners of slaves for their enormous investments in these chattels, but there was also the problem of how to deport the Negroes. Deportation was thought essential, as nobody knew how to cope with the presence of hundreds of thousands of illiterate and untrained blacks.[2]

When the appalling facts with respect to Gabriel's plans for a wholesale massacre of the whites became known, there were shudders throughout the commonwealth. There had been some amelioration of the unquestionably harsh laws of the colonial era affecting slaves, but the horrible slaughter in Haiti prior to Gabriel's attempted uprising had given pause to many Virginians, and a contrary trend set in. As early as 1795, for example, the General Assembly passed a law imposing a penalty of $100 on any person who assisted a slave in asserting a claim to freedom, if he failed to establish the claim. Another statute provided that no member of a society seeking the abolition of slavery could serve as a juror in a freedom suit.

Such statutes discouraged the Virginia Abolition Society, and it appears to have dropped out of sight, after the Gabriel Insurrection, along with the Maryland society, although both had been active as late as 1797.

And incredible as it seems, in view of the punishment meted out to the ringleaders in the Gabriel affair, there was another attempted slave revolt in Norfolk in 1802. A group of blacks conspired to rise on Easter Sunday and set fire to the town. A confession by one of the group, naming his fellow conspirators, led to their apprehension. Throughout most of April and May the militia remained on duty in Norfolk around the clock. One of the leaders was publicly hanged, following his conviction in court. The other principal plotter was given "a reprieve as he stood trembling under the gallows, and was conducted back to prison."[3]

As a result of these alarming events, the Southern abolition societies had all faded away by 1803, and only those in the North remained. Further expansion of schools set up for Negro children in various Virginia cities was discouraged.[4]

The problem of the free Negro gave increasing concern. Virginia's manumission act of 1782 had led to the emancipation of some 10,000 slaves within the following decade. Judge St. George Tucker's *Dissertation on Slavery* (1796) presented to the General Assembly a detailed and highly conservative plan for gradual emancipation over a long period. Despite Tucker's prominence and prestige, despite the fact that he was a man of immense learning, possessing a variety of talents almost rivaling those of Thomas Jefferson, his plan was not even discussed by the legislature.[5]

No free Negroes were involved in the Gabriel plot of 1800, but that attempted insurrection greatly increased the opposition to further manumissions. In 1806 the Assembly passed a law that any Virginia slave who was freed had to leave the state within twelve months. Neighboring states promptly passed laws forbidding free blacks to enter from Virginia. In fact, in the North free Negroes were nowhere welcomed and they were often hated.[6]

The Virginia statute of 1806 was later modified to permit local courts to give manumitted slaves special permission to continue to live in the Old Dominion, if they had performed some act of "extraordinary merit," or if they were persons of "good character, sober, peaceable, orderly and industrious." This loophole was the means by which many free Negroes were allowed to remain in the state, and they often made useful contributions. In the tobacco factories and the other industries which throve in later decades, free blacks were employed in large numbers. Furthermore, despite the many legal disabilities from which they suffered, and the suspicion and denunciation which were often visited upon them by the whites, they were permitted throughout the antebellum era to acquire, own and sell property. In fact, some of them owned slaves, and one owned no fewer than seventy-one. While there was much suspicion of the free Negroes, William B. Giles, who was notably independent in his views, defended them during his gubernatorial term (1827–30). The American Colonization Society was seeking to send such blacks to Africa, and Giles took the position that this class of citizens was by no means "so vicious, degraded and demoralized as represented by their prejudiced friends and voluntary benefactors." By the 1850s, the Northerner, Frederick Law Olmsted, recorded in his oft-quoted account of his journeys through the South, that at the current rate of wages, any "free colored man" might accumulate property faster in Virginia than any man in the North who depended solely on his labor.[7]

Competition for jobs between free blacks and non-slave-owning whites, especially in Tidewater and Piedmont Virginia, had caused interracial tensions for many years. Furthermore, the institution of slavery cast a stigma on labor which was almost as harmful to the poor white man as to the black. Work in the tobacco fields, for example, was considered to be the role of an "inferior race," and one which white men were often unwilling to assume. As for the owners of slaves, they considered manual labor degrading. Jefferson wrote that few of this class were ever seen to work with their hands. "For in a warm climate," as he put it, "no man will labor for himself who can make another labor for him." As for the "middling and lower classes" of Virginians, the Marquis de Chastellux, the French visitor to this country, declared that their "indolence and dissipation . . . is such as to give pain to every reflecting mind."

Black men, mostly slaves, built such roads and bridges as existed in the post-Revolutionary era and the early nineteenth century. On the very large plantations—which constituted an infinitesimal minority, since only a small fraction of the whites owned more than a few slaves, and the preponderant majority had no slaves at all—there were slaves with many skills. Such specialists as coopers, tanners, carpenters, shoemakers, blacksmiths and distillers were regularly found among the slaves on the great plantations.

Virginia's tobacco-plantation economy was suffering from a severe slump in the first four decades of the nineteenth century. This contrasted with the flourishing condition of "king cotton" in the lower South during nearly all of that period.

The upturn for the cotton growers had begun in the 1790s, with the introduction of a long-staple or sea-island grade of cotton. It was further stimulated by a series of inventions—the spinning jenny, the carding machine and Eli Whitney's "saw-gin." These devices and mechanisms made cotton production much more profitable. Added to the foregoing was President Jefferson's Louisiana Purchase in 1803, which provided a huge domain wherein cotton growing could be greatly expanded. Since this combination of circumstances brought a marked increase in cotton production, it also brought a demand for more slaves.

The slumping profitability of Virginia's tobacco plantations, along with those of Maryland and North Carolina, was due in the main to the manner in which tobacco exhausted the soil. Modern principles of crop rotation were largely unknown, and chemical fertilizers were non-existent. It was no longer possible for planters to move on to new lands, since practically all lands in the upper South had been pre-empted. Thus the plantation slave system in the tobacco states seemed, at least temporarily, to be undergoing a drastic decline. It was a situation which not only caused many planters to leave for the Deep South and southwest, where virgin lands for raising cotton could be had, but it also tended to make some of those who remained in the state more receptive to arguments for the gradual abolition of slavery.

On the other hand, Virginia now had a slave surplus, and these surplus slaves could be sold readily to the cotton planters. Good prices were paid for them, because of the demand. Thus the export of slaves from Virginia to the far South and the southwest compensated in large measure for the decline in the returns from raising tobacco. The fact that this profitable market existed tended to make some Virginia slaveowners less receptive to arguments for the abolition of slavery.

How well did Virginians treat their slaves? Albert Bushnell Hart of the Harvard faculty has written that "on good plantations there was indeed little suffering and much enjoyment." John Fiske, Ulrich B. Phillips and Francis Pendleton Gaines have expressed the view that the average master in Virginia and elsewhere was kind and considerate. Even persons who were cruel, selfish or sordid were not likely to maltreat severely a slave worth perhaps five hundred to fifteen hundred dollars. There were examples of maltreatment through whippings and other punishments, of course, but every slaveowner had a strong incentive to keep his chattels satisfied and in good health.

True, there is a school of thought, represented by Herbert S. Klein, that holds slavery in Virginia to have been unnecessarily harsh. Klein's comparative study of slavery in Virginia and in Cuba makes such points as that the Cuban legal codes "never forgot the legal personality of the Negro; the Virginian codes reduced the Negro to chattel slavery." Klein adds: "Without legal personality, the slave has no right to such things as personal security, property, marriage, or even parenthood. He may be granted these by a benevolent master, but he has no right to them, and this is crucial."

Klein also describes the disabilities under which the free Negro suffered in Virginia, and they were unquestionably considerable.

However, Cuba is not Virginia, and the Caribbean Island's slave system grew out of an entirely different cultural and religious environment and heritage. In salient respects the Cuban system was undoubtedly milder. One of the principal results is described by Klein as "heavy miscegenation," to the point where the majority of Cubans now classify themselves as "mulattoes," while many others are listed as "Negroes."

Miscegenation in the Old South, almost entirely between white men and black women, was an altogether deplorable feature of the slave system in Virginia and the other slave states. The visual evidence that it occurred is all around us today, but the percentage of racially mixed persons in Virginia and the rest of the South is only a fraction of that prevailing in Cuba.

As for the generally unfavorable appraisal of slavery in the Old Dominion given by Herbert Klein, we cite the contrary conclusion of Robert McColley, a native Kansan and University of California Ph.D., in his recent *Slavery and Jeffersonian Virginia*:

"Though chattel slavery was brutal, we must accept the testimony of honest men from all over the greater community of Western civilization that nowhere was it milder than in Virginia."[8]

NINETEEN

Thomas Jefferson and John Marshall

ENACTMENT by Congress in 1798 of the Alien and Sedition Laws during the administration of President John Adams who, like Washington, was a member of the Federalist party, was regarded by Jefferson, Madison and other opposition party leaders in Virginia as dangerous in the extreme. Members of this opposition party, then known as Republicans, were the forerunners of today's Democrats. At that time, they tended to be liberally oriented and, with certain exceptions, to emphasize States' rights, while the Federalists tended toward conservatism and to favor a stronger central government.

The Virginia leaders were stirred to action by the passage of the Alien and Sedition Laws. The former piece of legislation was aimed to a large extent against Europeans of radical leanings, especially those from France, where the French Revolution had just ended. It was estimated that 25,000 French refugees had come to this country, most of them strongly leftist Jacobins, with whom Jefferson and his Republicans were much more sympathetic than were Adams and his Federalists. The Alien Law, which expired in two years, gave President Adams the power to expel suspected foreigners. "Over a dozen shiploads of Frenchmen left the country in anticipation of trouble," but nobody was actually ordered out, except two Irish journalists.

The Sedition Law, designed to punish conspiracies against the government and libels against public officials, could have served a useful purpose, if it had been enforced with discretion. But the statute provided fines and imprisonment for anyone who spoke or wrote against the President or Congress "with the intent to defame" or to "bring them into contempt or disrepute." This phraseology was entirely too broad, and was an invitation to abuses by political partisans. When about two dozen men were arrested and ten convicted, including several Republican editors and a member of Congress, the wrath and indignation of the libertarian Thomas Jefferson knew no bounds. He and James Madison considered that both laws involved unconstitutional infringements on human rights.

The result was the Kentucky and Virginia Resolutions, which Jefferson and Madison drafted behind the scenes, in protest against the Alien and Sedition Laws. "The story of the drafting of these was a closely guarded secret for many years," writes Dumas Malone, by all odds Jefferson's foremost biographer, "and it cannot be fully told even now. Not until he had been several years in final retirement at Monticello was Jefferson's authorship of the Kentucky Resolutions made known. . . . Madison's authorship of the more moderate Virginia Resolutions came to public attention a little earlier."

If Jefferson, then Vice-President, had acknowledged his authorship of the Kentucky Resolutions, he might well have been charged with sedition and even impeached for treason. An atmosphere of hysteria prevailed at the time.

The Kentucky and Virginia resolutions were, in part, political documents designed to influence the upcoming presidential election, and in this they were highly successful. Jefferson was elected President in 1800, partly because of these resolutions, directing attention to the excesses of the Federalists.

The resolutions emphasized "States' rights." The Kentucky legislature declared in its pronouncement that whenever Congress palpably transcended its powers, as in the Sedition Law, a state had "an equal right to judge for itself, as well of infractions as of the mode and measure of redress." The Virginia legislature's resolutions introduced the concept of "interposing" the authority of the state between the wronged citizen and the government. This doctrine of "interposition" was to be revived a century and a half later by Virginia's racial segregationists, but to no avail.

It was in 1800 that the national capital was moved to Washington from Philadelphia, where it had been for the previous decade. George Washington, most of whose eight years as President had been spent in Philadelphia, after a brief sojourn in New York, preferred a site on the Potomac. Virginia and Maryland promised to make the necessary territory available, and Jefferson managed to get legislation through Congress fixing the site there.

A tract ten miles square, extending on both sides of the Potomac, was laid out, and called the District of Columbia. The cornerstone of the District's southern angle was laid in 1791 at Jones' Point on the Virginia side, at the extreme end of the northern lip of Great Hunting Creek. However, George Washington insisted that the public buildings be erected on the Maryland side of the river, lest he be accused of trying to enhance the value of nearby Mount Vernon. The portion of Fairfax County which was incorporated in the District of Columbia in 1789 was restored to the state of Virginia in 1847 and given the name of Alexandria County. Its name was changed in 1920 to Arlington County. The city of Alexandria, formerly known as Belhaven, was a part of the District during this interim, but was incorporated as a city under its present name in 1852.

President Adams, his Cabinet and members of Congress were highly unenthusiastic over their removal from comfortable Philadelphia to the raw, formless, mosquito-plagued capital on the Potomac, variously referred to as a "wilderness city," "capital of miserable huts" and "a mudhole almost equal to the great Serbonian bog." One result was that Gadsby's Tavern—on the Virginia side, and still standing in today's city of Alexandria—enjoyed a great boom. Termed "the best house of entertainment in America," Gadsby's was a haven for government officials while the swampy, malarial flats on the north side of the river were being cleaned up, and suitable structures were being erected for the federal establishment.

As John Adams's presidential term came to a close, he turned, in early 1801, to an already distinguished Virginian, John Marshall, and appointed him Chief Justice. Thomas Jefferson, who represented precisely the opposite school of political thought, was about to be inaugurated as Adams's successor, and Adams took pains to fill as many federal posts as possible before relinquishing the presidency to his Republican opponent. John Jay had declined reappointment as Chief Justice, so Adams urged Marshall, who was then Secretary of State, to accept the position. He agreed, and a new era in the history of the United States Supreme Court began. Marshall, who served as Chief Justice until his death in 1835, issued a long series of powerful decisions which helped to transform a handful of weak and quarreling states into a united nation.

A veteran of the Revolution who had fought in many battles and endured the horrors of Valley Forge, he had served with spectacular distinction some two decades later as one of three special envoys to France in the so-called "XYZ Affair." Then, as a Federalist congressman from Richmond, he had shown remarkable independence in casting the deciding ballot in favor of repeal of the obnoxious section of the Sedition Law, a favorite Federalist measure. He also voted to remove the teeth from the Disputed Elections Bill, under the original terms of which the Federalists could have stolen the approaching presidential election.

John Marshall was not only a legal genius, despite his almost nonexistent formal education in the law (six weeks at the College of William and Mary under George Wythe), but he was a delightfully congenial and convivial companion and host. His "lawyer dinners" in the Richmond home which he maintained throughout his entire term as Chief Justice, were famous. He loved the game of quoits and indulged his penchant for it frequently with Richmond friends.

He was notoriously, almost incredibly careless as to his dress, extremely absent-minded, as well as tall, loose-jointed and awkward. One visitor described his apparel as seemingly "gotten from some antiquated slopshop of second-hand raiment."

Marshall was a fast man with a quip, which can hardly have been suspected as he sat with immense dignity on the bench of the Supreme Court and handed down his epoch-making decisions. Challenged in a Philadelphia club to use the word "paradox" in verse, the tall, gangling jurist glanced through a door and saw several convivial Kentuckians. He came up almost at once with:

> In the Blue Grass region
> A 'paradox' was born,
> The corn was full of kernels
> And the 'colonels' full of corn.

The great Chief Justice also refused to take himself seriously. When a young attorney remarked to him that he had reached "the acme of judicial distinction," Marshall replied:

"Let me tell you what that means, young man. The acme of judicial distinction means the ability to look a lawyer straight in the eye for two hours and not hear a damned word he says."[1]

Marshall evidenced his judicial rectitude when he refused to have any part in the case of Martin vs. Hunter's Lessee, involving his brother's investments in Fairfax lands. The Supreme Court's opinion in favor of Martin, reversing the finding of the Virginia Court of Appeals, infuriated members of the latter tribunal. The Virginia court was dominated by Judge Spencer Roane, who, with the other Republican on the court, detested Marshall's Federalist views. The ruling of the Supreme Court, rendered in 1815, not only angered the Virginia court, but that body refused unanimously to obey the mandate of the nation's highest federal bench. Yet despite the United States Supreme Court's impotence in the face of this defiance, it did manage to get on the record a vital opinion fixing the pattern for the future relationship between our national and state courts.

Another Supreme Court case involving Virginia was that of Cohens vs. Virginia (1821). In this case, Marshall and his fellow justices held that Congress could lawfully pass an act permitting a citizen convicted in a state court to appeal to the United States Supreme Court, if he claimed that the state statute under which he was found guilty conflicted with the Federal Constitution or an act of Congress.

As Albert J. Beveridge says in his celebrated biography of Marshall:

"In conjunction with his [Marshall's] exposition in McCulloch vs. Maryland, it was the most powerful answer that could be given, and from the source of greatest authority, to that defiance of the National Government and to the threats of disunion then growing ever bolder and more vociferous."

The decisions of John Marshall were regarded as pernicious in the extreme by Thomas Jefferson, who occupied the presidency during Marshall's first eight years on the court. The two men were cousins, but they not only disagreed politically; they hated each other personally.

Jefferson believed deeply in the "rights of man," and he feared that the powerful central government which Marshall was helping to establish showed strong aristocratic if not monarchical tendencies. Jefferson was dedicated to the proposition that "all men are created equal," whereas Marshall shared the Hamiltonian view that "the people" were not to be trusted.

The two men were to clash head-on in connection with the trial of

Aaron Burr, at Richmond, in 1807. Prior to that time, Jefferson was busily engaged with various other affairs of state. Among these were such momentous matters as the Louisiana Purchase and the expedition of Lewis and Clark to the Pacific coast.

The Louisiana Purchase, termed "the greatest bargain in American history," added to the United States an enormous domain, extending from the Mississippi River to the Rocky Mountains, the exact boundaries of which were uncertain. But the twelve million dollars in cash paid Napoleon Bonaparte for this empire (plus a promise to assume three million dollars in claims which U.S. citizens had against France) was almost unbelievable. Jefferson had to "rise above principle" in putting through this deal, for as a strict constructionist Republican, who had always claimed that the federal government possessed no powers not expressly granted in the Constitution, he had to swallow hard. But he did so, and all future generations of Americans are in his debt.

Exploration of the Far West had long been a dream of Jefferson's, for he was anxious to discover a route to the Pacific and to learn of the western region's many natural wonders. He had directed two Virginians, Meriwether Lewis and William Clark, to embark upon an expedition to the West Coast before the question of buying Louisiana arose. The men were to ascend to the headwaters of the Missouri River and proceed from there. Consummation of the Louisiana Purchase occurred shortly after President Jefferson had arranged for this transcontinental trek, so that the two events complemented each other admirably.

Jefferson's insatiable curiosity concerning virtually every aspect of the world about him—so vividly exemplified in his *Notes on the State of Virginia*, written during the Revolution—could now be partially satisfied. Meriwether Lewis, a native of Albemarle County, the leader of the expedition, and William Clark, a native of Caroline and brother of George Rogers Clark, were admirably fitted to carry out the assignment. They set out from St. Louis in 1804 and returned there in 1806, having reached the Pacific near the site of today's Astoria, Oregon. Lewis and Clark brought back a great deal of valuable information, together with specimens of plants which delighted President Jefferson, and journals which are still consulted by students of the old West.

An apparent attempt by Aaron Burr to lop off that same huge region beyond the Alleghenies from the eastern United States and to estab-

lish a separate government there, with Burr at its head, was a sensational development of these years. Burr, a dark-eyed, dapper man of
the world, had killed Alexander Hamilton in a duel in 1804 and was
therefore a fugitive from justice. (Burr had almost been elected President over Jefferson in 1800, and when the close contest had to be
thrown into the House of Representatives for a decision, Jefferson had
won by a single vote on the thirty-sixth ballot.)

And now Burr was seemingly engaged in a desperate gamble termed
by Thomas P. Abernethy in his convincing study of the Burr trial "the
greatest threat of dismemberment which the American Union has ever
faced," except in the Civil War. Abernethy does point out that "disloyalty to the Union was not then looked on as heinous crime as it is
today," and he adds, "it was still widely acknowledged that states which
had voluntarily entered the compact could easily withdraw from it."
But Abernethy clearly regards Burr as guilty.

Burr was arrested, and his trial for treason in the Capitol at Richmond was the most famous case of its kind in American history. More
was involved than the guilt or innocence of Burr. The trial turned into
a bitter confrontation between President Jefferson and Chief Justice
Marshall. (The Chief Justice and other justices on the supreme bench
"rode the circuit" in that era as a part of their routine duties, which
explains Marshall's presiding over the Burr trial in Richmond.)

Neither Marshall nor Jefferson exhibited his best traits in this affair.
Jefferson was operating behind the scenes, in the hope of getting a
verdict of guilty. Marshall, for his part, was not wholly objective. He
chose as foreman of the grand jury John Randolph of Roanoke, a shrill
critic of Jefferson who sneered at the President as "St. Thomas of
Cantingbury," but who was also highly suspicious of Burr. Marshall
named Colonel Edward Carrington, his brother-in-law, as foreman of
the petit jury. The Chief Justice committed the further indiscretion of
dining, after the trial began, at the home of John Wickham, chief
counsel of the defense, with Burr as one of the guests.

Thousands of people poured into Richmond for the trial, including
youthful Washington Irving, one of numerous newspaper correspond-
ents. Andrew Jackson of Tennessee was there in his rough frontiersman's clothes. He defended Burr before street corner crowds and accused Jefferson of "political persecution."

The case was heard in the Hall of the House of Delegates at the
Capitol, a room inadequate to accommodate the crowds. These milled

around outside the door, where Houdon's statue of Washington looked down upon the scene. Fumes of tobacco and whiskey permeated the building. Tobacco juice was squirted copiously by spectators both inside and outside the improvised courtroom, not only on the floor but on the walls. Sandboxes were provided for the benefit of these gentry, but many were either poor marksmen or they made no effort to use the proffered receptacles.

Counsel for the defense were especially brilliant. Among them were not only John Wickham, the state's foremost attorney, but Edmund Randolph, former Secretary of State, U. S. Attorney General and governor, and Luther Martin of Maryland, whose legal talents were only exceeded by his consumption of alcohol. The prosecution was headed by an undistinguished U. S. District Attorney, George Hay, assisted by the able William Wirt, then on the threshold of his notable career, and Alexander McRae, Virginia's lieutenant governor.

The whole proceeding lasted for some four months, and near its close Justice Marshall produced a definition of treason which eliminated a substantial part of the prosecution's laboriously assembled evidence. District Attorney Hay was accordingly unable to put on the stand a whole array of witnesses. The case went abruptly to the jury, which took only twenty-five minutes to render its verdict:

"We of the jury say that Aaron Burr is not proved to be guilty under this indictment by any evidence submitted to us. We therefore find him not guilty."

President Jefferson was furious, and he sought to have Chief Justice Marshall impeached. Nothing came of it. The two men were to confront one another over the years as spokesmen for diametrically opposing political philosophies until Jefferson's death in 1826.

During the Burr trial, Jefferson had been having a running controversy with the British over their seizure on the high seas of members of the crews of American vessels who had deserted from British ships. The desertions may be explained, in part, by the fact that the pay for American seamen was much higher than that of their British counterparts.

Britain was in a death struggle with Napoleon and was unwilling to accept these desertions which were weakening her vitally important fleet.

Many Virginians, especially those in the Hampton Roads area, were outraged in June 1807, when the British frigate *Leopard* attacked the

American cruiser *Chesapeake* some ten miles off Cape Henry as the latter vessel was leaving for the Mediterranean. Commodore James Barron, commanding the *Chesapeake*, was unable to resist effectively, and when he made desperate efforts to do so, the British ship opened fire with her whole broadside. Three Americans were killed and eighteen wounded; the *Chesapeake* was riddled and had to lower her colors. The British came on board, carried off a British-born deserter, an American Negro, an Indian and a native white Marylander.

Great was the fury of the American people, especially those in Virginia. Volunteers from various Virginia cities stampeded to the colors, and the militia in the Hampton Roads area were called up. When one of the wounded sailors died, there was a mass turnout of Norfolkians, and thousands crowded Market Square for the arrival of the casket. A long procession marched behind it to the funeral in Christ Episcopal Church. Armed hostilities with Great Britain seemed imminent.

But Thomas Jefferson was opposed to going to war over this episode, although seizures and impressments of British deserters from American vessels on the high seas had been going on for quite a while, and they were to continue. He had felt for years that economic sanctions were an adequate substitute for armed conflict, and this was his chance to try out the theory.

He accordingly persuaded Congress to go along, and it passed the Embargo Act in a single day, late in 1807. All exports from America were prohibited, and various articles of British manufacture were refused entrance. American frigates were put in dry dock, and the defense of our coasts and harbors was entrusted to a fleet of small gunboats.

Norfolk's overseas trade, on which it depended so heavily, was brought to a sudden and complete halt, except for occasional smuggling. Jefferson's theory that American interests could be effectively defended with a fleet of minuscule gunboats was the subject of much ridicule. "From the dissection of a gnat to the construction of a man-of-war, our beloved chief is equally useful," sarcastically observed the Norfolk *Gazette and Ledger*. Tobacco, Virginia's major article of export, was hit hard, and the lack of a foreign market for this staple was grievous to the planters, who were in a period of depressed business anyway. Coal mines developed in the Midlothian area near Richmond, which had reached a production of 22,000 tons annually by 1798, were also damaged through the loss of overseas shipments.

Jefferson's embargo was a sad blunder, and this became increasingly apparent as the months passed. It had little or no effect in changing British policies, and it created a political backlash in the United States from New England to Georgia. In fact, there was serious talk in New England, whose ports were suffering severely, of a co-ordinated movement for nullification of the law. The result was that after the President had tried the futile policy for fourteen months, he and Congress agreed on its repeal. Jefferson signed the repealer three days before the end of his second presidential term. He retired thereupon to Monticello, and from public life. In his private capacity he was to remain active in many directions.

TWENTY

Madison, Monroe and a "Firebell in the Night"

JEFFERSON's eight years in the White House ended in 1809, after which his close friend and collaborator, James Madison, served for eight years. Then came James Monroe for eight more. The three were known as the "Virginia Dynasty." Thus, for nearly a quarter of a century, these Virginians were dominant in the national government. In fact, if Washington's eight years in the presidency be added, it will be seen that sons of the Old Dominion were in the White House for thirty-two of the first thirty-six years of this country's national existence.

Washington was, of course, a Federalist, whereas Jefferson, Madison and Monroe were all Republicans. Jefferson was the most influential of the foregoing triumvirate in determining policy; he was also the ablest politician, in the best sense of the term. Although he was now living permanently at Monticello, in accordance with his oft-expressed wish, there were no metes and bounds to the roving of his restless intellect.

Vilified and misrepresented as few men in our history have been, Jefferson managed to remain reasonably serene through it all, both in the White House and after his retirement. It took many years to get the truth to the American people, and some myths are still floating around. Jefferson was depicted in his time by enemies as a skulking and devious demagogue, who operated behind the scenes and was afraid to function in the light of day. He was also a "French Jacobin," which was roughly equivalent to calling a man a "Communist" a century and a half later; he was an "atheist" who would confiscate Bibles if he were elected President; he was the father of a brood of mulatto children.

Absurd as these allegations may seem, they were widely believed for generations. The canard concerning the mulatto children is still repeated, although the leading Jeffersonian scholars are confident that it is completely without foundation.

Jefferson did admit to an indiscretion in his youth, involving the wife of his friend John Walker. Walker, the son of Dr. Thomas Walker, was absent from home for several months, and Jefferson made improper advances to Mrs. Walker who rebuffed him. A generation later, Jefferson frankly declared: "When young and single I offered love to a handsome lady; I acknowledge its incorrectness."

Jefferson's Republican party dominated the national scene, beginning in 1800, and it also dominated the Virginia scene. The hegemony of the Jeffersonians in Virginia was maintained through a system of political control over local and state politics as complete as that maintained a century or more later by Thomas S. Martin and Harry F. Byrd.

The county courts were the central cogs in this early Virginia "machine," just as these same courts, and the officeholders around them, came to play a crucial role much later under Martin and Byrd. On these early courts sat justices of the peace—leaders in and usually respected members of their communities—who were appointed by the executive. Vacancies were filled on the recommendation of the remaining justices. The justices almost always made the decision as to who would run for the General Assembly. The Assembly, in turn, chose the governor who chose the justices! This circle within a circle was an admirable device for keeping perpetual political control. High above the justices, in regal dignity, sat the Virginia Court of Appeals, which exercised a sort of general supervision over the system of courts throughout the commonwealth. These judges were chosen for life by the General Assembly (whose members, as noted, were virtually elected by the justices of the peace).

For twenty-seven years, beginning in 1794, Judge Spencer Roane, one of the ablest jurists of his time, sat on the Court of Appeals. Only thirty-two years old when placed on this bench, he soon became its most influential member. He was, therefore, not only a powerful figure in legal circles but also in politics. Married to Patrick Henry's daughter and a long-time friend of Thomas Jefferson, he would have been named Chief Justice of the United States instead of John Marshall, if the post had been filled by Jefferson rather than by John Adams. Roane was a man of lofty principles, which appeared to harmonize well with his sincere conviction that the well-being of Virginia depended on the ascendancy of the Republican party—in Virginia and the nation.

He encouraged his cousin, a highly talented twenty-six-year-old book-store operator and former schoolteacher named Thomas Ritchie, to found the Richmond *Enquirer* in 1804. It was a zealous organ of President Jefferson's Republicans and became a power in the land. Roane, Ritchie and Dr. John Brockenbrough of the Virginia State Bank, all natives of Essex County, were a part of what was referred to as the "Essex Junto" or the "Richmond Junto," an agency of great political influence.

President James Madison was endeavoring to cope with the growing danger of war with Great Britain, following his induction into office in 1809, and the *Enquirer* was his ardent supporter.

One of the bitterest opponents of the oncoming conflict was John Randolph of Roanoke, who had gone to Congress in 1799, aged twenty-six, and whose transcendent abilities were such that he was appointed Republican floor leader two years later. At the time, he looked even younger than his years, but he was soon to become prematurely wrinkled. This, combined with a shrill voice that has been described as "flute-like," together with a body so tall and bony as to approach the grotesque, made Randolph a striking, even an astonishing figure in the House and Senate, in both of which he served. The bizarre effect was heightened when he appeared on the floor, as he often did, booted and spurred and brandishing a crop, with hounds yapping at his heels.

An attack of some disease when he was nineteen apparently rendered him impotent for life and accounted for his sopranolike voice. He suffered from almost constant ill health, and after 1818 was mentally deranged at times. Yet his genius was such, and his mastery of the biting phrase and the lightning riposte so great that he was feared by the other members of Congress as few of his colleagues were feared.

Almost brutally frank at times, and without a trace of hypocrisy, he proclaimed, "I am an aristocrat. I love liberty, I hate equality." Although highly conservative in his views in most respects, his will provided for the emancipation of his hundreds of slaves. An unbending advocate of States' rights, he declared that "asking one of the states to surrender part of her sovereignty is like asking a lady to surrender a part of her chastity."

"Clay's eye is on the presidency, and my eye is on him!", Randolph declared concerning the man who was one of several with whom he fought a duel. When a neighbor living near his Roanoke plantation in Charlotte County remarked, "Mr. Randolph, I passed by your front door this morning," Randolph replied waspishly, "I hope you will always continue to pass it, sir!" He described Thomas Ritchie, the editor of the *Enquirer*, as "a man of seven principles—five loaves and two fishes."

Another great figure of this era, likewise a stanch States' righter, was John Taylor of Caroline. He too opposed the War of 1812, for he saw it as tending to expand the powers of the central government.

A veteran of the Revolution, with extended service in the Virginia General Assembly and the United States Senate, of scrupulous integrity and dedicated to what he conceived to be the public weal, Taylor was an original thinker, and a knowledgeable critic of Alexander Hamilton's financial philosophy.

He wrote extensively and penetratingly, albeit in excruciatingly bad prose, in the fields of both economic theory and agricultural practice. V. L. Parrington terms him "the most original economist of his generation," but his stylistic shortcomings were such that John Randolph said concerning one of his pamphlets, "For heaven's sake, get some worthy person to do the second edition into English." Charles A. Beard asserts that Taylor's *An Inquiry Into the Principles and Policy of the Government of the United States* (1814) "deserves to rank among the two or three really historic contributions to political science which have been produced in the United States."

Taylor was a disciple of Jefferson in various matters, notably in his agreement with Jefferson's thesis that "those who labor in the earth are the chosen people of God." His concern for the well-being of agriculture as basic to all prosperity led to his widely read work, *Arator*. Taylor has been termed "the South's first agricultural reformer," and he advanced a novel theory as to Virginia's slave surplus. Instead of agreeing with the prevailing argument that Virginia's prosperity could best be promoted by the sale of surplus slaves to planters in the cotton states, he contended that the slave surplus was desirable and "the key to restoring [Virginia's] exhausted lands."[1]

Despite the opposition of such men as Taylor and Randolph, the United States was drawn into the War of 1812. Whether President James Madison, for all his erudition as a constitutionalist and political scientist, was a weak executive or a strong one, is debated by historians. The truth, as is so often the case, probably lies somewhere in between.

Britain's Orders in Council, which forbade U.S. ships to trade with France, with whom Britain was at war, or with any port under French influence, constituted a major grievance, but these were repealed almost immediately. Even more galling were the continued impressments of American seamen from American ships on the high seas for service on British warships.

The scene of hostilities for the War of 1812 was largely outside Virginia. However, the British attempt, in 1813, to take Craney Island, a key to the approach to Norfolk and Portsmouth by sea, was a noteworthy event of the conflict in the Hampton Roads area.

Governor James Barbour journeyed from Richmond to lend a hand in strengthening the defenses against the attack, which appeared imminent. Brigadier General Robert Barraud Taylor of Norfolk was in command of the 10,000 militia who were called out. The attack came in June, at which time the British assembled 2500 infantry and marines for the assault on Craney Island. It was defended by about 400 Virginia militiamen and 150 U.S. sailors, including naval gunners from the U.S.S. *Constellation*. When the British assault-force barges came within range, they were met with a hot fire which sank the admiral's barge and several others and killed and wounded many. Among the seriously wounded was Captain Hanchett, an illegitimate son of King George III. The British fell back and did not renew the attack.

Smarting under this defeat by a far smaller force, the British turned on the vulnerable town of Hampton. Again the Americans were overwhelmingly outnumbered, and this time they were unable to put up an effective defense. Hampton was taken, and the most monstrous atrocities were committed against the civilian population. Even Lieutenant Colonel Charles James Napier, the leader of the British invaders, wrote in his diary: "Every horror was perpetrated with impunity—rape, murder, pillage—*and not one man was punished.*" Some of this ruffianly behavior was chargeable to a group of French soldiers who had been captured by the British from Napoleon's forces in Spain and had been promised release after serving with the British fleet. But the

Hampton episode involved a series of barbarities which were wholly without excuse.[2]

When the British made their successful attack on Washington in 1814, and burned the White House and other public buildings, Virginia militiamen were again called into action. They responded in such numbers that Governor Barbour proclaimed it "the proudest day which Virginia has seen since the foundation of the commonwealth." So many turned out for the defense of Virginia against a possible British invasion that facilities were totally inadequate. As the governor expressed it, "with no shelter than the canopy of heaven, they stretched themselves on the naked earth, encountering every privation without a murmur." In another message, Barbour referred to the loss of slaves to the British "on the Eastern frontier," and he added: "The enemy leave no means unessayed to seduce them from their owners, under the delusive promise of liberating them, when it is now satisfactorily ascertained that they are consigned to the West Indies, sold to the planters there, and exposed to accumulated hardships."

Norfolk, as Virginia's principal seaport, suffered greatly during the War of 1812. The British blockade reduced the port's volume of both foreign and coastal trade. For a time, North Carolina's Albemarle Sound was left unguarded by the enemy, with the result that southeastern Virginia shipped its produce there, and on to foreign countries or to the southern ports of Wilmington and Charleston. But then all foreign trade was wiped out by the United States Government's embargo of December 1813. This even prohibited shipments of flour, wheat, meal and corn from Richmond and Petersburg to Norfolk, lest the British capture the cargoes as they crossed from the James to the Elizabeth River.

It was not until the Treaty of Ghent terminated hostilities on Christmas Eve, 1814, that Norfolk's ordeal came to an end. With peace declared, the harbor of Hampton Roads became once more the scene of bustling activity, and Norfolk's streets and wharves took on new life. Ships sailed again to all parts of the world and cargoes came pouring in. The upturn in maritime commerce was reflected in improved prosperity for other areas of Virginia, which thus recovered the markets for their products.

Norfolk had experienced a series of fires, beginning in 1799, the worst of which, on a snowy February night in 1804, destroyed not only hundreds of wooden houses in the district south of Main Street, from

Market Square to Town Point, but even spread into the harbor, where ships were set ablaze. A hundred more buildings were destroyed by fire in 1819, including many stores and homes, and in 1827 Christ Episcopal Church and sixty other structures were wiped out.

Coming in the wake of the burning of Norfolk in the Revolution, this was a shattering series of disasters. But it had its brighter side, for despite the great suffering and loss of life and property, the result was the rebuilding of much of the city and the substitution of brick for wood in most of the new construction. As the Norfolk *Herald* remarked in 1818, "Strangers were astonished at the improvement in our streets and buildings in the past eight or ten years." Mrs. Anne Royall, who visited Norfolk in 1828, wrote in *The Black Book*, her account of her journeys: "I expected to see an old, dirty-looking, clownish town. On the contrary . . . the houses are large and elegant, and many of them are surrounded by beautiful trees. . . . The streets are well paved, lighted, and the neatest kept in any town in the Union except Providence." By 1836 Norfolk had more miles of paved streets than any city in the South.[3]

Amos Bronson Alcott, the New England author and educator, wrote from Norfolk in 1820 that "hospitality is a distinguishing trait of the people, rich and poor." He added that "their polished manners and agreeable conversation ingratiate a traveller."

The uncivilized practice of dueling, which was becoming increasingly prevalent in Virginia and throughout the South—although it had been just about nonexistent during the colonial era—cost the lives of two noted men during these years. Colonel Armistead Thomson Mason, who had served as a colonel of Virginia volunteers in the Norfolk area during the War of 1812 and then had succeeded William B. Giles in the U. S. Senate, was killed in a duel with his brother-in-law, John Mason McCarty.

Commodore James Barron of Norfolk, who had been in command of the *Cheasapeake* in 1807 in her unfortunate encounter with the British *Leopard,* killed Commodore Stephen Decatur, hero of the Tripolitan naval actions in the Mediterranean, in a duel in 1820. Decatur made slurring references to Barron's conduct in the *Chesapeake-Leopard* engagement, and Barron accordingly summoned him to the so-called "field of honor." Decatur's and Mason's were among the many valuable lives that were needlessly sacrificed in the nineteenth century to the code duello.

Only "gentlemen" fought duels. If a gentleman considered that he had been insulted by one of the lesser breeds, the proper response was a caning or a horsewhipping. One argument advanced in favor of duels between gentlemen was that the alternative was assassination!

The period covered by James Monroe's presidential administration (1817–25) was known as the "Era of Good Feelings." This despite an economic depression and intramural brawling among Monroe's own Republicans which hardly spoke of widespread felicity within party ranks. Monroe did manage to create a sense of national unity, and his Republicans were so dominant almost everywhere that the Federalists were largely helpless.[4]

Monroe's personality and performance are more elusive than those of the other great Virginians who occupied the White House in the early years. Neither a philosopher nor an intellectual, and without conspicuous personal traits, such as Washington's statuesque grandeur or Jefferson's scintillating versatility, Monroe nevertheless had one of the most remarkable careers of them all.

It may well be that he held a greater variety of public offices than any man in American history. Consider the fact that he was twice a member of the Virginia General Assembly, twice governor of Virginia, served in both the U. S. Senate and House, was Secretary of State and Secretary of War, minister to three leading European powers as well as envoy extraordinary to France in connection with the Louisiana Purchase, President of the United States for two terms (elected to the second with only one dissenting vote) and delegate to the Virginia conventions of 1788 and 1829–30, over which latter gathering he presided.

This is an astonishing record. It can only mean that Monroe's solid virtues were widely appreciated and that he commanded respect from many directions. Best known for the Monroe Doctrine—which was as much the work of his Secretary of State, John Quincy Adams, as his own—he was also President at the time of the Missouri Compromise of 1820. Under this legislation, Missouri was admitted as a slaveholding state, but slavery was prohibited thereafter in all states situated north of Missouri's southern boundary.

The slavery issue was beginning to alarm thoughtful Virginians. The controversy over Missouri brought them to a realization that the same question would arise, perhaps in more virulent form, as other territories sought admission to the Union.

On the floor of the Virginia General Assembly the question was debated, and the potentially sundering effect of this issue upon the future of the Republic was recognized. Clearest of all in his prophetic vision was the venerable Sage of Monticello, who wrote from his mountaintop: "This momentous question, like a firebell in the night, awakened and filled me with terror. I considered it at once as the knell of the Union."

Slightly more than four decades later, Jefferson's dire prediction would become a grim reality.

TWENTY-ONE

East Is East
and West Is West

THE MOUNTING SECTIONAL CONTROVERSY in the United States had its rough parallel in the growing differences between the slaveholding and non-slaveholding areas of Virginia. Citizens of the northern states were concerned over the spread of chattel servitude into new territories, for they feared that they would be outvoted in Congress by the slaveholding states. Citizens of Virginia's Great Valley, where slaves were relatively scarce, and of the trans-Allegheny region, where they were even scarcer, felt that they were not only being outvoted, but that they were being discriminated against in other directions.

This sectional controversy between Virginia's Tidewater and Piedmont areas, on the one hand, and the upcountry, on the other, had its counterpart elsewhere, notably in South Carolina. Insofar as Virginia was concerned, it was to last until the Civil War, and it had much to do with the breakaway of West Virginia during that conflict.

Virginia's dwellers in the Valley and the transmontane regions called themselves "Cohees," a term thought to have come from "Quoth he," an expression of the early pietistic sects. The Westerners referred to the eastern Virginians as "Tuckahoes," a word which apparently came from the Indian name of a swamp root.

There was merit in the complaints of sectional discrimination advanced by the "Cohees" in the early 1800s. Prior to the Revolution they had been largely unconcerned over the fact that they were not represented in the House of Burgesses in proportion to their white population. But when the Revolution, in which they had played a most honorable part, was over, and thousands of additional settlers began pouring westward across the mountains, these citizens soon awakened to a realization that they were entitled not only to more representatives in the General Assembly, but also to a greater share in other governmental affairs at Richmond. In addition, they sought improved modes of communication, such as roads, canals, bridges and ferries.

During colonial times about the only internal improvements were those to facilitate the rolling of hogsheads of tobacco along the primitive roads to the wharves, sometimes as much as thirty or forty miles. Pre-revolutionary Virginia left the building of roads and bridges and the maintenance of ferries to the counties and to private individuals.

Once the hogsheads were got to the rivers, the planters were ingenious in their approach to the problem of water transportation. From five to ten hogsheads could be shipped downstream on a platform supported by two large canoes.

Then, in the early 1800s, the flat-bottomed bateau became the preferred vehicle. Although drawing only a couple of feet of water, it would support from five to eight hogsheads. Along the James one heard the rhythmic chant of the Negroes, as they steered these vessels to their destinations:

> Oh I'm gwine down to town!
> An' I'm gwine down to town!
> I'm gwine down to Richmond town
> To cyar my 'bacca down!

But much more was involved in the problem of Virginia communications than the transportation of tobacco, vital as that was to a substantial segment of the population.

The Westerners began clamoring for a constitutional convention to revise the organic law, and to give them not only better means of communication but also better political and economic opportunities. At a convention in Staunton, in 1816, called for the purpose of agitating these matters, it was pointed out that the white population beyond the Blue Ridge already exceeded that east of the range, whereas the latter area enjoyed a much greater representation in the legislature.

The Governor's Privy Council was regarded as an agency for the promotion of eastern interests, and its abolition was sought. The county courts, as cogs in a political mechanism dominated from Richmond, also were deemed to have excessive authority. The power of the sheriffs in some counties, and their tie-in with the court system, was another grievance.

Many Easterners also found these things objectionable, but correction required revision of the constitution; and that could only be accomplished by a constitutional convention. Once such a conclave was summoned, there was no telling where it would end, as every delegate would be free to raise any question he thought pertinent. The mood of the West was ominous.

Dependence of Westerners upon the East tended to be lessened in a limited way by the development of substantial salt production on the Kanawha River just after the turn of the century. A concern known as Kanawha Salines filled a genuine need and provided extensive employment. Salt was vital in that era for its preservative qualities, and of course was a flavoring ingredient.

Fully aware of the importance of developing better relations and communications with the western areas, the Virginia General Assembly appointed commissioners in 1812 "for the purpose of viewing certain rivers within this commonwealth." Chief Justice Marshall was named chairman, and as the court was in recess, he accepted. Still vigorous at fifty-six, and a lover of the rugged outdoor life, he spent months surveying the route from the James at Lynchburg all the way to the Ohio. The report, written by Marshall, provided valuable insights into the possibilities for developing a much greater traffic of both people and goods over the waterways linking the two great sections of the state.

In 1816, the year of the Staunton convention, protesting discrimination against the West, the General Assembly created a Fund for Internal Improvement and a Board of Public Works to administer it. The fund was altogether insufficient to meet the crying need for turnpikes, canals, bridges and other such facilities, but it was at least a gesture toward appeasing the mounting demand. The importance of providing better methods of transportation between the East and the West was an almost constant subject of discussion and debate in the Assembly during the succeeding decades.

The franchise was another matter of controversy. Virginia at that time was, with one exception, the only state among the twenty-four which limited the vote to freeholders, or owners of land. The West wanted the suffrage extended to all taxpayers, but this was rejected by the eastern legislators. Only about half of the Virginia freemen could vote.

There were widespread abuses. A freeholder could vote several times in a given election by purchasing freeholds at twenty-five dollars each in several nearby counties. By riding or driving furiously he could manage to cast a ballot in each of three or four political subdivisions. Residents of various eastern cities, in particular, were able in this manner to exercise greatly disproportionate influence in neighboring counties.

An indication of the overall discontent in the Valley and trans-Allegheny regions with existing conditions is seen in the recommendation of a committee of the General Assembly in 1818 that the seat of government be moved from Richmond to some point west of the Blue Ridge. Such a capital, the report said, would "present fewer incentives to *foreign ambition,* and less prospect to *internal insurrection,*" the latter being an obvious reference to the possibility of slave revolts. (In 1852, by the overwhelming vote of 88 to 35, the House would pass a resolution to move the capital from Richmond, but the plan would die in the Senate.)

The General Assembly was giving special attention in 1818 to the recommendation of the Board of Public Works that the James and Kanawha rivers be improved, and that a turnpike be built, connecting the two streams at their highest points of navigability. The House Committee on Roads and Internal Navigation declared unanimously:

"Should New River [which flows into the Kanawha] be rendered a safe and easy channel of communication between the Ohio and the commercial towns on the James River, the subject will assume a more important aspect . . . Not only will that part of our own state which lies on the Kanawha and the Ohio receive their supplies and send much of their produce to market through James River, but an immense tract of fertile country, a great part of the states of Kentucky and Ohio, will most probably give their commerce the same direction."

Two years later the Board of Public Works was recommending a similar link "between the Potomac and the Ohio . . . either by way of the Cheat or Youchiogany river." During these years there were also references to the possibility of linking the North Fork of the Holston with the New River, and of joining the Roanoke and the New.

By 1826, in another part of the state, an important project was going forward. Governor John Tyler reported that "the Dismal Swamp Canal, connected with the improvement of the Roanoke River, opens the prospect of extensive utility, presenting an improved navigation of upwards of 400 miles." He added that when the canal had been sufficiently enlarged to permit passage of vessels navigating Albemarle Sound, it would "open new prospects on Norfolk, our principal seaport, and offer immense advantages to the citizens of North Carolina and Virginia."

During these years the Board of Public Works was expending many thousands of dollars on improving the James and the Kanawha, and the turnpike designed to connect them.

In 1827 a brand-new element was injected into the situation with the incorporation of the Baltimore and Ohio Railroad. The arrival of the age of steam necessitated the making of a decision as to whether travel by rail would be preferable to that by water, and whether the link between the James and the Kanawha should be by rail rather than by turnpike. Another alternative, of course, was the building of a railway throughout the entire distance.

The B&O Railroad was granted permission to cross Virginia territory, but only after considerable objection, since some Easterners wanted to keep the railway out of the state. There was apprehension lest it divert business to Baltimore, Philadelphia and New York, and away from Tidewater Virginia.

A complicating factor arose with the realization that the plan to connect the Potomac and the Kanawha by means of a canal was federally sponsored. Strict constructionists among the eastern legislators accordingly began pushing the state and privately financed James River and Kanawha project, in which, temporarily, they had been losing interest.

The latter undertaking involved construction of a canal alongside the James from Richmond westward, since the river was not continuously navigable above the falls to anything but canoes, rowboats or bateaux. The canal would have to be paralleled by a towpath along which horses or mules would pull the canal boats.

Valuable guidance was supplied for this and other such projects in Virginia at the period by Colonel Claudius Crozet, a veteran of Napoleon's army who had been captured on the retreat from Moscow and had come to the United States following his release by the Russians. Crozet was named State Engineer for Virginia. He also was to be associated with the Virginia Military Institute from its founding in 1839, and to serve as president of its Board of Visitors.

In the mid-1820s the demands from the western part of the commonwealth were rising to such a crescendo that a constitutional convention became inevitable. It met at the Capitol in Richmond on October 5, 1829, and continued until early in the following year. Thomas Jefferson had always been scathing in his criticism of the Constitution of 1776, which now came up for revision. He felt that its provisions as to suffrage and representation were unfair to the West.

The convention of 1829–30 has been termed "the last gathering of the giants," for it included such venerable survivors of the Revolutionary era as Madison, Monroe and Marshall. Each would soon pass from the stage, but their fame was such that men rode hundreds of miles on horseback from neighboring states to see them in action, perhaps for the last time.

Madison, then seventy-eight, "dressed in black with an olive-colored overcoat, now and then raising his hand to his powdered hair," nominated Monroe as chairman of the convention, and the nomination was seconded by Marshall. Monroe accepted, but his health was such that he soon found it necessary to resign the chairmanship.

None of the three founding fathers took an active part in the discussions. Madison's intellect was still vigorous, but his voice was weaker than ever. His few efforts to make himself heard were so ineffectual that delegates left their seats and crowded 'round his desk, in order to catch his words.

Chief Justice Marshall, careless as always as to his appearance, was a sartorial anachronism, wearing the then outmoded silk stockings and knee breeches, with his hair in a queue. Ultraconservative, as was his wont, he was the most vigorous of the three, and his influence was used effectively on behalf of the retention of the much criticized, politically involved county court system.

But the Chief Justice and the two former Presidents were overshadowed by the man who, by common consent, commanded by far the most attention in that notable assemblage—John Randolph of Roanoke. Not quite so venerable as the three above-mentioned statesmen, he too was nearing the end, and he said publicly that death, for him, was not far away.

When it was reported that Randolph would reply to the first great speech of stentorian-voiced Chapman Johnson of Augusta, the "Ajax Telamon of the West," the galleries were so crowded that even breathing was difficult. However, the squire of Roanoke remained in his seat. The disgruntled throng accordingly melted away, "as much disappointed as though they had been to see a man hung, and had been cheated by the ill-timed clemency of the Governor."

But a few days later, when the galleries were practically empty, and Capitol Square was almost deserted, the tall, emaciated man with the eyes of well-nigh unearthly brilliance rose in his chair, and in his melodious treble, like the singing of a bird, intoned: "Mr. Speaker!"

"Never have I seen two words produce the same effect," wrote Hugh R. Pleasants, a reporter who witnessed the incident. "Where the crowd came from, or how they got the intelligence that Randolph had the floor, we could never learn. But it poured in like the waters of the ocean . . . persons running from all quarters."

Randolph made it clear that he was on the side of the conservatives, and he joined those who scorned the egalitarian creed popularized during the Revolution by the Jeffersonians. He declared that he did not consider Jefferson an authority on any subject except the best method of constructing a plow.

Another conservative who commanded a great deal of attention was the learned and eloquent Benjamin Watkins Leigh of Richmond. He also assailed the Jeffersonian dictum that all men are created equal, since, as he pointed out, slaves are men and are born daily into bondage. Leigh classed free-manhood suffrage with the other "plagues" which had arisen in the North—"the Hessian fly, the varioloid, etc." He had supervised the preparation of the Virginia Code of 1819 and was masterful in his analyses of the law and the constitution, always from the conservative viewpoint. Leigh was to be elected United States senator a few years later, and to serve with distinction.

One of his stanchest and most capable allies in representing the conservatives in the convention was handsome Abel P. Upshur of the Eastern Shore. Like Leigh, he was at the height of his career, and he provided powerful arguments against the contentions of the West. It was the era when speakers held the floor for hours, if not days. Upshur spoke for two days, but Chapman Johnson, to whom he replied, had shaken the rafters for nearly three.

Johnson and Philip Doddridge of Brooke County were the two major spokesmen for the transmontane region. Doddridge had grown up on the wild frontier, but had managed to obtain an excellent education. He was an accomplished speaker, and his arguments against the East were influential in creating sentiment for the subsequent separation of West Virginia from Virginia.

The vehemence of intersectional feeling was illustrated in the statement of Richard Morris of Hanover, whose genius, in the opinion of Hugh Pleasants, "was probably equal to that of any other man in the body, with the exception always of John Randolph." Morris declared that an emancipation act or a heavy tax on Negro slaves "would cause a sword to be unsheathed which would be red with blood before it found its scabbard." And Governor William B. Giles, ill and on crutches, and with the appearance of "a dying man," declared that "the forceful separation of Virginia must and will lead to the separation of the United States."

The outcome of the more than three months of deliberations and perfervid oratory was that the East granted somewhat greater representation in the General Assembly to the northern Piedmont and the Shenandoah Valley but rebuffed the trans-Allegheny region by actually giving it fewer representatives than it had already. There were concessions to the entire West in the extension of the suffrage to leaseholders and householders, in addition to the freeholders. The governor, who was granted somewhat more power, was still to be elected by the General Assembly, rather than the people. Membership in the Privy Council was reduced, but that agency and the governor would still appoint the county sheriffs and justices of the peace—one of the major abuses complained of, both East and West.

The constitution was ratified by a vote of the people of the commonwealth, but the trans-Allegheny region, roughly the present state of West Virginia, went almost solidly against it. The resentment there was intense, particularly over the fact that the area received a reduction in legislative strength. In fact, a writer in the Wheeling *Gazette* suggested that "the West call a convention of the West," and that commissioners be appointed "to treat with the Eastern nabobs for a division of the state—peaceably if we can, forcibly if we must." A person signing himself "Senex" declared in articles in a number of trans-Allegheny newspapers that nothing but dismemberment could bring relief. The Wheeling *Compiler* echoed that sentiment.

An important spokesman for the West in Richmond throughout this controversy was Thomas Ritchie of the *Enquirer*, a native of Tappahannock. His paper urged fairer treatment for the area beyond the mountains and expressed the hope that a Westerner would soon be elected governor.

Western indignation awakened the East to a realization that the Valley and trans-Allegheny regions would have to be given more attention. It was decided to push the James River and Kanawha Canal project. The turnpike movement, also designed to link the western regions with the East, was given new impetus. Incorporation of the Northwestern Turnpike Road in 1831, connecting Winchester and Parkersburg, was an early project. The state went in for large-scale borrowing for communications of various kinds, mainly railroads, but canals and turnpikes were included.

These policies were continued under the Whigs, who came to power with the election of Littleton Waller Tazewell of Norfolk as governor in 1834. The Whigs also gained a temporary majority in the General Assembly, ousting the Democrats (formerly known as Republicans, and now led by Andrew Jackson). The Whigs placed primary emphasis on the James River and Kanawha Canal as a means of appeasing the West. Internal improvements, along with protective tariffs and a national bank were important objectives espoused nationally by the Whigs, under the leadership of Henry Clay of Kentucky, a Virginia native.

The turnpike movement became especially active in the Shenandoah Valley at this time. A dozen or more of these roads were constructed between 1830 and 1840, under charters granted by the legislature. The turnpike from Harrisonburg over the mountains to Warm Springs was authorized in an Act of Assembly passed in 1830. The Valley Turnpike, most famous of all, from Winchester through Woodstock, New Market and Harrisonburg to Staunton, along the ancient Indian Trail and stage road, was incorporated in 1834. Stock was bought by private individuals or organizations, to the extent of three-fifths of the cost, and the State Board of Public Works supplied the remainder. From 1838 to 1841 the chief engineer for this turnpike was young Joseph Reid Anderson, later to become famous as the directing genius of Richmond's Tredegar Iron Works.

But turnpikes were not the answer to the grievances of the trans-Allegheny region. Neither, it now appears, was the plan to link the James River to the Kanawha by a turnpike or rail line. Transshipments from canal to turnpike or railway and thence to the Kanawha, or equally awkward arrangements for people or cargoes in the opposite direction, plus another transshipment via the James from Richmond to Norfolk, would have been extremely clumsy and complicated. Furthermore, the canal and the connecting line between it and the Kanawha were a long way from complete. In fact, they would never be completed. The canal finally got as far as Buchanan, in Botetourt County shortly before the Civil War. The Democrats, replacing the Whigs in 1845, after various political ups and downs, stipulated that Buchanan was to be the terminus, rather than Covington, the previously planned destination, and that a rail line would be built from that point to the Tennessee border and the Ohio River. This plan never came to fruition.

(For a delightful account of journeys from Richmond to Lynchburg on the "Jeems and Kanawha Canell," with its tobacco planters inhausting juleps on deck, spitting in the water, discussing politics and admiring the scenery; with its mules clop-clopping along the towpath, saluted by bullfrogs on the bank, and the *trahn-ahn-ahn* of the packet horn as the boat approached the locks, see George W. Bagby's "Canal Reminiscences.")

Jealousy between Richmond and Norfolk, as well as between the eastern and western sections of the state, was a factor in hamstringing the industrial and commercial development of the commonwealth. Richmond and the other towns at the fall lines of the rivers—Petersburg, Fredericksburg and Alexandria—wished to continue the emphasis on river and canal traffic. Their citizens, like many other Virginians, failed to realize that with the invention of the railway, a new era had dawned. The representatives of these urban areas, plus the surrounding territories which they were able to influence—by virtue of the freehold voting system already described, and otherwise—managed to delay railroad construction of the type that would have brought maximum development to the port of Norfolk. This last, of course, was a major reason for the above-mentioned shortsighted policy of the river ports, which feared Norfolk's competition.[1]

All plans for adequate railway communication in Virginia were blocked during the antebellum era, although some short lines were constructed here and there, including Colonel Crozet's notable tunnel through the Blue Ridge. But the Baltimore & Ohio was left in a strong position to build up the port of Baltimore, in competition with Norfolk. The B&O began drawing off the produce of the Shenandoah Valley, and it petitioned for authority to extend its line up the Valley and to the Ohio by way of the Kanawha. This alarmed Richmond, which was still wedded to the James River and Kanawha Canal concept. The General Assembly refused at its 1844–45 session to grant the B&O's request, despite petitions from the western part of the state.

Angry representatives from thirteen western counties accordingly met at Clarksburg. They made it clear that thereafter they would "vote against all appropriations for railways and canals in other parts of the state until our rights have been recognized."

This ultimatum so shook the East that in 1851 the state authorities permitted the incorporation of the Northwestern Virginia Railway, to connect Parkersburg with a point on the B&O near Clarksburg. The B&O soon got control of the new line, and work was completed in 1857. The result was that produce was funneled into the port of Baltimore from both the Shenandoah Valley and northwestern Virginia.

Not only had the General Assembly stood for many years athwart the path of adequate railways connecting lower Tidewater with the Ohio River, but the necessary locks at Richmond for the efficient operation of the James River and Kanawha Canal were not completed until 1854, about a decade and a half after they were supposed to have been ready. During that interval, cargoes had to be transferred across the gap by drays and wagons. Even when this laborious operation was completed, there was no assurance that Norfolk would get the western cargoes. They were often put on board ships which did not dock at Norfolk but continued on to Baltimore, Philadelphia or New York.

Many citizens of Norfolk were so irate over this entire situation that there were serious suggestions in the late 1840s and the 1850s that Norfolk secede and become a part of North Carolina. Both the Norfolk *Herald* and the Norfolk *Argus* made this suggestion in 1849, and the *Argus* repeated it in 1856.[2]

With lower Tidewater seething, the far western part of the state remained in near-revolt. During the 1840s there were repeated demands for another constitutional convention to correct the discriminatory provisions of the constitution adopted in 1829–30. One of the factors which aggravated this situation was the demonstration in the Census of 1840 that the white population of the trans-Allegheny region was approximately 271,000, or about 2000 more than the combined figure for the Valley, Piedmont and Tidewater.

This provided a glaring demonstration of the unfair representation accorded the West in the General Assembly. With more population than all the rest of the state, the transmontane region had only 10 of the 29 senators and 56 of the 134 delegates. The West demanded that this inequity be corrected, and it also demanded white manhood suffrage.

Another constitutional convention became inevitable. It met in October 1850, and did not adjourn until the following summer. The great personalities of a generation before were gone, and the level of debate at this "Reform Convention," as it was termed, was decidedly inferior—an indication of the drastic decline in the quality of Virginia's political leadership. The debates were also extremely bitter, at times. These acrimonious exchanges finally brought a compromise over legislative representation which met some of the West's major objections. The section beyond the Alleghenies was given 83 of the 152 seats in the House, or well over a majority, but only 20 of the 50 seats in the Senate. There was, however, the strong implication that the West would receive its rightful proportion in the Senate within about a decade and a half.

Every white male citizen was given the right to vote, another concession to the West, but a capitation tax was added, with half of the revenue allotted to schools. The governor, lieutenant governor, judges and numerous other state and local officials were to be popularly elected for the first time. Those who owned property in more than one city or county were limited to one vote.

All this must be considered a decided victory for the West. One result was that when the governor was chosen by popular vote in 1851, the choice was Joseph Johnson of Harrison County—a native of New York State—the first chief executive from the far side of the Alleghenies.

Western resentments were reduced, at least temporarily, by Johnson's election, but there were still substantial grievances. The discontent in Norfolk, as a result of policies which hampered that port's development, also remained alive until the Civil War. The outbreak of hostilities brought Norfolk and the surrounding area wholeheartedly back into firm and loyal co-operation with the Confederacy. By contrast, the reverberations of the guns at Fort Sumter were a tocsin sounding through Virginia's far western mountains and valleys, bringing tremors that caused those counties in a few years to break away and form a separate state.

TWENTY-TWO

The Sable Cloud

THE EVER-SMOLDERING CONTROVERSY over slavery threatened intermittently for decades to burst into flame. The late 1820s in Virginia had been relatively quiet, although Governor Giles spoke in 1829 in his message to the General Assembly of "a spirit of dissatisfaction and insubordination manifested by some of the slaves . . . from this place to the seaboard."

During the Convention of 1829–30 there had been no other special evidence that trouble was brewing. But in August 1831, Nat Turner's slave insurrection in Southampton County, in the southeastern corner of the state on the North Carolina line, was an alarm bell which roused the entire South.

William Lloyd Garrison's incendiary publication, *The Liberator*, had made its initial appearance in Boston, January 1, 1831, but there is nothing to indicate that this abolitionist journal had any part in bringing on the bloody butcheries that occurred some eight months later in Virginia. Garrison, ere long, would be blamed for the Turner uprising, and would infuriate the South with his tirades, but the attitude toward him in Boston itself in these years was such that he barely escaped being lynched in 1835 by a Boston mob, described as including "many gentlemen of property and influence."

Nat Turner, the slave who led the only uprising in Virginia history in which whites were massacred—there were occasional murders of individual masters and mistresses over the years—was a reasonably well-educated slave who had a kind and indulgent master. This made all the more terrifying to the people of Virginia and the South the fact that Turner, a part-time preacher who thought he saw visions, had gathered up a group of about sixty other slaves and embarked on an orgy of indiscriminate slaughter, beginning with his master and mistress and their baby. A hatchet and an ax were used in dispatching this gentle couple as they lay in their bed, after which the child's brains were bashed out against the brick fireplace. Guns, daggers, swords and razors also were employed in killing some fifty-five others, mostly women and children.

The rebellious blacks, some of whom were emboldened by stolen brandy, moved across the rural countryside toward the county seat, Jerusalem (now Courtland), slaughtering men, women and children as they slept, or as they begged for mercy or fought back. Terrified women were pursued from their homes and ruthlessly struck down; children were decapitated.

A staggering reverse for the insurrectionists came at the handsome home of Dr. Simon Blunt. Dr. Blunt gave his slaves the choice of fighting to protect the family or leaving. All remained loyal to him. The doctor, his young son and the overseer fired on the approaching blacks, and as the latter neared the house, the slaves of the Blunts leaped from hiding places armed with hoes and pitchforks and engaged the attackers. Turner and his followers fled, shaken by the realization that slaves had chosen to defend their master.

At the handsome Thomas home, the widow Thomas was warned of the approaching blacks. She and her children left hurriedly, in time to elude the oncoming Negroes. The latter did not loot the empty residence, but insisted that the slaves on the place follow them. One of the Thomas youngsters was George H. Thomas, aged fifteen, who would be known some three decades later as the "Rock of Chickamauga," one of the greatest of the Union generals in the Civil War.

The insurrection was over in forty-eight hours. Militia from neighboring Greensville County went into action, along with other militia units, soldiers from Fort Monroe and a contingent of U. S. Marines. The entire band of insurrectionists was soon killed or captured, with the exception of Turner. He was able to elude his pursuers for more than two months but was finally taken. He and fifty-two others were brought to trial. A score, including Nat, were hanged, and twelve were transported out of the state.[1]

Editor John Hampden Pleasants of the Richmond *Whig* had gone at once to the scene as a member of "Captain Harrison's troop of horse." In an unsigned article in the *Whig* for September 3, evidently

written by him, he expressed shock over the savageries and cruelties
perpetrated by both blacks and whites. Describing the scene at the
Vaughan house, where the family was massacred by the Negroes, he
declared that "a bloodier and more accursed tragedy was never acted,
even by the agency of the tomahawk and the scalping knife."

But Pleasants alluded "with pain" to the "slaughter of many blacks
without trial and under circumstances of great barbarity . . . generally
by decapitation or shooting." He went on to say that "to the great
honor of General Eppes [of Sussex County], he used every precaution
in his power, and we hope and believe with success, to put a stop
to the disgraceful procedures." Many of those slain had been innocent
of any wrongdoing.

A group of prisoners taken near Cross Keys were shot by troopers,
and their heads were stuck on poles. As for the body of Nat Turner,
it was "delivered to the doctors, who skinned it and made grease of
the flesh," according to William S. Drewry's The Southampton Insurrection. "His skeleton was for many years in the possession of
Dr. Massenburg. . . . Mr. R. S. Barham's father owned a money
purse made of his hide." Drewry rightly expresses disgust at such
"morbid and depraved procedures."

The General Assembly of 1831–32 which met a few months after
these gory events, spoke for a constituency which, quite understandably,
was in a state of alarm. For if so seemingly contented and well-treated
a slave as Nat Turner could lead such an uprising, what assurance
was there that similar rebellions would not occur at almost any time
and almost anywhere?

Governor John Floyd, who had previously favored gradual abolition,
was quick to react. In his message to the Assembly in December
1831, he urged revision of all laws intended "to preserve in due
subordination the slave population of our state." As a result, the
"black laws" were enacted, restricting the freedom of Negroes, whether
slaves or freemen, to assemble, to attend religious services, except
under certain conditions, and to carry firearms. More severe penalties
for violations were imposed. Even stricter laws were passed in other
southern states.

One major result of the Nat Turner insurrection was that it cleared
the air for the frankest discussion of the evils of the slave system
since the Revolutionary era. Plans for emancipation which before the
insurrection would have been considered fanatical and an echo of

northern abolitionism were brought into the open by legislators and the press. Both the Richmond *Whig* and the *Enquirer* advocated the immediate or eventual elimination of the slave system. Thomas Jefferson Randolph, grandson of Thomas Jefferson, came forth with a plan directing the General Assembly to consider a specific program for its gradual abolition, and the removal of the freed slaves from the United States. By contrast, a resolution offered by the conservatives forbade the legislature even to consider any plan for the abolition of slavery. The introduction of these contradictory proposals brought on a two-weeks' debate.

Tremendous interest was generated throughout the commonwealth and, indeed, the nation by this unprecedentedly forthright discussion in a southern state of the evils of slavery, and of serious suggestions for its elimination. The galleries of the Capitol were crowded.

There was unsparing denunciation of the institution by various prominent Assemblymen and equally vehement defense. The liberals denounced such cruelties as the break-up of families in the domestic slave trade, and argued that slave labor was more costly and less efficient than free labor. Thomas Marshall, son of the Chief Justice, excoriated the institution as "ruinous to the whites—retards improvement—roots out an industrious population—banishes the yeomanry of the country—deprives the spinner, the weaver, the smith, the shoemaker, the carpenter, of employment and support." Other opponents attributed the decline in the prosperity and prominence of Virginia in large measure to the slave system. They also raised the specter of further insurrections.

By contrast, slaveowners in the eastern and Southside counties referred scornfully to "that Fan-fanronade about the natural equality of man" and quoted the Scriptures in support of slavery. One of them actually asserted that slavery's "existence is indispensably requisite in order to preserve the forms of Republican Government."

The reformers agreed that abolition could only be achieved gradually, but this objective was abandoned, in the end, since the final consensus was that the time had not arrived to legislate on the subject. The majority view appeared to be that later on, when public opinion was ready, and better means for carrying out abolition had been formulated, the question should be broached in earnest.

The House did vote by the substantial margin of 79 to 41 in favor of a bill to deport and colonize free Negroes, with appropriations of $35,000 and $90,000, respectively, for the years 1832 and 1833, to pay for the deportations. Although the bill applied to free Negroes only, the Senate defeated it, 18 to 14.

The defeat of this particular bill should not be regarded as a shattering setback for the movement to abolish slavery, since it was so limited in scope as not to have been considered as "distinctly an anti-slavery measure." But its failure showed that the Senate, at least, was unwilling, at that time, to go even that far.

There was never a showdown during the session on the question of abolition, as such, although it has been stated by various writers that a proposal to free the Virginia slaves failed by a single vote. This is a myth.[2]

The fact remains, however, that the unwillingness of the session of 1831–32 to act affirmatively for gradual abolition was tragic in its consequences. For if Virginia had managed to produce an effective program for the ultimate achievement of this objective, the impact on the other slave states could have been far-reaching. As it was, the liberals became so disheartened that the conservatives took over. The South as a whole was to move thereafter toward enunciation of the absurd doctrine that slavery was a "positive good." Advocates of emancipation were scornfully termed "Negro-lovers."

The most important defense of slavery to appear at this time came from the pen of Thomas R. Dew, an extraordinarily able thirty-year-old professor at the College of William and Mary. It appeared not long after the legislature's adjournment, in the *American Quarterly Review* of Philadelphia, and was enlarged into a more comprehensive analysis entitled *An Essay on Slavery*. Dew's presentation of the pro-slavery position was seized upon and reiterated for decades by countless polemicists throughout the South.

The William and Mary professor went to the preposterous length of pronouncing slavery "perhaps the principal means for impelling forward the civilization of mankind." He scoffed at plans for its abolition, describing them as wholly impracticable, and as interfering with property rights. He marshalled Scriptural and other arguments in a manner that vastly impressed Southerners who were looking for excuses not to disturb the status quo.

For some years, as noted in Chapter Eighteen, Virginians had been making substantial profits from the sale of surplus slaves to the Deep South. The tobacco economy was languishing, whereas the cotton plantations were prospering and calling for more field hands. Virginia had them. Some Virginians, to their credit, "lived on the edge of bankruptcy rather than seek solvency through the sale of all or part of their 'people,'" according to Kenneth M. Stampp, the historian, while others, "more concerned about social prestige than about economic prosperity, feared to lose rank by marketing bondsmen." Some who sold their chattels were careful not to break up families, but others were less squeamish, and even bred slaves for the market.

Thomas Jefferson Randolph estimated during the debate at the session of 1831–32 that "the exportation [from Virginia] has averaged 8500 for the last twenty years," while Dew put the figure at 6000 annually for a more limited period. This bull market for Virginia's surplus slaves tended throughout the 1830s to offset the losses from Virginia's unprosperous tobacco culture and made it doubly difficult to revive the case for gradual emancipation.

A collateral result of the sale of thousands of Virginia bondsmen was that it lowered the slave population of the commonwealth, and thus tended to relieve the growing apprehension on the part of the planters that they would soon be hopelessly outnumbered by the blacks. But the specter of other and even bloodier Nat Turner insurrections haunted Virginia and the South for the remaining decades before the Civil War, especially since the abolitionists were actively seeking to foment such uprisings.

The appropriation of funds for the colonization of free Negroes, which was barely defeated in the Virginia Senate at the session of 1831–32, had been intended to further the objectives of the American Colonization Society, formed in Washington in 1816. An appropriation of $20,000 had been voted the society by the General Assembly in 1826, and private funds also were collected.

Virginians were more active in the society's affairs than citizens of any other state. U. S. Supreme Court Justice Bushrod Washington was the first president, and his colleague on the court, Chief Justice John Marshall, became president of the Richmond branch. Other Virginians who took leading roles included James Madison, James Monroe, John Randolph and the Reverend William Meade, later the celebrated Episcopal bishop.

At the opening meeting in 1816, presided over by Henry Clay, the Kentucky statesman made it plain that colonization was for free

Negroes, not slaves. He warned that the "delicate question" of emancipation should be avoided.

There were, nevertheless, vague hopes that the shipment of free Negroes to Africa would somehow lead to the ultimate elimination of the slave system. The notion persisted for decades that if enough slaves could be freed and colonized, the final result would be that all would go back to, or be forcibly deported to the land of their fathers, or elsewhere.

It was also contended that colonization was the best means of bringing Christianity to Africa and reducing the African slave trade by persuading the Africans to "drive off greedy slavers and welcome American traders seeking tropical products." One authority estimates that over a period of years, the organization saved an average of 20,000 Africans annually from being sold into slavery. The society also tended to promote national unity until about 1840, since all sections of the country were represented in its membership.

Liberia, on the western coast of Africa, was chosen as the place to which free Negroes should be sent. By 1830, about 1420 had been transported to that country.

The Nat Turner insurrection of 1831 revived interest in the colonization movement, even though the succeeding General Assembly refused, by a narrow margin, to make funds available for its promotion. There had been hopes that the federal government would appropriate money for the movement, but these proved vain. Another handicap was that the proslavery argument advanced by Thomas R. Dew, which appeared at about this time, was critical of colonization, and made it doubly difficult to persuade future Assemblies to give financial aid. In 1850 the General Assembly finally appropriated $30,000 a year for five years to support emigration. But the Civil War was approaching, and all these efforts were largely futile, since a grand total of fewer than 15,000 Negroes emigrated over the years, of whom the American Colonization Society was responsible for about 12,000.[3] Both Thomas Jefferson and Abraham Lincoln were advocates of colonization.

Virginia Negroes were prominent in the colonization movement. Lott Carey, who had taught himself to read and write and had been made supervisor in a tobacco factory, purchased his freedom and that of his family. He studied for the ministry, and was the spiritual leader of the first shipment of free blacks to Liberia in 1821. He was made Vice-Agent of the settlement. He died there suddenly seven years later.

Joseph Jenkins Roberts was also born a slave in Virginia. His emancipated parents had to leave the state, under the act of 1806 which forced free Negroes to leave within a year, and young Roberts went to Liberia in 1829. In 1841 he was made governor of the colony, and when Liberia became a Republic seven years later, he was chosen its first President. After the American Civil War, he was re-elected President, and is credited with averting a revolution at that time.

Meanwhile the controversy over slavery in Virginia continued. A new element in the politics of the state and nation was introduced with the rise of the Whig party. In Virginia, its sudden forward surge was closely bound up with the action of President Andrew Jackson in removing the deposits of federal funds from the Bank of the United States in 1833, an action which outraged many Virginians. The removal of the deposits was the chief bone of contention between the Democrats and Whigs of the state at that period. In fact, the very existence of the Bank of the United States had been a subject of heated debate off and on since Washington's administration.

Governor John Floyd was a Democrat, but he denounced "the disgusting prostitution of President Jackson" in removing the deposits, and Mrs. Floyd wrote her husband terming the President "a bloody, bawdy, treacherous, lecherous villain." As further evidence of the irrational feeling that existed, Lieutenant Governor Peter V. Daniel wrote a friend that "I am watched throughout the day; every door I enter, every person with whom I speak is a subject of jealous scrutiny . . . But d—— the contemptible slaves of the bank. I put them all at defiance."

The Virginia Whigs tended to belong to the middle and upper classes. They included many of the slaveowners and hence were strong in the Tidewater and Piedmont. Many were also supporters of Henry Clay's "American System" of high tariffs, so that there was Whig strength in manufacturing areas, including the region along the Great Kanawha, with its salt, iron and woolen industries. The sheep farmers of northwestern Virginia beyond the Alleghenies leaned toward Whiggery. By contrast, the Shenandoah Valley, with its so-called "Tenth Legion" of Democrats, and southwestern Virginia were both Jacksonian strongholds.

Littleton Waller Tazewell, as previously noted, became Virginia's first Whig governor in 1834. He was succeeded in office by two other Whigs, David Campbell and Thomas Walker Gilmer.

It was during the term of Governor Campbell that Whigs throughout the country began organizing to nominate William Henry Harrison
as their candidate for President. Harrison, who had been born in
Virginia at Berkeley plantation, had moved to the West and won fame
as an Indian fighter. His victory over the redskins at the Battle of
Tippecanoe in 1811 and his successful battle with them two years
later when Chief Tecumseh was killed, brought him national attention.
Although Henry Clay was far better qualified for the presidency,
Harrison won the nomination.

John Tyler, like Harrison a native of Charles City County, was
chosen as his running mate. Tyler, who had served as governor of
Virginia and was a traditional Democrat, was put on the ticket to
appeal to the States' righters of the South. Tyler had shown his
independence by resigning from the U. S. Senate rather than vote
to expunge a resolution censuring President Jackson. In that era,
the Virginia General Assembly frequently instructed the states' representatives in Congress as to how they should vote on a given issue.

The Whigs, in an orgy of demagoguery, presented Harrison as the
"log cabin and hard cider" candidate, under the slogan "Tippecanoe
and Tyler Too." The hero of Tippecanoe was a member of a great
Virginia family, the son of a signer of the Declaration of Independence,
and had not only been born on one of the colony's principal plantations, but was living at the time of his nomination at "North Bend,"
an extensive estate near the Ohio River—the name of which was
suddenly changed to "Log Cabin." In the campaign literature of the
Whigs he was metamorphosed into the humble candidate of the
plain people. Log cabins were erected at many politically strategic
points—seventeen of them in Virginia, "adorned with large numbers
of coon skins, gourds and cider barrels." For their Virginia meetings
the Whigs also "kept one live bear and three stuffed bear skins."
There was nothing properly describable as a platform on which Harrison
ran.

The Democrats, for their part, sought to depict Harrison as an
abolitionist, which was absurd, but no more so than the nonsense
which the Whigs disseminated concerning President Martin Van Buren,
who was seeking re-election. Van Buren was fantastically caricatured
as lolling in luxury in the White House, eating with gold spoons from
silver plate, riding about like an oriental potentate in a gilded coach

imported from Great Britain, and perfuming his whiskers with French *eau de cologne*.

Whatever may be said of this blatant appeal to the groundlings, it worked. Harrison and Tyler were elected by a large margin, although they lost Virginia by about fourteen hundred votes. But the Hero of Tippecanoe, then sixty-eight, contracted pneumonia and died only one month after entering the White House.

This brought Tyler into office. He was in the awkward position of being the first Vice-President to succeed to the presidency and of not belonging to the Whig party, which had elected him and Harrison. He also clashed early with Clay, who expected to be the dominant power in the Tyler administration.

But Tyler was a man of convictions. He proceeded to operate in accord with his own "strict constructionist" philosophy, and he proved an effective administrator, as well as a leader in obtaining the passage of desirable legislation. Among the events of his administration was the annexation of Texas, whose president was Virginia-born Sam Houston. Texas was brought into the Union because of fear on the part of the South that it would abolish slavery. However, the slavery issue was not paramount during Tyler's administration. His various achievements, which cannot be enumerated here, have been generally underrated.[4]

A tragedy of the Tyler administration was an explosion on board the U.S.S. *Princeton* which killed two Virginians in the Cabinet— Secretary of State Abel P. Upshur and Secretary of the Navy Thomas Walker Gilmer. Another victim was State Senator David Gardiner of New York. His attractive daughter Julia became President Tyler's second wife four months later.

Following the expiration of his term in the presidency, John Tyler retired to Sherwood Forest, Charles City County, reared a large family and lived the life of a country gentleman. On the eve of the Civil War, he sought earnestly to prevent the outbreak of hostilities, but when the die was cast, he voted for secession. A member of the Confederate Congress, he died during the conflict.

Zachary Taylor of Orange County was another Virginia-born President, but the slavery issue left him cold. Primarily a soldier, he was a mere infant when his family moved to Kentucky, which was a part of the Old Dominion for the next five years. Nearly all of his adult life was spent in the Army, and after participating in the

War of 1812 and the Seminole War, he made his great military reputation in the Mexican War. "Old Rough and Ready," as he was known, returned from the last-named conflict something of a hero, and although he had never voted in a presidential election, the Whigs nominated him for the presidency in 1848. He was elected over Democrat Lewis Cass of Michigan.

The slavery controversy was becoming increasingly bitter, and Henry Clay, John C. Calhoun and Daniel Webster were delivering memorable addresses on the subject in the twilight of their careers. The Compromise of 1850—involving agreements as to slavery in new territories and a Fugitive Slave Law—was in process of formulation, when President Taylor died. Almost overcome by the heat and a two-hour oration at a July 4 ceremony, incident to the building of the Washington Monument, he drank quantities of cold water and iced milk and ate cherries or cucumbers. Acute gastroenteritis followed, and five days later, thanks in part to the ministrations of a quack doctor, he was dead.

President Taylor had been in office only sixteen months. He was a slaveholder who did not defend slavery. Almost wholly lacking in political finesse, he was at the same time ruggedly honest. Taylor would not tolerate any talk of secession, and he informed southern fire-eaters that any such effort would be crushed. He even declared that, if necessary, he would crush it himself, at the head of the Army.

The battle between Whigs and Democrats in Virginia, with slavery as one of its major elements, was led for decades on the journalistic front by two great rival newspaper editors—Thomas Ritchie of the Richmond *Enquirer,* and John Hampden Pleasants, founder and editor of the Richmond *Whig.* At the time of the legislative session of 1831–32, the two editors were in substantial agreement as to the need for the gradual abolition of slavery, but they diverged thereafter on this issue, with Ritchie tending more and more to defend the institution. It was the era of personal journalism when editors were spokesmen for parties and wielded great influence, despite the small circulation of their papers.

When the reaction set in against the liberal views on human servitude expressed by many at the session of 1831–32, the General Assembly of 1835–36 passed what Clement Eaton has described in his valuable *Freedom of Thought in the Old South* as "the most intolerant law" that was ever placed on the Assembly's statute books.

It provided severe punishment for any member of an abolition society who entered the state to contend that "the owners of slaves have no property in the same, or advocate or advise the abolition of slavery." This extreme statute also declared that anyone circulating or printing a book, pamphlet or newspaper for the purpose of persuading slaves to rebel or denying the right of masters to property in their slaves was guilty of a felony. Postmasters were given inquisitorial powers over the mails.

Pleasants unlimbered his heavy editorial artillery against this legislative excrescence, saying that it violated some of the great constitutional safeguards of liberty of speech and the press. He went on to declare that the obnoxious law was "far worse than lynching."

The legislation was indeed extremely bad, but it was leniently enforced, for the most part, as was frequently the case with such laws in Virginia during the antebellum era. Two conspicuous examples may be cited. One involved the Reverend Jarvis C. Bacon in Grayson County, who maintained in 1849 that owners had no right of property in their slaves. He was given a small fine in the lower court which was remitted by the General Court. The other concerned Samuel Janney, a historian and schoolteacher in Loudoun County, who published a reply in 1859 to a statement by President William A. Smith of Randolph-Macon College, defending slavery as right in itself and as sanctioned by the Bible. Janney escaped with a mere cautionary word from the county magistrates, most of whom were slaveholders. He was a Quaker and a sincere abolitionist, albeit a well-mannered one, and he continued to criticize the slave system.

John Hampden Pleasants and Thomas Ritchie were the most notable editors of the nineteenth century in Virginia. Pleasants sought no public office during his twenty-two year editorship of the Whigs' party organ. Ritchie was more active politically during his more than forty years as editorial mentor to the Democrats, although he too never ran for elective office. He did serve for many years as the state's public printer.

Both men modified their views from time to time on various issues. Since "Father Ritchie," as he came to be known, was in the editorial chair for nearly twice as long as his rival, it was but natural that his editorial position underwent more alteration. Ritchie's shift from advocacy of slavery's abolition to a defense of the institution is a noteworthy example. Pleasants, however, remained a courageous advocate of gradual abolition, despite the drastic change in public opinion during the 1830s.

For years, Ritchie detested Henry Clay, and he is credited by some with having prevented Clay—and also John C. Calhoun—from attaining the presidency. Ritchie later became friendly with Clay. Although the *Enquirer's* editor grew reactionary in his defense of slavery, he was liberal in crusading for fairer representation for the state's western counties in the General Assembly, and the grant of the vote to non-freeholders (both of which reforms were also urged by Pleasants in the *Whig*).

Ritchie was a fervent advocate of better schools—even for women, a virtually unthinkable idea in that age—and he went so far as to hint that he might tolerate the idea of woman suffrage, which was still more unthinkable. Better farming was also one of his major concerns. His prominence was such and his influence in Democratic councils so great that a county in what is now West Virginia was named for him.

Ritchie retired as editor of the *Enquirer* in 1845, and moved to Washington, at the urging of President James K. Polk, to edit the newly established organ, the Washington *Union*. The *Enquirer* was turned over to his two sons. One of these, Thomas Ritchie, Jr., got into a heated altercation over slavery with the editor of the *Whig*, in which the young man called the forty-nine-year-old Pleasants a coward. Pleasants abhorred duelling and the code duello, but such was the sentiment of the time concerning the "code of honor" that he felt it necessary to summon Ritchie to the field. They met on the south bank of the James, near Manchester, and Pleasants was mortally wounded. He apparently made no real effort to wound Ritchie, and, in the words of Robert W. Hughes, a leading newspaperman of the era, "it was plain that he had practically immolated himself upon the altar of public opinion, and had given his own life, rather than take the life of another." An eloquent voice, which maintained to the last that slavery should be got rid of, had been silenced.

There were other such voices in Virginia at this period. Some attacked slavery on moral grounds, and others because they felt that it was woefully inefficient and in part responsible for the declining prosperity of Virginia, as well as for the state's loss of influence in the councils of the nation.

General John Hartwell Cocke of Bremo, Fluvanna County, was

anti-slavery on both grounds. He considered it "the great cause of all the great evils of our land." Cocke even welcomed the publication of *Uncle Tom's Cabin*, since he felt that it would hasten the end of human servitude.

In 1847 the Reverend Henry Ruffner, president of Washington College, offered a plan for gradual emancipation, commonly known as the "Ruffner Pamphlet," which caused a storm of controversy. He denounced "the consuming plague of slavery," argued that it was to blame for the drastic decline of Virginia's farming and manufacturing, and contended that "where slavery prevails, commerce and navigation cannot flourish." Ruffner was sneered at in eastern Virginia as an abolitionist—the most opprobrious epithet which could be applied to anyone.

John Minor Botts of Richmond, a center of controversy for decades, both before and after the Civil War, denounced human bondage in a speech at Powhatan Courthouse in 1850. He expressed pessimism as to the prospects for getting rid of it, but declared that any Southerner who came up with a feasible plan should be acclaimed as a public benefactor. Botts voted in Congress in 1856 to censure Rep. Preston Brooks of South Carolina for his ruffianly caning of the abolitionist Senator Charles Sumner of Massachusetts, while the latter was seated defenseless at his desk. But admiring officers and students of the University of Virginia presented Brooks with a gold-headed cane, and he was hailed as a hero throughout much of the South.

Other fearless critics of slavery in the 1840s and 1850s might be mentioned, including Robert E. Lee, who declared in 1856 that few would deny that slavery was "a moral and political evil in any country."

But there were many more during those years who defended the institution, including George Fitzhugh, most important of all, who will be treated at greater length in Chapter Twenty-four, and a number of leading clergymen. From the time when Cotton Mather, the eminent New England divine, wrote in his diary in 1706 that he considered the gift of a slave to him a singular blessing and a "mighty smile of heaven upon his family," there were clergymen who defended human bondage.

Typical of this group in Virginia during the mid-nineteenth century was the prominent Presbyterian, the Reverend Robert L. Dabney of the Union Theological Seminary faculty. "Domestic servitude," he wrote, "as we define it and defend it, is but civil government in one of its forms. All government is restraint; and this is but one form of restraint." He also defended slavery on religious grounds.

The Presbyterian Church split in the late 1830s into Old School and New School Presbyterians, with differences over both slavery and theological matters contributing to the rupture.

In 1844, bitter controversies broke out at the Methodist general conference, mainly because of sharp divergencies on the slavery question. Ministers whose views were not acceptable in certain parts of Virginia were forced to leave the state, church property was seized, mutilated and destroyed, and church entrances were, in some cases, guarded with shotguns. There were suits in the courts. A grand jury in Accomack County found the *Christian Advocate and Journal* of Baltimore to be an "incendiary sheet tending to excite slaves to insurrection," and moved to prohibit it from circulating in the area. A grand jury in Parkersburg, now West Virginia, made similar findings and took similar steps against the *Western Christian Advocate* of Cincinnati.

There was also an uproar among the Baptists over the slave question, and in 1845, the year in which the Methodists split asunder, the Baptists also broke into northern and southern segments. The Episcopalians managed to carry on their discussions of slavery more or less *sotto voce*, and no break occurred. Bishop William Meade was one of the few Episcopal clergymen who spoke out strongly on the issue. He attacked the institution in the *Southern Churchman* in 1856, although declaring that slavery is sanctioned in the Bible. The biblical argument was the one most used by southern ministers in their defense of the "peculiar institution." A great majority of leading southern clergymen of all denominations took the proslavery position in the 1840s and 1850s.[5]

Virginia laymen were likewise overwhelmingly in favor of the system, and they offered extraordinary arguments. That of Albert Taylor Bledsoe of the University of Virginia faculty was widely echoed. Bledsoe proclaimed that slavery did not deprive slaves of a natural right, since "they have a natural right to that government, to that supervision and control which, on the whole, is best for them; and such is slavery."

Nathaniel Beverley Tucker of the William and Mary faculty, was equally adamant. He urged secession as early as 1820. Tucker was a half brother of John Randolph and a novelist (*George Balcombe* and *The Partisan Leader*), as well as a teacher. He was greatly impressed with the proslavery views of Thomas Carlyle, as were many other Southerners. Tucker attended a convention in Nashville in 1850 to discuss the extension of slavery and related matters. He addressed the gathering in advocacy of disunion and the formation of a Southern Confederacy.

The free Negro was a subject of debate at this period. He was often denounced as worthless, trifling and criminal, and the crime rate among free blacks was indeed high. One explanation would seem to be that they were about 80 per cent illiterate, for it was illegal to teach them to read and write. The consensus among white Virginians was that the free Negroes rather than the slaves represented the principal threat to Virginia's well-being.

Yet John H. Russell declares in his book, *The Free Negro in Virginia*, that the average free black was "meek and submissive, and not inclined to rebellion." "Furthermore," he writes, "there are numerous witnesses of the forestalling of insurrections and the preventing of plots of slaves through the agency of free Negroes." He cites the thwarting by free blacks of a conspiracy by slaves in 1810 to set the town of Petersburg on fire, and a plot for insurrection in Goochland County in 1822. Not a single free Negro was found to be involved in the widely ramified plot organized by the slave Gabriel, and the four free Negroes implicated in the Nat Turner insurrection were not among the leaders.

Over against the denunciation of the free blacks we find such laudatory references to individual freemen as "a man of integrity and honesty," "honest and prosperous man," and "gentility, trustworthiness and skill." The Richmond *Whig* in 1845 termed the low-grade white a "far greater pest" than the free black. When Governor William ("Extra Billy") Smith repeatedly urged that all free blacks be expelled from the state, the *Whig* declared shortly after he went out of office that many free Negroes "in all relations of life" are "as respectful and good citizens as . . . the ex-governor . . . himself."

Unquestionably there was a substantial element of free Negroes who were both unwilling to work and criminally inclined. But numerous others were useful members of society, self-supporting and industrious. Luther P Jackson, the historian, writes that during the 1850s when Virginia, along with the rest of the nation, experienced a definite upturn in both industry and agriculture, Virginia's 54,000 free Negroes "could always find work, regardless of discriminatory statutes and white competition."

Slaves, too, were hired by industrial plants. This was especially true in Richmond where, on the eve of the Civil War, each of fifty-four corporations, mainly in the tobacco and iron industries, owned at least ten slaves. The Tredegar Iron Works pioneered in testing the adaptability of slaves to heavy industry. Joseph R. Anderson, the innovative head of the company, preferred to own the slaves in his plant, although he also hired them from various owners, as did other factories. He "stood ready to promote the advancement of any Negro slave who showed ambition," Luther Jackson declares. The Tredegar, unlike most Richmond industries, provided housing for its slaves. It also had a hospital for them, as did the Midlothian Mining Company.

Sexual intermingling between white men and black women on Virginia plantations was far too prevalent. Planters who were married family men, prominent in their communities and zealous churchmen, nevertheless had sexual relations with their slaves. Whether these women were willing or not made little difference; they had no choice. Then, too, the marriage bond between slave men and women was often a tenuous one and had no legal standing. The breakup of slave families through sale on the auction block also made for a lack of stability and morality. The 1860 census showed that there were 518,000 Negroes of "mixed blood" in the United States, or one-seventeenth of the country's black inhabitants.

A harrowing aspect of the antebellum scene in Richmond, Alexandria, Norfolk, Petersburg, Lynchburg, Williamsburg, Fredericksburg and other centers of population was the slave market. Here slaves were bought and sold, with grief-stricken parents separated from their children or each other. On other occasions, blacks who were being put on the block to be sold to the highest bidder seemed unconcerned. While many Virginians were loath to deal in human flesh, the system had become so deep-rooted and there had been so much rationalization by clergymen and other opinionmakers concerning slavery's supposed virtues that it required a special brand of independence, toughmindedness and courage to buck the tide.

The dependence of the larger plantations upon overseers introduced an element which has its deplorable aspects, although there are those who contend that the picture of the "brutal, unscrupulous, illiterate" overseer has been considerably exaggerated. The whipping of slaves by overseers for breaking rules of various kinds was a notorious aspect of the system. William K. Scarborough's recent study of the overseer indicates that a large number of transient overseers in the Lower South "generally inexperienced and incompetent," seem to have provided the excessively stereotyped image for the entire group. Scarborough concludes that hardly any of them were illiterate.[6] Kindly masters kept a sharp eye on their overseers.

The Reverend Nehemiah Adams, a New England abolitionist, came to the South in the mid-1850s fully prepared to find all the horrors that he had read and heard about. But the actuality was something quite different. He wrote:

"I feel like one who has visited a friend who is sick and reported to be destitute and extremely miserable, but has found him comfortable and happy. . . . We may wonder that he should be; we may prove on paper that he cannot be; but if the colored people of Savannah, Columbia and Richmond are not, as a whole, a happy people, I have never seen any." Adams did denounce the selling of slaves, whippings, and so on, as well he might, but what he observed in Richmond, for example, was precisely contrary to his expectations.

During this period, northern abolitionists continued their violent attacks on the domestic slave trade, but some of their fellow citizens in the North disagreed with them. In fact, the even worse African slave trade, illegal since 1808, was nonetheless continued, and slaves were smuggled in "by venturesome runners—many of whom were respectable New England church members," according to V. L. Parrington.

Antipathy toward the Negro in many areas beyond the Potomac and the Ohio was so intense that as early as 1831 the French scholar, De Tocqueville, observed that "the prejudice of race appears to be stronger in the states which have abolished slavery than in those where it exists." Negroes in the North were "Jim-Crowed" on all modes of transportation, or excluded from them entirely, compelled to occupy segregated areas in churches, theaters, hotels and restaurants, and denied the vote almost everywhere. They were mobbed frequently—five times in Philadelphia, for instance, between 1832 and 1849.[7]

Slaves who escaped from Virginia to "free territory" were presumably unaware of the almost universal disabilities and discrimination from which blacks suffered in those regions. The desire of slaves in Virginia and other states for freedom is obvious from such uprisings or attempted uprisings as those of Nat Turner and Gabriel. But the number who escaped to the North has apparently been greatly exaggerated. Furthermore, the importance of the much-publicized Underground Railroad as a means of aiding bondsmen to flee likewise has been magnified far beyond its rightful dimensions. Reviewing Larry Gara's *The Liberty Line: The Legend of the Underground Railroad*, C. Vann Woodward wrote in the *American Scholar*:

"By the time he [the fleeing slave] reached the helping hands of the Underground Railroad conductors—if he ever did in fact—he had already completed the most perilous part of the journey, the Southern part . . . Under analysis the 'flood' of fugitives diminishes to a trickle."

The U. S. Census Bureau estimated in 1860 that only 1000 of the 3,000,000 slaves held in 1850 were fugitives.

Edward Channing concluded, after examining original sources, that "there was much less organized system than has generally been supposed." Most of the escapes were made from Virginia and the other border states, but these escapes apparently were by no means numerous.

The Fugitive Slave Law of 1850, which was designed to recover and bring back slaves who had fled, was defied and violated in various parts of the North. Its practical effect was almost nil, Larry Gara writes. He adds that "there were probably not more than a dozen cases prosecuted under the act during its 14-year existence, although in some of those cases there were a number of defendants." A Virginia slaveowner reported in 1859 that it cost him more than six hundred dollars to recover a fugitive slave from Ohio. Another Virginian lost his life to a mob in Pennsylvania, attempting to return several slaves to his plantation.

In the cities and on the plantations there were some cruel, even sadistic masters. Such a master was an individual named Souther of Hanover County, who was arrested in 1850 for murdering one of his slaves. Souther not only flogged the man, and forced other slaves to join in the flogging, but he added to the agony with stamping, kicking and choking, plus torture by fire. For these incredible brutalities, Souther got five years in the penitentiary.

Virginia slaves were not always docile in the face of maltreatment; and obviously they were not all contented, even when treated well, as the cases of Nat Turner and various others prove. The Virginia State Library archives contain documents showing that between 1780 and 1864, 56 masters were murdered by slaves, plus eleven mistresses and seven overseers. There were 73 convictions for rape in Virginia during the 84-year period, and 32 for attempted rape. Ninety slaves were convicted of arson and 257 of burglary. A total of 109 were found guilty of assaults, attempts at murder "and the like" against whites.

Charles Dickens visited Virginia in 1842, and wrote on his return in scathing terms of the slave system. He noted "gloom and dejection" and an "air of ruin and decay wherever slavery sits brooding." But William Makepeace Thackeray visited the state in 1853, and his conclusions were otherwise. In a letter to a friend in England, he mentioned the impression of "happiness" given by the Negroes of Richmond; he spoke of the younger ones "trotting and grinning about the streets," while "the women are fat and in good case." But Thackeray went on: "Of course, we feel the cruelty of flogging and enslaving a Negro—of course they [the Virginians] feel here the cruelty of starving an English laborer, or driving an English child to a mine—Brother, Brother, we are kin."

Such, in some of its broader aspects, was slavery in Virginia. It was around this system of chattel servitude that the life of the commonwealth revolved during the antebellum era. It was, of course, nothing remotely resembling the hell of barbarism and savagery, of concubinage and lust depicted by William Lloyd Garrison and other frenetic northern critics, many of whom, including Garrison, had never bothered to come south, to let the facts interfere with their preconceived notions. Nor was the South under slavery, in the rhapsodical apostrophe of Thomas Nelson Page, "for all its faults . . . the purest, sweetest life ever lived," which "made men noble, gentle and brave, and women tender, pure and true."

Any civilization built on slavery was an impossible anomaly in a land dedicated to freedom and the rights of man. This was recognized by the founding fathers, who struggled to rid their country of the curse they knew slavery to be. They failed. Later, when the institution became woven into the warp and woof of the South's economy and.

social structure, its elimination was even more difficult. Like a sable cloud, it hung over Virginia and the nation, as periodic threats of disunion were heard, and intersectional animosities mounted. The Civil War was just beyond the horizon.

TWENTY-THREE

Education in the Antebellum Era

If Thomas Jefferson's plan for a system of popular education for the masses, as well as for the intellectual élite, had been put into effect, antebellum Virginia would have been second to none in this area of cultural advance. But after Jefferson's imaginative concept had been virtually nullified by the General Assembly in the late eighteenth century, its revival was never possible. Nor did the legislature, despite the repeated urgings of various governors and leading elements of the press, establish a statewide system of public schools before the Civil War. When a limited program was put into operation in the early years of the century, it was officially described as for the "education of the poor." With such a stigma upon it, many parents were quite naturally reluctant to enroll their children.

True, Virginia's overwhelmingly rural profile made the creation of an effective public school system much more complicated than was the case in more thickly populated states. Communication through the country districts of the Old Dominion over the few primitive roads was extremely difficult. There was, furthermore, the fact that many of the most influential planters educated their children in privately financed academies. These leading citizens often were lacking in enthusiasm for the establishment of public education for the less affluent, especially if it meant an increase in taxes. Also, there was reiterated testimony that many "poor whites" showed no desire for educational opportunities for their children.

It is important, however, to note the words of Prof. Paul Monroe of Columbia University Teachers' College, that in the northern states "few, if any, of the so-called free school systems of the antebellum period were in reality free." And he went on to say: "All were founded on a combination of appropriations from state and local funds with large contributions from the parents of the pupils in the form of rates for tuition."

Establishment by the Virginia General Assembly in 1810 of a Literary Fund "for the encouragement of learning"—a fund still in existence—was a promising beginning. The fund came from "certain escheats, confiscations and forfeitures." The legislature of the following year passed "An Act to Provide for the Education of the Poor," and stipulated that the sole purpose of the Literary Fund was to make available this type of schooling.

Yet, despite this limitation, there were developments within a few years that appeared to brighten greatly the prospects for a general system of public schools. Charles Fenton Mercer of Loudoun County offered a plan at the legislative session of 1815–16 which seemed destined to achieve this objective, and without any increase in taxes. Mercer's bill, which passed almost at once, provided that a $400,000 repayment to Virginia of a loan made to the federal government be credited to the Literary Fund, which had less than $50,000 at the time. Not only so, but repayments of other loans made to the national government, incident to the War of 1812, would also go into the fund, bringing its holdings to more than $1,000,000. This was sufficient to provide the basis for the establishment of a statewide system, open to all.

But at the following session of the General Assembly, the forces led by Mercer were the victims, ironically enough, of the drive generated by Thomas Jefferson for the establishment of the University of Virginia. Jefferson—whose spokesman in the General Assembly was Joseph C. Cabell—and Mercer were in entire accord as to the desirability of a statewide system of public education. But they differed radically as to how the system should be financed and implemented. Jefferson was opposed to using the Literary Fund for the schools. He preferred to force the localities to tax themselves for educational purposes by having the General Assembly establish ability to read as the prerequisite to citizenship.[1]

The forces led by Cabell and Mercer collided head-on in the legislature. Mercer, who spoke primarily for western Virginia, was outvoted by the Jeffersonian bloc which was intent on establishing the

(11) James Lafayette, a slave attached to General Lafayette in the American Revolution, performed extraordinary services as a spy. He was one of a number of Virginia slaves and free blacks who fought gallantly in the Revolution or did effective work as spies. James Lafayette, like a number of other blacks, was given his freedom and an annual pension for life by the Virginia General Assembly for his services. Lafayette greeted James warmly on the general's return to the U.S. in 1824. James Lafayette is shown late in life.

(12) John P. G. Muhlenberg, Lutheran pastor from the Shenandoah Valley, who became a leading general in the American Revolution.

(14) The Virginia Constitutional Convention of 1829–30, shown in a painting by George Catlin, was termed "the last meeting of the giants," since James Madison, James Monroe and John Marshall were all there. They were old men, and while each took part in the convention, the other younger members had the leading roles. John Randolph of Roanoke, who also had only a few years to live, attracted the most attention. Madison is shown addressing the chair, occupied by Monroe. Marshall is seated behind Madison, in the front row and slightly to Madison's left, and Randolph is the second figure on Monroe's left, middle row.

(13) *Left,* earliest known view of
the Capitol at Richmond (1802),
designed by Thomas Jefferson after the
Maison Carrée at Nîmes, France.
View shows how rugged the terrain in
Capitol Square was at that time.
The small structure on the right is a belfry.

(15) Silhouette of the brilliant and erratic John Randolph of Roanoke,
shows him on his stud farm.

University at Charlottesville, in accord with the long-cherished dream of the Master of Monticello. The planters of Tidewater and the Piedmont were, generally speaking, disenchanted with Jefferson's plan for local taxation to finance public schools and more favorably disposed toward his far-seeing program in the area of the higher learning. The university accordingly was chartered in 1819, and the creation of elementary and secondary schools open to all was postponed.

Establishment of the University of Virginia was, of course, a highly significant advance in the educational life of the commonwealth, and of the entire country, for that matter. Described by historian Herbert Baxter Adams of Massachusetts as "the noblest work of Jefferson's life," the institution opened its doors in 1825. Its invigorating influence upon education in the South exceeded that of any other university throughout the nineteenth century. Jefferson not only furnished his brainchild with buildings of internationally acclaimed architectural distinction, but he also designed a curriculum divided into separate "schools" and equipped with a novel "elective system."

In the words of Thomas P. Abernethy, "no early American save Mr. Jefferson would have dared to house a university in Roman temples, to employ a majority of foreign professors, to exclude the clergy and all their theologies." The venerable founder lived slightly more than one year after the university opened for its first session. He rejoiced to see his dream come true, but the last months of his life were saddened by the riotous behavior of the students. Their conduct grew even worse somewhat later, when Gessner Harrison, chairman of the faculty, was horsewhipped, and John A. G. Davis, his successor as chairman, was fatally wounded by a pistol-wielding undergraduate.

While Jefferson was indeed correct in describing himself as the "father" of the university, he carried his paternity to excessive lengths by prescribing textbooks for the law faculty which gave only one side of the continuing controversy over States' rights versus centralization. The "illimitable freedom of the human mind," which he had championed so often and so effectively, was thus denied to any professor who might be tempted to teach Hamiltonian heresies to the university's law students.

Meanwhile efforts to establish a comprehensive public school system were continuing. Governor David Campbell of Washington County, in his message to the Assembly in 1839, emphatically urged this as the state's "first, great and imperative duty." He asked for a $200,000 supplement to the Literary Fund, plus a general levy for the establishment and maintenance of eight thousand schools and the employment of four thousand teachers—certainly a modest complement of instructors. He also proposed a co-operative community plan whereby citizens would make a small contribution toward the education of their children, to avoid the "ignominy of charity."

The Census of 1840 shocked the state by revealing an exceptional degree of illiteracy. The total number of white illiterates was given as 58,732, or approximately one in thirteen, about evenly divided between the East and the West. This was much better than North Carolina's one in four, while Kentucky, Alabama and New Jersey also had higher rates than Virginia. But Connecticut, with the advantage of many towns and villages, had a grand total of only 526 illiterates and Massachusetts had 4500.

These revelations led to educational conventions in Clarksburg and Lexington in 1841 and culminated in larger gatherings at Richmond late in that year and in 1845. Both the Richmond *Whig* and the *Enquirer* were eloquent in their advocacy of strong measures to remedy the situation. Said the *Whig*: "That legislature would achieve immortal honor which would boldly mortgage the revenue of the state for fifty years to come, if nothing less would do it, for the education of the children of the commonwealth."

The western section of the state furnished the greater part of the energizing force toward a realization of these objectives, with Henry Ruffner, president of Washington College at Lexington, as the leading spokesman. He and others from that area resented the emphasis on the University of Virginia at the expense of the public schools. Ruffner produced a Plan for District Schools which was a pioneering effort and contained many of the features adopted in 1870, when his son, William H. Ruffner, became the first superintendent of the newly established public school system.

At the statewide convention held in Richmond in 1841, and attended by many eminent citizens of eastern Virginia, a memorial to the legislature was adopted, pleading for a comprehensive, adequately financed statewide system of public schools. The convention pointed out that "22,000 poor children and an indefinite number of thousands who are not poor, do not attend school at all." It added that those who do attend often do so "in miserable huts scarcely more comfortable than those you provide for your cattle."

Legislation to establish an adequate system was promptly introduced in the General Assembly, with U. S. Senator William Cabell Rives of Albemarle as the principal spokesman in its behalf. Rives had championed the cause of state-supported primary schools a quarter of a century before, and had been prominent as Senator, Representative and U. S. Minister to France. His address to the Virginia legislature was described as "strong, thrilling and eloquent." The bill he advocated passed the House with many votes to spare, only to be defeated by a narrow margin in the Senate.

Governor James McDowell of Rockbridge County returned to the attack the following year, with urgent recommendations for action. Superintendent Francis H. Smith of the Virginia Military Institute was one of his principal allies. Then in 1845, the second State Educational Convention met in Richmond and McDowell was the chairman. The eastern half of the commonwealth was again represented by many influential leaders. The principal Richmond newspapers and the *Southern Literary Messenger* gave strong support.

But the net result was a demonstration that it would be next to impossible to obtain the enactment by the General Assembly of a system of taxation for the benefit of the common schools, or to establish a school system with centralized direction. The General Assembly in 1846 passed legislation, but this did not provide for a State Superintendent or a State Board of Education. The raising of school revenues was left to the various political subdivisions.

Yet there was such momentum behind the drive in all parts of the Old Dominion that by 1855 there were systems of common schools in ten counties and four cities—more of them in Tidewater than in the trans-Allegheny region. Such systems were fully operative in the counties of Accomack, Elizabeth City, Norfolk, Princess Anne, Northampton and King George and in the cities of Norfolk, Portsmouth and Fredericksburg. In the trans-Allegheny region there were school systems in the counties of Washington, Jefferson, Ohio, Kanawha and the city of Wheeling. The most active of all was the Norfolk County and Portsmouth City system, it is stated by William A. Maddox in his valuable work, *The Free School Idea in Virginia Before the Civil War.* Maddox adds that "perhaps in no other state were the friends of education so energetic and persistent," but he concludes that, unfortunately, "in no state was more to be overcome."

A final effort to set up an adequate system of public education in the commonwealth was made by Governor Henry A. Wise of Accomack, who dominated statewide educational conventions held at Richmond in 1856 and 1857. Wise declared that "schools should not be a state charity, but the chief element of the freedom of the state." He urged upon the General Assembly an appropriation for schools of $250,000, but to no avail.

The Civil War lay just ahead, and the momentum generated in Virginia on behalf of a publicly financed system of education at all levels came to an abrupt halt with the opening of hostilities. The primary schools were suspended during the conflict, and revenues from the Literary Fund were used for military purposes, except for the usual appropriations from the fund to the University of Virginia and VMI.

The hundreds of small, privately supported academies throughout the state also became largely inoperative during the war. In the antebellum era they offered reasonably good, sometimes superlative, instruction, mostly of the classical variety, but often included some subjects of a more practical nature. Pupils were from the better circumstanced families. Total enrollment in 1860 was estimated at over 13,000, with 700 teachers.

Accommodations and equipment at these schools were usually far from lavish. If the classes were sometimes held in a substantial mansion, most classrooms were extremely primitive by modern standards. The boarding pupils usually lived in small structures of the plainest sort, often log cabins. Boys who traveled daily to the academies frequently did so on foot. William W. Minor recorded that when he was a student for six years at the Ridgeway School near Charlottesville, he "walked to school every day, arriving there by sunrise, winter and summer."

The classical emphasis was often notable at these schools, as at Winchester Academy in the Shenandoah Valley, where, in the early 1800s, students in the senior Latin class were always addressed in Latin by their teacher and required to answer in that language.

One of the most famous of the antebellum academies was Concord Academy, operated near Guiney's in Caroline County from 1835 to 1849 by Frederick W. Coleman. It consisted of a massive brick structure, surrounded by log cabins, the entire complex situated in a field, with no landscaping, shrubs or flowers, and accommodations, inside and out, of the most Spartan simplicity. "Old Fred," the headmaster, dominated the scene. His only rule and maxim was, "Be a man, be a gentleman." Instruction was completely informal and unscheduled, and Coleman and the other teachers would hold classes as the spirit moved. The duration of any given class was unknown in advance, with anything from thirty minutes to three hours as a possibility.

W. Gordon McCabe, whose own private school after the Civil War, at Petersburg and then at Richmond, was one of the most famous in the United States, has written concerning Concord Academy:

"Boys were knocked up at all hours of the night, sometimes long after midnight, and summoned to the recitation room by old Ben, the faithful Negro janitor, who equally feared and worshipped his master. A sharp rap at the door and the familiar cry, 'Sophocles, with your candles, young gentlemen,' would send the youngsters tumbling out of bed in the long winter nights, just as they had begun to dream of home or of certain bright eyes that had bewitched them in the 'long vacation.'"

The least pretentious of the prewar academies were called "old field," "hedge" or "forest" schools. Situated mainly in the western part of the state, they were designed to meet local needs, and the one-room schoolhouse was usually built of logs. Equipment inside was almost incredibly primitive, wooden benches without backs, no desks and a single rough table. Pupils were provided with slates and practically nothing else. Despite their crude facilities, these log schools, which have been compared to the "little red school houses" in other parts of America, served a useful purpose.

A few of the academies enrolled both boys and girls, but the sexes were usually taught in separate institutions. Courses offered the girls tended toward the "ornamental," and included music, drawing, painting, singing and French. Fairly often they studied such subjects as Latin and mathematics, but the antebellum "female" was not commonly supposed to be able to cope with these esoteric profundities. Chivalrous Virginians, and other southern males, preferred to worship at the feet of womanhood, and to limit the activities of the ladies to looking after their husbands' well-being and playing the harpsichord when they weren't occupied with raising babies by the

dozen. As Ellen Glasgow puts it in her novel, *Virginia,* the heroine's
education was "founded on the simple theory that the less a girl
knew about life, the better prepared she would be to contend with
it," and was designed "to paralyze her reasoning faculties so completely that all danger of 'mental unsettling' or even movement was
eliminated."

In fairness it should be said that women in Virginia before the
Civil War were often charged with heavy responsibilities in the
management of large households, which included not only their own
families but the well-being of the slaves. During the war, those
responsibilities were vastly increased, and they were discharged admirably.

Virginia's pioneer advocate of better education for women in the
antebellum era was James Mercer Garnett of Elmwood, Essex County.
In the 1820s, he opened a school for girls on his estate which became
famous throughout the Old Dominion, and even attracted pupils
from beyond the borders of the commonwealth. Garnett was an
evangelist for the cause, and in *Seven Lectures on Female Education*
he urged a wider recognition of the need for such schooling.

The huge slave population of Virginia, and other southern states,
had practically no organized educational facilities. Furthermore, Virginia's General Assembly passed a law in 1819 prohibiting the teaching
of Negroes, and many other states enacted similar legislation. After the
Nat Turner insurrection, it became more difficult to teach slaves,
as the white population reacted in terror to the threat of further
massacres. Nat Turner had been an educated slave, and it was feared
that such slaves would read the exhortations of the northern abolitionists for additional servile uprisings. These incendiary appeals for insurrections continued until the Civil War.

Yet the fact is that the laws forbidding the teaching of slaves
were frequently violated by masters and mistresses, and little was
done about it by the authorities. The affectionate relationship which
often existed between the planter's family and the slaves, especially
the house servants, led to this widespread ignoring of statutory pro-
hibitions. In fact, John Hope Franklin states that "Negro schools
are known to have existed in . . . Fredericksburg and Norfolk."

It may be assumed that these schools were of a strictly limited
character. For while slaves were permitted in a goodly number of
instances to acquire the rudiments of an education, there was no

disposition on the part of the vast majority of white Virginians or other Southerners to allow them to do more than that. In the words of Clement Eaton, "the paramount evil of Southern slavery was not that the slaves were mistreated physically, but that they were deprived of the opportunity to develop their capabilities fully." The same criticism can be applied to the prevailing attitude toward free Negroes, which was often more hostile than that shown toward the slaves. Many Virginians were unwilling to let free Negroes "learn to take care of themselves." It was widely felt that a maximum amount of control ought to be exercised over all blacks.

Negroes were shut out of higher education completely, of course. Yet insofar as the white population was concerned, Virginia's showing here was much better than it was in the development of the public schools. In the middle and late 1850s, for example, the state spent $50,000 more annually than Massachusetts on college level education. Not only so, but Virginia's college and university enrollment per white inhabitant in 1857 was one for every 666, as compared with one for every 944 in Massachusetts. In the preceding year, the University of Virginia had an enrollment of 558 as against Harvard's 361.[2]

But sectionalism in the Old Dominion was as regrettably evident in education as in other directions. At the University of Virginia during the 1840s, only about 10 per cent of the Virginia students came from west of the Blue Ridge; the young men from that section preferred to go to Ohio and Pennsylvania for their college training. The situation was even worse in 1857, when only 17 of 370 Virginians at the state university came from what is now West Virginia. The breakaway of that part of the commonwealth a few years later was being clearly foreshadowed.[3]

TWENTY-FOUR

Manners, Mores, Trail Blazers and Literati

As Virginia today becomes increasingly urbanized, it is difficult for us to envision the simple, rural, pastoral life of most Virginians in the years before the Civil War. There were no cities, in the modern sense. Richmond, in 1860, had under 38,000 inhabitants, while Norfolk, the next largest, had fewer than 15,000. There were such small towns as Petersburg, Alexandria, Lynchburg, Lexington, Abingdon and Fredericksburg, but Roanoke was still known as Big Lick and had only a few hundred people. Other towns and villages were scattered here and there, but the vast majority of the 1,600,000 white and black Virginians lived in the country, on farms, large or small. Nearly all roads were unspeakably bad, and homes were widely separated.

The large slaveowners, who might live miles away from their nearest neighbors, seemed "to drop their full-dress and constrained town-habits, and live a free, rustic, shooting-jacket life," a northern traveler reported. And William E. Dodd wrote that "it had long been a mark of distinction in a gentleman of Virginia to dress in shabby or last-year's suits." Many chewed tobacco.

Contrary to much popular misconception, most Virginia farms were of modest dimensions, with few, if any slaves. Only 114 Virginians owned as many as 100 slaves in 1860, and the white population of the state was over one million. Largest slaveowner of all was Samuel Hairston, who had about 1600 on various plantations, and "whose gardens at his homestead in Henry County were likened to Paradise."

Something over 11,000 Virginians owned as many as 50 slaves. Average holdings of both acreage and chattels in Virginia were smaller than in the states farther south, and the percentage of slaves in the total population of Virginia declined in the last three decades before the war from 48 per cent in 1830 to 30 per cent in 1860.

Almost everybody who was anybody in Virginia in the antebellum years was at least a "major," and the top echelon of male society was composed of "colonels." These honorary titles had no necessary relationship to military rank but were symbols of leadership, real or imagined. The British traveler, George W. Featherstonhaugh, relates an amusing anecdote, growing out of his visit to the slave states in the 1840s. It concerns the following conversation between a resident of Winchester and a ferryman:

" 'Major, I wish you would lead your horse a little forward,' which he did, observing to the man, 'I am not a major, and you need not call me one.' To this the ferryman replied, 'Well, kurnel, I ax your pardon, and I'll not call you so no more.' Being arrived at the landing place he led his horse out of the boat and said, 'My good friend, I am a very plain man, and I am neither a colonel nor a major. I have no title at all, and I don't like them. How much do I have to pay you?' The ferryman looked at him and said: 'You are the first white man I ever crossed this ferry that warnt jist nobody at all, and I swear I'll not charge you nothing.' "

Virginia hospitality, famous from colonial times, continued to be a salient characteristic. Henry Barnard of New England, who toured Virginia in 1833, and was typical of other travelers, wrote: "You would delight in this region, merely to observe the difference in manners and habits, and to experience the princely hospitality of the gentle-born families." He went on to describe the dinner he had enjoyed the evening before:

"Mrs. C. is at one end of the table with a large dish of rich soup, and Mr. C. at the other, with a saddle of fine mutton; scattered round the table you may choose for yourself—ham, beef, turkey, ducks, eggs with greens, potatoes, beets, hominy, etc., etc. On the second table cloth is the dessert, consisting of fine plum pudding, tarts, etc., etc. After this comes ice cream, West India preserves, peaches in brandy, etc. Off goes the second table cloth. Upon the mahogany table is set the figs, raisins and almonds, not to mention various wines."

Such a sumptuous table could not be set, of course, by a small farmer, but those farmers also were often hospitable, according to their means. "The cult of Southern hospitality" is described by the historian, Francis Butler Simkins, as "the part of the legend that was nearest reality." Edmund Ruffin, the agricultural pioneer, believed that the "hospitality of old Virginia," rather than agricultural backwardness, was the chief cause of economic adversity in the Tidewater region. He viewed with concern "the custom to give up to all our visitors not only the best entertainment but also the time, the employments and the habits of the host—and this not only to friends and visitors—but for every individual of the despicable race of loungers and spongers which our custom of universal hospitality has created."

Over against the prevailing testimony there is the experience related by New Englander Frederick Law Olmsted. He tells in circumstantial detail of how, in the mid-1850s, he journeyed from Lynchburg to Farmville on horseback and was taken ill. Over a period of several hours he stopped at the homes of five planters, explaining that he was ill and asking a lodging for the night, for which he was anxious to pay. He was turned away everywhere, usually with some such explanation as "We don't take in strangers." Finally, after dark, he was politely received at a country store and given a lodging. Olmsted's extended account of his journeyings through the South was praised by many at the time, both North and South, as objective and accurate. He was not anti-southern. During the Civil War he wrote to a friend: "Why do you want to be so savage with the Southerners? I think the slaveholders stand higher in the rank of civilization . . . today than English merchants or New York politicians."

Characteristic diversions of Virginians in the antebellum era were hunting, fishing and riding. Most Virginians were "outdoor types" who loved to go, gun in hand, in quest of quail, rabbit, deer or bear. They were often crack shots as well as expert horsemen. Fox hunting on horseback was a favorite sport.

Stephen Vincent Benét has given us a vivid vignette:

> The South . . . the honeysuckle . . . the hot sun . . .
> The taste of ripe persimmons and sugar-cane . . .
> The cloyed and waxy sweetness of magnolias . . .
> White cotton, blowing like a fallen cloud,
> And foxhounds belling the Virginia hills . . .[1]

The great majority of Virginians were more interested in active pursuits than in the contemplative life. The editor of the *Southern Literary Messenger* and R. R. Howison, the Virginia historian, agreed that they were not a reading people. Yet some of the larger mansions had substantial libraries. Conspicuous in those libraries were the works of Sir Walter Scott, whose novels, glamorizing the feudalism of the Middle Ages, appealed to many slaveholders. Few Virginians, or other Southerners, were tempted, however, to emulate Scott by writing for a livelihood. This was not the sort of thing in which a southern gentleman should engage. Politics and oratory were much to be preferred.

As for Virginia boys, George W. Bagby's description of their diversions before the war brings to life some of the homely pastimes and escapades of that long-gone day. Bagby wrote concerning the young antebellum Virginian:

"He must . . . make frog-houses over his feet in the wet sand, and find woodpecker nests. Meddle with the Negro men at hog-killing time, and be in everybody's way generally. Upset beehives, bring big wasp-nests into the house, and get stung over the eye by a yellow-jacket. Watch setting turkeys, and own a bench-leg fice and a speckled shoat. Wade in the branch, eat too many black-heart cherries, try to tame a catbird, call doodle bugs out of their holes . . .

"He must make partridge-traps out of tobacco-sticks; set gums for 'Mollie cotton-tails,' mash-traps and deadfalls for minks; fish for minnows with a pin-hook, and carry worms in a cymbling; tie Juney-bugs to strings and sing'em under people's noses; stump his toe and have it tied up in a rag; wear patched breeches, stick thorns in his heel . . ."

Reasonably well-to-do Virginians often went to the "springs" for all or part of the warmer months. Most of the "springs" were situated in the mountains, valleys and foothills of the Alleghenies on both sides of what is now the Virginia-West Virginia line.

Travel by stage coach and canal boat, and later by railroad, was a slow, prolonged and often arduous experience, and the problem of transporting an entire family hundreds of miles was enough to shake the most stouthearted. Yet the mountain resorts were well-populated during the season. Once the journey was negotiated it seemed almost necessary to stay a month or more, at the very least.

Since the first of the Virginia turnpikes to be completed crossed

Warm Springs Mountain, Warm Springs had an initial advantage over its rivals—the Hot, the White Sulphur, the Sweet, the Salt Sulphur and the Red Sulphur. Other springs would burgeon in the 1840s and 1850s, but in the 1830s these were the ones to which "society" flocked, not only from Virginia but from much of the Deep South.

In the early days, the expedition was undertaken largely for reasons of health—to bathe in the waters or to get away from the lowlands, where yellow-fever or cholera epidemics raged. Later the social aspects seemed paramount, and the benefits to be derived from bathing in mineral springs of various types were secondary. However, the Red Sulphur scored on the competition by advancing the impressive claim that its waters were the only ones known that could cure female sterility. Later the Red Sweet, not to be outdone, would announce that its own special springs held the surest guarantee of feminine fecundity.

The Hot, in the mid-nineteenth century, was a dismal place, inhabited only by invalids. The White, by contrast, was a gay haven, where the élite from all over the South gathered. This despite the fact that its sulphur water was described as having an odor "like a half-boiled, half-spoiled egg." Not only so, but some who had been drinking it claimed that silver coins in their pockets had turned black. Nevertheless, the White was the most prestigious of the prewar springs. There was dancing and flirting as the belles and beaux disported themselves, and the chattering matrons looked on approvingly. Trysts were held in the dusk at the columned springhouse. Planters smoked segars on the huge verandah and discussed the price of tobacco, cotton and Negroes.

In the 1850s Virginia and the rest of the South were enjoying special prosperity, and a whole batch of new springs opened up, including Yellow Sulphur, Grayson's Sulphur, Bath Alum, Montgomery White, Alleghany, Cotoosa, Jordan's White Sulphur, Capon, Orkney, Huguenot and Buffalo Lithia, to give a partial list. And there was Rockbridge Alum, a leader in prewar days which would achieve a later fame through its somewhat tenuous connection with James Branch Cabell's novel, *Jurgen*.

Some of the springs were in the Shenandoah Valley, but it seems logical to assume that those which were celebrated for gaiety were not excessively patronized by the Scotch-Irish Presbyterians who form so notable and valuable a proportion of the Valley population. The northern end of the Valley, in the Winchester-Berryville area, with its substantial infusion of Episcopalians, was psychologically attuned to the dancing and courting that went on at the springs, but the austerity of the Scotch-Irish was sometimes incompatible with such merrymaking.

John S. Wise, who was a cadet at the VMI during the Civil War and fought in the Battle of New Market, has described vividly and with perhaps pardonable exaggeration, the Lexington atmosphere of that time.

The Presbyterians of Lexington were "a type of humanity wholly new to me," Wise wrote in his notable memoir, *The End of an Era.* He went on to declare that "their impress was upon everything in the place." "The blue limestone streets looked hard," while the "red brick houses, with severe stone trimmings and plain white pillars and finishings, were stiff and formal." Moreover, "the grim portals of the Presbyterian church looked cold as a dog's nose."

The houses of these spiritual kinsmen of "Stonewall" Jackson are furnished with "straight up and down mahogany covered with hair cloth," and on the "black marble mantelpieces are cold, white wax flowers," Wise wrote. Upon the "Gothic table" is the family Bible, and chairs in hair cloth "stand stiff as horseguards' sentries about the walls." Hanging above them are pictures of Oliver Cromwell and the Rock of Ages.

The way to be "frisky" with a Presbyterian lass, Wise went on, was to "ask her to go to church." And he concluded with the fervent observation:

"For wild hilarity commend me to a coterie of strictly reared young female Presbyterians. An evening spent among them is like sitting upon an iceberg cracking hailstones with one's teeth."

The yellow fever and cholera epidemics from which many Tidewater Virginians fled to the mountains, occurred off and on during the nineteenth century. Yellow fever had been a problem in the eighteenth century, as well, and this lethal malady was to become epidemic on thirteen different occasions in Virginia. There were nine outbreaks in Norfolk, two in Portsmouth, and one each in Alexandria and Winchester. In addition to these "epidemics" there were "scares" in Richmond, Williamsburg, Hampton and City Point.

Nobody in that era knew what caused yellow fever, but it was obvious that the deadly sickness struck primarily around seaports and in other coastal areas. Walter Reed, a native of Virginia's Gloucester

County, would discover at the very end of the century that the scourge was mosquito-borne, and would thus become one of the world's great benefactors, but that was far in the future. For the time being, Virginians and other Southerners sought to cope as best they could with the recurrent epidemics.

The worst of them all overwhelmed Norfolk and Portsmouth in 1855, creating a carnival of horror aptly compared to the Black Death of the Middle Ages. Of Norfolk's 16,000 inhabitants, 6000 fled in terror. Practically all of the remaining 10,000 contracted the disease, and about 2000—or about one-third of the white population still in the city—died within three months. A similar proportion of Portsmouth's whites were wiped out. The Negroes in both cities got the malady too, but it was never as severe for members of that race and nearly all recovered.

The epidemic had broken out in midsummer, after a steamer from the West Indies put in at Norfolk with yellow fever on board. The disease spread rapidly to the city, and by the end of August, Norfolk "had become a great hospital." Ere long, seventy, eighty or even a hundred persons were dying daily, and it was impossible to bury them decently. Whole families were wiped out, the supply of coffins was exhausted and the gravediggers found that they could not keep up with the demand for graves. Mass burials became necessary.

Heroic doctors came down from the North to aid stricken Norfolk, and many of them gave their lives fighting the epidemic. More than half of the forty physicians from New York, Philadelphia, Baltimore and Washington who embarked on this errand of mercy made the supreme sacrifice. From Richmond and cities farther south came dozens of other volunteer physicians. Those from the deeper South had acquired a certain immunity from long contact with the disease, and few died. But the mortality among Virginia doctors was heavy; nearly half of those who went to Norfolk succumbed, and there were similar losses among Norfolk's and Portsmouth's own physicians. Other victims included Norfolk's mayor, the president of its Select Council, the postmaster and numerous leading business and professional men.[2]

On top of everything else, there was a smallpox epidemic throughout Virginia in the winter of 1855-56.

Norfolk had also been hit hard in 1832 by an outbreak of Asiatic cholera, in which four hundred died, three hundred of them Negroes.

When one adds these frightful ordeals to those already undergone by
Norfolk—the bombardment and burning in the Revolution, the great
fire of 1804, and Norfolk's trials during Jefferson's embargo and in
the War of 1812—it can readily be seen that few cities in our history
have suffered so much.

Insofar as cholera was concerned, however, Richmond was a worse
victim than Norfolk. In the 1832 epidemic, 498 Richmonders died.
There was another outbreak in the city in 1849, with hundreds of
cases and 129 deaths. In addition, thirty-one Negroes on Shirley
Plantation, Charles City County, succumbed in rapid succession. There
was another cholera epidemic in Richmond in 1854, with estimated
deaths of over two hundred.

The bewilderment of the medical profession and the public generally
in the face of this scourge may be seen from the fact that at the
time of the first epidemic, preventive measures were said to be: "Wear
a flannel shirt or jacket, flannel drawers and yarn stockings . . . never
permit any fruit at all to be in your house, or any vegetable except rice
and well-cooked potatoes." The Richmond *Whig* was firmly convinced
that the epidemic would continue until the City Council prohibited
the bringing to market of watermelons, cabbages and cucumbers.[3]

Medicine everywhere was in a relatively primitive state. Virginia
produced at least two remarkable pioneers, in addition to Dr. Walter
Reed.

One of these was Dr. John Peter Mettauer (1787–1875) of Prince
Edward County, whom one medical historian has pronounced "probably the most remarkable man the profession in this country has
produced," a man who "deserves to rank at the head of the surgeons
of this country up to his time." Operating during most of his career
without anesthesia and with equipment which today would seem
laughably inadequate, Mettauer performed successfully such difficult
operations as those for cataract, stricture of the urethra, vesico-vaginal
fistula, cleft palate and amputation of the breast. Patients and students
from all over the United States came to his infirmary and medical
school in rural Prince Edward County, near his alma mater, Hampden-
Sydney College. Despite his enormous professional competence, Mettauer was bewilderingly eccentric. He not only insisted on wearing
kid gloves during his lectures, but he always wore a stovepipe hat
during his waking hours—while lecturing, operating and at meals. He

was buried in the hat, and his coffin had to be made eight feet long, in consequence.[4]

Another great medical trail blazer was Dr. James Lawrence Cabell (1813–89). As professor of surgery at the University of Virginia for more than half a century, beginning in 1837, Cabell was not only a magnetic teacher but he was also ahead of Charles Darwin in publishing a work which recognized the theory of evolution. This was his *Testimony to the Unity of Mankind*, which appeared several months before Darwin's *Origin of Species*. Cabell also in large measure anticipated by many years Hugo de Vries' theory of mutations. He was, furthermore, the organizer and first president of the National Board of Health, and it was in the field of public health that he is said to have made his greatest contribution of all.[5]

Another Virginia pioneer, albeit in an entirely different sphere, was Matthew Fontaine Maury (1806–73), the "Pathfinder of the Seas." Maury was the founder of oceanography, the science by which currents are charted, the direction and force of the wind are determined, weather over the ocean is mapped, dangerous reefs are located, and so on. Mariners in all countries and all climes are eternally in his debt, as are passengers on ocean-going ships.

He was the first superintendent of the United States Naval Observatory, and under his direction it became one of the most important scientific agencies in the world. Maury was soon internationally famous, and his contributions not only to oceanography but to hydrography, astronomy and meteorology were recognized by kings, emperors and the Pope.

When the Civil War loomed, he sought by all possible means to promote discussion and arbitration between the sections. When this proved vain, he cast his lot with his native state, partly because of the debt he felt he owed Virginia for having provided a haven for his persecuted Huguenot ancestors.

In the war, he served as a commander in the Confederate Navy and made an invaluable contribution by inventing an electric torpedo which served as a formidable check against attacks on Confederate harbors. The Federal Secretary of the Navy stated after Appomattox that the North lost "more vessels by torpedoes than from all other causes."

Maury closed his career as a member of the faculty of Virginia Military Institute. The last four years of his life were spent there, and much of his talent and energy was consumed in efforts to rebuild devastated Virginia. He published a *Physical Survey of Virginia* and delivered addresses designed to promote agricultural development.

In the decade before the Civil War, Maury was one of the most internationally celebrated of living Americans, but few of the current generation outside Virginia have heard his name. Publication in 1963 of a definitive biography by Frances Leigh Williams has helped to bring Maury's achievements to public attention, but he is still, as Miss Williams says, one of the most "neglected figures in the history of American science."

Another neglected Virginia figure is Moncure Robinson (1802–91), a world-renowned railroad builder. His bridge over the James River, built in 1838 for the Richmond & Petersburg Railroad, was 2844 feet long. Four years previously Robinson had begun work on his masterpiece, the Philadelphia & Reading Railroad, which included a 1932-foot tunnel and a spectacular stone bridge. The Czar of Russia sought Robinson's services in 1840 as engineer in charge of the railway system being planned for the Russian empire. He declined. Robinson was a brother of Conway Robinson (1805–84), a highly regarded legal scholar and historian.

A pioneer of a different type was John Hartwell Cocke (1780–1866) of Bremo, Fluvanna County, who served as a brigadier general in the War of 1812. He was ahead of his generation in various respects. He was highly critical of slavery over a period of many years and a strong advocate of colonization. He paid no attention to the laws against teaching slaves to read and write. Recognizing the great obstacles in the way of ridding the South of slavery, he counted on economic forces to achieve that result in time, since he considered the institution to be not only immoral but highly inefficient.

Cocke was a pioneer in agriculture, and on his handsome estate, as well as on his Alabama plantations, he introduced new and scientific methods of farming. He was also forward-looking in the educational sphere, and was one of Thomas Jefferson's principal co-workers in the founding and building of the University of Virginia.

However, General Cocke has been termed a "puritan cavalier," for he tried to launch an antebellum "temperance" movement. Such doctrine was highly unpopular with Virginia gentlemen, accustomed as they were to their toddies and juleps. In fact, the Democratic State Convention of 1855 pronounced the rise of temperance societies a "damnableness" which had to be fought. Even Baptist clergymen in the late eighteenth and early nineteenth centuries had openly defended whiskey. For example, the Dover Baptist Association, in 1801, said liquor was "designed by Heaven as a blessing to man." At the same period "church members, and none more freely than the followers of Wesley [Methodists] bought and sold and drank strong waters," according to Lucian Minor, a leading temperance advocate.[6]

It is surprising, therefore, that General Cocke persuaded some of the state's foremost Episcopalians to join him in his quixotic crusade. Episcopalians in colonial days, and in modern times, have seldom been notable for prominence in furthering the objectives of the Anti-Saloon League, but in the mid-nineteenth century Cocke persuaded a substantial number of them to work with him in his effort to subdue the rum demon. Among those who did so were U. S. Senator William Cabell Rives, William M. Blackford, editor of the Lynchburg *Virginian*, and eminent members of the University of Virginia faculty, including John B. Minor, the noted professor of law, and William Barton Rogers, who later founded the Massachusetts Institute of Technology.

Cocke was against tobacco, too, and not only because it exhausted the soil and required more continuous labor than any other crop. He fought it because, in his view, its use produced "delirium tremens, nervousness, dyspepsia, insanity, indolence, the loss of teeth, discoloration of the skin, and dwarfishness."

There were other "puritan cavaliers" in Virginia, in addition to General Cocke, as is obvious from the number of prominent citizens who joined him in his efforts to bring "temperance." Then, too, the *Southern Literary Messenger* of Richmond was permeated for several years, beginning in 1837, with incredibly puritanical ideas concerning the proprieties which should prevail in the writing of fiction.

The plays and novels of Bulwer-Lytton, the English writer, sent the literary critic of the *Messenger* into spasms of apprehension, lest they "defile the mind of lovely and innocent woman." The critic made it clear that he had been "bred up on the simple manners of the 'Old Dominion,' where seduction is heard of only in romances and conjugal infidelity may be said to be unknown." After a number of tantrums of this sort, this highly sensitive Virginia *littérateur* concluded that he was opposed to the writing and reading of all novels, since they were a form of mental dissipation which kept the mind from serious and useful study.[7]

The foregoing cannot be considered typical of critical judgments in Virginia at that period, for novels continued to be read, and also to be written by Virginians. Edgar Allan Poe, who had edited the *Messenger* immediately preceding these apocalyptic outbursts, was of an entirely different mind. True, the content of the novels written and read by nineteenth-century Virginians was far more bland than that of today's fictional productions. Generally speaking, they were romantic rather than realistic, and their pages were suffused with a rosy glow. In particular, they were wont to romanticize slavery.

A man who blazed new trails in legal areas, although not in the field of imaginative literature, was William Wirt (1772–1834), Attorney General of the United States, following his appointment by President Monroe, and the "first Attorney General to organize the work of the office and to make a systematic practice of preserving its official opinions." Wirt had come to public notice in 1800 as counsel for the notorious scandalmonger, James Thomson Callender, in his trial for violation of the Sedition law. Six years later he was involved in the prosecution of Aaron Burr for treason. Wirt had literary ambitions, and in 1803 he published *The Letters of the British Spy*, which appeared anonymously in the Richmond *Argus*. His authorship soon became known, and this series of observations concerning Virginia by a non-existent British visitor was so popular that Wirt's desire for literary fame was greatly stimulated. His other major writing was his biography of Patrick Henry, to which he devoted more than a decade of spasmodic effort. While the book assembled many of the facts concerning Henry's life for the first time, they were so mingled with unsubstantiated tradition and fantastic laudation that Wirt almost ranks with Parson Weems as a purveyor of myths concerning one of the founding fathers. John Taylor of Caroline called the life of Henry "a wretched piece of fustian." Wirt was a Marylander by birth, but so much of his life was spent in Virginia, and his writings were so closely identified with the Old Dominion, that he deserves to be listed on any roster of those who made noteworthy contributions to the Virginia story.

A native of the commonwealth who wrote novels in the romantic tradition of Sir Walter Scott, but who did not romanticize or defend slavery, was William Alexander Caruthers (1802–46). Born in Lexington, Caruthers hated chattel servitude and did his best to lessen the antagonism between the North and the South. In his novel *The*

Kentuckian in New-York, he urged every Southerner to visit Gotham. Parrington terms Caruthers "a shrewd and kindly interpreter of both sections."

A Virginian who was especially distinguished as a writer in the sphere of economics was George Tucker (1775–1861)—not to be confused with his kinsmen, St. George Tucker (1752–1827), or Nathaniel Beverley Tucker (1784–1851), often referred to as Beverley Tucker. George Tucker is given a dozen pages by Jay B. Hubbell, a native of Virginia's Smyth County, in his definitive work, *The South in American Literature,* by far the most valuable and perceptive single book in the field. Tucker wrote a novel, *The Valley of Shenandoah,* and also a biography of Jefferson, but his chief claim to our attention lies in his writings on economics. Here his work was so exceptional that he has been termed the leading economic thinker during the first forty years of the nineteenth century. His major books were *The Laws of Wages, Profits and Rent Investigated, The Theory of Money and Banks,* and *Progress of the United States in Population.* Tucker argued that slavery was destined for ultimate extinction, since it was unprofitable. He was highly critical of the failure of Virginians to produce literary works of substance and wrote that "we have written fewer (and perhaps worse) books, and contributed less to the advancement of the arts, ornamental and useful, in Virginia, than any country on earth equally civilized." For all his levelheaded realism in several directions, Tucker defended dueling.

His novel of the Shenandoah Valley had few readers, but John Esten Cooke's romances of the Valley were widely read and did much to celebrate the virtues of that charming region. Cooke (1830–86) was both historian and novelist, but his work was marred by excessive haste in composition. He wrote his best novel, *The Virginia Comedians,* and two others during the year 1854 when only twenty-four, and while practicing law. His facility at turning out these romances was obviously enormous, but it worked in part to his detriment, as he was unwilling to revise and polish his work. Cooke wrote *Surry of Eagle's Nest,* another novel which attracted attention, in six weeks. He served on the staff of General J. E. B. Stuart in the Civil War, and his sketches of Stuart, Jackson, Ashby and others are vivid and engaging. Reviewing the state of Virginia letters since 1800, Cooke wrote that Virginia literature "is notable for its respect for good morals and good manners," and he went on to say that "it is nowhere offensive to delicacy or piety, or endeavors to instill a belief in what ought not to be believed."

A writer who was not bemused by such concepts was Edgar Allan Poe (1809–49). Although born in Boston, Poe called himself "a Virginian," for it was in Richmond that he spent most of his tragic life. Poe was an authentic genius, one of the few that this country has produced, and he left an indelible imprint upon American literature.

His life was filled with heartbreak, beginning with the death of his mother, Elizabeth Arnold Poe, a talented actress. She died, poverty-stricken in Richmond, December 8, 1811, two weeks before the dreadful "theater fire" destroyed the Richmond theater in which she had frequently appeared. The disaster took the lives of seventy-two persons, including Governor George W. Smith.

Elizabeth Poe's death left her two-year-old son, Edgar, an orphan. He was taken into the home of John Allan, a well-to-do merchant, and at first was treated with the utmost kindness by Allan and his wife. Soon, however, Allan became indifferent. Later he turned against Poe who, it must be conceded, had eccentricities of his own. The merchant cut his foster son off without a cent in his will, although he provided there for his own illegitimate children.

When Poe married, he and his adored wife, Virginia, and Virginia's mother, who was also his aunt, all starved together for years. Virginia finally died. Poe was not a heavy drinker, except spasmodically, but a small amount of alcohol, such as that contained in a glass of wine, affected him much more than it did most men. The widespread assumption that he drank constantly is incorrect. Poe's Gothic tales, with their macabre atmosphere, and some of his poems, with their spectral and unearthly magic, tended to heighten the impression that he wrote under the spell of alcohol or drugs. The fact is, however, that these unique stories and poems were the products of Poe's brilliantly imaginative and retentive mind. He is remembered, too, for several exquisite short lyric poems such as *To Helen* and *Annabel Lee*. In addition, as James Russell Lowell put it, he "lifted criticism from the abasement of sniveling imbecility into which it had sunk." A gifted editor, Poe made the *Southern Literary Messenger* the most important literary magazine in America during the one and a half years when he was at its editorial helm. But the publisher, Thomas W. White, was jealous of Poe's fame and unwilling to give him the title of editor or a free editorial hand. That, rather than his drinking, was the chief reason why White dispensed with Poe's services in January 1837. Poe left for the North. His life there was a constant battle with poverty and ill health. Although he was nationally famous as a writer and critic, his earnings were pathetically small. Professional writers had no more standing in New York and Philadelphia than they had in Richmond.[8]

Poe returned to Richmond for a visit in the summer of 1849, and was well received, even lionized. He remained until late September, when he left for Baltimore by steamer. He disappeared in that city and was found in a pitiable condition in a tavern. He died a few days later. Thus ended the star-crossed career of the greatest literary genius Virginia has produced.

One of his successors as editor of the Southern Literary Messenger was John R. Thompson (1823–73), who took charge of the magazine in 1847 at age twenty-four. Thompson had to struggle to keep the Messenger afloat. He deplored that southern publications were so little patronized by Southerners, "while thousands of dollars are sent by southern men to pay northern magazines to abuse them." Thompson wrestled with the problem until 1860, and James Southall Wilson has written that the period of his editorship "was that of the magazine's greatest influence and reputation." The Messenger was "the acknowledged representative of the South," and published the work of the leading southern writers. Thompson was also a minor poet of talent. As editor of the magazine he sought to avoid blatant sectionalism, and was largely successful. The conspicuous exception was when he erupted with fury over Uncle Tom's Cabin.

George W. Bagby (1828–83), who succeeded him in the editorial chair, was more bellicose. When Bagby took over in 1860, he called for the formation of a Southern Confederacy months before secession actually occurred. Bagby went into the Confederate Army as soon as war broke out, and somehow managed to sleep through the first Battle of Manassas. Ill health forced his retirement from the armed forces, and he devoted his remaining years to writing and lecturing.

Bagby viewed antebellum Virginia with considerable realism, eschewing the tendency in some quarters to glamorize and idealize a way of life which had its indubitable charm, but which fell considerably short of perfection. Bagby's writings, filled with both pathos and humor, were vastly popular in Virginia after the war, and thanks to a collected edition of his works, they have become more familiar to later generations of Virginians. But Bagby and his writings are little known beyond the borders of his native state. This despite the fact that he was, in the opinion of Thomas Nelson Page, "next to Poe, the most original of all Virginia writers." Some of his pictures of the life of antebellum Virginia and its people are so vivid as to be unforgettable. His "The Old Virginia Gentleman" and "John M. Daniel's Latchkey" (the latter a pen picture of a noted Richmond editor) are perhaps his best work. His "How Rubinstein Played," which Bagby termed "the most popular piece I ever wrote," has been copied in countless anthologies and school textbooks, often with the legend "Author Unknown."

Nathaniel Beverley Tucker (1784–1851) died a decade before the Civil War, but his novel, *The Partisan Leader*, which appeared in 1836, predicted that conflict. He was influential in creating a point of view congenial to secession, and his book has been described as "an obvious attempt to dramatize the philosophy of Calhoun."

However, the South's most potent propagandist for slavery in the 1850s was George Fitzhugh (1806–81) of Prince William County. He was an able spokesman for the doctrine beloved of the fire eaters that slavery was "a positive good." When the pernicious African slave trade was reopened, contrary to law, two or three years before the outbreak of armed hostilities with the North, Fitzhugh actually convinced himself that this abominable business of kidnaping and selling human beings was a benefaction to the victims since it provided a superior means of converting them to Christianity. He set forth his extreme views on slavery in two books, *Sociology for the South, or the Failure of Free Society* (1854), and *Cannibals All! or Slaves Without Masters* (1857). Fitzhugh attacked the *laissez-faire* doctrines of Adam Smith, and pronounced free capitalism under such auspices a dismal failure. He advanced the thesis that the answer was slavery, as practiced in Virginia and the rest of the South. Fitzhugh was a regular contributor to *De Bow's Review* of New Orleans, the widely read organ of southern business, and he also wrote for the Richmond newspapers.

Virginia's preoccupation with slavery in the decades before the war was a major reason why the state produced little important literature—nothing to compare with the output of Massachusetts during the period. The commonwealth—indeed the entire region—was on the defensive most of the time, and its leaders were largely absorbed in

answering the tirades of the abolitionists. Furthermore, the low esteem
in which professional writers were held served to discourage those
with literary ambition. There was also the fact that southern magazines
paid nothing for contributions. John R. Thompson told the students
of Washington College in 1850: "Anyone who would choose the
making of books as a means of support in this day, with his eyes
open to the bankruptcy of thousands before him might well, in my
judgment, be made the subject of a commission of lunacy."

The overwhelmingly rural character of Virginia, which had hardly
any substantial centers of population, and hence afforded little opportunity for people to gather and exchange ideas, was a salient handicap.
So was the absence of effective southern publishing houses. Most
books by Virginia authors had to appear under the imprint of a
northern publisher, if they were to appear at all. Southern magazines
had to struggle to survive. Virginians and other Southerners often
failed to patronize the work of their own writers, whether in books
or periodicals. Louis D. Rubin, Jr., a leading contemporary student
of the subject, does not regard these explanations and excuses as
adequate. He terms them "either rationalizations or symptoms of
something else."

Except for Poe, there was no Virginia writer of fiction, poetry or
drama from the Revolutionary, post-Revolutionary or antebellum eras
whose work is nationally recognized. In non-fiction, Jefferson's official
papers and letters, Madison's writings in The Federalist, and the pamphlets and speeches of other revolutionary statesmen are memorable,
but in history and biography no less than in the field of imaginative
literature, Virginia writers failed almost completely to attain national
stature.

In the fine arts, the story is the same. Virginia painters and
sculptors in the late eighteenth century, as well as in the years before
the Civil War and the post-bellum era, did not achieve first rank.
No Gilbert Stuart, no Augustus Saint-Gaudens sprang from the
Old Dominion. The explanation probably lies in the same set of
circumstances that stifled the growth of a creative literature.

There were, however, a number of artists of genuine talent. Several
attained wide recognition, and their works are admired today in
museums or other public places, or are treasured in private art collections or in private homes.

The earliest was Edward Peticolas (1793-c.1853), a member of a gifted family of artists of French extraction who fled from the Santo Domingo massacres and settled in Richmond. Peticolas studied abroad and returned to Richmond, where he came to be recognized over a considerable period as the city's foremost painter. He worked mainly in portraiture.

John Gadsby Chapman (1808–89), a native of Alexandria, has been termed "the first notable figure in American illustration." His work appeared in numerous important magazines and books during the 1830s and 1840s. Chapman abandoned his career as an illustrator in 1848 and departed for London. He soon moved to Italy, where he remained for a third of a century. He had been commissioned in 1837 to do a mural for the Capitol in Washington, and the not particularly successful "Baptism of Pocahontas" had been the result. This was the sort of commission he wanted, but he got no more of this type, and his work in Italy was not distinguished. He died in poverty in Brooklyn.

His son, Conrad Wise Chapman (1842–1910), did not achieve recognition during his lifetime comparable to that of his father, and he was beset by almost constant financial worries. He was in a mental hospital for several years, the expense of which wrecked his father financially. But Conrad Chapman's work came to be highly regarded after his death, and it has been shown in various important museums. One of these is New York's Metropolitan, which included thirty-one of his strikingly fine wartime paintings of Charleston, South Carolina— executed when he was stationed there as a soldier in the Civil War—in its 1935 "Life in America" exhibition. These paintings form a part of the permanent collection of Richmond's Confederate Museum, and an even larger collection of his work is at the city's Valentine Museum. Chapman's Mexican landscapes are also noteworthy. It is tragic that his genuine talent was so largely unappreciated during his lifetime. He died in Hampton and is buried there in the cemetery of St. John's Church. In the 1960s, both Chapmans were recognized with exhibitions in Washington's National and Corcoran galleries and Boston's Museum of Fine Arts.

William James Hubard (1807–62) was an Englishman who had a talent for cutting silhouettes in his youth and who came to America in 1824. Encouraged by Gilbert Stuart, he took up painting in oils and soon was executing excellent, small, full-length portraits of such statesmen as Clay, Marshall, Webster and Calhoun. He moved to

Virginia and married Maria Tabb of Gloucester County. Hubard painted many portraits of leading Virginians both in Gloucester and Richmond, including nine members of the Valentine family in the latter place. He spent most of the seven years which ended in 1860 making bronze replicas of Houdon's full-length Washington. When the war broke out, he used the Richmond foundry which he had constructed for the casting of these statues, to cast cannon and make explosives. A shell exploded there accidentally in 1862, and Hubard was fatally injured.

John A. Elder (1833–95), the son of a Fredericksburg bootmaker, manifested artistic talent in his youth. With the financial aid of Fredericksburger John Minor he studied in Europe. On his return, he was busily engaged in portrait painting in Richmond when hostilities erupted between the North and the South. Elder enlisted as a private. He was present at the Battle of the Crater, which is the subject of his best-known painting. His other vivid war scenes also were done at firsthand. After the war he painted many portraits of Confederate generals.

The war also furnished William Ludwell Sheppard (1833–1912) of Richmond with much material. He was studying in Paris when the conflict began, and he returned at once to enlist. After Appomattox, Sheppard began his artistic career in earnest, and he exhibited unusual competence and versatility. Battle scenes as well as landscapes, genre paintings, portraits and statues were all executed by him. Sheppard produced four monuments in Richmond—the Soldiers and Sailors Monument on Libby Hill, the A. P. Hill Monument on Hermitage Road, the statue of Governor William ("Extra Billy") Smith in Capitol Square, and the Howitzer's Monument at Harrison Street and Park Avenue.

The career of Alexander Galt (1827–63) ended tragically when, at thirty-six, he died from smallpox contracted in the Civil War army camps. Born in Norfolk and obviously gifted, Galt studied abroad and was Virginia's first important sculptor. He finished the "Bacchante," his most popular work, in Italy and returned to the United States in 1853. The following year the Virginia legislature commissioned him to do a full-length marble statue of Thomas Jefferson for the University of Virginia. (It was rescued from destruction there in 1895 when the Rotunda burned.) Galt served as aide to President Jefferson Davis during the war and did an excellent plaster bust of him.

Galt's great promise was never fully realized because of his untimely death, but Sir Moses Ezekiel (1844–1917) of Richmond, Virginia's foremost sculptor, was more fortunate. He lived well beyond the biblical threescore and ten, and was knighted by three European crowned heads—Emperor William I of Germany, and kings Humbert I and Victor Emmanuel of Italy. As a youth, Ezekiel attended the Virginia Military Institute, and he fought with the cadets at the Battle of New Market. Returning to VMI at the close of the war, he was graduated with honors and was on terms of close personal friendship with Robert E. Lee, then president of Washington College, and Mrs. Lee. A few years later he managed to get to Germany, where he was the first non-German ever to win the Michael-Beer Prize. This made it possible for him to study two years in Rome, where he spent most of the remainder of his life. He opened a studio in the picturesque Baths of Diocletian and kept it there for over three decades. His studio has been described as "something halfway between a salon and a showplace," and it was not only the scene of concerts but was a rendezvous for many celebrities. Sir Moses was a man of unusual charm and of marked artistic gifts. In addition to being knighted by three crowned heads, he was awarded the German Cross of Merit in Art. His bronze full-length statue of Thomas Jefferson, done for a Louisville, Kentucky, courthouse, a replica of which stands in front of the Rotunda at the University of Virginia, is perhaps his masterpiece. He did busts or full-length statues of other noted figures in America and Europe; his "Virginia Mourning Her Dead" ornaments the campus at VMI, and one of his works is in the Church of St. Margaret, adjoining Westminster Abbey.

Another noted Virginia sculptor was Edward V. Valentine (1838–1930). Born in Richmond, he too studied abroad—in Paris, Berlin and Florence. Persuaded by his father and brother to complete his European studies, he did not return to Virginia when the Civil War began. His celebrated German teacher, August Kiss, died in March 1865, and Valentine came back to Richmond in that year. His studio became a mecca for many famous personages, and he made statues of nearly all the Confederate heroes, most of them from life. His *chef d'oeuvre* is the recumbent statue of Robert E. Lee in the chapel at Lexington, a beautifully conceived and moving work. Lee's marble features, composed in sleep, seem to symbolize the tragedy which engulfed Virginia and the nation in the fratricidal conflict of the sixties.

TWENTY-FIVE

The Decline of Virginia

VIRGINIA in the mid-nineteenth century was far less influential in the councils of the South and the nation than it had been a few decades previously. From the predominant place that it had occupied since colonial times, the Old Dominion slipped almost suddenly into a secondary role. What is the explanation?

Several reasons may be advanced. One of them is the drain of thousands of Virginia's ablest and most adventurous sons and daughters, mainly to the less developed regions of the South and West. No fewer than 388,000 former citizens of the commonwealth were living in other states in 1850. Only 949,000 white and free colored people were still in Virginia. Since most of the emigrants left their communities to build new homes under actual or virtual frontier conditions, they tended to be the younger and more vigorous elements.

Among them were many men who later became famous, men whom Virginia could ill afford to lose. Richard Beale Davis has examined this list of expatriates and has come up with the astonishing fact that at least 227 men born in Virginia prior to 1810 served in Congress from other states. There were also such eminent persons as President William Henry Harrison, Stephen F. Austin, founder of Texas, and Sam Houston, its first president; Henry Clay, leader in Congress for decades, Secretary of State and candidate for President; William H. Crawford, Senator, Cabinet member and presidential candidate; John Penn and George Walton, signers of the Declaration of Independence from North Carolina and Georgia, respectively; Ephraim McDowell, pioneer in abdominal surgery; Cyrus McCormick, inventor of the mechanical reaper; nine governors of states and twelve governors of territories, to give only a partial list.[1]

Virginia was not only losing huge numbers of valuable citizens, but the state's rank in population was declining steadily. Until 1820, Virginia had the largest population in the Union, but in that year it fell to second place, and by 1860 had skidded to fifth. There were twenty-three members of Virginia's congressional delegation in 1810, but only eleven in 1860.

Why were Virginians leaving in such large numbers, while hardly anybody was moving into the state? One reason was that ours was a young and fast-growing country, and the future in the newly developed regions of the South and West, with their virgin lands, seemed well-nigh limitless. By contrast, the lands in the older sections of Virginia were becoming, or had become, exhausted.

They were exhausted largely because of the concentration on tobacco as the principal crop. It was a crop which depleted the soil rapidly, and since few people in that era had the least inkling of scientific farming methods, the results were catastrophic. Traveler after traveler in the Tidewater and Piedmont areas in the early years of the nineteenth century reported depressing scenes. The observations of Stephen Ravenel of South Carolina were typical. He was shocked to see "the slovenly farming, the unpainted houses and the ignorance of the lower classes." He added that the latter "are brutish in their manners and exceedingly vulgar . . . and in many instances can neither read nor write."

The general economic downtrend in Virginia was reflected in the sad decline of the College of William and Mary, which had experienced a drastic drop in enrollment, its buildings in a serious state of disrepair. South Carolina, on the other hand, was enjoying exceptional prosperity, owing to the boom in cotton, and this was to continue until the panic of 1819, which hit both South Carolina and Virginia. However, the Carolina planters managed to achieve a higher level of prosperity than those of Virginia until the Civil War.

The economic decline of Virginia was in some degree attributable to the aftermath of the Revolution. Many of the principal planters had been ruined by the war, and there had been considerable devastation in certain areas. Abolition of entails and primogeniture and disestablishment of the Anglican Church added to the general disorganization. Jefferson, Madison and Monroe were all in straitened circumstances in the first quarter of the nineteenth century. Some of this may well have been due to their rather extravagant and wasteful mode of living, but the economic climate played a part.

In the North there was much greater prosperity and a better living standard throughout the population. Lucian Minor of the William and Mary faculty took a trip to southern New England in the early 1830s and contributed a series of articles to the *Southern Literary Messenger*. He wrote from Northampton, Massachusetts: "Here is not a hundredth part of the abject, squalid poverty that our state presents. I have not seen a log house in New England; nor a dwelling house without one or more glass windows. And nine-tenths of the common farm houses are painted." At the end of his journey Minor declared: "No other six weeks of my life have had compressed into them half so much excitement, or half as much interest. Those Northern states have very far the start of us Virginians in almost all the constituents of civilization . . . They . . . possess better organized social and civil institutions. Their usages are more favorable to health, to virtue, to intelligence—and in their thorough, practical understanding of the word COMFORT . . . they are as far before us as we are before the Hottentots or Esquimaux."

Henry Ruffner, president of Washington College, expressed similar sentiments in 1847, when he said in an address, later published as the famous "Ruffner Pamphlet":

"In the free states are seen all the tokens of prosperity. . . . In the older parts of the slave states . . . are seen, on the contrary, too evident signs of stagnation or of positive decay—a sparse population— a slovenly cultivation spread over vast fields that are wearing out, among others already worn out and desolate; villages and towns 'few and far between,' rarely growing, often decaying, sometimes mere remnants of what they were . . . ; generally no manufactures, not even trades, except the indispensable few—commerce and navigation abandoned, as far as possible, to the people of the free states; and generally, instead of the stir and bustle of industry, a dull and dreamy stillness, broken, if broken at all, by the wordy brawl of politics."

The slave system was responsible for much of this backwardness. Slave labor was much less efficient than free labor. This was due, in part, to the fact that the slave usually had no incentive to work hard. On a few plantations there were rewards for slaves who performed well, but the average chattel was inclined to work as little as possible. He knew that he was a slave for life, anyway. So long as he could escape punishment for failure to perform his task he saw no advantage in excessive effort.[2]

Virginians were not only moving out of the state; they were also moving across the mountains into the western regions of the Old Dominion, where slaves were comparatively few. The census of 1850 showed that the white population west of the Blue Ridge was 90,000 greater than that east of the range. And the people of southwest and of northwest Virginia—now West Virginia—were often of fine Anglo-Saxon stock, proud and self-reliant and superior to the brutish type of eastern "poor white" described by Stephen Ravenel. There were "poor whites" in the mountains and valleys of the west, squatting on land they did not own, but the percentage was relatively small. The western Virginians were often self-respecting homeowners, living in their cabins or on their small farms, and asking no help from anyone.

Not only did slavery provide an inefficient system of labor, but the attacks on it from the North seemed to force Virginia and the rest of the South into a perennial posture of defense. In a period when New England was being swept by new ideologies and much of Europe was challenged by philosophical idealism, Virginia's thinking was largely static. Defense of the *status quo* against the assaults of outsiders became the chief concern of nearly all the leaders.

Youthful Jesse Burton Harrison, just back from Germany in the early 1830s, saw that Virginia needed to stop defending slavery and to get on with a plan for abolishing it. He published a reply in 1832 to Thomas R. Dew's defense of the institution. Harrison advocated a more forward-looking attitude on the part of Virginians who, he said, were too much inclined to bask in the glories of their forebears, instead of carrying the Old Dominion onward to new greatness. He also deplored what he felt to be the excessive desire of young Virginians to rush into politics. Harrison called, furthermore, for reform of the state's archaic system of education.

Backwardness in primary and secondary education—although not at the college level—accounted for much of Virginia's lack of advancement. In the words of the French historian and geographer, Jean Gottmann, the failure of Virginians "to maintain their eighteenth century leadership in the nation was to a large extent due to the feeble numbers of their educated élite." The percentage of illiteracy among whites in 1850 was 8.6, and only five of the thirty-one states had worse ratings. In 1845, Governor James McDowell, one of the most earnest advocates of better schools, called the situation "absolutely appalling." He referred to "the ruinous process of depopulation and impoverishment now at work," and said it would continue unless the legislature revised, amended and enlarged the state's "system of education and internal improvement." His plea was largely in vain.

Had it not been for certain spectacular advances in agriculture, Virginia's overall retrogression would have been even worse. Thanks to the ingenuity and leadership shown by several individuals, exhaustion and erosion of the soil were checked, and by 1850 there was a distinct upturn in the general level of farming.

Fielding Lewis, who married George Washington's sister, had been an early pioneer in the application of lime to Virginia's soil. John Alexander Binns of Loudoun County had used deep plowing, combined with the application of gypsum to the soil, to restore Loudoun's depleted lands, and had made the county the most productive in the state. The use of gypsum spread rapidly, and Avery O. Craven says in his trail-blazing work, *Soil Exhaustion as a Factor in the Agricultural History of Virginia and Maryland, 1606–1860*, that from 1800 to 1820 "no other single factor made such great changes for the better in the agricultural life of the two states."

Then came the researches and writings of John Taylor of Caroline, "the philosopher of political agrarianism." His contribution to better farming in the state was deemed the most important made by any individual up to that time. Taylor stressed the principle that "fertility of soil alone can give success." This could be achieved, he said, by "the return of manures of all kinds, animal and vegetable." In his influential book, *Arator* (1813), he advocated deep plowing and crop rotation.

Edmund Ruffin was Virginia's next agricultural pioneer, and his was the most far-reaching contribution of all. His *Essay on Calcareous Manures* (1832) caused a virtual revolution in farming practices in Virginia. In it he emphasized the significance of marl in the restoration of worn-out lands. John Rolfe had drawn attention to the properties of marl more than two centuries before, but Ruffin roused Virginians to a realization of its valuable qualities. His *Essay* ran through five editions, and the Year Book of the U. S. Department of Agriculture for 1895 called it "the most thorough piece of work on a special agricultural subject ever published in the English language." In

1833, Ruffin founded the *Farmer's Register*, a monthly journal designed to disseminate his ideas. It was termed by John Skinner, first editor of the *American Farmer*, "the best publication on agriculture which this country or Europe has ever produced." Ruffin is also authoritatively declared to have "a good claim to be called the father of soil chemistry in America." Ruffin, unfortunately, became involved in a bitter controversy with the bankers of the state after he had suffered financial losses in the panic of 1837. A man of strong, even violent, views on some subjects, he accused the bankers of "the tyranny of avarice, moral fraud and legalized swindling." This stirred up such a storm and caused so many cancellations of subscriptions to the *Farmer's Register* that he decided to stop publishing it in 1842. That, incidentally, was the year after the *Southern Planter* made its initial appearance, to continue in operation for more than a century and a quarter.

Ruffin contended in 1853 that properly marled land in Virginia had increased in value by 200 per cent. While marl was undoubtedly due a large share of credit for the great improvement noted in Virginia farming during the 1850s, the at least equally significant role of Peruvian guano should by no means be overlooked. Willoughby Newton, a leading citizen of Westmoreland County, pioneered in introducing this fertilizer to Virginia, and the results were sensational. Newton stated that the introduction of guano "was an interposition of Providence to save the country from total ruin." Guano was relatively expensive, whereas marl was ready to hand and cheap, but those who could afford the Peruvian fertilizer profited greatly from its application to exhausted lands. The farmers of the Northern Neck, fellow citizens of Willoughby Newton, were said to have become the richest agricultural population in America.

Thanks to the various innovations, such as the introduction of gypsum, marl and guano and the organization of agricultural societies to promote their use, soil exhaustion ceased to be a major problem in Virginia in the years immediately preceding the Civil War.

Diversification of crops and the raising of livestock for sale also were important factors in the rise of Virginia farming. Truck crops were grown in lower Tidewater, especially for export to the North. The growing of grain reached such proportions that, except for tobacco, it became Virginia's chief source of farm income. Orchards were planted in the Shenandoah Valley and the Piedmont.

Colonies of farmers came down from the North in the 1840s and

1850s and settled in a number of counties, ranging from Fairfax on the Potomac to the Tidewater counties of the southeast. The Fairfax colony received special attention and was the subject of a series of laudatory articles in the Richmond *Whig* and other papers in 1845. The series was by Samuel Janney of Loudoun, a Quaker who had long agitated against slavery. He pointed to the greatly superior farming methods of these "Yankees," who relied on scientific techniques, crop rotation and —last, but not least—free labor. The abandoned farms of Fairfax were soon producing in great variety and abundance, and land values skyrocketed.

Janney drew the probably sound conclusion that free labor was largely responsible, and he added that slavery ought to be abolished, so that the "retrograde movement which has so long been going on in the Eastern part of the state" might be arrested. Such a conclusion, in the climate of opinion then existing, was received with a decided lack of enthusiasm, to put it mildly. The Richmond *Examiner*, which had joyfully hailed the coming of the Northerners some years before, now sang a quite different tune. The editor was opposed to this "Vandal invasion of Virginia" with its "fragrant hordes of adventurers fresh from the . . . codfisheries of the Bay State" who would convert areas of the commonwealth into "a paradise of onions, squashes, string beans and 'liberty.'"

Manufacturing, like farming, experienced a decided upturn in Virginia in the 1850s. The Old Dominion had 4841 manufacturing establishments in the final years of the decade—fifth among all the states and first in the South. New York, Pennsylvania, Ohio and Massachusetts were still far ahead, but Virginia was making a definitely better showing. In the South, the state ranked number one in several categories, and it led the nation in tobacco manufacture. Richmond led the cities of the world in flour milling. The Tredegar Iron Works at Richmond was the foremost southern industrial establishment in the field. Norfolk, Petersburg, Lynchburg and other centers of population experienced a factory boom. The hiring of slaves by these factories increased, and this served as an outlet for the state's slave surplus. A greater outlet was in sales of slaves to the Deep South, where the demand remained high.

But despite the manufacturing and farming upturn of the eighteen-fifties, Virginia remained far behind states which, in earlier days, had

been far behind Virginia. Examples were given by Governor Joseph
Johnson in his message to the General Assembly in 1855:

"At the period of the War of Independence, the commerce of Virginia was four times larger than that of New York. In 1853, the imports
of the latter amounted to the enormous sum of one hundred and eighty
millions yearly, while those of Virginia were not quite $400,000. And
during that year, there were cleared from her [New York's] ports
9950 vessels to foreign ports, while from Virginia during the same
period 292, and the amount of goods imported was less than four
million dollars."

Governor Johnson went on to declare that Virginia's grievous decline could not be ascribed to superior natural advantages elsewhere,
since "Virginia has greatly the advantage over any portion of the North
in all the elements requisite to constitute a commercial and prosperous
community." He added sadly that "like the unfaithful servant, she has
failed to improve the talent entrusted to her care."

The inability of leading Virginians, especially those in Richmond,
Petersburg, Fredericksburg and Alexandria, the "river towns," to grasp
the vital necessity for developing railroads, is offered by some as an
explanation for the failure of Norfolk to realize its potential as a great
port. (See Chapter Twenty-one.) As Thomas J. Wertenbaker puts it
in his history of Norfolk:

"Had Virginia . . . placed her dependence upon railways and laid
out a wise and comprehensive scheme of construction, how different
would have been her history! Instead of squandering millions on
unwise projects her outlay would have been returned many times over
in increased commerce and manufactures; instead of rushing to disunion, she would have bound her Western counties with the bands of
economic interest . . . Starting with Norfolk, the state's only great
ocean port, a railway should have been built west to Petersburg, Richmond, Charlottesville, Staunton, Charleston and the Ohio River . . .
Then the north and south lines could have been added . . . Had this
been done the products of all Virginia . . . would have poured through
this system down to Norfolk . . . But this was not to be. The fall line
towns would not consent to connecting Norfolk with the back country.
Having developed under the old system of river navigation, they were
determined to maintain their ascendancy by legislative action."

Wertenbaker concedes, however, that the great success of the Erie
Canal in New York could well have brought to the "river towns" the

sincere conviction that equal success might be obtained in Virginia by developing the James River and Kanawha Canal, rather than the railroads. The fact remains that Virginia failed to advance commercially and industrially with anything like the speed that might reasonably have been expected. The same is true of the port of Norfolk, which never came close to realizing its potential in the antebellum years.

Virginia not only remained far behind the northern states in various categories of material and cultural advancement; it also lost the leadership of its own region to South Carolina. From the mid-1830s onward, Charleston rather than Richmond became the center from which emanated the prevailing views of Southerners on most issues of the day. Pre-eminent among those issues was slavery, and John C. Calhoun, with his aggressive championship of the "positive good" thesis, was the man to whom the South looked for guidance. There was no one in Virginia who exercised more than a fraction of his influence, and after his death in 1850 his soul went marching on.

South Carolina and Calhoun had set the tone in 1832 with the Ordinance of Nullification, and they soon came to dominate the thinking of the South. The lovely little town of Charleston, dreaming amid its live oaks and magnolias, never had more than 43,000 inhabitants, less than half of whom were white, but it was the powerful citadel of the fiery secessionists. Seldom in history has any small city exercised such influence over the ideas and attitudes of a vast region. The whole state of Virginia could not match it, and the secessionist views of the Carolinians were to prevail, as Virginia's relatively ineffective leaders sought vainly to avoid the holocaust which loomed ahead.

If the Old Dominion had not sustained so tragic a loss of prestige, its more conservative viewpoint might conceivably have prevailed. Peace rather than war might have been the final arbitrament, as intersectional tensions grew ever more ominous, and the sixties neared.

TWENTY-SIX

Fort Sumter and
John Brown's "Singing Bones"

THE JOHN BROWN RAID on Harpers Ferry in 1859 provided an ominous foretaste of coming events. Brown's announced plan to free the slaves, by organizing them into military units to fight their masters, and establish a Negro republic in western Virginia, roused the people of the Old Dominion to terror and fury and alarmed the entire South.

Brown was a fanatic whose family had a long record of insanity. His mother and one of his grandmothers died insane, and numerous other close relatives had been intermittently mad. Brown denied that he himself was thus afflicted. He led an expedition of six anti-slavery crusaders, including four of his sons, against five defenseless pro-slavery men in Kansas in 1856. The latter were dragged from their cabins and hacked to pieces with sabers, simply because of their attitude toward slavery. In view of Brown's history, his attempt at Harpers Ferry to set off the servile insurrection that the South had long dreaded, was not surprising.

A group of like-minded and extremely prominent New Englanders, terming themselves the Secret Six, had been furnishing Brown with money and arms for his activities in Kansas. They provided him with similar assistance for his climactic coup at Harpers Ferry.[1]

Virginia and the South were much concerned already over the increasing tension between the sections. There had been bitter recriminations in 1854 when a fugitive slave from Virginia named Anthony Burns was captured in Boston. Abolitionist Wendell Phillips had proclaimed to a cheering mass meeting in Faneuil Hall, "I am ready to trample any statute or any man under foot . . . when there is a possibility of saving a slave from the . . . officers of the law." A mob tried unsuccessfully to attack the courthouse and free Burns. With Boston draped in mourning and under martial law, Burns was escorted to the wharf by heavily armed troops and returned to Virginia, where he was chained on the top floor of Richmond's slave jail. He was later sold back into slavery for $905, after which a Virginia-born abolitionist redeemed him for $1300 and sent him North.[2]

Two years previously Harriet Beecher Stowe's *Uncle Tom's Cabin* had taken much of America and Europe by storm. It contained errors of fact, but it was a ringing philippic against slavery. The South was deeply disturbed over its possible effects, and the reaction in Virginia may be glimpsed from a letter of John R. Thompson to George Frederick Holmes, asking Holmes to review the book for the *Southern Literary Messenger*. "I would have the review as hot as hell-fire, blasting and searing the reputation of the vile wretch in petticoats who could write such a volume," Thompson said to Holmes. The latter, a noted scholar, author and teacher was not quite as "hot" in his critique as Thompson seemed to want, but he was caustic in his references to both the book and its author. Mrs. Stowe, he said, had, in writing it, strayed from the "place" allotted to females and had stepped "beyond the hallowed precincts—the enchanted circle—which encompass . . . [woman] as with a halo of divinity." Holmes also made unspecific denials of the book's factual accuracy, while proclaiming slavery "an institution natural, just and righteous . . . beneficial to both master and slave, and more especially the latter."

It was also during the 1850s that George Washington Lafayette Bickley, a physician who had written a history of Tazewell County, founded something called the Knights of the Golden Circle, dedicated to "the firing of the Southern heart." A meeting at White Sulphur Springs in 1859 gave impetus to this organization "with military trappings," designed to uphold "the constitutional rights of the South." Bickley planned to seize Mexico, with the aid of the Knights, legalize chattel servitude there, and annex Mexico to the United States, thus restoring to the Union the long lost balance in favor of slavery. The Knights claimed 115,000 members in 1860, including most of the leading officials of the southern states, but this is believed to have been

a serious exaggeration. The Knights of the Golden Circle vanished from
the scene with the outbreak of the Civil War.[3]

On the eve of that conflict, northern divines were calling for southern
blood. The Reverend Theodore Parker predicted a slave insurrection
in which "The Fire of Vengeance" would run "from man to man,
from town to town" through the South. "Who shall put it out?" he
asked. "The white man's blood." The Reverend George B. Cheever
of New York declared that rather than see slavery continued, "it were
infinitely better that 300,000 slaveholders were abolished, struck out of
existence."[4]

Indicative of the tension prevailing in Virginia is the fact that O.
Jennings Wise, son of Governor Henry A. Wise, fought eight duels in
two years just before the war. He was editor of the Richmond
Enquirer.

Thus it was in an atmosphere of febrile controversy, fed by differences over fugitive slaves, the opening of the African slave trade and
slavery in general, that John Brown launched his assault on Harpers
Ferry, with a view to setting the South aflame.

Brown and his little band of sixteen white men and six Negroes
crossed the Potomac at Harpers Ferry on the night of October 16,
1859. They seized the federal armory, killed the mayor and took several
leading citizens into custody, including Colonel Lewis W. Washington,
great-grandnephew of George Washington. Governor Wise ordered out
the militia and appealed to the federal government for aid. Brown
and his band barricaded themselves in the armory's engine house.
Colonel Washington, a prisoner inside the building, later pronounced
Brown "the coolest and firmest man I ever saw in defying danger or
death," and added: "With one son dead by his side, and another shot
through, he felt the pulse of his dying son with one hand and held
his rifle with the other."

Colonel Robert E. Lee was ordered to the scene with Lieutenant
J. E. B. Stuart as his aide, and a company of U. S. Marines. By the
time they arrived, Virginia volunteers from Charles Town had killed,
wounded or captured all but Brown and four others. Lee offered the
volunteers the "honor" of assaulting the engine house. They declined
—for fear of endangering the lives of Brown's hostages, according to
one version, and because they felt that professional soldiers were
"paid" to perform such missions, according to another. Lieutenant
Israel Green of the marines was accordingly put in charge of the

assault, and eighteen of his men battered down the door with a heavy ladder. The marines rushed in "like tigers," and laid Brown flat with blows on the head.

He was not seriously injured, however, and he answered questions calmly as he lay on a cot in the paymaster's office. Governor Wise said to him, "Mr. Brown, your hair is reddened by the blood of crime." "Governor," was the reply, "the difference between your tenure and mine is trifling, and I want therefore to tell you to be prepared; I am prepared. You all [referring to slaveholders] have a heavy responsibility, and it behooves you to prepare more than it does me."

Brown was brought to trial and was unruffled throughout. He admitted "a design on my part to free the slaves," but denied everything else. He was found guilty of murder, treason and inciting slaves to rebel. Before sentence was pronounced he made a statement which ended with these words: "I did no wrong, but right. Now if it is deemed necessary that I should forfeit my life for the furtherance of the ends of justice, and mingle my blood with the blood of my children and with the blood of millions in this slave country whose rights are disregarded by wicked, cruel and unjust enactments, I say, let it be done." Judge Richard Parker thereupon pronounced the sentence of death.

In view of the fact that nineteen friends and neighbors of Brown in Ohio sent affidavits to Governor Wise expressing the opinion that Brown was insane or unbalanced, it is hard to understand why Wise failed to carry out his original intention to have Brown examined by an alienist. Had this been done, Brown might well have been committed to an institution for life instead of being hanged. But Governor Wise allowed Brown to be executed on December 2. It was an epoch-making blunder, for the propaganda value of the hanging to the abolitionists was immense. Brown himself wrote that he was "worth inconceivably more to *hang* than for any other purpose."

Wise, an avid tobacco chewer who usually dressed in slovenly fashion, was in some respects a progressive leader. As a member of the constitutional convention of 1850–51, he had led in obtaining a wider suffrage and better representation in the General Assembly for the western areas of Virginia. He was a militant advocate of improved public schools. In his successful campaign for governor in 1854, he had defeated the Know-Nothing candidate and had thereby dealt a heavy blow to the Know-Nothing party, which sought to advance its

fortunes by arousing prejudice against Roman Catholics and foreigners. But Wise was a defender of slavery, and in his campaign for
governor he denounced his Know-Nothing opponent more pointedly
for his abolitionist views than for his anti-Catholicism. Wise's emotional
involvement in the slavery question may have influenced him unduly
in reaching his decision to hang John Brown.

While abolitionists made the most of the hanging northern opinion seemed overwhelmingly hostile to Brown, who might have brought
to the South horrors as dreadful as those of Santo Domingo. Abraham Lincoln and nearly all the northern newspapers condemned
him, but a small coterie of articulate extremists not only defended
him but compared him to Christ. Ralph Waldo Emerson referred to
Brown before his execution as a "new saint awaiting his martyrdom,
and who, if he shall suffer, will make the gallows glorious like the
cross." Louisa May Alcott called him "Saint John the Just," and
Henry David Thoreau saw him as "an angel of light." The Springfield,
Massachusetts, *Republican*, in sharp dissent from most of the northern
press, declared on the day after he was hanged:

"John Brown still lives . . . A Christian man, hung by Christians for
acting upon his convictions of duty—a brave man hung for a chivalrous
and self-sacrificing deed of humanity—a philanthropist hung for seeking the liberty of oppressed men. No outcry about violated law can
cover up the essential enormity of a deed like this."

Virginia and the rest of the South had the dubious satisfaction
of noting Brown's failure to persuade any Virginia slaves in the area
near Harpers Ferry to join his expedition. On the other hand, the
hanging of Brown and two of his black confederates roused the
abolitionists to redoubled activity, augmented the tensions between
the sections and lessened the chances for amicable adjustment. Moderates on both sides of Mason and Dixon's line found themselves in a
weakened position, while the more hotheaded citizenry held the center
of the stage.

One result was an increased demand for the use of textbooks in
Virginia schools and colleges written by Southerners. President William
A. Smith of Randolph-Macon College had called several years before
for the expurgation of abolitionist sentiments or innuendoes from all
such volumes. This argument was advanced anew by others, as intersectional feeling mounted.

A considerable number of Virginians had been attending northern colleges and universities, although hardly any Northerners had ever come south for educational purposes. The cry now arose that Virginians and other Southerners should stay south and not patronize "Yankee" institutions. In December 1859, a few weeks after John Brown's execution, more than 200 Southerners who had been studying in Philadelphia's medical colleges arrived in Richmond, and 140 of them promptly matriculated in the Medical College of Virginia. The group was welcomed to the city by the faculty and students of that institution, by the Town Council, military units and many citizens. A procession marched in triumph behind a brass band from the railroad station to Capitol Square, where Governor Wise addressed the students from the portico of the Mansion. "Let Virginia call home her children!" Wise proclaimed. "Let us employ our own teachers, especially that they may teach our own doctrines. Let us dress in the wool raised on our own pastures. Let us eat the flour from our own mills, and if we can't get that, let us go back to our old accustomed corn bread!" He was applauded loudly. The visitors then repaired to the Columbian Hotel, where a "beautiful collation" was served.

The extent to which intersectional relations had deteriorated may be seen in the words of Governor Wise to the General Assembly immediately following the hanging of John Brown. "We must take up arms," said the chief executive, "the issue is too essential to be compromised any more." He went on to note the ironic fact that "the first man killed [at Harpers Ferry] was a respectable free Negro who was trusted with the baggage of a railroad, and who, faithful to his duty, was shot running from the philanthropists who came to liberate the black race!"

And yet, despite the harebrained character of the raid, a raid that was doomed from the start, John Brown's bravery in the face of death gave his execution a symbolism that, less than two years later, would inspire the marching thousands of the northern armies. Two stirring songs, "John Brown's Body" and "The Battle Hymn of the Republic," would go far to convince the people of the North and the Union fighting men that theirs was a holy cause. And around the "singing bones" of John Brown, lying in the cemetery at North Elba, New York, would be woven legends that were to endure. They would make this fanatical, ruthless and indomitable foe of human servitude a hero,

a martyr and an oriflamme, as Union and Confederate armies clashed
in desperate combat:

> A straggler met him going along to Manassas,
> With his gun on his shoulder, his phantom-sons at heel,
> His eyes like misty coals.
> A dead man saw him striding at Seven Pines,
> The bullets whistling through him like a torn flag,
> A madman saw him whetting his sword on a Bible,
> A cloud above Malvern Hill.[5]

John Letcher had been elected governor of Virginia a few months
before the John Brown raid, and he took office January 1, 1860.
Letcher, a native of Lexington, had approved Henry Ruffner's "Pamphlet" of 1847, urging that slavery be abolished west of the Blue
Ridge. He was elected to Congress four years later and there won the
sobriquet of "Honest John, Watch Dog of the Treasury." But when he
ran for governor in 1859, Letcher was attacked for his "abolitionist"
views, and this became a leading issue of the campaign. Letcher stated
that he had abandoned his contention that slavery was a political
and social evil and that he had never considered it a moral evil. In
support of the latter point he cited the fact that he had owned slaves
in 1847, and since, by purchase rather than by inheritance.

Letcher did not share the secessionist views of his predecessor in
office, Henry A. Wise. He wanted Virginia to stay in the Union, if
this could be done honorably. In his inaugural address in 1860, he
proposed that the Virginia legislature invite the other states to a
national convention to discuss the mounting intersectional hostility
and to seek solutions. His suggestion was not heeded. When the General Assembly proposed such a convention in 1861, it was too late.

The controversy over slavery reached some sort of peak in 1860
when Representative Daniel C. DeJarnette of Caroline County declared on the floor of Congress that "for every master who cruelly treats
his slave there are two white men at the North who torture and murder
their wives."

The election in 1860 of Abraham Lincoln, the Republican nominee,
alarmed the South and was achieved without the aid of Virginia,
which gave him a grand total of 1929 votes, mostly from what is now
West Virginia. The Old Dominion was barely carried by John Bell of
Tennessee, the candidate of the newly formed Constitutional Union

party, made up of conservative former Whigs and Know-Nothings. The other candidates for President in 1860 were Stephen A. Douglas of Illinois, nominee of the Democrats, and John C. Breckinridge of Kentucky, chosen by the extreme wing of the Democratic party, which split off, under the hypnotic spell of Charleston's pro-slavery zealots.

Why were Virginia and the South so alarmed at the prospect of Lincoln in the White House? One of the major reasons was his "house divided" speech of 1858, in which he had said, "I believe this government cannot endure permanently half slave and half free . . . It will become all one thing or all the other." To the South, this meant that Lincoln, who was opposed to slavery, would move to abolish the institution, despite the fact that he said he had no right to do so, and the Republican platform reiterated that Congress had no such right. South Carolina and other states of the Deep South were determined to break up the Union and end the danger of any such attempt by the North.

Virginia stood aloof as Governor Francis W. Pickens of South Carolina declared that Lincoln had been elected "upon issues of malignant hostility and uncompromising war to be waged upon the rights, the interests and the peace of half the states of the Union." A South Carolina convention met in December 1860, before Lincoln was inaugurated, and on December 20, without a dissenting vote, passed an Ordinance of Secession. By February 1, the "cotton states" —Mississippi, Florida, Alabama, Georgia, Louisiana and Texas—had followed South Carolina out of the Union. The provisional government of the Confederate States of America was promptly formed at Montgomery, Alabama, with Jefferson Davis as President and Alexander H. Stephens as Vice-President.

Virginia was still hopeful of averting war. It led the way in calling a convention of all the states, to meet in Washington, February 4, and discuss the crisis. The members of the convention, presided over by the venerable ex-President, John Tyler, found that the situation had gotten out of hand and that they could achieve nothing. The seven seceding states had sent no representatives, while the Radical Republicans, at the other end of the political spectrum, rejoiced at the convention's failure.

Though Virginia's leaders were discouraged, they were still trying to prevent further disruption of the Union. The state convention which met at Richmond, February 13, struggled to find some means of avoiding the looming catastrophe. There were secessionist hotheads among its members, but under the chairmanship of John Janney of Loudoun it pursued a conservative and restrained course. As late as April 4, it voted 88 to 45 against secession.

But events were moving to an inexorable climax, with South Carolina leading the way. That state had begun maneuvering before Lincoln's inauguration for possession of the forts in Charleston harbor. The Carolinians demanded all federal property within their borders, as a vindication of their proclaimed sovereignty, and they proceeded to seize any such property that was undefended. Major Robert Anderson, U. S. Army, and his small garrison of federal troops were bottled up in Fort Sumter. The guns of that fort dominated the harbor and the city of Charleston, and South Carolina made strenuous efforts to persuade the government of President James Buchanan to surrender Sumter peaceably. These efforts were futile. By the time Lincoln was inaugurated, war appeared to be virtually inevitable. It may well be that Lincoln, realizing this, managed matters in such a way as to provoke the South Carolinians into firing the first shot. At all events, that is what happened, a fact which went far to unite the North.

Roger A. Pryor, an oratorical firebrand and Virginia congressman, who had been advocating disunion in the Old Dominion since Lincoln's election, urged the Charlestonians in a speech on April 10 to bombard Fort Sumter. If they did so, he declared, "just so certain as tomorrow's sun will rise upon us, just so certain will Virginia be a member of the Southern Confederacy." Pryor was chosen shortly thereafter to fire the first shot, but he declined, and Edmund Ruffin of Virginia accepted eagerly.[6]

Ruffin, the agricultural pioneer of former years, had developed a great admiration for all Charlestonians and a corresponding hatred for all "Yankees." The grim, humorless old man with the white hair hanging to his shoulders was ecstatic when Captain Cuthbert of the Palmetto Guards tendered him the awesome responsibility of launching hostilities. He would be bringing on a war in which hundreds of thousands would die, but such considerations did not trouble Ruffin, who expected the conflict to end in a few weeks or months with a southern victory. At 4:30 A.M. on April 12, the appointed signal flashed, and he pulled the lanyard on the "64-pound Columbiad" which sent the first shell arching through the dawn, to explode at the northeast angle of Fort Sumter's parapet. As the bombardment proceeded, the crinolined belles of Charleston thronged the Battery, cheering the soldiers on. Next day, Fort Sumter fell.

Even then, Virginia hesitated. In the early days of the century, when New Englanders talked of secession, Virginians had argued against it. At the time of the Louisiana Purchase, for example, four of New England's senators, led by Timothy Pickering, were so strongly opposed to the addition of this enormous area, which threatened to draw off New England's population and reduce its influence, that they saw dissolution of the Union as the only answer. Thomas Ritchie denounced these secessionists in the Richmond *Enquirer*. A decade later, during the War of 1812, when the Hartford Convention was toying with the idea of secession, Ritchie and other influential Virginians condemned the New Englanders for their "treasonable" efforts, as well as for their dangerous doctrines.

Colonel Robert E. Lee, writing to his son, W. H. F. ("Rooney") Lee, January 29, 1861, from a post in the far southwest, recalled these attacks on New England and declared: "I can anticipate no greater calamity for the country than a dissolution of the Union. It would be an accumulation of all the evils we complain of, & I am willing to sacrifice everything but honour for its preservation . . . Secession is nothing but revolution . . . If the Union is dissolved & the government disrupted, I shall return to my native State & share the miseries of my people & save in her defense will draw my sword on none."

While the Virginia convention was trying to make up its mind, the three leading Richmond newspapers, the *Examiner*, the *Dispatch* and the *Enquirer*, were all leaning toward secession. The *Examiner*, in particular, under the editorship of John M. Daniel, was vitriolic in its attacks on all moderates and conservatives. It termed them "old fogies" and "conceited old ghosts who crawled from a hundred damp graves to manacle their state and to deliver her up as a handmaid to the hideous chimpanzee from Illinois [Lincoln]."

What did the North propose to do, now that Sumter had been attacked? Even Wendell Phillips, the abolitionist leader, denied that Lincoln had any right to place a federal garrison in that fort, after it had been taken over by South Carolina. Horace Greeley, editor of the New York *Tribune*, the most influential anti-slavery paper in the country, declared that "the right to secede exists," and that the "erring sisters," the seven states that had seceded, should be allowed to "depart in peace."

The Virginia convention sent William Ballard Preston, A. H. H. Stuart and George Wythe Randolph to Washington for a conference with President Lincoln on April 13, in a desperate last-minute effort to ward off armed hostilities. Fort Sumter fell on that day.

News of the surrender of Sumter was received with feverish enthusiasm on the streets of Richmond, but the convention still demurred. The Fayette Artillery fired a hundred-gun salute in Capitol Square. That evening there was firing of rockets, burning of tar barrels, and general jubilation, but when the crowd surged over to the Governor's Mansion, "Honest John" Letcher received it calmly. He would not be swept off his feet by this hysteria and reminded the assembled shouters for secession that Virginia was still a part of the Union.

But on April 15, three days after the bombardment of Fort Sumter, President Lincoln issued a call for 75,000 volunteers from all the states to put down the rebellion. Virginia and her governor hesitated no longer. Unwilling to furnish troops to "coerce a sister state," the convention at Richmond voted on April 17, by 88 to 55, to secede. Of those supporting secession, fifty-five were from east of the Blue Ridge, ten from central and northern areas of the Valley, eighteen from the southwest and five from the northwest.

Sentiment for secession among the people of Richmond appeared to be overwhelming before the vote was taken. The *Dispatch* declared that the convention was "powerless to control or shape or alter the great stream of events." An out-of-town newspaper reporter who was in Richmond found that "disunion sentiment was at white heat." When Lincoln's call for 75,000 troops came, the *Examiner* roared: "Lincoln declares war on the South, and his Secretary demands from Virginia a quota of cutthroats to desolate Southern firesides." It was remarkable, under all the circumstances, that fifty-five members of the convention voted "no." Ratification or rejection of the convention's action by a vote of the people, was scheduled for May 23, but since the result was foregone, preparations for war went forward at once. (The subsequent vote for ratification was 128,884 to 32,134.)

On April 19, the Confederate flag flew from the Capitol flagpole, and a mile-long torchlight procession, greatest in the city's history, wound along Marshall, Broad, Franklin and Main streets, with bands blaring, voices singing, rockets bursting, and Roman candles illuminating the soft April night. The marchers stopped in front of the two adjoining hotels, the Ballard and the Exchange, to be harangued by orators. "I am neither a prophet nor the son of a prophet," one of them shouted, "yet I predict that in less than sixty days the flag of the Confederacy will be waving over the White House!" "In less than thirty days!" was the rejoinder from the crowd, and "On to Washington!" was the cry. The impetuous Virginia secessionists had somehow convinced themselves that one Southerner could whip three Yankees, and that the "weak, cowardly, money-loving North" wouldn't fight. They were soon to find out how wrong they were.

An embarrassing event occurred on Sunday morning, April 21. While Richmonders were sitting at worship in the churches, the alarm sounded from the Bell Tower in Capitol Square, signifying that an attack of some kind was imminent. The churches were emptied, and the bewildered citizenry were told that the federal sloop-of-war, *Pawnee*, mounting four guns, was steaming up James River from Norfolk, to bombard the city. Men rushed for their shotguns, pistols and sabers, and the Howitzers marched off down Main Street, to fire on the foe from the riverbank with their six-pounders. Chimborazo Heights was crowded with anxious and palpitating ladies, and there was general confusion. It turned out to be a false alarm, and the warriors and the ladies returned sheepishly to their homes. For years thereafter, *"Pawnee* Sunday" would be a joke in Richmond.

With secession awaiting only a perfunctory popular ratification, a commander had to be found for the military and naval forces of Virginia. The convention brought forward the name of Colonel Robert E. Lee, who had made a spectacularly fine record in the war with Mexico and had served as superintendent of the United States Military Academy. In fact, Virginia-born General Winfield Scott, Lincoln's Chief of Staff and the first U.S. officer to hold the rank of lieutenant general since George Washington, termed Lee "the very best soldier I ever saw in the field."

On April 18, Lee had been offered the command of the United States Army, but he had declined. In agony of spirit, he returned to stately Arlington, paced the floor for hours and then submitted his resignation from the Army. Unlike his fellow Virginian General Scott, who remained with the Union, Lee concluded that his chief obligation was to Virginia. Aged General Scott, with a distinguished record in the War of 1812 and the Mexican War, told Lee, "You have made the greatest mistake of your life, but I feared it would be so."

Mrs. Lee wrote a friend that her husband "has wept tears of blood over this terrible war, but as a man of honor and as a Virginian, he must follow the destiny of his state." It meant their financial ruin and giving up their beloved Arlington—situated across the Potomac from Washington, and hence vulnerable to seizure by federal forces. Lee was willing to make these sacrifices although, as he wrote his sister, he recognized "no necessity" for secession. (The home he abandoned, known today as the Custis-Lee mansion, is a national shrine, by act of Congress.)

Despite his strong opposition to Virginia's leaving the Union, Lee took the train to Richmond on April 22, in response to a request from Governor Letcher. He was wearing civilian clothes and a silk hat. On his arrival, he went to the Spotswood Hotel, and after having supper, walked through Capitol Square to the governor's office. There the governor told him that the convention had passed an ordinance calling for the appointment of a major general to command Virginia's military and naval forces, and had recommended him for the post. Lee accepted, although he was fully aware of the heavy odds against the South and pessimistic from the first concerning the chances for ultimate victory.[7]

What manner of man was this fifty-four-year-old former cavalry colonel upon whom had fallen so grave a responsibility? Most of us probably have a picture in our minds of a handsome, gray-bearded soldier of immense dignity, who seldom, if ever, indulged in levity of any kind, who was always the unruffled master of himself, and without even the most minor human frailties. Let it be made completely clear that there can be no question concerning the nobility of Lee, his courage and integrity, his brilliance as a military leader, his gentlemanliness or his deep religious faith. Yet there has been too much oversimplification of Lee's character and personality, just as there has been in the case of George Washington. Both men were supremely great, but they were not perfect, and both revealed human qualities that are seldom associated with them in the public mind.

Lee, for example, derived more than ordinary enjoyment from the company of pretty women throughout his life. He was quietly humorous in his contacts with them, and harmlessly flirtatious in his younger days, even after his marriage to unglamorous, ungregarious Mary Ann

Randolph Custis, great-granddaughter of Martha Washington. In writing to his friend, Jack Mackay, in 1835, he referred rapturously to the lovely ladies of Old Point, saying: "They are formed of the very poetry of nature, and would make your lips water and your fingers tingle." In the same year, writing to Captain Andrew Talcott, his commanding officer, concerning a bridal party in Alexandria incident to the wedding of Lee's brother, Smith, Lee said that when he was "relieved from the eyes of my Dame," meaning his wife, the "sweet innocent things" at the party "concluded that I was single, and I have not had such soft looks and tender pressures of the hand for many years."

In 1863, during the Civil War, Lee was riding down Franklin Street in Richmond to his temporary home at Number 707. He noticed young Beverley D. Tucker, later the Episcopal Bishop of southern Virginia, paying court on the front steps of the Triplett house to beautiful Mary Triplett, soon to become the great belle over whom the Mordecai-McCarty duel was fought. The grizzled commander of the Army of Northern Virginia dismounted from his horse, walked over to Mary Triplett, and bent down and kissed her. He then turned to Tucker and said, "Wouldn't you like to do that, sir?", got back on his horse and proceeded on his way.[8]

Lee was known to lose his temper on rare occasions. The terrific strain of the war told on him, and there were occasional lapses, as there had to be. Mary Boykin Chesnut tells of one such episode in her book, *A Diary From Dixie.* Mrs. Chesnut was a close friend of General Wade Hampton. In March 1864, she wrote that Hampton "came with his troubles; Stuart had taken one of Hampton's brigades and given it to Fitzhugh Lee." And she went on:

"General Hampton complained of this to General Lee, who told him curtly, 'I would not care if you went back to South Carolina with your whole division.' Wade said his manner made this speech immensely mortifying. . . . It seems that General Lee has no patience with any personal complaints or grievances. He is all for the cause, and cannot bear officers to come to him with such matters as Wade Hampton had come about."

One can sympathize with Lee, while regretting this particular outburst. As a matter of fact, he thought highly of Hampton, but at that time he was troubled sorely by failing health; by the death of a beloved daughter-in-law, while her husband, "Rooney" Lee, was a Union prisoner at Johnson's Island; and by the gigantic task of organizing to meet the massive spring offensive toward Richmond that General U. S. Grant was preparing, with vastly superior numbers and resources.

Such future problems and ordeals must have been on Lee's mind in April 1861, as he stood before the convention in Richmond and formally accepted the command of Virginia's forces. He had a black mustache then, and his physical vigor and "manly bearing" greatly impressed those who saw him. He had often been called the handsomest man in the Army, and he had an erect military posture which made him seem taller than his five feet eleven inches. He would soon grow a beard, but it would turn almost white with the cares and anxieties that came to him during the next four years.

Lee's reasons for declining command of the Union forces and resigning his Army commission have been noted. Although strongly against secession, he could not bring himself to "raise my hand against my relatives, my children, my home."

Was he fighting to protect and perpetuate slavery? There were leaders in the South, especially in the cotton states, who were undoubtedly doing so, but not Lee. He had pronounced slavery "a moral and political evil in any country," and he never owned a slave except the few he inherited from his mother, all of whom he emancipated many years prior to the war.

Were the other principal Virginia generals seeking to preserve the slave system? "Stonewall" Jackson never owned but two slaves, both of whom he purchased at their own request. He promptly accorded them the right to buy their freedom, and one accepted. The other preferred to remain as his house servant. Joseph E. Johnston never owned a slave, and like Lee, was much opposed to slavery. The same was true of A. P. Hill. J. E. B. Stuart inherited one slave and purchased one but freed both several years before the war. Fitzhugh Lee never owned a slave. Matthew Fontaine Maury, who termed slavery "a curse," owned only one, a woman who remained with the family until her death some years after the war.[9]

While there were Virginians, such as George Fitzhugh and George Frederick Holmes, who desired to preserve the slave system and who regarded it as a blessing, the majority disagreed. Since in 1860 three-fourths of all white Virginians owned no slaves, it is hard to believe that they risked their lives by the thousands to protect slavery.

What, then, was Virginia fighting for? She had been harassed for decades by tariffs and other economic measures that discriminated in favor of the North. She had endured the tirades of the abolitionists over the years. John Brown had tried to lead a slave insurrection against her people and had been applauded by prominent Northerners as a saint and a martyr. Virginians were tired of all this discrimination, hostility and abuse. They felt that their rights as citizens of a sovereign state were being violated. They sought earnestly to avoid secession and to remain in the Union, but President Lincoln's call for volunteers to put down the seceding states caused them to conclude that this was impossible. Jefferson Davis said, "All we ask is to be let alone," and that expressed the feeling of many.

True, the *controversy* over slavery was the principal cause of the war, but Virginia did not risk her sons, her wealth and her very existence for the preservation of a discredited institution in which most of her people had no direct interest. In the final analysis, Virginia simply was driven against her will to seek independence.

At all events, the Old Dominion had taken the fateful step of seceding, and she would now have to suffer the consequences. Those consequences would be felt for many decades.

TWENTY-SEVEN

Manassas to Sharpsburg

INVASION of Virginia, the most exposed geographically of the seceding states, would not be long delayed. General Lee was faced with the urgent task of whipping the Old Dominion's feeble and disorganized military and naval forces into shape to resist the anticipated attack. He had to improvise under great pressure.

John M. Daniel, the bellicose editor who had had a leading role in bringing on the conflict, was realistic as to the condition of Virginia's defenses. "The state's public means of resistance is simply nil," he declared. "Virginia has a few serviceable arms and scarcely any powder. The whole amount on hand is 200 kegs and 240 more ordered." Volunteers were coming forward in throngs, but they were mostly raw recruits and they had little with which to fight. One of the worst hazards was invasion of Virginia via Chesapeake Bay and the great rivers flowing into it. Naval forces to resist such an incursion were well-nigh non-existent.

Lee was confronted with the colossal problem of finding competent military and naval officers, organizing a general staff, mobilizing and training a force for defense, acquiring and distributing arms, ammunition and ships, and devising a defensive strategy that would be effective. At the outset, of course, he was commander of Virginia's forces only. More than a year would pass before he was given command of the Army of Northern Virginia, which included units from the entire South.

"The war may last ten years," Lee wrote his wife on April 30. He cautioned against the foolish optimism that prevailed in some quarters. Any notion that the conflict would end in weeks or months with a southern victory seemed to him almost insane. He knew the northern people well, he said, and they would never yield without a long and desperate struggle.

The Confederacy's survival for as much as four years was due in large measure to the military leadership provided by Virginia. Politically, as we have seen, the Old Dominion played a secondary role in the decades before the war, but with such brilliant commanders as Robert E. Lee, Thomas J. ("Stonewall") Jackson and J. E. B. Stuart, the state would leap to a predominant position once more.

For the present, however, Lee's name was not well known to the average Virginian. As for Jackson and Stuart, the former was still celebrated mainly for his eccentricities as a member of the Virginia Military Institute faculty, and the latter, with his jaunty panache and dazzling charisma, had not yet come to public notice.

The Federals moved on Norfolk at once. They scuttled several warships there, to prevent them from falling into Confederate hands, and burned various waterfront buildings and barracks. Fortunately, the dry dock was not damaged and other valuable structures remained largely intact. Some 1200 badly needed cannon were seized by the Virginians, along with 2800 barrels of powder. They began fortifying Norfolk and Portsmouth, as well as erecting defenses along some of the rivers.

The machine shops at Harpers Ferry, on the northern fringe of the state, were of vital importance. The Federal arsenal there had been set on fire, and few of the small arms it contained could be salvaged by the Virginia forces when they arrived on the scene. Luckily, the shops for the manufacture of such arms were not badly damaged. Lee decided that Harpers Ferry was so vulnerable to Union attack that the shops with their machinery must be moved gradually to Richmond. However, he directed that they be kept in operation where they were as long as any part of the machinery continued to produce arms. Major Thomas J. Jackson was put in charge at Harpers Ferry. Thus began the Civil War career of the redoubtable "Stonewall."

With innumerable problems pressing down upon him, Lee worked long hours at his headquarters in the Mechanics Institute on Ninth Street. It was hardly to be expected that even Robert E. Lee, confronted with such enormous obstacles, could maintain an equable temper at all times. The fact is that he did not do so, if we are to believe Edward C. Gordon, who held the posts of proctor, librarian

and treasurer of Washington College under Lee after the war, and
was one of Lee's most unrestrained admirers. Gordon wrote that "in
the Confederate Army it was an open secret that when he [Lee] was
organizing Virginia's forces at the beginning of the war, he was regarded by the militia and other colonels who brought their regiments
to Richmond as a sort of 'bear' that when aroused should be avoided
by wise people." Gordon added—in a chapter on Lee which is an
almost unrelieved paean of praise—that the general had "a fierce and
violent temper, prone to intense expression," over which he had "almost perfect control." Obviously, the control was not quite perfect, as
Gordon was frank enough to admit.[1]

When the official call for volunteers went out during the first week
in May, there was an overwhelming response from most sections of
the commonwealth, but there was the problem of how to train these
eager, but raw, recruits. The VMI cadets were brought to Richmond to
drill them and instruct them in the use of artillery. South Carolina
units, many of whose men had Negro body servants, arrived in Richmond, as did the Louisiana Tigers, with a goodly percentage of thieves
and cutthroats. Regiments and companies from these and other southern states were eager to confront the foe. There was little realization in
those early days of the long, hard road ahead.

Many Negro volunteers, both slave and free, came forward in the
early stages. They offered in a number of different communities to do
any work assigned them. In late April, for example, volunteering
Petersburg blacks gathered in the courthouse square, where white
speakers thanked them and presented them with a Confederate flag.
Responding, their spokesman, Charles Tinsley, a bricklayer, said: "We
are willing to aid Virginia's cause to the utmost of our ability. . . .
There is not an unwilling heart among us . . . we promise unhesitating
obedience to all orders that may be given us."

Throughout the war, Virginia Negroes worked on fortifications, in
armament plants, as employees of quartermaster and commissary departments in the distribution of food, clothing and equipment for the
fighting forces, as blacksmiths, carpenters, tanners, cooks and shoemakers. They mined coal, manned river boats and maintained the railways. They rendered indispensable service in the hospitals.[2]

On the other hand, there was, throughout the war, a strong tendency
on the part of slaves to flee to the Union lines, where thousands joined
the Union Army. "The arrival of Union soldiers in any part of the

South marked the beginning of a flow of humanity toward the Federal camp," Bell I. Wiley has written, "and in many cases, the flow was so great that it carried away the bulk of the male slave population." He cites the case of Shirley Plantation below Richmond, where this occurred.

As for Negro body servants, many privates as well as officers had them at the outset of the war. A factor here was the prevailing tendency of young aristocrats to volunteer as privates and to bring one of their slaves along. After the first year of the war, however, only officers were likely to be found with body servants. These servants usually remained loyal to their masters and relieved them of much drudgery. A salient activity of the body servant appears to have been the raiding of henhouses for his master's delectation.[3]

The shortage of adequate weapons was a condition in the South that was to continue throughout the war. Most of the scant supply of rifles in Virginia in the spring of 1861 consisted of obsolete flintlocks. There were not enough pistols and sabers for the cavalry units— although horses were in good supply—and artillery was antiquated and insufficient. The heavy naval guns and powder seized in Norfolk were priceless assets, but the supply of shells was woefully inadequate. This situation was but a foretaste of that which would confront the Confederacy thenceforth. Almost invariably, for the next four years, its soldiers would have to meet larger and better-equipped and supplied Union armies. Only the genius of the southern military leaders and the fighting qualities of the troops could compensate for these disparities. The South did have the advantage of defending its homes and firesides from invasion. Militarily, it also had "interior lines," and its people were more accustomed to the outdoor life and to the use of firearms.

Richmond became the Confederate capital in May, in response to an invitation from the Virginia convention. The formal inauguration of Jefferson Davis as President would be held the following February. Transfer of the government's headquarters from Montgomery was of debatable wisdom, since it placed the capital of the Confederacy in an area close to Washington, subject to attack by both land and water. The defense of vulnerable Richmond became a moral necessity, and strategic imperatives had to give way, at times, to considerations of prestige.

Relations between President Davis and General Lee were of crucial importance, in view of the vital roles of both men. Lee was one of the persons around Davis with whom the Confederate President never had a serious breach. Davis was a brave, high-minded, dedicated and in some ways able man, but he interfered too much in military matters, and he did not get along well with many of those under him. He was subject to great strain throughout the war, and he had digestive problems, as well as eye trouble and agonizing facial neuritis. These disabilities serve to explain much of the irascibility which he showed on occasion. He was also under almost constant snarling attack from John M. Daniel and Edward A. Pollard in the *Examiner*, which added greatly to his burdens.

Lee's military proficiency, together with his organizing and administrative ability, made it possible, within seven weeks, for him to put together units totaling 40,000 men. They were soon absorbed into the Confederate forces.

Disaffection throughout a large part of what is now West Virginia soon became manifest. There was angry opposition to secession in this region where so often there had been strong disagreement with the Piedmont and Tidewater.

At Big Bethel, on the lower peninsula between the James and the York rivers, there was a small skirmish, in which the Union forces were driven back. Units under General Benjamin F. Butler had sought to move toward the Confederate capital from Fort Monroe, then in Federal hands. This slight reverse did not silence the cry of "On to Richmond!"—a city described in the New York *Tribune* as "a den of conspirators, plotting the destruction of the republic." Soon the Union leadership was preparing for the invasion of northern Virginia.

General Irvin McDowell moved across the Potomac on July 16 with 35,000 men, some of whom wore the gaudy uniforms of the New York Zouaves and the cock-feather hats of the Garibaldi Guards. They were a motley army, not well trained, in most instances, but neither were the Confederates.

General Pierre Gustave Toutant Beauregard, "the magnificent Creole," commanded the Southerners, numbering about 20,000 and based on the important railroad junction of Manassas. He called for aid from General Joseph E. Johnston, who had some 10,000 men in the Shenandoah Valley. Johnston started toward Manassas. Together they would almost match McDowell in strength.

As McDowell advanced, the Confederates fell back behind a small stream called Bull Run. Johnston was hurrying to Beauregard's assistance. His First Brigade was commanded by an as yet largely unknown General Jackson, and that brigade was first to cross the mountains, a foretaste of the exploits for which Jackson's "foot cavalry" would become famous. The green, half-trained soldiers covered more than twenty miles, much of it uphill, in passing through Ashby's Gap. When a halt was ordered at 2 A.M., they fell to the ground exhausted. "Let the poor fellows sleep," Jackson said. "I'll guard the camp myself."

When Johnston arrived at Manassas, he was slightly senior to Beauregard, and hence took command. The battle which followed on July 21 is remembered for a series of blunders on both sides, with the South erring more grievously in the early stages. The Confederates' left flank was being rolled up, and they seemed about to suffer a disastrous defeat, when General Jackson and his men saved the situation by their heroic stand on the Henry House Hill.

General Barnard Bee of South Carolina rushed up to Jackson, as Bee's demoralized troops streamed toward the rear, and said, "General, they are beating us back!" "Sir," answered the always imperturbable Jackson, "we will give them the bayonet!"

Bee shouted to his fleeing men: "There stands Jackson like a stone wall! Rally behind the Virginians!"

The troops rallied, the tide turned, and Thomas Jonathan Jackson would be known ever after as "Stonewall." General Bee fell mortally wounded.

The fighting was by no means over. There was charge and countercharge as the men of the North and the South sweated and struggled through woods and fields, across streams and gullies in the July heat. The weird and blood-chilling "rebel yell," heard on many a field later in the war, first rent the air at this time.

Federal artillery got the range of the Henry House Hill, and Jackson might have been in serious trouble, had not a ruddy-bearded twenty-nine-year-old cavalry major named J. E. B. Stuart swept across at the head of his men and eliminated the infantry support for the batteries. More units from Johnston's forces were thrown into the fight at the psychological moment, and the Union Army was driven back.

Late in the afternoon, the Union retreat became a rout, believed to have been set off when a Confederate shell burst over a small bridge. This caused panic, especially among the congressmen, Cabinet members, clerks, curiosity-seekers and their ladies who had driven out from Washington, with picnic baskets, to witness the Confederate debacle which they considered inevitable. Senator Henry Wilson of Massachusetts made a precipitate departure on board an army mule, leaving behind the dancing pumps he had brought along for the scheduled "victory ball" in Richmond. The panic spread to the already demoralized Union troops, who joined the putative picnickers in headlong flight across the Potomac.

"Stonewall" Jackson asked for 10,000 men, that he might pursue the fleeing Federals into Washington. Longstreet had a fresh brigade which might have been used for a similar purpose. There was no pursuit. However, it is by no means certain that the Confederates could have taken Washington, despite the prevailing Union demoralization. McDowell still had an entire division that had not been engaged in the fighting, as well as portions of others that might have put up an effective resistance. The Southerners, furthermore, were suffering from battle fatigue. But a great Confederate opportunity may have been missed.

Although eager to lead an assault on the nation's capital, the devout General Jackson, hot and dusty from combat, suddenly realized that he had forgotten something. Next day he wrote his pastor in Lexington:

"In my tent last night, after a fatiguing day's service, I remembered that I failed to send you my contribution to our colored Sunday school. Enclosed you will find my check for that object."

"A fatiguing day's service!" That was Jackson's sole reference to one of the decisive battles in American history, a battle in which he had been a hero.

Exultation in Richmond over the victory was mingled with sorrow for the fallen. Trainloads of wounded arrived, and the bodies of the slain were brought back and laid to rest in Hollywood and Oakwood cemeteries. The "Dead March" from Saul echoed through the streets, and the mournful music was so prolonged and unending that a woman diarist wrote, "It comes and it comes, until I feel inclined to close my eyes and scream."

To less thoughtful Southerners, First Manassas proved that the war would end with a Confederate victory. Others were shocked into a realization that the triumph there had been dearly won, and that but for a fortunate turn of events, the battle might well have gone the other way.

As for the North, it was suddenly made aware that it was in for a long and bloody struggle. Elements of the northern press sought to arouse the people with preposterous accounts of mythical southern "atrocities." Consider the following from the Cincinnati *Enquirer:*

"Nothing in all this war has more deeply stirred the heart of the community than the dreadful barbarities inflicted by the rebel soldiers upon our fallen men in the retreat from Manassas. Every report confirms the shocking fact that they bayoneted our wounded soldiers all along the road for miles, cut them in quarters, kicked about their severed heads in fiendish sport, tied them naked to trees, tormented them with knives and many other barbarities never before heard of in a civilized community. . . . This worse than Fiji manner is attributable to the barbarism of slavery."

General Lee had remained in Richmond throughout the battle, since President Davis deemed his services at the capital to be essential. However, Lee had been to a considerable degree the organizer of victory, for it was he who had done the vital preliminary work that enabled the Virginia soldiery, constituting about one-fourth of those on the field, to go to the front with enough training and poise to meet the Federals on even terms. Lee also had a leading role in devising the strategy used by the Confederates in the engagement.

One week after the victory at Manassas, Davis sent Lee on a vaguely defined and well-nigh impossible mission in the mountains of western Virginia. He instructed Lee to iron out the differences between Generals Henry A. Wise and John B. Floyd, two temperamental former governors of the state, and General W. W. Loring. Each of the three had a separate command, and there was hostility and jealousy rather than co-ordination. Lee was without authority over these feuding prima donnas, although still the nominal commander of Virginia's forces. What was needed was a knocking together of heads rather than attempts at tactful persuasion, which latter approach was the only one available to Lee. His efforts proved futile. When many of Virginia's western counties went over to the enemy that winter, Lee got much of the blame. He accepted it uncomplainingly, as always. While he had been given a virtually insoluble problem, complicated by torrential rains and bottomless mud, a rougher and tougher man might have achieved better results. Lee's gentlemanliness, his humility, his unwillingness to be sharply categorical and critical in expressing his views, would plague him throughout much of the war.

When later he enjoyed the full authority that he lacked in western
Virginia in 1861, he would, on certain occasions, be too reluctant to
use it.

Lee returned to Richmond from his unglamorous and unsuccessful expedition into the mountains, wearing a beard for the first time.
Beards had become fashionable shortly before in the Crimean War,
and the Civil War generals adopted the style. Lee was greeted on
his arrival in Richmond by sneers from the press, which referred to
him derisively as "Granny" Lee and "Evacuating" Lee. It was strongly
hinted that he was timid and overcautious. No weight seems to have
been given to the fact that he was sent on a virtually impossible
mission. Stung by the criticism, Lee remarked sardonically that it was
a great mistake to have allowed "all our worst generals to command
armies, and all our best generals to edit the newspapers."

President Davis dispatched Lee to Charleston, South Carolina,
where he was given the job of fortifying that city and Savannah and
the various nearby coastal waterways against amphibious advances. It
was an important but uninspiring task, rendered doubly so by the
invidious comment of the *Examiner*. That newspaper expressed the
hope that Lee would prove more effective with the spade than he
had with the sword. Davis brought Lee back to Richmond in March.
His reputation with the public was in tatters, and few could have
foretold the future that awaited him. Fortunately, he retained the full
confidence of Davis.

Meanwhile, "Stonewall" Jackson, through no fault of his, had run
into serious difficulties that almost ended his military career. Jackson
had set out for Romney, in the mountains of what is now West
Virginia, on January 1, 1862. Major General Jackson's forces were
co-operating in bitter winter weather with those of Brigadier General
Loring, and after occupying Romney, Jackson ordered Loring to hold
it while he marched his men back to Winchester. Loring decided
that Romney was of no importance, and he and his officers petitioned
Confederate Secretary of War Judah P. Benjamin for permission to
withdraw from those frigid mountains to more comfortable quarters.
Benjamin, who was greatly gifted in many directions, but who was
wholly without experience in military matters, made an honest mistake
and granted the petition. It had been unwise, in the first place, to
give Benjamin the war portfolio. He had served briefly and with distinction as the Confederate Attorney General, and he was soon to

serve ably as Secretary of State. His action in overriding Jackson's orders without consulting him quite naturally outraged that stickler for proper military procedure. Jackson resigned from the Army and requested that he sent back to teaching at VMI.

The stir caused by this can well be imagined. Governor Letcher, Confederate congressmen and General Joseph E. Johnston promptly got into the act. Johnston wrote Benjamin that "the discipline of the army cannot be maintained under such circumstances." Although Jackson was so eccentric and grimly Calvinistic that some considered him insane,[4] the prevailing view was that his services in the Army were indispensable. Secretary Benjamin realized his error and was amenable to reason. The matter was smoothed over and Jackson stayed.

Shortly before this controversy arose, James M. Mason of Virginia and John Slidell of Louisiana, emissaries from the Confederacy to Britain and France, respectively, were taken forcibly from the British passenger ship *Trent* by an American man-of-war and lodged in a Boston jail. They had run the blockade, in the hope of getting European assistance for the South. A loud protest from the British Government secured their release, and they were allowed to proceed to London and Paris. Unfortunately, disasters to southern arms at Fort Henry and Fort Donelson on the Tennessee River lessened their chances of obtaining European aid.

These military reverses in the Confederate "West" occurred almost simultaneously with another at Roanoke Island, North Carolina, a fortified point strategically important to southeastern Virginia. The defense had not been adequately prepared, and Roanoke Island was taken by General Ambrose Burnside with "the first amphibian force used on the Western continent." General Henry A. Wise was in command of the Confederates, and his son, Captain O. Jennings Wise of the Richmond Light Infantry Blues, was mortally wounded in the disastrous action. Jennings Wise's funeral in Richmond, attended by a huge throng which included Confederate and Virginia dignitaries, awakened the people of the Old Dominion to the grim realities.

Manassas was fading into the past and Confederate arms were sustaining a succession of defeats. The one-year enlistments were expiring, and General George McClellan's invasion of Virginia via the peninsula would soon begin. Lee was the chief mover, in this critical situation, for the enactment of conscription by the Confederate Congress.

The provisions of the Conscription Act, when passed, were not as strong as Lee wanted. The upper and lower age limits were eighteen and thirty-five, whereas he preferred forty-five. Owners of twenty or more slaves were exempt, a provision which did nothing to raise the morale of those who owned just a few slaves or none at all, but in fairness it should be said that many large slaveowners enlisted voluntarily and fought well. The law also permitted the hiring of "substitutes," thus making it possible for reluctant warriors to pay somebody else to do their fighting—another highly dubious provision. But with enlistments expiring in a hundred Confederate regiments, the new legislation came just in time to prevent catastrophe, for McClellan was about to march up the Peninsula.

Then, as he was on the point of launching his invasion, a strange Confederate naval vessel, with armorplate made of railroad iron, moved ponderously out of Norfolk toward the Union fleet in Hampton Roads. She was the onetime Federal ship *Merrimack* sunk the year before by the Federals, but now raised by the Confederates, fitted out in this bizarre fashion, and rechristened the *Virginia*. There were several Negro slaves in the crew.

The massed Union warships, made of wood almost exactly like those that had fought half a century before in the War of 1812, fired broadsides at the intruder, but the cannon shot bounced harmlessly from the *Virginia*'s sloping armorplate. The Confederate ship closed in, rammed and sank the fifty-gun Union warship *Cumberland*, and then turned and went for the *Congress*. The last-named wooden vessel caught fire from the *Virginia*'s shelling and surrendered. Naval warfare had been revolutionized in a single day, and the navies of the world were suddenly obsolete. There was near panic in the Union Cabinet, and one member predicted that the *Virginia* would be shelling the White House "before we leave this room."

Such mobility on the part of the *Virginia* was impossible, since her slowness of movement was her greatest handicap. Furthermore, her seeming invulnerability was to be countered at once by the timely appearance of another revolutionary vessel, the *Monitor*. This Union ironclad was constructed along different lines. Described as a "cheese box on a raft," the *Monitor* had a revolving turret of iron, and drew only twelve feet of water to twenty-three for the *Virginia*.

When the *Virginia* moved out next morning with a view to wrecking the entire Union fleet, one by one, she found the *Monitor* standing athwart her path. The guns of both ships opened up, but neither was able to damage the other. After two hours of this futile bombardment, the *Virginia* tried unsuccessfully to ram the *Monitor*. Then the Confederate ship sought to move alongside so that her men could board the *Monitor* for hand-to-hand combat. The Federal vessel sheered off and dropped astern. After six hours, during which neither side did any appreciable damage to the other, the *Monitor* moved into water too shallow for the *Virginia* to follow. It was a drawn battle. Yet tactically it was a victory for the Federal ship, since she was still in being, and able to protect the Union fleet from destruction. The *Virginia* still barred McClellan from using the James, but he could proceed with his plans for invasion via the York. Furthermore, the Union blockade, one of the decisive factors in the war, would be drawn ever tighter, strangling the Confederacy by shutting off vital weapons, food, medicines and other supplies.

As if this wasn't enough bad news, there were the depressing tidings from Shiloh and Island No. 10 in the "West." Then suddenly Confederate hearts were lifted when Longstreet's infantry division and cavalry units under "Jeb" Stuart passed through Richmond en route to join Joseph E. Johnston's defenses on the peninsula. The bands played "Dixie," and ladies tossed flowers at the mudstained, often shoeless infantrymen. The latter took the daffodils and hyacinths and stuck them in their caps or their rifle barrels, as the crowds thronging the curb cheered, and the men responded with the rebel yell. There was the sound of bugles on the soft spring air as cavalrymen rode down Franklin Street, pretty girls waved handkerchiefs and threw kisses from windows, and the horsemen bowed in graceful acknowledgment. It was April 17, the first anniversary of secession. The enemy soon would be at Richmond's gates and many of the marching, laughing men would die; but violets perfumed the air on that golden morning in 1862, and the city would forget the mud and blood of war in the excitement of the hour.

McClellan was moving slowly toward Richmond, with about 105,000 men. He was informed by his intelligence that the Confederates opposing him numbered 200,000, whereas the actual figure was around 85,000. His faulty information was due in large measure to the inept performance of Allan Pinkerton, the famous detective, who was head of the U. S. Secret Service. Thanks partly to this circumstance, the Union commander hesitated to pursue an aggressive plan of attack.

As McClellan neared Richmond, he encountered the always swampy terrain on both sides of the meandering Chickahominy River, and this, added to the almost bottomless mud caused by spring rains on the primitive roads, was a further deterrent. However, Johnston, aware of his own numerical inferiority, retreated before McClellan, until the latter's advance units were within sight of Richmond's spires and within the sound of its church bells.

Norfolk, meanwhile, was taken over by the Federals. The virtually surrounded city could not be effectively defended, so it was evacuated. The Navy Yard was burned to prevent its falling into enemy hands, and shipping offshore was also destroyed. The armor-plated *Virginia*, which had made naval history, had to be burned to prevent her capture.

With the loss of this epoch-making vessel, the Confederate Navy was vastly reduced in capability, although Secretary of the Navy Mallory performed prodigies with very little. So did Commander Matthew Fontaine Maury, whose torpedoes, as noted in Chapter Twenty-four, were so very effective.

Following loss of the *Virginia*, Confederate fortifications were erected in frantic haste at Drewry's Bluff on the James below Richmond, with a view to preventing a Federal incursion. Federal warships, the formidable *Monitor* among them, steamed up the river on May 15, and opened a bombardment against the unfinished gun emplacements on the heights. The Confederate artillerymen there were devastatingly accurate, and the attackers were driven back downstream.

This gave encouragement to Richmond, as it faced what appeared to be an imminent Union assault by land. The Virginia General Assembly voted to put the city to the torch, rather than surrender, and citizens promised to burn their homes. There were plans for firing the Capitol and blowing up the statue of Washington in the square.[5]

Johnston attacked McClellan on May 31. In the ensuing Battle of Seven Pines, Johnston was severely wounded. Jefferson Davis named Robert E. Lee to succeed him in command. It was a turning point in the war, for now the Confederate forces in the Old Dominion would be led by one of history's greatest military geniuses. Lee promptly named the force defending Richmond the "Army of Northern Virginia."

There was no enthusiasm from the Army or the public over the appointment of Lee. He was still under a cloud, as a result of the unfair criticism following his unsuccessful efforts in the western mountains and his unexciting mission to fortify Charleston and Savannah. Not only so, but when he immediately put his soldiers to work building vital fortifications in front of Richmond, he was contemptuously dubbed the "King of Spades." His supposed excess of caution was contrasted with the *élan* and aggressive spirit of "Stonewall" Jackson. Actually, without Lee's masterful overall strategic concepts, Jackson's triumphs in the Valley would have been impossible.

Jackson, at that moment, was leading his troops in one of the most memorable campaigns in the annals of war. In the Shenandoah Valley his half-trained army was outmaneuvering and outfighting much larger Federal forces. Jackson moved with astonishing speed, and always with the element of surprise. In three weeks, from May 19 to June 9, beginning with a force of 6000 that was never larger than 19,000 he defeated, eluded or nullified Federal forces totaling 65,000.

Jackson hit Union General N. P. Banks like a thunderbolt at Winchester and drove him all the way across the Potomac, seizing enormous quantities of supplies in the process. This brought such alarm to the United States Government that President Lincoln, fearing an attack on Washington, wired McClellan that instructions to McDowell to join him were being countermanded. Those were the reinforcements for which McClellan had long been waiting in front of Richmond, and now they were gone. Jackson had thrown such consternation into the North that Lincoln even withdrew units from McDowell's command near Fredericksburg and sent them chasing the elusive "Stonewall" in the Valley. At the same time, he ordered General J. C. Fremont to assail "Old Jack"—aged thirty-eight—from another direction, while a third Union force was coming at him from still another. Jackson slipped between two of these attacking forces, and on successive days, at Cross Keys and Port Republic, gave each of them a bloody nose.

That ended Federal efforts to trap and smash Jackson in the renowned Valley Campaign—a classic studied in the military academies of the world. "Stonewall's" chief object—to prevent the reinforcement of McClellan by McDowell in front of Richmond—had been accomplished, although he had sustained a great professional and personal loss in the death of General Turner Ashby.

Through it all, the First Brigade was the spearhead of Jackson's lethal thrusts. Called the Stonewall Brigade from the time of its glorious baptism of fire at First Manassas, it was later compared to "the Macedonian Phalanx of Alexander, the Tenth Legion of Caesar, the Paladins of Charlemagne, the Ironsides of Cromwell, and the Old Guard of Napoleon." Its historian, James I. Robertson Jr., terms it with justice "the most renowned [brigade] in Confederate military history." Decimated by casualties during four years of fighting, during which it was usually given the most dangerous and difficult missions, only 210 of its 2600 original members would stack arms at Appomattox.

Jackson's Valley campaign was barely over when Colonel J. E. B. Stuart electrified the South with one of the most spectacular feats of the war. Lee had instructed him to scout in the rear of the enemy along the Chickahominy. On the morning of June 12, with 1200 men, including the gigantic Heros von Borcke, the Prussian dragoon who had run the blockade to fight for the Confederacy, Stuart moved. This was no time for flags and bugles, or for the minstrelsy of banjo-thrumming "Joe" Sweeny, who entertained Stuart's men in their lighter moments. Quietly and without fanfare, the horsemen trotted out of Richmond along the Brook Turnpike, and many who saw them guessed that they were heading for the Valley to reinforce Jackson. But they turned eastward beyond Ashland. Occasional enemy pickets were encountered as the scouting force penetrated deep into Union-occupied territory. In Hanover County, Captain William Latané's Essex Light Dragoons collided suddenly with Union cavalrymen. There was a sharp fight with sabers and pistols, and Latané was shot dead.

By the time Stuart had reached the vicinity of Old Church, he had gotten the information Lee wanted concerning the Federals. The normal course for Stuart would have been to return to Richmond over the route by which he had come. But the audacious cavalryman decided otherwise. He would ride entirely around McClellan's army and enter Richmond from the east. This he did, past Tunstall, Talleysville, and Charles City Courthouse, across McClellan's lines of communication and through areas where there were scattered units of Union troops and supply depots. He was back in Richmond June 15, bringing 165 prisoners and 260 captured animals—all with the loss of exactly one man, Captain Latané. This amazing feat, combined with the much more far-reaching victories of Jackson in the Valley, brought encouragement to the South at a time when a long series of reverses had greatly damaged Confederate morale.

But Lee, defending Richmond, was facing a force larger than his own—a well-equipped, well-armed and disciplined host, the most formidable yet put together on American soil. He boldly decided to bring Jackson secretly from the Valley, in an effort to destroy the Union Army. The risks were great, but Lee was never afraid of risks.

Jackson and his assistant adjutant general, Major Robert L. Dabney—an eminent Presbyterian clergyman unaccountably chosen for that post—left for Richmond in a closed railroad car. Getting out at Frederick's Hall they mounted horses after midnight and proceeded to their rendezvous with Lee. Jackson said his men could be in position on McClellan's flank at dawn on June 26, and all plans were made on that assumption. But Jackson and his men failed, for once, to meet a timetable. They were a day late, for reasons not fully explained, and Jackson himself arrived in a state of near-exhaustion from lack of sleep, a situation that would seriously damage his effectiveness throughout the Seven Days' Battles. He actually went to sleep one night at supper with a biscuit in his mouth.

Under these inauspicious circumstances, Lee launched the campaign. It involved battles at Mechanicsville on June 26, Gaines's Mill, June 27, Savage's Station, June 29, Frayser's Farm, June 30 and Malvern Hill, July 1. The muddy terrain along the Chickahominy swamps and in much of the rest of the area was a handicap for both sides, but Lee's maps were inferior to those of the Federals, strange as that must seem. The Federals also had greatly superior artillery and used it more effectively. Lee had to rely heavily on a single factory for his ordnance, the Tredegar Iron Works at Richmond, and such guns as he had were not deployed to the best advantage. Furthermore, Lee lacked an effective general staff.

One result of all this was that in almost every engagement, Lee launched attacks on McClellan at the points and under the circumstances that McClellan preferred. There was the Confederate slaughter when A. P. Hill attacked at Beaver Dam Creek, near Mechanicsville, on the opening day. There was the even greater slaughter at Malvern Hill on the final day, with similar examples in between.

"Stonewall" Jackson, utterly used up by a series of long, tiring rides to and from the Valley, combined with practically no sleep, was almost wholly ineffective throughout. One result was that Lee's golden opportunity at Frayser's Farm to destroy the Union Army was missed. Jackson, the man whose tremendous drive and dynamism made him a

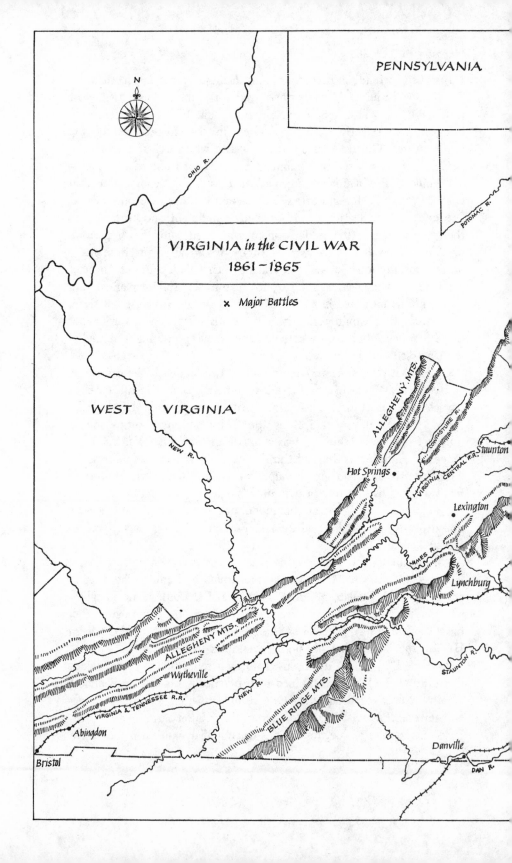

palacios

legend on two continents, suddenly seemed almost paralyzed, mentally and physically. He slept under a tree in broad daylight beside White Oak Swamp, instead of rushing to Longstreet's aid. When he woke up, he seemed in a trance, and totally unaware that the last chance to annihilate McClellan was slipping away.

After Malvern Hill—with its dreadful toll of southern youth, who charged fearlessly time and again in the face of massed Federal artillery—the rain came pouring down. Any opportunity that Lee had to pursue the Union Army effectively was made hopeless by the water and mud. McClellan succeeded in getting his battered forces to Harrison's Landing on the James, where, under the protection of Federal gunboats, he could not be reached. The following month, the Union commander abandoned his effort to take Richmond and began moving his troops by water to cantonments near Washington.

Confederate soldiers in bloody bandages had begun pouring into Richmond after the Battle of Seven Pines, and the flow of the wounded and maimed mounted with each engagement. Nearly 16,000 men in Lee's army were wounded during the fighting which began May 31 and ended July 1. By every available means of transport—wagons, ambulances, private carriages and public hacks—armless men, legless men, men with other dreadful injuries were brought groaning over the rough roads to the huge hospital on Chimborazo Heights, to the great Winder Hospital near the western edge of the city on Cary Street, and to dozens of smaller hospitals. Accommodations were swamped by this deluge of suffering Confederates, and many died for lack of attention. It was nobody's fault. The doctors worked almost around the clock. The women of Richmond, in particular, were eager to help and zealous in providing all possible comforts, often in their homes. But the need was too great to be met by the available personnel and facilities.

Yet, in the face of many handicaps and obstacles, Richmond had been saved. General Lee was no longer the "King of Spades"; on the contrary he was suddenly the idol of Virginia and the South. Lee's success in driving McClellan from the gates of the Confederate capital combined with Jackson's manhandling of several strong Union forces in the Valley convinced many Virginians that the South could never be defeated.

But Lee was not misled by such superficial thinking. In defending Richmond, he had lost some 11,000 of his best soldiers, including thousands of the bravest who had patriotically volunteered at the outbreak of war. They were either dead, wounded or otherwise out of action "for the duration," and they could never be replaced. The South's total casualties had been more than 4000 greater than those of the North, and the North had a nearly inexhaustible reservoir of manpower, not to mention arms, food, money and productive capacity. The South, by contrast, was using up its limited supply of men and materiel, its farm lands were being ravaged on a wider and wider scale, its railroads were being torn up, its currency was declining steadily in value, and the blockade was taking its deadly toll.

It might be supposed also that the presence of 3,500,000 black slaves in the South, 490,000 of whom were in Virginia, posed the constant threat of a servile insurrection. However, the Army of Northern Virginia could never have fought effectively, if there had been any real danger of a slave uprising in its rear, endangering the wives and children of the soldiers. No such uprising occurred throughout the four years of war. There were occasional minor conspiracies and plots, but they were promptly put down, with execution of those responsible.[6]

Booker T. Washington wrote after the war that "to defend and protect the women and children who were left on the plantations when the white males went to war, the slaves would have laid down their lives." He also stated that when the young masters on the Virginia plantation where he was a slave were killed or wounded, "the sorrow in the slave quarters was only second to that in the 'big house.'" Yet Washington declared that he had never seen a slave "who did not want to be free, or who would return to slavery."[7]

William H. Ruffner, State Superintendent of Public Instruction, said in his annual report for 1871 that "during the late war the Negroes of Richmond contributed thousands of dollars to sustain the Confederacy."

Yet the fact remains that many slaves, particularly the younger field hands, in Virginia and every other Confederate state, fled to the Union lines whenever the northern armies came within easy reach. Tens of thousands of them, including 5700 from Virginia, went over to the Federals and enlisted in the Union Army.[8] This not only meant added military manpower for the North, but it lowered agricultural production in Virginia and the rest of the Confederacy.

With Richmond saved from McClellan's invading force, Lee decided that the time had come to go on the offensive. This despite the fact that he might expect to be outnumbered and outgunned, as usual, unless he could, by superior generalship, bring greater numbers and firepower to bear at critical points.

Lee's adversary would be General John Pope, who had won a measure of fame in the West, and who took over in northern Virginia with bombast and braggadocio. In a statement addressed to the officers and men of his new command, Pope erupted:

"I have come to you from the West, where we have always seen the backs of our enemies; from an army whose business it has been to seek the adversary, and to beat him when he is found . . . I desire you to dismiss from your mind certain phrases, which I am sorry to find so much in vogue amongst you. I hear constantly of 'taking strong positions and holding them,' of 'lines of retreat,' and of 'bases of supplies.' Let us discard such ideas . . . disaster and shame lurk in the rear."

Pope added that "My headquarters will be in the saddle." This led to the wry observation on the part of some who were not charmed by his arrogance that he had "put his headquarters where his hindquarters ought to be."

Before Pope's main army became engaged with that of Lee, heavy fighting broke out between Jackson and Banks at Cedar Mountain. Jackson attacked Banks with superior forces, but Banks put up a terrific battle. At one point, the Confederates were hard pressed and falling back, with symptoms of an incipient rout. Grasping the situation in an instant, Jackson stormed into the melee on his horse—bareheaded, so as to be easily recognized—and with drawn sword shouted, "Rally brave men, and press forward! Your General will lead you! Jackson will lead you! Follow me!" The effect was electric, the retreat ended, and the Confederates achieved a narrow victory.

A week later, "Jeb" Stuart and his entire staff barely escaped capture at the hamlet of Verdiersville. They were surprised by Union cavalry and had to run for it through woods and fields. Stuart's famous plumed hat, by which he had come to be recognized, fell into Union hands. Much more serious was the loss of a dispatch case containing Lee's plan for attacking Pope.

But Stuart was soon avenged. At Catlett's Station, well in the rear of Pope's forces, "Jeb's" cavalry captured most of Pope's staff, his personal baggage, and his papers, containing his battle plans. Pope's dress coat was seized, and later displayed in a Richmond store window, with a card labeled "Headquarters in the saddle" and "the rear taking care of itself."

Lee and Jackson were now in a position to seek the destruction of the swaggering Pope, who had prophesied so dire a fate for their forces. They determined upon a highly risky operation, calling for splitting their numerically inferior army, in the face of the Federals, and sending nearly half of it on a fifty-mile encircling movement. The last-named hazardous maneuver was the sort of mission for which "Stonewall" Jackson and his "foot cavalry" had shown an especial genius.

Jackson's men didn't know where they were going when they were ordered to march at dawn on August 25, with scarcely any equipment, except their rifles. They were to stuff three days' rations into their haversacks and pockets. Many of the rations, as it turned out, were only half-cooked, the beef raw and without salt—and this in steaming August weather!

Yet Jackson's indomitable men executed the march on schedule, covering over fifty miles and passing through Amisville, Orleans, Salem (now Marshall), White Plains (The Plains), and through Thoroughfare Gap to Gainesville. En route, they had tried to remedy the glaring deficiency in their food supply by foraging along the road for green apples and green corn. The immediate effect on their digestive systems can be imagined, but they kept going somehow, and arrived on Pope's extreme right flank and in his rear. Pope, meanwhile, was wholly unaware of Jackson's whereabouts. He knew that "Stonewall" had disappeared, but that was all.

Jackson's men were astride Pope's main line of rail communications. They stopped a train, on which a U. S. Congressman with a broken ankle was traveling. Informed that the train had fallen into Jackson's hands, the congressman asked to be given a glimpse of the mighty "Stonewall." He was raised to the window just as Jackson went by, dusty and begrimed, his faded and ill-fitting uniform hanging loosely on his angular frame, and the usual frowzy cap over his eyes.

"O my God, lay me down again!" exclaimed the ailing statesman.

Jackson's men were utterly exhausted, but their commander found that Manassas Junction, only a few miles away, was a major Union supply depot. He must have it at once. Two regiments were ordered into action at midnight, and they stormed the position and took it. Next day, the magnitude of what they had taken became apparent.

Pope's enormous supply depot at Manassas Junction was a sight
for the tired eyes and a Mecca for the hungry stomachs of Jackson's
ragged, weary men. Like famished animals they descended on the vast
array of bulging warehouses, loaded freight cars and barrels of food
extending for miles. After subsisting for weeks on the most meager
rations, and marching great distances at high speeds with little rest,
their zest at finding this incredible array of food, drink and clothing
can well be imagined. With thousands of barrels of flour, salt pork
and corned beef to be had for the taking, as well as quantities of
such delicacies as lobster, candy, nuts and oranges, not to mention
whiskey, champagne and cigars, the problem of what to seize and
what to leave was almost insoluble. However, the men were happy
to load themselves up internally and externally to the limit of their
abilities. Teetotaler Jackson gave orders that they were not to have
any of the liquor and that the barrels were to be drained. "I fear
that liquor more than Pope's army," said "Stonewall." The boys
managed to acquire some of it, nevertheless. In addition to Jackson's
seizure of pork, flour and beef, huge quantities of ammunition fell
into his hands, as well as sorely needed ether, chloroform, shirts, soap,
toothbrushes, boots and blankets.

It now became necessary to deal with Pope's army, which was far
larger than Lee's. Longstreet moved along the same route that Jackson
had covered in marching around Pope, and on August 29 Lee ordered him to attack. The order was three times repeated, but Longstreet finally talked Lee out of it, and delivered the attack next day.
It came from the flank, and Pope was driven back, although not in
complete disorder. Jackson then drove his weary men against the
Federals at Chantilly in a violent thunderstorm.

The overall result of the fighting was that Pope pulled his forces
back to the Potomac. Virginia was once more almost completely
clear of the invader. Pope was relieved of his command, and McClellan
was put in charge once more.

Pope's army might have been destroyed, if Longstreet had attacked
on the day he was ordered to do so. This, however, is not certain. The
truly ominous fact is that Lee, for the first time, allowed a subordinate
to dispute his order. Less than a year later, at Gettysburg, Longstreet
would do it again, with results gravely serious for the Confederacy.

Lee had, for the present, removed the threat to Northern Virginia,
as he had removed the earlier threat to Richmond. In both instances

he had driven back forces larger than his own. But now he was in the presence of even larger armies, numbering at least 120,000, and he had only about 53,000. He could not stand still and wait to be overwhelmed; he must take the offensive before the enemy could envelop him. As with Danton in the French Revolution, Lee's motto was *l'audace, l'audace et toujours de l'audace!*

His audacious plan was to invade Maryland at once. In doing so he would be able to obtain badly needed supplies for his army, and he might catch the pursuing Federals off guard and wreck them in detail. He also hoped to arouse Confederate sympathies in Maryland. Lee planned to cut the line of the Baltimore & Ohio Railroad, and destroy the Pennsylvania Railroad bridge over the Susquehanna River near Harrisburg, Pennsylvania. Then, he said, "I can turn my attention to Philadelphia, Baltimore or Washington, as may seem best for our interests." He was hopeful of achieving so stunning a victory that world opinion would be influenced, and the Confederacy recognized as an independent nation.

At this critical juncture, the Army of Northern Virginia was short of everything except morale. When a regiment passed through Leesburg, a woman who was watching threw up her hands and exclaimed tearfully, "The Lord bless your dirty, ragged souls!" A boy sitting on a rail fence in Maryland described the soldiers in later years as "the dirtiest men I ever saw, a most ragged, lean and hungry set of wolves, yet there was a dash about them that the Northern men lacked; they rode like circus riders."

After wading across the Potomac, the Army headed for Frederick, with the bands playing "Maryland, My Maryland!" While in Frederick, the mythical episode of aged Barbara Frietschie's defiant Union flag-waving, embalmed for posterity in Whittier's poem, is supposed to have occurred. It never happened, but an episode that did occur, and that involved the finding by the enemy of Lee's written plan of campaign, may well have changed the whole course of the war. For an unknown Confederate staff officer left a copy of the plan wrapped around three cigars, and then lost the cigars. The entire package was picked up near Frederick when McClellan's troops arrived. The Federals were able to make their dispositions accordingly. Lee's ability, under such adverse circumstances, to stand off McClellan's much larger force, is evidence of his generalship and of the southern will to win.

He sent Jackson to take Harpers Ferry, and with it the Union garrison of 11,000. The Battle of Sharpsburg, or Antietam, which followed on September 17 was one of the bloodiest of the entire war, with terrible casualties on both sides. A. P. Hill came up from Harpers Ferry with vital Confederate reinforcements, which probably prevented a Confederate debacle. A more aggressive commander than McClellan would have followed up next day with further attacks on the southern forces, but he allowed Lee to withdraw across the Potomac into Virginia.

Lee had failed to reach his objective, and that failure had widespread repercussions. Many think of Gettysburg as "the high tide of the Confederacy," but Sharpsburg would seem to have a more valid claim. In the words of Clifford Dowdey, "politically, the war ended at Sharpsburg for the Confederacy . . . that was the last chance the Southern states had really to win independence."

Not only did the military situation tend to be "downhill" for the South from that time onward, but Lincoln seized upon the Confederate reverse at Sharpsburg as the opportunity he had been seeking to issue his Emancipation Proclamation. The proclamation freed not a single slave, since it specifically excluded all slaves in the border states or other areas under Federal control, such as the Virginia "counties of Berkeley, Accomack, Northampton, Elizabeth City, York, Princess Anne and Norfolk, including the cities of Norfolk and Portsmouth." Hence the proclamation was clearly a war measure, designed to defeat the South militarily. It was also a great propaganda coup, since it had the effect, throughout the world, of putting the Confederacy on the defensive with respect to slavery, and making the invasion of the South appear to be a "crusade for human freedom." One of the first results was to end all reasonable hope that Great Britain and France would recognize Confederate independence. If Lee had won at Sharpsburg and marched deep into Union territory, Lincoln would not have deemed the moment propitious for his Emancipation Proclamation, and European recognition probably would have come quickly, with incalculable results. But those three cigars, with their fateful wrapping, ended the possibility of a clean-cut Confederate victory in Maryland and a deep northern penetration.

Appomattox was more than two and a half years in the future, but Lee's last real chance of defeating the North was gone.

TWENTY-EIGHT

Fredericksburg to Appomattox

AFTER THE RETREAT from Sharpsburg, the Army of Northern Virginia spent some six weeks in the Winchester area, recuperating and regrouping. McClellan, only twenty miles away at Harpers Ferry, was overestimating Lee's strength, as usual. He termed Lee's army "greatly superior," when it was hardly half as large as his, with vastly inferior equipment and supplies. McClellan was immensely popular with his troops, but not with President Lincoln. The President accordingly replaced "Little Mac" with General Ambrose Burnside, whose sideburns have entered the language.

Burnside moved the Army of the Potomac toward Fredericksburg in mid-November. As the Union forces approached the town from the north, the Confederates were digging in along the south side of the Rappahannock River and on the heights above. Their position was a strong one, and their 78,000-man army was in fine fettle. It seemed hardly possible that Burnside would attack this entrenched force frontally, even though he had some 125,000 men and far superior artillery. Yet that is what he did.

Burnside attempted on the morning of December 11 to throw pontoon bridges across the river at and near Fredericksburg. When the heavy December fog lifted, General William Barksdale's Mississippi sharpshooters picked off the Federal engineers repeatedly, as they pushed across the stream. That stopped the pontoon-building. The Union generals could identify the houses from which the sharpshooters were operating, but they chose to blast the entire town with artillery, rather than direct their fire at those particular buildings. More than a hundred Federal guns opened up, indiscriminately destroying homes, stores and other structures, irrespective of the women and children inside. A substantial part of Fredericksburg was reduced to rubble.

But this didn't stop the Mississippi sharpshooters. Holed up in basements and behind piles of bricks, they were ready when the Federals went back into action on their pontoons. Again the riflemen picked off the engineers with deadly accuracy. Burnside concluded that the bridge could never be built in this way. He accordingly arranged to row masses of infantry across in small boats, and to take the losses. The Confederate riflemen killed and wounded many, but the great majority got over and established a bridgehead on the south riverbank. The Confederates had to withdraw to higher ground, leaving battered Fredericksburg to the invader.

Lee became convinced that the Federals were preparing to attack his positions in a major assault. Another day and night passed, and on December 13 the fog was thicker than ever. Visibility in the early morning was down to fifty or sixty yards.

But Confederate officers and men were able to discern the spectacular outlines of "Stonewall" Jackson, who had bloomed out suddenly in gaudy apparel. After becoming known throughout the Army for his dingy uniform and rusty, flat-topped hat, he appeared in a gold-braided dress coat given him by his friend "Jeb" Stuart, the only man anywhere who could tease "Stonewall" without offending him. The stern, dignified general also was caparisoned in new trousers, boots, saber and spurs, all given him by admirers, and in a new cap, with gilt braid, sent him by his wife, Anna. Jackson's metamorphosis caused glee among the troops. "Come here, boys!" exclaimed one snickering private, "Stonewall has drawed his bounty and has bought himself some new clothes."

Jackson and Lee stood on the heights above Fredericksburg and tried to see through the fog. They could hear drumbeats, bugle calls and commands behind the impenetrable mist—sure signs that the Federals were up to something big. Burnside, in fact, was about to hurl his men against the firmly dug-in Confederate forces on Marye's Heights above the town, with a stone wall and sunken road in front providing complete impregnability.

Burnside's plan for mass suicide began to unfold as noon approached and visibility improved. Brigade after brigade of blue-clad soldiers marched up the slope in the face of murderous artillery fire from gun emplacements on the heights and rifle fire from behind the stone wall. The Union men were brave beyond all reckoning, and they went down by squads, platoons and companies, their bodies piled so high that oncoming Federal troops had difficulty making their way over the corpses. By nightfall, the carnage was ended. Burnside had lost 9000 men killed and wounded in the futile series of charges and 3600 more along the rest of the front. The Confederates had lost only 5300, all told.

The antique gallantry of these Union troops was in glaring contrast to the disgraceful behavior of others in smashed Fredericksburg. As Bruce Catton, historian of the Army of the Potomac, puts it, they "unleashed upon this historic town the spirit of unrestrained rowdyism . . . the very essence of jackbooted vandalism." Catton quotes a Pennsylvania soldier as writing: "The city had been rudely sacked; household furniture lined the streets. Books and battered pictures, bureaus, lounges, feather beds, clocks, every conceivable article of goods, chattels and apparel had been savagely torn from the houses and lay about in wanton confusion." Fires were made from broken furniture, pianos "were utilized as horse troughs."

Burnside did not renew the attack on Lee's positions. Reeling from his huge losses, he retreated under cover of darkness. Lee had won a victory, but it was in no sense decisive, for he had been unable to follow it up. Not only so, but the Union Army's dead and wounded could be readily replaced, whereas the South's manpower was limited.

The fighting was over until spring, and both armies went into winter quarters. Part of the winter was spent by the Confederates in building fortifications along the Rappahannock. Poker and other card games, chess, marbles and snowball battles helped to while away the hours in the huts occupied by the troops. There were amateur theatricals and similar entertainment, including banjo numbers by Stuart's irrepressible Sweeny and his entourage. Once when Sweeny was twanging and singing in front of his tent, with a jug of liquor much in evidence, General Lee happened by. "Gentlemen," said he, "am I to thank General Stuart or the jug for this fine music?"

Pickets of the two armies—on opposite sides of the Rappahannock—sometimes became friendly. They would make swaps across the stream —southern tobacco for northern coffee, for example—with tiny boats of bark carrying the little cargoes over. Real coffee was a rarity in Virginia, thanks to the blockade, and many other things were scarce. The soldiers' diet was so limited that Lee feared scurvy. He sent foragers into the countryside to gather up sassafras buds, wild onions, garlic, lamb's-quarter and poke sprouts. The sturdy and nourishing black-eyed pea was one of the principal reliances of the Confederate Army.

In Richmond and other Virginia cities, civilians were hungry and ill-clad. Prices had risen to such a degree that food and clothing were excessively expensive. Governor Letcher took note of this in his message to the General Assembly in January 1863. He said that "a reckless spirit of money making seems to have taken entire possession of the public mind . . . avarice has become a ruling passion . . . patriotism is second to love of 'the almighty dollar.'" Citing the fact that soldiers in the Confederate ranks were being paid only eleven dollars a month, the governor went on to say that for their families "the price of everything (even the necessaries of life) is put up to the highest point, and those who have not the pecuniary ability to pay these prices must suffer." President Jefferson Davis wrote a letter to Governor Letcher denouncing "the shameful extortion now practiced upon the people by men . . . who were worse enemies of the Confederacy than if found in arms among the invading forces." In December 1863, Letcher declared that "the crime of extortion . . . is daily growing in magnitude and importance . . . it embraces to a greater or less extent all interests—agricultural, mercantile and professional," and is "bold, heartless, remorseless and definitely insolent in its exactions." He recommended "all proper and legal means" to break up these practices, but a year later Governor William Smith was deploring the situation all over again. No effective steps were ever taken to bring to heel the extortionists and profiteers. There were similarly cold-blooded and greedy individuals in other southern states, and the same sort of thing had happened, North and South, in the American Revolution.

J. B. Jones, whose *Rebel War Clerk's Diary* affords so useful an insight into conditions in Richmond, recorded on March 3, 1863: "There are some pale faces seen in the streets from deficiency of food; but no beggars, no complaints. We are all in rags, especially our underclothes."

A month later, on April 2, "bread riots" broke out in Richmond. Mrs. Roger A. Pryor, wife of the Confederate general, saw a commotion in Capitol Square and asked a girl on a bench what was going on. She replied: "We are starving. As soon as enough of us get together we are going to the bakeries and each of us will take a loaf of bread.

That is little enough for the government to give us after it has taken all our men." Mrs. Pryor said the girl's arm was "a mere skeleton."

Soon thereafter hundreds of women, some of them armed with pistols or knives, converged on the Main and Cary street shops and wholesale houses. Several large grocery establishments were looted of bread, beef, hams, butter and other articles of food. The rioters then expanded their operations over a distance of some ten blocks and began breaking into jewelry stores, millinery shops and so on. They carried off diamonds, hats and other articles, in addition to food. Mayor Joseph Mayo, Governor Letcher and President Davis appealed to the mob without effect, until Davis stated that they would be fired on by troops within five minutes if they did not disperse. That ended the affair. There were no similar disorders in the city for the remaining two years of the war, although shortages of all kinds grew steadily worse.

One problem was that blockade runners which managed to get through the ever-tightening cordon of Union ships, all too often brought in luxuries, on which huge profits could be made, instead of sorely needed food, medicines, drugs, machinery, guns and ammunition. Shiploads of liquors, cigars, perfumes, and silk stockings—slipped in through Wilmington, North Carolina, almost the only southern port free of complete Federal control in 1863—were not what Virginia and the South required in this crisis. In Richmond's forty gambling establishments, situated mainly in the area below the Exchange Hotel at Fourteenth and Franklin streets, the smuggled brandy and cigars, the silks and satins found a ready market, and the food was superb. Nearby was Locust Alley, a block-long red-light district, but prostitutes operated in many other areas. Venereal disease was widespread and crime flourished. Deploring the influx of undesirable characters, the Richmond *Whig* for April 30, 1863, described the city as "a den of thieves, extortioners, substitutes, deserters, blacklegs and Cyprians."[1]

Richmond's hospitals were crowded with wounded—about 60 per cent of all wounded Confederates were treated in the city. With acute shortages of drugs, medicines, surgical instruments, bandages and nearly everything else, ingenious expedients were essential. The juice of the green persimmon was used as a styptic, a penknife often had to serve as a scalpel, bent prongs of table forks were pressed into service in delicate procedures incident to skull fractures, and a piece of soft pine wood proved effective in probing for bullets. Cotton-seed tea, thoroughwort and willow bark were made to serve for scarce quinine, American hemlock for opium, watermelon seed for flaxseed, peanut oil and cotton-seed oil for olive oil, hops and motherwort for laudanum, dandelions for calomel, Jamestown weed for belladonna, and blood root and wild cherry for digitalis. Amazingly good results were achieved, despite the grievous handicaps, especially at the great Chimborazo Hospital under Dr. James B. McCaw. Through this hospital, the largest in the world, passed 76,000 patients and the mortality rate of slightly over 9 per cent was not equaled until World War II.[2]

Measles was the greatest enemy of the troops. Diseases consequent to and traceable to measles "cost the Confederate Army the lives of more men and a greater amount of invalidism than all other causes combined." Typhoid and malaria were other scourges. Nine-tenths of all recruits suffered from diarrhea.

Amputations of legs and arms were carried on under the most difficult conditions, often without anesthetics. Many of these mutilations were unnecessary. Practically all gunshot wounds of the femur and wounds which penetrated the joints were erroneously deemed to be fatal, unless there was immediate amputation.[3]

Richmond was suffering in 1863, but Norfolk was suffering still more, for it had been occupied by the Federals since May 1862, and was to remain under Federal occupation until the end of the war. Its trade vanished, its schools closed, its streets became filled with holes and covered with filth, its newspapers were put out of business and journalistic mouthpieces for the occupying forces took their place.

Negro slaves were recruited by the Union authorities. They were organized into regiments, drilled in the streets, and used for garrison duty in Norfolk, as well as for punitive expeditions into the nearby countryside. When the Emancipation Proclamation became effective, January 1, 1863, the blacks paraded in honor of the occasion. Negro women trampled and tore the Confederate flag, and an effigy of Jefferson Davis was buried in the cemetery.

All this was deeply offensive to the people of Norfolk, who reacted indignantly and sometimes violently. The most conspicuous example of the latter response involved Dr. David Minton Wright, and was the cause of a double tragedy. Dr. Wright, an admired and beloved physician who had been heroic in his treatment of patients during the deadly yellow-fever epidemic of 1855, was standing on the sidewalk when a company of Negroes, commanded by a young white officer,

Lieutenant A. L. Sanborn, passed. The spectacle aroused Dr. Wright, who must have been greatly overwrought, for he approached Lieutenant Sanborn with clenched fists and exclaimed, "Oh, you coward!" Sanborn halted and said to Wright, "You are under arrest," whereupon Wright drew a pistol and fired twice at the Union officer, wounding him fatally. It was a rash and inexcusable act.

Dr. Wright was tried for murder by a special military commission, convicted, and sentenced to death. Penelope Wright, the condemned man's daughter—later Mrs. Alexander W. Weddell, mother of the U. S. Ambassador to Spain and the Argentine—almost succeeded in enabling her father to escape. Bravely she changed clothes with him in his cell, and the ruse was not detected until he was on his way to freedom. He was brought back, and later was hanged in the middle of the race track at the Norfolk Fair Grounds. Thousands watched, as was the custom in those days, but "few old citizens could be recognized," since the "better classes" were said to have stayed at home.

Dr. Wright went to the gallows "touched with inner serenity . . . in an indescribable sense the victor over his own destiny," according to Lenoir Chambers, the Norfolk editor and biographer of "Stonewall" Jackson, but his death cast a pall over Norfolk for years. And Norfolk's ordeal was far from over. It included the arrival in November 1863, the month following Dr. Wright's execution, of General Benjamin F. Butler as commander of the Department of Virginia and North Carolina, with headquarters at Fort Monroe.

The general's exploits in New Orleans had caused him to be known to citizens there as "Beast" Butler, and his reputation had preceded him when he arrived in Virginia. He was particularly zealous in his determination to recruit, drill and train Negroes for army duty. He directed that these Negroes receive "the most summary punishment" for any breaches of discipline. He was also extremely strict with white Norfolkians and he condoned excessive strictness in his subordinate's treatment of the whites. Butler was militarily incompetent and personally unscrupulous. His highhanded, unsupervised and widely ramified financial operations in the Norfolk area have never been fully understood by investigators. He certainly used his position to enrich his friends and probably himself, as well.[4]

Norfolk's depression and gloom under Federal occupation was even greater than that of the Virginia cities which were still free, but as early as the winter of 1862–63, southern morale was on the downgrade. More than 30 per cent of the soldiers were absent without leave from the Confederate armies, although a large percentage of these simply wandered off for some relatively trivial reason. Others deserted because their starving and freezing families sent them heart-rending appeals that they would die without immediate help. For these families, food, clothing and firewood were all in very short supply. Some deserters were executed by firing squads, but vastly more simply drifted back after short absences and went unpunished. Some stayed at home permanently; in rural areas, especially in the mountains, it was difficult to pursue them.[5]

The shortage of horses for the cavalry and artillery was growing acute. Early in the war, the quality of the horses in the Confederate service was high and they were well-fed. But as the years wore on, many of them were killed in the fighting, and fodder for the surviving animals became increasingly scarce. They had to "make do" with the sort of meager rations that were available to the troops. It was easy to tell when Confederate cavalry had been in a given neighborhood, for the bark had been gnawed from the trees by the underfed horses. Henceforth dependence would have to be placed on animals that were usually weak from lack of nourishment. The cavalry, the "eyes and ears" of the Army, and the vitally important horse-drawn artillery, would both be operating under these grievous handicaps. The Union armies, by contrast, were completely equipped with well-fed, vigorous animals.

In addition to all this, General Lee's health was beginning to decline. He was not sleeping well, he had contracted a throat infection, and he was experiencing severe pains in his back, arms and chest. There was the possibility of serious heart trouble. Lee seemed to recover, but he began tiring easily. He was only fifty-six, but he looked at least ten years older.

Thus, with an ailing commander-in-chief, unprecedented desertions, and far from adequate rations and equipment, the Army of Northern Virginia faced the approach of spring. The season would bring upon that army massive assaults from overwhelmingly more numerous and better armed and supplied Union forces.

General "Fighting Joe" Hooker had replaced the inept General Burnside as commander of the Army of the Potomac. Spring found Hooker on the northern side of the Rappahannock with 130,000 men, "the finest army on the planet," as he put it. Lee faced him across the river with an army less than half as large. By the end of April, Hooker had his force over the stream, in the area west of Fredericksburg near Chancellorsville. Hooker announced bombastically to his troops that "our enemy must either ingloriously fly or come out from behind his defense and give us battle on our own ground, where certain destruction awaits him."

This high-flown rhetoric did not intimidate Lee. He determined, despite the tremendous odds, to attack. The result was one of the military masterpieces of all time.

Lee and Jackson held their final conference in the woods on the night of May 1–2, about a mile and a half from Hooker's headquarters in the tavern known as the Chancellor House. This onetime large residence and its dependencies constituted "Chancellorsville," which sounded like a town or village, but wasn't. Lee decided to divide his small army into three parts—a most dangerous expedient, since he could be inviting destruction in detail. But as was so often the case, Lee knew the mind and temperament of the opposing commander, and was able to predict his reactions and movements. This made it possible for Lee to take risks that otherwise might have been disastrous.

Lee placed one part of his army at Fredericksburg, facing east toward Union forces under Sedgwick, while a second part was left facing Hooker. The third part, actually half of Lee's entire army, was sent on a secret fourteen-mile flanking movement led by Jackson. This last was the crusher.

The march was made by some 28,000 men through the rough, thinly settled region known as the Wilderness. It proceeded along narrow lanes and byways, through leafy woods bright with dogwood and redbud blooms, and into thick undergrowth that threatened, at times, to stop all forward progress. The very difficulty of the movement contributed greatly to its success, for the Federals never dreamed that such a march was possible. Hence complete surprise was achieved.

Hooker's right flank, under General O. O. Howard, was lolling about in the afternoon sunshine, the men playing cards, smoking and sleeping, totally oblivious to the fate that awaited them. Jackson moved up close in the woods and gazed upon the scene, only a few hundred yards distant. "His eyes burned with a brilliant glow" as he prepared, like an avenging angel, to put his unsuspecting foe to the sword.

It was about 6 P.M. when Jackson launched his assault. By then, the Federals were cooking supper, with arms stacked, unaware that any Confederates were within miles. Suddenly the sound of bugles echoed through the silent forest, followed by the eerie and blood-chilling rebel yell. Rabbits, foxes and deer came pouring out of the thickets into the Federal lines, and behind them "Stonewall" Jackson's men came crashing through the timber. Howard's exposed flank was rolled up in confusion and wild disorder, as Confederate rifle fire and canister tore through the ranks of the surprised, disorganized and fleeing Federals.

General Hooker was relaxing on the front porch of the Chancellor House with a couple of aides, serenely confident that all was well, and that this time he had Lee in a trap. Suddenly the sound of strange firing from his right caused a staff officer to take out his glasses and look down the road.

"My God, here they come!" the startled officer exclaimed, as Union soldiers, guns, wagons and ambulances came hurtling toward him in pellmell flight, kicking up clouds of dust. General Hooker sprang on his horse and tried to rally the fugitives. It was too late. They were in headlong retreat and there was no stopping them.

As night fell, some of the Federals managed to pull themselves together, and to organize resistance at certain points. Jackson, the light of battle in his blue eyes—one of his nicknames was "Old Blue Light"—was pressing his advantage. He ordered A. P. Hill's division forward and rode with part of his staff to reconnoiter the Union lines. An officer in the party, thinking that Jackson was exposing himself to an excessive degree, asked, "General, don't you think this is the wrong place for you?" Jackson replied, "The danger is all over—the enemy is routed."

The party went forward in the deepening darkness. Shadowy forms were moving about in the woods, and it was impossible to tell whether they were Federals or Confederates. As Jackson and his staff rode back toward their own lines, they were fired on by a North Carolina unit that mistook them for Union soldiers. Jackson's left arm was shattered in the furious fusillade, and a ball passed through his right hand. In great pain, he was carried to a field hospital, where his arm was amputated just below the shoulder by young Dr. Hunter McGuire.

Meanwhile, "Jeb" Stuart took field command of the victorious Confederate forces in Jackson's stead. Although his experience had been exclusively with the cavalry, he carried out his new duties effectively. Characteristically, he rode to the front, where shells were exploding and bullets whining, and gave the men the watchword, "Remember Jackson!" Then he galloped along the lines and sang in his rich baritone, "Old Joe Hooker, won't you come out of the Wilderness?"

Hooker's men had put up a brave resistance here and there, but they had been outgeneraled, and they were thoroughly beaten. Yet Lee, once again, was unable to take full advantage of his stunning victory. The wounding of Jackson had taken from him the one man who might have followed up the triumph effectively. The loss of his most brilliant lieutenant, coupled with the small size of his army, made it impossible for Lee to harvest the fruits of his master stroke.

In addition, the news from "Stonewall" Jackson was soon to plunge the entire South into gloom. He had been taken to the modest residence of the Chandler family near Guiney's Station, Caroline County, and he seemed to be recovering from his wounds. Then suddenly pneumonia set in. Jackson's wife hurried with their seven-month-old daughter to his bedside. By then he was extremely weak, but there was still hope for his recovery. Three days later he was sinking fast, and the end was near. Devoutly religious as always, Jackson said calmly that if it was God's will, he was ready to go. Mrs. Jackson knelt beside his bed and told him that he could not live beyond the evening. When this was confirmed by Dr. McGuire, the general said, "Very good, very good; it is all right." Informed that the whole Army was praying for him, he replied, "Thank God, they are very good to me."

He became delirious and sank into a coma, but then cried out suddenly, "Order A. P. Hill to prepare for action! Pass the infantry to the front! Tell Major Hawks—" He was unable to finish the sentence. A few minutes later he spoke again, and quietly and clearly uttered his last words: "Let us cross over the river and rest under the shade of the trees."

The death of "Stonewall" Jackson was the heaviest blow the South had received since the guns boomed at Sumter. He, more than any man, was the hero of the Confederacy.[6] His body was brought to Richmond, where it lay in state both in the Capitol and the Governor's Mansion. Thousands passed the bier, many of them weeping, and gazed for the last time upon the face of the great captain. His body was taken to Lexington by railway and canal boat and buried in the cemetery there.

At such heavy cost, the victory at Chancellorsville was won. It now devolved upon Lee, without the invaluable help of Jackson, to attempt a bold stroke that might conceivably win independence for the South. Despite dwindling men and resources, he determined upon another invasion of the North. He hoped, among other things, to replenish his supplies.

The Army of Northern Virginia set out one month after Chancellorsville, heading for Maryland and Pennsylvania. There was grumbling in other southern states that Virginians were too prominent in the upper echelons of the command. In the list were not only Robert E. Lee, his son W. H. F. ("Rooney") Lee, and his nephew Fitzhugh Lee, both brigadiers, but also "Jeb" Stuart, A. P. Hill, Jubal Early and Richard S. Ewell. "Bald Dick" Ewell, with his high-pitched voice and wooden leg—the leg was amputated after Second Manassas—was given command of Jackson's old corps. Despite fine qualities, he lacked initiative.

The Confederate troops were a ragtag lot as they crossed into northern territory. Shoes were either badly worn or non-existent, shirts didn't match trousers, and hats or caps were conspicuous by their absence. Rations were scant, yet morale was high.

En route to Maryland, Stuart fought a desperate engagement with Union General Alfred Pleasonton at Brandy Station or Fleetwood Heights—the biggest cavalry battle ever fought on American soil. Neither side could be termed the victor, but Stuart did manage to prevent the Federals from learning of Lee's northward movement. Gigantic "Rooney" Lee, described as "too big for a man and not big enough for a horse," was severely wounded.

Stuart's close call at Brandy Station may account for his apparent desire to make a spectacular compensatory coup during the northern invasion. As usual, he was given considerable latitude by Lee, and he went off on a long raid, with the result that Lee had no idea where he was for nearly a week. The Confederate commanding general, in consequence, got no information from Stuart during that time as to the location or movements of the Union Army.

The Confederates under Lee and the Federals under George G. Meade, who had replaced Hooker, stumbled into one another near the town of Gettysburg. Almost at once the absence of "Stonewall" Jackson was felt by the South. Lee ordered Ewell to attack the Federals on Cemetery Hill and to take the position, "if practicable." Ewell decided that it wasn't practicable and did nothing. Almost certainly, Jackson would have assaulted the hill at once, with probable success.

Those were the "dread heights of destiny" from which, two days later, the firmly entrenched Federals would pour down deadly volleys and decimate Pickett's charging veterans in the climactically crucial event of the battle.

Ewell made an ineffective attack on Cemetery Hill next day. Then came another, and even more fatal delay. Longstreet was directed by Lee to assail the Federal flank on Big Roundtop, but he argued with Lee for several hours before doing so. The assault failed, perhaps more because of the grudging manner of its execution than because of the lapse of time.

It was now the third day, and Lee's opportunity was slipping away. He had virtually no alternative but to assail Meade's strongly fortified position on Cemetery Hill, and even then sullen Longstreet demurred. Finally the attack was launched, and Pickett made his virtually impossible charge against Cemetery Ridge, across nearly a mile of open territory, in the face of devastating artillery and musket fire.

There were 4500 Virginians in that charge out of a total of 15,000 Confederates, including the historic First Virginia, most famous of all Virginia regiments, which traces its origins back to early colonial times. It had fought under George Washington in the French and Indian War, under Andrew Lewis at Point Pleasant, and under Washington's overall command at Trenton, Princeton and Yorktown. What was left of the First Virginia after Pickett's charge—it sustained 80 per cent casualties—would fight on through to Appomattox.

Pickett's three Virginia brigades were commanded by Brigadiers Lewis A. Armistead, Richard S. Garnett and James L. Kemper. They formed the assault force on the right end of the line. In a grand display of raw courage, the brigades moved out toward the Union positions and up the fire-swept slope, with most of their commanding officers on horseback, and the Confederate battle flags fluttering in the hot July sun.

Exploding shells, solid shot and canister raked them from in front, and enfiladed them from the flank, while concentrated musket volleys poured down upon them. Officers and men fell by scores and hundreds as the avalanche of iron and lead ripped great gaps in their ranks. Yet on they came! The carnage among the Confederate color-bearers was frightful, for when one fell, another leaped forward to seize the flag and hold it aloft. Pickett, with his long hair and flamboyant mustachios, followed close behind the charge on his black horse.

Generals Garnett and Kemper were hit as they rode up close to the Federal lines. Garnett was killed and Kemper was gravely wounded. General Armistead, who led his men on foot, yelled, "Give them the cold steel!" as he jumped over the stone wall on the crest of Cemetery Ridge. He put his hand on a smoking Federal cannon, and fell with a mortal wound.

Only 150 men climbed over the wall with Armistead. The rest had fallen or had stopped at the wall to fire over it. These remnants were promptly attacked from three sides by fresh Union forces.

Some survivors of Pettigrew's and Trimble's fine North Carolina, Tennessee and Virginia brigades, with a few Mississippians, under the overall command of A. P. Hill, also made it to the top of the ridge, after suffering casualties comparable to those of Pickett. They, too, were engulfed by the oncoming Federals, and forced to fall back.

The Confederates retreated over ground covered with their dead and wounded. Only slightly more than a thousand of Pickett's 4500 Virginians were able to make their way back, and about five hundred more managed to crawl or be carried down by stretcher-bearers—some fifteen hundred in all.

Thus ended the Battle of Gettysburg. Because of a succession of blunders, for most of which Lee was not responsible, another opportunity had gone. Yet Lee, with characteristic magnanimity, took all the blame.

The retreat in the pouring rain, with hundreds of wounded groaning in agony in their rough, lurching wagons, calling for water in the muggy heat, and imploring God to let them die and end their suffering, was as terrible as anything on the battlefield. Finally Lee crossed the Potomac and was once more back on Virginia soil. He was faced with the certainty that new attacks were being prepared by the inexhaustible armies of the North.

Not only so, but on July 4, the day after Pickett's charge, the whole South received the melancholy news that Vicksburg had fallen. The Confederacy was now cut in two, since the entire Mississippi River was in Federal hands. It was an even more far-reaching blow than the reverse at Gettysburg.

Virginia also had been cut in two, but in a wholly different manner. The establishment of West Virginia as a separate state was officially proclaimed by President Lincoln, effective June 20. This part of the Old Dominion had been at odds with the eastern section for so long that the breakaway held few surprises. The process had begun early in the war. Sentiment in the northwestern counties was strongly pro-Union, and most of the region was overrun by Union forces. In fact, soon after the passage of Virginia's Ordinance of Secession, a group of unconditional unionists from those counties met in Richmond to discuss separation from the rest of the state.

A powerful force in behalf of such action was the Wheeling *Intelligencer,* under the editorship of a young Ohioan named Archibald Campbell. Constitutional questions as to the legality of secession from Virginia were brushed aside on grounds of political and military expediency, and a "governor" and "legislature" were chosen. Following Lincoln's proclamation of statehood, the so-called restored government of Virginia established headquarters in Alexandria. Love for the Negro played no part in the decision to separate, as is obvious from the fact that the new government promptly excluded all Negroes, whether slave or free, from the newly formed state. About 35 per cent of Virginia's territory was lost in the breakaway, and 25 per cent of its population.

As the winter of 1863–64 approached, the people of Virginia tightened their belts again. Thousands of their ablest and most patriotic young men had been killed on the battlefield or maimed for life. Food and clothing were becoming increasingly scarce as prices skyrocketed. J. B. Jones, the indefatigable diarist, wrote in July that "we are in a half-starving condition." A few months later he related that "we are a shabby looking people now—gaunt and many in rags."

Yet there was a certain amount of feasting and merry-making in Richmond as late as the winter of 1863–64, even in the Confederate White House. Mary Boykin Chesnut tells of a supper in the White House which included ices, chicken salad, oysters and champagne. She herself had been giving similar suppers occasionally, and her husband, Colonel Chesnut, reproved her several times. There was hardly any of this after January 1864.

Constance Cary Harrison wrote that "every crumb of food better than ordinary, every orange, apple or banana, every drop of wine or cordial procurable went straightaway to the hospitals." She added that "many of the residents had set aside at least one room of their stately old houses as hospitals, maintaining at their own expense as many sick or wounded soldiers as they could accommodate."

The great majority of Virginians were, indeed, suffering, and the breakdown in transportation was one of the major reasons. The railroads were being steadily ripped up or seized by the northern armies. Many were out of commission, and all were operating with inadequate or worn-out equipment. It was impossible to haul sufficient quantities of men, munitions, supplies and food under such circumstances.

Lack of adequate transportation was one of the major handicaps of Richmond's Tredegar Iron Works. Despite the ability and ingenuity shown by its directing head, Joseph R. Anderson, the company could not get enough pig iron and other raw materials. Anderson launched a statewide campaign to reopen small charcoal furnaces, and many of these were got back into operation. Even so, the Tredegar, mainstay of the entire Confederate war effort, was never able, throughout the four years, to function at more than one-third capacity.

The labors of Joseph Anderson to keep production of heavy ordnance going were matched in the sphere of small arms and equipment by Josiah Gorgas, Confederate chief of ordnance. Gorgas was a genius in his field. Where Anderson relied heavily on slave labor in his plants, as did many other factories during the war, Gorgas supplemented the force in his laboratories and arsenals by employing white women.

The women of Virginia and the South made a contribution to the war effort which is not fully appreciated. With their menfolk absent in the Army, they were left at home to look after their children, often with extremely meager incomes and inadequate food and clothing. Under great emotional strain, constantly dreading the news from their loved ones at the front, they took over the management of their households and carried on. Some worked full or part time in vital war installations, as in the case of those employed by Gorgas. Many were active in hospitals. For most women, it was a sufficiently difficult task to keep their families together, in the absence of husbands, sons and brothers. Even the caustic bachelor, John M. Daniel, praised the women of Virginia in the *Examiner* for their contribution to the war.

The loyalty of the great majority of slaves who remained on the plantations—thousands fled to the Union lines, as we have seen—was a striking phenomenon of the war years. The absence of most able-bodied white men in the armed forces must have tempted many slaves to revolt, but few actually made the effort, and those were promptly put down. The white women of Virginia and the South, generally speaking, were protected faithfully by the black men who served them.[7]

Lead and salt were essential to the Confederacy, and vital supplies of both were in southwest Virginia—near Wytheville and Saltville, respectively. Two weeks after the Battle of Gettysburg, about a thousand Union cavalrymen swooped down on the area with a view to capturing Wytheville, disrupting rail traffic to the lead mines and salt-refining facilities, and perhaps putting the mines and refineries out of commission. Mary Elizabeth ("Molly") Tynes, aged twenty-six, was caring for her invalid mother near Jeffersonville, now Tazewell, when she learned the intentions of the Federals. She rode all night across the mountains to Wytheville, a distance of some forty-one miles, through rough and difficult terrain, and despite hazards from bears, wolves and panthers. She arrived at dawn, almost exhausted, her clothes torn and her face and arms scratched, but in time to give the warning. The Union cavalrymen were driven off and the lead and salt were saved. Unfortunately, in December, Union General George Stoneman wrecked the salt works and captured and burned thirteen trains on the railroad spur leading to Saltville.

With Virginia's supplies of salt and dozens of other necessities strained to the utmost, the problem of feeding Union prisoners of war was a huge one. Some 4000 Federal officers were crammed into Richmond's Libby Prison on the riverbank, and about twice as many privates were in the prison camp on nearby Belle Isle. Congestion was so great by late 1863 that 4000 prisoners were transferred to Danville, where they were confined in converted tobacco warehouses. Sufferings of the prisoners in both cities were often intense from lack of adequate food, clothing, medicines, blankets and sanitation. Yet Confederate soldiers in the field and many civilians behind the lines were suffering similarly. The principal difference between the northern and southern prison camps was that the North had ample supplies of food, clothing, medicines and blankets, but it refused to make them available to Confederate prisoners. A higher percentage of deaths occurred in the northern prisons than in the southern, according to official U.S. figures, but in the northern camps much of this could have been prevented. There were sadistic and inefficient prison officials on both sides of Mason and Dixon's line, but it was impossible for the sinking Confederacy to provide the sort of care for prisoners that was available in the North but not offered.[8]

A cavalry raid on largely undefended Richmond, designed to free the war prisoners, was attempted in March 1864 by Colonel Ulrich

Dahlgren whose troop was a part of General Judson Kilpatrick's force. Dahlgren came down the James River valley from the west, with about three hundred men. On the outskirts of the city he was met by the hastily thrown together and lightly armed Home Guard, composed of overage men and young boys, also numbering about three hundred. The Home Guard drove off Dahlgren with rifle fire. He veered around Richmond and was killed in King and Queen County by other local forces. Papers said to have been found on his body told of a plot to burn Richmond and murder Jefferson Davis and his cabinet. These papers were almost certainly forged.

Tragedy struck at the Confederate White House in the following month, when little "Joe" Davis, aged five, fell from the high porch on the rear of the building and was killed. President Davis, afflicted in recent days and weeks with agonizing pain in his face which seemed, at times, to threaten total blindness, walked the floor all night in grief. When the body of the little boy was taken to Hollywood, hundreds of children heaped flowers on the grave.

This overwhelming sorrow came to the Davises just when the Confederacy stood facing the certainty that Union armies would soon be hammering at the gates. Lee was preparing to confront General U. S. Grant, the new supreme commander of all the Federal forces, who had taken Vicksburg the previous year. On top of all else, Lee's health was growing worse.

Grant crossed the Rapidan, May 4, and "On to Richmond!" was again the cry. He had 120,000 men as against 60,000 to 65,000 for Lee. The two forces met in the Wilderness, near the old battlefields of the year before. It was a bitter struggle in densely wooded country, with the undergrowth catching fire from exploding shells and many of the wounded burning to death. Longstreet was wounded accidentally by a bullet fired by his own men, as had happened to Jackson almost exactly twelve months previously, and not far from the same spot. Lee's most experienced corps commander was now out of action for an indefinite period.

Grant tried a flanking movement, but as was to happen several successive times, Lee moved quickly and kept his army between the invaders and Richmond. The next battle was near Spotsylvania Courthouse and was one of the most sanguinary of the war. At the Bloody Angle, north of the courthouse, trees were cut down by the hail of bullets. The battle was notable, too, for the initiation of trench warfare, with both sides digging in. Lee's losses in the engagement were only about one-third of Grant's, but Grant could afford them and Lee couldn't. The Confederates gathered up 120,000 pounds of northern lead on the battlefield.

While Lee was still in the vicinity of Spotsylvania Courthouse, Grant sent "Phil" Sheridan's cavalry against Stuart, who had been hovering on Grant's flanks and reporting his movements to Lee. Units of the two opposing cavalry forces met near Yellow Tavern, six miles north of Richmond.

Riding their bony and underfed horses, the Confederates were being hard-pressed by Sheridan's well-mounted troopers. Stuart, always in the van, his plumed hat at a jaunty angle, his yellow sash about his waist and his red-lined cape flowing, rushed into the melee firing his pistol and rallying his men. A sergeant from a Michigan regiment, who had been unhorsed in the fierce hand-to-hand fighting, fired at the big officer. The bullet struck Stuart in the stomach and passed through his liver. In great pain, he was gotten to an ambulance, which somehow eluded the Federals and brought him to Richmond. Despite his agony, he refused brandy, having promised his mother long ago never to touch it.

They took him to the home of Dr. Brewer, his brother-in-law, at 206 West Grace Street, a spacious brick house where roses bloomed. When word spread in the Confederate capital that General Stuart, the *beau sabreur* of the Army of Northern Virginia, was dying, crowds gathered in the street and on the sidewalk. Many were in tears. The sound of battle to the North echoed through the city like rolling thunder.

The thirty-one-year-old general was told that his wound was mortal. "God's will be done," he said quietly. He hoped to see his wife once more. She was trying frantically to reach his bedside from Hanover County, but Federals were between her and Richmond, and her route was long and circuitous. When she arrived, the great cavalryman was dead.

Lee had lost the man on whom he had relied to keep him informed of Union movements, and the people of Virginia and the South had sustained one more shattering blow. Grant made it known that he would "fight it out on this line, if it takes all summer." It would take all summer and all winter, too, but the northern hosts were not to be denied.

Three days after Stuart's death on May 12, an engagement took

place at New Market in the Shenandoah Valley that brought renown
to the cadets of the Virginia Military Institute. Union General Franz
Sigel was raiding in the Valley and was opposed by Confederate
General John C. Breckinridge. They clashed at New Market, and some
240 VMI cadets, the eldest under eighteen, were a part of the Confederate force. The boys had marched through rain for four days to get
into the action. They charged gallantly and captured an enemy flag.
About a dozen were killed and twoscore wounded. Sigel was driven
from the Valley, but a month later General David Hunter was raiding
there. He burned the VMI, destroying it completely, with the exception
of the superintendent's living quarters. The libraries of both the institute and of nearby Washington College were wrecked, and "every
particle of philosophical apparatus broken to pieces." Half a century
later the U. S. Congress would make an appropriation of $100,000 in
partial payment for the damage to VMI.

The daring Confederate ranger, Colonel John S. Mosby, was operating with a small force across much of Northern Virginia during 1864.
The previous year, at the head of a handful of men, he had performed
the amazing feat of seizing the sleeping Union general, E. H. Stoughton,
with about a hundred of his soldiers and many horses at Fairfax
Courthouse. Now he was keeping the Federals off balance with his
sudden pounces. Mosby was slight of build, piercing of eye, quick of
brain, and an accomplished Greek and Latin scholar. His ingenuity and
cold nerve enabled him to outwit and outfight far larger forces in what
came to be known as "Mosby's Confederacy." It extended across the
upper end of the state, from the Potomac to the Shenandoah Valley.
One exceptional accomplishment among many during 1864 was the
"Greenback Raid," in which Mosby's rangers seized a train near
Harpers Ferry carrying approximately $173,000.

In mid-May, Lee was still barring Grant's path to Richmond. After
the battle of Spotsylvania, the northern commander tried once more
to outflank his opponent, but Lee moved alertly and interposed his
army between the Federals and their objective. He inflicted a serious
defeat on them at the Battle of the North Anna. Grant then crossed
the Pamunkey; the Chickahominy was now the last stream between
him and the Confederate capital. He was less than ten miles from the
city's outskirts.

The two armies met near a little crossroads called Cold Harbor. Lee
had a violent intestinal attack that made it impossible for him to ride

Traveller—he had to move about in a carriage—but he saw to it that his army was well dug in. In fact, his line was shrewdly designed to take advantage of every natural obstacle, every ravine, hillock, stream and bog, so that a searing cross fire could be laid down from several directions against any assaulting force. What followed was hardly less than mass murder.

The Union attack was ordered for dawn on June 3. As the men moved out, a sheet of flame leaped from end to end of the Confederate trenches and the ground shook with the roar of exploding shells and the crash of solid shot. Hundreds of Federals went down in the first volley, and thousands more joined them within a few minutes. The ground in front of the Confederate earthworks was covered with the dead and dying, many of them horribly mangled. Grant lost 7000 men, dead and wounded, in half an hour, and the toll of Federals for the day was 13,000. Lee lost not more than 1500, and probably fewer than that.

Yet Grant had plenty of men left, and they were well-fed and well-equipped. On the day after the carnage at Cold Harbor, General Meade was entertained near the battlefield by General W. F. ("Baldy") Smith, famous for his hospitality. Champagne was served, although it was certainly no victory celebration. Overnight guests in "Baldy's" tent were customarily awakened by a servant bearing a champagne cocktail.[9]

Richmond also was being threatened from the east, and if the Union general in charge had been anybody other than the bungling "Ben" Butler, the city would doubtless have fallen much sooner. Butler mismanaged the Army of the James badly. He could have taken Petersburg in the spring of 1864, thereby curtailing the war by almost a year. Lee was preoccupied with Grant and Petersburg was wide open. Yet Butler wasted time trying to make up his mind, after which he let himself be bottled up at Bermuda Hundred by a much smaller Confederate force. He stayed bottled up until he was relieved of his command when the war was nearly over.

Only a month had passed since Grant's Army of the Potomac crossed the Rapidan on its drive toward Richmond, and it had lost 55,000 men, 46,000 of them killed or wounded. This was almost as many men as Lee had in his whole army. There was a real question whether the North would accept such colossal losses much longer.

Grant decided that going through or over the Army of Northern Virginia was next to impossible. However, if he could go around it and cut Richmond's rail communications with the South and the Shenandoah Valley, the city would have to fall for lack of supplies. Lee's army also would be fatally weakened. Grant saw the seizure of Petersburg, on the railroad line from the South, as a vital part of this plan. He accordingly determined to bypass Richmond and lay siege to Petersburg, while sending tough "Phil" Sheridan to spread desolation through the Valley, "the granary of the Confederacy," and at the same time to tear up the Virginia Central Railroad with its link to Richmond.

Grant executed this flanking movement around Lee with great skill, and so swiftly that he almost got Petersburg in the process. The city was saved by the hurriedly organized resistance of a brave band of old men and boys. A tablet in Blandford Church tells of ". . . the Citizen Soldiers of Petersburg, the gray haired sires and beardless youth who . . . laid down their lives near this venerable church in successful defense of our Altars and Firesides." This was magnificent, but nothing could prevent the siege. Grant settled down in mid-June in front of Petersburg, and both armies dug trenches furiously.

In late June, the Federals began driving a shaft under Elliott's salient in the Confederate line. When the shaft had reached the desired spot, some five hundred feet from the starting point, kegs of powder were carried in. Early in the morning of July 30 the fuse was lighted. There was a tremendous explosion, and men, guns, rocks and clods were blown high into the air. The Federals saw a huge smoking gash in the earth, sixty feet across and thirty feet deep, containing Confederates, both alive and dead, and the assorted debris thrown up by the blast. A gap five hundred yards wide yawned in the southern defenses, and if the Northerners had taken quick advantage of it, they could have broken through and won a smashing victory. But they muffed the opportunity. A Union division moved uncertainly into the crater, followed by the other units. They got bogged down, and the Confederate defenders on both sides of the opening were given time to recover from the initial shock. As the southern defense stiffened, the confused mass of Federals became more and more hopelessly jammed together in the great hole, where they were perfect targets for both rifle and mortar fire. After several hours, during which the Confederates picked off or bombarded the Federals with deadly accuracy, General William Mahone's Confederate brigade counterattacked fiercely with the bayonet and drove the disordered remainder back to their own trenches. The whole operation was a total fiasco for the North. It had lost 4000 men, and Lee's lines in front of Petersburg were unbroken.

In the Shenandoah Valley, General Jubal Early was having considerable success and was even threatening Washington and moving into Pennsylvania. His burning of Chambersburg, Pennsylvania, was resented in the North, but the South retorted that it was in retaliation for Union General Hunter's burning of the Virginia Military Institute.

Early's successes were terminated by Sheridan. The latter not only defeated him but launched a systematic plan of destruction in the Valley. Sheridan tabulated his accomplishments as follows:

"The whole country from the Blue Ridge to the North Mountains has been made untenable for a rebel army. I have destroyed over 2000 barns filled with wheat, hay and farming implements; over seventy mills filled with flour and wheat; have driven in front of the army over 4000 head of stock, and have killed and issued to the troops not less than 3000 sheep. A large number of horses have been obtained. . . . Lt. John R. Meigs, my engineer officer, was murdered beyond Harrisonburg near Dayton. For this atrocious act, all the houses within an area of five miles were burned."

It can readily be seen that the once lush and beautiful Valley of the Shenandoah had been turned into something resembling a smoking ruin. Sheridan boasted that a crow flying over it would have to take his rations with him. Union General William T. Sherman, whose "March to the Sea" through Georgia was about to begin, would hardly be more ruthless.

Supplies of food for Virginians were growing increasingly short. The soldiers in the trenches in front of Petersburg were among the chief sufferers. Union General "Ben" Butler wrote in his autobiography after the war that "the fact is incontestable that a soldier of our army would have quite easily starved on the rations . . . served out to the Confederate soldiers before Petersburg." He also commented on the "lank and emaciated condition of the prisoners," adding that they were not only grievously short of food but of clothing as well. Those in the Petersburg trenches passed much of the winter, one of the coldest on record, in snow and sleet.

As for the citizens of Petersburg, they believed that they were nearer actual starvation than those of Richmond. In addition, they were suffering bombardment by Federal guns.

Yet with all the hunger in the front lines and behind them, there was "plenty of food, if energetic action had been taken to concentrate it for the army," William L. Royall wrote in his *Reminiscences*. He quoted Major Lewis Ginter, one of Richmond's most prominent and respected citizens, as telling him after the war that he was sent by General Lee to North Carolina in the winter of 1864–65 in search of food and clothing for the army. Ginter told him, Royall said, that he "found warehouses bursting with grain and meat" in Danville and also in North Carolina, but that he couldn't arrange for trains to haul these supplies. Speculators apparently had bribed railroad officials to let them use the dwindling amount of rolling stock for their own purposes. A train of nine Richmond & Danville cars arrived in Richmond in December 1864, loaded with food, but only two of them were for the hard-pressed government. The others went to individuals. In the following month, Major S. B. French, of the Bureau of Subsistence, complained that whereas he had received more than a dozen telegrams from agents in Georgia and North Carolina telling of large shipments of corn, none had arrived.[10]

To corruption was added inefficiency. J. B. Jones recorded in his diary that in late January 1865, General J. D. Imboden wrote a letter to General Lee "exposing the wretched management of the Piedmont Railroad," and showing that "salt and corn in immense quantity have been daily left piled in the mud and water and exposed to rain."

Lee wrote the able Virginian, J. A. Seddon, Secretary of War, concerning the "alarming frequency" of desertions from the Confederate Army, and ascribed it to "insufficiency of food and nonpayment of troops." He remarked later that he had been "up to see the Congress and they do not seem to be able to do anything except eat peanuts and chew tobacco."

Wives and children of the troops were suffering severely from lack of food, clothing, firewood and money in the last winter of the war. Many wives were writing their husbands imploring them to come home. Often the husband, recognizing that the Confederate cause was hopeless, left his post and headed back to his anguished family. President Davis "emphatically announced" in September 1864, that two-thirds of the Army were absent from the ranks. This included the wounded, the sick and others absent for legitimate reasons, but there was a vast deal of desertion. In southwest Virginia, which early in the war appealed to be more secessionist in sentiment than the rest of the state, a secret organization calling itself the Heroes of America had been stimulating desertion since 1863, with devastating results. It was officially estimated in February 1865, that more than 100,000 deserters were scattered throughout the South.[11]

In the midst of such widespread defeatism, the tenacious and brave Confederate soldiers who fought on, despite the odds, are all the more to be admired and respected.

In February 1865, President Davis sent three commissioners, including Robert M. T. Hunter, president pro tem of the Confederate Senate, to a conference with President Lincoln at Fort Monroe, to discuss peace terms. It soon became clear that no agreement was possible. President Davis insisted quixotically on northern recognition of southern independence, and Lincoln insisted on preservation of the Union and the disarming of the South.

In desperation Lee, who was now commander-in-chief of all Confederate forces, urged his government to arrange for the enlistment of 200,000 slaves in the Army; the slaves to be freed after the war. This idea had been discussed for some months; the Richmond *Enquirer* had urged the plan the preceding October.

Lee believed that black combat troops would make a valuable contribution to the Confederate cause. Blacks wearing the Union uniform had been decidedly ineffective at the Crater, but so had the white Union troops in that engagement. General "Baldy" Smith had praised Negro troops highly for their success in a subsequent fight with the Confederates in front of Petersburg. Union General George H. Thomas had paid tribute to the soldierly qualities of blacks who fought in the Battle of Nashville.[12]

Lee's little-known and seldom-publicized letter to the Confederate Congress, urging the enlistment of Negroes, was in part as follows:

"I think we could at least do as well with them as the enemy, and he attaches great importance to their assistance. Under good officers and good instructors, I do not see why they shouldn't become good soldiers. They possess all the physical qualifications, and their habits of obedience constitute a good foundation for discipline. They furnish a more promising material than many armies of which we read in history. . . . I think those who are employed should be freed. . . . The best course to pursue . . . would be to call for such as are willing to come with the consent of their owners."[13]

The proposal had been defeated before in the Senate, but Lee's letter brought about reconsideration and adoption on March 8. However, it was then too late for the measure to have any effect on the course of the war.

Events were moving to their inevitable climax, as far larger Union forces converged on the dwindling Confederate Army defending Petersburg and Richmond. Sheridan was brought by Grant from the Valley and Sherman was coming up through the Carolinas. A last-ditch Confederate attack on Fort Stedman, one of Grant's strong points in his line around Petersburg, failed. Then came the shattering Union victory at Five Forks on April 1. After cutting the rail line from North Carolina, hard-driving Sheridan also cut the Southside Railroad to Lynchburg, while inflicting heavy losses on the Confederates and taking many prisoners. There was sharp fighting all that day, in which A. P. Hill was killed. Grant ordered a general assault on the Petersburg lines next morning.

Lee saw that Petersburg was falling and that Richmond could not be held. He sent this word to President Davis on Sunday morning, April 2. Davis was attending services in St. Paul's Episcopal Church, and on receiving the message he left at once, tense and pale. The news spread rapidly that Richmond was about to be evacuated. The pervading gloom contrasted with the bright sunshine that dappled Capitol Square.

Davis and his Cabinet boarded trains for Danville, taking with them the Confederacy's small supply of gold and many official papers. Warehouses in Richmond were set afire by the retreating Confederates to prevent their contents from falling into Federal hands, and the James River bridges were put to the torch. A strong wind sprang up and spread the flames. Soon the entire business district from Main Street to the river was an inferno with tongues of fire leaping into the sky. Many residences were burning, and terror-stricken people fled for their lives.

The conflagration raged through the night of April 2–3, while mobs looted. They dipped whiskey from the gutters, where it had been poured by authorities. The arsenal and armory blew up, as the roaring blaze reached the powder and ammunition. At 2 A.M., eighty-year-old Mayor Joseph Mayo and a small delegation set out in a couple of dilapidated hacks, drawn by starving horses, in an effort to find a Federal officer outside the city who could accept its surrender. They carried a piece of wallpaper, on the unflowered side of which they set forth their formal request to the Federals to take over, put out the flames and restore order.

The Federals came quickly and they behaved admirably. General Godfrey Weitzel, standing on the Capitol steps and looking down into "a gigantic crater of fire," ordered General Edward H. Ripley to put out the conflagration as soon as possible, and to stop the looting. Ripley's men fell to, and did extremely effective work. They were highly considerate of Richmond's citizens and protected the women from molestation. Flames scorched the home of crippled Mrs. Robert E. Lee on East Franklin Street. General Weitzel sent a conveyance to take her to a place of safety, but she refused to leave. "It is impossible to describe the kind attention of the Union soldiers," she told her husband later.[14]

President Lincoln entered smoldering Richmond with a small party on April 4. He held his young son "Tad" by the hand as he walked through the streets from the wharf, with only Admiral D. D. Porter and a small guard of sailors for protection. A crowd of exultant Negroes accompanied him to the Confederate White House. There the tired President rested, and received several Confederate officials. He then drove about the stricken city, which was still covered with cinders and smelled of smoke, with twenty blocks of its most valuable business property gutted. This done, Lincoln returned to his ship.

The Army of Northern Virginia, meanwhile, was in its death agony. Lee's last hope was for a union with General Joseph E. Johnston's forces in North Carolina, but Lee was being pressed relentlessly from several directions. His men were almost without food and were reduced to purloining handfuls of corn from their famished horses and mules. A Confederate debacle occurred at Sayler's Creek on April 4, and Lee lost about half of his army. Grant's victorious forces hemmed in the pitiful remainder, numbering about 9000, and the Confederates' last desperate effort to break out of the tightening ring failed.

There was nothing left for Lee but surrender. He met Grant on April 9 at the quiet little village of Appomattox. The meeting took place in the house of Wilmer McLean who had been living, ironically enough, on the Manassas battlefield four years before and had moved his family to seemingly safe and remote Appomattox to get away from the fighting.

The terms agreed to by Grant were unusually generous. No mention was made of Lee's sword, so it was not surrendered. Grant stated that Confederate officers and men who gave their word not to take up arms again would be permitted to return home. Those in the cavalry or artillery who owned horses would be allowed to take them along for spring plowing. Grant also provided 25,000 rations for the half-starved Confederates.

When word spread that surrender had come, hardened but exhausted southern soldiers wept openly. Men who had won the admiration of the world for their fortitude under fire and their courage against titanic odds, who had endured the smoke and flame of Pickett's charge and the carnage at the "Bloody Angle," threw themselves on the ground and sobbed uncontrollably.

Lee's great self-control failed him, too, as he rode back to his headquarters. Officers and men pressed about him, trying to touch their beloved commander or his horse. His deep voice trembled and his eyes filled with tears as he told them over and over to go home, plant their crops and obey the law.

Next day, Lee's noble "Farewell to the Army of Northern Virginia" was read to the troops. And on April 12 what was left of that proud force of fighting men marched, dry-eyed, up the hill toward Appomattox Courthouse for the formal surrender. There they found two Federal brigades lining the road, with General Joshua L. Chamberlain, winner of the Medal of Honor for heroism at Gettysburg, in command.

Chamberlain, like Grant, was magnanimous in victory. As the Confederates strode past, en route to surrendering their flags and stacking their arms, the Union general ordered a soldierly salute, which was returned at once by General John B. Gordon, the Confederate commander, and his men. It was, as Gordon wrote later, "a final and fitting tribute from Northern to Southern chivalry."

With the surrender of the Army of Northern Virginia, the war, to all intents and purposes, was over. The remaining Confederate armies in other parts of the South soon realized that their cause was hopeless.

More than any other Confederate state, the Old Dominion had furnished the leadership in the conflict, and independence had not been achieved. Yet Virginia, in defeat, had carved her name high on the scroll of valor and sacrifice.

TWENTY-NINE

Reconstruction

VIRGINIA had been the chief battleground of the war, and the physical devastation there was greater than in any other southern state. In huge areas bridges were down, roads cut up, homes severely damaged or destroyed, barns and fences burned or otherwise wrecked, crops trampled and cattle driven off. Much of Richmond, Abingdon, Wytheville and Bristol had gone up in flames, and Fredericksburg and Petersburg had been heavily bombarded. Large stretches of the Shenandoah Valley were a virtual desert, thanks to the prolonged fighting and the systematic destruction carried out by Sheridan. The section of the state east of the Blue Ridge and south of Washington, and extending to the east and south of Richmond, was in only slightly better case. A great deal of it had been fought over for years. The area from Alexandria to Manassas was described by John T. Trowbridge, a Northerner who visited the state almost immediately after the war, as showing "no sign of human industry, save here and there a sickly, half-cultivated corn field . . . the country for the most part consisted of fenceless fields abandoned to weeds, stump lots and undergrowth." Near Richmond he saw what had been "one of the finest farms in Virginia . . . showing the ruin and dilapidation of war . . . the windows were broken, and the garden, outhouses and fences destroyed." It was typical of many other such homes in the path of the invading armies.

In addition to this wholesale devastation, the keystone of Virginia's and the South's economic system had been knocked out with the elimination of slavery. Entirely new economic approaches had to be devised. This would have been sufficiently difficult, under normal circumstances; it was doubly so in the wake of defeat and demoralization. On top of all else, Confederate currency and bonds were absolutely worthless.

Even worse than the physical wreckage and the loss in material assets was the killing or maiming of thousands of Virginia's youth—those who would have been the leaders of the oncoming generation. Of about 170,000 who served in the regular armed forces, 15,000 lost their lives. The dead lay in graves from Manassas to Appomattox, and many of the living stumped about on wooden legs or with empty sleeves. Some overcame their crippled condition, and served in important posts after the war, but an entire generation of young men had been practically shot to pieces on the battlefields, with the result that the task of recovery was doubly great.

A bleak future loomed ahead for the commonwealth. Its people had sacrificed to the uttermost, had suffered for four years, and in the end had sustained a total defeat. If near-despair gripped Virginians for some months after the surrender, that is hardly surprising. They were stunned and scarcely knew where to turn. Many veterans were suffering from war-induced psychoneurosis, which was not then understood.

Perhaps the most significant glimmer of hope in the almost unrelieved gloom was the example set by General Robert E. Lee. He had ridden Traveller from Appomattox to Richmond in a drenching rain to join his family. Even the northern troops who garrisoned the former Confederate capital saluted when the forlorn little group rode up to the house at 707 East Franklin Street.

From that time forward, Lee urged all who consulted him to stay in Virginia and to work for the building up of the old commonwealth. "Abandon all these local animosities and make your sons Americans" was the counsel that the former commander of the Confederate armies gave to scores who sought his advice. Thousands of Southerners left the country and emigrated to Mexico or to Central and South America. He discouraged this. "Virginia has need of all her sons and can ill afford to spare you," Lee wrote to one of these emigrants.

The assassination of President Lincoln on April 14, two days after the surrender, added to the woes of Virginia and the South. Nearly all civil and military leaders of the Confederacy condemned and deplored the murder. General George E. Pickett's reaction was typical: "The South has lost her best friend and protection in this her direst hour of need."

Had Lincoln lived, his generous and understanding policy toward the conquered region might well have prevailed. But this was not to be. Vice-President Andrew Johnson was unable to hold the northern Radicals in check.

Relations in Virginia between Negroes and whites were amicable, on the whole. Despite the near-chaos in the first months, with some 360,000 Virginia Negroes homeless and drifting about—the great majority east of the Blue Ridge—there was surprisingly little violence, and a minimum of interracial bitterness. Many former slaves made their way to the cities.

Sometimes they aided their impoverished onetime owners. Booker T. Washington wrote that after the war there were "many instances of Negroes tenderly caring for their former masters and mistresses who . . . had become poor and dependent." He added: "I know of instances where the former masters of slaves have for years been supplied with money by their former slaves to keep them from suffering." Myrta Lockett Avary related that a Virginia family received their "first green-backs" from a former dining-room servant. He had found employment elsewhere on gaining his freedom, but brought five dollars to his erstwhile mistress at the end of the first week, and said he would continue to aid her in this manner each week thereafter. He declared that he would be "proud" if she didn't try to pay him back.[1]

At times, the burden fell the other way, and poverty-stricken whites denied themselves to care for their destitute former slaves.

The calm which prevailed in several Virginia cities was noted by Harvey M. Watterson, who was dispatched to the Old Dominion by President Johnson in early June 1865, and asked to report on conditions. He wrote the President from Richmond that "you may walk the streets for days and not witness one act of disorder or violence." He added that "prominent citizens of Petersburg and Lynchburg do not hesitate to avow that property is as safe in those cities as before the Rebellion." He quoted a "leading citizen of Lynchburg" as saying: "A more gentlemanly and more humane set of officers, and I may add, of soldiers, never occupied an enemy's country. Not one dollar's worth of private property was molested, nor any outrage of the most trivial character perpetrated."

In Norfolk, the situation was less happy; friction arose between the blacks and the Union soldiers, rather than the native whites. As in other eastern Virginia cities, Norfolk's black population had swollen to abnormal proportions. There were several riotous encounters between the blacks and the Union troops—which the northern press described, fantastically, as unprovoked attacks on Negroes by white citizens of Norfolk. As a matter of fact, the latter had much better relations with the blacks than the Union troops did. However, anti-southern elements in the North, notably in Congress, fed upon these false reports in the northern newspapers.[2]

There were riots also in Alexandria, which, like Norfolk, had been occupied by Union forces since early in the war.

In the desolation that gripped much of Virginia, it was hardly surprising that many white citizens were "unreconstructed" and remained so. Bitter old Edmund Ruffin, who had fired the first gun in the bombardment of Fort Sumter, and then had witnessed the downfall of the Confederacy and his own financial ruin, shot himself immediately after committing to paper his "unmitigated hatred . . . of the perfidious, malignant and vile Yankee race."

Obnoxious Union directives contributed to the prevailing misery. One which prohibited the wearing of Confederate buttons caused real hardship, since many veterans had no clothes except their battered uniforms. Ingenious Virginia women sewed black cloth over the buttons, thereby making them usable, and at the same time conveying the thought that the wearers were in mourning.

Brilliantly versatile Innes Randolph, perhaps with tongue in cheek, penned the oft-quoted bit of verse entitled *The Good Old Rebel*. Randolph, a four-year veteran of the war, expressed amusingly the rancor felt by some former Confederate soldiers. The first two stanzas give the general tenor:

> Oh, I'm a good old Rebel,
>   Now that's just what I am;
> For this "fair land of Freedom"
>   I do not care a damn.
> I'm glad I fit against it—
>   I only wish we'd won,
> And I don't want no pardon
>   For anything I've done.

I hates the Constitution,
This Great Republic, too;
I hates the Freedmen's Bureau
In uniforms of blue.
I hates the nasty eagle,
With all its brag and fuss;
The lyin', thievin' Yankees,
I hates 'em wuss and wuss.

The devastation wrought by the armies in the tobacco- and wheat-growing regions greatly retarded agricultural recovery. There was an almost total failure of the wheat crop in 1865 and a partial failure in 1866. Not only that, but the tobacco growers were grievously handicapped by the fact that whereas most of the Negro field hands had been working on the tobacco crop before the war, it was now difficult to get them back on the farms. The raising and curing of tobacco is a long and demanding process, and a tobacco grower could not risk having his workers wander off elsewhere before the intricate business was completed. Given the chaotic situation affecting the former slaves, it was both complicated and hazardous to raise the leaf in the years immediately after Appomattox.

In general, the planters had much land but practically no money. They accordingly devised the tenant and share-crop systems, under which the onetime slaves agreed to work the farms in return for a quarter to a half of the crop.

The value of Virginia's farms plunged downward in 1865, and land that brought $150 an acre before the war could be bought for two dollars. Farming was done on a smaller acreage than in the antebellum era, which was inevitable, given the elimination of the slave system. Between 1860 and 1870, the number of Virginia farms with at least one thousand acres fell from 641 to 317. Overall recovery was so slow that by 1870 the farmers of Virginia were hardly better off than they had been five years previously. A ray in the gloom was the revival of the cattle industry in southwest Virginia, owing to the rising demand for beef in the urban centers.

In manufacturing, the outlook was dismal. Virginia had been by far the leading manufacturing state of the South in 1860, but factory output had not reached prewar levels by 1870. Virginia was the only southern state of which this was true. The principal reasons for its

slow rate of recovery would seem to lie in the greater wartime devastation visited upon the Old Dominion.

Total monetary losses of all kinds sustained by the people of the
state during the war and reconstruction were estimated at $457,000,000
in a report adopted by the House of Delegates in 1877. Major
elements in this total were: personal property, $116,000,000; realty,
$121,000,000; internal improvements, $26,000,000; state's interest in
banks, $4,000,000; slaves and other property, $163,000,000. Thus a
state with somewhat fewer than 700,000 white and 500,000 black
inhabitants had sustained losses approaching half a billion dollars, in
an era when such a sum was of almost inconceivable magnitude.

General Robert E. Lee counseled his old soldiers and all other
Southerners to try to overcome these huge losses and the tragedy of
defeat by hard work and obedience to authority. He and Mrs. Lee
were occupying Derwent, a modest house in Powhatan County, in
August 1865, when he was invited to become president of Washington
College at Lexington. The college had been looted in the war and
was almost in a state of collapse. Lee turned down lucrative business
offers of various sorts, but accepted the position at Lexington at a
salary of $1500 a year. Characteristically, he hesitated to do so for
fear that the institution might suffer from having his name associated
with it.

Lee's health had been deteriorating since his illness in 1863. He
had a serious heart condition, and although only fifty-eight in 1865,
he looked far older, and his hair and beard were almost white. Yet
he plunged into his new duties with enthusiasm and worked long
hours at his desk. Enrollment soon increased astronomically to around
four hundred, with students coming from all over the South and
from northern states as well.

In addition to managing the affairs of the college and keeping
in close personal touch with the faculty and the hundreds of students,
Lee carried on an extensive correspondence with people throughout
this country and in Europe. He did this with virtually no secretarial
help.

He was indicted for treason, but General Grant agreed with him
that paroled prisoners of war, of whom Lee was one, could not be tried
for treason, so long as they observed their paroles. Lee applied to
President Andrew Johnson for a pardon, and Grant added his own
"earnest recommendation" that the pardon be allowed. Lee later signed

the oath of allegiance, when he found that this was required. However, when the Fourteenth Amendment was adopted in 1868, it provided that a two-thirds vote by Congress was necessary to the removal of such a disability as Lee's. In 1971 Senator Harry F. Byrd, Jr., introduced legislation designed to restore posthumously Lee's rights of citizenship.

Lee refrained from all criticism of the federal government and the northern people. This was in glaring contrast to the barrage of attacks on the "Yankees" and all their works that emanated from such "unreconstructed" individuals as George Frederick Holmes, Robert L. Dabney and George Fitzhugh.

Lee's five-year career as head of Washington College was notable for the example he set in this respect, and also for the educational pioneering that went forward there under his leadership. He stressed the need for less emphasis on the classics and a greater concern for more practical types of instruction that would be useful in building up the shattered South.

Pursuant to this theory, courses in commerce and business, in agriculture and journalism were projected. It is not known just how much of this trail-blazing was due to Lee's own imaginative concepts, and how much to his faculty. Some of the courses never really got off the ground, but certainly the direction was admirably forward-looking and well-calculated to aid in bringing the New South into being.

Despite his lifelong military career, Lee was well-read in ancient and modern languages, as well as in the English classics. Some of his correspondence is sprinkled with quotations from Voltaire and Cervantes, Shakespeare and Goethe. At Washington College he astonished students of Greek by addressing them in that language. He questioned a student of Spanish so narrowly concerning his course that the youth suddenly became aware that Lee knew more Spanish than he did.[3]

Lee's health was growing progressively worse, and on a trip to the far South the attentions showered upon him by an adoring people left him nearly exhausted. Not long after his return, he was stricken with his final illness, and he died October 12, 1870, aged sixty-three. Like "Stonewall" Jackson, Lee called on A. P. Hill in his delirium. His last words were "Strike the tent!"

Lee's calming influence during the years after Appomattox did much to reconcile the southern people to the grim realities. If the idol of the South had sought to arouse antagonism toward the national government, the results could well have been catastrophic. The Old Dominion's relatively brief period of reconstruction might have been much harsher and more prolonged.

Virginia's first provisional governor after the surrender at Appomattox was Francis H. Pierpont, who, during the war, had been governor of the "restored" state, i.e., the part under Federal rule, with the "capital" at Alexandria. Pierpont, a native of what was later West Virginia, had been an ardent anti-slavery and Union man in the antebellum era. After the close of hostilities, however, he demonstrated a realistic appreciation of the difficulties faced by Virginia, and made an earnest effort, as head of the government in Richmond, to alleviate the sufferings of the people. For example, he said, "It is folly to suppose that a state could be governed under a republican form of government, wherein a large portion of the state, or nineteen-twentieths of the people are disfranchised and cannot hold office."

As for the enfranchisement of the former slaves, William Lloyd Garrison, the rabidly militant abolitionist, had written in 1864: "When was it ever known that liberation from bondage was accompanied by a recognition of political equality? Chattels personal may be instantly translated from the auction block into freemen; but when were they ever taken at the same time to the ballot-box and invested with all political rights and immunities? . . . it is not practicable." Charles Sumner, another New England abolitionist, recommended educational qualifications as a prerequisite to voting by the freemen, most of whom were illiterate.[4]

Eight northern states refused between 1865 and 1868 to allow Negroes to vote, despite the small number of blacks in those areas. Negroes were permitted to have the franchise in only five northern states, in each of which there were practically no colored citizens.

The Virginia General Assembly which met in late 1865 was conservative and composed mainly of old-line Whigs. It superseded the small legislative body that had met in Alexandria during the war, and it had no intention of enfranchising the blacks. It did promptly remove the restrictions on voting by Confederates imposed by the Alexandria legislature.

The newly constituted Assembly also proceeded to adopt a Vagrancy Law, designed to give a degree of control over the thousands of freedmen who were drifting about aimlessly. They were looking for the "Forty acres and a mule" promised them in the North, and for other vaguely defined benefits. The nebulous state of mind of many of these guileless and uninformed individuals is aptly described in the following lines:

> An old grey field hand dimly plods through the mud,
> Looking for some vague place he has heard about
> Where Linkum sits at a desk in a gold silk hat
> With a bag of silver dollars in either hand
> For every old grey field hand that comes to him,
> All God's chillun got shoes there and fine new clothes,
> All God's chillun got peace there and roastin'-ears,
> Hills of barbecue, rivers of pot-licker,
> Nobody's got to work there, never no more.[5]

The Vagrancy Law adopted by the General Assembly early in 1866 was not as harsh as similar statutes passed in other southern states, but it could be used unfairly by the whites, and it provoked hostile outbursts in the North. The absurd claim was advanced there that Virginia and other southern states were trying to bring back slavery. The reaction in the North to the law was so pronounced that General A. H. Terry, military commander for Virginia, ordered that it not be enforced. John T. Trowbridge, the visitor from prosperous and unscarred New England—where provisions for taking care of superannuated mill hands were non-existent—was outraged by the lack of arrangements in wrecked and impoverished Virginia for taking care of superannuated former slaves.

The same Virginia General Assembly that passed the Vagrancy Law adopted legislation for the legalization and protection of marriages between blacks—rites for which there had been no legal sanction in slavery times. All slave marriages that had taken place before the war also were legalized by the Assembly, and the children of such unions were declared legitimate.

The Freedmen's Bureau was established in Virginia by the Federal authorities to feed, protect and educate the former slaves. The head of the bureau was former Union General O. O. Howard, a conscientious but naïve man. His assistant commissioner for Virginia was Orlando Brown, another ex-general in the Union Army, likewise well-intentioned. However, these high-minded individuals were capable of unwise actions. So were the idealistic northern schoolteachers who came to Virginia and other southern states to instruct the freedmen. Their zeal was immense, and they succeeded in providing much-needed schooling for a good many thousands of blacks. On the other hand, their supercilious attitude toward the South did much to create antagonism. In addition, they were so provocative as to prescribe *Uncle Tom's Cabin* as reading material in the schools, and to arrange for celebrations on the anniversary of the fall of Richmond. Furthermore, they named Virginia schools for the detested General Benjamin F. Butler and for Toussaint l'Ouverture, the bloodstained onetime ruler of Haiti.

Yet valuable Hampton Institute, founded by the dynamic Samuel Chapman Armstrong, had its origins in the work of these dedicated northern pedagogues. Five other normal schools for blacks also were founded as a consequence of their leadership. One of these was the Richmond Normal and High School, and another was the Charlottesville Normal School. Similar schools of a less permanent character were begun at Alexandria, Lynchburg and Danville.

The Freedmen's Bureau and its imported teachers, mostly women, managed to bring about the erection of more than two hundred schoolhouses during the bureau's five years of life, and to teach some 50,000 young Negroes to read and write. A good many of the latter seem to have learned quite imperfectly, but a beginning had been made. The bureau also had fed thousands in the first months and provided medical attention.

The Freedmen's Bureau was charged, on the one hand, with being an adjunct of the Republican party, and on the other was criticized by the Radicals in that party for being "too moderate." Regulations forbade its participation in political affairs, but some of its officers took part in such affairs, nevertheless. One means of doing so was through the Union League, a secret society which made special efforts to control the Negroes, and particularly their votes, for the greater glory of the Republican party. Meetings were held at night, often in total darkness. The League was well organized in Virginia and it exercised tremendous influence over the blacks. It created animosity between the races.

There was much natural kindliness on the part of white Virginians toward the Negroes, and this feeling was widely reciprocated. Union League agitators helped to undermine this state of things. They had a fruitful soil to work in when, for example, the *Religious Herald*, organ of Virginia's largest religious denomination, the Baptists, pronounced the blacks "naturally indolent, extravagant and careless," and as "fitted [only] for slavery," heavy manual labor, or such domestic work as cooking, washing and house cleaning.[6]

The General Assembly of 1866 was urged by Governor Pierpont to approve the Fourteenth Amendment, but the lawmakers refused by a nearly unanimous vote. Nine other southern states also refused. All ten states were soon penalized by the congressional Radicals, who decreed that they should lose their identities and be termed "military districts." Virginia became Military District Number One, and Union General John M. Schofield was named commander. Like Governor Pierpont, Schofield was an honest and understanding man.

However, the good offices of these officials were soon to be largely nullified. Such characters as the Reverend James W. Hunnicutt, a cold-eyed, hard-bitten mob orator, and Judge John C. Underwood, a sincere Unionist and foe of slavery, but a fanatical critic of the Confederacy, did much to undermine the progress that might have been made.

Hunnicutt was a native of South Carolina who lived in Fredericksburg before the war, where he edited a religious paper. He was not only a slaveowner but an advocate of secession. After Appomattox, however, he blossomed as a fiery foe of the Virginia whites and a violently partisan advocate of wholesale Negro enfranchisement. A reporter for the New York *World* wrote of Hunnicutt that "none who gaze once upon that countenance, so full of cunning and malignity, can ever forget it." The New York *Times* declared that "it is time for good men of all parties to discountenance and disown him."

Judge Underwood, a native New Yorker, had married a cousin of "Stonewall" Jackson before the war, but it would be difficult to find a more vicious critic of all things Confederate. He established a dairy farm in Virginia's Clarke County in the antebellum era. However, he became so unpopular as a result of his aggressive anti-slavery views that he was warned to leave the state, which he did.

Appointed United States district judge for Virginia, Underwood presided over proceedings in connection with the intended trial of Jefferson Davis. The former President of the Confederate States had been confined by the Federal authorities for two years at Fort Monroe, during the first part of which he had been put in irons and subjected to other inhuman treatment.

Judge Underwood delivered a charge to the grand jury sitting at Norfolk on the case of Jefferson Davis in May 1866, that was nothing less than a tirade. Among other things, he said that the Confederacy had "burned towns and cities with a barbarity unknown to Christian countries, scattered yellow fever and smallpox among the poor and helpless, and finally struck down one of earth's noblest martyrs to freedom and humanity," namely Lincoln. Of Richmond he declared that "licentiousness" ruled there to such a degree that "probably a majority of the births were illegitimate."

This outburst brought a prompt response from the Virginia press. The Petersburg *Index* termed His Honor an "absurd, blasphemous, cowardly, devilish, empirical, fanatical, ghoulish, horrible, ignorant, jacobinical . . . Yankeeish zero," while the Richmond *Whig* termed him a "dirty demagogue" and "monster." The judge retorted with some scathing observations concerning the Richmond newspapers, blaming them for "the murders, lusts, assassinations, violent and ungoverned passions" of the capital city. The *Whig* roared in reply that Underwood was an "ignorant blockhead" and an "indisputable ass."

Jefferson Davis was brought to Richmond in May 1867, for trial on the charge of treason for which he had been indicted the previous year at Norfolk. Whereas he had been extremely unpopular in the declining months of the Confederacy, reverential citizens lined Main Street and silently bared their heads as he passed. It was a mark of respect, even affection, for the man who had led them for four fateful years, and who now appeared broken in health by his long confinement.

Davis went to the courtroom in the postoffice building, in full expectation of being tried. Charles O'Conor of New York, one of several northern lawyers who came down to represent him, requested that the trial proceed. But counsel for the government answered that the case could not be heard at that term of court. Judge Underwood, now relatively mild-mannered, gratified Davis and his counsel by announcing that the defendant would be admitted to bail in the sum of $100,000. Among those who thereupon signed the bail bond were Horace Greeley and Gerrit Smith, two of Davis' bitterest northern foes in former years.

There were shouts, cheers and rebel yells, as the former Confederate President, now grayer and older in appearance than when he left burning Richmond two years before, emerged from the building.

He drove in his carriage to the Spotswood Hotel. As he entered the door, there was deep silence, and at a command "Hats off, Virginians!" thousands of men massed on the sidewalk and in the street, uncovered.

Davis was never brought to trial. Meanwhile the ineffable Hunnicutt was appealing blatantly for the Negro vote, with a view to making it an important adjunct of the Republican party. Hunnicutt had denied in 1864 that racial equality was either possible or desirable, but three years later he had reversed his position. In a harangue to Negroes he declared: "The white race have houses and lands. Some of you are old and feeble and cannot carry the musket but can apply the torch to the dwellings of your enemies. There are none too young— the boy of ten and the girl of twelve can apply the torch."

Hunnicutt summoned the Republicans of the state to meet in convention at Richmond in April. Of the 210 delegates, 160 were Negroes. The purpose of the gathering was to elect a "loyal governor and loyal congressmen."

Dr. Thomas Bayne, a loquacious and apparently able Negro delegate from Norfolk, first came to prominence at this Republican convention. He would be equally prominent at the state constitutional convention some months later, and the subsequent legislative session. Bayne was a center of controversy, and he would be ridiculed, at times, by the Richmond press, but emotion and partisanship were involved in the newspaper reports and comments of that era, and one finds it impossible to rely upon them in all respects. Bayne was a former slave who was taught dentistry by his Norfolk master, but then escaped to New Bedford, Massachusetts, where he practiced his profession and was elected to the city council. He returned to Norfolk after the war. He is authoritatively described as "the most spectacular, the most radical and one of the most hated of the Negroes in politics." He was small, garrulous and "bouncy," and "pure African" in color and features. His black cutaway, spotless white cravat and well-shined shoes made him sartorially conspicuous.

The treatment that Bayne and other Negro delegates received in the Richmond newspapers was not always unfavorable. For example, the *Dispatch* declared that "the debate today showed the colored men infinitely superior to their white confrères," and mentioned Bayne first on the list. "There were more brains in the colored leaders than in the white riff-raff," said the paper. The *Enquirer* pronounced some of the Negroes "intelligent looking men and neatly attired."

The press had great sport, however, with the bad grammar of some of the blacks. The *Dispatch* quoted one of these delegates as saying, "Dis convention is a equal convention, and we all has equal and illegal rights here."

Hunnicutt was in complete control of the April conclave of the Republicans, and also of the one held in August, which was brought together to consider the program of the earlier gathering. The Republicans endorsed "all acts passed by Congress," however, extreme. Furthermore, when a white delegate offered a resolution asking Congress not to confiscate the lands of everybody who served in the Confederate forces, he was shouted down. John Minor Botts, a respected member of the party who had served a jail term in Richmond for his Union sympathies, tried to exercise a moderating influence on the Republican wild men, but was unsuccessful. The leading New York newspapers were critical of the convention's actions. The *Tribune* declared that "to organize a campaign on the Hunnicutt plan is to abandon any hope of a permanent Union party in the South." The *Herald* asked, "Shall this continent be given up to barbarism for a fanatical experiment and a party scheme?"

An idea of Hunnicutt's viewpoint may be obtained from his demagogic appeal to some 2500 persons, mostly black, who convened in Capitol Square in connection with the August convention—as quoted in the Richmond *Dispatch* and the Richmond *Enquirer* for August 2:

"We tell the strangers that if they want to come with us they will have to swallow a bitter pill. They must swallow the Constitutional Amendment, the Civil Rights Bill, the Sherman-Shellabarger-Wilson Bill, the Supplementary Bills, every Reconstruction Act, the Iron-Clad Oath, the 17th of April platform, Wardwell, Hunnicutt and the nigger: yes, the nigger—his head, his feet, his hide, his tallow, his bones and his suet! Nay, his body and soul, they must swallow, and then, perhaps, they can be called Republicans."

Despite the insulting character of the foregoing, most Negroes followed Hunnicutt. Some white employers struck back. For instance, the Lynchburg *News* expressed gratification over the fact that "150 Negroes employed by the Wythe Iron Mines, all of whom voted the straight out radical ticket, were discharged."

In the deliberations of the Republican convention and those of the state constitutional convention soon to take place, the so-called carpetbaggers and scalawags played a significant role. The carpet-

(16) Depiction by Currier & Ives of an idyllic scene on a southern plantation.

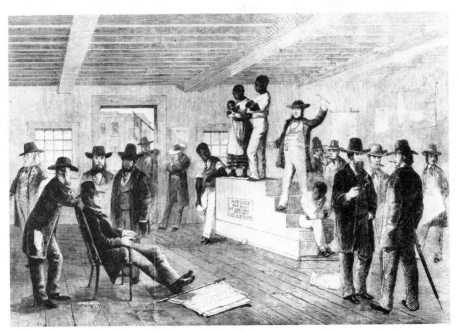

(17) A less idyllic scene from the *Illustrated London News*, showing a slave auction in Virginia.

(18) *Left*, Edmund Ruffin, famous agricultural pioneer, who fired the first gun against Fort Sumter in April 1861, shown next day in the uniform he wore at the time. He killed himself soon after Appomattox, rather than be governed by what he termed "the perfidious, malignant and vile Yankee race."

(19) *Right*, Stonewall Jackson is shown in this stirring statue by Charles Keck, which stands near the courthouse in Charlottesville and is one of several fine pieces of statuary in that city and at the University of Virginia.

(20) An oil portrait of Robert E. Lee, aged about 24, in the dress uniform of a lieutenant of engineers, by William E. West.

(21) *Left*, J. E. B. Stuart, the "Beau Sabreur" of the Confederate Army. The great cavalryman was killed at age 31.

(22) *Right*, General William Mahone, stormy petrel of Virginia politics for decades after the Civil War, in which he had served gallantly as the "Hero of the Crater." Mahone weighed about 100 pounds, had a squeaky voice, and was so fastidious as to his clothes that his tailor said he would rather make dresses for eight women than one suit for the general.

baggers were whites who came down from the North after the war. Some of them were sincere idealists who sought in various ways to uplift the blacks; others were slick, unscrupulous grafters. Horace Greeley described the latter group as "stealing and plundering, many of them with both arms around Negroes, and their hands in their rear pockets, seeing if they cannot pick a paltry dollar out of them." The scalawags were native Virginians who were co-operating cynically with the Radical Republicans in order to profit thereby, financially or otherwise.

Delegates to the Virginia constitutional convention were elected in October 1867. Under acts passed by Congress, many former Confederates were prevented from voting and practically all of these were excluded by the "test oath" from holding office. Seventy-two Radical Republicans were elected as delegates, 25 of them Negroes, to 33 Conservatives. The latter group, which included former Democrats and Whigs, had come together shortly before, in the hope of putting a brake on the excesses of the Radicals.

Judge Underwood was chairman of the convention, which met in the Capitol at Richmond in December 1867, and got down to serious business in early 1868. The Richmond press promptly termed the gathering the "Mongrel Convention," the "Convention of Kangaroos," the "Black Crook Convention" and the "Bones and Banjo Convention."

The convention was certainly unlike anything seen before in Virginia. Thirteen of the delegates came from New York, others from Ohio, Massachusetts and Pennsylvania, two from England, two from Canada, and one each from Scotland and Ireland. The majority of the white Radicals were northern men who had come to the Old Dominion with the Union Army. In addition to these carpetbaggers there were native scalawags. As for the Negro members, all but one were Virginia natives, and all were born in the antebellum era when it was illegal to teach blacks to read and write. Despite the latter handicap, about half of them had managed to learn at least these rudiments, and some were men of unusual ability and excellent presence. Most were property owners.[7]

Hunnicutt's influence waned as the convention got under way, but such vindictive individuals as John Hawxhurst and Orrin Hine, both native New Yorkers, were active and potent in the deliberations. Dr. Thomas Bayne and Lewis Lindsay were perhaps the most influential Negro members. Lindsay, a Richmond delegate, like Bayne spoke militantly and often. He was later the leader of a well-known Richmond brass band. J. W. D. Bland, who represented Prince Edward and Appomattox is described by James Douglas Smith, a leading student of the convention, as its "most thoughtful and able Negro member." Bland was only thirty years of age, but he showed courage and a capacity for dispassionate analysis. He was killed two years later, along with sixty-one other persons, in what was known as the Capitol Disaster. Part of the Capitol's second floor collapsed on April 27, 1870, during a largely attended Supreme Court hearing incident to a contested Richmond mayoralty election. Bland was then a member of the Virginia Senate. The General Assembly sent resolutions of condolence to his widow and an official delegation to his funeral. It also made an appropriation toward the funeral expenses.

The Radicals in the constitutional convention wrote the disfranchising clauses and the "iron-clad oath" into the organic law, over vigorous objections from white Conservatives. The Conservative leader was twenty-five-year-old Eustace Gibson, a native of Culpeper County, then living in Giles County, who battled valiantly but vainly on the floor, despite constant pain from wounds sustained in the war. Northern General Schofield also appeared before the convention to urge the elimination of these clauses, but to no avail.

The disfranchising provisions denied the vote to all former Federal or state officials who had fought for the Confederacy. The "iron-clad oath" required state and local officers to "recognize and accept the civil and political equality of all men before the law," and to swear that they had "never voluntarily borne arms against the United States."

These provisions of the constitution were assailed by the Conservatives. They declared that under the provisions, there would be "universal Negro suffrage" with "all Negroes eligible to office." Excluded from exercising the ballot would be all whites proscribed from office by the Fourteenth Amendment, while election of the vast majority of local officials would be by popular vote, with nearly all leading whites banned from the polls. The Conservatives also contended that the General Assembly districts had been laid out in such a way as to make Negro majorities inevitable in both the Senate and House. The Conservatives summed up by saying that the new constitution would mean that the blacks would hold "every office" and that Virginia would be under "Negro rule."

A minor factor in the Virginia situation at this period was the newly organized Ku Klux Klan. Various historians declare erroneously that the Klan did not appear in the state after the war. True, it was never a controlling element, nor was it ever guilty of the outrages perpetrated in other states farther to the south, where E. Merton Coulter, the eminent Georgia historian, says Klansmen "shot, hanged, burned and drowned Negroes, carpetbaggers and scalawags." However, the organization did function on a small scale in certain Virginia areas. Its first appearance seems to have been in northern Virginia in the spring of 1868, when it was reported to have beaten a Negro. During the "Underwood Convention," as it was called, the Klan threatened to hang Hunnicutt from the tail of Washington's horse in the Capitol Square, and to clip Dr. Bayne's "superfluous tongue and ears." This was mere bluff and bluster. In the Appomattox area, "the favorite tactic was to don white sheets and ride horseback," primarily with a view to frightening the blacks away from the polls. In the York-town-Williamsburg region during the same period, a crippled New England missionary was "dragged from his bed and over the ground to the woods and terribly beaten." The "Yankee Teacher" who told of this outrage also related that the Klan had been active in her neighborhood in less sinister ways, with a view to terrorizing the Negroes. She related the following concerning the hooded KKK: "One of them held out a skull to one of our men [a Negro], and asked him to please to hold it while he fixed his backbone! Another in some way disposed of a whole bucket full of water; our Aleck . . . asked how anyone could drink so much, and the 'sperit' cried aloud 'Wait till you've been in hell for a year!'" The Klan seems not to have functioned in Virginia after 1868.[8]

It appears almost certain that the blacks would have gained political control of the state, if the entire "Underwood Constitution" had been approved by the people and put into effect. It also seems clear that the blacks were unprepared to discharge such responsibilities. They had just emerged from two centuries of slavery, during which they had been permitted few opportunities to develop their capacities, and had been forbidden to obtain even a rudimentary education.

General Schofield, who commanded Military District Number One, recognized the inequity of the proposed constitution. He wrote General U. S. Grant in the spring of 1868, stating that no satisfactory Union party could be organized on any such basis. He urged that the constitution be allowed to "fall and die where it is," and that another convention be called to draw up a constitution "fit to be ratified by the people of the state, and approved by Congress and the country at large." General Schofield ordered the referendum on the constitution postponed.

The Conservatives imagined, incorrectly, that the northern congressmen and people would not permit Virginia to fall beneath the sway of the Radicals and their Negro allies. Every northern state that had voted on Negro suffrage since the war had rejected it. However, many in Congress and the North were determined to force upon Virginia a governmental polity which they themselves had refused to accept.

In this critical situation a group of Virginia leaders, headed by Alexander H. H. Stuart of Staunton, a member of President Millard Fillmore's cabinet before the war, decided to offer a compromise. They would make no objection to Negro suffrage if the disfranchisement and test-oath clauses in the Underwood Constitution could be voted on separately from the main body of that document. This proposal for "universal suffrage and universal amnesty" by the so-called "Committee of Nine" was violently opposed by some white Virginians, who were unable to bring themselves to accept unlimited Negro suffrage, and even regarded the proposal as "treason." However, Stuart and his committee went ahead, and they gained the approval of President Grant, after his election. He commended the compromise to Congress, and Congress accepted it.

The Conservatives, with some Negroes among them, began an intensive effort to win the referendum, and to elect a Conservative governor and legislature. A valuable ally in this battle was General William Mahone, "The Hero of the Crater" and a masterful politician, of whom much more would be heard in the ensuing two decades. Mahone's strategy was designed to divide the Republicans, who were committed as a party to support the entire Underwood Constitution.

He succeeded, through behind-the-scenes maneuvering, in getting the Republicans to nominate Dr. J. D. Harris, a Negro physician from Hampton, for lieutenant governor. Mahone's purpose was to split the Republican vote, since he reasoned that many white Republicans would not cast their ballots for a ticket on which a black was running. The head of the ticket was former Union General H. H. Wells, a New Yorker, who was provisional governor of Virginia, succeeding Pierpont, and a competitor of Mahone in railroad development.

The second part of this clever strategy involved getting the Republican moderates to name a separate and more conservative Republican ticket, and to have the Conservative party endorse it. The Republican moderates accordingly nominated for governor, Gilbert C. Walker, another New Yorker, who had moved to occupied Norfolk during the war, and for lieutenant governor, John F. Lewis, a Union sympathizer and member of the pioneer Lewis family in the Shenandoah Valley. Walker was not a "carpetbagger," in the usual sense. He was one of several substantial northern businessmen who had settled in Norfolk during the war, and had stayed on because they felt that the city and the surrounding region offered excellent opportunities for growth and expansion. When Walker was chosen by the moderate Republicans as their gubernatorial candidate, the Conservatives were prevailed upon to abandon their futile effort to elect a Conservative and to get behind Walker. The Committee of Nine, whom Walker had aided substantially in their successful effort to enlist Grant's support for the Committee's compromise plan, were influential in bringing Conservative support to Walker. A. H. H. Stuart and Colonel John B. Baldwin, of Augusta, the two leading members of the committee, were especially helpful in this regard.

The ultraconservatives were extremely reluctant at first to go along with the plan, but most of them relented and joined the campaign. It was one of the hardest fought contests in Virginia's political annals, with both sides resorting to improper tactics. The Union League and its allies swung the vast majority of the Negroes behind Wells and Harris, but a small minority of blacks supported Walker and Lewis. Several members of this latter group of Negroes were nominated for the General Assembly by the Conservatives. The Union League's effectiveness in the contest was lessened by the refusal of many farmers to employ Negroes who belonged to the organization. White employers in the cities also threatened to discharge Negroes who voted for the Wells ticket.[9]

A few days before the election, some 250 Conservative Negroes of Richmond held a barbecue and invited a number of leading white members of the party. Although they were risking physical retaliation from other Negroes—such retaliation was meted out in several known instances—[10] they displayed a banner upon which appeared a picture of a white man and black man shaking hands, and beneath it the words "United We Stand, Divided We Fall." A short time thereafter a suspension bridge on which many were standing, and which connected two James River islands, collapsed. Several persons were killed and a large number injured. Among the dead was the Richmond banker, Colonel James R. Branch, a leading white Conservative.

Candidate Wells had backed the disfranchisement and test-oath clauses of the constitution at the opening of the canvass. However, he discovered the magnitude of the opposition, and before the election on July 6, 1869, he announced that he was against these drastic restrictions on the political activities of most white Virginians.

The campaign strategy of the Conservatives paid off. The disfranchisement and test-oath clauses were defeated by approximately 124,000 to 84,000. The rest of the Underwood Constitution was ratified by a well-nigh unanimous vote, and Walker defeated Wells by about 119,000 to 101,000. In addition, the General Assembly chosen in the same election was overwhelmingly Conservative. In a legislature of 180 members, the Conservatives had a majority of 70. There were 27 Negro members, three of whom were Conservatives.

It was a shattering defeat for the Radicals, and for their scalawag and carpetbag cohorts. A waggish Charlottesville merchant announced a sale of waterproof carpetbags for anyone crossing the Potomac going north.

There was jubilation throughout Virginia. Gilbert Walker, the handsome, dark-eyed thirty-seven-year-old governor-elect, received loud acclaim in Norfolk on election night, as he appeared on the balcony of the Atlantic Hotel. He congratulated Virginia on her deliverance from "vampires and harpies." Bonfires were lighted, the band played "Dixie" and there was much rejoicing. Next day Walker traveled to Richmond and was met at the station by a huge throng, which followed him to the Spotswood Hotel. He spoke to massed thousands from the balcony.

With the disfranchising and test-oath clauses removed, the Underwood Constitution should have been reasonably acceptable to most Virginians. True, its political parentage was not what they would have preferred, since Judge Underwood was still widely hated, and the Radicals had dominated the convention that drafted the document. On the other hand, the Underwood Constitution had some excellent features, notably the requirement that a statewide system of public schools be established. It called for a written secret ballot, instead of voice voting or voting by a written ballot open to inspection by election officials at the polls. Heaviest taxes were placed on landed property, of which Negroes and carpetbaggers possessed little or none; taxation was made equal and uniform for various types of property. There was a provision for dividing counties into townships that was of dubious value; seemingly it was included by the Radicals in the hope that they could get control of government in the counties. On the whole, however, the constitution, as finally ratified, had its distinctly redeeming features.

When the newly elected and conservatively dominated General Assembly met in October, it carried out promptly, and almost unanimously, the demand of Congress for ratification of the Fourteenth and Fifteenth amendments to the U. S. Constitution. These amendments were designed to protect the former slaves in their voting rights and their other rights as citizens. Ratification of the amendments signalized the end of reconstruction, insofar as Virginia was concerned. Federal troops would remain in some states of the Deep South until 1877.

Virginians bade a glad farewell to Military District Number One in January 1870. The Federal garrison was withdrawn and the commonwealth's representatives were permitted to take their seats in the U. S. Senate and House. Governor Gilbert C. Walker and his government were given complete control of the state.

Virginia was back in the Union, after four years of sundering civil war and five years of Reconstruction. Thousands of her most vigorous sons were dead, and her once prosperous people were impoverished. She would slowly fight her way back, but the effects of her ordeal would be felt for generations.

THIRTY

The Era of Mahone

VIRGINIA was back in the Union, but tempestuous years lay ahead. The dominant personality of those years would be a dyspeptic former Confederate general weighing about a hundred pounds, with a squeaky voice, bizarre taste in dress, rare executive ability and great political prescience. He was William Mahone, whose exploits at the Battle of the Crater and elsewhere in the war had brought him the high commendation of General Robert E. Lee.

General Mahone's fine military record was achieved despite digestive problems that made it necessary for him to take an Alderney cow and chickens with him on all his campaigns. Only five feet five inches tall, gaunt and scrawny, he had long hair and a full beard. His military dress was foppish, his fingers were delicately tapered like a woman's, and his feet small and narrow. His commands were given in a "voice that was almost a falsetto tenor." Yet Mahone's division was described as "in better fighting trim" at Appomattox and as having "surrendered more muskets" there than any division in Lee's army. A member of that division called its commander "the biggest little man God Almighty ever made."[1]

"Billy" Mahone was the son of a Southampton County tavern-keeper. He was a graduate of the Virginia Military Institute, where he studied engineering. At the institute he developed great virtuosity as a poker player, and he is said to have won large sums from his fellow cadets. After graduation in 1847, he entered the burgeoning railroad business, for which he revealed extraordinary capacity and an imaginative approach. By 1861 he was president, chief engineer and superintendent of the substantial Norfolk & Petersburg Railroad.

Following Appomattox, Mahone went back into the railroad business, with a view to consolidating some of the short lines that had grown up before the war. His objective was to merge several roads into a single rail link between Norfolk, Petersburg, Lynchburg and Bristol. He succeeded, by 1870, in getting legislation through the General Assembly authorizing these mergers and creating the Atlantic, Mississippi & Ohio, of which he was chosen president at the almost unheard-of salary for that day of $25,000. The legislation had passed after a bitter contest lasting for years, in which the rough-and-tumble political infighting of the era was much in evidence, and bribery apparently was resorted to by both sides. Opponents of the consolidation, among whom Richmond business and financial interests were conspicuous, felt that Mahone's A.M.&O. railroad would build up Norfolk and the Southside and Southwest at the expense of the rest of the state. There was much criticism of Mahone's salary as president of the road. Jokers opined that A.M.&O. stood for "All Mine and Otelia's." Otelia was Mrs. Mahone. They had thirteen children.

"The Hero of the Crater," as we have seen, was one of the most influential backers of Gilbert C. Walker in the latter's successful fight for the governorship in 1870. In that contest Mahone provided the financial sinews of war for Walker's victory. Walker signed the bill authorizing the creation of the A.M.&O., but he soon threw his support to two measures, at least one of which was highly objectionable to Mahone. This provided for the sale to private interests of Virginia's substantial prewar investments in railroads. The other, a law covering Virginia's state debt known as the Funding Act, may have been acceptable to the general.

Allen W. Moger points out in his exceptionally authoritative book, *Virginia: Bourbonism to Byrd*, that the two bills were interrelated, and he adds: "Students of this period substantially agree that the legislation was procured by an unholy combination of the forces of the bankers, brokers, speculators and railroads . . . assisted by a few excellent men who were influenced by a desire to protect what they believed to be the essential credit and unsullied honor of the commonwealth." Moger adds that "some votes were bought, and many leaders most concerned about the state's honor and recovery had direct financial interest in one or both of these pieces of legislation." Governor Walker was among those with such a financial interest.

The bill providing for the sale of the state's railroad stock was strongly backed by the Baltimore & Ohio and Pennsylvania railroads, bitter rivals of Mahone and his A.M.&O. The two northern lines wished to purchase control of certain Virginia railways, with a view to erecting a system rivaling Mahone's. The latter declared that if they suceeded, southern Virginia would become a "howling wilderness." He fought the plan with all his resources.

The General Assembly before which this dramatic confrontation occurred was not conspicuous for ability or dedication. It was the product of the hectic and corrupt politics of that day, and was not infrequently termed "Virginia's worst legislature." The Conservative party, which included former Democrats and Whigs, had a large majority in both branches. The Negro members, totaling twenty-seven, were greatly outnumbered by the whites.

Sale of the state's rail stock may have been wise, under all the circumstances, but the commonwealth sustained huge losses in the process, while certain private interests reaped large profits. The only state-owned rail stock not disposed of was that in the Richmond, Fredericksburg & Potomac.

The Funding Act, with provisions for handling the state debt, was passed by the same General Assembly. It was to be a center of controversy for many years, as Virginians wrangled over the soundest and most honorable means of dealing with obligations assumed by the state prior to the Civil War in order to finance the construction of canals, turnpikes and railroads. By 1870, the debt had mounted to $45,000,000. Governor Walker and leaders of like mind in the legislature succeeded in ramming through the Funding Act, whereby Virginia would pay off two-thirds of the debt. The remaining one-third would be assumed, it was hoped, by West Virginia, and interest-bearing coupons instead of bonds were provided for this portion. For Virginia's two-thirds, holders of old bonds would receive new ones bearing 6 per cent interest. Negotiable coupons would serve to guarantee the interest, and would be detachable annually for payment of all taxes and other obligations due the state.

While fairly plausible arguments could be made for this arrangement, the sums required for payment of the debt, under its terms, were so large as to leave the state with insufficient funds to meet the ordinary expenses of government. The public schools, in particular, were left with wholly inadequate financial resources.

When the people of the state became fully aware of the meaning of this legislation, and of that under which the state's railroad securities had been sold, there was a widespread hostile reaction. Of the 132 members of the House of Delegates, only 26 were re-elected the following autumn. The new legislature repealed the Funding Act, but Governor Walker vetoed the repealer.

Virginia Supreme Court Justice Waller Staples held, in a minority dissent involving the debt question, that the Funding Act was unconstitutional—in part because it diverted to other purposes funds specifically designated in the constitution for education. Judge Staples was from Christiansburg and his opposition to the act was in accord with sentiment throughout the southwest. Frank S. Blair, prominent Wythe County attorney, also spoke for that region when he declared, in words that were to be quoted thereafter, "Honor won't buy a breakfast."

Virginia's "honor" was the principal consideration with many sincere citizens, who believed that the Old Dominion was obligated to pay every cent of the debt incurred before the war, plus interest, although they felt that West Virginia should assume its rightful share. Those who disagreed asserted that the vast majority of Virginians had suffered colossal and irreparable losses in the war, and that it was hardly fair to expect them to shoulder the enormous burden of the state's prewar obligations, especially in view of the fact that most of the bonds were held in the North or in England. It was asked, furthermore, why if an individual could legally take out bankruptcy, it was so outrageous for a state to take comparable action, when its economy had been wrecked, its currency rendered worthless, and its countryside devastated by the very people to whom a large percentage of the debt was owed.

Most of those who took this view were not asking for repudiation of the debt, but for a reasonable reduction. They were predominantly from the rural areas, mainly the western regions of the state including the Shenandoah Valley. As for the Negroes, they had had no part in contracting the debt in the antebellum years, and they quite naturally saw no justice in their having to pay any part of it now. Leading advocates of paying in full included many members of the old, established families, the better circumstanced citizens both in the cities and on the large plantations, together with the whites in the black belt.

Governor Walker's ardent espousal of the Funding Act and of the railroad securities sale endeared him to Virginia's ultraconservatives or "Bourbons," but rendered him *persona non grata* to Mahone. A wide breach developed between the two men.

Walker's break with Mahone, combined with the governor's espousal of the two above-mentioned unpopular measures, caused him to lose much of his influence in the closing years of his gubernatorial term. While his role in "redeeming" the commonwealth from the Radicals in the election of 1869 had been of far-reaching importance, some of his major policies as governor were highly debatable, and his personal financial operations were suspect. Following his governorship, he served two terms in Congress from the Richmond district, after which he returned to his former home, Binghamton, New York, where he died.

Virginians looked forward in the gubernatorial campaign of 1873 to electing "one of their own," preferably a former Confederate general. They found their man in James Lawson Kemper of Madison County. Speaker of the House of Delegates for two terms before the war, handsome, black-bearded General Kemper still limped from the nearly fatal wound he had sustained while leading his brigade in Pickett's charge at Gettysburg.

The campaign of 1873, in which Kemper was the Conservative standard-bearer, against Robert W. Hughes, the Republican nominee, was acrimonious. The Republicans and Hughes were allied with the Negroes, and Hughes was accordingly denounced by Kemper and others as a "Judas" and "worse than a carpetbagger." Yet Kemper was more fair-minded and objective on the race question than most public men of his day, and while repudiating all notions of "social equality" for the blacks, he stood firmly for their equality before the law. Some of his more violent partisans in the campaign sought to simplify the issues, and to consolidate them into one overriding question: "Shall we be governed by Negroes?" There had never been any real possibility of "Negro rule" in Virginia after the victory of the Conservatives in the constitutional referendum of 1869, but this demagogic tactic of pretending that the blacks were about to take over the state would be used by white politicians for decades. The number of blacks in the General Assembly of 1873 was only 17, as against 27 two years before, and it was to decline steadily thereafter until 1891, when there would be no Negroes in the state's lawmaking body. While the blacks held local offices in a number of Virginia cities, notably Petersburg and Danville, and they finally succeeded in electing one black congressman for a single term, the whites were in no real danger of losing control of the commonwealth after 1869.

Governor Kemper demonstrated exceptional courage early in his administration when he vetoed a bill that would have abolished the election of city officials in Petersburg—many of whom were black—and given their appointment to a municipal judge chosen by the General Assembly. Kemper vetoed the bill for various reasons, among them that it "deprived citizens of Virginia, many of them Negroes, of their inalienable right of self-government without due process of law." There was an initial outburst of indignation, but sentiment soon turned in the governor's favor throughout both the state and nation. He was overwhelmed with congratulations.

Another issue involving the race problem arose the following year in connection with the unveiling in Capitol Square of the statue of "Stonewall" Jackson "presented by English gentlemen" to the commonwealth. Negro militia units asked permission to march in the parade, but fire-breathing General Jubal A. Early objected violently. He had taken the oath to "support our infernal, lying constitution," in order to vote for Kemper for governor, but he now wrote Kemper that Negro participation in the parade would be "an insult to all Confederates who have any respect for themselves left." Kemper replied that the black units would march, that the program was fixed, and that "all hell can't change it." He urged Early, furthermore, "for God's sake" not to come to the ceremony. Early came anyway. As matters turned out, the Negro units did not show up, although they were expected. Perhaps this was because they had marched two days before in the procession which bore the body of General George E. Pickett to Hollywood Cemetery. General Joseph E. Johnston was one of those who had strongly urged that they be permitted to take part in Pickett's funeral ceremonies.

Governor Kemper's views on the state debt were more flexible than those of "Bourbons" whose minds were completely closed to any arguments that the amount should be scaled down. He pronounced the Funding Act a "disastrous mistake," but said it would have to be implemented, unless the holders of state bonds voluntarily agreed to reduction. He argued repeatedly for a reasonable readjustment, but was never able to bring this about.

He was charged with shortchanging the public schools and acting in the interests of the bondholders. This Kemper strongly resented, but he did back the state auditor when that official distributed a dividend to bondholders, while withholding funds required to be paid the schools, under the constitution. There was simply not enough money to do both, and Kemper had to decide one way or the other. The governor was on record as urging all Virginians to support the policy of free education, but he also felt that the provisions of the Funding Act had to be carried out, so long as there had been no voluntary scaling down of the debt.

Kemper was a controversial figure in various ways. For example, many of his associates charged him with ingratitude. A man of unimpeachable integrity, he stressed his determination to avoid even the appearance of favoritism. His executive duties were performed under almost constant pain caused by the Union Minié ball lodged at the base of his spine, and this made him seem irritable and unapproachable. One student of his career explains much of the criticism by saying that some of his disappointed followers "had expected him to perform the impossible feat of turning the clock back twenty years."

Mahone was in partial eclipse during the Kemper administration, although he had been the chief fund-raiser for the Kemper campaign in 1873. The money panic of that year caused him to lose control of the A.M.&O., which was subsequently placed in the hands of receivers. But with the campaign of 1877, the hundred-pound "king of the lobby" bounced back into the political arena. He became a candidate for the gubernatorial nomination, and assumed the lead for the first time in urging "readjustment" of the state debt.

Mahone's free railroad passes and his similar financial favors, combined with his backstage wirepulling and other political maneuvering, had made him a conspicuous, if somewhat sinister figure. Yet few questioned the potency of his influence.

Dressed in his invariable peg-top trousers and Prince Albert type coat, with a gray slouch hat most of the time, and a "hundred-dollar Panama" in summer, Mahone was quickly recognized in any gathering. He was so fastidious a dresser and so hard to please that his northern tailor was said to have remarked: "I would rather make dresses for eight women than a suit for the general."

There were several aspirants for the Conservative nomination for governor when the party convention opened in Richmond on a sweltering August day. Free liquor was much in evidence. Mahone led on the first ballot, but concluded that his opponents would combine to defeat him, so he threw his support to Colonel F. W. M. Holliday of Winchester, "the one-armed hero of the Shenandoah Valley." Holliday was nominated.

Mahone had been under the impression that Holliday was more definitely in favor of readjusting the debt than any of the rival candidates. This despite the fact that Holliday had not committed himself. Furthermore, he made no speeches during the campaign. When the General Assembly met, following Holliday's election, it became apparent that he was a stanch defender of Virginia's "honor," as the term was then used. James Barbour of Culpeper successfully sponsored a bill to modify the terms of the debt settlement and provide more money for schools. It passed, despite such statements as that of John W. Daniel of Lynchburg, soon to become a U. S. Senator, that he would rather see a bonfire made of every schoolhouse in the state than see the Barbour bill on the statute books. Although he had indicated in a public letter before the convention that the debt was a matter for the legislature, not the governor, to handle, Holliday vetoed the measure, and in doing so expressed views that were then all-too-prevalent among leading Virginians. The governor declared that "our fathers did not need free schools" and he pronounced them "a luxury . . . to be paid for by the people who wish their benefits."

Such sentiments were in accord with those expressed in 1875 by Prof. Bennett L. Puryear of Richmond College in articles published in the *Planter and Farmer* over the pseudonym "Civis." Any extension of governmental functions through the public schools would "relax individual energy and debauch public morality," he declared, and he added that the menial classes neither needed nor could benefit from formal education. Three years later, the Reverend Kinloch Nelson, a prominent Episcopal clergyman, pronounced the public schools "essentially communistic." Matthew Fontaine Maury had referred in a public address in 1870 to "this system of common schools that has been thrust upon us."[2]

It was partly because of such attitudes that almost half of the

schools failed to operate in 1878–79. In 1879 the school system was
unable to collect from the state $1,500,000 legally due it. Yet the
Conservative party had pointed to the schools in the gubernatorial
campaign of 1873 as its greatest accomplishment, and the Republican
party had endorsed Superintendent William H. Ruffner's administration. Governor Kemper told the Educational Association in 1876 that
Virginians should not regard the operation of a system of public education as a debatable question.

The system in Virginia during the 1870s consisted almost entirely
of elementary schools, and in rural areas these schools usually had
only one teacher.

Counties were forbidden by law to use state funds for high
schools. The few such schools were not adequate in preparing graduates
for college. A University of Virginia professor complained as late
as 1891 that there was a wide gap between the senior classes in the
high schools and the entering class at the university.

Pupils were segregated by race in the public schools, a policy of
which Superintendent Ruffner approved. He felt that the Negroes,
just out of slavery, were in a relatively primitive state of civilization,
and that they therefore required separate schools. He also was sure
that if any effort were made to educate the races together, white
hostility would destroy the none-too-strong school system.

Invaluable financial help was received from the Peabody Education
Fund, established after the war by George Peabody, a New England
philanthropist, as a "gift to the suffering South." Dr. Barnas Sears, the
fund's general agent, had his headquarters in Staunton. Sears was
partial to the Virginia system, which received $233,000 from the fund
between 1870 and 1882, one-fifth of the total contribution to all
southern schools. The Virginia school law of 1870, for which John
B. Minor, professor of law at the University of Virginia, served as
consultant, was regarded as a model. Minor was an enthusiastic
backer of public schools over a period of about fifty years.

The plight of Virginia's schools in the 1870s, combined with
Governor Holliday's veto of the Barbour bill, had substantial repercussions, even among the holders of bonds for the state's public debt.
The latter, for the first time, evidenced a willingness to accept modifications in the terms of the Funding Act, under which the schools and
other governmental services were being starved. When the General
Assembly convened in early 1879, sentiment was veering toward re-

medial action. The result was passage of the "McCulloch Act," which provided a reduction in the interest rate on the debt, and a possible lightening of the load imposed by obligations assumed in connection with the one-third assigned to West Virginia. There were other presumed benefits, although some observers regarded them as worse than nothing.

"Billy" Mahone, meanwhile, had been busy mobilizing sentiment for "forcible and irrepressible Readjustment of the state debt." He no longer regarded voluntary readjustment as adequate, and decided upon the more drastic approach. Outright repudiation was never a part of his plan. He launched the Readjuster movement formally at a convention in Richmond on February 25–26, 1879. Most of those in positions of authority in the state were "Funders" and almost unanimously opposed his program. Mahone had bought control of the Richmond *Whig*, but the other leading newspapers were strongly, even violently against readjustment. The Richmond *Dispatch* published a "blacklist" of Conservatives who had joined forces with Mahone to scale down the debt.

Mahone and his Readjusters realized that the elections of 1879 would be crucial, and they began mobilizing their forces for the showdown. The Funders, on their part, did likewise.

In addition to Mahone, there were other conspicuous leaders of the Readjusters. One of these was John E. Massey, who had been a Baptist preacher, but decided to enter politics, and was a powerful factor in the campaign of 1879. "Parson Massey," as he was called, termed himself "the father of the Readjuster movement," and he was certainly one of the pioneer advocates of this policy. Furthermore, his almost unparalleled ability as a stump speaker and master of repartee, especially before rural audiences, won many votes. He would break later with Mahone, after the latter thwarted his ambition to be governor and U. S. Senator, but he would serve as lieutenant governor, state auditor and state superintendent of public instruction, despite Mahone's hostility. In the last-named office he would be charged with profiting heavily from book contracts, but would sue for libel and win a favorable verdict in a Norfolk court, following a widely publicized and sensational trial. Massey lived for many years at Ash Lawn, the Albemarle County home of James Monroe.

Another stanch advocate of readjusterism in the campaign was H. H. Riddleberger of the Shenandoah Valley. Editor of the strongly Demo-

cratic *Tenth Legion Banner,* Riddleberger entered the General Assembly
in 1871, and was at first a Funder. But he later concluded that the
"privileged classes" were in control of things, and he switched.
Riddleberger was the most influential and prominent Readjuster in
the Valley during the campaign of 1879.

The Richmond *Whig,* Mahone's organ edited by W. C. Elam, was
a power in the 1879 campaign, and served as a vehicle for answering
the bitter assaults of nearly all the other newspapers. Elam, a North
Carolina native, is said by Charles C. Pearson, in his *Readjuster
Movement in Virginia,* to have used "insinuation, virulent personal
attacks, and often deliberate misrepresentation." He fought a duel with
Colonel Thomas Smith of Fauquier County over an editorial statement
in the *Whig* that upon the collapse of the Confederacy "the President,
Governor and the whole bomb-proof corps grabbed the remaining
swag and sneaked away." After the duel, Elam is said to have denied
having written that particular editorial, which reflected on Smith's
father, "Extra Billy," Virginia's wartime governor.

The Funders included in their ranks most of Virginia's "best people."
Both sides sought the Negro vote, but the Readjusters had easily
the more effective arguments, and the blacks supported them overwhelmingly. The Readjuster appeal to the Negroes went approximately
as follows:

"Put us in office and we will keep your schools open, pay your
teachers, provide for your higher education, abolish the whipping post,
and remove your insane from jails to a well-equipped asylum."

The Funders fully expected to win, and when the election returns
showed that the Readjusters had gained a clear majority in both
branches of the General Assembly, they were sadly shocked.

Final returns showed 82,000 votes for the Readjusters and only
61,000 for the Funders. The Readjusters won 56 of the 100 seats
in the House and 24 of the 40 in the Senate. They were the
beneficiaries of a serious economic depression. Their votes came mainly
from the Negroes and the western sections.

The Funder press, which had repeatedly misrepresented the position
of the Readjusters as "repudiation," declared—as paraphrased by historian Charles C. Pearson—that "rascality had won; the Negro was
the cause; and the world must know that taxpayers and *real Virginians*
had voted to pay the debt."

Mahone was riding high. When the newly elected General Assembly met in December 1879, the term of Colonel Robert E. Withers in the U. S. Senate was expiring. Senators at that time were elected by the state legislature, and Withers was the Funder candidate to succeed himself. The Readjuster steam roller promptly eliminated him and chose Mahone, who would take his seat in March 1881.

The Readjusters, meanwhile, made another effort to scale down the state debt, and H. H. Riddleberger successfully sponsored legislation to that end. The bill was vetoed by Governor Holliday, who pronounced it "contrary to the spirit which has ever moved and inspired the traditions of the commonwealth." Mahone and his followers saw clearly that they would have to place one of their own in the governor's mansion at the next election, if their program was to succeed.

When the 1881 Readjuster convention met to nominate the party's candidate for governor, William E. Cameron of Petersburg and Parson Massey of Albemarle were the leading contenders. Mahone, for some reason, did not want Massey as chief executive, and he ended by throwing his support to Cameron, who was nominated. Cameron's Funder opponent was John W. Daniel of Lynchburg.

The campaign of 1881 was an extremely vigorous one. Cameron and Daniel met several times in joint debate. Daniel's earlier statement that he would rather see every schoolhouse burned than to see Virginia repudiate her debt, was an issue that was not allowed to die. By contrast, the Readjusters pointed to their stanch support of the schools.

The outcome was another great Readjuster victory. Mahone and his followers not only put William E. Cameron in the governorship by a margin of just under 12,000 votes, but they won majorities in both legislative branches.

These results had been achieved, in part, with the aid of President Chester A. Arthur, who had taken office in September 1881, following President James A. Garfield's assassination. Arthur threw his influence behind the Readjuster ticket in Virginia, in return for a drastic action by Mahone. The "Hero of the Crater" turned Republican.

This loudly denounced apostasy on the part of Mahone was one of the most controversial events of the era. The United States Senate was evenly divided between Republicans and Democrats when Mahone took his seat there. Elected to the Senate as a Readjuster, rather than as a member of either of the major national parties, the question was which party he would align himself with in the organization of the upper house. Taking the position that he was free to decide, and that he was elected to the Senate to represent the people of Virginia, rather than any political group, he chose to cast his lot with the hated Republicans. For doing so he was branded by the Funders as "a traitor to his state, his section and his party."

Nevertheless, his action paid off in various ways to the benefit of Virginia. For one thing, Mahone was given extremely influential committee appointments in the Senate. For another, the backing of President Arthur in the state election of 1881 undoubtedly contributed to the sweeping Readjuster victory and made possible that party's enactment of measures which, despite the cries of outrage and dismay from the ultraconservative Bourbons, redounded to the well being of the commonwealth.

Mahone's motives in all this were by no means immaculate. He was anxious to build a machine that would maintain a steely grip on the state for an indefinite period. His political methods, furthermore, were slippery. In addition, he became increasingly arrogant and dictatorial.

The benefits of his policies to Virginia were soon to be realized. When the General Assembly convened, Riddleberger introduced another bill for readjustment of the state debt, similar to the one Holliday had vetoed. The bill passed and Governor Cameron signed it. The long and acrimonious controversy over this matter was nearing an end. The Funders were still adamant in denouncing the legislation as "repudiation," but advocates saw it as based on the principle that "the state's creditors should be compelled to share in the general loss occasioned by war and reconstruction."

The Funders were shocked again a year later when the U. S. Supreme Court handed down a ruling which, in effect, validated the settlement provided in the Riddleberger Act. This was so heavy a blow to the Conservative leadership that they felt compelled to accept the settlement and to end their prolonged agitation of this particular issue.

The plan provided for the payment by Virginia of a total debt of about $21,000,000, for which new bonds known as "Riddlebergers" would be issued, bearing 3 per cent interest. The remaining one-third of the debt would, it was hoped, be assumed by West Virginia. However, not until 1918 was a settlement of this latter question reached. In that year, the U. S. Supreme Court held West Virginia

liable for one-third of Virginia's *pre-Civil* War debt. The amount
was fixed at about $14,000,000. Payment was made by the West
Virginia legislature over a period of two decades, with the final in-
stallment in 1939.

Enactment in 1882 of legislation that led to a final settlement
of the long-debated debt question was only the first of a series of
far-reaching accomplishments in that year by the Readjuster-dominated
General Assembly. The Funders, by contrast, had not been notable
for awareness of the state's pressing needs, for they had been predominantly concerned with paying the debt, even if vital state services
suffered or were wrecked in the process.

But the General Assembly of 1882 moved promptly to provide a
different emphasis. Public education was the most essential area of
activity crying for attention, and the Readjusters enacted laws to
correct this situation by providing much more adequate financing.
The Literary Fund, established long before to aid the schools, was
bolstered with an appropriation of $379,000, while an additional cash
payment to schools of $400,000 was voted, plus quarterly payments of
$25,000. Schools for blacks, with black teachers, were given special
attention. On a higher level, the Normal and Collegiate Institute
for Negroes was established at Petersburg, with $100,000 appropriated
for its construction. The Central Hospital for mentally afflicted blacks
also was got under way at Petersburg, and $100,000 was provided
for its physical plant. Operating funds for both institutions were made
available.

The whipping post was abolished. This had been used primarily
against Negroes; anyone who had been whipped was automatically
barred from voting. Another measure especially welcome to the blacks,
as well as to the "poor whites," was abolition of the one-dollar poll tax.

Taxes on corporations were increased. These levies had been extremely low, and control over corporations, especially railroads, was
nominal. Under the new scale of taxes and assessments, corporations
paid more nearly in proportion to their ability. Relief for owners of
real estate was provided in the form of a cut in the realty tax from
fifty to forty cents per one hundred dollars of assessed value.

Another benefit came to the farming population—which constituted
by far the major percentage of Virginia's people—in the form of
larger appropriations to the Virginia Agricultural and Mechanical
College at Blacksburg. This important center of learning, later Virginia

Polytechnic Institute, had been established in 1872, and was languishing
for lack of funds.

Two-thirds of Virginia's Morrill Act endowment had been allotted
by the General Assembly to the Blacksburg institution at its founding,
and the remaining one-third to Hampton Normal and Agricultural
Institute. Under the Morrill Act of 1862, Congress had made available
to each state thousands of acres of the federal domain with which
to endow agricultural colleges. After the war, Washington College and
the Virginia Military Institute designed a joint technical program,
in the hope of obtaining these funds, and the University of Virginia
offered to create an agricultural college with the same object in view.
But the legislature voted to send the money to Blacksburg and Hampton. Governors Walker and Kemper had declared that business enterprise and industrial progress were the keys to the Old Dominion's
prosperity, and they regarded the Virginia Agricultural and Mechanical
College as especially important in this connection.

When, about a decade later, the General Assembly of 1882 enacted
a whole series of laws for the educational advancement of the commonwealth, as well as its social advancement, Virginia moved ahead of
the other southern states in these fields. Not only so, but in putting
through this program, the Readjusters kept the promises they had
made in the campaign the year before.

Yet it should be stressed that there was another and much less prepossessing side of the coin. U. S. Senator Mahone's ruthless and highhanded methods in securing the foregoing legislation made him suspect,
and caused him to be rightfully denounced as a political spoilsman and
an autocrat.

He was rapidly consolidating his hold. H. H. Riddleberger had
been elected to the U. S. Senate, replacing John W. Johnston. This
gave the Readjusters both senators, several congressmen, the governorship, and majorities in both branches of the General Assembly, plus
federal and state patronage. Mahone was the undisputed boss of this
widely ramified machine.

The Mahone-controlled legislature refused to re-elect any of the
justices of the Virginia Supreme Court, as well as three-fourths of
the circuit and corporation court judges. Most of these jurists had
been Funders, and Mahone decreed that they had to go. But this
was by no means all. Boards of educational and charitable institutions

were ousted on a wholesale scale, as Funders were replaced with Readjusters. Some of these changes were for the better; many were not.

Worst of all was the discharge of William H. Ruffner, the able and devoted head of the public school system, and his replacement with Richard R. Farr. Ruffner, a son of the distinguished Henry Ruffner—whose "Ruffner Pamphlet" blazed new trails before the Civil War—had struggled valiantly, against heavy odds, to build up the schools for both races. Named the system's first superintendent in 1870, on the recommendation of Robert E. Lee, a strong advocate of public schools, Ruffner was widely respected. But Mahone was determined for some reason to get rid of him, and after a dozen years in office he was dropped.

On the other hand, the Readjusters were responsible for significant improvements at the University of Virginia, long a citadel of Funder sentiment. Many friends of that institution were filled with apprehension and alarm when the General Assembly passed a law providing for the replacement of its Funder Board of Visitors with an all-Readjuster board. Yet the results were almost wholly salutary. James T. Moore demonstrates in the *Virginia Magazine of History and Biography* (January 1970) that the new board "won the cooperation of three hostile groups—the students, the faculty and the Democratic legislature," and "brought about a new spirit of innovation and efficiency." In accord with "their entire state policy," the Readjusters "did not attempt revolutionary or destructive changes in either the state government or the University," but sought, rather, "to modernize both, to make them more responsive to the changing needs of the state." At the university, their objectives were admirably realized.

Yet their program for the commonwealth would have been far more acceptable if Mahone had not used such brazen methods. He openly demanded that officeholders contribute a fixed percentage of their salaries to the Readjuster's "war chest"—5 per cent for state employees living in Richmond and 2 per cent for federal employees. In addition, businessmen who received state contracts were expected to do their share toward financing party activities.

Mahone also required Readjusters who held office to follow him blindly. Written pledges to "vote for all measures, nominees and candidates . . . as the caucus may agree upon" were frequently required. It was this which caused the bolt of the so called "Big Four,"

who refused to accede to Mahone's demands. The four were Senators
S. H. Newberry of Bland County and Peyton G. Hale of Grayson
County, formerly Conservatives, and B. F. Williams of Nottoway
County and A. M. Lybrook of Patrick County, formerly Republicans.
By voting together in the closely divided Senate, they could defeat
any measure of Mahone's by a majority of one, and they were
instrumental in voting down a number of his extreme proposals.
Parson Massey, who had broken with Mahone, worked with the
"Big Four" in fighting extremist measures sponsored by the "boss."
As Massey put it in his *Autobiography*, if these bills "had become
laws Virginia would not only have been made irretrievably Republican
. . . Mahone would have been vested with autocratic power in, and
over, her."

In that same year, Massey ran for congressman-at-large on the
Conservative ticket. The Mahoneites nominated Republican Read-
juster John S. Wise, a VMI cadet who had been wounded at the
Battle of New Market, and son of former Governor and Confederate
General Henry A. Wise. Massey was bitter in his denunciation of
"Mahoneism," and Wise hated Massey. In this savage confrontation,
Wise was victorious by some 5000 votes. The following doggerel
issued from the Mahone camp:

> Down midst de Funders
> Hear Dat mournful sound!
> All de Funders am a-weeping
> Poor Massey's in de cold, cold ground.

To what extent did Mahone depend upon the Negro vote for his
victories, and what were his views and those of Readjusters on the
race issue? Mahone stated in 1883 that "the Readjuster party in
Virginia is composed of 110,000 colored and about 65,000 white
voters."[3] It is not surprising, in view of the Readjusters' reliance on
the black vote, that the Conservatives stressed race in their campaigns.
Although "Negro rule" was far from a fact in Virginia at the time,
it was obvious that Mahone owed much to his black supporters.
Would he, therefore, accord them greater concessions than most white
Virginians of that era were willing to accept?

Mahone and his party were frequently on record as opposing
"social equality," mixed schools and racial intermarriage, and they
regarded the Negroes as members of an inferior race. On the other

hand, the Readjusters were strongly in favor of granting the Negro his political rights, and they showed their further concern by putting into effect measures which accorded the blacks better educational facilities and social services. But Mahone's biographer, Nelson M. Blake, quotes with approval the statement that Mahone no more contemplated Negro domination than did the "Bourbons." However, the Readjusters had to have the black vote in order to win elections and put their program into effect. They got that vote and they organized it into a genuine political force.

Mahone and his followers rewarded the Negroes with appointments to office. During the era of Republican dominance in Virginia, following the Civil War, the Negroes had received few political plums. U. S. Senator Mahone and Governor Cameron now saw to it that they were more considerately treated. Yet Readjuster leaders were careful not to give the blacks top positions, either in the state or the federal service. As Cameron wrote Riddleberger, "our people in this section expect and are willing that Readjuster Republicans and true colored men shall receive a larger proportion of the subordinate patronage . . . and it should be so in other sections."

Negro doorkeepers were named at Richmond for the Senate and House, Governor Cameron chose a black as his messenger, Negroes were given clerkships in some state offices, and a number of colored guards were named at the State penitentiary. Blacks were given the opportunity to teach black children in the schools. The most important federal post awarded a Virginia Negro was that of assistant postmaster at Norfolk, and there were a number of appointments to clerkships and other minor positions in the federal service. Blacks were also given appointments in the localities. In Danville, the most conspicuous example, they elected a majority of the town council, under a charter granted by the Readjuster legislature. In Danville, too, all the justices of the peace were black, as well as nearly half of the police force.[4]

The elections of 1883 were approaching, and the Conservatives decided that it was time for a determined effort to "redeem" the state from "Mahoneism." They accordingly adopted a new approach. Instead of holding their convention in Richmond they moved it to Lynchburg. They also arranged to provide special representation for the Shenandoah Valley and the southwest, both hotbeds of Readjusterism. In addition, they formally changed the name of their party from Conservative back to "Democratic"—although they had campaigned in 1881 as "Conservative Democrats"—and they chose a new state chairman. He was John S. Barbour of Culpeper, a long-time foe of Mahone on both the political and the railroad fronts, and an organizer of great gifts.

The resurgent Democrats, in convention assembled, accepted the Riddleberger debt settlement. They also expressed wholehearted support for public schools that would educate both races. Mahone's dictatorial rule was, of course, denounced.

After the Lynchburg convention adjourned, Chairman Barbour began setting up the Democratic organization throughout the state. It was a masterpiece of thoroughness and efficiency, and it extended down to the precinct level. Committees were given responsibility for registrations and similar necessary details, with regular reports to headquarters. The Lynchburg *News* claimed that Peter J. Otey of that city, rather than Barbour, did most of the work in framing the plan before it was put into operation.

The Democrats and the Readjusters prepared feverishly for the elections, and both sides resorted to improper and highhanded methods. The Readjusters might have won, had not a riot in racially tense Danville three days before the voting played directly into the hands of the Democrats. Whether members of that party shrewdly provoked the shooting for political purposes, is unknown. This was charged by the Readjusters, but positive proof was not forthcoming. At all events, there was gunplay in which four Negroes and one white were killed. This was a godsend to the Democrats, who seized upon it and claimed that here was irrefutable evidence of the fruits of "Mahoneism." The government of Danville, it was argued, had fallen under the sway of the blacks, thanks to a Readjuster-approved charter— a result frequently forecast by the Democrats.

Lurid accounts of the riot, broadcast by the Democrats to every corner of the state on the eve of the election, greatly exaggerated the crisis in Danville. White voters in all sections accordingly were influenced to vote "against Mahone," and a triumph for the Democrats resulted. They won about two-thirds of the seats in both branches of the General Assembly, and Mahone's hold on the state government was broken. The diminutive former general would be squeaking orders to his henchmen for several more campaigns, but he had reached and passed the high-water mark of his political power. Mahone was once termed "the most influential political figure in Virginia since the days of Thomas Jefferson," but his supremacy had ended.

When the newly-elected General Assembly met, it demonstrated that it did not intend to repeal the progressive reforms instituted by the Readjusters, but it also revealed a determination to seize the engines of power. Readjuster Governor Cameron was still in office, so the Democratic majority in the legislature transferred much of the appointive authority to itself. It also launched investigations into the activities of Readjuster officeholders, and uncovered incompetence, petty graft and excessive partisanship.

Election machinery was overhauled in such a manner as to place it under Democratic control. Congressional districts were rejiggered to the marked advantage of the Democrats. The General Assembly passed a resolution demanding that Mahone resign from the U. S. Senate. The grounds alleged were of a highly partisan character, and Mahone paid no attention.

The popularity of the reforms that he had successfully sponsored in Virginia was attested by the reluctance of the legislature to tamper with them. The Riddleberger debt settlement remained in effect, as did the larger appropriations for educational and charitable purposes, the more liberal franchise provisions and the reformed tax laws. The whipping post was not brought back. Laws affecting the politically powerful railroads were tightened. It can readily be seen that in pursuing these policies the Democrats were busily engaged in divesting themselves of their ultraconservative "image."

But they were determined to retain control, and to that end they enacted the Anderson-McCormick election law. They were fully aware that their one-sided victory in the election of 1883 was largely due to the Danville riot and the accompanying emphasis on the race issue. The new law was so written as to "perpetuate the rule of the white man in Virginia," according to the strongly approving Richmond *Dispatch*. Historian Charles E. Wynes has termed the law "an open invitation to fraud and corruption."

Supplementing and strengthening the political machinery it provided was the "courthouse clique" system which had been operative in Virginia since the early 1800s. (See Chapter Twenty.) Somewhat modified over the years, it now revolved to a considerable degree around the Democratic party's county chairman, who got his orders from the state chairman. These party functionaries, operating in conjunction with a Democrat-controlled General Assembly, were able to dictate appointments to the county electoral board, and through it the election judges and clerks. Allen W. Moger has pointed out that through these "election officials and the use of money and local pressure," the county chairman "was able to see that only his men were chosen as treasurer, sheriff, clerk of the court, commissioner of the revenue, member of the legislature and supervisor."

The presidential campaign of 1884, in which Grover Cleveland faced James G. Blaine, provided the next test for the two major parties in Virginia. Mahone decided to conduct the contest under the banner of the Republican party, and to subordinate the role of the Readjusters. It seemed to be impossible to carry on a political campaign in those days without a substantial degree of corruption. This one was no exception and both sides were guilty. Cleveland won the state by 6000 votes, and the Democrats also triumphed in eight of the ten congressional races. Cleveland promptly began ousting Republican postmasters and other U.S. officeholders in Virginia.

Despite this setback, Mahone made a desperate effort to retain the governorship in 1885. Tossing off orders to the Republicans in the manner of an Eastern potentate, he chose John S. Wise as the party nominee. Wise was exceptionally adept as a stump speaker. The Democrats selected Fitzhugh Lee to oppose him. Lee was popular and articulate, had been a Confederate general, and was a nephew of "Marse Robert." To add strength to the ticket and a diversified appeal, the Democrats named Parson Massey as their candidate for lieutenant governor.

The campaign was less acrimonious than others during the era, and was characterized by barbecues, joint debates, "mounted processions" and similar events. It was claimed that Lee was capitalizing on his relationship to his uncle by riding on a saddle used by the famous Confederate commander, but this was untrue. Furthermore, Lee said he wished his name was Smith, in order that he might be judged on his own merits, and at the same time get the support of all the Smiths.

Lee won by about 16,000 votes, and great was the rejoicing among the Democrats over the "redemption" of the state government from the Readjusters. Mahone claimed that the election had been stolen, saying that the Democrats had "absolute control" of the election machinery. It is remarkable, all things considered, that the Republicans, led by Wise and Mahone, were able to give the Democrats, led by Lee and Barbour, so close a run.

Parson Massey was elected lieutenant governor, and the Democrats gained greatly increased majorities in the General Assembly. The newly chosen Senate had 29 Democrats and only 11 Republicans, while the House had 72 Democrats and 28 Republicans. There was now only one Negro in each branch.

"Fitz" Lee's inaugural ball in Richmond the night of January 1, 1886, launched a new era in Virginia. The Democrats were at last returned to power, and Mahone had been ousted. Governor Lee, a gallant cavalry general under "Jeb" Stuart, was magnetic and popular. He and hundreds of other Democrats and their gaily bedecked ladies danced all night in the First Regiment Armory to the music of two brass bands. One of the latter played a march especially composed in honor of the new chief executive. It opened, appropriately, with cavalry calls.

A note of intersectional amity was sounded in the attendance of the Joel Parker Association from New Jersey, an organization of Union Civil War Veterans. Multitudinous toasts were drunk with these erstwhile foes, and there was unabashed admiration for their ability to "partake of their collation."

Mahone's service in the U. S. Senate was terminated as soon as the newly elected Democratic legislators could vote on the matter. John S. Barbour, the organizer of victory in this and previous campaigns, aspired to Mahone's seat but he encountered sharp competition from John W. Daniel, the "Lame Lion of Lynchburg," who limped from a war wound. A youthful railroad attorney named Thomas S. Martin first came to statewide notice as Daniel's campaign manager. Thanks largely to Martin's astute management, Daniel defeated Barbour, and was chosen senator, effective in March 1887. Barbour was disappointed, but he gained his objective in 1888 when he was elected to succeed Riddleberger.

Fitzhugh Lee's policies as governor were based on more flexible thinking than that of some previous executives. Although he was a member of a great Virginia family, Lee was not a typical "Bourbon." Mahone had tried to raise specters of "Bourbon reaction" during the campaign, but to little avail. Lee was youthful in outlook and open to suggestions. He regarded the debt question as settled, and he believed in supporting the public schools. He was also in favor

of developing the state agriculturally, and was responsible for outlawing fraudulent fertilizers and enlarging the Department of Agriculture. He favored intensified industrialization. No less than $100,000,-
000 in new capital is said to have come into Virginia during his governorship.

Fitzhugh Lee's more enlightened outlook was, in part, a legacy of
the Mahone regime. Whatever may be said in criticism of Mahone,
and there is plenty to be said concerning his political methods and
his dictatorial propensities, he had shaken Virginia's ruling group out of
its lethargy. That group was now more receptive to new ideas, less
determined to maintain the status quo.

After 1889, the Democrats held the governorship, large majorities
in the General Assembly, both seats in the U. S. Senate and most of
those in Congress. Enclaves of Republican strength would remain in
southwest Virginia, the Shenandoah Valley and a few other areas,
of more limited extent, but the Democrats would retain control of
the state government, the legislature and both Senate seats for more
than three-quarters of a century. Mahone's subsequent attempts to
regain power came to nothing.

The Negro vote was no longer solidly Republican. Mahone charged
that Fitzhugh Lee had gained his entire majority in 1885 through
fraud in seven Black Belt counties, all of which he carried. After
that election, the Democrats gained strength among the Negroes of
eastern Virginia.

John Mercer Langston, a Virginia-born Negro who was then
serving as the first president of the Virginia Normal and Collegiate
Institute at Petersburg, decided to run for Congress in 1888 from
the Fourth or Black Belt district. Three other Negroes had sought unsuccessfully to win this seat, beginning in 1872. Langston felt that the
time was now ripe.

He was the son of Ralph Quarles, a white Louisa County planter,
and Lucy Langston, his former slave of mixed Negro and Indian
blood, to whom he had given her freedom. Quarles and Lucy died a
few years after Langston's birth, and at age five the boy was removed
to Ohio, where he grew up. He studied law and became the first
Negro admitted to practice before the United States Supreme Court.
When the Civil War broke out, he was active in recruiting colored
troops for the Union Army. At the end of hostilities, he was named
inspector general for the Freedmen's Bureau. He then taught law

at Howard University in Washington, becoming dean of the law school and acting president of the institution. He was named U. S. Minister to Haiti in 1877, and in 1886 was chosen the first president of the Virginia Normal and Collegiate Institute.

When Langston decided to make a bid for Congress as a Republican from Southside Virginia, he found William Mahone, the fading leader of Virginia's Republicans, ranged in solid opposition. Mahone felt that the time had not come for a Negro to serve in Congress from the Old Dominion, and that if one did so, it would hurt the Republican cause in the state. He also seems to have had a personal dislike for Langston.

But the latter was not deterred. The district contained many more Negroes than whites, and he felt that he could win without Mahone. This despite the fact that Mahone managed to line up a number of Negro leaders in the district against Langston.

Mahone put up Judge Robert W. Arnold as the official Republican nominee, and the Democrats named Edward C. Venable. The Democrats were in control not only of the state government but of the precinct election machinery practically everywhere. Langston drew the race issue sharply, and called on the blacks to support him. The Democrats trotted out the usual claim that they were fighting to save southern civilization. Both sides employed the customary fraudulent election techniques. When the votes were counted, Venable was given 13,310, Langston 12,657 and Arnold 3207. Langston contested the count, and after a long-drawn-out battle before a congressional committee and the House itself, he was declared the winner. By that time his term had only a few months to run.

Soon after being sworn in, Langston made an intemperate, even incendiary speech to his supporters, in which he hinted strongly at violent revolution, if that should become necessary, and advocated the "commingling of white men's blood and black men's blood" to produce a superior civilization. These sentiments did little to endear him to his white constituents.[5] He ran again for Congress in 1890, but lost to a white Democrat, J. F. Epes, by more than 3000 votes.

Langston settled in Washington and resumed the practice of law. He wrote his autobiography, *From the Virginia Plantation to the National Capital*, which is "almost unrelieved in praise of the author."[6] Yet Langston's high estimate of his own abilities was, in considerable degree justified.

Whether Langston's congressional candidacy greatly intensified interracial animosity in Virginia is open to question. Some contend that it did. At all events, race relations deteriorated in the years following his successful effort to become a congressman.

Mahone's attacks on Langston cost the Republican boss many of his black supporters, and he lost many of his white supporters, as well. Nevertheless, he decided to seek the governorship in 1889. Campbell Slemp of Lee County was his running mate for lieutenant governor.

Mahone's Democratic opponent was Philip W. McKinney, an eminent Farmville lawyer who had run unsuccessfully for attorney general eight years before. Mahone was able to retain most of the Negro vote, despite his efforts to defeat Langston, for he had made special appeals to the blacks over a long period. But some of the principal Republican leaders broke with him. John S. Wise, William E. Cameron and others signed a circular declaring that "the defeat of William Mahone is essential to the salvation of the Republican party." Cameron added later that "The politicians known as Mahoneites . . . are only acquainted with three elements of management—force, fraud and finance." Wise declared that "the only way Mahone will bury the hatchet is in the head of every one who opposes him."

Despite these discouragements, Mahone put on the most vigorous campaign of which he was capable. Both sides were vituperative in their statements. Mahone again denounced the "Bourbons" and their reactionary views. The pro-McKinney Lynchburg *Virginian*, for its part, appraised the contest as a "fight between intelligence, virtue, religion and the material interests on the one hand, and vice, venality, corruption and unscrupulous rapacity on the other."

With his following sharply divided, Mahone's cause was hopeless from the first. He was defeated by nearly 43,000 votes. This stunning setback not only ended what little influence Mahone had left, but was a severe reverse for the Republican party. It would be generations before the party regained its influence in Virginia.

The Negroes also became politically powerless over a long period. The General Assembly which met in 1891 contained not a single Negro. In 1892, Joseph R. Holmes of Charlotte County, a black who had served in the Underwood convention more than two decades before, decided to run for the legislature. He was shot dead by a white man in the audience he was addressing. This outrage ended efforts of the blacks to run for the Assembly from that area.

With McKinney's landslide election as governor in 1889, the "Era of Mahone" may be said to have ended. Mahone died six years later. The pint-sized ex-general had been a dominant figure on the political scene in Virginia for more than a decade and a half, and for several years he had been the state's political czar. But power went to his head, and his totalitarian techniques alienated thousands who might have been won over to his side. In addition, some of his stanchest white friends and most influential allies broke with him, as did many Negroes.

Yet if the Era of Mahone was over, it had left an indelible imprint upon the commonwealth. There would never again be the widespread indifference to the public schools that existed when the little general came upon the scene a few years after the Civil War. Nor would Virginia ever again be rent asunder in controversies over the public debt, with essential services shunted aside while lawmakers, public officials and business leaders wrangled over the best means of dealing with the problem. True, there would soon be sharp retrogression in the prevailing attitude toward the Negro, but his education would remain a matter of sufficient public concern for it to be recognized as a continuing responsibility of the state. The same would be true of the state's duty to care for the Negro insane. The whipping post would never be brought back.

William Mahone had his grave faults along with certain conspicuous virtues. His name, even today, provokes shudders in some circles. The fact remains that, with all his shortcomings, he brought lasting benefits to Virginia during his stormy career.

THIRTY-ONE

Fade-Out of the "Bloody Shirt"

WITH HUNDREDS OF THOUSANDS killed or maimed on both sides of the Potomac and the Ohio, it is not surprising that bitterness lingered for years after the war. In the North there were the Thaddeus Stevenses and the Ben Wades to keep alive intersectional animosities, and in Virginia there were the George Fitzhughs, the Robert L. Dabneys and the Jubal A. Earlys.

After serving briefly as a judge of the court in the hated Freedmen's Bureau at Richmond, George Fitzhugh reverted to his prewar posture of belligerent antagonism toward the North. "Cruel, persecuting, revengeful, envious radicalism cannot mar the beauty and fertility of our fields . . . nor crush out our just pride and self-respect," he wrote. As for the blacks, he stooped to the absurdity of saying: "There never lived one single full-blooded Negro who could manage successfully all the details of a large farm. Nay, there never was a Negro or a North American Indian who could manage his own family."

The Reverend Robert L. Dabney's aversion to "Yankees" was as irreconcilable as Edmund Ruffin's had been. He declared in 1870 that he would never forgive the Northerners. "What, forgive those people who have invaded our country, burned our cities, destroyed our homes, slain our young men, and spread desolation and ruin over our land? No, I do not forgive them," this minister of the gospel declared.

The outbursts from Virginia's purveyors of antagonism were matched in the North by those in *Harper's Weekly*. It specialized in assaults on Southerners "who had betrayed their trust," and had forced "Union soldiers to rot in Andersonville and Libby prisons."

Fortunately, these intersectional rantings were not typical. The example of tolerance and Americanism set by Robert E. Lee outweighed a hundred jeremiads from lesser spirits who seemed incapable of forgiving or forgetting.

In New England, James Russell Lowell, who had been one of the foremost anti-slavery writers in earlier days, adopted a much more understanding tone with the coming of peace. In his ode on the centennial of George Washington's taking command of the Continental Army at Cambridge, Massachusetts, he said, in part:

> Virginia gave us this imperial man. . . .
> What shall we give her back but love and praise
> As in the dear old unestranged days
> Before the inevitable wrong began? . . .
> If ever with distempered voice or pen
> We have misdeemed thee, here we take it back. . . .

Five years later, another Revolutionary anniversary served as the theme around which the tattered bonds of friendship between the sections could be knit together again. When the centennial of the surrender of Cornwallis at Yorktown was observed there in 1881, Massachusetts historian Robert C. Winthrop sounded a strong note of reconciliation. And James Barron Hope of Norfolk, Virginia's official laureate for the occasion, wrote:

> Give us back the ties of Yorktown
> Perish all the modern hates!
> Let us stand together, brothers,
> In defiance of the Fates;
> For the safety of the Union,
> Is the safety of the states![1]

Much credit for the success of the centennial at Yorktown must go to Michael Glennan, editor of the Norfolk *Virginian,* who began agitating in 1879 for the celebration, and roused the state and nation to the importance of a suitable observance.

George W. Bagby's writings from New England in 1880 helped to pour balm on intersectional wounds. Southerners in antebellum days had often gotten the impression that most New Englanders who came South were peddlers trying to sell them "red-flannel sausages, wooden nutmegs and wheelless clocks." Bagby was commissioned by the Baltimore *Sun* to visit Connecticut and record his impressions. He was surprised, among other things, to encounter "no sniveling divines." He also paid tribute to the thrifty propensities of the Connecticut citizenry in the following:

"There is a marked difference between the spitting of Yankees and the spitting of Southerners. Economical even in his expectoration, the Yankee holds his quid half a day, ejecting at long intervals a meagre drop or globule, rarely squirting and never spattering. . . . The very salivary glands of these people are labor-saving."

On the more serious side, the Virginian "learned that the Southerner, not the Northerner, was most guilty of hard-feelings." As he circulated in a crowd on New Haven common, he heard "one speaker after another get up in defense of the South." "Deeply moved," Bagby concluded that reconciliation was not only possible but inevitable. In the last year of his life, in an address at Trenton, New Jersey, entitled "Yorktown and Appomattox," Bagby—who as editor of the *Southern Literary Messenger* had called for Virginia's secession months before it was actually voted—issued a plea for reconciliation and peace.[2]

Intersectional fraternization in the early postbellum years was not easy at the White Sulphur Springs, where a few faint glimmerings of gaiety were visible as early as 1867. When General Robert E. Lee made the first of three annual visits there in that year, a former governor of Pennsylvania and his party were shunned by the assembled Southerners until Lee warmed the frigid atmosphere by walking over to the lonely group and introducing himself. Later, as animosities died, there were easy relations between visitors from the North and those from the South.

The hotel at the White was badly down-at-heel, but it was gradually gotten back into full operation, while the same process went forward at such other springs as the Rockbridge Alum and the Allegheny. Not until the early 1890s would the Hot Springs be metamorphosed from a mecca for invalids into a great resort, with the old hotel rejuvenated at a cost of a million dollars and rechristened The Homestead.

Meanwhile in the 1870s and 1880s, the White became a center of joyful relaxation, with three reigning Virginia belles holding the center of the stage: Mary Triplett, with her blonde "cameo-like beauty"; May Handy, divine of face and form, and the delightsome Mattie Ould, whose witty ripostes were widely quoted. At first there had been a great scarcity of young men at the springs, for those who had survived the war were often working hard at almost any job they could get. But a few years later a fair number of these Virginia gallants were able to break away from their mundane tasks and catch the wheezing, puffing Virginia Central train to White Sulphur Springs. Conspicuous among them was Jo Lane Stern, active in the Virginia National Guard, of whom it was said, "He would rather lead the german than the Old Guard at Waterloo."

"Grand fancy masked balls" and other such diversions in which Southerners and Northerners joined without inhibitions, were led with gusto and aplomb by Stern. The White was in its postbellum heyday, and control of the hotel had been bought by William A. Stuart, owner of extensive herds of cattle in Virginia's southwest. The regally beautiful Irene Langhorne appeared at the resort in 1889, aged sixteen, to send renewed palpitations through the ranks of the eager young men. The seal and superscription was placed upon the final union of the sections when Miss Langhorne—whose sister Nancy would become the first woman elected to Britain's House of Commons—was married in St. Paul's Episcopal Church, Richmond, in 1895, to Charles Dana Gibson, the Massachusetts artist whose "Gibson Girl" was all the rage.

Such evidences of growing North-South cordiality were the culmination of a series of events. One of these was an address of Woodrow Wilson, delivered in 1880 when he was a student at the University of Virginia, wherein he declared: "I yield to no one precedence in love for the South, but *because* I love the South, I rejoice in the failure of the Confederacy." He went on to say that "the perpetuation of slavery would, beyond all question, have wrecked our agricultural and commercial interests, at the same time that it supplied a fruitful source of irritation abroad and agitation within."

Ulysses S. Grant, in the early 1880s, contributed $500 toward the erection of the Home for Confederate Soldiers at Richmond. Then, in 1884, finding it impossible to attend a fair in Richmond to raise additional funds for the home, the former commander of the Army of the Potomac wrote wishing the committee in charge success in its efforts to erect "for all the brave men who need it a home and rest from cares." He added: "The men who faced each other in deadly conflict can well afford to be the best of friends now, and only strive for rivalry in seeing which can be the best citizens of the grandest country on earth." When Grant died the following year, the Virginia Democratic Convention adopted resolutions of sorrow.

The acrimonies of former days were receding to such a degree that members of a Boston post of the Grand Army of the Republic were cordially received and feted in Virginia in 1886. After stops in Luray and Natural Bridge, the G.A.R.s came to Richmond where they were hospitably entertained by their foes of more than two decades before—Governor Fitzhugh Lee and members of R. E. Lee Camp, United Confederate Veterans. The silken United States flag which the Richmond Grays had carried from their founding in 1844 until 1859, was formally presented to the visiting northern veterans.

The ardently pro-southern writings of Thomas Nelson Page were becoming so popular in the North that onetime anti-slavery zealots there were beginning to wonder if they hadn't been misinformed concerning the "peculiar institution." The talented novelist and short-story writer drew so mellow, magnolia-scented and moon-drenched a picture of the South "befo' de war" that many Northerners were convinced. Page's gallery of handsome colonels and lovely damsels, waited on by adoring "uncles" and "mammies" and surrounded by happy-go-lucky, dancing, banjo-strumming "darkies," seemed so positively idyllic that who could find fault? His works were eagerly sought by northern magazine and book publishers, along with those of Joel Chandler Harris and other southern writers. The result was that a much more favorable picture of the antebellum South began to emerge. It was, of course, a too favorable picture, since the darker side of slavery was seldom stressed, or even mentioned, in these literary excursions.

Perhaps the climax of all this came when Thomas Wentworth Higginson, who had commanded a regiment of Negro troops in the Union Army during the Civil War, and had been one of the most militant abolitionists, read Page's *Marse Chan*—and wept. Page's artistry had temporarily overcome Higginson's deep convictions; the Massachusetts reformer actually shed tears over the death of a slave-owner![3]

While the "bloody shirt" was still waved in Congress, on occasion, by belligerent Northerners, who exhorted their followers to "Vote as you shot," the trend, by the 1880s, was in the other direction. Veterans of both the Union and Confederate armies who wrote reminiscences usually spoke with respect of their erstwhile foes and sought to promote intersectional amity. George Cary Eggleston showed such a spirit in his *A Rebel's Recollections,* as did John S. Wise in his *The End of an Era.*

An address by J. L. M. Curry to the sixth reunion of the United Confederate Veterans at Richmond in 1896 served to strengthen further the friendly feeling between the North and the South. It also put the patriotism of former Confederate soldiers in a properly favorable light. Curry, a native Georgian who had served in the Confederate Army, and then had taught at Richmond College for thirteen years, had succeeded Barnas Sears as agent for the Peabody Fund for Southern Education, and was a national figure. He declared to the U.C.V. that "recognition of the glorious deeds of our comrades is perfectly consistent with loyalty to the flag and devotion to the Constitution and the resulting union."

The following year a native Virginian, William P. Trent, then on the faculty of the University of the South at Sewanee, Tennessee, published what has been termed "the most important literary biography in Southern history." It was a life of William Gilmore Simms, the South Carolina novelist, and it contained drastic criticisms of the antebellum South, some of which were extreme. It was, however, an incisive and perceptive study, and it helped to convince the North that there were unterrified voices below the Potomac. It also shook many Virginians and other Southerners out of their complacency. However, the book brought down upon Trent such a barrage of criticism from his native state and other areas of the South, that in 1900 he accepted a high-ranking professorship at Columbia University, New York City.

Another situation conducive to improved intersectional relations was the widespread desire of northern capitalists to invest in southern business and industry. This trend began immediately following the Hayes-Tilden electoral settlement of 1877, and by 1880, these aggressive gentlemen were convinced that great opportunities for profitable enterprise were to be found in the Old Dominion. Impecunious local citizens, for their part, often welcomed them with open arms and loud hosannahs. Virginia was the richest state in the South at the period; yet its per capita wealth was more than $100 below that of Kansas, the poorest non-southern state. Virginians were happy to have wealthy investors from New York, Hartford, Philadelphia and Pittsburgh contribute toward a rectification of this imbalance, even though a large percentage of the profits usually was drained from the state.

Many of these investments by outlanders paid off in spectacular fashion, especially at the western and eastern ends of the commonwealth. The discovery of rich coal deposits in southwest Virginia caused capitalists to pour millions into coal mining and railroad building. The Norfolk & Western, formerly the Atlantic, Mississippi & Ohio, sent its coal trains roaring across Virginia and into the port of Norfolk. The numerous towns and factories that sprang up along its line, especially in the southwest, were other major factors in the state's development at this period. Roanoke grew in half a dozen years from the village of Big Lick into a booming young city. Norfolk's forward leap was also notable.

Similar near-miracles were happening just across the great harbor of Hampton Roads from Norfolk, thanks to the drive and enterprise of Collis P. Huntington, the northern and western railroad magnate. Huntington acquired the Chesapeake & Ohio and extended it from Richmond to the small village of Newport News. There he built not only coal and freight piers but a shipyard which soon became the famous Newport News Shipbuilding and Dry Dock Company. The rise of Newport News as a bustling port and shipbuilding center had begun. Furthermore, the essential stimulus provided by Huntington contributed importantly to the intersectional *rapprochement* that was taking place.

This process was accelerated by the South's eager co-operation in the Spanish-American War, which began in 1898. A call for 3000 Virginia volunteers went out, and within forty-eight hours 15,000 came forward. A second call for 1670 was promptly filled. Fitzhugh Lee was one of two former Confederate generals appointed from civilian life as major generals in the United States Army. Lee served in Cuba.

His selection for this honor was hardly surprising in view of the prevailingly cordial North-South climate, and the generous posture of President William McKinley. The President, himself a Union veteran, declared in Atlanta in 1898 that the care of Confederate graves was a national duty.

The North's increasingly sympathetic attitude toward the South with respect to the race problem was another significant factor in bringing the sections together. In the years that followed the end of Reconstruction, northern leaders of public opinion frequently expressed understanding for the South's point of view. As early as 1883 the U. S. Supreme Court declared that federal courts could not secure Negro rights supposedly guaranteed by the Fourteenth and Fifteenth amendments.

The *Century*, the *Atlantic*, *Scribner's* and *Harper's* began vying with one another in the publication of the works of such southern contributors as Thomas Nelson Page. E. L. Godkin, the influential editor of the *Nation*, spoke for many non-Southerners when he pronounced the South's racial "difficulties . . . far greater than those of the North," and urged patience and sympathy for the region. Richard Watson Gilder, editor of the *Century*, and numerous other prominent Northerners echoed these sentiments.

A rift in the lute of intersectional amity threatened to occur in 1890, when Senator Henry Cabot Lodge of Massachusetts introduced his so-called "Force Bill." Republican leaders in the North, of whom Lodge was one, had become annoyed, if not alarmed, by Democratic successes, especially in the election of Grover Cleveland as President in 1884, and by the increased Democratic representation in Congress from the South. The latter phenomenon was undoubtedly due, in part, to the elimination of Negro voters by fraudulent means. The would-be Negro voters in Virginia and the other southern states, most of whom were Republicans, accordingly asked their party's leaders to protect their right of franchise. Hence the "Force Bill."

The measure provided for the appointment of federal supervisors at the polls, representing both parties, when as many as five hundred voters asked for this. The bill passed the House and was narrowly defeated in the Senate. James Bryce, the British author, said the prevailing view in the North was that such legislation was "an attempt to overcome nature by law." Paul H. Buck feels that this analysis of northern sentiment is correct, and that it was hostility in the northern states to the Lodge bill which resulted in its defeat. He asserts that when the Republicans failed to pass this measure, they "tacitly accepted the fact of white supremacy in the South."

The career of Booker T. Washington was a major factor in bringing about a more sympathetic feeling in the North with respect to the South's attitude on the race question. Washington's address at the Atlanta Exposition in 1895, in which he set forth his view of the Negro's proper role, was received with enormous enthusiasm and made Washington a national figure overnight. He was already influential in important circles, both North and South, having founded and established Tuskegee Institute in Alabama in the face of almost insuperable odds, after working his way through Hampton Institute. But his Atlanta speech added greatly to his fame.

In that address, this Virginian who had been born a slave enunciated the interracial doctrine that "in all things that are purely social we can be as separate as the fingers, yet one as the hand in all things essential to mutual progress." He also said: "It is important and right that all privileges of the law be ours, but it is vastly more important that we be prepared for the exercise of these privileges. The opportunity to earn a dollar in a factory is worth infinitely more than the opportunity to spend a dollar in an opera house."

Booker T. Washington was saying that the Negro, as of 1895, was primarily in need of a chance to support himself and his family, and that the acquisition of industrial skills at that stage was more important than studying liberal arts or pushing for political or social equality. He convinced leaders in all sections that this was the proper approach to the Negro question. Northern foundations and philanthropists concluded that Washington was a man on whom they could rely for advice in distributing their largesse, and they began clearing their donations through him. The same arrangement was made as to federal patronage when Theodore Roosevelt entered the White House in 1901. Roosevelt lost little time in having Washington to lunch—an event which caused a storm of outraged disapproval in Virginia and throughout the South. Undeterred, "T.R." made Washington his consultant on all Negro appointments to federal office during his seven years in the presidency. He also consulted the Negro leader on many appointments of white Southerners. President Taft likewise sought his counsel on many appointments.

Washington was sharply criticized by a minority of black leaders who felt that he was an "Uncle Tom" who was consigning Negroes to permanent second-class citizenship. They argued that his advice, if followed, would lead to relegation of the blacks for an indefinite period to the lowly status of manual workers without access to full-scale political or other rights. There was a certain amount of jealousy behind these criticisms, since other Negro leaders envied the influence of what they termed the "Tuskegee machine." There were also honest misgivings over Washington's policies, as well as doubts as to the desirability of concentrating so much power in the hands of one man.

As for the charges that Washington was an "Uncle Tom," the fact has gradually emerged that while he did indeed express highly conciliatory sentiments to white persons in public, he was active for years behind the scenes in attempts to break down segregation and otherwise to obtain full rights for the Negro. In fact, he spent large sums from his own pocket—about $4000 in one two-year period, he said—in financing court tests and other efforts to achieve equality. He persuaded Giles B. Jackson, a prominent Negro lawyer in Richmond, to launch a legal fight in 1901 against the enactment of a Jim Crow law on Virginia railroads. Soon after Washington's death in 1915, the *New Republic* published an article by him attacking segregation.[4]

Whatever one thinks of the hypocrisy involved in talking one way in public on a pressing issue and another quite different way in private, the fact remains that Washington would have been in a hopeless position if, in the 1890s or early 1900s he had openly launched a drive for complete citizenship rights and full equality for the Negro. Public opinion in all parts of the United States was far from ready for such doctrine. So Washington followed policies acceptable to his day and generation, and became one of the most influential Virginians in history. He was the first Negro elected to the Hall of Fame in New York City. The slave cabin in Franklin County, Virginia, where he was born has been reconstructed and is visited by many tourists. His autobiography, *Up From Slavery*, is still read as an inspiring chronicle of achievement.

The intersectional good will that Washington fostered was highly important in the late nineteenth and early twentieth centuries. North-South relations were beginning to improve when he became active as a speaker and publicist. By enunciating a doctrine of race relations acceptable to the great majority on both sides of Mason and Dixon's Line, he promoted understanding and served as a helpful interpreter of southern mores to other areas of the nation.

However, he was unable to prevent the substantial disfranchisement of the Negro in Virginia and the other southern states near the turn of the century. Nor could he ward off the enactment of Jim Crow laws where few, if any, had been enacted before. Yet he was undoubtedly the most influential figure the Negro race in the United States had produced up to his time.

Men of good will both north and south of the Potomac—among whom Booker T. Washington was conspicuous—were responsible for the fact that the "bloody shirt" was coming to be less and less in evidence. The rancors and enmities of war and Reconstruction were fading from memory.

THIRTY-TWO

Daniel, Martin, Glass
and Free Silver

THE SUDDEN RISE of a quiet, relatively unknown country lawyer named Thomas S. Martin to a position of dominance in Virginia politics for a quarter of a century, was a major phenomenon of the 1890s.

He was the son of John Martin, an Albemarle County justice of the peace who managed the woolen mills at Scottsville. "Tom" Martin was small of stature and inclined to shyness in his youth; yet he showed qualities of determination and self-reliance. He was a VMI cadet during the Civil War, but did not get into the Battle of New Market, since he was confined to the institute infirmary with a severe cold. After the war he attended the University of Virginia for two sessions, but his father died and he became the chief support of his mother and his brothers and sisters. He read law, mainly at night, and was admitted to the bar. He began practicing in his native town of Scottsville, and soon became known throughout the immediate area. By the early 1880s his reputation as a lawyer in Albemarle, Fluvanna, Buckingham and the city of Charlottesville was such that he was retained by the Chesapeake & Ohio Railroad as its attorney for those four political subdivisions.

It was the era when railroads were developing and expanding, and when they were subject to little or no effective control by the state or national governments. Railroads were deep in politics in Virginia and other states. The fact was to be more and more significant as railroad attorney "Tom" Martin became increasingly active on the political scene.

His masterful and successful management of John W. Daniel's candidacy for the U. S. Senate before the General Assembly of 1885—senators were then elected by the legislature—brought him forcefully to the attention of political insiders. Daniel defeated the powerful John S. Barbour in that contest. But Thomas S. Martin was merely a name to most Virginians when, in 1893, he announced his own candidacy for the Senate in competition with Fitzhugh Lee.

Lee was one of the two most popular men in Virginia, the other being Senator Daniel. He had not only made an impressive record as a Confederate general; he had recently completed a successful term as governor. A contest before the General Assembly between such a man and a small-town lawyer who had never run for public office appeared to be no contest at all.

Martin, however, was far from being a political nonentity. More than half of the General Assembly had asked Governor McKinney in 1892 to appoint him to fill out the term of Senator Barbour, but the governor had named General Eppa Hunton. Martin, furthermore, had been offered a seat on the Virginia Supreme Court of Appeals.

Hunton was chosen in 1893 to fill out Barbour's unexpired term, but did not offer for reelection. Martin and Lee sought to succeed him. Martin and his agents had been busy for many months, and when the time came, they were ready. Martin was an organizing genius who worked quietly behind the scenes and spoke but seldom in public. He and his friends used railroad money to line up votes in the General Assembly against Lee. Candidates for the legislature were aided with their campaign expenses, in return for promises to support Martin. Other aspirants for the Assembly were assured of certain coveted committee assignments by Martin men in the lawmaking body, if they would agree to back the Albemarle candidate.

The showdown for the Senate came, and the state was shocked with the news that Martin had led Lee on every ballot and been nominated on the sixth. In his first campaign, Martin had unhorsed one of "Jeb" Stuart's most famous cavalrymen. It seemed incredible. Without the judicious distribution of railroad money, it could hardly have happened.[1]

Race was not an issue in the Martin-Lee contest, but race relations were in an uncertain state in the nineties. Lynchings were fairly frequent, and talk was being heard in political circles concerning the desirability of passing restrictive legislation affecting the franchise and providing separate accommodations for Negroes on railroad trains and street cars, in restaurants, theaters and so on. Enactment of legislation making available "separate but equal" facilities on trains and in waiting rooms was recommended by Governor McKinney in his message to the General Assembly in 1891. McKinney was regarded as unfriendly by the Negroes.

However, he backed up the authorities of Roanoke City in 1893, when they called out the militia to protect a Negro, and the soldiers fired on the lynch mob, killing eight and wounding more than a score, including Mayor Henry S. Trout. The mob had refused to heed warnings that they would be fired on if they persisted in trying to storm the jail. The Negro was spirited away by officers, but was overtaken, hanged and shot, and his body burned.

This was one of the rare, if not unique, instances in the late nineteenth century in the South where the militia shot down white mobsters. Many would-be lynchers were stopped in their tracks during the era by the mere threat that the military would open fire. But in far too many other instances the troops were not there to protect the black, and the mob had its way. Governor Charles T. O'Ferrall of Rockingham, who succeeded McKinney, denounced the crime of lynching, and boasted that only three such episodes had taken place during his administration, whereas there had been sixty-one in the state in the preceding fourteen years. The great majority of the victims were, of course, Negroes. O'Ferrall pointed out, however, that only about one-third of those lynched were even charged with rape or attempted rape.

He urged two successive general assemblies to pass a law requiring every county or city where a lynching occurred to pay into the treasury of the state, for the benefit of the public schools, $200 for each thousand of its population, the total not to exceed $10,000. O'Ferrall also urged severe penalties for any officer who allowed a prisoner to be taken from him by a mob "without exhausting all means to prevent it." His recommendations were deemed unacceptable. Not until the administration of Governor Harry F. Byrd some three decades later would strong anti-lynching legislation be enacted.

In addition to calling out troops to prevent the slaying of Negroes by mobs, O'Ferrall sent the militia to the southwestern coal mines during a strike, for the protection of non-striking miners. He was denounced in some quarters as an enemy of labor, but most of the state's newspapers backed him.

Highly unorthodox views on the race issue had been expressed several years before by Prof. Noah K. Davis of the University of Virginia, in an article in the *Forum* (April, 1886.) He opposed social intermingling but wrote: "We want in Congress men of capacity, honesty, strength. Color is nonessential . . . The time may come when a Negro shall be our Secretary of State; and who will be foolish enough to object? . . . We shall see, or our children shall see, white servants and laborers under Negro employers. . . . Brains, not color, must settle rank."

A Virginian who assailed the South's doctrine of "white supremacy," while demanding an end to segregation in the schools and everywhere else, was Lewis H. Blair, a prominent Richmond businessman and Confederate veteran. His fellow citizens were startled in 1887 when Blair began a series of articles in a New York magazine, setting forth his unorthodox views. Two years later those views appeared in more extended form in a book published in Richmond entitled *Prosperity of the South Dependent Upon the Elevation of the Negro*. One result was a demand from the Richmond Democratic Committee that Blair resign from that body. For a decade or more he was a storm center of controversy. Then, in the early years of the twentieth century he reversed his position in every respect. At that time, he demanded "segregation of the Negro who as a lower form of man should be made a 'ward of the nation.'" The reasons for this extraordinary about-face are not clear.

Approximately when Blair's book appeared, in 1889, the town of Rocky Mount was set on fire and twenty-six stores and dwellings were burned. Four Negroes were convicted of having set the blaze and were sentenced to be hanged. The sentence was carried out for three of the defendants, but one of them confessed on the gallows that he had lied in charging the fourth, Nannie Woods, with complicity. He stated that she was in no way connected with the crime. Instead of pardoning her, Governor McKinney commuted her sentence to life imprisonment. When Governor O'Ferrall took office Nannie Woods had been in prison for five years. O'Ferrall pardoned her at once.[2]

A harbinger of better days in the field of race relations during these years was the founding at Lawrenceville, in Virginia's Southside, of

St. Paul's Normal and Industrial Institute. The founder was a young Negro deacon in the Episcopal Church, James Solomon Russell. The institute opened its doors in 1888 with meager equipment and small enrollment, but gradually grew and prospered. Its progress was due mainly to Russell's ability and dedication. He was the first Negro elected a bishop in the Episcopal Church, an honor he declined, to remain at St. Paul's, which was affiliated with that church. When he died in 1935, Archdeacon Russell was hailed as one of the great leaders of his generation in Virginia. In the intervening years, St. Paul's College has given added emphasis to the liberal arts and it is offering the B.A. and B.S. degrees.

Virginia Union University at Richmond, another predominantly Negro center of learning, began operations in 1899, when there was a merger of two institutions established in 1865 by the American Baptist Home Mission Societies. Like St. Paul's, Virginia Union offers liberal arts, and it also provides graduate religious instruction.

For educational and other reasons, Governor McKinney became convinced during his administration that it was important for the state to erect a library building to serve as a repository for the thousands of books, manuscripts, reports and other records of the commonwealth. The General Assembly appropriated $200,000 for the purpose. The building was not completed until 1895, when McKinney had been succeeded by Governor O'Ferrall.

At that time the volumes and documents had to be transferred from the Capitol to the new structure. Without anything remotely approaching adequate investigation, the state authorities decided that much of this material was worthless and contracted with a junk dealer to haul it away. Chutes were constructed from the upper floor of the Capitol to facilitate the operation. Irreplaceable official papers going back many years and rare old volumes were catapulted into the junk wagons. The junk dealer was said to have complained that the ancient documents had so many wax seals on them that his men had to spend time stripping them off, in preparing the papers for the mill. More than half a bushel of such seals were seen in a heap in the dealer's yard or scattered on the ground. Important gaps in the holdings of the Virginia State Library today may be traced to his horrendous negligence.

Another development of this era was the final demise in Virginia of the savage practice of dueling. It had been declining and was virtually extinct, when suddenly, in 1893, Joseph Bryan, publisher of the Richmond *Times* and generally considered Richmond's leading citizen, was summoned to "the field of honor." The challenge came from Jefferson D. Wallace, a lawyer and member of the City Democratic Committee who deemed himself aggrieved by something that had appeared in the *Times*. Bryan replied that he considered dueling "barbarous and absurd" and turned the matter over to the police. They promptly arrested Wallace, since dueling had long been illegal. The charge against Wallace was not pressed, but dueling in Virginia was dead. It was killed when a man of character and standing, such as Joseph Bryan, denounced it publicly for the barbarity that it was and refused to accept a challenge. Bryan had been a gallant member of Mosby's raiders in the Civil War and nobody questioned his courage. He was deluged with congratulations from all over the state.

There was ferment in Virginia during these years, extending to the grass roots, and growing out of a long period of depressed farm prices. This condition was accentuated by the depression and panic of 1893. The farmers were in a state of near-revolt, and there was uneasiness, if not alarm, in the business community.

Money had become extremely scarce in rural Virginia after the 1873 panic of twenty years before, and farmers were deeply in debt and often unable to get credit. They frequently had difficulty in buying even the simplest clothing. Country women in parts of Virginia felt it necessary to economize on shoe leather by walking to town barefoot, and putting their shoes on when they arrived. Income taxes on Virginia farmers were almost non-existent, but the suffering agriculturalists paid land taxes and other levies to the state which seem to have made their burden proportionately greater than that of the more affluent businessmen.[3] Farmers were having their problems throughout the United States. Some who tried to go west, in search of better days, returned sadly disillusioned and carrying signs bearing the words, "In God we trusted; in Kansas we busted."

Conditions in Southside Virginia were especially depressed, as the region was still wedded to the one-crop tobacco economy, and tobacco prices were down. Leaf production in Virginia actually dropped between 1880 and 1890. So dreary was the outlook and so low the wage scale on farms in the Southside that it seemed impossible to get white immigrants to come in. Pay for competing black field hands averaged less than ten dollars a month, and such workers were said to be able to feed themselves on corn and bacon for about fifteen dollars a year.

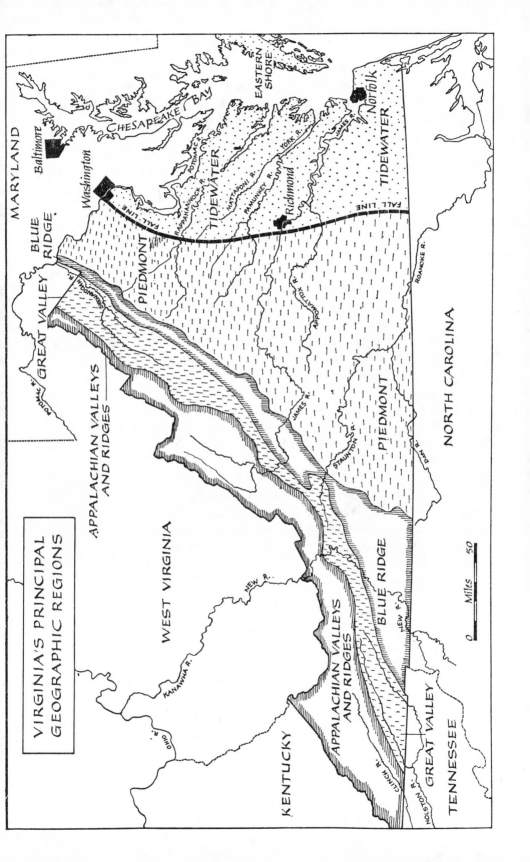

VIRGINIA'S PRINCIPAL GEOGRAPHIC REGIONS

Negroes greatly outnumbered whites in the region, tenancy and share-cropping were widely prevalent, and living conditions for the blacks were often appalling. The dead hand of the past hung heavily over the worn-out lands.[4]

In contrast to the Southside's one-crop economy, there was diversification in other areas of the state. Truck farming and peanut growing were intensively developed in lower Tidewater, while cotton was cultivated in Southampton County. Fish and oysters yielded income to dwellers around Chesapeake Bay. Lumbering was a significant industry in the central Piedmont and on the peninsulas between the James and the Potomac. In the Shenandoah Valley and the southwest, cattle and sheep raising was becoming a major industry, dairy farming was prospering, and in valleys of the mountainous southwest, Burley tobacco was grown. Purebred horses were raised in the northern Piedmont, especially in Loudoun County. In fact, Loudoun, with its well-diversified crops and scientific procedures, claimed the best farming and the highest yields in Virginia.

Coal was discovered in Tazewell County in 1873, and a decade later the Norfolk & Western began carrying this high-quality bituminous fuel to eastern Virginia. Excellent coal deposits were discovered in other counties of the southwest, and this great resource of the state was tapped on a huge scale. Norfolk and Newport News would become two of the world's leading coal ports. By the end of the century, Norfolk would be connected with the interior by eight railroads and with all parts of the globe by twenty-six steamship lines. It was also the country's largest peanut market and one of its leading cotton ports.

Machinery manufacture, tobacco manufacture and flour milling were foremost Virginia industries in the nineties. Richmond's flour mills were producing 3500 barrels a day and exporting the product to all points of the compass. The Tredegar Iron Works was going full blast again, and the Richmond Cedar Works was "the most extensive woodworking plant in the world." The introduction of the cigarette proved a boon to Richmond, where the industry became concentrated. Lynchburg, by contrast, was a victim of the changed habits of tobacco users. Chewing went out of fashion, with the result that Lynchburg's substantial plug industry went down the drain. The cuspidor was no longer a ubiquitous article of furniture.

But although there were many clear evidences of progress, Virginia as a whole was by no means prosperous. The commonwealth was battling its way back from adversity and defeat, and much remained to be done.

Many of Virginia's vigorous young men had left for the North and West, where they would often become successful and take positions of leadership. Others returned to the Old Dominion after working as laborers. J. B. Harrison, a northern journalist who toured the South in 1881, saw a number of these Virginians in Texas. He described them as "sons of the best families" who told him that they couldn't take such menial jobs at home. One said it would be "too much of an affliction for my family, and I should lose caste with my lady friends." They planned to return after they had saved enough money to get a start at home on a level that they would not find humiliating. Apparently these young Virginians had left the state a decade or so after the war. Immediately following Appomattox the returning Confederate soldiers had to fall to and take any jobs they could get. Some bestirred themselves at once as farm laborers, hitching up their spavined horses to the plow and planting crops. Others left their wrecked homesteads and went to work in town as "watchmen, brakemen, street-car drivers, foremen in factories," according to Thomas Nelson Page, who said "there was no feeling of indignity."

Some who returned to Virginia in the eighties and nineties from Texas or other states may have become involved in the speculative development of numerous towns in the western part of the state, especially along the railroads. A number of these were sound enterprises, but there was an artificially stimulated boom psychology in others, followed by heavy losses to investors.

The Lexington area was involved to a special degree. Lexington itself put on a drive to convince all and sundry that it had the potential to become an important manufacturing center. There was a synthetic real estate boom as an accompaniment of this concept, and a steel works was built. The whole thing blew up in the early nineties, and was greatly intensified when the Bank of Lexington closed its doors, on the discovery that its cashier, one of the town's foremost civic leaders and pillars of the church, had absconded with $180,000 of the bank's assets.

Another collapse took place at nearby Buena Vista, where promotion and speculation were even more uninhibited, the get-rich-quick fever took full possession, and a furnace, a foundry and a woolen mill were constructed. There was avid investment in lots in response to representations only loosely related to the facts. It was another case of "boom and bust."

Similarly at Glasgow, a few miles away, investors from as far distant as England, including the Duke and Duchess of Marlborough, were induced to buy lots. Fitzhugh Lee, who had completed his gubernatorial term a short time before, was president of the company, and announced the patronage of the English nobility with obvious pride. He apparently believed that the investment was a sound one. Again there was total collapse, with large losses to all involved.

Such serious setbacks as these, coming as they did on the eve of the panic of 1893, were enough to keep much of the state in turmoil. The farmers were especially distraught, and were looking for leaders. They found them among the Virginia aristocracy, a circumstance that gave the farm revolt in the Old Dominion a special cachet not duplicated elsewhere, and served as a brake on radicalism.

The hard-pressed farmers had begun organizing quietly in 1885. They met in Richmond and formed the Farmers' Assembly. Colonel Robert Beverley of Blandfield, Essex County, a large landowner of ancient lineage, was chosen president. The Farmers' Assembly hoped to operate within the Democratic party. Its conservative leadership was a virtual guarantee that the organization would not indulge in unseemly agitation, and would confine itself to serving as a sounding board before the legislature.

This mild approach was not productive of relief. By 1888 the more aggressive Farmers' Alliance held its first meeting in Luray, with delegates from five counties. Two years later the fast-growing Alliance met in Lynchburg, with 94 counties represented. By then there were 113 sub-Alliances in Virginia, listing 30,000 members. The Farmers' Assembly went out of existence soon thereafter, leaving the Alliance to spearhead the drive for remedial action. Major Mann Page, than whom there was no more aristocratic Virginian, was president. The equally patrician Colonel Randolph Harrison edited the Alliance's official organ, while the Ruffins of Hanover County were active in the movement.

Discriminatory practices of the railroads were among the chief grievances. Major R. C. Kent of Wytheville, leader of the Alliance forces in the General Assembly and a Princeton University graduate, introduced a bill at the 1890 session to establish a strong railroad commission with power to regulate. It was defeated, and the Richmond

State said with truth that the farmers had failed in their attempt through lack of organization and cohesion.

Kent made another effort at the legislative session of 1892, but the bill, as passed, was weak. The Alliance had failed again; satisfaction for the farmers obviously could not be obtained from the Democratic party. The stage was set for the entry into Virginia of the Populist party.

Populist rumblings had been heard from the Midwest for years, but Virginia's Democratic leadership was slow to grasp the magnitude of the oncoming storm. Alliance lecturers had stirred the state's farmers to a realization that middlemen, price fixing and railroad rates were operating against their interests, and many were receptive to appeals for drastic action.

The Populist party platform went far beyond anything the Virginia Alliance had demanded. At their convention in Omaha in 1892 the Populists called for free coinage of silver, abolition of national banks, creation of a larger supply of paper money, government ownership of railroads, direct election of senators, the eight-hour day, and adoption of the income tax, which last was regarded by conservatives as "communistic."

Only a month or two before the Omaha convention, "Sockless Jerry" Simpson, the rampaging Alliance congressman from Kansas, had been in Virginia helping to organize the farmers. William Jennings Bryan of Nebraska—whose father had been born in Virginia, at Sperryville, and migrated west—also had spoken in the state. Soon thereafter, and only a few weeks before the Populist convention met at Omaha in July, a call was issued for a third party convention to be held at Richmond. James G. Field, a one-legged Confederate veteran from near Gordonsville who had served as Attorney General of the state was chosen permanent chairman. Delegates to the Omaha convention were selected. A speaker expressed the gathering's distaste for the conservative Democrat, Grover Cleveland, by saying, "Strong Republican tickets have been nominated at Minneapolis and Chicago, headed by Harrison and Cleveland, respectively." The Populists, inside and outside Virginia, were violently against Cleveland, mainly because of his opposition to free silver, probably the central demand in the Populist platform. These farmers wanted inflation, and they saw in free silver a way to get it. Farm prices were low in terms of the dollar, while manufactured goods had not declined proportionately in value.

At Omaha the Populist platform was adopted with enormous enthusiasm, and each plank "brought mounting delirium in the packed hall." Then came the nomination of a presidential candidate, and James B. Weaver, a Union veteran from Iowa, was the choice. To give the ticket sectional balance, Confederate veteran James G. Field of Virginia was named for Vice-President. "Tears were in the eyes of many," as they viewed this evidence of fading intersectional antagonism.

The Weaver-Field ticket was not well-received by the Virginia press. The *Virginia Sun*, the Populist organ edited by Charles H. Pierson, an Englishman living in Caroline County, gave it sympathetic treatment, but the bulk of the state's newspapers were highly critical. Field was attacked for having been a Mahone sympathizer. The argument also was made that a vote for Weaver-Field was half a vote for the Republican, Benjamin Harrison, and hence half a vote against the Democrat, Cleveland.

Weaver and Field scheduled a rally for Richmond in October. Weaver was refused rooms at the Exchange Hotel, the Howitzers' band broke its contract to play, at the last minute, and eggs were thrown. On the platform at the rally were not only Weaver and Field, but the Kansas cyclone, Mrs. Mary Lease, "of 'raise less corn and more hell' fame." The dignified Mann Page presided. Many of the one thousand persons who attended apparently did so from curiosity. Few converts seem to have been made.

Free silver was the principal issue in other states, but in Virginia the Democratic leadership chose to play it down. Cleveland, the party nominee, was on the "wrong side" of the issue, since he stood for gold. The popular and admired Senator Daniel, leader of the silver bloc in the state, had fought the nomination of Cleveland. He and the rest of the Democratic leadership of the commonwealth fell in reluctantly behind the choice of their party, and said as little as possible about silver. Cleveland carried the state by a handsome margin against Harrison, while the Weaver-Field combination polled only 12,190 votes, mostly in the Southside.

The Populists were undismayed, and in 1893 they nominated Edmund Randolph Cocke for governor against the Democrat, Charles T. O'Ferrall. Cocke was a grandson of Edmund Randolph, and his family had entertained General and Mrs. Robert E. Lee at Derwent for several weeks after Appomattox. He was a convinced free silverite. O'Ferrall, as a member of Congress, had proclaimed himself for silver.

The Populists assailed conditions in Virginia, and attacked the election laws as dishonest and discriminatory, as they undoubtedly were. They called for graduated state and national income taxes and taxation of non-resident corporations doing business in the state. They deplored the involvement of the public schools in politics, and urged greater financial support for them.

The Republicans chose not to nominate a candidate for governor, and a majority of them probably supported Cocke. He got over 81,000 votes, but O'Ferrall was an easy winner with about 130,000. The race issue was again paramount, and played into the hands of the Democrats, who depicted the Populists as the party of "Mahone and the Negro." Not a single Negro had attended the Populist Convention, but Mahone did control most of the black vote, and he had been quoted as saying that "the Republicans will support the Populists." That was enough to damn Cocke in the minds of many. In addition, the Democrats had practically all the money, and they had control of most of the electoral machinery. Whether Cocke's votes were counted honestly is open to grave question.

Electoral fraud had, in fact, become so notorious and widespread that the General Assembly of 1894 passed the Walton Law, designed to correct some of the more glaring defects in the Anderson-McCormick Law of a decade before. Sponsors of the Walton Law were careful to leave the Democrats in control of the electoral machinery. They also left loopholes large enough for corruption to continue. Disfranchisement of the Negroes was facilitated. More than half of the black population was still illiterate, and the new law made it possible for election officials to eliminate large numbers of these Negro voters. In the black belt, where fraud was especially prevalent, a Democratic practice was to hire Negroes to attend Republican rallies and hiss so loud and long that the speaker gave up and left the stand.

Virginia was in turmoil as the presidential election of 1896 drew near. Senator Daniel, the eloquent "Lame Lion," with the scars of half a dozen Civil War wounds on his body, was the dominant figure in the state, and the chief spokesman for "free and unlimited coinage of silver at 16 to 1." Daniel was a handsome man, and a stemwinding orator whose rolling sentences, especially on Confederate themes, held audiences spellbound for hours. In his younger days he had written a legal textbook on "Negotiable Instruments" which received unbounded praise from legal scholars in all parts of the United States.

The Democrats of Virginia met at Staunton in June, and the party's silver wing was in complete control. Senator Daniel was the center of attraction, and it was obvious that the delegates would ratify his silver platform enthusiastically.

But Senator Martin was yet to be heard from. He had been thunderously silent concerning free silver, and was generally believed to be opposed to it. His unwillingness to discuss the question led a Roanoke paper to term him "Thomas the Silent . . . who resembles the Irishman's flea; when you catch him he is not there."

There was vast curiosity at the Staunton convention concerning the position to be taken by Martin, who had been elected three years before with heavy support from the railroads—which were dead against free silver. Virginia's congressional delegation stood eight to two in favor of it, and nearly all the other leading public men in the state took the same position.

In response to cries from the convention floor that he take the rostrum, Martin came forward. Unlike Daniel, Martin was never an orator, and he seldom made speeches. On this occasion he found further silence to be impossible.

Martin gave a hint of his position at the outset of his remarks by assailing Grover Cleveland, the advocate of gold, as a "party wrecker." He then said, "There are none, I take it, within hearing of my voice who do not know that . . . the Democrats of Virginia will declare for free and unlimited coinage of silver." This declaration was greeted with salvos of applause. Martin went on to say that he had not agreed "in all respects" with the policy of the silver bloc, but added, "I find no difficulty in placing myself with the Democrats of Virginia." As a matter of fact, he found great difficulty in doing so, and he well knew that his corporate backers would be quite unhappy over his action. But politically his course was wise, for the sentiment for free silver in much of the Old Dominion, as well as in many other states, was hardly short of hysterical.

At the Democratic National Convention a few weeks later in Chicago, Senator Daniel was chosen temporary chairman, as well as a member of the steering committee. His ringing keynote address was entirely concerned with the currency question, and it set the stage for William J. Bryan's "Cross of Gold" speech. The latter deliverance by the "Boy Orator of the Platte" sent the delegates into spasms of enthusiasm. None was more carried away than delegate Carter Glass, who rushed forward to grab the Virginia standard and join the parade for Bryan. Glass was then the redheaded and fiery young editor of the Lynchburg *News*, and a leading advocate of free silver. He not only urged this panacea upon the country in numerous editorials; he loudly denounced Grover Cleveland, the "gold cormorants" and the "banded money sharks" of Wall Street. Championing the "toiling millions," Glass at Chicago was a member of the resolutions committee which framed the platform. He urged that instructions be given the incoming President to convene Congress in special session, immediately following the inauguration, to pass free coinage legislation.[5]

A group of conservative Virginians, led by Joseph Bryan, were greatly aroused by the happenings at Chicago. Bryan's Richmond *Times* declared that the platform adopted there "abounded in nonsense and anarchy in equal proportions." The "Cross of Gold" speech was a "studied piece of sophomorical rodomontade."

The group of "Gold Democrats" or "Gold Bugs" held a convention in Richmond, with Joseph Bryan presiding. A platform endorsing the gold standard was adopted, and President Cleveland was defended. Among the Democrats who bolted and joined the opposition to William J. Bryan were former Governor O'Ferrall, previously a free silverite; Basil B. Gordon, former chairman of the Democratic State Committee; Beverley B. Munford, prominent Richmond attorney, and Judge John T. Goolrick of Fredericksburg.

Shortly after the Virginia convention, the "National Democratic" party met at Indianapolis and adopted a gold platform. Its nominees were John M. Palmer of Illinois and Simon B. Buckner of Kentucky. The Virginia bolters backed this ticket.

The campaign that followed was one of the most exciting in the state's history, and feeling ran high. The Richmond *Times* which led the fight on Bryan, sustained a heavy loss in circulation, and was on one occasion in danger of being attacked by a mob of irate free silverites, who were restrained by the police. Friends shook their fists in one another's faces as they argued vehemently on street corners. Speakers were hissed from platforms. Large employers announced that many employees would have to be discharged, if Bryan was elected, and at least one declared that those who were retained would get a cut in wages. Senator Daniel led the fight for Bryan in Virginia, and Bryan spoke in Richmond to what was described as the largest political gathering in Virginia history.

When the votes were counted, Bryan was found to have carried the state by under 20,000 majority over McKinley. Palmer and Buckner got only slightly more than 2000 votes, despite the fact that they appeared to be well-financed. It was evident that most Democrats who opposed free silver had voted for McKinley.

The Populists had backed Bryan, since the Democratic candidate and platform were in tune with Populist ideas, especially in the area of currency reform. But the campaign of 1896 was the climax of Populist effort in Virginia. Many of the party's leaders rejoined the Democrats in that contest, and it was difficult to woo them back into Populist ranks again. Little was heard of the Virginia Populists thereafter, but the party had played a role in helping to focus attention on agrarian grievances.

As the free-silver issue subsided, Senator Daniel became less concerned with this approach to the country's ills. Senator Martin had never been in favor of it and was happy to drop the subject. As for Carter Glass, he was to change so completely in later years that his biographers, Smith and Beasley, do not so much as mention that in his early days he was one of the most militant of all the advocates of free silver, or that he repeatedly attacked the bankers who fought the plan as robbers and oppressors of the poor.

THIRTY-THREE

Montague's Election
and a New Constitution

AN OUTBREAK of yellow fever in Hampton at the turn of the century showed that Virginia was still subject to this dreadful scourge, which had caused so many thousands of deaths over the years. Simultaneously the disease broke out among American troops in Havana. This latter event led to the appointment of a commission of medical officers from the U. S. Army to seek the cause of the mortal malady, and if possible to find a cure. Virginia-born Walter Reed was named head of the commission. He was the scholarly son of a Methodist minister, and a graduate of the University of Virginia medical school.

Major Reed went to Cuba with the commission and engaged in a series of experiments. Considerable risk was involved, and one member of the commission was bitten by an infected mosquito and died. Others were made ill. But the disease was definitely traced to a specific type of mosquito, and work was begun at once leading to its eradication. Within a year, yellow fever was virtually wiped out in Cuba, and ere long it had been wiped out everywhere. Walter Reed, the man most responsible, died in 1902 of a ruptured appendix, just when the fruits of his epoch-making discovery were being harvested.

J. Hoge Tyler of Pulaski County was governor at the time, having succeeded Charles T. O'Ferrall. He was the last of seven high-ranking Confederate officers to hold the governorship. Tyler was severely tested when an issue arose involving the use of Negro troops from Virginia in the Spanish-American War. Two battalions of these troops were among the first Virginians to volunteer when the call went out in 1898. There were also two white battalions. The question was whether the black units would be permitted to serve under their black officers. Tyler was subjected to great pressure by those who wanted him to designate white officers in their stead, as had been done in Alabama. For example, Joseph Button, clerk of the State Senate, wrote in opposition to retention of the black officers, "I assure you that feeling against you is intense; for God's sake do not take such a step." But Tyler felt that removal of the Negro officers solely because of their race would be unfair, and also that it would violate the laws of Virginia and the Fourteenth Amendment. Unfortunately, the pressure was such that he ended by putting a white colonel over the black officers. This led to such bickering and ill feeling that the black soldiers preferred to return to civilian life. They were accordingly mustered out of service.

The defeat of Fitzhugh Lee by Thomas S. Martin for the U. S. Senate in 1893 had given rise to a desire on the part of the more progressive elements of the Democratic party for the election of senators by a vote of the people, rather than by the state legislature. Congressman William A. Jones of Warsaw was the leader in this movement, and he was chiefly instrumental in arranging a meeting in Richmond on May 10, 1899, for the purpose of framing "such measures as may be deemed best to promote the election of senators . . . by direct vote of the people." Jones and his associates in calling this "May Conference" insisted that it was not aimed at any individual, and was not intended to advance anybody's political fortunes. Martin was convinced, however, that the basic purpose was to oust him from the Senate, and his contention was not entirely without foundation. At the same time, some of the movement's sponsors were undoubtedly sincere in believing that the people should be permitted to choose their senators.

The convention asked the Democratic Central Committee to "order a state primary or a state convention to . . . nominate the senatorial candidate to be elected in November, 1899." Since the committee was completely dominated by Martin, this request was promptly denied. Congressman Jones, who had been seriously considering running against Martin, thereupon backed away from the contest. Others also declined to make the race, but Governor Tyler decided to do so.

Tyler was not a strong candidate, for he did not enjoy the united support of the anti-Martin forces. His lack of strength became more evident when the Martin machine went into high gear. First, it put on a series of "snap" conventions for the choice of legislative candidates, which nominated pro-Martin aspirants for the General Assembly before Tyler's men knew what was happening. In Norfolk County, only forty-eight hours' notice was given, and in 21 legislative districts Tyler was denied the privilege of having his candidacy presented. The Martin-controlled Democratic Central Committee, headed by J. Taylor Ellyson, actually threatened to read out of the party all legislative candidates who were pledged to support Tyler. The committee also made it plain that no party campaign funds would be available to Tyler supporters.[1] The outcome was foregone. When the Democratic caucus met, the vote was 103 to 27 in favor of Martin.

Yet Tyler's effort had not been entirely futile. The campaign had kept the issue of electoral reform before the public, and when Tyler delivered his next message to the General Assembly, he reiterated his support of the direct election of senators and their nomination in primaries. The contest of 1899 had been a salutary lesson to the anti-Martin faction. That faction was made aware of the necessity for hard work, better organization and greater alertness to the tactics of the opposition.

The election of Andrew J. Montague, then of Danville, as attorney general in 1897 had advanced the reformist cause, although at that time Montague had not broken with Martin, and his position on various salient issues remained to be spelled out. Like most Virginia politicians of the day, he was for free silver. His four-year service as attorney general brought his name before the public, and at the same time, he sat as one of three members of the State Board of Education, under the system then prevailing. The board appointed school superintendents throughout Virginia, and this gave Montague more political leverage than he enjoyed by virtue of his post as the commonwealth's principal legal officer. The attorney general had less power at that time than he does today. In addition to serving as a leader in calling the May Convention of 1899, Montague also was outspoken in his advocacy of a constitutional convention.

Agitation for a convention had begun in the latter part of the nineteenth century, and the question had been submitted to a vote of the people in 1888. The advocates were trounced 63,125 to 3698. Another bill calling for a referendum in 1897 was gotten though the

General Assembly. This time the proposal was defeated 83,435 to 38,326. The growth of Populism was credited with frightening many voters into casting a negative ballot. It was feared, in the words of the Richmond *Times,* that "Kansas ideas would be introduced into the organic law." However, proponents of a convention, including Montague, were encouraged, and they renewed their efforts. Early in 1900, the legislature passed a bill providing for a referendum in May of that year.

A principal argument for a convention was that elections in Virginia had become so shot through with fraud that something had to be done. No fewer than twenty congressional elections had been officially contested between 1874 and 1900. Vote buying, ballot-box stuffing and assorted varieties of political thievery were notoriously widespread.

Carter Glass, one of the convention's most vociferous advocates, declared repeatedly that suffrage limitation was its primary purpose. Disfranchisement of the Negro, he said, would "simplify the race problem and end political rascality." It is important to note that although hardly more than a generation had passed since the end of the Civil War, many leaders of public opinion in the North subscribed to the doctrine that Negroes were inferior to whites, and that their voting rights should be severely limited. The *Atlantic Monthly,* for example, declared in an editorial in 1901: "If the stronger and cleverer race is free to impose its will on 'new-caught sullen peoples' on the other side of the globe, why not in South Carolina and Mississippi?" And noted professors John W. Burgess and William A. Dunning of Columbia University published books backing up the South's position. The former rejoiced that the Republican party "has at last virtually accepted the ideas of the South" with respect to "the political relations of the races," while the latter pronounced "the enfranchisement of the freedmen" a "reckless . . . species of statecraft."[2]

Elimination of surplus officeholders and achievement of economy in government were seen as other major objectives of the convention. Glass declared in his Lynchburg *News* that a convention was the "one hope of salvation . . . from the corrupt, costly and intolerable domination of an officeholding despotism." He joined with other Virginia editors in unsparing, and excessive, denunciation of the Underwood Constitution of 1869. The Richmond *Dispatch* termed it "the miserable apology to organic law which was forced upon Virginians by carpet-baggers, scalawags, Negroes, supported by federal bayonets."

The Democratic State Convention of 1900 met in Norfolk, and although Martin and Congressman Claude Swanson, another organization leader, were silently opposed to a constitutional convention, they apparently saw which way the political winds were blowing. The Democrats at Norfolk endorsed the convention with only six dissenting votes. The Republicans were opposed, since they suspected, and rightly, that many of their dwindling company of followers, both white and black, would be disfranchised.

The statewide referendum took place on May 24, 1900, and while the turnout was extremely small, the vote was for a convention, 77,362 to 60,375.

Andrew J. Montague had announced his candidacy for governor in January. He had gone along with some of the more dubious political practices then prevalent in Virginia, but he would now break openly with the Martin organization, and with his fellow townsman, Claude Swanson, then serving his fifth term as congressman from the Fifth District. Prior to that time, he and Swanson had co-operated politically. The Martin organization would soon get behind Swanson as Montague's opponent for the governorship.

"Jack" Montague was born in 1862 in Campbell County, where his parents happened to be "refugeeing" during the Civil War, but he grew up at Inglewood, Middlesex County, the family farm on the Rappahannock. His father was Lieutenant Governor Robert Latané Montague, who had presided over the secession convention after the resignation of John Janney, and then had served in the Confederate Congress. His mother was Cordelia Gay Eubank of King and Queen County. The younger Montague was redheaded, like his father, but apparently without the hot temper usually associated with red hair. Like his father, too, he was called "The Red Fox of Middlesex." He was a fluent and convincing speaker, but he seems to have been considerably less effective in the rough and tumble of political debate.

In his campaign for governor, Montague espoused such progressive causes as party primaries, better schools and roads, and the responsibility of employers for injuries to their employees. He thus placed himself in the forefront of the liberal movement in the state, insofar as these issues were concerned. At the same time, he assailed Martin and his followers for their machine methods and their refusal to espouse forward-looking programs.

Claude Swanson had been following the Martin line, and hence had been passively or actively in opposition, or indifferent to, the above-mentioned reforms. But before the campaign was over, he was advocating the nomination of the governor in a primary. He also fell into line behind better schools and roads, while promising to sign an employer's liability bill, if one were passed. Swanson was always shrewd in his diagnosis of popular movements, and usually quick to "get on the bandwagon," if that seemed to his political advantage. Years later, a colleague in the U. S. Senate said he was the only man he had ever seen who could "keep both ears to the ground at the same time."

Swanson challenged Montague to joint debate, but despite Montague's top-flight reputation as a speaker, he refused. However, the paths of the two candidates crossed at Boydton, and it was impossible for Montague to avoid engaging Swanson in a discussion of the issues before some two hundred persons. The aggressive Swanson may have bested him, although it is difficult to tell at this distance. Be that as it may, Montague did not meet Swanson thereafter on the hustings. Montague's campaign speeches gave the impression of sincerity and dignity, but he was at his best when occupying the platform alone.

At all events, he made steady progress in the harvesting of delegates to the Democratic State Convention which would choose the gubernatorial nominee. The times were propitious for new approaches to public questions, and Montague was the beneficiary of this trend. Senator Martin worked hard behind the scenes for Swanson, and Senator Daniel also backed him. Yet more than a month before the convention met at Norfolk, Montague was seen by all to be the winner. This was so obvious when the gathering opened that Swanson's name was not even presented. He proved a good loser, and was loudly applauded as he congratulated and shook hands with his victorious opponent.

Montague's campaign against the Republican nominee, Colonel J. Hampton Hoge of Montgomery County, was a vigorous one. Hoge, for his part, attacked the Democrats, alleging corruption and inefficiency. But the Republicans were badly divided and they were no longer a real threat, except in the southwest. Nor did they wish to be known any further as "the party of the Negro." At the convention which nominated Hoge there were only fifty black delegates. Speakers openly expressed satisfaction over this circumstance, to the embarrassment of the delegates in question.

The Republicans had little chance of winning, in any event. They were opposed to holding a constitutional convention, and opinion in the state was running the other way. But they received their *coup de grace* when Republican President Theodore Roosevelt entertained Booker T. Washington at lunch shortly before the election. Montague's liberalism did not extend to the race problem, and he joined in the orgy of demagoguery that exploded over the South. Montague stated that "the white race" was "by divine right . . . entitled to supremacy . . . one race must guide . . . one must be guided." The Republican party, he proclaimed, "loves a Negro better than a white man." President Roosevelt could "lie in the gutter," if such was his wish, a Virginia newspaper declared, but white supremacy must be maintained.

As a result of this episode, the Virginia Republicans expected the worst. Hoge polled only 81,366 votes to 116,683 for Montague. The latter lost his own Fifth District—where Swanson apparently did little to help—but he carried the nine other districts as well as all eighteen Virginia cities and sixty-six counties. Youthful "Jack" Montague was the first postwar governor of Virginia who had not served in the Confederate forces.

Republican strength was now concentrated largely in the mountainous Ninth District, where the Slemps, father and son, were about to obtain a foothold that would keep the district Republican for two decades. "Swarthy, squat" Campbell Slemp of Turkey Cove, Lee County, had served in the House of Delegates as a Readjuster, and in 1902 he was elected to Congress from the Ninth. He was re-elected twice more, and when he died during his third term, his son, C. Bascom Slemp, was chosen to succeed him. Bascom Slemp was elected thereafter for seven successive terms.

Politics in the southwest was even wilder and woollier in that era than in other parts of Virginia, and the "feudin' tradition" persisted. Intimately related to the notorious frauds that were perpetrated by both parties, were two serious shooting affrays. Republican James A. Walker of Wytheville, sole surviving commander of the Stonewall Brigade, was defeated for re-election to Congress in 1898 by Judge William F. Rhea of Bristol. Walker contested the election, and while taking depositions in Bristol the following year, he fired at Rhea's attorney, William Hamilton, in a heated argument. Walker missed, but

Hamilton shot back, wounding him twice. Then in Scott County in 1903, there was a violent election dispute at Fairview precinct. Shooting began, and when the smoke had cleared, two Democrats lay dying on the floor and two Republicans had been wounded.

Such gunplay growing out of allegations of electoral crookedness, many of which were justified, highlighted the need for change, either at the hands of the General Assembly or the constitutional convention. When the one hundred members of the convention were chosen in the various districts, the Democrats elected 88 and the Republicans 12, with 10 of the Republicans coming from the western section of the state. There were no Negro members. This last is hardly surprising, since the principal objective of the convention was to disfranchise the black voter. At that time, neither party was angling openly for black support, although there was much undercover buying of Negro votes and other comparable skulduggery.

The Richmond *Times* had been engaged in a seven-year crusade against electoral fraud, with the underlying thesis that most of it revolved about the black voter. Many sincere whites had somehow convinced themselves that this thesis was correct, and had reached the remarkable conclusion that it would be fair to the black voter virtually to eliminate him in the interest of "honest elections."

The Negro in Virginia had had his ups and downs during the postbellum years. The Jim Crow system, it should be noted, came to the Old Dominion from the North. "The Northern Negro," in the words of C. Vann Woodward, "was made painfully and constantly aware that he lived in a society dedicated to the doctrine of white supremacy and Negro inferiority." Abraham Lincoln himself had declared in 1858 that he had never been "in favor of bringing about in any way the social and political equality of the white and black races."

Virginia Negroes were not Jim Crowed in the modern sense until the turn of the century. Thomas Wentworth Higginson, the former abolitionist, had visited Virginia, South Carolina and Florida in 1878. He "compared the tolerance and acceptance of the Negro in the South on trains and on street cars, at the polls, in the courts and legislatures, in the police force and militia, with attitudes in his native New England, and decided that the South came off rather better in the comparison." In 1884, he checked again, and arrived at similar conclusions.

The conservative Richmond *Dispatch*, which later took a very different attitude, declared in 1886 that "nobody here objects to sitting in political conventions with Negroes," or to "serving on juries with Negroes." It went on to say that Negroes were sitting in both branches of the General Assembly, as they had a right to do. At that time, Virginia blacks rode on trains and streetcars in the same manner as the whites, with no segregation. Occasionally, but only occasionally, they were not segregated in restaurants, bars, theaters and railway waiting rooms.

By the early nineties, demands were beginning to be heard that the races be separated, and that the blacks be almost completely disfranchised. Not long before Virginia's constitutional convention met, the New York *Times* declared: "Northern men no longer denounce the suppression of the Negro vote [in the South] . . . the necessity of it under the supreme law of self-preservation is candidly recognized."[3]

It was in such an atmosphere that the constitutional convention met. The General Assembly, by a majority of one vote, had decreed in 1900 that the races must be segregated on railroad cars. Similar legislation for streetcars and steamboats was passed in 1901. The convention would now address itself to achieving the Negro's well-nigh total separation from the ballot box, although, of course, disfranchisement of black citizens was not its sole objective.

The convention assembled in the old Hall of the House of Delegates at the Capitol on June 12, 1901. Its members were not comparable in brilliance or prestige to those who had sat in such conventions of the past as those of 1788 and 1829–30, but among them were men of considerable ability and substance. Included were Senator John W. Daniel, Carter Glass, ex-Governor William E. Cameron, R. Walton Moore of Fairfax, William A. Anderson of Rockbridge, Eppa Hunton Jr. of Fauquier, A. Caperton Braxton of Staunton, and Preston Campbell of Abingdon, aged twenty-seven, the youngest member.

The anti-Martin wing of the Democratic party was dominant in the deliberations, as soon became apparent. It had been widely predicted that Senator Daniel would be chosen chairman, but his closeness to Senator Martin militated against him, and former U. S. Congressman John Goode of Bedford was elected. The venerable Colonel Goode, who was aligned with the anti-Martin Independents, had served in the secession convention of 1861, in the Confederate Army and the Confederate Congress. The secretary of the convention

was young Joseph Button of Culpeper, a close ally of Martin. Senator
Daniel was chosen chairman of the committee on the elective franchise,
deemed the most important of all the committees. The other most
important ones were headed by Independents, as follows: committee
on corporations, A. Caperton Braxton; on the judiciary, Eppa Hunton
Jr.; on the executive, William E. Cameron; legislative committee,
R. Walton Moore.

Senator Daniel, at the outset, may have preferred his vital franchise
committee chairmanship to presiding over the convention. However,
he probably regretted having accepted this responsibility, for it involved the knottiest problems of all. After struggling with them for
several months, he became ill and had to retire completely from the
convention from October until March. A major share of his duties fell
upon Carter Glass, who also was in frail health and had to have a
severe operation. Yet Glass, whose small frame was far from robust,
under the best of circumstances, pulled himself together, and by a great
act of will and determination, played a decisive role in the final working
out of the franchise provisions.

Elimination of the Negro vote to the maximum degree possible
was the intention from the outset, a fact made abundantly clear by
Glass. He termed Negro enfranchisement "a crime to begin with and
a wretched failure to the end," and stated that "the unlawful but
necessary expedients employed to preserve us from the evil effects of
the thing were debauching the morals and warping the intellect of
our own race." A major problem was how to exclude the blacks without excluding large numbers of illiterate whites. The delegates from
the Shenandoah Valley and the southwest, where the Negro problem
was almost non-existent, were concerned with seeing that white men
could still vote. Economic issues, such as discriminatory railroad rates,
rather than the franchise, were of primary interest to these westerners.

After prolonged discussion of various restrictive proposals, such as
the property clause, the grandfather clause, the "understanding" clause,
literacy tests and so on, it was decided that one set of requirements
would be made applicable for the first two years, and that other
provisions would apply thereafter. What was known as the "temporary
understanding clause" included a requirement that the would-be voter
give a reasonable explanation of any section of the Constitution, unless
he had paid property taxes to the state of at least one dollar, or was
a Confederate or Union veteran or the son of one. It applied to all who

had registered prior to 1904, and local registration boards were given sweeping authority to decide whether the applicant's explanation was "reasonable." Since many such boards were determined above all else to eliminate Negro voters, the results can well be imagined. Despite the professed desire of the convention to purify Virginia politics, this was not exactly the sort of purification that might be expected to promote that objective.

A poll-tax requirement was introduced for all who registered in 1904 or thereafter. The $1.50 tax had to be paid for the three preceding years, six months prior to the general election, in an era when $1.50 had far greater purchasing power than it does today. Persons who became interested in a given contest after the six months' deadline could not participate in the election or the primary which preceded it. It was an admirable device for holding down the number of voters, both white and black. A would-be registrant after 1903 also was required to apply "in his own handwriting, without aid," giving his name, age, address and so on, and to "answer on oath any and all questions affecting his qualifications as an elector, submitted to him by the officers of registration." This last was susceptible to serious abuse, although in recent years evidence of such abuse has seldom been forthcoming. Both provisions remained for more than half a century as part of Virginia's organic law, until voided by the federal courts and the Congress in the 1960s.

The effect of the permanent franchise provisions in the new constitution, drafted mainly by Democrats, was not only to eliminate most of the black voters, but also large numbers of whites, especially those in the mountain districts of the southwest, a majority of whom just happened to be Republicans. There, in the Ninth District at the turn of the century, one voter in every 4.2 could neither read nor write, and nearly all were white. Paradoxically, the illiteracy rate among the few blacks in this particular district was only one in twenty-one. In the state as a whole, more than 50 per cent of the Negro males of voting age were illiterate, as compared with 12 per cent of the adult male whites. Blacks outnumbered whites in thirty-five counties, and they constituted nearly 36 per cent of the state's population of about 1,850,000.[4] The overall effect of the new franchise requirements was to cut the total vote in half, as shown by the number of Virginians who cast ballots in the presidential elections of 1900 and 1904.

The Republican partisan, William C. Pendleton, told in his *Political History of Appalachian Virginia* of being an eyewitness to the efforts of unlettered mountaineers to register after the adoption of the new constitution. He spoke of the "horror and dread visible on the faces of the illiterate poor white men, who were waiting to take their turn before the inquisition," and added that "it was still more horrible to see the marks of humiliation and despair that were stamped upon the faces of . . . men who had been refused registration, and who had been robbed of their citizenship." Large numbers of both Republicans and Democrats in the district were turned down by the registration boards.

A controversy in the constitutional convention comparable in intensity to that concerning the franchise erupted over the control of corporations. The era of the "robber barons" was fresh in memory and "Teddy" Roosevelt was addressing himself intensively to the problem of the "trusts." Railroads were among the worst offenders, and it devolved upon the Virginia convention's committee on corporations to devise appropriate means of curbing them, along with other combinations of corporate wealth.

A. Caperton Braxton, the chairman of the committee, was an admired Staunton attorney, but few were prepared for the spectacularly able manner in which he discharged his responsibilities. The railroad lobby descended upon the convention in full force determined to prevent any sort of effective regulation, and it was joined by representatives of other corporations who vowed eternal allegiance to the principle of *laissez faire*.

Braxton had prepared himself thoroughly, and he checkmated these lobbyists at virtually every point. Called a "wild anarchist" and the possessor of a "warped mind"—because he had said, for example, that the time had come for a decision whether "the people or the railroads would control the government of the commonwealth"—he pressed steadily forward. Leading newspapers, fantastically prophesying doom, predicted that if a regulatory commission for corporations were set up, it would mean "a state of chaos" and an end to prosperity in Virginia.[5]

Despite all this sound and fury, the recommendations of Braxton's committee were adopted by the convention almost exactly as written. They provided for the establishment of a State Corporation Commission with power to regulate railroads and other corporations. This represented an entirely new departure in the machinery of government, and conferred on the commission a wider jurisdiction than that enjoyed by any similar state agency in this country, before or since.[6] The dire predictions of "chaos" have, of course, not been remotely borne out. And while the commission has been subjected to occasional criticism, the corporations have been, and are, among its stanchest supporters, while the public has benefited greatly.

Establishment of the commission and adoption of new and more stringent voting requirements were the most important actions of the convention. That body also provided for the popular election of the secretary of the commonwealth, state treasurer, commissioner of agriculture and superintendent of public instruction, an unwise arrangement that would be changed a quarter of a century later during the administration of Governor Byrd, when each of these officials was made a gubernatorial appointee. Monthly court days were done away with. These had provided opportunities for generations of rural citizens to gather at the various courthouses, there to talk politics, chew tobacco, whittle, swap lies and trade horses. Twenty-four circuit courts were created to replace the county courts.

The convention adjourned June 26, 1902, more than a year after it had convened. However, it had been in actual session for less than ten months.

The question now was whether a Democratic party pledge to allow the people to vote for or against the new constitution, would be honored, and whether an act of the General Assembly requiring such a vote, would be obeyed. Strong sentiment had developed for proclaiming the document without a vote. It was feared that if the constitution were submitted for approval to the old electorate, many of whom it disfranchised, the vote would be in the negative. Some favored submitting it to the new and reduced electorate.

Carter Glass was the author of the plank in the Democratic party platform, adopted in 1900 at the state convention of the party in Norfolk, which pledged that the constitution, when framed, "shall be submitted to a vote of the people for ratification or rejection." This plank was included with a view to persuading the voters to cast their ballots for a convention in the referendum which was about to take place, and they did so vote, as we have seen. When the General Assembly met in 1901, and provided for the election of delegates to the convention, it stipulated that the constitution to be adopted "shall be submitted to the qualified voters of the commonwealth." Yet State Senator Glass, ignoring his authorship of the plank pledging submission, argued at the legislative session that submission was not necessary. He contended, furthermore, that if the constitution were submitted, it should be to the new and restricted electorate, and declared that this had been his understanding of what the party pledge of 1900 meant. As Glass expressed it, "no body of Virginia gentlemen could frame a constitution so obnoxious . . . that I would be willing to submit its fate to 146,000 ignorant Negro voters." Neither the party promise nor the legislative act stated whether the constitution was to go before the old or the new body of voters, but there can be no question that both meant that it should be submitted to one or the other. Yet the convention ended by not submitting it to either, and simply proclaimed the document. From a strictly legal standpoint, this may have been defensible, since a constitutional convention is normally regarded as sovereign and all-powerful, but moral and ethical considerations are something else again. Whether the convention would have been held at all, if the people had not been induced to vote for it by the party pledge of submission, will never be known. Whether the constitution would have been ratified, if voted on, is also unknown.[7]

The failure of the convention to honor the pledges made for submission caused challenges to be filed in both the state and federal courts. The Virginia Supreme Court of Appeals upheld the finding of the lower courts that the newly framed constitution was "the only rightful, valid and existing constitution in the state." The United States Supreme Court also refused to intervene, saying that what had been done "cannot be undone by any order of the court."

So the constitution went into full force and effect. The electorate had been sharply curtailed and would remain so for more than sixty years, thanks mainly to the poll tax, to political apathy and to the strength of the Democratic "organization." The Negro had been disfranchised to such an extent that any small threat to white control of the state's affairs which he represented, was eliminated.

If the Independents, who were mainly responsible for holding the constitutional convention and who dominated its deliberations, imagined that they would thereby strengthen their position, their expectations were not realized. The small electorate played into the hands of the Martin organization, which was more readily able to control it, and proceeded to consolidate its grip on the state. True, the level of political morality improved and except in limited areas the widespread and perennial corruption of the postbellum era did not return. But after the election of Andrew J. Montague as governor in 1901, there were no other major breaks in the hegemony of the Martin organization until the election of Westmoreland Davis in the untypical three-cornered race of 1917.

The constitutional convention of 1901–02 had passed into history, but the impact of its deliberations and conclusions, both good and bad, upon the political and social life of the state would be long-lasting.

THIRTY-FOUR

A Gettysburg for the Progressives

VIRGINIA in 1900 was more than 85 per cent rural, but farms were much smaller than in the antebellum era, owing to the shortage of field hands. Richmond, with 85,000 population, was the largest city. Virginians were recovering from the shock and humiliation of a defeat that had occurred more than a generation before, but whose traumatic effects were still evident, both in the material realm and in the realm of the spirit.

Many imposing homes that had been surrounded by substantial acreage before the Civil War, with orchards and gardens, stables and smokehouses, were down-at-heel or in a state of near-collapse. Large areas had grown up in weeds, broom sedge and slash pines. Low-income whites, who had never had much of anything, were living in some of the decaying mansions. These sallow-complexioned, undernourished citizens were still eking out a bare existence, often despite the ravages of hookworm, pellagra or malaria. The Negroes were at the bottom of the heap, and the competition for jobs between them and the most disadvantaged whites was sometimes bitter. Lynchings were all too frequent, although much less so than in states farther to the south. A number were prevented when governors called out the militia.

Transportation facilities in the rural areas were about as they had been a century before. Horses or mules pulling carriages or wagons, or oxen pulling carts, were the principal means of travel from the family home to the neighbor's, to the country store or the rural post-office. Almost all roads were unspeakably bad, with deep mud in wet weather and choking clouds of dust at other times. If a train trip was desired, the coaches were often dirty and cinder-bestrewn, hot in summer and cold in winter.

The first commercially successful electric streetcar line in the world began operations at Richmond in 1888, and by 1900 the trolley had replaced horse-drawn cars there and in many other cities. A. Langstaff Johnston of Richmond was the builder of the original line.

Automobiles were almost unheard-of. A steam Locomobile, fueled by kerosene and riding on solid rubber tires, which chugged along Norfolk streets in 1899, is thought to have been the first automobile operated in the state. A decade would pass before the motorcar was a significant factor in transportation. A man who purchased a car in 1900 with a view to driving it from Staunton to Norfolk, provided he could manage to negotiate the endless succession of ruts, bumps and mudholes, had to ship it by freight train, since one of the counties through which he had to pass would not allow automobiles to use its roads. Autos were considered nuisances, and they were also regarded as playthings of the rich. Virginia-born Woodrow Wilson, president of Princeton University, warned the students there in 1907 against the "snobbery" of motoring. Nothing has done more to "spread socialistic feelings" in the United States than this "arrogance of wealth," he declared.[1]

The beginnings of a movement for statewide prohibition of alcoholic beverages occurred in 1901, with the organization of the Anti-Saloon League of Virginia. The goal of drying up the entire commonwealth was kept carefully under wraps at the time, and "local option" was declared to be the objective. The Reverend James Cannon, Jr., a Methodist divine of enormous ability, vast energy and devious methodology was the Virginia league's long-time executive head and most gifted impresario. He would be a powerful factor in the politics of the state for a decade and a half.[2]

In 1903 the General Assembly passed the Mann Act, sponsored by State Senator William Hodges Mann of Nottoway County. It provided stringent regulations for the licensing of saloons in places with fewer than 500 inhabitants, and had the almost immediate effect of closing more than 500 saloons in Virginia's country districts, thereby reducing the total number in the state to about 2500. Cannon had framed the legislation with Mann, and had mobilized the Methodist and Baptist churches in its behalf. He was to mobilize them again and again, as the manifest evils of the old-time barroom were depicted in lurid hues from hundreds of pulpits.

These years also witnessed the emergence of Virginia's two foremost novelists—Ellen Glasgow and James Branch Cabell. In addition, Mary Johnston, whose historical romances were widely popular, published her first best seller, *To Have And to Hold*, in 1900. Father John B. Tabb, a lyric poet of exceptional wit and grace, had come to public notice somewhat earlier; his *Poems* (1894) would reach seventeen editions.

Miss Glasgow's first novel, *The Descendant*, (1897), was considered a daring work for a young Virginia woman, reared in the genteel tradition. Its hero was not only a "poor white," but illegitimate, as well. This was contrary to what was considered by many in that era to be in good taste, and one of Miss Glasgow's elderly kinsmen remarked despairingly, "It is incredible that a well-brought-up southern girl should even know what a bastard is."

With *The Battleground* (1902)—termed by critic Louis D. Rubin, Jr., "in its time, shocking in its harsh realism"—Miss Glasgow embarked upon "a social history of Virginia from the decade before the Confederacy." Its major theme was "the rise of the middle class as the dominant force in southern democracy."

James Branch Cabell, whose *The Eagle's Shadow* appeared in 1904, was a writer of an altogether different type, but he too helped to shake Virginia out of its ancient ways. His beautiful, if mannered, style has been the object of much admiration, and his imaginative flights into the legendary medieval realm of Poictesme exhibit both an opulent fancy and a graceful irony. Parrington terms Cabell "one of the great masters of English prose, the supreme comic spirit thus far granted us . . . individual and incomparable."

Thus it will be seen that Virginia was beginning to stir with new ideas and new life in the early 1900s, even though the pall of defeat still hung over the commonwealth. While a vast deal remained to be done, there were signs that the state was moving slowly out of the doldrums. One of those signs was to be found in the programs and politics of Governor Andrew J. Montague.

He was a progressive thinker on public questions and an enemy of the Martin organization. His advocacy of election by primary, of positive programs for better schools and roads, and of employers' liability for injuries to employees was in advance of positions taken by his political rivals.

Unfortunately, Montague leaned over backward and took the extraordinary position that he ought not to fight aggressively for the passage of measures proposed by him to the legislature. Not a forceful leader, at best, he felt that as a matter of principle he should do no more than set forth his proposals in formal addresses to the General Assembly. "As governor I do not think I should undertake to favor in advance bills which are likely to come before me for approval or disapproval," he declared. The result was that except for the employers' liability bill, which had been endorsed by the Democratic State Convention, little of his program was enacted into law.

In addition to the fact that he suffered from this manifest handicap, he did not have the united backing of the progressive faction of his party. Other members of that faction had ambitions for higher office, which conflicted with his—notably his known desire for a seat in the U. S. Senate. Montague, furthermore, was perhaps too conscientious for his own political good in making appointments. For example, Caperton Braxton, the influential "father" of the State Corporation Commission, sought to persuade the governor to name E. S. Goodman, traffic manager of the Richmond Chamber of Commerce, to the commission. Braxton wrote a friend that his efforts got nowhere with Montague, and that they were like "singing psalms to a dead horse." On top of all else was the fact that a majority of the General Assembly was against Montague from the outset. His successor in the governorship, Claude Swanson, would capitalize on this situation and obtain the enactment of forward-looking measures that Montague had been unable to get through the hostile legislature.

The Assembly defeated a bill backed by Montague which provided for the party primary as a means of nominating candidates. But Senator Martin apparently saw the direction of the political winds, for when the Democratic State Convention met in 1904, it endorsed the primary with hardly a ripple.

This meant that when Martin came up for re-election the following year, he would face the voters in a primary, instead of going before the Martin-controlled General Assembly, as in the past. Montague announced his candidacy for Martin's seat, and the battle was on.

Martin's reputation was that of a "business senator" who did most of his work in committees, made scarcely any speeches on the floor, and was zealous in attending to requests from constituents. Montague did not regard him as worthy to rank with the statesmen who had represented Virginia in the Senate in past years. Yet the fact remains that Martin impressed many, including some of his former critics, with his ability and his conscientious devotion to duty.

Montague sought to make Martin's earlier opposition to nomination by primary the principal issue of the campaign. This issue was highlighted when the two men met in joint debate at King George Courthouse. Martin's lack of experience as a public speaker was expected to work greatly to Montague's advantage, but Martin held his own quite well. In fact, the impression seems to have prevailed in much of the state that he had somewhat the better of the argument during the three-hour discussion. Montague challenged him twice subsequently to renew the debate, but Martin declined.

Montague was handicapped throughout by the fact that several leading progressives, notably former Governor Tyler, John Goode and Caperton Braxton backed Martin, while others, including Carter Glass, remained neutral, and still others, Attorney General William A. Anderson among them, did little or nothing to help. Congressman William A. Jones was absent in the Philippines.

The Martin machine, with its statewide organization, ground relentlessly on, and when the ballots were counted, Martin was seen to have won in a landslide. He polled nearly 47,000 votes to about 36,000 for Montague, and carried all ten congressional districts, about two-thirds of all counties and cities, and such supposed Montague strongholds as Richmond and Danville. The electorate had spoken, and its verdict admitted of no misinterpretation. It was a sad blow for "Jack" Montague.

The Negro vote in this contest was inconsequential. Registration and poll-tax provisions of the constitution of 1902 had eliminated the great bulk of the black electorate. Of the estimated 147,000 Negroes of voting age in 1900, only 21,000 were on the registration lists late in 1902. By 1905, when the capitation tax became effective, it was believed that fewer than half of the 21,000 registered blacks had met this requirement.

Methods used by ignorant white registrars to prevent Negroes from voting are vividly illustrated in letters received in 1902 by Congressman Henry D. ("Hal") Flood of Appomattox. One of these follows:

"We hope to get most of our men registered. We have knowed

[knocked] out some white reps [Republicans] and paralyzed the negroes. I do not think that we knocked any democrats but we will lose one or two. They may not aplly."

And another of these registrars wrote Flood:

"All right will sirtainly do my best to get the Democratic voters to register & vice versa I am one of the registrars their seems to be verry little interest taken in the registrations but I think they are awakening to the necesity prety fast There wont be no negro registered that aint entitled to You bet."[3]

During Montague's campaign for the Senate, he had been involved in the climactic events of a drive for better public education that had begun in the late nineties. This movement received great impetus from the so-called "Ogden Movement," in which Robert C. Ogden, a wealthy northern merchant and president of the Hampton Institute board of trustees, furnished much of the inspiration and financing. A series of annual meetings at Capon Springs, West Virginia, beginning in 1898, and known as the Conference on Southern Education, launched the drive. These conferences were participated in by a number of leading Virginians.

Virginia's public schools were somewhat better than those in any other southeastern state, on the basis of accepted indices, but they were greatly below the national average. Schools in the Old Dominion were open 119 days (about four months) during the session of 1898–99, but there was no compulsory attendance law, so that thousands of children didn't bother to go or were put to work by their parents. Nearly all the schools were elementary, and there was only a handful of four-year high schools. However, in average daily expenditure per pupil, value of school property per child of school age, and salaries paid teachers, Virginia led all the southeastern states, and Virginia schools were open for more days during the school year than in any state except Georgia. Facilities for Negro children were everywhere far inferior to those for whites.[4]

As a candidate for governor in 1901, Montague had stressed better schools as the principal plank in his platform. During the previous year the Richmond Education Association had been formed in the home of Mrs. Benjamin B. (Lila Meade) Valentine. She and Mrs. Beverley B. (Mary-Cooke Branch) Munford, another leader in the association, were zealous and dedicated trail blazers thenceforth in many constructive efforts in education, health, labor legislation and women's rights.

The sixth in the series of annual Southwide educational conferences, begun at Capon Springs, West Virginia, was held at Richmond
in 1903. The Southern Education Board had been established in 1901,
and had appointed as its Virginia agents Henry St. George Tucker, of
the Washington and Lee law faculty, former member of Congress and
one of the organizers of the original Capon Springs conference, and
Dr. Robert Frazer, president of the Virginia State Normal School at
Farmville. They began at once making plans for the conference in
Richmond, which was to meet in April 1903. Governor Montague
lent his wholehearted co-operation. Robert C. Ogden brought his
usual trainload of educators, philanthropists and other interested persons. After three days in Richmond, the group adjourned for further
meetings at the University of Virginia and Hampton Institute.

Great enthusiasm on behalf of better education was aroused by
this conference. One of its leaders was Dr. Charles W. Dabney, president of the University of Tennessee and son of the Reverend Robert
L. Dabney, whose violent opposition to public schools in the late
nineteenth century has been noted. Charles Dabney's forward-looking
attitude was in direct contrast to that of his father, and his two-
volume work, *Universal Education in the South*, is the standard history
in the field. In it he declared that in the early 1900s "the chief obstacles
to the development of public schools in the South were poverty, prejudice and politics." He rejoiced that Virginia's constitution of 1902
removed the "politics" to a considerable degree from the state's system.

Governor Montague, whose father had likewise been a caustic critic
of public schools, called a meeting of leading citizens in 1904 to consider the educational, economic and civic interests of the commonwealth. After a two-day session, they formed the Cooperative Education
Commission—soon to change its name to Cooperative Education
Association. The organization worked with the Rockefeller-financed
Southern Education Board, which helped to underwrite its activities.
Dr. Samuel Chiles Mitchell, of the University of Richmond, one of
the great teachers of his time as well as one of the most advanced
thinkers, was unanimously elected president.

When the Cooperative Education Association met at Norfolk in
November of that year, it adopted a resolution requesting Governor
Montague and Dr. Edwin A. Alderman, who had just become the first
president of the University of Virginia—replacing the time-honored

"chairman of the faculty"—to lead a statewide campaign for better schools. Plans for the famous "May Campaign of 1905" were under way.

The May Campaign was an unqualified success, and much interest in an improved public school system was aroused. Whereas the original intention was for Montague and Alderman to do all the speaking, this was changed, and one hundred prominent citizens from various walks of life spoke at courthouses, in town halls and at country crossroads. More than one hundred meetings were held in ninety-four counties. As matters turned out, Alderman did not speak at all during May, although he opened the campaign with an address at Richmond in March. It was stated that he was suffering from throat trouble. However there is the suspicion that he felt it necessary to withdraw because of opposition to his participation from his Albemarle neighbor, Senator Martin. The latter's good offices were extremely important to the University of Virginia, since his "organization" controlled the appropriations by the state to that institution. Martin gave lip service to the May Campaign but he was never strongly committed to the public schools. He suspected, furthermore, that Montague, who was then running against him, was using the school campaign to gain votes. While Alderman failed to participate in the speaking during May, he did deliver several addresses on public education in the fall.[5]

The May Campaign engendered a spirit of optimism among Virginians. The state was more prosperous than during the nineties, when the panic of 1893 cast its shadow over the land. There was to be a business slump in 1907, but in the years immediately preceding it there was special buoyancy and hope.

One reason for the sanguine outlook in the educational sphere was the election by the voters of Joseph D. Eggleston, Jr., as state superintendent of public instruction. He was later to become president of Virginia Polytechnic Institute and of Hampden-Sydney College, and his incumbency as head of the public school system was highly productive.

Eggleston was the first popularly elected head of the system, and Claude Swanson was chosen governor in the same election (1905). Swanson had become a complete convert to the cause of improved schools, and he and Eggleston worked well together.

The General Assembly that met in 1906 was ripe for the enactment of school legislation. The May Campaign had set the stage for impressive advances, and Swanson was able to take advantage of the momentum thus aroused. He achieved notably, not only in education but in other spheres, for he had a friendly legislature, the lack of which had served to thwart his predecessor.

A deluge of school bills inundated the lawmakers, and most of them passed. The Mann high school act appropriated, as a supplement to local funds, $50,000 annually for the establishment of high schools. Since there were only about seventy-five high schools in Virginia at the time, only ten of which gave four-year courses, the need was obvious. This $50,000 appropriation was doubled two years later, and within a decade there were hundreds of high schools. The quality, in most instances, left much to be desired, but a meaningful start had been made. Then there was an act appropriating an additional $200,000 per year for the salaries of primary and grammar school teachers. Nor was the higher learning neglected. The annual appropriation to the University of Virginia was raised from $50,000 to $75,000, while $85,000 additional was made available for improvements. The College of William and Mary, which had fallen on evil days, following the burning of the main building during the Civil War, and had been largely inoperative during much of the postbellum era, was taken over by the state in 1906.

A normal school for women was opened at Harrisonburg in 1909, another at Fredericksburg in 1911, and a third at Radford in 1912. The first such institution, for Negroes, had been established at Petersburg in 1882, and in 1884 one for whites had been opened at Farmville. However, the Petersburg institute for blacks provided courses for both male and female schoolteachers, and it also included other academic offerings.

Schooling for Negroes in the early 1900s was on a different plane from that provided for whites, largely because of the emphasis placed by Booker T. Washington and his followers on the importance of trade education for the race. Hollis B. Frissell, who succeeded Samuel C. Armstrong as head of Hampton Institute, had said in 1901: "We have felt for many years at Hampton that the study of books in the case of the blacks was of secondary importance; that the question of decent living and intelligent industry was the main feature." Armstrong shared this view.

There were 148,950 illiterate Negroes in Virginia in 1910, and 83,961 illiterate whites. No less than 23 per cent of the total population could neither read nor write.

The health of Virginians was another concern of Governor Swanson.

Under his prodding, the General Assembly revamped the State Board of Health, and provided an annual budget of $40,000. The governor then chose Dr. Ennion G. Williams as the state's first health commissioner. Dr. Williams, one of the most dedicated public servants in Virginia history, performed prodigies with limited finances both in the eradication of disease throughout the commonwealth, and in the improvement of sanitary conditions in the schools. Catawba Sanitarium for tubercular patients was constructed, as well as a hospital for the blind, deaf and mute.

Tens of thousands of Virginians were suffering from hookworm. The malady made them feeble, lazy and stupid, and a prey to other diseases. The Rockefeller Sanitary Commission launched a five-year campaign in 1910 designed to eradicate hookworm, especially in the South, and by the end of the period great progress had been made. The public health authorities in each state then took over, and hookworm was all but wiped out. It still persists to a minor degree in Virginia and other states.

Malaria was next on the agenda of the Rockefeller Commission, and again great progress was made. When effective methods were introduced for controlling the breeding of the mosquitoes which carried and spread the ailment, malaria was eliminated as an indigenous threat to Virginians. However, soldiers and sailors returning from overseas in various wars have imported the malady. The third major curse of the South that has practically been wiped out in the state is pellagra. It killed hundreds of Virginians annually during the early years of the century, but once inadequate diet, lacking in vitamins, was found to be the cause, an effective attack was mounted.

The sad state of Virginia's roads was of prime concern to Governor Swanson. He selected St. Julien Wilson as Virginia's first highway commissioner. The highways were appallingly inadequate for carriages and wagons, and even more so for the oncoming automobile. The governor lent support to the "better roads movement" organized during his term, and addressed a statewide Good Roads Convention attended by more than seven hundred persons.

A board of charities and corrections, twice recommended by Montague, became a reality under Swanson. A fisheries commission was established, and the governor ordered the first geological survey of the commonwealth.

Swanson demonstrated independence of Senator Martin when he

forced a showdown with the railroads over rates. He threatened to call a special session of the legislature, and compelled the carriers to back down.[6]

Services of the State Department of Agriculture were expanded during Swanson's administration, but more important was the launching of farm demonstration work and boys' and girls' club work, under the stimulus of the Cooperative Education Association and School Superintendent Eggleston. T. O. Sandy of Burkeville, a VPI graduate, was named state agricultural agent, and demonstration work was done for both races. The General Assembly of 1908 provided for an agricultural high school in each congressional district. Farming for boys and domestic science for girls were stressed. Poultry and canning clubs for girls were begun by Miss Ella G. Agnew, who was named in 1910 as the first state home demonstration agent in the United States. Boys' corn clubs were organized in Virginia, after Dr. Seaman A. Knapp had come to the state and explained the similar work he had been doing farther south.

This demonstration work can be given a large share of the credit for the fact that, by 1940, Virginia farmers came nearer to producing sufficient food for their families and feed for their livestock than those of any state in the Union. Also, the 4-H Clubs, which were an outgrowth of the boys' and girls' clubs, were important factors in raising the level of rural living in the Old Dominion.[7]

Living standards, as well as educational and cultural standards in Virginia and the South as a whole, were elevated through the work of Dr. James Hardy Dillard, father of Hardy C. Dillard, retired dean of the University of Virginia law school who was named in 1970 to a seat on the Court of International Justice at The Hague. Dr. Dillard's family owned hundreds of slaves in Nansemond County before the Civil War, but he devoted the final decades of his life to an effort to "transform the average white man's attitude toward the Negro." In 1908, Dillard resigned a comfortable and pleasant post as dean of the college of arts and sciences at Tulane University, and a leading position in the New Orleans community, to work with the rural Negroes in Virginia and the other southern states. At that time, he took charge of the Jeanes Fund, which had been endowed by a wealthy Philadelphia woman with a view to improving Negro schools in the country districts of the South. Two years later he agreed to add to this the management of the Slater Fund, established by a well-to-do New Englander for the benefit of southern Negro education.

Dillard, with characteristic generosity, spoke of Jackson Davis, then school superintendent of Henrico County adjacent to Richmond, and Miss Virginia E. Randolph, a Negro teacher in one of the county's Negro schools, as "the inventors of the real Jeanes Plan." Davis, who later rendered important service with Rockefeller's General Education Board, had noticed the effective work of Miss Randolph, a largely self-taught master of the domestic and industrial arts, in making her school superior to the other black schools in the area. "Her school was in perfect order, windows washed, floor scoured, yard cleaned . . . cookstove well polished, where the children cooked vegetables and meat for a hot lunch." Miss Randolph asked permission of Superintendent Davis to visit some other schools in the county in order to aid them in teaching the children how to make better homes. It was gladly granted. The results were such that Davis told Dillard about them, and the latter made Jeanes funds available so that the system might be extended to other areas of Virginia. It worked so well that it became the standard approach to the problem throughout the South, and "supervising teachers" traveled over the region. Dillard described a county with "25 or 30 little country schools for colored children, most of them one-room schools open five or six months a year . . . some with 60 or 70 children in a room," and added: "Think of the difference it makes to . . . [their] teachers, most of them earnest, hardworking, doing the best they can to teach a little reading, writing, arithmetic and geography . . . to have a bright, sympathetic, well-trained teacher come to see them two or three times a month, sometimes spending a day, sometimes two or three days."

Dr. Dillard's sane and constructive contribution to the Negro's advancement was recognized in many ways, including the naming of Dillard University in New Orleans in his honor. Tribute to Miss Randolph's service was paid in 1970, when her body was moved to a modest museum on the site of the one-room school in Henrico County where she began her teaching career. Events of her useful life are recalled there by means of documents, personal items, memorabilia, letters and a bronze bust.

A few years before Miss Randolph's work came to the attention of Jackson Davis, agitation had begun for an exposition in 1907 commemorating the three hundredth anniversary of the Jamestown settlement. The Association for the Preservation of Virginia Antiquities had endorsed the idea as early as 1900. At that time it seemed to be generally assumed that the exposition would be staged in Richmond. However, the Norfolk *Dispatch* led in advocating Hampton Roads as the proper site, and its view prevailed. Fitzhugh Lee was chosen president of a company formed in 1902 to make plans and raise funds, and a mile-long frontage at Sewells Point overlooking Hampton Roads was selected. But Congress was slow in making an appropriation, and difficulties were experienced in raising the needed $1,000,000 from private sources. Fitzhugh Lee died in 1905, and former Congressman Henry St. George Tucker was chosen to succeed him.

As often happens with such enterprises, construction was well behind schedule. When the opening date, April 26, arrived, with President Theodore Roosevelt as the chief attraction, the grounds were far from ready. Five months would pass before they were. When everything was finally in place, the exposition was regarded as "architecturally, scenically, educationally and entertainingly superior and in some respects unique," according to the late editor and author, Lenoir Chambers.

An interesting and successful feature was the Negro exhibit, organized by Giles B. Jackson of Richmond, and underwritten to the extent of $100,000 by the Virginia General Assembly. It was planned and executed by an entirely black organization, and it displayed Negro achievement in many areas, including industry, education and art. The exposition's official Blue Book praised this exhibit highly, as did President Roosevelt, who stopped off in Richmond to congratulate Jackson.

The presence in Hampton Roads of the Atlantic Squadron of the United States fleet lent special dignity to the exposition. Also anchored there for a time were "monster ironclads" from England, France, Germany, Japan and half a dozen other countries.

From the beginning the exposition had many problems. It was relatively inaccessible, and attendance was disappointing. Within a week after it closed, it was placed in the hands of receivers. A decade later, in World War I, the site would be used as a part of the great Norfolk Naval Base.

"Harry" Tucker, who had taken charge of the enterprise under great handicaps, following "Fitz" Lee's death, decided to run for governor in the election of 1909. His opponent was William Hodges Mann. The liquor issue was becoming increasingly acute, and Judge Mann was a vice-president of the Virginia Anti-Saloon League, the organization that was spearheading the "dry" crusade. Mann was a political ally of Senator Martin, whose "organization" stalwarts were often wholly out of sympathy with anything that smelled remotely of prohibition. In order to pacify his rebellious followers, Martin sought assurances from Mann. Admonishing him to be "clear and specific," Martin arranged a conference at which Congressmen James Hay and "Hal" Flood were present. At this time, Mann assured them "in the most unmistakable terms" that he was opposed to prohibition, and that he would veto any act providing for statewide prohibition, unless the legislature that adopted it had been elected on that issue. Martin passed these glad tidings to his cohorts, and they began falling in line—some with decided misgivings.

Tucker was an opponent of the Martin organization, but, like many who were affiliated with that political juggernaut, he was for local option and against statewide prohibition. He sought to capitalize on the liquor issue, and when he and Mann met in joint debate, he demanded to know how Mann would vote, if there were a statewide referendum. Mann was reluctant to reply, but he finally acknowledged that in such a case, he would vote for a statewide law. As with the Reverend Dr. Cannon—who led the fight for statewide prohibition after saying for years that he favored "the principle of local option"—Judge Mann had at first proclaimed that he thought each locality should be allowed to decide the question for itself. However, when pressed, he had to admit that, in reality he favored the exact opposite of this, namely, statewide prohibition. No wonder Senator Martin was "extremely annoyed."[8]

Norfolk was a crucial spot, and there the wheelhorses in Martin's machine were whiskey men and brewers. Norfolk, furthermore, had been notorious for its hard-boiled politics and crooked elections. Two successive congressional contests in that district had been ruled invalid by the House of Representatives. Gambling was also a characteristic of the Norfolk scene, and gun toting was not unknown. It is hardly surprising that the gubernatorial candidacy of a vice-president of the Anti-Saloon League was received by this constituency with something less than enthusiasm. Yet the potency of the Martin operation was such that the unhappy liquor dealers of Norfolk contributed $10,000 to the Mann war chest in the final week of the campaign, in response to an urgent appeal from the senator, who was "exceedingly uneasy" as to the election's outcome. Then at the polls the liquor boys and

their customers voted in accordance with the "word," as passed down
from on high. Thus did the teetotaling, bone-dry candidate sweep
wringing-wet, convivial Norfolk by better than two to one. Mann also
ran much better than anticipated in Richmond and other saloon-in-
fested centers of population. In the state as a whole, he defeated
Tucker by a majority of 5078. The whiskey vote apparently made the
difference.[9]

Tucker's defeat was a setback for the independent faction that had
been trying to break the hold of what was often known as the Martin
"Ring." Two years later, in 1911, a still more serious challenge was
hurled at the Ring.

Senator Martin was up for re-election, and the death in 1910 of
Senator Daniel—who had served for five consecutive terms—had
created a vacancy. Governor Mann offered Daniel's seat to Congressman Henry D. Flood, with the understanding that Flood would run
in the 1911 primary. However, Congressman Claude Swanson let it be
known that he would run in 1911, even if he had to oppose "Hal"
Flood. The risk of a vicious political bloodletting between two organization stalwarts was too much for the Martin machine to take, and
Flood was persuaded to decline. Mann then appointed Swanson.

It soon became apparent that Martin and Swanson would have opposition. Congressman William A. Jones announced that he would
oppose Martin, and Congressman Carter Glass followed almost at
once with an announcement of his candidacy against Swanson. The
two independents lost little time in delivering caustic assaults on their
opponents. Jones blasted the "corrupt, vile, selfish and miserable machine." Glass, almost always vitriolic in his attacks on those with whom
he disagreed, assailed Swanson for "extravagance and mismanagement
of his governorship," and for being party to an "unholy alliance between the preachers and the barkeepers." He also charged Swanson
with purchasing American Tobacco Company stock, knowing that
taxes were about to be lowered on tobacco by Congress—a charge
which apparently was not without substance.[10]

There was strong personal dislike between Martin and Jones. Glass
and Jones sought repeatedly but unsuccessfully to draw Martin and
Swanson into a public debate. Martin gave as his excuse for refusing
that he had not spoken to Jones for twelve years, and that he would not
enter into a debate with a man whom he disliked so intensely.

Jones attacked Flood for sending out postcards to voters on which was inscribed the pungent legend, "Jones and Glass have about as much chance for the Senate as a celluloid dog has of catching an asbestos cat in hell."

Jones sprang a surprise by producing several unpublished letters having to do with the Martin-Lee contest of 1893 and the lobbying by railroad interests in Martin's behalf. While they did not completely prove that Martin's election over Lee was achieved by means of railroad money, the strong implication was there. The Richmond *Times-Dispatch* concluded on the eve of the election that Martin was unfit to represent Virginia in the Senate because of this, and that Swanson was unfit because of his transactions in tobacco stock. Other leading newspapers which had been supporting the two men also reversed their stands.

Yet Martin and Swanson had by far the better of it on election day, and Jones and Glass went down to a shattering defeat. Martin swamped Jones by 65,000 to 31,000, in round numbers, while Swanson crushed Glass, 67,000 to 28,000.

How did this happen? For one thing, the electorate had been severely reduced in size by the new constitution. There were probably fewer than 100,000 active Democrats who went regularly to the polls. This small bloc could be more readily controlled by a well-organized machine than was possible with the much larger pre-1902 electorate. Thus the independents who dominated the constitutional convention of 1901–02, ironically enough, had played into the hands of the opposition. The Richmond *News Leader* estimated on the day after the election that there were 8000 to 10,000 officeholders around the courthouses or in federal posts who were beholden to the Martin organization. This solid phalanx was able to send the Martin-Swanson team far down the road toward victory. It was a preview of the techniques that would be employed over and over to keep the Martin organization, and after it the Byrd organization, in power.

The senatorial primary of 1911 was a Gettysburg for the Virginia progressives. Coming as it did in the wake of the 1909 gubernatorial primary in which Mann defeated Tucker, and the 1905 senatorial primary in which Martin demolished Montague, it was a staggering setback. Prospects for smashing the Martin machine were growing dimmer and dimmer.

Yet it was not a Gettysburg for progressivism in Virginia, since the machine had shown its ability to adjust to the changing tides of public opinion. Important advances in education, highways, health and agriculture had been made under the auspices of the organization. Its capacity for acceding to popular demands for more and better services just in time to prevent a popular revolt was one of the secrets of its long and almost uninterrupted reign.

THIRTY-FIVE

Wilson, War, Prohibition, Machine and Anti-machine

THE PRESIDENTIAL CANDIDACY of Woodrow Wilson in 1912 seemed to offer the Virginia progressives one last chance to even matters with the Martin organization. When Martin aligned himself in bitter opposition to the political aspirations of Virginia's native son, the independents sought to capitalize on the situation.

Martin strongly disliked Wilson, partly, it appears, because of Wilson's record as governor of New Jersey in crushing the machine there, and also because of his reputation as the "scholar in politics." Josephus Daniels, who became Wilson's Secretary of the Navy, relates the following episode, as described to him by Edwin A. Alderman:

"Alderman told me that at his table at the University, when Wilson was his guest, a verbal combat between Wilson and Martin reached such heights of passionate ferocity as he never imagined could dominate two such leaders. He had to intervene and change the subject."[1]

This was before the Democratic National Convention met at Baltimore. At that convention, Martin threw his influence against Wilson, and withheld the support of the majority of the Virginia delegation until the forty-second ballot, when Wilson's nomination was inevitable. Closely allied with Martin in his opposition to Wilson was Thomas Fortune Ryan, the New York multimillionaire, who was the son of a tenant farmer in Nelson County. Ryan was a member of the Virginia delegation.

After Wilson's nomination, Martin, a loyal Democrat, fell in behind him and helped him carry Virginia. But Wilson made a speech shortly thereafter in his native city of Staunton which offended Martin all over again. The President-elect spoke of men who had opposed his nomination, who did not "believe in the state's Bill of Rights," and who would have to be "mastered." Then he turned almost directly toward "Hal" Flood and declared that one of these men was present. When Senator Martin heard of this he was irate. Wilson's scarcely disguised attack on him and his organization at Staunton opened old wounds.

However, it gave encouragement to such Virginia independents as Carter Glass and Henry St. George Tucker, who had backed Wilson throughout the convention fight, and who now were hopeful that Wilson would turn to them as his acknowledged spokesmen and patronage dispensers in Virginia. These hopes were vain. Wilson could not afford to offend the organization men who occupied highly strategic positions in Washington. Martin himself was chairman of the Senate Appropriations Committee, Swanson was chairman of Senate Public Buildings and Grounds and ranking member of Naval Affairs, of which he would later become chairman; Flood was chairman of House Foreign Affairs, and Hay chairman of House Military Affairs. Two independents, Jones and Glass, were chairmen, respectively, of House Insular Affairs and House Banking and Currency —an extraordinary group of prestigious committee chairmanships from a single state.

Wilson's "New Freedom" and its accompanying legislation would have been jeopardized if he had bypassed Martin and his followers in the Senate and House and assigned all patronage to their opponents in the Old Dominion. Wilson decided, therefore, to divide the Virginia patronage between the state's machine and anti-machine groups, giving each its "fair share." However, there was so much squabbling and disagreement that the president ended by allowing the Martin faction to distribute most of the political plums. It was another severe setback for the independents. Some of them were so discouraged that they gave up and decided to make their peace with the Martin wing of the party.

Martin was working at this time in close communion with the Anti-Saloon League, whose Virginia branch was still enjoying the indefatigable leadership of the Reverend James Cannon, Jr. The *entente cordiale* between the machine and the league, established during the

Mann-Tucker gubernatorial campaign of 1909, was to continue, despite ups and downs, until Martin's death.

The "drys" were girding up their loins for a final assault on the citadel of rum, both in Virginia and the nation. Cannon throughout his career did the work of two or three ordinary men, and he was almost demoniacal in his driving determination to dry up the Old Dominion. It was known that a law providing for a statewide referendum could not pass at the legislative session of 1912. The House approved such a bill at that time by better than two to one, but nobody was surprised when the Senate defeated it, 23 to 15. A number of Martin stalwarts in the Senate voted with the "wets." However, by the time 1914 arrived, several of these had reversed their positions, under the spell of the Reverend Dr. Cannon's political thaumaturgy.

In 1914 the House again voted overwhelmingly for a referendum, but the bill passed the Senate only by virtue of a resort to heroic measures. A 20-to-20 tie was achieved there by dragging a hard-drinking senator out of bed, despite his sufferings from an alcoholic carouse the night before, and adding his "dry" vote to the total of 19. This put the issue squarely up to Lieutenant Governor J. Taylor Ellyson, who was personally well over on the "wet" side. Ellyson had been pledged in advance by the farseeing Cannon to vote "dry," in the event of a tie. He kept his pledge, and the bill passed 21 to 20. The era of the amphibious statesman—that notorious species which voted "dry" and drank "wet"—had dawned for Virginia.

The referendum was set for September 22, 1914, and both sides made extensive preparations. The Anti-Saloon League, the Woman's Christian Temperance Union and the Methodist and Baptist churches were arrayed in one camp, while facing them were most of the daily newspapers—whose motive, according to Cannon, was the retention of their liquor advertising—the Local Self-Government Association of Virginia and the Personal Liberty Association. The two last-named organizations included many persons to whom Cannon was wont to refer as "high society folks." The doctor, who wielded an acid pen, was fond of ridiculing them for the pernicious example they set, as they lounged about in their exclusive clubs, partaking of highballs and juleps.

Some years previously, the Richmond *Times-Dispatch* had enunciated the dictum that "every man has a right to drink liquor to his comfort." This was seized upon by Cannon, who hung on the *Times-*

Dispatch and other opponents of prohibition the sobriquet of "Bold, Brave Boys of the Bottle." Their motto, he added, was "Give us liquor or give us death!"

There was never much doubt of the referendum's outcome. The emotional appeals of the "drys" were much more effective than the sober statistical analyses and protestations of the "wets." The prohibitionists attributed virtually all the evils of society and of mankind to alcohol, and promised to bring in a millennium wherein babies would no longer lack shoes and fathers would never more fill drunkards' graves, if Virginians would vote right on September 22. When the ballots were counted, it was found that statewide prohibition had carried easily—94,000 to 63,000. Men, women and children sang hymns, and even wept and became hysterical, as the glad news was received.

When the General Assembly of 1916 convened, it was faced with the duty of prescribing the precise conditions under which prohibition should be carried into effect. Cannon's exhibition of political potency had catapulted him into a position of immense power and prestige. Appointments to several legislative committees—those having to do with what Cannon termed "moral legislation"—were submitted to him for approval or rejection. Throughout much of the session he occupied a seat on the floor of the Senate. At times he prompted speakers who were discussing prohibition from the "dry" point of view, although this was in violation of the rules. The legislation, as finally passed, allowed every householder to obtain from outside the state one quart of liquor, three gallons of beer or one gallon of wine per month. These concessions to anti-prohibitionist sentiment were made with Cannon's entire approval. He was always careful not to get ahead of public opinion.[2]

Prohibition took effect in Virginia October 31, 1916. A newspaper estimated that from $1,000,000 to $2,000,000 was spent by Richmonders in storing up alcoholic beverages against the oncoming drought. There was a notable lack of drunkards, for as the same paper put it, "those who were laying in a stock had no intention of getting unsteady on their feet, as they wanted to get their precious supply home intact."

After the new law had been in effect for a year, all three strongly anti-prohibitionist Richmond newspapers, surprisingly enough, pronounced it a great success. And when nationwide dry legislation became effective a few years thereafter (wartime prohibition in 1919

(23) James W. Hunnicutt, radical Republican, who urged Negroes to set fire to the homes of whites during Reconstruction, and whose harsh and unforgiving attitude toward those who had fought for the Confederacy was condemned in the North. A reporter for the New York *World* wrote that "none who gaze once upon that countenance, so full of cunning and malignity, can ever forget it."

(24) John Mercer Langston, the only black ever elected to the U.S. Congress from Virginia. The son of a white planter and a slave, Langston rose to be U.S. Minister to Haiti, first president of Virginia Normal and Collegiate Institute at Petersburg and Dean of the Howard University Law School, before being elected to Congress for one term.

(25) Trolley car on the earliest commercially successful electric line in the world, first operated in Richmond in 1888.

(26) *Below,* Booker T. Washington, the most distinguished black leader in Virginia history, and adviser to Presidents Theodore Roosevelt and William H. Taft. Openly conciliatory toward white leadership, Washington worked secretly to break down the segregation system.

(27) *Right,* Robert Russa Moton, who succeeded Booker T. Washington as head of Tuskegee Institute, and raised standards there. He also was a leader in founding the Negro Organization Society, and in other progressive movements.

(28) *Far right,* U.S. Senator Thomas S. Martin, most influential political leader in Virginia for the quarter of a century preceding his death in 1919. The "Martin machine" was as potent in its day as the "Byrd machine" in more recent years.

(29) Governor Harry F. Byrd and
Harry F. Byrd, Jr., the latter in
the uniform of a member of the
governor's staff (1928).

(30) *Below,* Rear Admiral Richard E. Byrd
being welcomed at Richmond's
Broad Street Station in 1930 on his return
from the South Pole, by John Stewart
Bryan, newspaper publisher and later
president of the College of William and
Mary. More than 4000 people were
at the station, and Byrd was greeted with a
13-gun salute by the Richmond Howitzers.

and the Eighteenth Amendment in 1920), it was clear that Cannon had been wise in allowing Virginians a quart a month. For national prohibition shut off that quart, and the moonshiners and bootleggers moved in at once. Thousands of otherwise law-abiding citizens began violating the law.

Henry Carter Stuart, one of the great landowners of southwest Virginia, was governor at this time. He had a record of political independence, had served in the Constitutional Convention of 1901–02, and on the State Corporation Commission, and had run unsuccessfully in the Ninth District against C. Bascom Slemp for Congress in 1910. The popular Stuart had begun in 1911 lining up support for the governorship, and by 1913, the year of the primary, he was far in the lead. The organization felt that the part of wisdom was to let him have the nomination without a contest. Relations between Stuart and the organization were harmonious thereafter.

Stuart had put tremendous effort into his campaign against Slemp in 1910. His lack of opposition for governor three years later was, to some extent at least, a reward for his having made this fight. The organization leaders turned out in force and spoke in the district in support of his congressional candidacy. Among them were Martin, Swanson and Flood, along with such independents as Glass, Jones, Tucker and Montague. President Theodore Roosevelt delivered an address at Bristol in Slemp's behalf. It was estimated that each side spent from $100,000 to $250,000—an enormous sum for a single congressional district. The usual southwest Virginia electoral skulduggery was resorted to by backers of both candidates. When it was all over, Slemp was found to be the winner by 227 votes. The election machinery was almost entirely in the hands of the Democrats, which made Slemp's victory all the more remarkable.

World War I burst upon the nation during Governor Stuart's administration, and Virginia was even more involved than the average state, owing to its proximity to Washington and to the complex of military and naval installations around Hampton Roads. Shipments overseas from Norfolk, Portsmouth and Newport News had reached huge proportions during the years immediately preceding this country's entry into the war in 1917. With the construction of the Norfolk Naval Base, largest in the country, and the adjacent Army Supply Base, also the nation's largest, the Hampton Roads area underwent tremendous expansion.

Coal was the principal export during the war years, and more than 10,000,000 tons were shipped from Norfolk and Portsmouth in 1917, with much additional tonnage from Newport News. Pocahontas coal from southwest Virginia was admirably suited to the use of steam-driven ships, and this high-grade commodity poured onto the Hampton Roads docks over the railroads. Huge quantities of coal were shipped overseas, or by water to domestic ports for the war factories, especially those in New York and New England. In addition, Norfolk and Portsmouth sent to American ports thousands of tons of fruits and vegetables, tobacco, petroleum products, cotton and seafood. Hundreds of thousands of tons of Chilean nitrates were brought into Norfolk during the conflict, together with iron and steel articles and many other raw materials and finished products. But exports greatly exceeded imports.

Members of the American Expeditionary Force, 288,000 of them, sailed from Hampton Roads during 1917–18. With them went ships loaded with every kind of equipment and supplies, from horses and mules to airplane parts and blankets, uniforms and canned goods. Trains rumbled onto the docks loaded with men or machines, and these were hurried onto the transports for shipment to France.

Elsewhere in Virginia there was enormous wartime activity. A few miles from Petersburg, Camp Lee had been constructed in three months, with facilities for accommodating and training 45,000 men. Here the 80th Division, which included thousands of Virginians, was whipped into shape for action on the battle front. The soldiers on leave flooded into Petersburg and Richmond.

The city of Hopewell grew from nothing during the war years. A guncotton factory had been built near City Point prior to the outbreak of war in Europe, and when the cannon began booming, additional factories sprang up, and there was an influx of thousands of workers, for whom accommodations were found with the utmost difficulty. But Hopewell came through this ordeal and developed as an important industrial center.

As a city where thousands of sailors were on leave, Norfolk had special problems common to all such ports. It also suffered severely, along with the rest of Virginia, during the extremely cold winter of 1917–18. The harbor was frozen over for the first time in many years, and ocean-going traffic to and from foreign lands was nearly paralyzed for months. The severe nationwide influenza epidemic of the following winter also took a heavy toll in the area around Hampton Roads, as well as throughout the state.

The epidemic broke out on Friday, September 13, 1918, at Camp Lee. Within four weeks more than 500 had died there. In early October, Richmond authorities closed all churches, schools and theaters, and the John Marshall High School was converted into an emergency hospital for 1000 patients. Roanoke instituted similar emergency measures. Over 50 persons died in Pulaski in a single week, and 75 more in Lynchburg in nine days. Masks over the nose and mouth were worn widely. There were fantastic reports—such as are prevalent in wartime —that the Germans were spreading "flu" germs. The worst was over by Armistice Day, November 11, but the malady continued throughout the winter. A total of 11,641 persons died of it in Virginia. Warwick County was hardest hit of all, followed by Fairfax and Prince William counties.

Virginia supplied twenty-one separate military units in the American Expeditionary Force, many of them attached to the 29th and 80th divisions. The number of volunteers was quite large. Some Virginia National Guard units had gained experience in the Mexican border troubles of 1916, and the entire guard went overseas as the 116th Infantry and the 111th Field Artillery. These regiments gave an excellent account of themselves in the Meuse-Argonne offensive. About 1200 Virginians lost their lives in the war. Sergeant Earl Davis Gregory of Chase City was the state's Medal of Honor Winner. The Virginia Military Institute, which had furnished so many leaders in other wars, was again conspicuous in helping to bring victory in this one.

Woodrow Wilson, who led the nation through the conflict with the Central Powers, had lived in Virginia for the eight months following his birth in the Presbyterian manse at Staunton, after which his father, the Reverend Joseph R. Wilson, accepted a call to a church in Augusta, Georgia. However, Wilson considered himself a Virginian. Asked during the presidential campaign of 1912 whether he regarded himself as a Virginian or a Georgian, he replied, "I am a born Virginian," and when the questioner pointed to the short time he had lived in the state, he replied, "Yes, but a man's rootage is more important than his leafage." In addition to his birth in Staunton, Wilson had attended the University of Virginia law school, where, as he often stated in later life, Prof. John B. Minor influenced his thinking enormously. Wilson's father had taught for four years at Hampden-Sydney College.

Wilson is in some ways a much misunderstood man. Widely regarded as austere, solemn and stern, if not arrogant, and as lacking a sense of humor, he was, in fact, a raconteur and mimic of rare talent. He actually danced cakewalks with New Jersey senators, and hornpipes on station platforms while campaigning for the presidency. True, he could also be scornful of those with whom he disagreed, and if a caller at his office was a person with whom he felt no *rapport*, he might seem to the visitor to be an "incarnation of Jonathan Edwards," the hellfire-and-brimstone New England preacher. But with congenial spirits Wilson was a delightful companion, a teller of many humorous anecdotes and an author and reciter of limericks.[3]

Wilson was a casualty of the war, as surely as the men killed in the trenches. True, he made a serious mistake when he refused to accept any amendments or reservations to the Convenant of the League of Nations, but he was so deep in his dedication that he was unable to see the wisdom of making concessions. Fearing that ratification of the League would fail in the Senate, he embarked in 1919 on a coast-to-coast speaking tour, despite warnings from his physicians that the trip might be fatal. He was virtually exhausted when the tour began, and was plagued by raging headaches. In September he made his famous prophesy: "I can predict with absolute certainty that within another generation there will be another world war if the nations of the world do not concert the method by which to prevent it." Soon thereafter came his inevitable breakdown, followed by a paralytic stroke. Wilson was an invalid until his death in 1924. It was during this period that he broke with friends of long standing—Colonel Edward M. House, Private Secretary Joseph R. Tumulty and Secretary of State Robert Lansing. His lengthy illness and paralysis would seem inevitably to have affected his judgment and his mental processes. Allowance should have been made by the public for the circumstances under which these breaks with old friends occurred, but such was not the case. Woodrow Wilson had his faults, but he has been criticized for some of the wrong things. At all events, he is often ranked as one of our half-dozen greatest Presidents.

Negro Americans do not share this latter judgment. Many of them voted for Wilson in 1912, after he had assured them that he wished to see "justice done to the colored people in every matter; and not mere grudging justice, but justice executed with liberality and cordial good feeling." Yet, according to historians Carter G. Woodson and

Charles H. Wesley, Negroes were eliminated during Wilson's first term "from all higher positions in the government and segregated in the civil service." In addition, according to historian John Hope Franklin, "the first Congress of Wilson's administration received the greatest flood of bills proposing discriminatory legislation against Negroes that has ever been introduced in an American Congress." Most of the bills failed to pass, but the blacks were bitterly disappointed over Wilson's attitude. They held indignation meetings throughout the country.

Fearing that trouble might break out on the return of the black troops from overseas, Wilson sent Robert Russa Moton, a native Virginian who had succeeded Booker T. Washington as principal of Tuskegee Institute, to talk to the Negro troops. Moton praised them in the highest terms for their contribution to the war, but some who heard him claimed that he warned the soldiers that they could not expect to find in the United States the democracy they were enjoying in France, and that when they returned they would have to be content with the same position they had always held in the American scheme of things. There is nothing remotely like this in his own account of what he said to the Negro soldiers in France, but many blacks believed that he made these statements. Dr. Moton was unpopular with some black citizens, as a result. Yet he made a significant contribution to Negro .advancement and to interracial good will. He had been a leader in the formation of the Negro Organization Society in 1912, with its motto of "Better Schools, Better Health, Better Homes, Better Farms." Out of this grew National Negro Health Week. The Virginia society also raised $2000, and persuaded the General Assembly to establish the Piedmont Sanatorium for tuberculous blacks at Burkeville in 1914. Then, as head of Tuskegee, Dr. Moton insisted upon higher standards, and the institution began to do accredited college work in teacher training, agriculture and business practice. Moton's book, *What the Negro Thinks*, which appeared in 1929, won the Harmon Award for distinguished Negro achievement. His handsome home, Holly Knoll, in Gloucester County, is now the Moton Conference Center.

Blacks had been leaving Virginia and other southern states after World War I. The census of 1920 showed that the North and West had 330,000 more Negroes in that year than a decade previously. The exodus would become much more massive in succeeding decades.

Virginia's gubernatorial primary of 1917 turned out to be a three-way

affair. There were two prohibitionist candidates and one anti-prohibitionist. Lieutenant Governor J. Taylor Ellyson, long-time chairman
of the State Democratic Committee, who had never been suspected of
being a teetotaler, and Attorney General John Garland Pollard, who
was a complete abstainer, were the "drys." The "wet" was Westmoreland Davis, who never touched alcohol, but who believed in local
option, and promised, if elected, to uphold and enforce the prohibition
law.

The liquor issue obscured all others, and the fact that the Reverend
James Cannon, Jr., and his ally, Senator Martin, united behind Ellyson
added piquancy to the contest. This was the more true, since Cannon
and Pollard had a long record of personal antipathy for one another,
and there were acrimonious exchanges between them. Cannon shut
Pollard out of his newspaper, the Richmond *Virginian*, and refused
to publish Pollard's statements at the vital stage of the campaign, even
as paid advertisements. The "wet" press declared that one of the prime
issues of the contest was "ecclesiastical kaiserism."

Davis said little about the liquor issue, and was content to rest on
the fact that the Anti-Saloon League had pronounced his record "very
unsatisfactory." Many Democrats were tired of seeing Cannon regnant
on Capitol Hill and virtually dictating "moral" legislation to the
General Assembly, so they backed Davis. The latter also ran strongly
with the farmers, for he had bought the *Southern Planter* and had
crusaded in its columns for various progressive agricultural measures.
Davis got about 39,000 votes to 27,000 for Ellyson and 22,000 for
Pollard. The Davis victory was due primarily to the fact that the
prohibitionist vote was split. The winning candidate was comparatively
unknown in Virginia, although his mother was a Virginian and he
attended VMI. He had moved back to the Old Dominion from New
York in 1903 and settled on a handsome estate near Leesburg, after
amassing considerable wealth as a lawyer in Gotham. He was an
independent in politics, and had never run for public office. His
nomination, which was tantamount to election at that period, was a
heavy blow to the Martin organization.

The Davis victory was misconstrued in some quarters as a stunning
setback for prohibition. It was nothing of the sort. The General
Assembly of 1918 could hardly wait to ratify the Eighteenth Amendment, and it did so overwhelmingly in both branches. It even tried to
be the first state in the Union to ratify, but Mississippi won the race

by three days. Two years later, the Assembly did manage to turn out of the post of State Prohibition Commissioner the Reverend J. Sidney Peters, Cannon's intimate friend and former business associate. However, Peters was succeeded by Harry B. Smith of Culpeper, whose aridity in all directions was total.

Governor Davis was not only conscientious in calling for the enforcement of prohibition, but in his final message to the General Assembly he actually recommended an amendment to the Virginia constitution requiring all elective and appointive officers of the state to take an oath that they had not violated the prohibition laws, and that they would not violate them, as long as they held public office. Nothing further was heard of this proposal.

Davis instituted valuable reforms, especially in the areas of fiscal management and prison administration. The "executive budget" he introduced was widely praised and was copied in eight other states by 1922. A State Purchasing Commission was established without creating additional offices, and Davis declared that it had saved over $400,000 almost at once in purchases of coal for state institutions.

The state penal system was overhauled, under the leadership of LeRoy Hodges, whom Davis appointed as chairman of the State Prison Board. Greatly improved medical care was provided, especially for the many prisoners who were suffering from venereal disease. Striped uniforms were eliminated, and prisoners were allowed to read newspapers for the first time. Industries were established in the prison for the manufacture of articles used by state institutions. The notorious convict-leasing system, under which prisoners were leased to private industry with little or no regard for their welfare, was abolished. There were complaints against brutal guards, but the overall improvement was great.

Passage of the workmen's compensation law, under which corporations were held responsible for injuries to their employees, a measure advocated by all three candidates for governor in 1917, meant the creation of a State Industrial Commission to administer it. As head of this commission, Davis appointed young Robert H. Tucker, of the Washington and Lee faculty. It was the first of many valuable public services rendered by Dr. Tucker.

The death of Senator Martin in 1919 removed from the political scene a man who had been enormously influential in Virginia affairs for a generation. His passing left a vacancy in the Senate for Governor

Davis to fill. Despite the dubious aspects of Martin's election over Fitzhugh Lee in 1893, he was a man of personal integrity who had a great capacity for influencing his associates in the Senate.

Although he was out of sympathy with much that President Wilson was doing in the area of social and economic reform, Martin was always a loyal party man, and he felt obligated to push the President's program. Despite warnings from his doctors, he worked long, exhausting hours in discharging his duties as Senate majority and minority leader and chairman of the Senate Appropriations Committee. During the war, he was especially zealous and effective in putting through vitally important money bills.

In some ways "Tom" Martin was an authentic political genius. He was at his best in the committee room or in adjusting differences between the two branches of Congress over a given piece of legislation. He enjoyed the confidence of his fellow senators to an extraordinary degree, and his other associates were equally loyal and admiring.

Despite the huge federal funds that passed through Martin's hands in his influential position, and the opportunities he enjoyed for increasing his income, he died a poor man. Richmond friends, knowing that he was financially embarrassed, made up a purse of $50,000 during his final illness. He declined to accept it.[4]

With Martin's Senate seat vacant, Governor Davis decided to appoint Carter Glass, then Woodrow Wilson's Secretary of the Treasury. Glass had a long record of opposition to the Martin organization—which was, of course, a major reason why Davis chose him. He was also the most eminent Virginian of his generation, with the exception of President Wilson, and he had been the dominant figure in the passage of the crucially important Federal Reserve Act, without which, some believe, the First World War could not have been financed. In leading the fight as a congressman for this legislation, Glass had been opposed by many bankers and other moneyed interests, and this was another reason for regarding him as a man of liberal views.

Before naming Glass, Davis had an extended conversation with him on a November night in 1919 at Morven Park, the Davis estate near Leesburg. According to Davis, Glass told him that he felt more strongly hostile to the Virginia Democratic machine than ever, and that he would fight it as long as he lived. Shortly thereafter, Davis appointed him to the Senate. Glass took his seat in early 1920.[5]

Only a short time elapsed before Glass was turning away from

Davis and in the direction of Claude Swanson and Henry D. Flood, Martin's heirs as leaders of the machine. Flood and Swanson, for their part, set out deliberately to woo Glass away from Davis. It was important to get the peppery little Virginian into the organization, if possible. Although Glass had run against Swanson for the Senate in 1911, Swanson entered with enthusiasm upon the business of flattering and wooing him. Davis was known to be planning to run against Swanson in 1922, and it was important to Swanson that he neutralize the influential Lynchburger or bring him over into the organization camp.

A significant initial step was to see that Glass was placed in nominaion for the presidency at the 1920 Democratic National Convention at San Francisco. This was some six months after he had been seated in the Senate. Davis was suspicious that Glass was flirting with the organization. The governor went to the convention with a room reserved next to that of Glass, but noted on his arrival that Glass had moved. Andrew J. Montague, another independent, expected to nominate Glass for President, but he found, on reaching San Francisco, that Glass was not speaking to him. Glass was placed in nomination for President, but not by Montague. His name was put before the convention by his former foe, Congressman "Hal" Flood. Glass was one of twenty-three nominees.

When Glass came up for election in 1920 for the remainder of Senator Martin's term, the organization allowed him to have the nomination unopposed. The process of winning him over was proceeding apace. The results were apparent in 1921 from the following entry in Glass' diary: "Swanson . . . is bigger than I thought him when it comes to forgetting and forgiving. Why should this not be pleasant? *It is.*" The next year Swanson was assuring Glass that there would again be no opposition from the organization when he ran for the full Senate term. "Certainly not from my friends," said the jovial, backslapping Swanson. "I am telling them all I intend to support you. And I mean active, effective support." Two weeks later Swanson said, "We will stand together, Glass, and if anybody wants to break this combination, let them try it."

All this brought Glass more firmly into the ranks of the machine. He rationalized his desertion of Davis and his newly acquired affiliation with the latter's enemies by advancing the contention that there was no longer a machine. In a letter to Flood, Glass wrote: "Montague and

I complained of the machine when there was a machine. . . . Montague had been elected to Congress without factional agitation or opposition; I have been elected to the United States Senate without opposition. . . . On the other hand, the late Senator Martin and Senator Swanson were re-elected without any factional opposition; thus factionalism in the Democratic party apparently has disappeared."

If factionalism had disappeared, it was remarkable that a hotly contested struggle for the governorship between Henry St. George Tucker and E. Lee Trinkle had just been fought, with the allegedly defunct machine successfully backing Trinkle and the independents backing Tucker. Westmoreland Davis, furthermore, was preparing to run against Claude Swanson for the Senate in 1922 and once again the machine would prove that it was a most lively corpse.

Where did Carter Glass stand in the Davis-Swanson contest? He went to Europe, and took no active part. However, he reportedly passed the word that he believed Swanson, with his experience, would be a more valuable Senate colleague than Davis.[6]

Swanson had many advantages over Davis in the race, in addition to the fact that he was backed by the organization. He had been in public life much longer and had made an excellent record, especially as governor. Endowed with an outgoing personality, he was a far more adept campaigner and speaker than the somewhat cold and withdrawn Davis. Another factor was a letter from President Wilson declaring that Swanson's "help was invaluable throughout the period of the war." Then, too, Swanson enjoyed the highly effective support of young Harry Flood Byrd, who had been named chairman of the State Democratic Committee shortly before, as successor to his uncle, "Hal" Flood, who had died. Undeterred by the fact that he was chairman of what some regarded as a non-partisan committee, Byrd devoted his exceptional energy and ability to the support of Swanson. The impact of these various factors was devastating to Davis. He polled only 37,800 votes to 102,000 for Swanson. Davis was embittered by this smashing defeat, which meant his permanent retirement from public life. He would become a harsh, and at times unfair, critic of the administrations of governors who came after him.

With Davis eliminated, Tucker defeated, and Glass won over, the machine was strengthening its position in various directions. Andrew J. Montague had gone to Congress in 1912 from Richmond, where he would remain for twelve consecutive terms. He, too, would soon be in the organization fold. Montague was sponsored at various times for Cabinet posts and for a seat on the U. S. Supreme Court, but none of these materialized. Henry C. Stuart also had been won over by the machine. Congressman William A. Jones of Warsaw, the other major figure in the opposition ranks, had remained an independent, but he had died in 1918. Jones, who served fourteen terms in Congress, was the foremost leader there in urging independence for the Philippines. A bill that he sponsored, and that passed in 1916, laid the foundations of independence for the islands—which finally became a reality in 1946. The handsome Jones Bridge in Manila commemorates the Virginia congressman's valiant championship of Philippine freedom.

The Tucker-Trinkle contest of 1921 was between a man widely known throughout Virginia and one not at all well known outside his native southwest. "Harry" Tucker had been president of the American Bar Association, had served in Congress and had come close to winning the governorship in 1909. Lee Trinkle was a state senator from Wytheville who had run unsuccessfully against Bascom Slemp for Congress in 1916. Tucker was tall, white-haired and patrician in appearance, while heavy-set, square-jawed Trinkle was a wearer of innumerable lodge pins and an inveterate "booster."

But although Trinkle was not yet well known to the average citizen, he was a first-rate campaigner. He was also a man of ability. He had stood first in his class at Hampden-Sydney and been voted the most influential student at the University of Virginia. As a member of the state senate, he had supported prohibition and was personally "dry," whereas Tucker had opposed it and was personally "wet." Trinkle had strongly favored woman suffrage and Tucker had fought it.

Tucker announced his candidacy early, and he obtained many commitments of support before Trinkle got into the contest. But the machine did not intend to let Tucker have the nomination unopposed. He had refused to accept Bryan and free silver in 1896, had bolted, and had been an independent Democrat ever since. Trinkle accordingly was brought out in opposition as the organization's anointed candidate, and once the word was passed, many of those who had told Tucker they would support him went over to his opponent. The machine was functioning on all cylinders. When the votes were counted, Trinkle was found to have won by a majority of 22,500.

Then came the contest with the Republicans in the general election. While the outcome was never in doubt, the Democrats knew they had been in a fight. For the Republican standard-bearer was the able Richmond attorney, Henry W. Anderson, who put on a vigorous campaign and ventilated the issues more thoroughly than had been done for many years.

The platform on which Anderson ran called for "an exclusively white Republican party in Virginia." This was a specific spelling out of policies introduced more than a decade before under the aegis of Bascom Slemp. This "lily-white" emphasis was designed to get away from the earlier association of the Republicans in the public mind with Negroes and Reconstruction. The platform also called for poll-tax repeal, election-law reform, the right of labor to organize and bargain collectively, better schools and roads, and a business administration.

The poll-tax repeal and election-law reform planks played into the hands of the Democrats, who promptly advanced the argument that such changes in the voting would greatly increase the black vote. Thus the rawhead-and-bloodybones of "white supremacy" once more were dusted off and brandished before the electorate.

The Negroes, for their part, were greatly discouraged by the Republican attitude, which included a pledge that blacks would not be given public office or be allowed to participate in party councils. Calling themselves the "lily-blacks," they nominated an all-Negro ticket headed by John Mitchell, Jr., Negro banker and editor of the Richmond *Planet*. This move was opposed by P. B. Young, editor of Virginia's other leading Negro weekly, the Norfolk *Journal and Guide*.

Anderson's incisive statewide canvass put the Democrats on the defensive, and made it necessary for them to explain, and if possible to justify, many of the practices they had followed over the years. The explanations they offered seem to have satisfied the voters, for Trinkle defeated Anderson by a record-breaking two-to-one majority. Mitchell, the "lily-black" nominee, got only about 5000 votes out of a total of 210,000.

So Trinkle came into the governorship as the hand-picked candidate of the Democratic organization. However, he was to demonstrate a modest degree of independence in office—independence which ultimately caused the organization to force him into political outer darkness. This would be the fate of other Democrats who insisted on using their own judgment occasionally, instead of taking orders.

Trinkle, for example, appointed LeRoy Hodges, who had been private secretary to Westmoreland Davis, as his budget director.

Hodges was in every way competent to discharge this responsibility, but retention of a man who had been in the inner circle of an anti-organization administration was not acceptable to the machine's leadership.

Trinkle also got into trouble with that leadership on the issue of bonds for roads. State Senator Harry F. Byrd, who was rising fast in the organization, although U. S. Senator Swanson was still the recognized leader, was vitally interested in the roads question. A legislative commission on highways, of which Byrd was a member, had recommended in 1918 that the state constitution be amended to permit the issuance of highway bonds—which was directly contrary to Byrd's later position on this question. Byrd also was co-sponsor at the 1918 session of a joint resolution to amend the organic law in accordance with this recommendation. But at the session of 1920, when the amendment came up again for ratification, Byrd voted against it.[7] He had changed his mind as to the desirability of the state's issuance of general obligation bonds—for roads or anything else. Pay-as-you-go would be the guiding star of his philosophy throughout the remainder of his long career. Despite Byrd's opposition, the road-bond amendment passed in the popular referendum of November 1920, by a majority of 61,000.

Trinkle opposed bonds the next year when he ran for governor. Yet when the legislature met in 1922, he favored bonds, and he spoke in various parts of the state in their behalf. He then called a special session of the General Assembly for 1923, and recommended that a specific bond issue for roads be referred to the voters, and that pay-as-you-go be the policy in the interim. Byrd, meanwhile, had made up his mind definitely that road bonds were bad. The legislature voted to hold a referendum on a $50,000,000 bond issue in November 1923, and Byrd was galvanized into action as leader of the opposition.

Virginia's roads at that time were atrocious. The Automobile Club of America actually urged motorists in 1921 to bypass the state. Even so, things were not quite as bad as they had been in 1912. In that year, a group of men set out from Bristol in an Overland car with a view to traveling to Washington. They finally made it, with the aid of picks, shovels and extra axles. In 1916, Governor Stuart received word that citizens in the vicinity of Dumfries, between Fredericksburg and Washington, had blown up a stretch of newly built road in order to preserve their towing business.

Harry Byrd was fully aware of the sad state of Virginia's roads, but he had become sincerely and irrevocably convinced that the way to remedy the situation was through paying for the needed highways by means of the gasoline tax and automobile license fees, rather than by going into debt. He took charge of the anti-bond battle with great energy, and organized the commonwealth from stem to stern. Arrayed against him were the Virginia Good Roads Association, the Virginia Bankers Association and most of the daily newspapers. The stalwarts of the organization were on his side, as were many rural Virginians, whose reluctance to vote for anything that threatened higher taxes was well known. Also in the anti-bond camp was Governor Trinkle, who had changed his mind once more. Similarly Henry C. Stuart who had advocated bonds in 1922, now accepted the presidency of the Pay-As-You-Go Roads Association. A musical comedy could almost be written on the gyrations of Virginia politicians at this season on the subject of road bonds.[8]

The outcome of the referendum was a victory for the anti-bond forces by a majority of about 46,000. The public career of Harry Byrd, who organized the triumph, was well underway.

Governor Trinkle presumably was pleased by the results of the referendum, but he had run afoul of Byrd in the course of his various changes of front. He also came under fire from Byrd, a member of the State Finance Committee, when it was announced that there was a deficit of $1,700,000 in the state treasury. Trinkle attributed it to the business depression, but neither Byrd nor the press was convinced, and the governor came under heavy attack. Being exceptionally thin-skinned, this was a great trial for him.

George P. Coleman, a capable and conscientious public servant, was highway commissioner under Governors Stuart and Davis. He was retained in the post for a time by Trinkle, but he was an ardent bond advocate and, in addition, he and Byrd were personally unfriendly. The General Assembly of 1922 reorganized the highway department with a view to demoting Coleman. He was placed under the chairman, a newly created position. Trinkle named Henry G. Shirley, one of the top men in the United States, to the new office, and was acclaimed for making so excellent a selection. Coleman resigned.

Another casualty of the bond fight was State Senator C. O'Conor Goolrick of Fredericksburg, one of the ablest and most progressive members of the legislature. Goolrick was a leading advocate of road bonds. The machine brought out W. Worth Smith of Louisa against him and defeated him for re-election. It was an example of the unwillingness of the machine to tolerate dissent.

A couple of alleged scandals in the Trinkle administration brought considerable criticism on the governor, as did his propensity to "boost" all things Virginian. Unwilling to admit that the Old Dominion was backward in important respects, Trinkle declared in an unguarded moment that people who talked about "poor old Virginia" should be "shot at sunrise." This deliverance was gleefully seized upon by the press, which delighted to torture the sensitive chief executive. Thomas Lomax Hunter, a former member of the legislature and later a newspaper columnist of considerable renown, wrote:

> O Virginia,
> Where are thy men of might, thy
> Grand in soul?
> Gone glimmering through the
> dream of things that were.
> The state which once had a man as
> Governor who said, "Give me liberty or give
> me death" now has one who cries
> "Shoot him at sunrise."

Woman suffrage had been written into the U. S. Constitution in 1920, with the adoption of the Nineteenth Amendment, but that amendment was never ratified by the Virginia Assembly. This despite an eleven-year campaign by a group of prominent and able Virginia women.

After spasmodic earlier attempts in Virginia to obtain votes for women, Mrs. Orra Gray Langhorne of Lynchburg, who was also active in promoting the whites' understanding of the blacks, organized the Virginia Suffrage Association in 1893, with most of its membership in Lynchburg. Nothing much came of this. Then in 1909, several years after Mrs. Langhorne's death, a meeting was held in the Richmond home of Ellen Glasgow, the novelist. Out of this grew the Equal Suffrage League of Virginia, with the dynamic and versatile Lila Meade Valentine as president. Mrs. Valentine had been involved in various movements up to that time, but after 1909 she concentrated much of her attention on women's suffrage.

She and her associates were faced with the argument that adoption of woman suffrage would mean giving votes to black women, and this, it was feared by various conservatives, including the leaders of the Martin machine, might mean a serious dislocation of the status quo. In response, suffrage league officials contended that the poll tax and literacy tests would serve powerfully to limit the vote of lower income groups in both races. Nevertheless, the fear that "white supremacy" might be endangered could not be overcome by the arguments of the lady suffragists. There was also the claim of the opponents, including some prominent members of the weaker sex, that woman's place was in the home, and that females ought not to descend from the pedestal on which southern chivalry had enthroned them, to become embroiled in the sordid concerns of politics. There was also the contention that voting qualifications ought to be determined by the respective states, rather than by the federal government.

Senator G. Walter Mapp and E. Lee Trinkle, also a state senator at that time, were sympathetic to the cause of women's votes, but there was no legislator sufficiently concerned to provide purposeful leadership. President Wilson sent a telegram in 1919 urging Virginia to ratify, but to no avail. The untiring work of such women as Miss Adele Clark, Miss Lucy R. Mason, Mrs. John H. Lewis and Mrs. Mary-Cooke Branch Munford, not to mention Mrs. Valentine, was without tangible result. After ratification of the Nineteenth Amendment over Virginia's unyielding opposition, the Equal Suffrage League became the League of Women Voters, which has been a highly useful civic agency since that time.

While these events were in progress, some of the same women who worked for the suffrage were actively engaged in efforts to obtain the admission of women to the University of Virginia. This movement began in 1910 and continued for eight years, with Mrs. Mary-Cooke Branch Munford as the leader throughout.

The controversy centered around the proposal to establish a co-ordinate college at Charlottesville. President Alderman and most of the faculty favored it, but the great majority of students and alumni were opposed. Advocates argued, with considerable logic, that the state university ought to be open to all qualified citizens of either sex. Opponents, however, contended that the University of Virginia took pride in its peculiarly masculine atmosphere, and that this would be destroyed by the admission of women.

Women could attend the normal colleges at that period, but no other state institution was open to them. There were several excellent privately supported institutions for women. Randolph-Macon Woman's College at Lynchburg belonged to the same system as Randolph-Macon College at Ashland, both of which stood high in the educational world. The Lynchburg institution was first in the South to discard the narrow concepts of the antebellum "female institute." It was also the first southern woman's college admitted to membership in the Southern Association of Colleges and Secondary Schools, and the first to be awarded a chapter of Phi Beta Kappa. Highly regarded Sweet Briar College had been in operation for some years when Mrs. Munford began her crusade, and Hollins, founded in 1842, was another fine institution.

But these were relatively expensive, and besides, taxpayers argued that their daughters were entitled as a matter of right to attend the state university. The argument was accepted by the Virginia Senate at several sessions of the General Assembly, but was rejected by the House. Finally, in 1918 both branches went part way, and admitted women to the University of Virginia's graduate and professional schools. At the same session, it was decided to admit women to the College of William and Mary on an equal basis with men. In 1944, Mary Washington College at Fredericksburg became the co-ordinate college for women of the University. Finally, in 1970, when the devoted Mrs. Munford had been in her grave for more than three decades, the University of Virginia opened its doors to women in all departments.

THIRTY-SIX

Harry Byrd, the Depression and the New Deal

THE METEORIC RISE of Harry Flood Byrd to a position of undisputed leadership in Virginia's Democratic party was the most impressive political phenomenon of the 1920s in the Old Dominion. Byrd was to captain the organization which dominated Virginia's political life for the next forty years. Descended from the Byrds of historic Westover, he was the son of Richard Evelyn Byrd, who had enjoyed the perhaps unique distinction of being elected unanimously as Speaker of the Virginia House of Delegates at the beginning of his second term in that body. Harry Byrd's uncle was Congressman Henry D. Flood, of Appomattox, Senator Martin's right-hand man. Possession of such influential kinsmen was certainly no handicap to Byrd, but he could never have achieved the pre-eminent position that was his, had he not exhibited exceptional ability, great industry and a remarkable capacity for inspiring confidence in and influencing other men.

The fledgling Byrd left school at fifteen to try and salvage his family's virtually bankrupt Winchester *Star*. The boy achieved the incredible by getting the paper back on its feet. He then entered the apple-growing business. In the latter field, he and his brother, Thomas B. Byrd, became operators of the largest privately owned apple orchards in the world.

Harry Byrd was twenty-eight when he entered the Virginia Senate in 1916. He made an excellent record, not only by virtue of his strict attention to business, but also because of his engaging and outgoing personality. He was not exactly handsome, but his expansive and winning smile caused him to be compared to the "Laughing Cavalier," the famous painting by Frans Hals. He was a teetotaler almost to the end of his life, but extremely companionable. He learned much of his politics from his father and uncle.

Byrd's victory in the 1923 bond referendum election catapulted him into public notice and into a position to compete with Senator Swanson for the leadership of Virginia's Democrats. It was not until he became governor three years later that he achieved this leadership, but the foundations had been laid.

When Byrd was a delegate to the marathon Democratic National Convention of 1924 in New York, he happened to get into a taxicab with the Reverend Dr. James Cannon, Jr., who by then had become Bishop Cannon. The bishop told Byrd that he had better not run for governor in 1925, since "we have decided to elect Walter Mapp." Byrd had not planned to run in that year, but he stated later that the bishop's attempt to dictate gubernatorial candidacies in Virginia made him "so mad" that he decided to run.

Senator G. Walter Mapp of Accomack, the Cannon candidate, was a long-time member of the machine and an able legislator who was personally "dry" and the chief spokesman for the Anti-Saloon League in the General Assembly. He was a forward-looking man in most respects, with progressive ideas concerning the needs of Virginia.

But he was no match for Harry Byrd. The latter was an inferior speaker with a singsong delivery and a somewhat thin voice, but he had innumerable contacts all over the state, especially in the rural courthouses. The organization had to choose between two of its members, Mapp and Byrd, and Byrd had the inside track. The machine went into high gear in his behalf, and he was nominated by a whopping 40,000 majority. In the November election, his majority over nominal Republican opposition was even larger.

Byrd came into the governorship in 1926 at a time when the organization was on the defensive because of Virginia's backwardness, and in danger of losing its hold on the state. He knew the situation was precarious, and that he would have to move aggressively, with a sweeping program of reform, in order to keep control. He had been careful during the campaign not to disclose the magnitude of his plans, since public opinion had not been adequately prepared. He was largely content to lay down general principles—such as the need for "greater economy and efficiency," which could mean almost anything. In fact, so unspecific were Byrd's pre-election pronouncements, except in limited areas, that a prominent attorney asked why he hadn't included the Lord's Prayer and the Ten Commandments in his platform.

But after his election the young governor convinced the most hardened courthouse politicians that he meant business. Not only so, but he convinced them that his "program of progress" was essential to their political salvation. The results in the legislature were amazing. A whole series of far-reaching bills went through both branches with hardly any opposition, some of them unanimously. A measure providing for the elimination of one of the two politically powerful commissioners of the revenue in each of the ninety-nine counties passed the Senate unanimously, with only eight negative votes in the House. A similar bill had been badly defeated only two years before. Governor Byrd showed that a strong leader with great state-wide popularity who seizes the proper moment to present a meaningful program can secure its adoption.

Also at the session of 1926, Byrd set in motion his plan to reorganize the sprawling state government, with its nearly one hundred bureaus, boards and departments, into something much more compact and more readily manageable. The New York Bureau of Municipal Research was retained to survey the situation and make recommendations. Its suggestions were submitted to a screening committee of Virginians headed by William T. Reed, a Richmond tobacco manufacturer and confidant of Byrd, after which the General Assembly of 1928 consolidated the various agencies into a dozen departments, at an increase in efficiency and a substantial saving.

Another significant improvement successfully sponsored by Byrd was the adoption of the "short ballot," which limited to three the number of state officials chosen by popular vote. These are the governor, lieutenant governor and attorney general. The necessary constitutional amendments were approved by wide margins at two sessions of the General Assembly, but it was only by virtue of majorities in the Shenandoah Valley and the southwest that the amendments squeaked through in the popular referendum.

Appropriations to roads, education and mental hospitals during the Byrd regime were unprecedentedly large, and the tax structure was revised to provide complete segregation of tax subjects between the state and the localities. Another object of the revision was to attract new industries to Virginia, and the results were little short of astounding. Byrd declared that in the "fiscal year 1927 Virginia made the largest industrial progress of any state in the Union," with $265,000,000 added to the state's industrial capital.

Yet Governor Byrd was far from being a tool of "big business." On the contrary, he moved with great effectiveness against certain corporations, notably the oil companies and the Virginia subsidiary of the American Telephone and Telegraph Company. His collision with the oil companies concerned the price of gasoline in Virginia, which was higher than in some nearby areas. Over the companies' violent protest, Byrd rammed a bill through the legislature requiring them to furnish the governor with their wholesale and retail gasoline prices in Virginia and the other states. He would publicize these prices, if it seemed desirable. His encounter with the telephone company concerned its plan to put increased rates into effect before this was authorized by the state's highest court. He forced the company to back down by threatening to call a special session of the legislature and amend the law permitting rates to go into effect before the court had acted.

Byrd, furthermore, obtained passage by a well-nigh unanimous vote of the strongest anti-lynching law enacted by any state up to that time. There hasn't been a lynching in Virginia since. The state's record in this respect has always been one of the best in the South, but Byrd declared that it was "intolerable" that there should be any lynchings at all.

There was no law at the time requiring segregation of the races in theaters, public auditoriums and other places of public assembly, although separation by custom prevailed. For years, Hampton Institute had been having addresses and performances in its auditorium before mixed audiences. The Newport News *Daily Press* suddenly erupted with a demand that there be a law to prevent this. An organization called the Anglo-Saxon Clubs, headed by composer and concert pianist John Powell, the greatest musician Virginia has produced, spearheaded the drive. The law was passed and Governor Byrd allowed it to become law without his signature.

Byrd was a great lover of the out-of-doors, and a hunter and hiker who kept himself in fine physical shape virtually until the end of his life. He was chiefly instrumental in making the Shenandoah National Park a reality, although the concept originated in the 1890s with George Pollock, a dedicated conservationist. As governor, Byrd procured the creation of the State Conservation and Development Commission, and under the chairmanship of William E. Carson, that agency took the lead in establishing the park. With its beautiful and picturesque Skyline Drive, which joins the spectacular Blue Ridge Parkway at the park's southern end and continues along the spine of the mountains into North Carolina, it is one of the grandly impressive drives of the world.

Another action of Governor Byrd foreshadowed much that was to come after: he obtained a constitutional amendment forbidding the issuance of general obligation bonds by the state for any purpose, except under the most limited conditions. This superseded the much more liberal constitutional provision for highway bonds that he himself had sponsored in 1918. The restrictive amendment would remain in the state's organic law until it was finally removed in 1970.

Further evidence of Byrd's fiscal conservatism, as well as of his efficient management of public funds, is seen in the fact that whereas he found a deficit in the state treasury of $1,368,000 when he took office, he left with a surplus of $4,250,000. The surplus would have totaled $5,500,000 had not taxes been reduced by nearly $1,300,000 midway of his term.

His achievements as governor, both as an exemplar of efficiency and economy, and as a man of independence and courage who tackled would-be lynchers, on the one hand, and powerful corporations, on the other, won him national acclaim. He was regarded as a youthful progressive, a fact somewhat difficult to grasp for those who knew him only in his ultraconservative later years.

In 1928, when Byrd was at the height of his influence, Governor Alfred E. Smith of New York was nominated for President by the Democrats. This came as no surprise, but when it happened, Byrd and the other Democratic politicians in Virginia were faced at once with a critical situation. Smith was not only a well-known foe of prohibition, but he was also a member of the Roman Catholic Church. It was doubtful if the Democrats would be able to carry Virginia, with Smith as the nominee. His opponent was Herbert Hoover, who was a world-renowned humanitarian and a member of President Coolidge's cabinet, as well as a Protestant with an acceptable record on prohibition. Hoover was no dry crusader, but he was to hail prohibition sonorously as an "experiment noble in motive and far-reaching in purpose," which seemed to satisfy the Anti-Saloon League.

"Al" Smith might have won in the Old Dominion, however, had it not been for the devastatingly effective campaign mounted against him by Bishop Cannon, who was said by his ancient enemy, William Randolph Hearst, to have "the best brain in America, no one excepted."

The bishop was a sincere prohibitionist; he was also a flagrant anti-Catholic, and had been one for at least two decades. While denying again and again that he was actuated by religious bigotry in his fight against Smith, he evidently did not regard Roman Catholics as Christians, and he had referred to their Church on at least one occasion as the "mother of ignorance, superstition, intolerance and sin."[1]

The Ku Klux Klan had been revived a few years before, and was attacking Catholics, Jews and Negroes, but it never got much of a foothold in Virginia. The activity of the Klan, plus Hoover's lily-white policies, and a belief among the Negroes that Smith was on the side of the underprivileged, caused many Virginia blacks to vote for Smith.

There was enough latent anti-Catholicism in the commonwealth, especially in areas where Roman Catholics were completely unknown, for Cannon to play upon it day after day and week after week with misleading and false charges, and to raise fantastic fears in the minds of thousands. The year 1928 was a far cry from 1960, when the "religious issue" was apparently buried once and for all with the election of John F. Kennedy.

Bishop Cannon combined his assaults on Smith's Catholicism with equally determined assaults on his "wetness." It was the era when Virginia's moonshiners were in their heyday, and the burbling of stills smote gently upon the ear in mountain fastnesses and lowland swamps. It was also the era when the ubiquitous bootlegger waxed rich, and when Mrs. Mabel Walker Willebrandt, who had served for eight years as Assistant Attorney General of the United States in charge of prohibition enforcement, admitted that liquor could be obtained "at almost any hour of the day or night, either in rural districts, the smaller towns or the cities." The charred keg and the Mason jar became standard items of equipment in many homes, basements exuded the exhalations of homemade beer and wine, and hip flasks were widely toted. Judges on the Virginia bench, deacons in the churches, and many other leading citizens had few scruples about violating the prohibition law. Yet there was strong "dry" sentiment in the Old

Dominion, especially in country areas, and this, combined with the anti-Catholicism stimulated by Cannon's barely camouflaged jehad against that church, was enough to swing the state to Hoover by 24,000 majority. Cannon operated on a South-wide basis, and his candidate also carried North Carolina, Florida and Texas, none of which had gone Republican since the nineteenth century.

With Virginia in the Republican camp for the first time in generations, the political situation was chaotic. And Bishop Cannon was "feeling his oats" in an unprecedented manner. He demanded that Governor Byrd, Senator Glass and the other Democratic leaders apologize publicly for the things they had said about him and his fellow Virginians who voted for Hoover. His demand was met with cold silence.

It was clear, however, that Cannon might be in a position to dictate the choice of Byrd's successor as governor in 1929. Fearful of such a result, Byrd and his associates cast about for a candidate who was unassailably dry, who was a member of one of the two great Protestant evangelical denominations, the Methodists and the Baptists, and who was personally obnoxious to Cannon. They found their man in Dr. John Garland Pollard, head of the School of Government and Citizenship at William and Mary, a leading Baptist layman, a former attorney general, and a candidate for governor in the three-way contest of 1917. Pollard had a long record of independence from the machine, but he and Byrd were anxious to demonstrate that Virginia had gone Republican for quite special reasons—certainly not in repudiation of Byrd's "program of progress." Above all, they were determined to show that it would be unthinkable to turn the state over to Bishop Cannon.

G. Walter Mapp, who had been defeated by Byrd four years before, announced again for governor, but having supported Smith, he was not acceptable to Cannon, despite his long prohibitionist record. Rosewell Page, a state official who had supported Smith, also got into the race.

The bishop and his "Anti-Smith Democrats" met in Roanoke and nominated Dr. William Moseley Brown, a thirty-five-year-old professor at Washington and Lee University who had backed Hoover. The Republicans then met in Richmond and also nominated Brown.

At this juncture, the press carried the astonishing news that Cannon, who for many years had denounced gambling in all its forms, had been one of the largest customers of Kable & Company, a bankrupt New York bucket shop, then in the hands of the authorities. In addition, he had been an avid plunger. The firm had bought for him stocks worth $477,000 and had sold them for approximately $486,000, all for a total payment by the bishop of $2500.

The public had barely digested these remarkable statistics when it was greeted by publication of the fact that the Reverend Dr. Cannon had been officially termed a "flour hoarder" during World War I.

Methodism was rocked from stem to stern by these revelations, and Cannon was thrown on the defensive. He composed an enormously long apologia entitled "Unspotted from the World," which the critic and publicist H. L. Mencken puckishly termed the bishop's "bull *Immaculatum . . . ab hoc saeculo*." In this vast manifesto Cannon contended that he had merely been buying stocks "for investment on the partial-payment plan," that he was innocent of the flour-hoarding charge, and that this was nothing but another venomous attempt by wets and Roman Catholics to destroy his reputation.[2]

Would Virginians who had followed the bishop's lead and voted for Hoover in 1928 be eligible to take part in the Democratic gubernatorial primary of 1929? Under the state's election laws, as interpreted up to that time, persons who voted for a Republican were not allowed to participate in choosing a Democratic nominee the following year. However, Virginia's Attorney General John R. Saunders came up with a ruling that enabled the Democrats who had cast their ballots for Hoover to enter the primary and vote for one of the Democratic candidates for governor. Saunders held that a voter's action in a national election did not determine his status in a state primary. The "Hoovercrats" were accordingly welcomed back into the Democratic fold. The ruling was to be reiterated by several succeeding attorneys general, when Virginia Democrats voted for Republicans for President of the United States. It was a major reason why presidential candidates of the GOP were able to carry the state in the 1950s and 1960s.

Bishop Cannon urged all anti-Smith Democrats to stay out of the August primary and support William Moseley Brown in November. Only a limited number did so. Cannon's archenemy, Pollard, won overwhelmingly, getting 70,000 more votes than Mapp and Page combined, the biggest margin in the history of Virginia primaries.

The bishop responded with a six-column blast denouncing Governor

Byrd and the other Virginia leaders who had failed to apologize
to him. He also dragged in the religious issue all over again. Then
suddenly he announced that he was sailing for Brazil, which was one
of the areas of the globe included in his episcopal see. This was
interpreted to mean that he had abandoned hope for his candidate,
Brown, which was doubtless correct. When the votes were counted
in November, Pollard was found to have won by a smashing 70,000
majority. The outcome was regarded as a resounding endorsement
of Byrd's "program of progress," and a repudiation of Cannon, the
Republicans and the die-hard anti-Smith Democrats.

Governor Pollard, an even-tempered man who chuckled frequently,
remarked on the dismal, rainy day of his inauguration that it was
"a proper kind of a day for ducks and Baptists." He had expected
to develop and expand the Byrd program in certain respects. But
neither he nor Byrd was aware that the terrific stock market crash of
October and November, 1929, portended perhaps the worst depression
in American history. Bankrupt businesses, plummeting farm prices,
bread lines, soup kitchens and millions of unemployed were to charac-
terize the American scene for years. The "roaring twenties," with their
flappers and Stutz Bearcats, their bathtub gin and loud "whoopee,"
were to fade from memory and give way to ruined speculators, closed
banks, jobless men selling apples and hungry women and children.

Virginia was less hard hit than most, but the depression there was
exceedingly severe. Fortunately, per capita wealth was higher in Virginia at the onset of the depression than in any of the former Confederate states, and 51 per cent of Virginia homes were owned,
compared with the national average of 47 per cent. The state's
economy was well-balanced between agriculture, manufacturing and
trade. The percentage of the farm population with modern tools and
conveniences was higher than in any of the southern states, except
Florida and Texas, Virginia had a better ratio of subsistence farmers
than most, her agriculture was more diversified, and she had the
lowest farm-tenancy rate in the South except Florida. On the other
hand, production value per Virginia farm worker was among the
lowest in the nation.[3]

With economic conditions growing steadily worse throughout the
United States, the nation was staggered in the summer of 1930 by
one of the most catastrophic droughts in its history. Virginia's rainfall
for the year was only 60 per cent of normal, crops were ruined, and

many cattle starved for lack of feed and water. Harry Byrd, as head of the Virginia Drought Relief Commission, was quick to demand federal aid for relief of distressed Virginians. He did not suggest that the state of Virginia provide funds for her own sufferers.

Governor Pollard was coping with this emergency when a textile strike in Danville on September 29, 1930, brought further woe. Some four thousand workers left their jobs in the Danville mill, perhaps the most progressive factory of its kind in the South, with better wages and more humane working conditions than were generally found elsewhere. There had been violent textile strikes, with several killings, in the Carolinas and Tennessee, and the United Textile Workers called the strike in Danville when a 10 per cent wage cut was announced because of depressed economic conditions. The "stretch-out system," under which additional work was piled on the mill hands, was another grievance. Riots in November caused Governor Pollard to order out three companies of the National Guard, at the urgent request of the local authorities. Sporadic violence continued into January. The economic depression and other factors made it almost inevitable from the first that the union would lose the strike. The mill hands voted on January 29 to end the walkout, although their demands had not been met. Many were not rehired, since the mill was suffering severely from the business debacle.

All of Southside Virginia, famous as a tobacco-producing and marketing center, was hard hit at this period. Tobacco prices skidded to $6.63 per 100 pounds, lowest since 1920. This, combined with the failure of several South Boston banks and the intensified business depression in nearby Danville, as a result of the strike, created dismal conditions. The director of a Danville tobacco warehouse said, "We find men actually weeping after they have had to sell their tobacco at prices that will mean nothing less than complete disaster." It was estimated that half of the able-bodied workers of Halifax County were jobless.

Parents in this and other areas were not sending their children to school, for they had no money with which to buy them clothing and shoes. The coal mines of the southwest were hardly operating at all, and conditions for the miners and their families were grim. The bottom of the depression was reached in 1932, and there was a sharp increase in urban unemployment during the first six months of that year. Overall unemployment in 1932 averaged 100,000 members of the work force, with a peak of 145,000 in July. This was estimated to be 19 per cent of the state's laboring force, as against more than 30 per cent for the whole country. Virginia wheat was selling for fifty cents a bushel, lowest price in 132 years, while the tobacco crop was the smallest since 1876, although the price had gone up two dollars.[4]

The cities were the scene of much suffering, but in Richmond and Norfolk the situation was not as bad as might have been expected. In Richmond this was largely due to the city's well-balanced economy, and to the fact that the important tobacco industry was not greatly affected by the depression, since smokers didn't stop smoking, but merely switched to cheaper brands. In Norfolk there was the Navy, which spent around $20,000,000 a year in the city. Banks were going under throughout the United States, but in Norfolk none did so, and in Richmond only one failed to open, after President Roosevelt closed and opened the nation's banks. Although the situation was acute in many rural areas, numerous urban dwellers went back to the farms, where food and shelter of sorts were often obtainable. As a result, the number of Virginia farmers grew by 16 per cent from 1930 to 1935.

In Richmond, an Unemployed Council was organized in 1932 by a northern Communist who had come to town for the purpose. Few paid any attention until Mayor J. Fulmer Bright began arresting and hounding the little band of agitators, derisively termed "Joseph Stalin's Army of Northern Virginia." The arrests were frequently in violation of constitutional rights. There was a peaceful "hunger march" in the snow around City Hall, and the leader was clubbed on the head and arrested. This sort of thing went on for months. Those taken into custody by the police were usually convicted in police court, but nearly all were acquitted in the appellate court.

Unemployment during this period was especially high for Negroes, but even when they had jobs, the pay scale was extremely low. In 1936, for example, 7946 tobacco workers, all but 192 of whom were black, got an average of $6.40 per week. Foremen in the same plants, all white, averaged $63 a week. A strike in 1938 resulted in increases of $1.00 to $1.25 a week for the stemmers, with time and a half for overtime. There were comparable increases for the other Negro employees. In the Chesapeake Bay region, oyster shuckers got $1.00 a day for shucking a minimum of twelve gallons. In Norfolk, Negro workers around the docks earned $.25 an hour, with no extra pay for overtime, and this had been the going wage there for many years. A study in Lynchburg in 1937 of wage levels for black domestics showed the average for servants to be $4.00 a week, with meals and lodging included, where desired, but with a work week of eighty to ninety hours. Even making allowances for the fact that the dollar in the mid-1930s would buy nearly three times as much as in 1970, the foregoing scales of pay for blacks were all unconscionably low.[5]

Governor Pollard believed with Harry Byrd that the way to cope with a depression was to reduce expenditures. Pollard cut his own salary 10 per cent early in 1932 and recommended that all state salaries be slashed similarly for a period of one year. It was the first of several cuts in pay and in other state outlays. The governor boasted, meanwhile, that Virginia's bonds were selling at a better rate than those of the United States or any other state, and that the debt of the Old Dominion had been reduced by 12½ per cent while the national debt had risen by 400 per cent.

Byrd suggested in 1932 that the state take over the county feeder-road system, at a saving to the counties of $3,400,000. This was done, and it was helpful to the counties but not at all to the suffering cities. The Norfolk *Virginian-Pilot*, conscious of Byrd's fondness for building roads, carried an editorial by its Pulitzer Prize-winning editor, Louis I. Jaffé, headed "Highwayolatory as a State Religion." The paper noted that Byrd's scheme did little or nothing for schools, colleges, public health and mental hospitals, and that the cities were left holding the bag.

Henry W. Anderson, the Republican leader, urged a special session of the General Assembly and diversion of 10 per cent of the gasoline-tax receipts for relief purposes. Governor Pollard refused, saying that this would discourage private charity. Anderson retorted that "the people cannot eat roads or be clothed in our modern god of concrete."

Establishment by the Congress in 1933 of numerous emergency federal agencies, with a view to ameliorating some of the worst features of the depression, put thousands to work and set the country on the slow upward climb to better conditions. President Hoover had relied principally on the Reconstruction Finance Corporation to funnel federal moneys into the states for relief purposes, but President Roosevelt came up, in the first "hundred days," with a whole series of recommendations designed to cope with the crisis.

Harry Byrd had just been named to the U. S. Senate by Governor
Pollard, following Senator Swanson's appointment as Roosevelt's Secretary of the Navy. Byrd supported the Administration's emergency
measures enacted in the "hundred days," but he soon became disenchanted when the President forgot his promises to economize and
embarked on a huge spending program. Byrd voted thenceforth
against nearly everything on Roosevelt's domestic agenda.

Byrd had been an enthusiastic supporter of Roosevelt's platform in
1932, since it promised greater federal economy and a return to States'
rights. Hence he often referred to himself jokingly in later years as
"one of the original New Dealers." At the 1932 convention his own
name had been presented by Virginia for the presidency, but Roosevelt
had been nominated on the fourth ballot. Byrd at that time was an
admirer of F.D.R., and was widely mentioned as a cabinet possibility,
as were Swanson and Glass. Reports that Byrd was preparing to
run against Swanson, if Swanson offered for another term in 1934,
seem to have angered the latter. When Roosevelt tendered Swanson
the Navy portfolio, he accepted, but he then refused to resign promptly
from the Senate, so that Byrd might obtain seniority over fifteen other
incoming freshmen senators.

Swanson's ungracious refusal, despite urging by newspapers and
others that it would be to Virginia's advantage, as well as Byrd's, for
Byrd to have as much seniority as he could get, was clear evidence that
there had been a breach between the two men. It was never healed.
Byrd continued to dominate Virginia politics from Washington, while
Swanson remained aloof and concentrated on his cabinet responsibilities. He was almost completely inactive on the Virginia political
scene until his death in 1939. Swanson was nearly seventy-one when
Roosevelt appointed him to the cabinet, and ill health plagued him
almost constantly thereafter.[6]

Governor Pollard called a special session of the General Assembly
for August 1933, with a view to co-operating in the recent creation of a
federal public works program and also bringing Virginia abreast of
fast-developing events in the area of liquor control. The Twenty-first
Amendment, repealing the Eighteenth, or prohibition, Amendment,
had passed both houses of Congress, and would have to be voted on
by the people of the respective states. Legalization of beer was also on
the General Assembly's agenda.

The Virginia referendum was held in October, and Virginians who had been voting "dry" until a short time before, were caught up in the stampede for repeal that was sweeping the country. They cast approximately 100,000 ballots for repeal of both federal and state prohibition laws and only 58,000 against.

Although Senator Byrd had voted for the National Industrial Recovery Act (NRA), one of the pieces of emergency legislation adopted during the "hundred days," he regarded it as probably unconstitutional. Senator Glass, who was bitter in denunciation of the entire Roosevelt New Deal from the very beginning, was to describe NRA as "not only unconstitutional, but . . . administered with a degree of brutality that has created a reign of terror."

As Byrd and Glass expected, NRA and other alphabetical creations of the New Deal were declared unconstitutional by the U. S. Supreme Court. Many of these hastily put together agencies were also wasteful and inefficient, and Byrd and Glass, given their well-known views, could be pardoned for criticizing them because of this, as well as because they represented a tremendous extension of federal power. Yet the emergency was great, and the state of Virginia was doing relatively little to cope with it.

Work relief, rather than the dole, was the federal program to aid the jobless, and various newly created federal agencies were got into operation. Virginia limited its relief program to putting the unemployed to work on the highways, most of which money would have been spent on the roads anyway. The Old Dominion's relief problem was less severe than almost any other, but it was bad enough, and the commonwealth put nearly all of the burden on Uncle Sam.

William A. Smith, a Petersburg engineer, was director of the Virginia Emergency Relief Administration, which was set up in 1933, and he made a good record, under difficult circumstances. Matching funds were not required from the state. The result was that from 1933 through 1935, the Federal Emergency Relief Administration paid out more than $26,000,000 for relief in Virginia, which was over 90 per cent of the state's relief bill. The money went principally to improvements around the schools, but smaller sums went to better sanitary facilities, malaria control, airport projects, parks, streets and so on. There were nearly 52,000 FERA relief cases in Virginia (approximately 250,000 people) at the peak in May 1935. The total dropped soon thereafter. The highest percentage of rural cases was in southwest Virginia, while among the cities Bristol and Hopewell led, percentagewise, with Richmond and Norfolk showing the largest total number on relief. Negroes accounted for 36 per cent of those on FERA relief rolls in Virginia, which was substantially more than the percentage of blacks in the population.

The large group of marginal farmers was suffering less than some other elements, since it had so little to begin with. Tenants, mostly on the less prosperous farms of central Virginia, and mountaineers in the southwest could usually eke out some kind of existence, even in bad times. Arnold Toynbee, the British historian, had written that the Appalachian "mountain people . . . suffer from poverty, squalor and ill health," and he compared them, with some exaggeration, to the "Rifis, Albanians, Kurds, Pathans and Hairy Ainus." Many of these mountaineers, of sturdy stock, together with other long disadvantaged rural Virginians, were quick to see the opportunities for self-improvement in the federal programs. Large numbers were eligible for relief, and they got on the rolls and took advantage of the chances which they saw for improving their lot.

The state of Virginia refused to contribute money for direct relief during the life of FERA. Its officials argued that the commonwealth was taking other means of alleviating the sufferings of the people. They mentioned a reduced state budget, a lighter local tax load as a result of the state's having taken over the county feeder roads, use of the State Highway Department as a relief agency to administer funds provided by the federally funded Reconstruction Finance Corporation, and $1,600,000 of state money appropriated to provide work for the jobless on the highways. Other states were appropriating funds for both direct relief and highway construction. Virginia's political leaders felt that the first objective should be to maintain the fiscal soundness of the state government and the integrity of the individual unemployed, whose characters, they feared, would be undermined by the huge federal relief system. The Richmond *Times-Dispatch* and the Norfolk *Virginian-Pilot* frequently took Senator Byrd and his Virginia leaders to task for their ultraconservative attitudes.

After FERA came the Works Progress Administration (WPA) and the Public Works Administration (PWA). WPA put needy persons to work on the less expensive, but nonetheless useful, projects, such as construction of smaller buildings, improvements to schools and other public structures, the laying of sewers, drainage and so on, with each project limited to $25,000. Unemployed Negro women on WPA were chiefly responsible for laying out azalea gardens at Norfolk which later became the famous gardens known throughout the United States. Some out-of-work professional people were given employment on writers' projects, art work, musical composition and cataloguing. Many of their productions had no permanent value, but some were distinctly worth while, as for example, the WPA-sponsored books, *Virginia: A Guide to the Old Dominion* and *The Negro in Virginia*.

PWA concerned itself with more massive and permanent types of construction, such as libraries, dormitories and hospitals. Among the more important projects may be mentioned the Alderman Library at the University of Virginia, the Medical College of Virginia hospital, and the Virginia State Library, for each of which PWA put up nearly half the cost. Some $30,000,000 of PWA money were spent in Virginia on such projects, under the able direction of General James A. Anderson, later the state highway commissioner.

Establishment of the Rural Electrification Administration (REA) proved a boon to rural Virginians, only 7.6 per cent of whose farms were electrified in 1934. The first REA co-operative was set up at Bowling Green in 1936, and others were rapidly established. Four years later, largely as a result of the constructive work of these agencies, 21 per cent of Virginia farms had electricity. By then, half of these agricultural customers were being served by REA and the others by the power companies, whose extensions into the countryside had been greatly stimulated. Within another decade nearly all of Virginia's farmers, along with those in the rest of the country, could enjoy the benefits of electric lights, improved living standards and reduced work loads.

The Tennessee Valley Authority (TVA) was another New Deal creation of the mid-1930s. Its overall impact on the extreme southwestern tip of Virginia, the only part of the state within the authority's boundaries, was much less than in some other states. Yet the TVA was useful to about five thousand Virginia farmers who treated nearly 250,000 acres with TVA fertilizers. TVA flood control had little effect on Virginia's Powell, Holston and Clinch rivers which drain into the Tennessee, and it was not until 1945 that TVA began serving power to some five thousand customers in Bristol. A decade later, sales of power were expanded through the Powell Valley Electric Cooperative at Jonesville. Critics of TVA have always argued that it represents an unwarranted infringement upon private enterprise,

especially in the field of electric power. On the other hand, TVA has
done a good deal to stimulate private business by raising the purchasing power of the region, and by inventing new types of machinery
and new processes.[7]

A popular and useful federal agency was the Civilian Conservation
Corps (CCC), which put unmarried, unemployed youths in camps to
do conservation work for six months. Over eighty camps were established in Virginia by 1937, at least a dozen of them for Negroes.
Some educational instruction was supplied, and the young men worked
out of doors, in healthful surroundings, planting millions of trees,
building hundreds of small bridges, digging gullies to halt erosion, and
so on. The CCC created six state parks in various sections of Virginia,
and these were subsequently turned over to the commonwealth. These
parks, worth some $5,000,000, became the property of the state, at a
total cost to it of $100,000.

The Agricultural Adjustment Administration (AAA) had been established in 1933, and it was this agency which first caused Byrd to
break openly with Roosevelt. Byrd concluded that entirely too much
power was given to the Secretary of Agriculture, and he exclaimed
in 1934, "We do not want a Hitler of American agriculture." Yet
G. F. Holsinger, head of the normally conservative Virginia Farm
Bureau Federation, termed the AAA "the most important piece of
legislation ever enacted in behalf of agriculture." The Virginia Grange
also supported the new agency. As for the rank-and-file farmers, they
gave it overwhelming approval. The flue-cured tobacco and wheat
growers of Virginia voted by lopsided majorities in favor of the production controls established for their crops. Senator Byrd adhered
stanchly to his beliefs, despite the fact that the trend in the state
and nation was the other way, and in doing so ran great political
risks. He succeeded in eliminating some of the features of the AAA
which he found objectionable, with the result that the bill, as finally
passed, was probably strengthened. However, the Supreme Court pronounced the AAA unconstitutional in 1936, so new approaches had
to be devised. The Soil Conservation and Domestic Allotment Act
was the result. Most Virginians were pleased with this legislation, and
Senator Byrd voted for it.

Governor Pollard, meanwhile, was endeavoring to deal with the many
problems confronting him, and he managed important governmental
reforms. He brought about the establishment of an efficient accounting

and auditing system, under the leadership of T. Coleman Andrews—afterward U. S. Commissioner of Internal Revenue—as auditor of public accounts, and his successor, L. McCarthy Downs. Andrews stirred things up in the counties, where his thorough, non-political audits revealed that some forty county officials were short in their accounts for a total of more than $1,100,000. Most of this was in the counties of Arlington, Bath and Lee. County treasurers were mainly responsible for the overall situation, but in most cases no misappropriation of funds was involved. The treasurers had indulged in the practice of "holding out tax tickets" i.e., failing to report tax delinquencies, as a favor to taxpayers, and making themselves liable for the funds until each taxpayer met his obligations. The practice was stopped by the newly instituted regular audits. Three county officials received prison terms.

Appointment of a Commission on County Government, with Dr. Robert H. Tucker as chairman, and that commission's report, recommending optional forms of improved county government, was another advance during the Pollard administration. Governor Byrd's constitutional revisions had opened the way for this step, and the General Assembly adopted forms recommended by the commission.

For some three decades, little progress was made, and only a handful of counties, mostly urban, opted for the new forms. But then a much greater disposition for change was manifested, and by January 1, 1970, thirty-eight of ninety-six counties had appointed a central administrator or authorized such action. As for the cities and towns, the city manager form originated in Staunton in 1908, and all thirty-eight Virginia cities had it in 1970, while twenty-four of the twenty-five towns above 3500 population had town managers.

Establishment of the State Compensation Board to fix the salaries of county fee officers throughout the state was another important development. Governor Byrd had initiated a thorough study of the fee system, a delicate matter, since the county officers concerned were the bulwarks of the machine in the rural areas. Yet the need for action had been apparent for decades, since the income of these officers was often excessive, and the system was basically unsound. In 1922, no fewer than fifty-one of them were getting higher incomes from fees than any state official, including the governor. The State Compensation Board was composed of three men, and its long-time head was E. R. Combs, who had been a machine wheel horse for

Byrd in the southwest, and had been brought to Richmond by him as state comptroller. A quiet, courteous man who worked largely behind the scenes, Combs was generally considered second only to Byrd in the hierarchy of the organization. It was never proved that any salary was raised or lowered by the compensation board for political reasons, but the mere existence of such an agency, authorized to fix salaries within certain prescribed upper and lower limits, served as a powerful "persuader" to keep the boys in line for the machine.

The much-admired Virginia Museum of Fine Arts, the first State Art Museum to be established in this country, was founded during the Pollard administration. The governor gave enthusiastic support to the venture, and managed to get together $100,000 from private sources and the federal government to match an equal sum contributed by John Barton Payne. Judge Payne, a native of what is now West Virginia, grew up in Fauquier County, and served in Woodrow Wilson's cabinet and as head of the American Red Cross. He had given the state of Virginia his million-dollar collection of paintings in 1919, and these constitute the nucleus of the museum's fine collection, valued in 1970 at $20,000,000. Much of the museum's spectacular progress has been due to the imaginative direction of Leslie Cheek, Jr. It has a broad cultural spectrum, which includes music, drama and the dance. Its art mobiles and its numerous chapters or affiliates have given it unusual acceptance throughout the state.

In an address to the General Assembly, Governor Pollard spoke of Virginia's pride in Richard Evelyn Byrd, the flier who was "attracting the admiration of the world." Richard was a brother of Harry Byrd, and was then on his first expedition to the South Pole. He had helped Charles Lindbergh in substantial ways to prepare for his solo flight to Europe in 1927, but had got little except criticism for his good sportsmanship. Uninformed persons felt that Byrd was "too timid" about taking off himself, and that he had let Lindbergh get ahead of him.[8] Dick Byrd later was promoted to admiral, and his services to his country in peace and in war, in aviation and in polar exploration are universally recognized.

Fewer Virginians were on relief during the 1930s than citizens of almost any other state. Many dwellers in the Old Dominion like to believe that they are self-reliant and desirous of making their own way, without help from any governmental agency.

One Virginian who gave a notable example of this quality at the bottom of the depression was Robert Porterfield of Abingdon. Desirous of providing employment for out-of-work actors from New York and other theatrical centers, Porterfield opened what he called the "Barter Theatre." Admission was in commodities rather than specie. Hams, apples, geraniums or canned goods were accepted at the box office. Profits for the first year totaled $4.30, plus assorted jellies and an overall increase in weight of 305 pounds for the troupe, but Porterfield had kept the actors fed and working. After surmounting the first difficult year, he went on to build one of the most significant theatrical organizations on either side of the Atlantic. Barter became the first state theater in this country, and it has trained some leading actors and actresses. By invitation, it presented *Hamlet* on the original site—Elsinore Castle in Denmark—the only U.S. troupe to receive this accolade. Barter also has brought live theater for the first time to dozens of rural Virginia communities.

Governor Pollard was succeeded in 1934 by George C. Peery of Tazewell, a strong, silent, rangy and handsome man from the southwest. Peery had "redeemed" the Ninth District in 1922 from the Republicans, and then had served on the State Corporation Commission. Whether he could have won back the Ninth in a contest with the old master, C. Bascom Slemp, is unknown, for Slemp had retired in 1922, after seven consecutive congressional terms, to devote himself to politics on the national level.

Slemp was the dominant factor in Virginia's Republican politics for the quarter of a century ended in 1932, although toward the end of that time his leadership was sharply disputed by Henry W. Anderson of Richmond, a high-minded and idealistic man who did not share Slemp's fervent predilection for political "pie." Slemp's "Dear Ben" letters, which got into the *Congressional Record*, to his great embarrassment, were proof that he collected money from appointees to postmasterships and other federal posts. The letters were addressed to Ben R. Powell of Gretna, the GOP's patronage dispenser for the Fifth Congressional District. Powell later became angry with Slemp when the latter denied him the Gretna postmastership. Powell turned the damning correspondence over to Congressman Thomas W. Harrison of Winchester, who put it in the *Record*.[9]

Slemp who served as leading adviser on the South's politics to Presidents Harding, Coolidge and Hoover, and was private secretary to Coolidge, hoped for a cabinet appointment from each of the

three. The "Dear Ben" letters are thought to have kept him from
getting it. Slemp evidently felt that he had earned a place in Hoover's
cabinet, after he had collaborated with Bishop Cannon to smash the
solid South. But his hopes in this regard were not only thwarted; he
found his influence in Virginia drastically reduced by the fact that
whereas his own Ninth had for many years been Virginia's only
Republican district, two more districts had gone to the GOP in
the Hoover landslide. These were the Seventh, or Shenandoah Valley
district and the Second, or Norfolk-Portsmouth district. This meant
that Slemp was no longer virtually the sole dispenser of Republican
patronage for Virginia. Then in 1932 came the Roosevelt landslide.
The "Sage of Turkey Cove" was so frustrated by this series of reverses
that he retired almost completely from politics. When Henry A. Wise
of Accomack ran for the Senate against Harry Byrd, Slemp is understood to have done little or nothing to help Wise. In fact, Slemp
was hostile to both Henry Wise and Henry Anderson, neither of
whom shared his avid interest in political jobbery.

Slemp's remaining years were spent in attending to his extensive
business concerns and collecting items having to do with the history
of southwest Virginia. He also was active in the late 1920s in the
establishment of the University of Virginia Institute of Public Affairs.
He contributed $1000 to the institute in each of three successive years,
and aided in raising other funds for it.[10]

Slemp's political decline and fall occurred at about the time George
Peery entered the governor's mansion in 1934. Peery found the depression slightly abated, but it was still serious. Nevertheless, he suggested a $1,000,000 raise in taxes, for the benefit of the public
schools, and the legislature concurred. This was more than offset by
a $1,800,000 reduction in auto license fees.

Peery noted in his message of 1936 to the General Assembly that
the federal government would make no more grants to the states for
direct relief. He recommended, therefore, that $1,000,000 of state
funds be appropriated for each of the next two years, the money to
be spent in the localities, with each locality required to match the
amount allotted to it. This was in addition to the work on the highways.
The federal WPA would also continue to provide many jobs.

Governor Peery proposed that the General Assembly postpone enactment of old-age-assistance legislation, to implement the federal program,
until more study could be given the matter, and wasteful practices

held to a minimum. The result was that Virginia did not set up old-age-assistance machinery for two more years. It was the last state in the Union to do so.

As for unemployment insurance, Peery urged that the lawmakers enact the necessary legislation in 1936, so that Virginia might be in a position to take part in the program, under the federal Social Security Act, at no cost to the state. But the Virginia Manufacturers' Association put on such a campaign of opposition that the General Assembly failed to act. The result was that when the Supreme Court refused to pronounce the unemployment insurance law unconstitutional, the governor had to call a special session of the Assembly, at a cost of $70,000, to pass the implementing statute.

The Virginia legislature failed again at the session of 1938 to come up to its usually high standard. The Alcoholic Beverage Control Act had been passed in 1934, and two years later the lawmakers requested the University of Virginia and the Medical College of Virginia to provide a scientific study of the effects of alcohol in moderation and excess upon the human system, for use in the public schools. The 184-page study, duly produced by Dr. J. A. Waddell and Dr. H. B. Haag of the two medical faculties, was pronounced by the State Board of Education "a most valuable contribution . . . scientifically sound and very scholarly." The board recommended that ten thousand copies be struck off and distributed to schools and libraries. But a few extracts from the report got into the press before the legislature of 1938 convened, and these caused the Anti-Saloon League and the Woman's Christian Temperance Union to mobilize for action. They noted that the report contained the statement that small quantities of alcohol "may favor digestive activities" and that such quantities "do not directly affect the heart or the blood vessels." There was also the dire declaration that "we cannot abolish drinking by legislation nor frighten a person into sobriety." That was enough. The report contained numerous and emphatic warnings against overindulgence, but an avalanche of mail descended on the desks of the legislators, demanding that the entire report be destroyed. Only one or two members of the Assembly had read it but the oldest lawmaking body in the Western world bowed to the demands of the professional drys. All copies of the document were promptly and solemnly shoveled into the Capitol furnace.

Further excitement was caused in Virginia during these years by

President Roosevelt's "court-packing plan." In it he proposed legislation authorizing him to enlarge the Supreme Court by up to six members, if seventy-year-old justices refused to retire. The initial reaction in Virginia was almost unanimously unfavorable, but in a few weeks Congressman John W. Flannagan of Bristol—who had "redeemed" the Ninth District from the Republicans in 1930 and was to serve nine consecutive terms—and Congressman Clifton A. Woodrum of Roanoke announced that they favored the plan. So did the Virginia Farm Bureau Federation as well as many labor unions. The plan was beaten in Congress, after the court began taking a more liberal view of New Deal measures, and conservative Justice Willis Van Devanter decided to retire.

Senators Byrd and Glass were strongly opposed to this plan, as well as to practically everything else the Roosevelt administration was doing. Glass termed the "court-packing plan" this "frightful proposition . . . utterly destitute of moral sensibility." Byrd called the administration "the most wasteful and bureaucratic form of government that has been known in our history," and denounced the "crackpot legislative ideas of those holding important public positions." When the dollar was devaluated and the gold standard abandoned, Glass pronounced the action "worse than anything Ali Baba and his forty thieves ever perpetrated."

Virginia experienced a decided economic upturn between 1935 and 1940. No fewer than 510 new manufacturing plants came into operation in the state during that period. Between 1929 and 1937, the value of the Old Dominion's industrial products increased nearly 22 per cent, highest increase in the Union, and by 1937 all manufacturing indices in Virginia for 1929 had been exceeded. During the same years, Richmond's industrial output jumped 44 per cent, making it the fastest-growing industrial center in the country. The year 1937 was marred, however, by fifty strikes in various parts of Virginia, brought on by increased industrialization, enactment of the Wagner labor relations act, interunion rivalries, and improved business conditions. There was little violence. An economic setback occurred in Virginia in 1938, owing to the nationwide recession of that year, but the forward movement was resumed shortly thereafter.[11]

Virginia's remarkable industrial and business advance in the latter half of the 1930s was explained in various ways. For one thing, the state had enjoyed relative stability during the worst depression years, with scarcely any disorder. In 1935, five hundred armed men forced the unloading of potato trucks at Painter, Accomack County, claiming that the price the potatoes were bringing was wholly inadequate. This and the minor riots in Danville at the time of the textile strike of 1930–31 were about the only occurrences of the sort. Virginia's favorable tax system, its sufficient supply of labor, at relatively low wage rates, its plentiful raw materials, mild climate and good transportation facilities were all considered significant factors in furthering the industrial boom, but the political leaders attributed the boom and the state's success in weathering the depression mainly to their conservative fiscal policies. Pay-as-you-go thenceforth became for them an unshakable article of faith. It would endure as long as Senator Byrd lived.

How were Virginia's Negro citizens faring at this period? They had come through the depression moderately well. Roosevelt's New Deal had helped to gain them their share of relief money and jobs. Furthermore, the Roosevelt policies, with emphasis on the less privileged, had won the great majority of the blacks over to the Democratic party. And in the Old Dominion, thanks to several court cases, Negroes were able by 1936 to vote in Democratic primaries, from which they had previously been barred. James O. West, a black citizen of Richmond, filed the first of these suits in 1928, and others were filed a few years later by W. E. Davis and L. E. Wilson, both of Elizabeth City County. The net result was that Negro participation in primaries was upheld by the Virginia courts. The blacks did not vote in large numbers, however, primarily because of apathy. The poll tax was also a barrier to the polling booth for some black citizens.

Negro business was not as flourishing in Virginia as it had been several decades previously, since white competition had become sharp. Richmond was considered "the most important center of Negro business activity in the world" from 1890 to 1920, according to *The Negro in Virginia*, which points out that "there were livery stables, shoe stores, haberdasheries, barber shops and restaurants operated by Negroes for white patrons." Blacks also operated "the most efficient laundry in the city." A total of twenty-seven banks were established in the state by Negroes during the early years of the century, but in 1939 only three were left. Two of these, the Consolidated Bank and Trust Company of Richmond and the Danville Savings Bank and Trust Company were operating successfully in 1970. The Richmond institution, oldest Negro bank in the United

States, grew out of the St. Luke's Penny Savings Bank, founded by
Mrs. Maggie Walker, the first woman in the United States to be
president of a bank.

In the late 1930s Negro farmers were producing a large share of
Virginia's crops. They raised about 30 per cent of the tobacco and
corn, half of the cotton, three-fifths of the peanuts and a quarter of
the potatoes. Many of them were opposed to mechanization, however,
and regarded tractors and such as "lazy man's tools." A mule was
greatly to be preferred. These attitudes are far less prevalent today.

A number of Virginia-born Negroes were nationally known in these
years for their achievements as scholars, editors, singers, artists or actors. Carter G. Woodson, a native of Buckingham County, founded
the Association for the Study of Negro Life and History as well as
the *Journal of Negro History.* He was the author of more than a
dozen historical works dealing with the Negro in the United States.
Charles S. Johnson, born in Bristol, was founder and first editor of
the nationally circulated journal of Negro life, *Opportunity,* and was
the author of half a dozen books on the Negro. He would become
president of Fisk University. Abram L. Harris, Ira DeA. Reid and
Ambrose Caliver, Virginia natives, made reputations as authors of
books on Negro life. P. B. Young was for decades one of Norfolk's most
prominent and public-spirited citizens. His Norfolk *Journal and Guide*
was notable for its constructive and well-written editorials. Luther P.
Jackson, a native of Kentucky and an admired member of the Virginia
State College faculty for nearly three decades, made a number of
valuable contributions to the history of Virginia blacks.

Leslie G. Bolling and George H. Ben Johnson, both of Richmond,
achieved national notice, Bolling as a sculptor in wood and Johnson
as a painter. Charles S. Gilpin, another Richmonder, was hailed for
his performance in the title role of Eugene O'Neill's notable dramatic
success, *Emperor Jones.* Dorothy Maynor of Norfolk had begun her
musical career to reverberating acclaim, and Serge Koussevitzky, conductor of the Boston Symphony, had pronounced her "a native
Flagstad." Camilla Williams of Danville also was launching her distinguished career as a singer. She became the leading soprano of the
New York City Opera Company, and won praise for her artistry all
over the world.

Richmond's golden age of literature may be said to have occurred
in the 1930s when Ellen Glasgow, James Branch Cabell and Douglas

Southall Freeman had become internationally renowned. There were other native Virginian writers in that era, including Willa Cather, born in Winchester but removed to Nebraska, the setting of nearly all her novels; but Glasgow, Cabell and Freeman were clearly pre-eminent among those who lived and wrote in the Old Dominion.

Richmond's literary renaissance had been stimulated in the preceding decade by *The Reviewer*, a little magazine founded by Emily Clark and Hunter Stagg. It had a small circulation but it published contributions from a number of nationally known writers, while introducing others who became nationally known.

Miss Glasgow and Cabell were at the height of their fame in the mid-1930s, and Freeman was approaching his peak, for *R. E. Lee* had appeared and been hailed as one of the masterful biographies in the English language. *Lee's Lieutenants* was not far away. Louis D. Rubin, Jr., the eminent critic, viewing the novels of Glasgow and Cabell and the biographical writings of Freeman, termed them "all in all, as distinguished a literary performance as one American city will perhaps ever know."

"No other state has been so faithfully reflected in a series of novels" as is Virginia in Miss Glasgow's "social history," Jay B. Hubbell has written. Miss Glasgow achieved her place in the front rank of American letters despite the fact that, as she wrote late in life, "for many years, I had rarely known what it meant to be free from pain." Deafness was another of her trials, but she was a sparkling conversationalist, and she entertained charmingly in her antebellum home at One West Main Street.

Cabell entertained occasionally, but he was no conversationalist, nor did he ever speak publicly. At a dinner given in his honor by the Virginia Writers' Club, he made no response when the tributes had been concluded. This was due to an innate shyness, rather than to any lack of appreciation. He was an artist with the written, rather than the spoken, word—"the Debussy of prose," as one critic has phrased it.

Freeman, by contrast, was a facile talker and public speaker, with an enormous fund of information on almost all subjects. He worked with practically no let-up during his waking hours the year 'round. As editor of the Richmond *News Leader* for a third of a century, biographer and historian, lecturer and commentator, he was, in truth, a Virginia institution.

It was somewhat ironic that Virginia should have experienced such literary pre-eminence just when her economic fortunes were at so low an ebb. The hard-pressed citizens of the commonwealth took pride in the brilliant writings of Freeman, Glasgow and Cabell, and they came through the depression with fewer scars, both material and psychological, than were suffered by the people of most other states. One reason was that Virginia's relief agencies were more efficiently managed, with less waste and a greater return on the dollar, than many others. True, in some cases there was doubtless too great a reluctance to put needy persons on the rolls, but the traditional self-reliance of Virginia's people may have more than counterbalanced this factor. At all events, the Old Dominion emerged from the ordeal in relatively good shape, with her agriculture showing a good recovery and her industry roaring ahead.

THIRTY-SEVEN

The "Organization" Rebuffs Two Challengers. Virginia in World War II

THE FIRST CITIZEN of Richmond to be elected governor of Virginia was James H. Price, who was chosen to the office in 1937. He was not the preferred candidate of the Byrd organization, but his state-wide popularity was such that he was unbeatable. Several political trial balloons were sent aloft by the machine on behalf of others, but these promptly collapsed.

Jim Price was endowed with an attractive and dignified, yet out-going, personality, a fine physique, a handsome face, gray hair and an erect bearing. He happened to be born just over the line in West Virginia, but he had dwelt in the Old Dominion since finishing high school. He was particularly active in Masonic circles, and this gave him a large state-wide acquaintance. He had served seven terms in the House of Delegates, and had then been chosen lieutenant governor in the crucial campaign of 1929, when John Garland Pollard was elected governor over the "Hoovercrat" candidate.

When Senator Byrd and his inner circle found that all trial balloons for possible opponents of Lieutenant Governor Price had barely gotten off the ground, and that he could not be defeated, "the word" was passed just before Christmas 1936. A number of organization leaders promptly made well-publicized and almost simultaneous leaps for the Price bandwagon. Byrd himself was not in the group, but it was clear that the machine had decided reluctantly to support the Richmonder. So great was Price's popularity that there was also an amusing "coattail campaign," wherein each of the candidates for lieutenant governor and attorney general in the 1937 primary sought to prove that he had shown more enthusiasm for Price than his opponent.

Price had never been a member of the machine's Sanhedrin. In addition, he was more "New Dealish" than Byrd, and lacking in enthusiasm for the all-out anti-Roosevelt stance of the Byrd organization. On the other hand, he was more conservative than Roosevelt.

On January 31, 1938, Price announced the appointment of LeRoy Hodges as state comptroller and chairman of the State Compensation Board, replacing in both positions E. R. Combs, Byrd's *alter ego* and spokesman in the organization. Price also ousted other stanch organization men from the posts of director of the motor vehicle division, director of purchasing and printing, and state treasurer, and he replaced six of the seven members of the Advisory Legislative Council. The war was on.

And yet Governor Price did not go far enough in dismantling the Byrd machine at the seat of government to weaken it appreciably. He merely succeeded in infuriating its leaders. The fact is that Price did not have the temperament for a showdown fight with Byrd, nor was he an organizer. Furthermore, there was a machine majority in both branches of the General Assembly, so that the governor could not put through legislation that the organization found objectionable. The result was that his program was cut to pieces. As an example of the manner in which measures in which he was interested were manhandled, consider the fact that Delegate Francis P. Miller, a leading Price supporter, was given a grand total of five minutes by Speaker Ashton Dovell to explain the merit system bill he had introduced, and on which he and the Advisory Legislative Council had worked for two years.

Governor Price evidenced a greater receptivity than his predecessor to federal assistance in caring for the old, the blind, the unemployed and the disadvantaged. He also favored public housing and obtained the legislature's approval of the federal program. His attitude on these matters and his friendship with the Roosevelt administration made it possible for him to obtain large PWA grants for public buildings. Price was likewise greatly interested in education, and he succeeded in raising public school teachers' salaries appreciably. He brought into his administration non-political technicians, such as Dr. Rowland Egger of the University of Virginia as budget director, and Dr. Dabney S. Lancaster as state superintendent of public instruction.

Price appointed the Virginia Defense Council in May 1940, only a few hours after President Roosevelt named the National Defense Commission. The war in Europe was reaching a crescendo and Hitler's panzers were slicing through the low countries and France. After the Japanese attack on Pearl Harbor in December of the following year, Price used the few remaining weeks of his term to strengthen further the state's preparations for the conflict. A Virginia Aircraft Warning Service was set up, with a state-wide network of more than one thousand observation stations. Virginia was one of three states said by a federal official to be "doing the best defense jobs in the nation."

Price pioneered in the entire country by urging mayors to appoint at least one Negro to draft boards, especially in areas of large Negro population. He also named the Reverend J. Alvin Russell, Negro president of St. Paul's Polytechnic Institute, to the State Defense Council.

President Roosevelt sought to give Price control of federal patronage in Virginia. The governor received a conspicuous rebuff when he urged the appointment of Judge Floyd H. Roberts of Bristol to the U.S. district court. Senators Glass and Byrd pronounced the appointment personally objectionable, and the Senate rejected Roberts overwhelmingly, out of "senatorial courtesy." No effort was made to prove him unqualified.

Price was a democratic and unpretentious man. He placed his own telephone calls, using the words "This is Jim Price at the governor's office," not "This is Governor Price." Great reluctance to say "no" was probably his most serious fault. It prevented him from becoming a forceful and aggressive leader. His sudden death from a stroke in 1943 at age sixty-one shocked the state.

There was no real heir to Price in the anti-organization group. Colgate W. Darden, Jr., of Norfolk, representing the Byrd wing of the party, was the organization's choice for governor in the 1941 primary. Such diverse leaders as Byrd, Francis P. Miller, Congressman

John W. Flannagan, an all-out New Dealer, and Westmoreland Davis endorsed Darden well in advance of the voting. He had no opposition worth mentioning from the Democrats, while the Republicans, who during this period were almost completely impotent, made only a perfunctory effort. Their candidate was Benjamin Muse of Petersburg, a former Democrat and liberal in the General Assembly who had bolted to Alf Landon in the presidential campaign of 1936.

Darden, a former congressman and state legislator, was the first citizen of Norfolk to become governor in over a century. He was endowed with unusual ability and personal charm, and a forward-looking viewpoint on the issues before the commonwealth. Despite his endorsement by the Price wing, he lost no time in replacing most of the important Price appointees in the state government. He also capitalized on the progressive program of his predecessor by putting through the General Assembly several measures which the machine-dominated legislature had refused to pass for Price. A conspicuous example was the program of enlightened penology, including a system of probation and parole, which Darden regarded as the most important single achievement of his administration. Price had striven vainly to obtain most of this program.

Darden devoted a great deal of attention to education. The Denny Commission, headed by Dr. George H. Denny, former president of Washington and Lee University and the University of Alabama, was created by the General Assembly, on the governor's recommendation, to formulate a plan for the improvement of the public schools. It proposed sweeping changes, most of which were enacted into law, with Darden's approval. The schools had been called "undemocratic" in management and operation, indifferent to the "three R's," lacking in facilities for vocational education and poorly staffed. The compulsory education law was not being adequately enforced. Facilities for Negroes were grossly inadequate, and improvements were said by the commission to be essential. Additional funds for the public schools were recommended, and substantial increases were provided.

Governor Darden made a special effort to eliminate as many one- and two-teacher schools as possible. A State Planning Board study, made at his request, showed more than 100,000 children enrolled in 2276 such schools in ninety-seven counties, with the totals fairly evenly divided between white and black children. Darden estimated that it would cost from $50,000,000 to $60,000,000 to provide the buildings needed for consolidations that would reduce these one- and two-room schools to fewer than fifty. He urged that the money be made available.

Darden also addressed himself intensively to improvements in higher education, especially with respect to the University of Virginia. He was particularly desirous of creating a better relationship between the state university and the public schools, and he pointed out that only about 10 or 11 per cent of Virginia's high schools were sending graduates to the Charlottesville institution. He was able to improve this percentage by instigating changes at the university, albeit the percentage of increase was less than he had hoped for. Later, as the successful president of the university for twelve years, he would improve it still further.

Since black students were not admitted to the state university or to the other state institutions of higher learning, with the exception of Virginia State at Petersburg, Governor Darden approved the recommendation of a committee that Negro medical and dental students be sent to Meharry College in Nashville, Tennessee, with their education subsidized by the commonwealth of Virginia. He also urged that Virginia State be placed under an all-Negro board of visitors and that the Petersburg Colony for the treatment of feeble-minded Negroes and the Piedmont Sanatorium for tuberculous Negroes at Burkeville be placed under the management of all-Negro staffs. Darden also recommended repeal of the poll tax.

Overshadowing all strictly domestic questions as Darden took office was the Second World War, and much of his time was devoted to coping with the problems that arose by virtue of Virginia's greater than average involvement. About fifty military and naval installations, more than in any other state, were within Virginia's borders, and those around Hampton Roads were of special significance. The Virginia State Guard, organized as the Virginia Protective Force, was authorized when the National Guard was called into federal service. It carried on for five years, and then was demobilized. The governor thanked it in his final address to the General Assembly for "a task well done."

Virginia sent more than 300,000 men and women into the armed forces during the four years of conflict, and about 9000 gave their lives. Ten Virginians were awarded the Medal of Honor, among them General Alexander A. Vandegrift of Charlottesville, who led the U. S. Marines in their desperate and crucially important victories over the Japanese on Guadalcanal and Bougainville. He was later commandant of the U. S. Marine Corps.

Virginia Military Institute men were again conspicuous in every theater. Most famous of all was General of the Army George C. Marshall, born in Pennsylvania but widely related in Virginia. Other VMI men included Lieutenant General Lemuel C. Shepherd, U. S. Marines, of Norfolk, who had been wounded three times as a young lieutenant in World War I. He commanded the Sixth Marines in the Pacific in World War II, and was much decorated. General Shepherd was commandant of the Marine Corps after the war. Lieutenant General Lewis B. ("Chesty") Puller, a native of West Point, Virginia, a VMI man often called the most decorated marine in history, with five Navy crosses, fought across the Pacific in the island landings and then covered himself with more glory in the Korean war. Lieutenant General Leonard T. Gerow of Petersburg, a VMI graduate, was in overall command of the Omaha Beach landings of June 6, 1944, and then led the Fifteenth U. S. Army.

In the first wave of the D-day assault on Hitler's "Fortress Europe" —made in the face of almost point-blank German cannon, rocket and machine-gun fire from the heights above—were Virginia's 116th Infanty and 111th Field Artillery of the 29th Division, the only non-regular units chosen for the assault wave. They suffered huge casualties in getting a foothold on the shell-scarred beach. Members of the 116th came from cities and towns of the Piedmont, the Shenandoah Valley and the Southside, while those of the 111th were mainly Richmonders and Fredericksburgers. The little town of Bedford contributed no fewer than forty-six men to the 116th, and only half of them returned. These and other Virginia units fought their way across France and across the Pacific.

Back in the Old Dominion, citizens supported the men on the front lines by buying war bonds, taking part in civilian defense, collecting scrap metal and co-operating in the rationing of food, clothing, gasoline, tires and fuel.

The expansion of military and naval installations in the Hampton Roads area was colossal. As early as November 1941, on the eve of Pearl Harbor, the population of Norfolk had nearly doubled, and both then and later there was not enough of anything—houses, food, water and schools. The Naval Base and the Navy Yard at Portsmouth were expanded enormously, as was the great shipyard at Newport News, which was turning out aircraft carriers and other warships at top speed.

Thousands of sailors on leave crowded into Norfolk and created additional problems for the harassed municipality. Disreputable dives on East Main Street were heavily patronized. National magazines published lurid accounts of Norfolk's supposedly inadequate preparations for taking care of this chaotic and festering situation, which grew worse after the United States entered the war. A Navy Department investigation found, however, that much of the criticism was unfair, and that Norfolk had performed well under extreme difficulties.

The danger of attack by the Axis powers, especially Germany, on the vitally important and highly concentrated installations in the Hampton Roads area, gave particular concern. Possible bombing from the air or U-boat forays from the sea had to be guarded against. Hundreds of ships damaged by German or Italian submarines limped into Hampton Roads for repairs. Thousands of survivors of sinkings were brought to the Norfolk Naval Base.

Most of the task force which invaded North Africa in late 1942 sailed from Hampton Roads. As the war wore on and the Allies were able to cope more effectively with the submarine threat, shipments out of Norfolk and Newport News to Europe were greatly increased. Coal cargoes were stepped up, and as the Germans were being driven back in Western Europe, huge quantities of food and other supplies were shipped across the Atlantic for the rehabilitation of the devastated lands.

Radford, chosen as the site of a large munitions plant, was swamped with an influx of 20,000 workers, three times the city's population. Blackstone's population was only one-fifth of the total personnel in nearby Camp Pickett. Camp Lee near Petersburg was reactivated from World War I. Camp Peary was constructed near Williamsburg for the Seabees, who built airfields and other necessary installations on Pacific islands. Amphibious warfare for the Pacific landings was perfected at Little Creek. A vast area of Caroline County was taken over for Camp A. P. Hill, where the U. S. Army held maneuvers. The U. S. Marine base at Quantico was expanded.

The perennial problem of what role the black soldiers would play in the armed forces gave concern throughout the conflict. These soldiers were not fully integrated into the various branches of the service, but were, of course, subject to the draft. The National Association for the Advancement of Colored People wanted all races mingled together in the different units, with black officers commanding some of them.

"Most white Americans are puzzled and alarmed by the impatience and bitterness of large sections of our Negro population," a writer in a national magazine said in 1944. Fantastic rumors were abroad, in Virginia and other southern states. The blacks were buying up all the ice picks and "switch blades" in town, with a view to a wholesale massacre of the whites under cover of darkness, according to one of these. Then there were the mythical "Eleanor Clubs," named for Mrs. Eleanor Roosevelt, wife of the President, whose interest in Negro progress was well-known. Members of these "clubs" were supposed to have vowed to abandon domestic service as degrading, and to have as their slogan "Every white woman in her kitchen by Christmas."

A South-wide effort to promote better race relations was under way. It was instigated by two Negro leaders in Virginia, Dr. Gordon B. Hancock of Virginia Union University, and P. B. Young, Norfolk newspaper publisher. They had brought together a group of black leaders from all over the South at Durham, North Carolina, in October 1942, and had formulated a list of objectives. A group of white leaders met in Atlanta and approved this "Durham Manifesto." Delegates from both groups then met at Richmond in June 1943. Out of this came the establishment of the Southern Regional Council, with headquarters in Atlanta. It carried on the movement for better opportunities for the blacks, but was never able to enlist a wide enough cross section of white Southerners to be really effective. Interracial bitterness continued, both inside and outside the armed forces.

In an effort to defuse racial antagonisms on the domestic front, and in fairness to harassed black citizens, the Richmond *Times-Dispatch* suggested editorially in late 1943 that Virginia abandon segregation on streetcars and buses. It was the first paper in the South to urge this step; and although it circularized the principal southern newspapers with its proposal, the only southern daily that gave support was the small Kinston, North Carolina, *Free Press*.

The surrender of the Germans in May 1945, was greeted with delirious joy throughout Virginia. When the Japanese gave up in

August, there was additional celebrating. The titanic struggle had ended and Virginians could begin getting back to normal.

One deplorable evidence of normalcy was another stolen election in southwest Virginia. A shocking scandal in Wise County broke almost simultaneously with the end of the war. It involved the contest for lieutenant governor in the August 1945 primary between L. Preston Collins and Charles R. Fenwick. Fenwick was announced as having won by 572 votes. Suspecting shady practices in Wise, Collins demanded an investigation. When inspection of the twenty-six Wise County poll books was sought, it was found that twenty-four of them had been stolen. Judge Julien Gunn of Richmond, who was sitting in the case, thereupon declared that the county was "impregnated with political crooks and ballot thieves," and awarded the election to Collins, since 3300 of Fenwick's majority had come from Wise. No one suspected Fenwick of any part in this skulduggery, but it was one more bit of evidence that much of southwest Virginia, for all its good qualities in other directions, was incorrigibly addicted to stealing elections. In fact, the grand jury which investigated the matter, without indicting anybody, found that "most of the illegal acts have been a result of precedent and practice, over a number of years, possibly as many as 20 or 25, although no complaint seems to have been called to the attention of the court at any time."

Two years previously, there had been a similar scandal in adjacent Dickenson County. This one revolved around absentee ballots, which —along with poll tax payments—were for many years vehicles of corruption in the elections of the southwest. The Republicans claimed that in the Dickenson County election of 1943, the Democrats had won all the county offices by the fraudulent use of absentee ballots. This had come to be a common practice. The "black satchels" in which political agents carried hundreds of absentee ballots to voters, and marked them, on the pretext that the voters were to be absent on election day, were notorious. In the Dickenson case, Judge Joseph L. Cantwell of Bristol declared that the election was carried on "as though done with the purpose of seeing that no election vices be left undone." He spoke of "shocking and flagrant violations of the law," and added that "the absentee ballot was misused in almost every conceivable way."

Illegal block payments of poll taxes by both parties also were a widespread phenomenon in counties of the southwest. Politicians would deposit sums of money for the payment of these taxes for the faithful—in counties where the treasurer was a member of the party furnishing the money. The treasurer was usually a Democrat, and that party always dominated the electoral boards in the various counties and cities. There was one Republican on each board, but there were always two Democrats. With the abolition of the poll tax as a prerequisite to voting, this method of violating the election laws, used by both parties when they had the opportunity, is no longer possible.

Governor after governor denounced electoral fraud and pointed to absentee ballots as a chief source of the evil. Strenuous efforts were made on the floor of the legislature to correct the situation by passing laws with teeth in them, but for decades nothing effective was done. Finally, in 1970, the General Assembly passed a law that should effectively thwart the operations of the "black satchel" brigade.

The refusal of the Democratic organization over a period of generations to do anything to stop these absent-voter and poll-tax frauds is something which has never been satisfactorily explained. Political morality in Virginia is of so high an order in other respects that this long-continued lapse is the more disturbing. The crookedness was confined almost entirely to one section of the state, but much more determined efforts should have been made to stop it.

The same 1945 primary which brought the Collins-Fenwick contest witnessed the nomination of Lieutenant Governor William M. Tuck of Halifax for governor. Bill Tuck was a salty, jovial, paunchy former member of the state senate who had an undistinguished record in that body and the House of Delegates. It was probably because he had no important legislation to his credit over a period of some twenty years and was known primarily as a genial handshaker that Senator Byrd did not give Tuck "the nod" before he announced his candidacy for governor. After Tuck got into the race, and more particularly after he had shown that he was a forceful and competent executive with ideas of his own who would not be pushed around, Byrd backed him strongly. Tuck's opponent in the primary was Moss A. Plunkett of Roanoke, an independent Democrat who was known from the first to have no chance. Tuck won handsomely.

Meanwhile, Senator Carter Glass, who had been ill and bedridden for years, and who had not answered a Senate roll call since 1942, died on May 28, 1946, aged eighty-eight. His final years were anti-climactic, for he should have resigned when he found himself unable to carry on his duties. There were public calls for his retirement, but he stayed stubbornly on, while confined to his bed at his Lynchburg home. It was a sad finale for a distinguished career. His leadership in obtaining the Federal Reserve System placed the nation forever in his debt.

When Glass died, former Governor Colgate W. Darden, Jr., could have had his seat, but he declined it. A contest then developed before the Democratic convention between Congressman Howard W. Smith of Alexandria and Congressman A. Willis Robertson of Lexington.

Smith, an ultraconservative in the Byrd tradition, had been singled out for "purging" by President Roosevelt in 1938. His opponent for the House of Representatives was little-known William E. Dodd, Jr., son of the noted historian. Smith had incurred F.D.R.'s wrath by his anti-New Deal attitudes, especially in connection with an administration-backed wage bill. Governor Price warned that "Dodd hasn't a prayer," but the effort to elect him persisted, and Roosevelt invited him to the White House. The result was foregone. Smith was nominated by a huge majority.

Robertson, the other candidate for the vacant Senate seat in 1946, was no liberal, but he was regarded as less conservative than Smith. He had entered the Virginia senate in 1916, served in World War I and came out with the rank of major, and then returned to the state senate. He was patron there of the Robertson Act, under which the first $14,000,000 was obtained for the newly created state highway system. In 1926, he was named the first head of the just-established State Commission of Game and Inland Fisheries, and in 1932 was elected to the House of Representatives. He was re-elected for six more terms.

The contest in the Democratic convention of 1946 between Robertson and Smith for Glass's Senate seat was spirited. Robertson won. He would remain in the Senate and Smith would remain in the House for two more decades, and each would take an important position of leadership.

Bill Tuck had entered the governorship the preceding January, and in his inaugural address he had stressed the danger that the states would become subservient to an all-powerful federal government. He would voice alarm over this possibility throughout his public career. A colorful phrasemaker, Tuck declared that the national government was under the dominion of "tormenting minions of vice and venality . . . thimbleriggers and flugelmen."

Blimplike in his physical contours, and weighing around 230 pounds, a tobacco chewer, smoker of big cigars, and devourer of collards, chitlins and turnip greens, this man endowed with a Falstaffian wit and Falstaffian dimensions moved purposefully into the governor's mansion. His outward joviality, reminiscent of Walter Scott's "Friar Tuck," and his virtuosity as a raconteur may have contributed to the notion that he had no convictions of his own. This turned out to be one of the prime misconceptions of the decade.

In order to discourage strikes by state, city, town and county employees, Tuck put through a law making it illegal to re-employ any public worker for one year after the worker had struck. He also procured passage of a resolution declaring it to be "against public policy" for any public official to bargain with a labor union. There were howls from labor leaders that Tuck was Hitler and Mussolini rolled into one. Soon they would howl still more loudly.

For a strike on the Virginia Electric and Power Company system was threatened, and Governor Tuck vowed that he would seize and operate the company, if this became necessary to maintain service. Advised by the attorney general that he had no such right, he protested that everybody around him seemed to be "dying of the can'ts."

On the eve of the scheduled walkout, he called for induction of 1600 Vepco employees into the unorganized state militia. Whether Tuck had the right to take such action was highly questionable, but he took it and averted the strike.

In January 1947, he summoned the legislature into special session, saying that this was imperative to provide a $6,500,000 increase in funds for salaries of public school teachers. He also used the session to obtain legislation restricting organized labor. One bill, designed to prevent interference with vital services of public utilities, made it possible for the governor to seize and operate any utility where such interference was threatened. Another outlawed union membership as a necessary condition for employment, and was known as the "right-to-work-law."

Six utility companies—power, telephone and transportation—were seized by Tuck during his four-year administration, pursuant to the authority conferred upon him by the above-mentioned statute, and service was maintained in each instance. The procedure was a drastic one, but Tuck claimed that "these results were obtained without impairing the rights of either management or labor or in any way interfering with the orderly processes of collective bargaining." Labor leaders disagreed fervently.

The furor over this legislation had hardly died down when Tuck decided to call for an increase in corporate and individual income taxes. He said this was necessary in order that Virginians might be provided with a better grade of education, health and welfare. There were loud ululations from various quarters, especially from leading newspapers, chambers of commerce and other business groups normally supporting the organization. As Tuck ruefully declared later, "They called on me to preach the sermon, and I preached, but when I passed the collection plate, the congregation ran out on me." Yet he refused to be diverted from his objective. His tax program was passed overwhelmingly by the legislature, and public services that had been starved got an infusion of badly needed additional funds. He also obtained a one-cent raise in the gasoline tax to "get the schoolbuses out of the mud."

Governor Tuck was much less successful when he tried in 1948, with the specific approval of Senator Byrd, to stack the cards against President Truman and in favor of the Virginia machine in the presidential election of that year. This was far from being the organization's finest hour. The bill it sponsored was a monstrosity.

The measure would have given the State Democratic Committee or the State Democratic Convention the power to decide for whom Virginia's electoral vote would be cast in the presidential contest. The decision could even be reached before the election. Furthermore, the names of the Democratic nominees could be kept off the ballot entirely. This proposal evoked such formidable opposition from almost every quarter that the bill's sponsors did a quick backtrack—like a man "retracting in a patch of sneeze weed," to use one of Bill Tuck's favorite expressions. A milder substitute was brought forward and passed. Under its terms, Virginia electors could bolt the Democratic party's national ticket, but the authority has never been used.

A third, or States' rights party, stressing ultraconservative attitudes on the race question, nominated Governor Strom Thurmond of South Carolina for President. This party, derisively dubbed the "Dixiecrats," polled 43,000 votes in Virginia, mostly in the Southside. It was apparently just enough to swing the state to Truman against the Republican nominee, Thomas E. Dewey, who trailed Truman by under 29,000 votes.

Governor Tuck decided that it was time to make a survey of the state government, with a view to achieving greater simplification and economy. The firm of Griffenhagen and Associates of Chicago was retained to study the problem and make recommendations. Its conclusions were then submitted to a Virginia commission, headed by former Congressman Thomas G. Burch of Martinsville. There were entirely too many employees in the state government, and the Burch commission sought to bring about improvement. Yet its modest recommendations were cut to pieces by the machine-dominated legislature, and the net result was that little was accomplished. The organization leaders never tired of deploring the swollen bureaucracy and the centralization in Washington, but they were not greatly interested in reducing the similarly swollen bureaucracy and centralization in Richmond.

Tuck deserves praise for putting an end to the flogging of prisoners in the state prison system. He was also responsible for a gradual phasing out of the chaining of prisoners in the convict road camps. And although as a dedicated devotee of country music he could hardly have been expected to embrace the cause of the fine arts, he put through the General Assembly a $1,000,000 appropriation for the state art museum.

"The Tuck years belong to the golden age of Byrd organization hegemony in Virginia," J. Harvie Wilkinson III writes in his admirable book, *Harry Byrd and the Changing Face of Virginia Politics.* After Tuck went out of office, the political skies were less serene. "Crisis and dissension" wracked the organization through the 1950s, Wilkinson points out.

Signs of this deterioration were not long in coming. State Senator John S. Battle of Charlottesville was the organization's anointed candidate for governor, but he was faced with serious opposition. Francis Pickens Miller of Albemarle, the ablest anti-organization candidate in many years, entered the race. In addition, Horace H. Edwards of Richmond, a somewhat independent member of the organization, and former chairman of the State Democratic Committee, was running. A fourth candidate was Remmie Arnold, a highly conservative Petersburg fountain-pen manufacturer.

Francis Miller, onetime Rhodes Scholar at Oxford, a colonel on Eisenhower's staff in World War II, a cultivated student of world affairs and articulate critic of the Byrd machine, mounted a most effective campaign. He had been a member of the House of Delegates and hence was privy to the workings of Virginia politics. The organization was vulnerable on various counts, and Miller made the most of these vulnerabilities.

He threw such a scare into the machine that Senator Byrd leaped into the fray, something he seldom did in state elections. He was seriously alarmed. Byrd called Miller "the CIO-sponsored candidate." Miller said Byrd had raised "a false issue," and was seeing "CIO ghosts," but Byrd and Battle kept emphasizing that the CIO backed Miller. They undoubtedly won votes by this tactic, although the CIO was not at all powerful in the state at the time.

Byrd and Battle also came up with the slogan, "A Vote For Edwards Is a Vote for Miller," which was devastating in its effect on the Edwards candidacy. Edwards had built up a considerable following, even within the organization. He had served as mayor of Richmond and was familiar with the ills of the cities. He advocated a 2 per cent state-wide retail sales tax.

Edwards' following began leaving him in droves when the Byrd-Battle-Combs combination put the screws on the officeholders in the courthouses. Scores, if not hundreds, of telegrams rained down on Edwards, withdrawing support which the senders had promised him. He was in a hopeless position.

Battle still had to cope with Miller and was in real danger of defeat. At that juncture Major Henry A. Wise, a former member of the Republican National Committee, publicly urged his fellow Republicans to enter the Democratic primary and vote for Battle. This highly unorthodox procedure was winked at by the Democratic high command, which let it be known that these voters would be welcomed. Republicans had been entering Democratic primaries for many years and voting for Byrd-backed candidates, but it was done quietly—never so blatantly as this. The GOP had a primary of its own in 1949 for the nomination of state officers—their first primary in history—but realizing that the Republicans who were running had no chance in the general election, thousands of that party's adherents ignored their own primary and entered that of the Democrats. Fewer than 9000 votes were cast in the Republican primary as against

316,000 in the Democratic. Since Battle's plurality over Miller was just under 24,000, it seems probable that Battle owed his nomination to the GOP. Miller estimated that over 30,000 Republicans entered the Democratic primary and voted for Battle. While in a two-way contest between Battle and Miller, Battle might have won without Republican help, with Edwards and Arnold in the race, the pro-Battle Republican vote apparently was decisive.

When John Battle took office in 1950, the General Assembly was strongly controlled by the organization, despite the political ferment in the state. He was able, therefore, to present and put through a program. It was predominantly addressed to the shortcomings of the public schools.

The time was ripe for such an effort, and Battle was an effective, if easygoing, leader. Tall, dignified, handsome and gray-haired, sometimes called Lincolnesque in appearance because of his brooding expression, John Battle was the very model of a Virginia governor. He had served for two decades in the General Assembly and had risen to the chairmanship of the powerful Senate Finance Committee and the Advisory Legislative Council.

The Tuck tax increases were bringing in more money than had been anticipated, and there was a substantial surplus in the state treasury. So Battle recommended that $75,000,000 be set aside from this surplus during the next four years for the construction of public school buildings. The localities had previously been held responsible for all such construction, but the governor felt the emergency to be such that this precedent should be ignored. He also successfully opposed requiring the localities to put up matching money, and $45,000,000 was made available for the first two years of his administration, with the remaining $30,000,000 appropriated for the second two years. Although matching was not required, the localities did, in fact, put up more than $69,000,000 toward the carrying out of the 414 school-construction projects involved in the program. They also made such generous appropriations for other school projects that no less than $243,000,000 was spent from all sources for public school construction during the four years of Battle's administration.

The issue of teacher pay also arose at the session of 1950, and Delegate Robert Whitehead of Nelson County, uninhibited and forthright leader of the anti-organization forces, sought to add an extra $1,000,000 for pay increases to the large ones already made. There was plenty of money in the treasury to do this, but the move was defeated, after prolonged debate, on the specious plea that to add this item would unbalance the budget. What the organization was really afraid of was that Whitehead would gain political credit, if the increase were granted, and would run for governor. Whitehead, as a practical politician, was not oblivious to such considerations, but he was an unusually high-minded man—"the conscience of the House," some called him. As matters turned out, he never did run for governor, for he lacked the necessary funds, but he kept the organization on its toes, and was a salutary influence. His homespun oratory, replete with similes and analogies from his rural background, was extremely effective. He was indeed a formidable antagonist, "a d'Artagnan in debate," as Guy Friddell says in his delightful book, *What Is It About Virginia?*

Governor Battle pointed to two aspects of Virginia's health program that were "unique in the nation." One was the medical-examiner service, under which the state's chief medical examiner investigated more than 7000 deaths in 1953, over 20 per cent of all the deaths in Virginia—a program "recognized nationally as the most complete and best example of such a system in the United States." The other was the facility for the treatment and rehabilitation of alcoholics established at the Medical College of Virginia.

Periodic efforts to repeal the poll tax had been made since the 1930s, but all had been defeated. A frightfully complicated plan passed at two sessions of the General Assembly but was soundly beaten by the people in 1949. Another effort was made in 1950, but although a relatively simple repealer passed the House, it was killed in a senate committee.

Another event of the 1950 session was the enactment of State Senator Harry F. Byrd, Jr.'s automatic income-tax-credit law. The Tuck tax program had made Virginia a "high tax state," it was charged, and Byrd, Jr.'s plan was designed to afford a certain degree of relief. In effect, it provided that if general-fund revenues for a given fiscal year exceeded budget estimates by a specific percentage, individual and corporation income taxpayers would receive a refund by that percentage of their income tax bills.

The result was that in the next five years, $25,000,000 was returned to individuals and corporations. This money would otherwise have gone toward remedying some of the state's glaring deficiencies in the fields of education, health and welfare. These refunds seemed to many to be a good idea at the time, but some undoubtedly changed their minds. The need to spend this money on state services or facilities is seen in the fact that in 1950, Virginia had the lowest percentage of high school attendance in the nation, next to the highest percentage of high school dropouts before graduation, and next to the smallest percentage of children of school age in school. The state was also at or near the bottom in the percentage of college-age population in college. The automatic tax refunds made it all the more difficult later on for Virginia to catch up with the rest of the country.

In another area, the trend in Virginia was more encouraging. The 1950 census showed that for the first time, there was a large in-migration of whites. The in-migration had begun on a small scale in the decade after 1930, but in the succeeding decade it became much more pronounced, with the result that 169,000 more whites entered Virginia than left it during the ten years ending in 1950. From 1870 to 1930 the trend had been the other way. However, predominant numbers of blacks continued to leave Virginia through-out all these years, and the number of black women going elsewhere was so large that the Old Dominion became "the only state in the Union with more males than females, and increasingly so, in the total population," Jean Gottmann points out in his excellent work, *Virginia In Our Century.*

The Korean War broke out in the summer of 1950, and Governor Battle reactivated the State Council of Defense from World War II. Hundreds of local defense councils and five regional councils were established, together with hundreds of ground observation posts for the detection of hostile aircraft. A Virginian, Walter S. Robertson, played a conspicuously able role in bringing about an end to hostilities. As assistant secretary of state for Far Eastern Affairs, Robertson, one of the leading Virginians of his generation, went to Korea and pre-vailed on crusty old President Syngman Rhee, after weeks of argument, to agree to an armistice with the North Koreans. Robertson was a delegate thereafter to numerous international conferences and also to the United Nations General Assembly.

Another citizen of the Old Dominion who rendered exceptional service during these years was Rear Admiral Lewis L. Strauss. He made a distinguished record in World War II and as chairman of the

Atomic Energy Commission. Although he never attended college, he was elected president of the Institute for Advanced Study at Princeton, New Jersey. His autobiographical book, *Men and Decisions*, is a fascinating account of a remarkably fruitful and dedicated career.

Senator Byrd was up for re-election in 1952, and Francis Miller, who had given John Battle such a scare three years before, entered the primary against him. In the words of James Latimer: "Miller ran against the Byrd machine and Byrd's conservative record, while Byrd ran against Harry Truman, the CIO and northern liberals. Miller said the CIO-labor charge was a 'pure phony' and 'red herring.' Byrd said Miller was a Trumanite, big-spending wastrel." Byrd won by a whopping majority, 216,000 to 128,000, in round numbers. Miller had performed a service in this campaign and that of 1949 by pointing out some of the machine's and the state's manifest shortcomings.

As in so many Virginia primaries that had gone before, the total vote was very low. This was due, in part, to apathy, in part to the organization's usual invincibility, in part to the poll tax, with its requirement that it be paid three years in a row six months before the general election. For example, in the gubernatorial primaries from 1925 to 1945, the organization candidate had only to get from 5 to 7 per cent of the adult population in order to win. In actual fact, the winners in those years polled from 6.2 to 11.2 per cent, but even these fantastically low percentages were well in excess of what was needed for victory. It was this which caused V. O. Key, Jr., to remark in his *Southern Politics*, "By contrast, Mississippi is a hotbed of democracy."

The Democratic State Convention met immediately after the Byrd-Miller primary, and was fully prepared to endorse U. S. Senator Richard B. Russell of Georgia for President. But on the day the gathering met, the delegates read in their morning papers that Russell had come out in favor of liberalizing the Taft-Hartley Law, restricting the activities of labor unions. This "heavie newes," as Captain John Smith would have phrased it, caused a virtual cascade of Russell-for-President buttons into the nearest wastebaskets. The shocked and disillusioned delegates decided to go uninstructed to the party's national convention at Chicago.

On arrival there, they found themselves, as usual, out of sympathy with the party's leading candidate and eventual nominee, Adlai Stevenson. Since 1912, Virginia delegations at Democratic National Conventions had supported the nominee only twice on the first ballot. These exceptions occurred in 1916, when Woodrow Wilson was up for renomination, and in 1936, when Franklin D. Roosevelt was being renominated for a second term.

The Virginia delegation at Chicago ran into trouble getting themselves seated. Northern Democrats had managed to provide a "loyalty oath," pledging each state delegation to support both nominees and platform. Virginia, South Carolina and Louisiana all refused to take this oath. It was then modified to provide only a promise that the names of the nominees would appear on the ballot in the respective states. This also was refused. The Virginians contended that such a pledge might be taken as obligating them to support the nominees and platform—hardly a rational position. The delegation had its back up and was determined not to promise anything at all.

If Governor Battle had not assumed a more conciliatory stance in a brief address to the convention, the Virginians might never have been seated, and they might even have been thrown out. Battle and former Governor Tuck started for the platform almost simultaneously as debate waxed hot over the "loyalty oath." Tuck had in his hand a sizzling declaration of defiance which almost certainly would have ended the delegation's participation in the conclave. But Battle got to the platform first, and the content of his remarks and the manner of their delivery greatly impressed the delegates, as well as the nationwide television audience. He said Virginia would not take the loyalty oath, as a matter of principle, but assured the convention that Virginia law guaranteed the nominees a place on the ballot. The Battle declaration was followed by a motion that the Virginia delegation be seated, and it carried. Tuck never delivered his torrid blast. He and Byrd were strongly suspected of wanting to be either not seated or actually thrown out, but Battle thwarted any such plan by winning the race to the platform. When the governor returned to Richmond, he received a hero's welcome.

Battle endorsed Adlai Stevenson for President, as did Senator Robertson, Congressman Howard Smith, Attorney General Almond and others. But no word came from Senator Byrd. Finally he delivered a radio address in mid-October flaying the administration of President Harry Truman and pointing out that Stevenson had not "repudiated Trumanism." Hence, he added, "I will not, and cannot, in good conscience, endorse the national Democratic platform or the Stevenson-Sparkman ticket." Byrd did not urge support of Dwight D. Eisenhower, the Republican nominee, but the effect was the same. The general with the infectious grin swept Virginia. Four years later, Byrd would remain completely mum, and "Ike" would carry Virginia again. Then in 1960, Byrd once more pursued a policy of "golden silence," and Richard M. Nixon carried the Old Dominion for the GOP against John F. Kennedy. Byrd was silent in 1964, but Lyndon Johnson carried the state over Barry Goldwater, with the greatly enlarged Negro vote providing Johnson's margin of victory. Virginia went Republican in 1968, when Nixon bested Hubert Humphrey, but Byrd was then dead.

Governor Battle endured a severe emotional ordeal over the nationally publicized case of the "Martinsville Seven." It involved seven Negroes who raped a white woman in Martinsville, and were sentenced to die. There was a determined effort by sincere persons to obtain a commutation to life imprisonment, but the governor did not intervene. He said many years later in an interview with Carl Shires of the Richmond *News Leader,* as part of Shires's fine series of interviews with living governors:

"I tried to figure out a way to keep a couple of those younger men from being electrocuted. But they were as guilty as the rest. . . . There had been judicial review all the way up to the U. S. Supreme Court. I could not intervene. . . . And several of those who came to see me read the case history and told me they were sorry they had intervened. All seven men died in Virginia's electric chair. I've slept with a clear conscience. The law had spoken."

Throughout his administration, Battle continued his emphasis on progress in the public schools. In addition to the $75,000,000 made available from the state for construction, he was instrumental in putting the schoolteachers, along with other state personnel, under federal social security. He also blazed a new trail by making Virginia "the first state to adopt a clearly defined policy for teaching fundamental subjects in the public schools," namely, the three R's.

His school program was formulated on the assumption that the schools would remain segregated as between white and black. The U. S. Supreme Court's epoch-making decision of May 17, 1954, outlawing segregation in the public schools, was only a few months away when Governor Battle's term came to an end.

THIRTY-EIGHT

The Era of "Massive Resistance"

THE SUPREME COURT'S decision on school segregation in *Brown* v. *Board of Education* overshadowed everything else in the four-year term of Governor Thomas B. Stanley, who followed Governor Battle in 1954. Stanley had come up the political escalator, serving three terms as speaker of the House of Delegates and six years in Congress from the Southside's Fifth District.

He came from Stanleytown, Henry County, and was a wealthy furniture manufacturer who had made generous contributions to the Democratic party and its candidates over the years. Affable and amiable, he had built up such a following that he was chosen by organization leaders to carry the party banner in the 1953 gubernatorial primary. He was successful there, but then ran into heavy weather in the election when opposed by Theodore Roosevelt (Ted) Dalton, a Republican state senator from Radford.

Dalton was a tall, attractive, articulate candidate with a specific and moderate program. Stanley was a tall, well-meaning, inarticulate candidate whose vague and bumbling pronouncements heralded a program of "sound business administration and no increase in taxes." As the campaign progressed, it became evident that Stanley was in trouble. In October Francis P. Miller, who had been the victim four years before of a wholesale entry into the Democratic primary by Republicans who voted for his opponent, turned the tables. He said publicly that most Democrats were under no legal obligation to vote for Stanley. Miller stated that he himself would stand by his loyalty oath to support the Democratic nominee, but he praised Dalton and virtually urged Democrats to cast their ballots for him.

Dalton, at this juncture, wrecked his chances by advocating the issuance of $100,000,000 in highway bonds. These were revenue bonds, redeemable out of gasoline tax revenues, and the bonds would not have been a general obligation of the state. But Senator Byrd, who was champing at the bit and greatly worried lest the Republicans capture the governorship, seized upon this as a pretext for entering the campaign. He virtually took over, and charged that Dalton wanted to "junk pay-as-you-go." In the final week it almost appeared to be a contest between Byrd and Dalton. The senator's last-minute intervention turned the tide and Stanley won. But Dalton got 45 per cent of the vote, highest up to that time for any Republican gubernatorial candidate in this century.

Stanley's inaugural address brought him further trouble. Having promised no increase in taxes, he advocated a one-cent hike in the gasoline tax. He did this, he said, because of information not available to him during the campaign. Various organization leaders were taken by surprise, and those who had promised that there would be no tax increase were embarrassed and indignant. They promptly put the governor's gas tax proposal to sleep in the General Assembly.

The unhappy chief executive also was confronted with a first-class revolt in the legislature, led by the Young Turks, a group of House members who had supported Robert Whitehead's heretical effort in 1950 to add $1,000,000 to the appropriation for raises in public school teacher pay. They were now on the warpath again, in an effort to repeal the Byrd automatic income-tax-credit law. A total of $7,000,000 was scheduled to be returned to the taxpayers in 1954 under this law. The Young Turks were determined to make this money available for Virginia's inadequately financed public services, and to repeal the law, if possible. Ably led by former Rhodes Scholar Armistead Boothe of Alexandria, and such other members as George Cochran of Staunton, Stuart Carter of Fincastle and Walter Page of Norfolk, these men who were mostly in their thirties and forties considered themselves members of the Byrd organization. However, they were not interested in taking orders from the machine to vote contrary to their convictions, and they believed that the time had come to stop starving the state's schools, colleges, hospitals and welfare services.

Their revolt stalled the legislative machinery in the closing days, and ended, after prolonged battling, in a compromise. About one-third of the $7,000,000 was made available for public services and the other two-thirds went back to the taxpayers. But it was the beginning of the end for the Byrd automatic income-tax-credit law. The law was repealed at the next session of the General Assembly, as it should have been.

The Young Turks who brought this about had been penalized for their revolt in 1950. Speaker E. Blackburn Moore of Berryville, a Byrd intimate of many years who served as speaker for a record-breaking nine terms, had given some of them inferior committee assignments. After their apostasy in 1954, the penalties inflicted through committee assignments and otherwise were more drastic. Insofar as the machine was able to do it, they were shut out of practically all chance for higher office. Several of them accordingly retired from public life in disgust. The treatment given these knowledgeable and forward-looking young Virginians by the inner hierarchy was one of the organization's greatest blunders. The machine could have conciliated them and groomed them for future political preferment, at great advantage to itself. Its failure to do so left the organization with few promising young leaders who could take over when the rapidly aging upper echelon—Byrd, Tuck, Smith, Combs and Robertson—retired. Furthermore, the harsh treatment meted out to these Democratic legislators caused many young and aspiring Democrats to join the Republican party.

As for the Supreme Court's segregation decision of 1954, the Young Turks were much more flexible in their attitude than were Speaker Moore and the other organization leaders. However, at the outset, Governor Stanley received the decision calmly, saying that he contemplated no precipitate action. He also stated that "views of leaders of both races will be invited" in approaching the problems created by the court. But the governor's objective attitude was short-lived.

Southside Virginia, whence had come Stanley's winning margin in his contest with Dalton, was dead against any compromise over segregation. That largely rural, sparsely populated and none too prosperous section had a greater percentage of Negroes than any other. The Southside had provided the Democratic machine for many years with a heavy proportion of its winning majorities in state elections, and the organization's top leadership, from Byrd on down, recognized its debt to the region below the James. The Southside's disproportionate influence in state affairs had long been a political fact of life.

Senator Byrd is reported to have joined the Southsiders in pronouncing Governor Stanley's low-key approach to the court's decision wholly unacceptable. It seems logical to assume that the governor "got the message." Within a week of the court's ruling, Stanley had kept his promise to invite the views of leading blacks, but only in a technical sense. He summoned such Negro leaders as Oliver W. Hill, Dr. R. P. Daniel and P. B. Young to his office, but he asked them to ignore the court's findings and to urge all Virginia blacks to accept continued segregation. Needless to say, they refused. That was the extent of Stanley's consultation with Negro leaders.[1]

A few weeks later, he assumed a militant posture by saying publicly, "I shall use every legal means at my command to continue segregated schools in Virginia."

Former Governor Tuck, then representing the Southside's Fifth District in Congress, the same district that Stanley had represented, expressed himself on the issue:

"There is no middle ground, no compromise. . . . If the other [Virginia areas] won't stand with us, I say make 'em. . . . If you ever let them integrate anywhere, the whole state will be integrated in a short time."

The Southside's philosophy was soon to be expressed in the manifestoes of a newly formed organization, the Defenders of State Sovereignty and Individual Liberties. The Defenders are not to be confused with Ku Kluxers or similar types of night riders believing in violence and murder. Headed by Robert B. Crawford, a mildmannered Farmville laundry owner, with J. Barrye Wall, gentlemanly editor and publisher of the Farmville *Herald*, as another influential member, they were conservative and restrained in their approach. The Defenders were not even willing to tolerate the waving of the Confederate flag as a symbol of resistance to authority. But they exemplified and expressed the Southside's unyielding opposition to integration in any form. All the original officers of the Defenders were Southsiders and the first thirteen chapters were located in that section. Headquarters were opened in Richmond, and the organization expanded to other parts of Virginia. At the end of two years, it had sixty local chapters with about 12,000 members. They spoke for Virginia's hard-core resisters.

Governor Stanley's next move was to appoint a commission charged
with recommending "legal means" by which the Supreme Court's
ruling could be circumvented and integration prevented. He had
indicated that he would name a biracial commission, and he was
urged to do so by various groups, including the Virginia Council of
Churches. Armistead Boothe and Ted Dalton also advocated this course
in a joint statement. But other counsels prevailed. State Senator
Garland Gray of Sussex County, a stanch Southside segregationist
and influential legislator, had been active in arousing sentiment for
"holding the line" against the court. He favored a commission composed exclusively of state legislators.

Stanley not only followed Gray's advice in this respect, but he
named Gray chairman of the commission. He also loaded the thirty-
two-member body with legislators from the Southside, other sections
of the state being given lesser representation. Since there were no
Negroes in the General Assembly, the decision to appoint only
assemblymen automatically eliminated all blacks from consideration.
David J. Mays, Richmond lawyer and historian, was named commission
counsel.

The Gray Commission, as it came to be known, held one long
public hearing at Richmond's Mosque on November 15, 1954. The
session continued for eleven hours and more than one hundred speakers
were heard. This was the only public hearing held by the commission,
which soon began closed-door deliberations lasting for nearly a year.
Its plan was finally unveiled on November 11, 1955. The terms must
be regarded as relatively moderate, when one considers the more
drastic stand soon to be taken by the General Assembly.

The Gray Commission actually accepted a limited amount of integration. Its principal insistence was that no child be *required* to attend
an integrated school. The plan was based on the principle of local
option, and it sanctioned the mixing of races in the schools, if
local authorities chose to integrate. At the same time, it provided
machinery designed to hamper and thwart integration. The scheme
included a state-administered pupil-assignment plan, ostensibly not
based upon race, under which pupils could be assigned to a given
school on the basis of individual health, aptitude, availability of
transportation, and "the welfare of the particular child as well as the
welfare and best interests of all other pupils attending a particular
school." The latitude allowed under these criteria was obviously great.

The plan also provided tuition grants of public funds for the education of children who chose to attend private non-sectarian schools, or public schools in another jurisdiction.

The Gray Commission recommended that the compulsory-attendance law be amended to provide that no child be forced to attend a school in which the races were mixed. It also urged a special session of the General Assembly for amending Section 141 of the state constitution, to legalize tuition grants. That section made no provision for using state funds to underwrite attendance of pupils in privately financed schools. The brief session of the legislature was held, and machinery was set in motion for amending the constitution. The legislature arranged for a popular referendum on January 9, 1956, to determine whether to hold a limited constitutional convention for the legalization of tuition grants.

The organization leadership, from Byrd on down, got behind the plan. But Byrd issued a thousand-word statement in which be carefully refrained from endorsing local option, while approving tuition grants. This notable omission should have been the tip-off for much that followed. Colgate W. Darden, Jr., urged the organization leaders to promise support of free public schools, but except for ex-Governor Battle, few in the machine's top echelon were interested in such a pronouncement.

Opposition to the proposed constitutional amendment was scattered, poorly financed and ineffective. Over against the solid phalanx of machine supporters in the courthouses and elsewhere throughout Virginia, and the proamendment Defenders, stood a hastily thrown together Society for the Preservation of the Public Schools, headed by State Senator Armistead Boothe. Many clergymen worked with Boothe and his associates, as did a number of labor leaders. The Norfolk *Virginian-Pilot* was the only widely circulated newspaper which espoused their cause; almost the entire white press was militantly in the other camp.

The Richmond *Afro-American* urged a negative vote by all Negroes, and the blacks went almost solidly against the amendment. Dr. E. B. Henderson of Falls Church, vice-president of the Virginia State Conference of the NAACP, reported that 2071 Negroes in nine northern Virginia counties readily signed a statement opposing all forms of segregation in public life. He said that less than one per cent of those asked refused to sign.

Dr. Dabney S. Lancaster, former state superintendent of public instruction and president emeritus of Longwood College, was in charge of the information center opened by the amendment's advocates. Congressman Watkins M. Abbitt, from the rock-ribbed Southside, was co-ordinator, while Delegate W. Tayloe Murphy of Warsaw, like Lancaster a moderate on the race issue, was chairman of the speakers' bureau. Richmond banker Thomas C. Boushall, another moderate, was in charge of fund-raising.

The referendum-information center issued a statement on December 31 stressing that under the Gray plan each city, county and town would decide whether it wanted full integration, partial integration or no integration. The statement was signed by Lancaster, Abbitt, Murphy and Boushall, former Governors Darden and Battle, and a number of others. The natural assumption by any reader was that the assignment and tuition-grant proposals were parts of a comprehensive plan to be put into effect by the General Assembly. With such a program, those regions of Virginia where the black population was relatively small could adopt a different school policy from that of the Southside and other areas where this population was large. Many signers of the declaration, who had acted in good faith, were greatly embarrassed a few months later when the legislature took a contrary course.

In the referendum on January 9, the advocates of a convention to legalize tuition grants won by a majority of better than two to one, with the biggest majorities coming from the areas with the largest black population. This despite the fact that almost all the Negroes who participated voted "no."

Before the convention met on March 5, the General Assembly convened in regular session. Whereas the state had appeared to be moving in the direction of partial compliance with the Supreme Court's decision, events during the legislative session showed that strong forces were pulling it in the opposite direction.

A remarkably effective campaign for "interposition" in the Richmond *News Leader*, conducted by its talented editor, James J. Kilpatrick, was a major element in bringing about the changed direction of the commonwealth. William W. Old, a Chesterfield county lawyer, had published a pamphlet in August 1955, exhuming the doctrine of interposition from political battles of the late eighteenth and early nineteenth centuries. Under it, the state was supposedly able to "interpose"

(31) John Powell, internationally known concert pianist and composer.

(32) The MacArthur Memorial in Norfolk, where General Douglas MacArthur is buried. It contains many mementoes and decorations of the famous leader. The building is the old Norfolk City Hall and Courthouse, erected in 1847.

(34) Launching of U.S. carrier *John F. Kennedy*
at the yards of the Newport News Shipbuilding and
Dry Dock Company, one of the world's foremost shipyards.
It is the builder of some of the most famous warships
and transatlantic liners in history, including the nuclear
carrier *Enterprise* and the liner *United States*,
holder of the transatlantic blue ribbon.

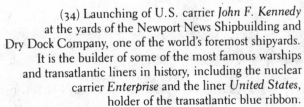

(33) Wild and rugged Breaks Interstate Park on the Virginia-Kentucky line, showing the largest canyon east of the Mississippi, where the Russell Fork River cuts through the Cumberland Mountains. The canyon is five miles long and 1600 feet deep. Most of the park is in Virginia's Dickenson County.

(35) Dr. Paul Freeman, distinguished conductor of many major symphonies in this country and abroad. In 1970, he was named conductor-in-residence for the Detroit Symphony.

(36) Camilla Williams, noted operatic singer, who has had major roles in operas throughout this country and around the world, where she has performed to great acclaim.

its sovereign authority between itself and the federal government. The commonwealth had "interposed" its authority in 1798, when Virginia's General Assembly passed a resolution of interposition in refusing to obey the Alien and Sedition Laws. The doctrine had not been invoked since the Civil War. Kilpatrick seized upon it, dramatized it, and ran a series of editorials, beginning in November 1955, and continuing until February 1956.

There was something approaching hysteria in the Assembly's attitude on this subject. Many inside and outside that body believed that interposition would prevent integration in the public schools. Such was not Kilpatrick's view. He wrote a friend in late 1955, soon after his crusade was launched, that the federal courts would probably brush the resolution aside. At about the same time he wrote another friend, "It never was thought by any of us that interposition was a substitute for the legislative program." After the controversy was over, he said, "I never did understand interposition to mean effective nullification." Kilpatrick also wrote in 1970, "the primary justification was to relieve community tensions and to cool incipient violence by elevating the level of public debate."[2] Whether it achieved the last-named objective is highly questionable.

Robert Whitehead was one of the small minority in the General Assembly who heaped scorn on the whole interpositionist concept. Whitehead termed it "nullification nonsense," and he added: "The lightning flashed, the thunder struck and a chigger died!"

But his oratory was without effect. The legislators had become bemused by interposition, and the school question in all its ramifications was almost the only subject discussed during the sixty-day session. The Senate passed an interposition resolution by 36 to 2 and the House followed 88 to 5.

Fortunately the resolution was toned down, after its introduction, and much of the nullificationist element was removed. In its final form it pledged the Old Dominion "to take all appropriate measures honorably, legally and constitutionally available to us, to resist this illegal encroachment upon our sovereign powers." Attorney General J. Lindsay Almond ruled a few days after its passage that the resolution was not a legislative enactment having the force and effect of law, and that it could not be asserted as a defense in court. But it had the undoubted effect of hardening Virginia's resistance to the Supreme Court's segregation ruling. It also had that effect

in four or five other southern states, which followed the example of
the Old Dominion by passing resolutions of interposition, at least
one of which was both defiant and nullificationist.

The fate of the local-option feature of the Gray Plan was becoming
uncertain. Speaker Moore let it be known that he would introduce a
resolution providing, in effect, that the lawmakers would do nothing
in preparation for the 1956–57 school term. Almost simultaneously,
Senator Byrd declared that "massive resistance is the best course for us
to take." Thus was born the phrase "massive resistance." It would be
heard many times thereafter.

The Richmond *Times-Dispatch* attacked Speaker Moore's proposed
resolution at once as "a breach of faith." The paper pointed out that
the people of Virginia had been told in advance of the January
referendum that the various political subdivisions would enjoy local
option "with respect to integration in their schools, beginning with
the session which opens in September." But now, the paper went on,
Moore says he will seek to prevent local option from taking effect
next fall. The *Times-Dispatch* termed it "a cynical piece of business,"
and led the fight in opposition. The following week it published extracts from papers in all sections of Virginia denouncing Moore's proposed resolution. The Richmond paper reiterated its criticism in other
editorials.

The Moore resolution was introduced, nevertheless, and it passed
the House, 62 to 34. Considering the power wielded by the speaker
and the rest of the organization's hierarchy, the adverse vote was
large. When the resolution reached the senate, it was killed, 4 to 1,
in committee. In partial extenuation of Moore and Byrd, it should
be said that neither man promised *personally* before the referendum
was held to back the entire Gray Plan, and that Byrd pointedly
omitted all mention of local option in his prereferendum statement.
However, the whole weight of the Democratic organization had been
thrown behind a "yes" vote, and Dabney Lancaster said Governor
Stanley had told him, in persuading him to accept the direction
of the referendum-information center, that the pupil-assignment and
tuition-grant plans were to be treated as inseparable parts of the
program. "Lancaster and other moderates like him had been betrayed
by Defenders and organization politicos who came to them for help
and ended by using them as a front," Robbins L. Gates writes.[3]

Despite the defeat of the Moore resolution, it was increasingly clear that the machine was determined to ditch local option. Little time was lost in setting the process in motion. Great pressure was applied, and Governor Stanley, who had "wholeheartedly" endorsed the Gray Plan when it was announced some months before, now found that it was gravely defective.

Delegate Robert Whitehead summed up the posture of affairs when he said: "The Supreme Court of the United States reversed itself. Next Governor Stanley reversed himself. Now the Gray Commission has reversed itself. This leaves the situation in a state of profound confusion."

A constitutional convention of forty delegates met at Richmond on March 5 to carry out the mandate of the January 9 referendum. John C. Parker, prominent Franklin attorney, was chairman. The convention voted unanimously to amend Section 141 and thus to legalize tuition grants. H. D. Dawbarn of Waynesboro offered a resolution endorsing local option, but it was killed in committee.

Governor Stanley summoned the General Assembly to meet in special session on August 27, 1956—the third meeting of that body within ten months. What was known as the "Stanley Plan" was set before the members. It included thirteen bills, the most significant of which required the governor to close any school under court order to integrate, and to cut off all state funds from any school which tried to reopen in obedience to the order of the court. Several leading participants in the referendum campaign of the preceding December and January—Darden, Lancaster, Boushall and Murphy— appeared in opposition to the plan, and in favor of local option. Such outstanding members of the Gray Commission as Delegates J. Randolph Tucker, Jr., and FitzGerald Bemiss of Richmond and Senator Robert F. Baldwin of Norfolk were in agreement with them, and refused to be stampeded.

A determined effort was made in both branches of the General Assembly to eliminate the fund-withholding provision of the Stanley program. Considering the amount of near hysteria in the legislature, and among the people generally, the effort received a surprisingly large vote. In the House it failed by only 59 to 39 and in the senate by only 21 to 17. But it failed, and the Stanley Plan was obviously headed for adoption. Senator Byrd was throwing all his weight behind it, and this, combined with the furor over the bogus issue of interposition, had reversed the state's direction. The racial attitudes of most whites in Virginia's black belt, comprising only a small fraction of the state's population, had been imposed on the entire commonwealth.

This would mean the closing of some schools, after all preliminary steps in the Stanley Plan had been taken. For with state funds withheld, a locality would face two main choices: (1) it could try to operate segregated schools, using only local funds or (2) it could close its schools, and, under other provisions of the plan, provide tuition grants from state and local funds for private, nonsectarian schooling of all children, where private facilities were available.

The school session of 1956–57 passed without bringing this legislation to a final test, and Governor Stanley went out of office midway of that session. No Negro pupil had entered a white public school during his administration, a fact in which he took pride.

However, when interviewed in 1967, he said he regarded his greatest accomplishment as governor to have been the improvements he brought about in the system of mental hospitals. Some one thousand employees and four thousand beds were added, the food service was greatly improved, and larger capital and operating funds were made available. The $20,000,000 additional in capital funds for the hospitals was part of a $51,000,000 onetime windfall achieved by advancing the time for payment of individual and fiduciary income taxes from the fall to not later than May 1.

Stanley's successor was J. Lindsay Almond, who had served as attorney general for nearly a decade. The son of a railway engineer, he had grown up on a farm in Orange County, and had managed, despite financial stringencies, to graduate from the University of Virginia law school. Fascinated in his youth by the political oratory which reverberated around the courthouses, Almond sought to imitate it, and ultimately developed a similarly orotund, polysyllabic style of public speaking, based on a vocabulary of startling dimensions and accompanied by forceful gestures and the shaking of his white mane. His style might be termed "Orange Courthouse, *circa* 1910 (when the William Jennings Bryan influence was running high)," according to Charles McDowell, Jr., the witty and whimsical *Times-Dispatch* columnist.

Almond had served as a respected judge in Roanoke, had been elected to Congress, and was serving there in 1948 when Virginia Attorney General Harvey B. Apperson died. Leaders of the organization persuaded Almond to give up his seat in Congress and, at a one-third cut in salary, take over as attorney general. He was anxious to serve later as governor, and he made the sacrifice. He was at that time in the good graces of the machine, although his endorsement of President Harry Truman for re-election probably did not strengthen his position. Yet his endorsement was mitigated by the extraordinary language in which it was tendered in a Norfolk speech. "The only sane and constructive course to follow," Almond said, "is to remain in the house of our fathers—even though the roof leaks, and there be bats in the belfry, rats in the pantry, a cockroach waltz in the kitchen and skunks in the parlor."

Two years later, Almond committed the political *faux pas* of writing a letter endorsing Martin A. Hutchinson, who had run against Harry Byrd for the Senate in 1946. The endorsement was for a post on the Federal Trade Commission. Byrd was much annoyed, and he gave "the nod" for governor to Tom Stanley in 1953.

During Stanley's four years, Almond handled the state's cases in the courts. As a lawyer of marked ability, he realized that Stanley's program for maintaining segregation had its serious vulnerabilities. Yet Almond struggled as best he could in manning the state's legal defenses. Emotionally, he sympathized with what Stanley was trying to do, but intellectually he knew that the day would almost certainly come when the entire jerry-built structure would collapse.

Near the end of Stanley's term, Almond announced his candidacy for governor, without consulting Senator Byrd. The latter definitely preferred Garland Gray, who had done a complete somersault in his approach to the school segregation issue, in full view of the public, along with most members of the commission he headed. Almond, however, had built up such a state-wide following as attorney general that Gray promptly withdrew. After that, Byrd was friendly, at least for the time being.

Almond's Republican opponent was Ted Dalton, who had made so good a run against Stanley four years before. He might have made another excellent showing on his platform calling for preventing school closings and liquidating massive resistance. However, Almond was far superior to Stanley as a campaigner, and Republican President Eisenhower's intervention at Little Rock, Arkansas, with federal bayonets at the height of the canvass wrecked whatever chances Dalton had. His share of the vote fell seven points below the 45 per cent he got in the previous contest. With the schools almost the only issue,

Little Rock was too heavy a burden for him to carry. "Little Rock knocked me down to nothing," Dalton said ruefully after the campaign. "It wasn't a little rock, it was a big rock."

Almond had campaigned as a total backer of massive resistance. He came into the governor's office with that image. The tone and pace of his pronouncements may be grasped from the following typical sample of his lush prose style:

"Encompassed by the iron will of an arrogated power, buffeted upon the storms of an uneven contest, pierced with the daggers of political expediency and battered by the unholy alliance of a conspiracy to destroy the constitution, Virginia, true to the faith of the founding fathers and refusing to desecrate her heritage, must never recede in this struggle to preserve her rights, nor suffer her voice to be stifled in the councils of the nation." No speech writer produced that; it is authentic Almond.

A sensational development of early 1958 was Senator Byrd's sudden announcement that he would not run for re-election later that year. He had promised Mrs. Byrd, then an invalid, that he would retire. It was a political bombshell of megaton proportions. Both branches of the General Assembly adopted resolutions, without a dissenting voice, urging Byrd to reconsider. Congressman Tuck and ex-Governor Battle made wide-ranging plans to run for Byrd's seat, on the assumption that his decision to retire was final.

The outpouring of appeals that Byrd reconsider—from admirers throughout the state and nation, as well as the Virginia legislature—had their impact, but even more persuasive, it now appears, was the prospect that Tuck and Battle were squaring off for a political donnybrook which might have torn the organization to shreds. With the fight over massive resistance already subjecting the machine to exceptional strains, this would have been too much. Byrd announced that he had decided to run for re-election, with Mrs. Byrd's concurrence.

When the schools opened in September 1958, the Stanley school-closing laws came into play at several points. Warren County in the Shenandoah Valley was ordered by the court to integrate, whereupon Warren County High School at Front Royal was closed and removed from the public-school system, by order of Governor Almond. He had never favored the school-closing laws, but they were on the books.

Shock waves from the unprecedented event in Warren were reverberating through the state when two Charlottesville schools, Lane High and Venable Elementary, were closed for the same reason. Next came the much more comprehensive closings in Norfolk, involving nearly 10,000 students.

In each of these areas efforts were made to organize private schools to take care of the pupils who were without educational facilities. In Warren County and Charlottesville, a majority of the displaced students were accommodated in makeshift quarters, until more permanent quarters could be obtained. In Norfolk the situation was catastrophic, since thousands of pupils in six junior and senior high schools were without any schooling.

The public schools shut down in these three localities remained closed throughout the fall. Four thousand residents of Charlottesville signed a petition in October, urging support of Governor Almond's firm stand. A somewhat meaningless informal referendum in Norfolk in November, with an extremely light turnout, showed some 60 per cent against reopening the schools on an integrated basis. In January, the Norfolk City Council actually went beyond the state law and voted to withhold funds for the operation of any public-school grades above the sixth, a move which would have ended schooling for about five thousand blacks. A federal court promptly enjoined the council from putting this shocking plan into effect. Almond had opposed it as "a vicious and retaliatory blow against the Negro race."

The Norfolk *Virginian-Pilot*, with Lenoir Chambers as editor and William Shands Meacham lending valuable support as associate editor, ably set forth the case against the school closings. The *Virginian-Pilot*, alone among major dailies in the state, had opposed massive resistance throughout the entire controversy. For his leadership in this fight Chambers was awarded a Pulitzer Prize.

The Virginia press was overwhelmingly in favor of keeping the schools segregated, as long as that could be done legally, but leading newspapers said after the school closings that a new policy and a new direction would have to be found. They had been willing to support the buying of time by the use of legal devices, in order that the impact of so far-reaching a decision as that in *Brown* v. *Board of Education* might be cushioned and disorder and violence held to a minimum. But when it became obvious that all available legal maneuvers had been exhausted, and that public education was endangered, the press bowed to the edicts of the courts and urged that they be obeyed.

Business leaders throughout the state also became alarmed, lest the uproar and shutting down of schools damage the economic progress of the commonwealth. A group of prominent businessmen and industrialists met with Almond at about this time, and pointed out that new industries would not wish to settle in areas where there was great uncertainty as to the availability of adequate educational facilities. They felt, too, that Virginia's "image" was being severely damaged by massive resistance.

Time was running out. The courts were about to speak, and they did so on January 19, 1959. The Virginia Supreme Court of Appeals, in *Harrison* v. *Day*, outlawed school closing and held, by a vote of 5 to 2, that "the state must support such public free schools in the state as are necessary to an efficient system, including those in which the pupils of both races are compelled to be enrolled and taught together, however unfortunate that situation may be." On the same day, a three-judge federal district court in Norfolk held, in *James* v. *Almond*, that Virginia's statutes calling for shutting down the public schools violated the Fourteenth Amendment, and denied to citizens "the equal protection of the laws."

This was clearly the time for Governor Almond to signalize a change of direction for Virginia. He had anticipated just such rulings for months. Yet he chose to go on the radio with a ripsnorting, defiant speech that surpassed almost any that had gone before. Referring in lurid terms to the "livid stench of sadism, sex immorality and juvenile pregnancy infesting . . . mixed schools," the governor shouted, "Let me make it abundantly clear for the record now and hereafter . . . I will not yield to that which I know to be wrong. . . . We have just begun to fight!"

Congratulations poured in from Senator Byrd and the other hard-core resisters. Almond had lifted their hopes for yet another round of legal gimmicks with which to thwart integration. There were none to be had, of course.

Almond in after years was at a loss to understand why he made what he termed "that damn speech." He was "tired and distraught" and not thinking clearly, he said. His intention had been to assure Virginians that he was doing everything possible to preserve segregation, but he inadvertently gave the impression that he knew of "some way to prevent any mixing of the races in the public schools, when nothing of the sort was possible."

Only eight days after he had delivered himself of this unfortunate rodomontade, Almond went before the General Assembly and made it clear that the line against any integration could no longer be held. All that could be done now, he calmly told the lawmakers, was to minimize racial mixing in the schools. The massive resisters were thunderstruck, and Almond was sneeringly referred to by some of them thereafter as "Benedict" Almond.

He pressed forward, nevertheless, with his new and more moderate program. It included a different type of tuition grant, and stronger laws against violence, together with repeal of the compulsory-education law. Also there would be a commission to study the situation and recommend any further legislation that might be deemed desirable.

Then, on February 2, 1959, twenty-one black children quietly entered the formerly white schools of Norfolk and Arlington. There was heavy police protection, and there were no threats or shouted obscenities, such as disgraced some other states, under similar circumstances.

Almond's more moderate legislative approach was still merely on paper, and getting it through the Assembly would take some doing. Massive resisters tried to organize for a fight to the end.

When the commission, headed by Senator Mosby G. Perrow, Jr., of Lynchburg, a moderate, made its report, the central recommendation was for "freedom of choice," or local option. In order to get this through the senate, it was necessary to adopt the novel expedient of having the senate resolve itself into a Committee of the Whole. Lieutenant Governor A. E. S. Stephens of Isle of Wight, a Southside county, made the crucially important ruling upholding the motion to go into a Committee of the Whole. This would enable the entire senate to vote on Almond's package of legislation, instead of having each bill put to sleep in the old guard-dominated Committee on Education. Stephens' ruling "enraged" those who favored continued resistance, according to James Latimer, the *Times-Dispatch's* superlative political reporter. Among them were Senators Garland Gray, Mills E. Godwin, Jr., and Harry F. Byrd, Jr. It was barely upheld by a majority of one, thanks to the vote of Senator Stuart Carter of Fincastle, who had undergone major surgery but was brought into the chamber on a stretcher to provide the whisker-thin margin of victory. This broke the back of the resistance.

Almond's "freedom of choice" legislation was adopted, albeit by extremely narrow majorities in the senate and somewhat larger ones in the House. Speaker "Blackie" Moore had managed years before to secure the establishment of a State Pupil Placement Board for the assignment of pupils to schools, but this was abolished and local school boards were given back this power. In putting through this legislation, the governor had the support of the more liberal members of the Democratic organization, including a number of former Young Turks, the anti-organization group in both houses, and the Republicans.

Almond's legislation substituted token integration for massive resistance—and thus returned in substantial measure to the Gray Commission's program of four years before. Senator Byrd never forgave him for this, and for not going "the last mile," i.e., to jail. Yet going to jail as a gesture of defiance and all-out resistance would have been the height of futility, and would have meant certain defeat in the end. Virginia would have been the victim of another federal power play, as happened in Arkansas, Mississippi and Alabama, with federal troops enforcing the orders of the court, and the Old Dominion's reputation for obedience to law irreparably damaged. Lindsay Almond is to be thanked for the courageous leadership he gave in avoiding so great a catastrophe. He himself arrived at his final decision to uphold the law by a tortuous route, and after making inflammatory speeches which he later regretted. But as a good lawyer, a political realist and a patriotic Virginian he took, in the end, the only sensible course.

As J. Harvie Wilkinson III puts it, Almond "emerged from his anguished political and personal decisions as the forerunner of a more modern and moderate Democratic party in Virginia." In so doing, "he pioneered policies and coalitions which Albertis Harrison held and Mills Godwin extended in the gubernatorial races of 1961 and 1965." In other words, Governor Almond laid the groundwork for the striking progress in many directions subsequently achieved by Governors Harrison and Godwin.

After his gubernatorial term had ended, Almond was nominated by President Kennedy for the U. S. Court of Customs and Patent Appeals. Senator Byrd kept the nomination from coming to a vote for many months, but finally allowed it to go through. Despite this uncalled-for harassment, Almond remained an admirer of the senator. Byrd felt sincerely that Almond had betrayed Virginia to the integrationists, and he did not speak to Almond from early 1959 until his own death in 1966. Yet in 1967, when Almond was asked to name the greatest Virginian in public life during his era, he named Harry Byrd. "That's the way I feel," he said simply, "and it may surprise some people."[4]

After Governor Almond put through the "freedom of choice" legislation in 1959, he sought to obtain the enactment of a 3 per cent retail sales tax at the regular session of 1960, accompanied by a cut in the personal income tax. His effort was defeated, mainly by the same group that had been fighting him on his school program. But additional funds had to be found somewhere, in order to balance the budget, and these came from higher levies on liquor and beer, as well as from a three cents per pack tax on cigarettes, the first such tax in Virginia history. Known in his youth as a boxer with a "Sunday punch," Almond could be aggressive, and he rammed these levies through.

Another achievement of his administration was the leadership he showed in laying the groundwork for the greater industrial development of the state. He called the first state-wide industrial conference, attended by more than seven hundred business leaders. The Virginia Industrial Development Corporation was established, and the modernization and expansion of the port facilities of Hampton Roads also was begun. Much larger appropriations for industrial advertising were made available.

With the enactment of Almond's "freedom of choice" legislation, the era of massive resistance came virtually to an end. The one exception was in Prince Edward County, which occupied a special status, since this black belt county was one of the five original defendants in the NAACP's school segregation cases before the U. S. Supreme Court. The county was ordered by that tribunal in May 1959, to desegregate its schools in September. Responding to the overwhelming desire of the county's white population, the board of supervisors decided to abandon public education. It made no appropriation for public schools, and those institutions accordingly did not open at the time specified by the court. The white children of the county were accommodated in private academies.

For four years, the Negro boys and girls of Prince Edward were

without schools. Finally, in 1963, the Prince Edward Free School
Foundation was established with federal funds. Colgate W. Darden,
Jr., was chairman of the trustees, and experienced educators from
throughout the nation went to the county to aid the young blacks to
the extent that this was possible. As a matter of fact, the lost years
could never be fully made up, and that was the tragedy of Prince
Edward. After the foundation had been functioning for twelve months,
the Supreme Court ordered Prince Edward to reopen its public
schools, and it obeyed. In October 1970, only forty-six white boys
and girls were attending these schools. All the others remained in
privately financed Prince Edward Academy.

However, reports from the county indicated that a new spirit of
co-operation and a renewed concern for public education were in
evidence. The bitterness of earlier years had abated, a Negro had been
appointed to the school board, and a new superintendent of schools
had been chosen. But there could never be full compensation for the
lost school years of Prince Edward's black boys and girls.

The end of the era of massive resistance aroused mixed emotions
in the minds and hearts of Virginians. Some felt it to have been worth
all the effort that had gone into it, since it had "bought time" for the
radical adjustment in race relations that had to come. Others regarded
the era as a stain on the good name of the commonwealth and best
forgotten.

There was an unverified report that someone high up in the organization hierarchy remarked at the height of the resistance that
"this policy will keep us in power for another twenty-five years." If
the statement was made, it was based on one of the worst political
miscalculations of modern times in Virginia. For the Democratic machine headed by Senator Byrd was on the verge of breaking up in the
early sixties, and it did break up shortly thereafter. A primary result of
the fight over massive resistance was to split the Byrd machine into
factions, and to accelerate its collapse.

If a different policy had been followed, such as that outlined by the
Gray Commission in its original report, the results might well have
been more fortunate, not only for Virginia as a whole, but for the
Byrd organization. Token integration, such as the Gray report proposed, worked reasonably well in North Carolina and other southern
states in those early days, without the closing of schools. If Virginia

had taken this road at the outset it would have set a better example to the nation, and at the same time there would, in all likelihood, have been adequate opportunity for adjustment to the new and difficult dispensation.

THIRTY-NINE

Virginia: The New Dominion

DESPITE the end of massive resistance, the controversy over integration was far from over. It would continue into the indefinite future. However, blacks in moderate numbers were being admitted to the public schools without violence of any kind. Virginia was the only state on the Atlantic seaboard from Florida to Massachusetts where the National Guard did not have to be called out between 1954 and 1970 to quell interracial disturbances. Richmond, the onetime Confederate capital, achieved the transition in schools and other areas so smoothly that Arthur Krock, writing in the New York *Times*, called it "a model for every town, city and county in the United States." Richmond's excellent record in integrating its schools was mainly due to an extraordinarily capable and courageous pair of leaders—H. I. Willett, city superintendent of schools, who had just served a term as president of the American Association of School Administrators, and Lewis F. Powell, Jr., chairman of the city school board, who served shortly thereafter as president of the American Bar Association.

Yet in Richmond and elsewhere throughout the state most white citizens were not happy over the situation. It was difficult for many Virginians to revolutionize their racial attitudes and their thinking over so brief a span. There were times, furthermore, when serious trouble seemed on the verge of breaking out. But it never did, and the riots and the mayhem, the burnings and the lootings that took place in so many states did not occur in Virginia. Nor was any part of the commonwealth taken over by federal troops.

Lindsay Almond's successor as governor in 1962 was Albertis S. Harrison, the handsome, platinum-topped attorney general, who was an organization man from Brunswick County in the Southside, but who was a good enough lawyer to know that massive resistance couldn't last. He was viewed askance by the all-out resisters, since he had tended to side with Almond in the bitter infighting that took place at the session of 1959. As he was clearly the strongest and best-qualified of the organization's gubernatorial aspirants, he was tapped by the inner circle. Harrison was another example of the high caliber of men chosen by the machine for office. It was the organization's insistence on men of integrity and stature that kept it in power for so long.

Harrison would not win the governorship without a contest, however, for Lieutenant Governor A. E. S. Stephens announced his candidacy. If Robert Whitehead had not died suddenly the year before, he might have opposed Harrison. Stephens, who had trained with the organization, repudiated some of its orthodoxies in 1959, as we have seen, when he ruled that the senate could go into a Committee of the Whole. He deviated still further during his campaign against Harrison, criticizing the organization for its failure to cultivate and promote its knowledgeable and aspiring young men. He then made the grievous blunder of denouncing Senator Byrd in a speech at Winchester before the senator's friends and neighbors. Byrd promptly released a letter to the press in which Stephens had solicited his support and had termed him one of the great Virginians of his time.

There never was any doubt as to the outcome. Harrison won handily, as did those on the ticket with him—Senator Mills E. Godwin, Jr., of Nansemond County for lieutenant governor, and Senator Robert Y. Button of Culpeper for attorney general. Godwin defeated Senator Armistead Boothe, and Button defeated T. Munford Boyd, a greatly beloved blind member of the University of Virginia law faculty.

Since Albertis Harrison came into the governor's office without the albatross of massive resistance around his neck, he could address himself to the pressing problems of the commonwealth. That had been virtually impossible for his predecessor while the state and its people were being swept up in the furor over racial integration. Plenty of such problems were lying around for the new governor's attention.

He struck a much-needed note in his inaugural address, when he said: "If I were to fix one goal for Virginia during the final decades of this century, it would be the expansion of the minds of our people within the tradition of the Virginia character. And if I were to venture even the gentlest criticism of our beloved state, it would be that in times past we have not expanded sufficiently our intellectual, cultural and social horizons."

Harrison approached the state's problems in a quiet and methodical manner, precisely the reverse of that of the flamboyant Bill Tuck and without the stem-winding oratory of Lindsay Almond. He concluded that the state's basic need was much greater industrial expansion. By satisfying that need he felt that the commonwealth would be able to travel a substantial distance toward the broader horizons which he envisioned.

Greatly increased state revenues as a result of prosperity, a large surplus in the treasury, and bigger than expected returns from the newly enacted state withholding tax on incomes were helpful in the desired direction. Harrison escalated the intake by bringing in more and more industries. Increased vocational and technical education was an integral part of the effort, as was the proposed deepening of the James River channel from Richmond to Hampton Roads, from twenty-five to thirty-five feet. Taking a broad view of the river project, Harrison said it was certain that the port of Hampton Roads "with its vast servicing facilities, also will benefit." A legislative commission created by the General Assembly in 1962 reported that the valuable seed-oyster beds on the lower James would not be damaged, a judgment confirmed by the Virginia Institute of Marine Science.

During the four years of Harrison's term, more than a billion dollars was invested in Virginia by private industry in new and expanded plants, adding 177,000 new jobs. Per capita income rose from $1894 to $2373, giving Virginia first rank among the southeastern states. Virginia's employment rate remained among the very best in the nation, although there was 8 to 10 per cent unemployment in the six coal-producing counties of southwest Virginia.

The state was getting predominantly high-wage industries, calling for increasingly better levels of skill and knowledge. With this in view, the governor launched a totally new program of technical education beyond the high school, together with a greatly expanded community and branch college service in every section of Virginia. Thus Harrison paved the way for the establishment under his successor of a comprehensive system of community colleges. Creation of this system was recommended in 1965 by the Virginia Higher Education Study Commission, of which Senator Lloyd C. Bird of Chesterfield County was chairman. This notable report was a landmark in the advancement of education in Virginia. Taken in conjunction with the advisory service rendered by the increasingly important State Council of Higher Education, the stage was set for meaningful progress. The Council of Higher Education came into its own under the able five-year directorship of Dr. Prince B. Woodard.

Governor Harrison provided much the largest appropriations for public schools and institutions of higher learning in the state's history up to that time. The emphasis he placed on higher education was also seen in a special item in the budget to enable the colleges and universities to raise professors' salaries to the national average. He arranged, furthermore, for funds to aid in attracting exceptional scholars to their campuses.

Preservation of unspoiled areas of the state for recreational purposes was the object of a commission appointed by the governor, and headed by Senator FitzGerald Bemiss. This commission rendered an extraordinarily comprehensive and valuable report in 1965, and the 1966 General Assembly created the State Commission of Outdoor Recreation, of which Bemiss was chairman and Elbert Cox, who had made an excellent record with the National Park Service, became director. At the same session, the Assembly appropriated $4,470,000 for the purchase of large tracts of land for parks and other recreational purposes, a sum which was virtually matched by the federal government. By late 1970, approximately $17,000,000 additional had been made available from the state and federal treasuries, and seven new state parks had been established. Twenty-eight regional or local park projects were in various states of readiness, and a total of over $7,000,000 had been provided for them from the same two governmental sources.

By recommending special taxes, Governor Harrison laid the groundwork for state participation in financing the new system of interstate highways spanning the commonwealth largely paid for by the federal government.

During the Harrison administration, and especially during the year 1964, several things happened to shake the Byrd organization. The Twenty-fourth Amendment to the U. S. Constitution became effective, and it banned the poll tax as a prerequisite to voting in federal elections. Two years later the U. S. Supreme Court banned the tax in Virginia's state elections, thus wiping out one of the organization's most valuable means of keeping the electorate small and therefore controllable.

The same tribunal ruled in 1964 that seats in both branches of a state legislature had to be apportioned on a population basis. Virginia had a much better record than most states in this respect, but its assembly districts were laid out in a manner to give disproportionate representation to the rural areas, usually Democratic organization strongholds. The General Assembly acted in 1964, and transferred eleven seats in the 140-man legislature from rural to urban constituencies. Northern Virginia, adjacent to Washington, acquired six of these seats, while the other five went to the fast-growing region around Hampton Roads. An inexorable trend toward ultimate political domination by the urban and suburban areas was under way.

The year 1964 also witnessed the first defeat for the Byrd organization in a state Democratic convention. It was, furthermore, a personal defeat for Senator Byrd. The issue was whether to endorse President Lyndon Johnson for another term. Byrd had expressed himself in vehement opposition to such an endorsement, mainly because of Johnson's stand on civil rights. Yet, after a tempestuous session, punctuated by yells, boos and catcalls, the assembled Democrats finally voted by a slight margin to endorse Johnson. "We won, boys, we won!" shouted exuberant Representative Pat Jennings, who was serving his sixth term from the anti-Byrd Ninth District of southwest Virginia. "It's been a long dry spell, but we won!"

In the presidential campaign that fall between Johnson and Barry Goldwater, both Governor Harrison and Lieutenant Governor Godwin remained "regular" and endorsed the Democratic ticket. They also boarded the Lady Bird Special, the train on which Mrs. Johnson was campaigning through Virginia on behalf of her husband. In doing so, they called down upon their heads fervent imprecations from ultraconservative Virginia politicians, but they solidified their positions with other elements. It was, in fact, one of the things that made Mills Godwin unbeatable when he ran for governor the following year.

Johnson carried Virginia, a state that had gone Republican in every other presidential election since 1952, and would be swept by Nixon four years later. From 100,000 to 150,000 Negroes are estimated to have voted in the 1964 presidential contest, practically all of them for Johnson. They provided his margin of victory.

Almost at the end of Harrison's gubernatorial administration, in

November 1965, Harry F. Byrd, seventy-eight and in failing health, announced his retirement from the U. S. Senate. He had been elected for six consecutive terms, more than anyone in Virginia history. He was genuinely ill, and the fact that the Byrd machine was distintegrating had nothing to do with his decision to retire. He died the following October of a malignant brain tumor.

As a member of the Senate since 1933, Byrd had battled against prevailing trends, even when his course was highly unpopular in Virginia. Quantities of half-baked and extravagant legislation were introduced in Congress over the years, and much of it was subjected to Byrd's devastating analysis. He served for a quarter of a century as chairman of the Joint Committee on Reduction of Non-Essential Expenditures, and in that capacity probably saved the taxpayers billions.

A conspicuous example of his ability with fiscal matters is seen in a letter he wrote to Marriner S. Eccles, chairman of the board of the Federal Reserve System, in response to Eccles' contention that government debts and deficits are good in themselves. Byrd's communication, which appears in the *Congressional Record* for January 16, 1939, shows that he wielded a pungent pen. He not only dealt effectively with Eccles' arguments but dug up quotations from Eccles' own addresses in which the Federal Reserve official answered and contradicted himself.

A poor speaker in his early days, Byrd gradually developed a more adequate platform technique. Never an orator or phrasemaker, he impressed his audiences with the solid content of his speeches and the sincerity with which they were delivered. In a debate with the scholarly and articulate Senator Paul H. Douglas of Illinois before the American Academy of Political Science in 1950, on the subject "American Democracy and the Welfare State," Byrd obviously was judged by the discriminating audience to have had the better of it. This is shown by the frequency with which the words "laughter" and "applause" are sprinkled through the transcript of his remarks, whereas they appear much less frequently in those of Senator Douglas. Furthermore, Byrd received a standing ovation at the close, while Douglas did not.

Harry Byrd was much more conservative than most leaders of his era, too conservative, in fact. He was against nearly everything that was happening in Washington on the domestic front—while supporting most administration proposals in the area of foreign affairs. Having come up the hard way in his youth, he had trouble grasping the fact that many persons lacked his ability and drive, and that even those with ambition and competence could be trapped by circumstances beyond their control. Yet none could question that he had the courage of his convictions.

In his personal integrity Byrd set an example for all men in public life. He even refused to accept over $200,000 in federal soil-conservation payments, to which he was fully entitled, on the ground that he had voted for the law under which the payments would be made. He steadfastly declined to sell a single apple to the federal government from his enormous orchards.

As head for some four decades of the Virginia machine, a "julep-cooled antique," in the words of a magazine writer, Byrd was mainly responsible for the high caliber of the state's public servants. To him, more than to any man, is due the fact that politics in Virginia during his time was almost totally free of even the suspicion of crookedness, thievery or graft. The only exceptions worth noting were the local election frauds, mainly in the southwest.

Byrd hated the word "machine." He described the political faction he headed as "a loose organization of friends who believe in the same principles of government." But this "loose organization" was capable of functioning with tight cohesion, if not ruthlessness. In addition, Byrd's almost lifelong adherence to the principle of pay-as-you-go put Virginia in a straitjacket, and starved the state's public services. Pay-as-you-go became a sacred cow, and woe to the candidate for office in Virginia who sought to tinker with it.

Numerous persons who disagreed with Senator Byrd in Washington admired, respected and liked him. A gracious host, charming companion and courteous foe—although capable of occasional demagoguery —[1] he was almost worshiped by many. Yet large numbers of working-class citizens, especially Negroes, detested him. They felt that he did not have their interests at heart.

When he died at his handsome home, Rosemont, near Berryville, it was indeed a turning point in the history of the state.

Upon Byrd's retirement from the Senate, Governor Harrison had appointed State Senator Harry F. Byrd, Jr., to succeed his father, until the general election the following year. That election was to be a fateful one in various respects, for Harry Byrd, Jr., was not only running, but Senator A. Willis Robertson was up for re-election, as was Representative Howard W. Smith. With the Byrd organization already shaky, its leader hopelessly ill, and these key figures going before the electorate, 1966 would be memorable in Virginia's political annals.

Harry Byrd, Jr., had served eighteen years in the senate of Virginia. He was chiefly notable there for his sponsorship of the automatic-tax-refund law, and for his leadership among the massive resisters. Throughout his public career he had dwelt in the shadow of his illustrious father, whom he resembled in many ways and whose philosophy he shared. He had the senior Byrd's warmth in personal contact with those he found congenial. As editor of the Winchester *Evening Star* and publisher of the Harrisonburg *News-Record* he was an experienced and competent newspaperman.

A new and stricter federal civil rights law became effective in 1965. Under its terms, federal registrars could be sent to states in which fewer than 50 per cent of the citizens of voting age had cast their ballots in the previous presidential election. Since Virginia's percentage of participation had been only 41, the implication was that citizens there had been prevented from voting through literacy tests and other devices. Such an implication was unjustified, insofar as Virginia was concerned. The U. S. Civil Rights Commission had reported in 1961 no "significant racially motivated impediments to voting" anywhere in the state, and the NAACP had reached a similar conclusion a few years previously. When Negro organizations put on a registration drive in Southside Virginia in 1965, they found few serious hindrances to their activities. The only one of any slight importance seems to have been occasional difficulty in locating registrars at convenient times or places. No federal registrars were sent into Virginia under the civil rights law, although they were dispatched to several other southern states.[2]

Voting was now wide open to illiterates. Fortunately, the illiteracy rate for Virginians fourteen years and over had been reduced to 3.4 per cent by 1960.

Lieutenant Governor Mills Godwin was ambitious to succeed Albertis Harrison as governor, and he announced his candidacy in January 1965. His record as a foremost "massive resister" and as a leader in defeating a sales tax four years before did not handicap him as he prepared to espouse programs and policies that would carry Virginia into the new age. He performed a virtual political miracle by getting the conservatives as well as the liberals behind him. The Byrd organization leadership endorsed him, evidently on the assumption that he would not stray too far from the principles and policies laid down by Virginia's senior U. S. Senator. At the same time the Virginia AFL-CIO and Negro leaders backed him, apparently on the theory that his heart was in the right place, and that they might expect him to be more co-operative than previous organization governors, few of whom had had support from labor unions and blacks. Godwin made no apologies for his past record. Discussing his position on massive resistance several years later, he said, "No man could have survived in public office, especially in Southside, if he was 'soft' on integration." He also argued that when Lindsay Almond proposed a sales tax, the time was not ripe for it.

Democrats of all factions backed Godwin so solidly that he had no opposition in the primary. In the general election he was opposed by A. Linwood Holton, Jr., a forty-one-year-old Republican attorney from Roanoke, and by William J. Story, Jr., a member of the John Birch Society and former superintendent of schools for South Norfolk, who was the nominee of the newly formed Conservative party. Holton put on an aggressive campaign. As a progressive member of the GOP, he attacked the failure of the Democrats to provide adequate public services. Story, the Conservative candidate, proclaimed that both Democrats and Republicans were "slowly moving down the road to socialistic, Communistic, Marxist control" of Virginia. The Democrats, under Godwin would, it appeared, help to destroy the American way of life. Godwin's ride on the Lady Bird Special the previous year would never be forgiven.

Godwin was taunted by Holton concerning his record on massive resistance. He replied that it bought valuable time during which Virginians were able to adjust to conditions that had to come, but for which there had been inadequate preparation.

He was moving steadily away from the standpat policies he had previously followed and in the direction of those which would enable Virginia to cope with what he called "the whirlwind of change." He recognized the essential necessity for improved public services, and for providing the funds to pay for them.

The people of Virginia were ripe for such doctrine, and when the votes were counted in November, Godwin had won handily, although the Conservatives prevented him from getting a majority. He polled nearly 48 per cent of the vote, Holton nearly 38 per cent, and Story a surprising 13.4 per cent. Most of the 75,000 who backed Story were from the Southside, and many of them would be among the 321,000 Virginians voting for George Wallace of Alabama for President in 1968 against Nixon and Humphrey. Holton's showing for governor in 1965 was a creditable one, especially since his Republican backers spent far less money than the Democrats.

The primary and election of 1965 were sufficiently unusual, but those of 1966 were even more so.

State Senator Armistead Boothe announced against Harry Byrd, Jr., for the U. S. Senate. Boothe had been manhandled to such a degree by the machine leadership for a number of years that he was driven to assume much greater hostility toward the organization than he would otherwise have shown.

He gave Byrd the fight of his life, and almost defeated him. A seasoned and relaxed campaigner, quick in repartee and endowed with a ready wit, he jabbed at Byrd and parried his thrusts. Boothe got the Negro, the labor and the liberal vote. When the ballots were counted, he was found to have come within 8225 votes of winning, in a record-breaking primary turnout of over 434,000.

Senator A. Willis Robertson was opposed in the same 1966 primary by State Senator William B. Spong, Jr., of Portsmouth. Robertson was seventy-nine years old, had been in politics for half a century, was known throughout Virginia, and had never been defeated for public office. Spong was forty-five, had served with ability in the General Assembly for a dozen years, but was little known beyond the confines of lower Tidewater.

Despite his advanced years, Robertson was in remarkably fine physical and mental condition. A football star and hammer-throwing champion in his college days, he became an avid huntsman and fisherman who believed in a drastic regimen of daily exercise. Charles Houston, veteran Richmond *News Leader* columnist, noted in 1965 that Robertson not only read fine print without glasses, but "his biceps are like steel, his legs like oak saplings, and his abdomen as undentable as a brick wall."

Robertson had been born in 1887, a short distance beyond the Virginia line in Martinsburg, West Virginia. In the same town only a few blocks away and two weeks later a baby named Harry F. Byrd saw the light. Thus, by one of the most extraordinary coincidences in history, these men who were to serve together for two decades in the U. S.

Senate from the same state were born at almost exactly the same time and place in another state.

As a congressman and senator, Willis Robertson became an authority in several fields—foreign trade, the tariff, banking, currency, taxation and conservation. He shared much of Harry Byrd's antagonism to excessive spending and centralization, but was never a member of the Byrd machine's inner circle. Of all his activities, he regarded those in the sphere of wildlife conservation as perhaps the most important. "I would be happy," he once declared, "if history records my efforts in behalf of conservation as a worthwhile contribution to my day and generation." He was particularly concerned for the preservation of the forests from destruction and the rivers from pollution, and in this was ahead of his time. In 1946 he received the *Field and Stream* Award as the nation's premier conservationist.

His rival, Bill Spong, achieved a record of moderation during his dozen years in the General Assembly. He was a Young Turk, and as such had been willing to buck the organization. He was chairman of a commission on public education, created during Governor Stanley's administration, and in that capacity was chiefly responsible for an extremely thorough and valuable study of the needs of Virginia's public schools.

The contest between Robertson and Spong was a lively one and the result was in doubt until the last ballot was counted. Since Spong was not well known throughout the state, he spent much of his time pumping hands in every corner of the commonwealth. In his speeches, he relied on a sober presentation of the facts, expressed in an almost startling drawl. Robertson, by contrast, was an orator in the style of a century ago, often speaking without a manuscript, and interlarding his remarks with quotations from the classics and homely anecdotes, while accompanying his words with emphatic gestures.

Robertson's advanced age damaged him with the electorate. So did contributions made to his campaign by bankers. As chairman of the Senate Banking and Currency Committee Robertson impressed and aided the bankers, and they supported him. The extent of their support was exaggerated during the campaign, but it helped to explain the final outcome. Robertson lost to Spong by 611 votes.

The third momentous contest of that same July 1966 primary was between eighty-three-year-old Congressman Howard W. Smith of Alexandria, seeking renomination for his nineteenth term from the

Eighth Congressional District, and delegate George C. Rawlings, Jr., of Fredericksburg, his young, noisy and liberal challenger. Smith, an honest, highly respected ultraconservative former judge, was perhaps to the right of Harry Byrd, Sr., in his political views. When it was pointed out to him that he had voted against two-thirds of the administration's bills, he remarked wryly that maybe he ought to apologize for supporting the other third. As chairman of the powerful House Rules Committee for many years, he was denounced by liberals for holding up their legislation. He was even charged with deliberately absenting himself on his Fauquier County farm at critical moments. Governor Mills Godwin said jokingly at a dinner in tribute to Judge Smith that "no other man has made the judicious use of a dairy farm an instrument of national policy."

The Negro vote, the labor vote and the liberal vote all went to Rawlings, as they did to Boothe and Spong. Rawlings nosed out Smith by 645 votes. Smith's long career was at an end, but Rawlings did not get to Congress. William L. Scott, a Republican lawyer from Fairfax, defeated him. Thousands of conservative Democrats voted Republican in the election and turned the tide. The same thing happened when W. Pat Jennings was defeated by Republican William C. Wampler in his campaign for a seventh consecutive term from the Ninth District of southwest Virginia. In both cases, conservative Democrats backed the nominee of the GOP against his liberal Democratic opponent. The Republicans now held four of Virginia's ten congressional seats. Republican sentiment was rising in the state as the Byrd organization grew weaker.

The group of political thinkers in the Neanderthal tradition calling themselves the Virginia Conservative party had a major degree of responsibility for the defeat of Willis Robertson and Howard Smith, and for the narrow escape of Harry Byrd, Jr. The Conservatives urged their followers to stay out of the primary, since Robertson and Byrd had failed to resign from the "foul and filthy" Democratic party, and hence were not deserving of support. This played directly into the hands of the more liberal Spong and Rawlings, whose narrow margins over their opponents could be attributed to the fact that Conservatives who would have voted for Robertson and Smith, had they entered the primary, did not vote at all. The Conservative party apparently took pride in accomplishing the retirement from public life of two of the most influential conservatives in Congress.

This same group, it will be recalled, had opposed Mills Godwin when he ran for governor the preceding year, since Godwin, it appeared, was somehow vaguely tainted with the "communist conspiracy." Actually, of course, Godwin was firmly rooted in the Virginia tradition, and determined to make modern Virginia worthy of its great past. Few had ever heard him mention the fact, but the Godwins came to the colony even earlier than the Byrds, and were prominent and influential there in the seventeenth century.

When Mills Godwin was inaugurated as governor in January 1966, he wore thermal underwear against the icy blasts, but his program was warmly received by the legislators and the people. That program was one of the most comprehensive and ambitious in Virginia annals, and the political climate was ripe for change. Godwin had just enough affiliation with the old order in Virginia politics to be able to hold its support, and just enough *rapport* with younger elements to enlist their backing. The Byrd organization had counted on rural voters for the bulk of its strength, but the state was rapidly becoming urbanized, and Godwin would show a clear recognition of this fact by making a special appeal to the cities and their fast-growing suburbs.

Adoption of a sales tax was the first order of business, if Virginia, both urban and rural, was to receive the public services its people were demanding, and if the commonwealth was to avoid falling hopelessly behind its sister states. Schools, colleges, hospitals, health, roads, welfare and recreation all needed huge infusions of additional money.

Albertis Harrison and Mills Godwin were close political friends, and as Harrison's term neared its end, he had conferred with the lieutenant governor on policies and programs. This was particularly true with respect to a sales tax. Enactment of such a levy had been discussed for about a decade and a half, and now the time had come to put it on the books. Fifteen municipalities had enacted sales taxes of their own, and if this kept up the one remaining important untapped source of state revenue would be pre-empted, and it would probably be impossible ever to get a state sales tax through the General Assembly. So Governor Harrison recommended a 2 per cent tax, with half of the receipts going to the localities. These terms differed from those to be proposed by Governor Godwin, but the basic idea was similar.

Godwin and his progressive program were confronted at the outset by the fact that Speaker Blackburn Moore still sat enthroned in the House, Senator Garland Gray still presided over the powerful Democratic caucus, and other old-time Byrd conservatives, in their sixties, seventies and eighties, held crucial committee chairmanships. The governor managed to retain the good will of these organization stalwarts, while, with masterful expertise and timing, he moved to the middle of the road. As part of that shifting process, he gave appointments and other recognition to urban assemblymen who in earlier years had been passed over by the machine leadership because of their slightly unorthodox views.

Godwin's superb handling of the lawmakers paid off in various ways, including an achievement seemingly unique in Virginia history. He not only got through a 2 per cent sales tax, with a 1 per cent additional optional tax for the cities and counties, effective July 1, 1966, but he also obtained the passage of another 1 per cent state levy, effective July 1, 1968. This last amounted to usurping the prerogatives of the next General Assembly, but it enabled the governor to make long-term plans with the assurance that adequate financing would be forthcoming.

Another conspicuous achievement of Governor Godwin at the legislative session of 1966 was the laying of the foundations for a system of two-year, low-tuition community colleges, offering vocational, technical and liberal arts courses. The state had long been at or near the bottom in the percentage of its young citizens in college, and unlike most other states, it had no community colleges. A system of twenty-two such institutions was projected in legislation adopted in 1966. Dr. Dana B. Hamel was named head of the system, and Eugene B. Sydnor, Jr., chairman of the board. Under their knowledgeable direction great progress has been made, and by the end of 1970, no fewer than sixteen of these colleges, with 38,000 students, over 2300 of them from minority groups, were actually in operation. Enrollment was well ahead of forecasts, and 120,000 students were expected by 1980.

A tremendous infusion of additional funds for the four-year state-supported colleges, as well as for the public schools, was another salient achievement of the 1966 session. In his inaugural address, Godwin had said that Virginia "is of the nation, and it is by the nation's standards that we are now called upon to judge her." He was seeking to bring the lagging commonwealth to a position competitive with rival states, many of which were likewise putting forth heroic efforts and appropriating unprecedentedly large sums for educational purposes. It was impossible, of course, to close the yawning gap at a single legislative session, or several sessions, but a real start had been made.

In the autumn of 1966, Godwin called a state-wide Conference on Education, designed to carry Virginia forward to new heights. Held in Richmond's Mosque on October 5, it was the largest gathering of its kind in Virginia history. Official delegates from every corner of the state filled the entire auditorium, while many interested citizens thronged the mezzanine. Much enthusiasm was manifested.

Governor Godwin delivered an inspirational address in which he declared that "it is time to shed the comfortable arguments, the warm and familiar excuses, the pleasant encumbrances of the old ways, for we know in our hearts that they will not serve us now." The "old ways," with their prime emphasis on balancing the budget, no matter how many Virginians were denied state services, were on the way out.

This became doubly apparent when Thomas C. Boushall, prominent Richmond banker, proposed abandonment of the long sacroscanct pay-as-you-go method of financing. Boushall suggested that the state constitution "be promptly amended to permit the issuance of bonds limited to use in public educational affairs." The jettisoning of pay-as-you-go had been advocated at the 1964 session of the General Assembly, and had won a surprising degree of support. Boushall's suggestion, coming from so respected and responsible a source, was the beginning of a state-wide debate, and gave great impetus to the movement for the issuance of general obligation bonds by the commonwealth.

The state-wide Conference on Education at Richmond was followed by eight regional meetings, at each of which Godwin spoke. He was building grass roots support for his program.

With schools, colleges, hospitals and highways calling constantly for more revenue, despite the receipt of many millions from the sales tax, the time had come for the final climactic assault on the citadel of pay-as-you-go. The first steps were recommended by Godwin to the 1968 legislature—that Virginia make use of the limited borrowing authority already in the constitution, and that a commission be appointed to revise the entire document. The constitution, as written, allowed the issuance of $81,000,000 worth of general obligation bonds, if approved by the General Assembly and the voters. Although this provision had been included in the organic law in 1928 with the specific approval of Governor Harry F. Byrd, it had never been used, and many ultraconservatives shuddered at the thought of thus "plunging the state into debt." But Mills Godwin put the weight of his popularity and power behind the move, declaring that if this step was not taken, Virginia's progress would come to "a grinding halt." The General Assembly approved the proposal and also provided for the creation of the commission to revise the constitution. That fall the $81,000,000 bond issue was thumpingly endorsed, almost 2 to 1, by the voters.

The Commission on Constitutional Revision, with former Governor Albertis Harrison, then a justice on the Virginia Supreme Court of Appeals, as chairman, had set to work meanwhile to rewrite the constitution, with liberalization of the severe restrictions against bond issues as a major objective. When the task was completed, a special session of the General Assembly in 1969 reviewed and ratified the results. There emerged a streamlined document, replacing the verbose constitution of 1902 with one hardly half as long. In addition, reasonably safeguarded provisions for the issuance of general obligation bonds were included.

In another section, the legislature added a requirement that the Assembly meet annually instead of biennially. This new constitution went before the people in 1970, after Godwin had gone out of office, but with the firm support of his Republican successor, Governor A. Linwood Holton, Jr., and practically every other important leader in both the Republican and Democratic parties. It was ratified overwhelmingly.

Mills Godwin had taken Virginia out of the rut in which she had been wallowing for decades. He had not only obtained passage of a sales tax, but he had put over an $81,000,000 bond issue and liberalized the constitution to permit other bond issues. As James Latimer expressed it, "Ten years ago no Virginia politician in his right mind would have believed any governor in his right mind would have advocated or tried all these things." Yet, Latimer went on, Godwin realized all three objectives "with an amazing minimum of opposition, rancor and political flak."

Among far-reaching developments in the educational sphere had been the appointment in 1966 of a legislative commission, headed by Edward A. Wayne, president of Richmond's Federal Reserve Bank, to consider the advisability of combining the Medical College of Virginia with Richmond Professional Institute into an urban university, designed specifically to meet the needs of an urban community. The commission rendered an exceptional report, recommending that the plan be carried out, and Virginia Commonwealth University was born. By the end of 1970 it was going forward steadily under President Warren W. Brandt and had over 14,000 students. Its Health Sciences Division (MCV) had performed heart transplants on several patients, one of whom was at that time the longest surviving such patient in the world.

The University of Virginia observed its 150th anniversary in 1969 with an appropriate program. Under President Edgar F. Shannon, Jr., the institution's academic standing was advancing dramatically and its graduate and research facilities were attracting scholars from many lands. The Alderman Library's usefulness was especially enhanced by the Clifton Waller Barrett collection of American literature, probably the greatest such collection on the globe, and the McGregor collection on American history. A first-rate University Press, available to scholars throughout the state, was established and was publishing the papers of George Washington, along with incisive studies of the contemporary scene.

The College of William and Mary exhibited significant characteristics of a university, under President Davis Y. Paschall. It began offering the Ph.D. degree in several disciplines, including history, psychology and certain sciences, while continuing to operate its law school. Entrance requirements and scholastic standards were markedly raised.

In 1970 Virginia Polytechnic Institute became Virginia Polytechnic Institute and State University, a name reflecting its greatly enlarged role in the life of the commonwealth. Under President T. Marshall Hahn, Jr., the institution notably strengthened its graduate and undergraduate offerings in business, arts and the sciences, and underwent an overall upgrading and broadening of its curriculum.

Dr. Hahn served with diligence and insight as chairman of the Metropolitan Areas Study Commission, created on Governor Godwin's recommendation. The many problems arising from the population explosion in certain sections of Virginia were pressing for attention. These were particularly acute in the metropolitan areas—the conglomerates which included a core city and surrounding regions, bringing difficulties and perplexities new to the state.

The "urban corridor," extending from Washington, D.C., southward through Fredericksburg and Richmond to the Hampton Roads area,

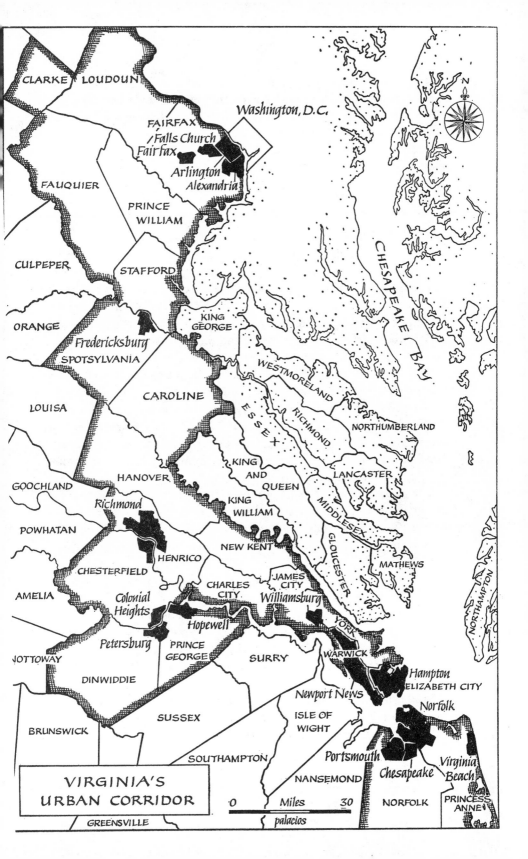

CLARKE · LOUDOUN

FAIRFAX
Falls Church
Fairfax
Arlington
Alexandria

Washington, D.C.

FAUQUIER

PRINCE
WILLIAM

CULPEPER

STAFFORD

ORANGE

KING
GEORGE

Fredericksburg

SPOTSYLVANIA

CAROLINE

WESTMORELAND

RICHMOND

E S S E X

NORTHUMBERLAND

LOUISA

KING
AND
QUEEN

LANCASTER

GOOCHLAND

HANOVER

KING
WILLIAM

MIDDLESEX

Richmond

NEW KENT

POWHATAN

HENRICO

GLOUCESTER

MATHEWS

CHESTERFIELD

CHARLES
CITY

JAMES
CITY

Williamsburg

AMELIA

Colonial
Heights

Hopewell

YORK

Petersburg

PRINCE
GEORGE

SURRY

WARWICK

NOTTOWAY

DINWIDDIE

Hampton
ELIZABETH CITY

Newport News

Norfolk

ISLE OF
WIGHT

NORTHAMPTON

BRUNSWICK

SUSSEX

Portsmouth

Chesapeake

Virginia
Beach

SOUTHAMPTON

NANSEMOND

NORFOLK

PRINCESS
ANNE

VIRGINIA'S
URBAN CORRIDOR

0   Miles   30

palacios

GREENSVILLE

CHESAPEAKE BAY

N

and embracing a number of urbanized counties along the way, contained something like 57 per cent of the state's population, including the six largest cities. Jean Gottmann, the eminent French geographer, coined the word "Megalopolis" to describe the heavily populated and industrialized belt from Boston to Washington, including part of Virginia's northern fringe. It seemed only a question of time before Megalopolis extended through Richmond and on to Norfolk, Portsmouth and Newport News. Virginia's projected population in 1980 is put by some as high as 6,000,000, with three-fifths living in the urban corridor. Yet there is evidence that many rural families are choosing to remain in the Virginia countryside. The steady trend toward the cities has been slowing down.

The impact of the federal government on the urban corridor is tremendous. This is pointed out by A. E. Dick Howard, the University of Virginia's brilliant young law professor, who directed the publication of *Virginia's Urban Corridor*, under the university's auspices, and who was a crucially important factor, as executive director of the Virginia Constitutional Revision Commission, in the adoption of the state's revised constitution. "Northern Virginia is what it is largely because of the growth of Washington, D.C.," Howard writes in his introduction. "Similarly on both sides of Hampton Roads . . . military bases and other government operations are mainstays of the area's economy. Nowhere else in Virginia is the federal government in such a pivotal position to influence the development and solution of area problems."

The corridor also is becoming increasingly important in the political life of the state, a process accelerated in 1971 through the reshuffling by the General Assembly of congressional and assembly districts to take account of the shifting population. And while the Negro and labor union votes are large there, so is the Republican vote. Of the twelve Republicans elected to the General Assembly in 1969 for the first time, eleven were from that heavily urbanized section.

The Hahn Metropolitan Areas Study Commission devoted nearly two years to formulating its comprehensive report on the problems of the urban corridor and the state's other greatly congested urban areas. Its findings and recommendations were communicated to the legislature in 1968.

Establishment of regional planning districts was a salient accomplishment which grew out of the report. In addition, the State Division of Planning was reconstituted as the Division of Planning and Community Affairs. This agency formalized the planning districts and trained 1500 local officials in modern community planning and administration.

Unfortunately, political considerations prevented the adoption of much of the Hahn report. An important proposal that was rejected called for creation of a Commission on Local Government, with broad powers to restructure political subdivisions and rearrange their finances. The commission did articulate to some degree the extra service demands which devolve upon cities in the modern era, and it encouraged the state to take over certain highway and welfare costs. The commission hoped to provide politically acceptable solutions for such problems as those surrounding annexation and merger, but these were not forthcoming.

In the matter of merging urban counties and cities, Tidewater Virginia had managed, despite the difficulties, to achieve greater success than any other section of the United States. For centuries Virginia has had a system unique in this country, but similar to that in England, under which counties and cities are entirely separate political entities, a situation that evolved gradually. No other American state has this plan on a state-wide basis, although some individual cities are separate from the counties surrounding them. Efforts to merge counties and cities have encountered great obstacles in most of Virginia and throughout the nation, since citizens of the counties usually vote against merger. But in lower Tidewater there has been success in three instances. In 1952 the voters of the city of Hampton and Elizabeth City County elected to merge, and the county went out of existence as a governmental unit. Ten years later, the voters of the city of Virginia Beach and Princess Anne County decided to come together under the name of Virginia Beach. In the same year, 1962, the city of South Norfolk and Norfolk County merged as a municipality, under the name of Chesapeake. All three of these mergers resulted in completely consolidated cities. The last two were consummated to avoid annexation by Norfolk of the territory involved.

The frightful death toll on the highways of Virginia, and everywhere else, caused the creation of the Virginia Highway Safety Commission in 1968, with Overton Jones, associate editor of the Richmond *Times-Dispatch*, as the able chairman. It is the policy-making wing of the simultaneously established Virginia Highway Safety Division, a full-time government agency. Every city and county in the state is required to have a local highway safety commission, and the state division works with each of them. Regional conferences for training purposes are a part of the program. All phases of traffic safety are within the purview of the division, and the program established by the General Assembly and developed by its dynamic director, John T. Hanna, is perhaps the most complete and far-reaching in its particular field to be found in any state.

One of Governor Godwin's problems was the lack of enthusiasm exhibited for his administration by black citizens. They had cast many votes for his election, but they felt that he was proceeding too slowly in appointing them to important positions and otherwise incorporating them into the life of the state. He did, in fact, proceed too deliberately, but he finally named about thirty-five blacks to membership on boards and to other responsible positions, far more than any of his predecessors. The huge increase in public school appropriations which he sponsored also was beneficial to the Negroes. On the college level, the governor recommended and the General Assembly provided the largest per capita appropriations for almost totally black Virginia State College that had been made available to any state-supported institution of higher learning. Norfolk State, which has a much larger enrollment than Virginia State, the parent institution, became independent in 1969. Restrictions applied previously with respect to all capital appropriations for building college dormitories—which had had to be financed with revenue bonds—were waived for Norfolk State. Two large dormitories were constructed.

Godwin indirectly championed the cause of the blacks when he lashed out at the Ku Klux Klan, which was beginning to hold rallies in cowpastures and other such places of rendezvous on the Southside. The governor pointed out that cross burning was a felony under Virginia law—except on private property with permission of the owner —and he offered $1000 for information leading to arrests and convictions. Several arrests were made, and one man got three years. When Marshall Kornegay of North Carolina, the grand dragon, called on the governor to protest what he termed "harassment," Godwin told him in no uncertain terms that he would not hesitate to call out all eight hundred state troopers and the National Guard to break the back of the Klan in the commonwealth. That just about wrote finis for the klaverns, kludds, kligrapps and klonvocations in Virginia.[3]

Industrial development, already booming, was given added impetus under Mills Godwin. He not only made annual trips to New York and Chicago, where he appeared before large groups of top-flight business executives, but he led two expeditions to Europe to promote the state's foreign trade. On these journeys Godwin's unusual ability as a speaker on both formal and informal occasions, combined with his poise and his attractive personality, made many friends for Virginia. A foreign-trade office was opened in Brussels, where the State Port Authority already was represented, and where the State Department of Agriculture was soon to begin promoting livestock sales. Results from all this were not long in coming. Virginia's industrial growth went forward at an unprecedented rate.

The port of Hampton Roads, with its spectacular natural advantages, was a prime beneficiary of these trends. The volume of foreign trade there jumped markedly. Total exports from Hampton Roads, consisting overwhelmingly of coal, have far exceeded, for many years, those of any other port in the United States. This is by no means true of imports, but import volume is mounting, and in 1970 Hampton Roads ranked second only to New York on the eastern seaboard in the new import traffic in containers. Under this modern method, sharply promoted by greatly increased state appropriations for port development, goods are shipped in sealed metal containers which offer faster and cheaper service.

The foregoing fits in with the projected deepening of the James River downstream from Richmond. If the plan is found to be economically feasible, it is expected to benefit not only the Norfolk-Portsmouth-Newport News area but the entire state. The U. S. Army Corps of Engineers began a survey in 1970 to determine its economic practicality, with the expectation that the survey would take two years. Meanwhile the Virginia Port Authority was at work co-ordinating and unifying Virginia's ports.

Governor Godwin sought in every way to promote an increased tourist trade for Virginia. On his trips inside and outside the United States he publicized the commonwealth's manifold attractions—scenic, historic and cultural. Unprecedented sums for tourist advertising were appropriated by the General Assembly. In 1969 Virginia's tourist trade reached a billion dollars a year for the first time, according to one analysis. It fell somewhat short of that total when another method of computation was used.

Greatest of all the lodestones for tourists in Virginia is Colonial

Williamsburg, which recreates a vanished way of life with such near perfection as to attract visitors from all over the globe. The restoration of the colonial capital, begun by John D. Rockefeller, Jr., in the 1920s and constantly expanded and improved, is perhaps the most complete, accurate and painstaking such enterprise to be found anywhere. The pigsties and cowsheds of two hundred years ago, with their swarms of flies, are not in evidence today, but Virginia's eighteenth-century civilization comes alive in the taproom at the Raleigh Tavern, in candlelight flickering from crystal chandeliers in the Palace, and in the restored House of Burgesses where Patrick Henry bade defiance to the mightiest power on earth.

Tourists by the hundreds of thousands bring only a temporary increase in Virginia's population, but the number of permanent inhabitants is mounting. Final figures for the 1970 census show an overall rise of 681,545, or 17.2 per cent, and a total population of 4,648,494, fourteenth in the nation. Norfolk is still the largest city, with Richmond second, followed by Virginia Beach, Newport News, Hampton, Portsmouth, Alexandria and Roanoke, in that order. Twelve cities lost population during the decade while twenty-five gained, and some of the gains were due to annexation of adjacent territory or to mergers. Among the counties, thirty-nine showed losses and fifty-five gains, while one showed no change, the losses being accounted for in some instances by annexation of county territory. Population dropped in the counties of Accomack and Northampton on the Eastern Shore, where the economic impact of the unique seventeen-mile long Chesapeake Bay Bridge-Tunnel had not yet been strongly felt. A sharp decline occurred in southwest Virginia, where automation of the coal mines and the switch of some consumers to oil or gas curtailed job opportunities.

Although the mountain counties of the southwest lost population during the decade, it should be only a question of time before that beautiful region is back on the road to progress and prosperity. The ten-year program initiated in 1961 by President John F. Kennedy for all thirteen states of Appalachia, projecting a total expenditure of $10,-000,000,000 in federal, state and local funds, actually got under way in 1965. In most of the southwestern Virginia counties involved in the program, levels of health, education and transportation have been definitely raised. Federal appropriations for Virginia totaled over $61,000,000 by 1971, and the federal commission estimates that five times this sum was generated by other federal, state and local agencies. A prime difficulty lies in the remoteness of so many Appalachian dwellers from the outside world. Immured in their coves and hollows, with nothing remotely describable as roads to link them with the population centers, they sit on their sagging cabin porches with their squirrel rifles, content to follow their ancient ways.

But there are many energetic and ambitious citizens of southwest Virginia, and they are moving to get their rugged section out of the doldrums. Much remains to be done. The portion of Interstate Highway 81, which extends from Roanoke to Bristol, is a factor in this effort, for it is having a far-reaching impact on life in areas which were once remote. So are the roads being built in the counties by the Appalachian Regional Commission. Efforts to promote industry also are significant. Duffield Industrial Park, representing the combined efforts of Lee, Scott and Wise counties and the city of Norton, evidences the up-and-coming spirit in that part of Virginia. Its establishment was aided greatly by the Appalachian Commission.

The southwest also is acquiring important additional recreational and tourist attractions. Wholly aside from the renowned Barter Theatre at Abingdon, and "The Trail of the Lonesome Pine" pageant at Big Stone Gap, based on the novel by John Fox, Jr., there are exciting new park developments. Mount Rogers National Recreation Area, centering on 5710-foot Mount Rogers, the state's highest peak, is within a day's drive of nearly one-third of the nation's population. This huge recreational facility extends from New River on the east side of Grayson County westward through Jefferson National Forest for nearly one hundred miles. It comprises 154,000 of the 575,000 acres in the forest. Adjacent to it on the south is Mount Rogers State Park, with about five thousand acres. Two privately operated resort-type developments are planned, together with a winter sports site on nearby White Top mountain (5540 feet). Amphitheaters with screen, sound and light for nature lectures, are a part of the scheme, together with six camping grounds. Dedication of some of the latter began in 1970. There are foot and bridle paths, and the Appalachian Trail, which stretches from Maine to Georgia, passes through the area.

Other scenic and recreational attractions in the southwest are certain, in time, to help in making that picturesque part of Virginia better known. There is Natural Tunnel State Park in Scott County, which is preserving the remarkable tunnel there. On the border between

Haysi, Virginia, and Elkhorn City, Kentucky, is Breaks Interstate Park. Its most spectacular feature is the biggest canyon east of the Mississippi, a cleft five miles long and 1600 feet deep, cut through the mountains by the Russell Fork River. And on the very edge of the southwest, the Blue Ridge Parkway winds along the crest of the range from Roanoke southward through Floyd and Carroll counties into North Carolina. Thus Virginia's "mountain empire," with its crags and waterfalls, its forests and upland meadows, its trout streams and shimmering lakes bids fair to become one of the continent's garden spots. There men and women, weary and distraught with the cares of urban living, can breathe the clean air of the hills and drink from the unpolluted waters.

Richmond, long noted for its conservatism, was showing exceptional *élan*, as it moved into the new age. Not a single major office building had gone up there between 1930 and 1960. Then almost suddenly, tall structures began piercing the sky on nearly every hand, until the downtown area was transformed. A civic center, built around a new city hall and a huge coliseum, attracted widespread attention. An ultramodern expressway system was being got under way. A gift of $50,000,000 to the University of Richmond by pharmaceutical manufacturer E. Claiborne Robins was an event of no uncertain magnitude. The city's forward surge, its superior race relations and its smooth transition from segregation to integration caused it to be chosen twice—in 1950 and 1966—as an "All-American City" by the National Municipal League and *Look* magazine.

Norfolk, too, was bounding ahead in a manner befitting the state's largest city. It was first in the nation to take advantage of the federal housing act of 1949, and the result was the demolition of slums or other inferior housing over an area covering hundreds of acres. Honky-tonks, tattoo parlors, beer joints and other cheap hangouts on East Main Street for sailors and their girls were wiped out, and in their stead rose a modern business district with broad boulevards and nineteen- and twenty-two-story bank buildings. An elaborate civic center, with a new city hall, coliseum and public library are other striking features. Norfolk, an "All-American City" in 1960, was chosen by the federal government several years later as one of the first participants in the Model Cities program. It was the first community between Baltimore and Atlanta to have a symphony orchestra. In late 1970 it was given the Walter P. Chrysler, Jr., multimillion-dollar art collection.

It is the home of recently established and rapidly growing Old Dominion University, with over 9600 students in 1970, as well as Norfolk State College, with more than 5200, largest predominantly Negro institution in Virginia. During World War II, according to Norfolk's own admission, the city was "dull, dirty and corrupt." The transformation since that time has been little short of amazing.

The state of Virginia was moving forward in cultural realms. Her standing there was, in some respects, not as high as in former times, but in others it was higher. In painting, for example, the state had a number of Virginia-born artists of national reputation. There were at least eight of these—Robert Gwathmey, Julien Binford, Bernard Perlin, Charles Smith, Nell Blaine, Bernard Martin, Jewett Campbell and Cy Twombly. Many leading Virginia-born writers have been mentioned earlier in these pages. They form a highly respectable company. One who has not been mentioned is William Styron, a native of Newport News, certainly one of the most talented novelists of our time. Tom Wolfe, born in Richmond, has achieved recognition as one of our most incisive and amusing social commentators.

In music, Dr. Paul Freeman, a Richmond-born Negro in his mid-thirties, had received acclaim in 1970 as a conductor of many major symphony orchestras on both sides of the Atlantic. After attending Armstrong High School in Richmond and Virginia State College, Freeman was awarded the B.M., M.M. and Ph.D. degrees by the Eastman School of Music in Rochester, New York. He then won two international awards, and at age thirty-two was chosen as conductor for the fiftieth birthday celebration of the Swedish composer Blomdahl at Malmö in 1967. He was named in 1970 conductor-in-residence of the Detroit Symphony. Another accomplished Richmond-born black musician is twenty-five-year-old Isaiah Jackson III, conductor of New York's Youth Symphony Orchestra, and assistant director to Leopold Stokowski, conductor of the American Symphony.

Virginia has not produced a Nobel Prize winner, but there are eight winners of the Pulitzer Prize, living and dead. These are: in biography, Douglas S. Freeman, for *R. E. Lee*, 1935, and *George Washington*, 1958, the latter a posthumous award shared by Mary Wells Ashworth, coauthor of Vol. VII; and David J. Mays, *Edmund Pendleton*, 1953. For the novel, Ellen Glasgow, *In This Our Life*, 1942; William Styron, *The Confessions of Nat Turner*, 1968. For newspaper editorials, Louis I. Jaffé, Norfolk *Virginian-Pilot*, 1929; Virginius Dabney, Richmond *Times-Dispatch*, 1948, and Lenoir Chambers, Norfolk *Virginian-Pilot*, 1960. William H. Fitzpatrick, editor of the Norfolk *Ledger-Star*, won a Pulitzer Prize in 1951 for editorials written for the New Orleans *States*.

Virginia's Negro population is taking an increasing role in the political, economic and cultural life of the commonwealth. The blacks are moving into the cities, where their proportion of the population is mounting, as the whites move to the suburbs. On the other hand, their percentage of the state's total population is shrinking slowly. It was 22.2 in 1950, but by 1960 it had fallen to 20.6, and by 1970 to 18.6.

Virginia's foreign-born population constituted only 1.2 per cent of the whole in 1960, against the national average of 5.4 per cent. Arlington County and other northern fringe areas of the state contain the bulk of Virginia's foreign-born. The state's preponderantly Anglo-Saxon background goes far to explain the conservatism of Virginians and their adherence to British principles of liberty and democracy, handed down over the centuries from the time of Magna Carta.

As Mills Godwin approached the end of his term as governor, he could look back with great satisfaction upon his accomplishments. Every major recommendation made by him to the General Assembly in 1966 and 1968 had been approved by that body.

But a personal tragedy marred his final years in the mansion. Becky, his adopted daughter and only child, was struck by lightning on the sands at Virginia Beach in August 1968, and fatally injured. She was almost fifteen, and adored by Governor Godwin and his lovely wife, Katherine. Despite this catastrophe, both carried on bravely. When one year later, hurricane Camille dumped twenty-seven inches of rain on a section of Nelson County within a few hours, and almost equal amounts on adjacent regions, at enormous cost in lives and property, Governor Godwin toured the stricken area several times, fully conscious from his own experience of the sorrow that had come to so many bereaved families. No fewer than ninety-two lives were lost in Nelson, plus nineteen more in Rockbridge, two in Goochland and one in Louisa. The raging waters broke through the dikes protecting low-lying areas of Richmond, and for the first time in decades part of lower Main Street was inundated to a depth of five feet.

When one considers the far-reaching character of the reforms which

Mills Godwin translated into reality during his four years, one can only conclude that his was one of a handful of truly exceptional gubernatorial administrations in the long history of Virginia, and second to none in modern times. It is a somewhat ironic fact, however, that although Godwin's accomplishments were nothing short of sensational, the Democratic organization, through no fault of his, had disintegrated before he went out of office. The large influx of new voters, especially Negroes, brought in as a consequence of federal court decisions and statutes, and the reapportionment of the state, combined with the growing independence of the electorate and the steady rise of the Republican party, destroyed the bases on which the power of the machine rested.

The Democratic primary of 1969 and the ensuing election provided convincing evidence that the Byrd organization was no more. There were contests for governor, lieutenant governor and attorney general, and the organization candidates were defeated by wide margins, both in the first primary and the run-off. Lieutenant Governor Fred G. Pollard of Richmond, the most conservative aspirant for governor, got only 23.3 per cent of the vote the first time around and was eliminated. William C. Battle of Charlottesville, a son of former Governor Battle and a personable moderate who had served successfully as U.S. ambassador to Australia, led Henry E. Howell, Jr., of Norfolk in the first primary by 4339 votes. Howell, with the slogan "Keep the Big Boys Honest," spent much of his time campaigning against the Virginia Electric and Power Company. The big winner was thirty-three-year-old State Senator J. Sargeant Reynolds of Richmond, candidate for lieutenant governor, who polled nearly 64 per cent of the vote against three opponents, one of whom was endorsed by what was left of the machine. Governor Godwin did not publicly back anybody in the first primary, but he came out solidly in opposition to Howell. He supported Battle in the run-off against Howell. Battle won by about 18,600 votes.

Virginia's Democrats went into the ensuing election campaign badly split. There had been ill-concealed animosity between the Godwin wing of the party and the Howell wing since the party's state convention at Salem in 1968, when Godwin was booed and hooted by liberal elements. And now Bill Battle, tired from two strenuous primary contests, was faced with a formidable, aggressive and well-

financed Republican candidate, A. Linwood Holton, Jr., a native of
Big Stone Gap and a graduate of Washington and Lee and Harvard.

Holton was a young, vigorous and attractive campaigner. He carefully refrained from attacking Godwin's program, but proclaimed "It's
Time For a Change," i.e., the GOP ought to be given a chance to show
what it could do, since there had not been a Republican governor
since William E. Cameron. Cameron was elected as a Readjuster in
1881, but became a Republican when the Readjuster party reorganized
as the Republican party three years later.

Holton had been regional co-ordinator for Richard Nixon in the
latter's successful presidential campaign of 1968, and Nixon came to
Virginia on the eve of the gubernatorial election and spoke for Holton.
The AFL-CIO and the Crusade for Voters, a black organization,
endorsed the Republican candidate for governor, in the hope of wiping
out the last vestiges of the Byrd machine. Godwin backed Battle
strongly, but Howell sulked and made no speeches for the candidate.
Thousands of conservative Democrats voted for Holton as did many
Howell followers. He defeated Battle, 481,000 to 416,000. Holton did
not carry the other two Republicans on the ticket with him, however.
Their Democratic opponents were easy winners—J. Sargeant Reynolds
for lieutenant governor over H. D. Dawbarn of Waynesboro, and
Andrew P. Miller of Abingdon, son of Francis Pickens Miller, for
attorney general over Richard Obenshain of Richmond. (However,
young Lieutenant-Governor Reynolds, whose appeal to the voters in
every election had been phenomenal, and who was the front runner
for governor in 1973, would die in June, 1971, after a courageous battle,
of a malignant brain tumor.) In the General Assembly, the Republicans won much the largest number of seats they had had in the
twentieth century—24 in the House of Delegates out of 100 and seven
in the Senate out of 40. There were three Negroes in the General
Assembly, two from the Richmond area and one from Norfolk, all
Democrats.

"The Key to the Holton victory clearly was his ability to win urban
votes, both in the state's largest cities and in its developing suburban
complexes," Dr. Ralph Eisenberg of the University of Virginia wrote.
Since more than 59 per cent of the total vote came from the urban
corridor and the two metropolitan areas lying outside the corridor,
the significance of Holton's strength in those areas is evident. Another
factor here was the manner in which Holton was able to cut into

Battle's support from black voters. Holton also made an appeal to youth. Of twenty-two mock elections on Virginia campuses, he had won twenty.

A disturbing aspect of the campaign lay in the enormous amount of money spent by the twenty candidates for statewide office in the primaries and the election. They acknowledged total outlays of $2,700,-000, including $500,000 spent by Holton, As numerous political expenditures never get into these computations, the overall sum was considerably higher, perhaps as much as $4,000,000.

In his inaugural, Governor Holton stressed his intention "to make today's Virginia a model in race relations," and he moved almost at once toward this objective. He chose thirty-six-year-old William B. Robertson, a black, as a member of his executive staff. About a year later he named thirty-eight-year-old Ernest D. Fears, Jr., as the first Negro head of a state-wide Selective Service System in the United States. In between he appointed more Negroes to state boards and other responsible posts than any previous governor. He also moved toward obtaining more and better jobs for blacks in both the public and the private sector.

Governor Holton gained favorable nationwide publicity, and some criticism in Virginia, when he escorted his thirteen-year-old daughter to an overwhelmingly black Richmond public school and enrolled her for the session of 1970–71, when, as governor, he could have sent her to another public school. His two other children of school age were similarly escorted by Mrs. Holton and enrolled in another predominantly black school. However, Holton objected to the busing of school pupils across town for the sole purpose of promoting race mixing, and under his leadership the state of Virginia intervened as a "friend of the court" in appealing a lower federal court pro-busing order.

Serious breakdowns of discipline were reliably reported to exist in certain urban schools, as a result of these court orders, and the educational process there was severely hampered by this and by a decline in teacher morale. In some schools, however, the adjustment was achieved smoothly. In Richmond and in Norfolk, which also was hit by a busing order, thousands of parents either transferred their children to private schools or refused to send them anywhere. The Richmond City School Board filed suit in federal court, asking that tribunal to combine its school system—approximately 66 per cent black at the end of 1970—with those of adjacent Henrico and

Chesterfield, with their much smaller black enrollments. The counties in question resisted strongly. Many white Richmonders had moved to Henrico and Chesterfield to get away from the Richmond school situation.

Conditions were said to be generally more peaceful in rural regions than in the cities, even where the black population was large. In preponderantly black Surry County there was no disorder, but white parents simply refused to send their children to the public schools. All six hundred of them were enrolled in private academies or taken out of school entirely. Government tuition grants, which had helped to sustain many private schools in the 1950s and 1960s, had been outlawed by the federal courts in 1968. Yet privately financed centers of instruction, usually day schools, continued to proliferate across Virginia. The number of Virginia pupils in such centers, inside and outside the state, totaled about 56,000, an increase of around 10 per cent for the session of 1970–71 over the previous session, while in Richmond the increase was nearly 20 per cent, according to the State Department of Education. Compulsory education laws were beginning to be enforced in this confused situation, but no one could be certain concerning the final outcome of all this until the U. S. Supreme Court had spoken.

The old, established preparatory schools, such as Norfolk Academy, which goes back to 1728; Episcopal High School, founded in 1839; Woodberry Forest, established after the Civil War; St. Christopher's, St. Catherine's and Collegiate in Richmond, all high-ranking centers of instruction, and others of almost comparable reputation, were having to turn away many applicants who were pounding on their doors in view of the unsettled conditions in the public schools. The private preparatory schools had made their reputations under such great headmasters as Robert W. Tunstall at Norfolk Academy; Launcelot M. Blackford and Archibald R. Hoxton at Episcopal High; Carter Walker at Woodberry, and Churchill G. Chamberlayne at St. Christopher's. A great headmistress was Miss Virginia Randolph Ellett of St. Catherine's.

Virginia's half-dozen military preparatory schools were having trouble filling their enrollments, apparently because of the pacifist sentiment that was rising in the United States and other countries. The too prevalent mood of permissiveness also seemed to work against the military schools, with their strict discipline.

In the Virginia General Assembly, a new spirit of co-operation between the Democrats and Republicans was manifesting itself. The process had begun in 1968, when Speaker John Warren Cooke of Mathews County appointed Republicans to several important committees for the first time. He followed this two years later by giving the minority party representation on all major committees. The 1970 legislature, in which the Democrats had large majorities in both branches, considered various Republican-sponsored bills on their merits. For example, Governor Holton's proposal for a thorough survey of the state government and its agencies and institutions, with a view to effecting economies and greater efficiency, was approved. William L. Zimmer III, prominent Richmond attorney, was named chairman, and he assembled a group of fifty-seven business and professional leaders from throughout the commonwealth. The study was privately financed, and Warren King & Associates of Chicago were retained as consultants. A 206-page report was the result. It estimated that implementation of all the recommendations could bring an annual saving of $61,000,000 in the current operating budget, plus a net one-time saving of $12,000,-000 and a net one-time cost avoidance of $18,000,000 more. The governor and the General Assembly would have to pass on these proposals, and the amount of actual saving remained to be determined.

Holton's appointments to public office during his first year were generally commendable. He went outside the state to get several of the most important officials, since he did not find what he regarded as the needed competence within Virginia's borders. He tended to choose relatively youthful appointees, and he retained a number of the most efficient Democrats. Holton requested and got stronger air and water pollution control laws, and his appointments to the State Water Control Board and the State Air Pollution Board added muscle to those two significant environmental agencies. The governor and his party had a significant role in the enactment of legislation which, at long last, drastically amended the absent-voter law to end the mail-ballot racket that for generations had been notorious in southwest Virginia.

U. S. Senator Harry F. Byrd, Jr., ran for his first full term in 1970. He chose to offer as an independent, since the State Democratic Central Committee voted to require all candidates to take a "loyalty oath" which, in his view, bound him to support the Democratic nominee for the presidency in 1972, no matter who that nominee might be. His reasons for this interpretation of the oath were not clear, but at all events he left the party, at least temporarily, and did not enter the Democratic primary. Candidates in the primary were former Delegate George C. Rawlings, Jr., of Fredericksburg, Delegate Clive L. DuVal of Fairfax and Prof. Milton Colvin of Washington and Lee University. The voters stayed away from the polls in droves, and Rawlings won by an extremely narrow margin.

In confronting Rawlings in the election, along with Delegate Ray L. Garland, Roanoke Republican, Harry Byrd, Jr., put on a masterful campaign. He had matured greatly since succeeding his father in the Senate, and had demonstrated that he was more open-minded in his views and less rigidly wedded to ultraconservative doctrine than the elder Byrd. Endowed with personal magnetism and able to come through effectively on television, Harry, Jr., could now speak for himself, without having his every utterance interpreted as reflecting his father's position. Thousands of Democrats had stayed out of the primary to support him, and he polled 54 per cent of the total vote, leaving only 46 per cent for his two opponents combined.

It was a famous victory. In the same election, Republicans captured six of the state's ten congressional seats, the first time they had done that well since 1886. In each of the six districts, the Republicans defeated a liberal Democrat, and at least three of the four Democrats who retained their seats in the other districts were conservatives. All this, combined with Byrd's one-sided triumph, leads one to believe that the people of Virginia are more conservative than liberal. Yet they are not as conservative as they once were, or they would never have ratified the abandonment of pay-as-you-go and other necessary reforms. Nor would they have elected a Republican governor whose platform was in some respects more liberal than those on which the dominant Democrats had been running for decades. Further evidences that times were changing are seen in the General Assembly's decision in 1968 to permit sales of liquor by the drink, under local option, and in approval by the people in 1970 of a constitutional amendment to let the General Assembly decide whether to have pari-mutuel betting at race tracks. In the past, both proposals had been repeatedly voted down by the legislature.

Hence it will be seen that the ancient commonwealth, long known as the Old Dominion, might today be more appropriately termed the New Dominion. In almost every area—political, racial, educational, industrial and cultural—Virginia has entered a new era. The Byrd machine is defunct, and the state's politics have become fluid and uncertain. The racial situation has been totally transformed. In the educational realm, more than a score of new two-year community colleges are either already in operation or nearly so. The state's industrial development has gone forward at unprecedented speed, and the population explosion in the urban corridor is spectacular.

Greater receptivity to new ideas on the part of the average Virginian is manifest. Arnold Toynbee, the British historian, wrote in the 1940s that "Virginia makes the painful impression of a country living under a spell, in which time has stood still." About a decade later, Jean Gottmann, the French geographer, said he felt that the salient characteristic of Virginia was "resistance to change." But after another decade had gone by, Gottmann was writing that "much change has developed in the economy, and the society of the Old Dominion . . . [has] grown definitely younger and more modern."

Thus, centuries after the first settlers planted their colony at Jamestown in blood, suffering and death, Virginia, torn in the Revolution and crushed in the Civil War, is on the move. The New Dominion is challenging her sister states and showing evidences of youthful vigor and resolve. It seems altogether probable that the now-developing Virginia will be a blend of the old and the new such as few states can provide—a modern civilization in which the gracious manners of antebellum days will be combined with a forward-looking spirit, and a determination that no worthy citizen of the commonwealth shall lack the opportunity to realize his full potentialities. The great Virginians of the past strove mightily to found a nation and provide blessings for their posterity. They would, it seems safe to say, applaud the vital and alert commonwealth of today, so rich in promise for all her people.

NOTES

CHAPTER ONE – *Into the Storm*

1. *The Three Worlds of Captain John Smith*, Philip L. Barbour, 105.
2. *Economic History of Virginia*, Philip Alexander Bruce, Vol. I, 100–1, 120, 123.
3. *The Soul of a Nation*, Matthew Page Andrews, 53 (footnote).
4. Barbour, op. cit., 5, 38–39, 394.
5. *Old Virginia and Her Neighbors*, John Fiske, Vol. I, 36.
6. *Shakespeare of London*, Marchette Chute, 62.

CHAPTER TWO – *Starvation, Disease and Indians*

1. *Virginia, the Old Dominion*, Matthew Page Andrews, 34–35. *The Soul of a Nation*, Andrews, 198–99.
2. *The Three Worlds of Captain John Smith*, Philip L. Barbour, 157.
3. "The First Epidemic in English America," Gordon W. Jones, *Virginia Magazine of History and Biography* (hereafter VMHB), January 1963.
4. Barbour, op. cit., 153.
5. From *Western Star* by Stephen Vincent Benét, c. 1963, Rosemary Carr Benét, reprinted by permission.
6. *Colonial Virginia*, Richard L. Morton, Vol. I, 17–18.
7. *Virginia in Our Century*, Jean Gottmann, 287; *Economic History of Virginia*, Philip Alexander Bruce, Vol. I, 112–18, 120–21; *Tobacco Coast*, Arthur P. Middleton, 52, 55–57, 59.
8. Morton, op. cit., Vol. I, 25–26.
9. Ibid., Vol. I, 26–27.
10. *The Story of Virginia's First Century*, Mary Newton Stanard, 99, 100; *The Literature of Virginia in the Seventeenth Century*, Howard Mumford Jones, 18, 19.
11. Morton, op. cit., Vol. I, 31–32.
12. *The Soul of a Nation*, Matthew Page Andrews, 200–1; *Virginia's Mother Church*, George MacLaren Brydon, Vol. I, 17.

CHAPTER THREE – *Tobacco, Pocahontas, the First Assembly and the First Negroes*

1. Pocahontas was living in Henrico at the time, and it is known that the Reverend Alexander Whitaker, rector of the Henrico church, baptized her. He would not have performed the ceremony, had it taken place at Jamestown, since the Reverend Richard Buck, the Jamestown rector, would have done so.
2. *Colonial Virginia*, Richard L. Morton, Vol. I, 52.
3. *The Soul of a Nation*, Matthew Page Andrews, 277 and note. *The Negro Almanac*, 1967 ed., 1–2.
4. *Colonists in Bondage*, Abbot Emerson Smith, 297–98.

CHAPTER FOUR – *A Massacre and a Martinet*

1. "That Mythical First Thanksgiving," Virginius Dabney, *Saturday Evening Post*, November 29, 1958.
2. *Virginia's Mother Church*, George MacLaren Brydon, Vol. I, 57, 58, 59.
3. *Medicine in Virginia in the Seventeenth Century*, Wyndham B. Blanton, 33–34.
4. "The Thrusting Out of Governor Harvey," J. Mills Thornton III, VMHB, January 1968.

CHAPTER FIVE – *Governor Berkeley's Golden Years*

1. *Virginia in Our Century*, Jean Gottman, 287–88.
2. *Economic History of Virginia in the Seventeenth Century*, Philip Alexander Bruce, Vol. II, 134.
3. *Hening's Statutes* Vol. II, 192, (hereafter *Hening*).
4. *Patrician and Plebeian in Virginia*, Thomas J. Wertenbaker, 91–99. *The South in American Literature*, Jay B. Hubbell, 90.

CHAPTER SIX – *Requiem for a Rebel*

1. *The Writings of Col. William Byrd of Westover in Virginia Esqr.*, John Spencer Bassett, ed., xi. *From Slavery to Freedom*, John Hope Franklin, 70.
2. *Black History: A Reappraisal*, Melvin Drimmer, ed., 29, 30, 32–33. *The Negro in Our History*, Carter G. Woodson and Charles H. Wesley, 64, 66–67. "The Business of Slave Trading," Simon Rottenberg, *South Atlantic Quarterly*, Summer 1967, 415. Franklin, op. cit., 42, 43.
3. *Medicine in Virginia in the Eighteenth Century*, Wyndham B. Blanton, 154, 156–57.
4. *The First Gentlemen of Virginia*, Louis B. Wright, 102, 103. "Virginia's

Benefactors of Education: Benjamin Syms and Thomas Eaton," Donald Ransome Taylor, *Virginia Journal of Education*, January 1963.
5. *Colonial Virginia*, Richard L. Morton, Vol. I, 234, 237. *Virginia under the Stuarts*, Thomas J. Wertenbaker, 147.
6. Wertenbaker, op. cit., 154; Morton, op. cit., 238–39.
7. *South and Southwest*, Jay B. Hubbell, 206, 207, 227.

CHAPTER SEVEN – *The Capital, the Commissary and Spotswood*

1. *Colonial Virginia*, Richard L. Morton, Vol. II, 417 and note.
2. *Virginia, the Old Dominion*, Matthew Page Andrews, 190. Morton, op. cit., 491–92.
3. Morton, op. cit., Vol. I, 216 (note), 302.
4. "The Route Followed by Governor Spotswood in 1716 Across the Blue Ridge Mountains," Delma R. Carpenter, VMHB, October 1965.

CHAPTER EIGHT – *Gooch, Carter, Byrd and the Clergy*

1. *The Planters of Colonial Virginia*, Thomas J. Wertenbaker, 129. *Colonial Virginia*, Richard L. Morton, Vol. II, 522–23.
2. Morton, op. cit., 524–25.
3. Wertenbaker, op. cit., 159–60.
4. *Illustrated English Social History*, G. M. Trevelyan, Vol. II, 36–37.
5. *The Present State of Virginia*, Hugh Jones, ed. by Richard L. Morton, 254, footnote, with numerous references to authorities.

CHAPTER NINE – *Pioneers Beyond the Mountains*

1. *A History of the Valley of Virginia*, Samuel Kercheval, 253, 261, 267, 274–75. *A History of Southwest Virginia*, Lewis P. Summers, 124.
2. Kercheval, op. cit., 388–89 and note.
3. *The Virginia Germans*, Klaus Wust, 39.
4. *Virginia's Mother Church*, G. MacLaren Brydon, Vol. II, 70, 83. *History of the Valley of Virginia*, Samuel Kercheval, 180.
5. *The German Element in the Shenandoah Valley of Virginia*, John W. Wayland, 87, 272. *Colonial Virginia*, Richard L. Morton, Vol. II, 542–44. Bill Garrard in Richmond *Times-Dispatch*, August 31, 1952. Klaus Wust, letter to the author.
6. Brydon, op. cit., Vol. I, 192–93, 196; Vol. II, 70.
7. Kercheval, 306.

CHAPTER TEN – *French, Indians and Washington*

1. *Colonial Virginia,* Richard L. Morton, Vol. II, 616–17.
2. *George Washington,* Douglas S. Freeman, Vol. II, 336–38, and footnote, 338.
   Vol. VII, 506 and footnote. *Myths and Men,* Bernard Mayo, 45. *Sally Cary: A Long Hidden Romance of Washington's Life,* Wilson Miles Cary, 7, 8, 9.
   First in Their Hearts, Thomas J. Fleming, 19, 20, 23, 28, 30, 31.

CHAPTER ELEVEN – *A Young Man Named Patrick Henry*

1. *Edmund Pendleton,* David J. Mays, Vol. I, 178. "The Attempt to Separate the Offices of Speaker and Treasurer in Virginia, 1758–1766," Jack P. Greene, *VMHB,* January 1963.
2. *The Byrds of Virginia,* Alden Hatch, 214.

CHAPTER TWELVE – *Stamps, Tea and Long Knives*

1. *The South in the Revolution,* John R. Alden, 109.
2. *The Virginia Experiment,* Alf J. Mapp, 340–41. *Soil Exhaustion as a Factor in the Agricultural History of Virginia and Maryland, 1606–1860,* Avery O. Craven, 27–28.
3. *A Seed-Bed of the Republic,* Robert Douthat Stoner, Roanoke, Roanoke Historical Society, 59.

CHAPTER THIRTEEN – *Richmond, Norfolk, Williamsburg and Philadelphia*

1. *Patrick Henry, Patriot in the Making,* Robert D. Meade, 16, 55–56. *Patrick Henry, Practical Revolutionary,* Robert D. Meade, Appendix I, address of Hugh Blair Grigsby at College of William and Mary, July 4, 1859.
2. *The Letters and Papers of Edmund Pendleton,* David J. Mays, ed., Vol. I, Pendleton to Richard Henry Lee, 132.
3. *The Negro in the American Revolution,* Benjamin Quarles, 13.
4. *Richmond College Historical Papers,* Vol. I, 119. R. K. Meade to Everard Meade, *Southern Literary Messenger,* Vol. XXV, 24 (footnote).
5. *A History of the South,* Francis B. Simkins, 85. *The Virginia Experiment,* Alf J. Mapp, 427.

CHAPTER FOURTEEN – *The Rocky Road to Yorktown*

1. *The Life of George Rogers Clark*, James A. James, 291–92, 298–99, 436, 461–62.
   Article on Clark in Dictionary of American Biography (hereafter DAB).
   "A Sword for George Rogers Clark," Walter Havighurst, *American Heritage*,
   October 1962. *The Wilderness Road*, Robert L. Kincaid, 147.
2. *Hening*, XIII, 102. *The Negro in the American Revolution*, Benjamin Quarles,
   88.
3. *Slavery and Jeffersonian Virginia*, Robert McColley, 88.
4. *Acts of 1812*, CXXXVI. Quarles, op. cit., 88.
5. *Hening*, XII, 380–81; XIII, 619.
6. "Jack Jouett's Ride," Virginius Dabney, *American Heritage*, December 1961.
   "From Cuckoo Tavern to Monticello," Virginius Dabney, *The Iron Worker*,
   Summer 1966. *Jefferson, War and Peace, 1776 to 1784*, Marie Kimball, 138–
   39; 172, 173, 174. *Jefferson the Virginian*, Dumas Malone, 364, 365, 366.

CHAPTER FIFTEEN – *Religious Freedom Wins, Public Education Loses*

1. *History of Slavery in Virginia*, James C. Ballagh, 23. *The Peculiar Institution*,
   Kenneth M. Stampp, 25.
2. *Medicine in Virginia in the Eighteenth Century*, Wyndham B. Blanton, 128–29,
   294.
3. *Virginia's Mother Church*, G. MacLaren Brydon, Vol. II, 384, 415.

CHAPTER SIXTEEN – *The Battle for the Constitution*

1. *The American States During and After the Revolution*, Allan Nevins, 486.
2. *George Washington*, Douglas S. Freeman, Vol. VI, 86.

CHAPTER SEVENTEEN – *Washington's Climactic Role*

1. Sketch of Salomon in DAB by James H. Peeling.
2. *George Washington*, J. A. Carroll and Mary Wells Ashworth, Vol. VII, Appendix
   VII–2, 637–47.

CHAPTER EIGHTEEN – *Slavery in Virginia and a Thwarted Revolt*

1. *From Slavery to Freedom*, John Hope Franklin, 209; *Edmund Pendleton*, David
   J. Mays, Vol. II, 327–29. *The Negro in Our History*, Carter G. Woodson and
   Charles H. Wesley, 177–78. *A History of Slavery in Virginia*, J. C. Ballagh,
   92. *Slavery and Jeffersonian Virginia*, Robert McColley, 107–13.

2. *The Road from Monticello,* Joseph C. Robert, 10, 12. *Antislavery in Virginia, 1831–1861,* Patricia P. Hickin, 123, 204, 244, 248, 343–46, 559.
3. *Norfolk, Historic Southern Port,* Thomas J. Wertenbaker, 140.
4. *Anti-Slavery in America,* Mary S. Locke, 109–10. *From Slavery to Freedom,* John Hope Franklin, 160.
5. Locke, op. cit., 128–30. *White over Black,* Winthrop D. Jordan, 574.
6. *The Free Negro in Virginia,* John H. Russell, 71. *Abraham Lincoln,* Albert J. Beveridge, Vol. II, 50.
7. *Free Negro Labor and Property Holding in Virginia,* Luther P. Jackson, 6, 27–28, 31, 69.
8. For a comprehensive and enlightening discussion of the supposed superiority of Latin-American slavery to that in the American South, and the appalling brutalities practiced under the Latin-American system, plus other significant data, see Chapters 2 and 3 of C. Vann Woodward's *American Counterpoint.*

CHAPTER NINETEEN – *Thomas Jefferson and John Marshall*

1. *The Life of John Marshall,* Albert J. Beveridge, Vol. IV, 82–83.

CHAPTER TWENTY – *Madison, Monroe and a "Firebell in the Night"*

1. "John Taylor of Caroline, Continuity, Change and Discontinuity in Virginia's Sentiments Toward Slavery, 1790–1820," Keith M. Bailor, VMHB, July 1967.
2. "Low Tide at Hampton Roads," Parke Rouse, Jr., U. S. Naval Institute Proceedings, July 1969.
3. *Norfolk, Historic Southern Port,* Thomas J. Wertenbaker, 142–43, 145.
4. "James Monroe and the Era of Good Feelings," Harry Ammon, VMHB, October 1958.

CHAPTER TWENTY-ONE – *East Is East and West Is West*

1. *Norfolk, Historic Southern Port,* Thomas J. Wertenbaker, 191–95. *Representation in Virginia,* J. A. C. Chandler, 46 (footnote), 47.
2. Wertenbaker, op. cit., 196–202. *Sectionalism in Virginia From 1776 to 1861,* Charles H. Ambler, 243.

CHAPTER TWENTY-TWO – *The Sable Cloud*

1. *The Peculiar Institution,* Kenneth M. Stampp, 132–34. *The Land They Fought For,* Clifford Dowdey, 12–22. *The Negro in Virginia,* compiled and edited by the WPA, 178–81. *The Road from Monticello,* Joseph C. Robert, 3–4,

and footnote. *The Road from Monticello* contains the most authoritative and thorough discussion of the entire historic session of 1831–32.
2. Ibid., 34.
3. *From Slavery to Freedom*, John Hope Franklin, 236.
4. *Oxford History of the American People*, Samuel Eliot Morison, 456–60, 554–56. Article on Tyler in *DAB* by Thomas P. Abernethy. *The Virginia Plutarch*, Philip A. Bruce, Vol. II, 166–70.
5. *Freedom of Thought in the Old South*, Clement Eaton, 271.
6. *Writing Southern History*, Arthur S. Link and Rembert W. Patrick, eds., chapter by James C. Bonner, 159–60.
7. *North of Negro Slavery*, Leon F. Litwack, quoted by C. Vann Woodward in "The Antislavery Myth," *American Scholar*, Spring 1962.

CHAPTER TWENTY-THREE – *Education in the Antebellum Era*

1. *The Free School Idea in Virginia Before the Civil War*, William A. Maddox, 55–59.
2. *Freedom of Thought in the Old South*, Clement Eaton, 196–97.
3. *Sectionalism in Virginia from 1776 to 1861*, Charles H. Ambler, 275, 282.

CHAPTER TWENTY-FOUR – *Manners, Mores, Trail Blazers and Literati*

1. From *John Brown's Body*, Stephen Vincent Benét, 1928.
2. *Norfolk, Historic Southern Port*, Thomas J. Wertenbaker, 210–16. *Medicine in the Nineteenth Century*, Wyndham B. Blanton, 225, 229, 230, 232, 233. *The South in the Building of the Nation*, Vol. VII, Robert M. Slaughter, 367–68.
3. Blanton, op. cit., 238–43, 262.
4. Ibid., 35–37. Slaughter, op. cit., 361–62. Sketch of Mettauer in *DAB* by Louise F. Catterall.
5. Blanton, op. cit., 24–25, 351. Sketch of Cabell in *DAB* by G. H. Genzmer.
6. *Liquor and Anti-Liquor in Virginia*, C. C. Pearson and J. Edwin Hendricks, 38 (footnote), 42, 118 (footnote), 140.
7. *Virginia in History and Tradition*, R. C. Simonini, Jr., ed.; chapter by Gardner B. Taplin, 43, 46.
8. *The South in American Literature*, Jay B. Hubbell, 529, 540. "The Personality of Poe," James Southall Wilson, *VMHB*, April 1959. "Acid for an Inkstand," Ulrich Troubetzkoy, *Iron Worker*, Autumn 1966. *Edgar Allan Poe: A Critical Biography*, Arthur Hobson Quinn, 77, 113, 116–17, 136, 173.

CHAPTER TWENTY-FIVE – *The Decline of Virginia*

1. "The Jeffersonian Virginia Expatriate in the Building of the Nation," Richard Beale Davis, VMHB, January 1962.
2. *The Growth of Southern Civilization, 1790–1860*, Clement Eaton, 66. *The Cotton Kingdom*, Frederick Law Olmsted, 98, 104–5, 602–5. *Memorials of a Southern Planter*, Susan D. Smedes, 54–55.

CHAPTER TWENTY-SIX – *Fort Sumter and John Brown's "Singing Bones"*

1. *The Burden of Southern History*, C. Vann Woodward, 45–51. *John Brown, A Biography*, Oswald Garrison Villard, 187–88, 508–10.
2. *The Negro in Virginia*, compiled and edited by the Works Progress Administration, 131.
3. *The Militant South*, John Hope Franklin, 125–28.
4. Woodward, op. cit., 58–59.
5. From *John Brown's Body*, Stephen Vincent Benét, 1928.
6. *The Secession Movement in Virginia, 1847–1861*, Henry T. Shanks, 198. Sketch of Pryor in DAB by James E. Walmsley. *Edmund Ruffin*, A. O. Craven, 216–17.
7. *Patriotic Gore*, Edmund Wilson, 333. *The End of an Era*, John S. Wise, 429.
8. *R. E. Lee*, Douglas S. Freeman, Vol. I, 118, 133. "Lee and the Ladies," Douglas S. Freeman, *Scribner's* magazine, November 1925.
9. *Virginia's Attitude Toward Slavery and Secession*, Beverley B. Munford, 156–58.

CHAPTER TWENTY-SEVEN – *Manassas to Sharpsburg*

1. *General Robert E. Lee after Appomattox*, ed. by Franklin L. Riley, 78–79.
2. *The Negro in the Civil War*, Benjamin Quarles, 35–36. *The Confederate Negro*, James H. Brewer, 165–67.
3. *Southern Negroes, 1861–1865*, Bell I. Wiley, 8, 9, 134–35, 136 (footnote).
4. *R. E. Lee*, Douglas S. Freeman, Vol. II, 40. *Stonewall Jackson*, Lenoir Chambers, Vol. I, 514.
5. *The Beleaguered City*, Alfred Hoyt Bill, 124–25.
6. *A History of the South*, Francis B. Simkins, 241. Wiley, op. cit., 82–84.
7. *Up from Slavery*, Booker T. Washington, 12–15.
8. Wiley, op. cit., 310–11.

CHAPTER TWENTY-EIGHT – *Fredericksburg to Appomattox*

1. *Experiment in Rebellion,* Clifford Dowdey, 257. *Four Years in Rebel Capitals,* T. C. DeLeon, 313–14, 316–17. *Ironmaker to the Confederacy,* Charles B. Dew, 207–9. *The Beleaguered City,* Alfred H. Bill, 156, 304. *The Confederate State of Richmond,* Emory M. Thomas, 68–69, 126.
2. Clifford Dowdey, op. cit., 305.
3. *Medicine in the Nineteenth Century,* Wyndham B. Blanton, 273, 279–80, 284, 286.
4. *Norfolk: Historic Southern Port,* Thomas J. Wertenbaker, 244–54. "Notes on Life in Occupied Norfolk, 1862–1865," Lenoir Chambers, *VMHB,* April 1965. Article on Benjamin F. Butler by Carl R. Fish, *DAB. A Stillness at Appomattox,* Bruce Catton, 206–10, 329.
5. *The Land They Fought For,* Clifford Dowdey, 238.
6. *The South to Posterity,* Douglas S. Freeman, 14. *Stonewall Jackson,* Lenoir Chambers, Vol. II, 458–59.
7. *Southern Negroes, 1861–1865,* Bell I. Wiley, 82–84.
8. *Virginia, the Old Dominion,* Matthew Page Andrews, 519. "Houses of Horror, Danville's Civil War Prisons," James I. Robertson, Jr., *VMHB,* July 1961. "Libby Prison, the Civil War Diary of Arthur G. Sedgwick," William M. Armstrong, *VMHB,* October 1963. *Some Reminiscences,* William L. Royall, 63. *Experiment in Rebellion,* Clifford Dowdey, 380–81.
9. *A Stillness at Appomattox,* Bruce Catton, 182–83.
10. *Virginia Railroads in the Civil War,* A. J. Johnston II, 226–27.
11. *The Life of Johnny Reb,* Bell I. Wiley, 144–45. "Disloyalty in the Confederacy in Southwestern Virginia, 1861–1865," Henry T. Shanks, *North Carolina Historical Review,* April 1944.
12. *The Negro in the Civil War,* Benjamin Quarles, 299, 310–11.
13. Jones, John B., *A Rebel War Clerk's Diary,* Vol. II, 432–33, Howard Swiggett, ed.
14. *The Beleaguered City,* Alfred H. Bill, 276–78. *Four Years in Rebel Capitals,* T. C. DeLeon, 398, 400–1. *Dixie After the War,* Myrta L. Avary, 15, 24–25. *Robert E. Lee, the Complete Man,* Margaret Sanborn, 247–48.

CHAPTER TWENTY-NINE – *Reconstruction*

1. *Up from Slavery,* Booker T. Washington, 14. *Dixie After the War,* Myrta Lockett Avary, 150–51.
2. *Norfolk: Historic Southern Port,* Thomas J. Wertenbaker, 256–57.
3. *Robert E. Lee,* Margaret Sanborn, Vol. I, 122; Vol. II, 277–78.
4. *Black History: A Reappraisal,* Melvin Drimmer, ed., 294–95, quoting C. Vann Woodward's article in *Journal of Negro Education.*
5. From *John Brown's Body,* Stephen Vincent Benét, 1928.
6. "Virginia Baptists and the Negro, 1865–1902," W. Harrison Daniel, *VMHB,* July 1968.

7. *Negro Office-Holders in Virginia, 1865–1895*, Luther P. Jackson, 1–43, 47–56.
8. " 'Life in Virginia' by a 'Yankee Teacher,' " Margaret Newbold Thorpe, Richard L. Morton, ed., VMHB, April 1956. *Republicans, Rebellion and Reconstruction*, Richard G. Lowe, 301. "The Freedmen's Bureau and Negro Education in Virginia," William T. Alderson, *North Carolina Historical Review*, January 1952. *Negroes in Virginia, 1865–1867*, J. P. McConnell, 72–73. *Virginia During Reconstruction, 1865–1870*, James D. Smith, unpub. Ph.D. diss., 415.
9. *The Political History of Virginia During Reconstruction*, H. J. Eckenrode, 124–25.
10. *The Negro in the Reconstruction of Virginia*, A. A. Taylor, 270.

CHAPTER THIRTY – *The Era of Mahone*

1. *William Mahone of Virginia*, Nelson M. Blake, 62–65, 151. *The End of An Era*, John S. Wise, 325–26.
2. *The Virginia Conservatives*, Jack P. Maddex, Jr., unpub. Ph.D. diss., 602–3, 610.
3. *To Carry Africa into the War*, James T. Moore, unpub. M.A. thesis, 159.
4. Ibid., 154–56.
5. *Forgotten Prophet: The Life of John Mercer Langston*, unpub. Ph.D. diss., William F. Cheek III, 336. *Race Relations in Virginia, 1870–1902*, Charles E. Wynes, 43.
6. Cheek, op. cit., 378.

CHAPTER THIRTY-ONE – *Fade-Out of the "Bloody Shirt"*

1. *The Road to Reunion*, Paul H. Buck, 55, 66, 137, 139. I am indebted to Mr. Buck for much material used in this chapter.
2. "The 'Old Virginia Gentleman' in New England," Cecil D. Eby, Jr., VMHB, January 1962.
3. Buck, op. cit., 235.
4. *Lift Every Voice*, Dorothy Sterling and Benjamin Quarles, 16–26. *Black History*, Melvin Drimmer, ed., 346–53, quoting August Meier's *Booker T. Washington: An Interpretation. From Slavery to Freedom*, John Hope Franklin, 387–90. "Uncle Tom? Not Booker T.," Jacqueline James in *American Heritage*, August 1968.

CHAPTER THIRTY-TWO – *Daniel, Martin, Glass and Free Silver*

1. *Thomas Staples Martin*, James A. Bear, unpub. M.A. thesis, 144, 156–57, 162. "Thomas S. Martin: Committee Statesman," Paschal Reeves, VMHB, July 1960. "From Copy Desk to Congress," Harry E. Poindexter, unpub. Ph.D.

diss., Vol. I, 186–92. *Virginia: Bourbonism to Byrd*, Allen W. Moger, 103–5, 111–21. I am indebted to Mr. Moger for much material in this and other chapters covering the period 1870–1925.

2. *Race Relations in Virginia, 1870–1902*, Charles E. Wynes, 114–15.
3. *The Virginia Conservatives*, Jack P. Maddex, Jr., 482, 496–97.
4. *Populism in the Old Dominion*, William DuB. Sheldon, 2–5.
5. Moger, op. cit., 147, 158.

Chapter Thirty-three – *Montague's Election and a New Constitution*

1. "The May Movement of 1899," Raymond H. Pulley, *VMHB*, April 1967. *Life and Career of J. Hoge Tyler*, Thomas E. Gay, Jr., unpub. Ph.D. diss., 186. *Old Virginia Restored*, Raymond H. Pulley, 114–15.
2. *Origins of the New South*, C. Vann Woodward, 325.
3. *The Strange Career of Jim Crow*, C. Vann Woodward, 34–36, 38, 73.
4. *The Negro in Virginia Politics*, Richard L. Morton, 5, 150.
5. *From Bourbonism to Byrd*, Allen W. Moger, 234–35. *Political Career of Allen Caperton Braxton*, Victor D. Weathers, unpub. M.A. thesis, 65–68.
6. "Creating the Virginia State Corporation Commission," Thomas E. Gay, Jr., *VMHB*, October 1970.
7. *The Virginia Constitutional Convention of 1901–02*, Ralph C. McDanel, 114–15. *From Copy Desk to Congress*, Harry E. Poindexter, unpub. Ph.D. diss., Vol. II, 402–3 and footnote. Moger, op. cit., 198–99, 200. *Origins of the New South*, Woodward, 341–42.

Chapter Thirty-four – *A Gettysburg for the Progressives*

1. *Norfolk: Historic Southern Port*, T. J. Wertenbaker, 319–20. *Oxford History of the American People*, S. E. Morison, 889.
2. *Dry Messiah*, Virginius Dabney, 56–58.
3. *The Negro in Virginia Politics*, Andrew Buni, 21.
4. *Separate and Unequal*, Louis R. Harlan, 9 (footnote), 10–13.
5. *Bourbonism to Byrd*, Allen W. Moger, 247–48. *The Virginia Phase of the Ogden Movement*, Marjorie F. Underhill, unpub. M.A. thesis, 78 (footnote). *Edwin A. Alderman*, Dumas Malone, 205.
6. *Claude A. Swanson of Virginia*, Henry C. Ferrell, Jr., unpub. Ph.D. diss., 206, 210, 211.
7. Underhill, op. cit., 114.
8. "Prohibition and Virginia Politics," Robert A. Hohner, *VMHB*, January 1966.
9. *Salt Water and Printer's Ink*, Lenoir Chambers, 216–21. *Prohibition and Virginia Politics*, Hohner, unpub. Ph.D. diss., 102 and footnote.
10. Ferrell, op. cit., 238.

CHAPTER THIRTY-FIVE – *Wilson, War, Prohibition, Machine and Anti-Machine*

1. Daniels, Josephus, *The Wilson Era—Years of Peace*, 520–25.
2. Dabney, Virginius, *Dry Messiah*, 99–101.
3. Dabney, Virginius, "The Human Being" in *The Greatness of Woodrow Wilson*, Em Bowles Alsop, ed., 17–21, 25, 27.
4. Horn, Herman L., *The Growth and Development of the Democratic Party, in Virginia, since 1890*, unpub. Ph.D. diss., 459. Conversation with Thomas S. Martin, Jr.
5. Moger, Allen W., *Bourbonism to Byrd*, 324 and footnote, 325. Kirby, Jack T., *Westmoreland Davis*, 150–51.
6. Moger, op. cit., 326–27.
7. Hawkes, Robert T., Jr., *Political Apprenticeship of Harry F. Byrd*, unpub. M.A. thesis, 24. *Senate Journal*, 1918, 26, 29. Willis, Leo S., *E. Lee Trinkle and the Virginia Democracy*, unpub, Ph.D. diss., 96.
8. Willis, op. cit., 75–76, 100, 114. Moger, op. cit., 335–36.

CHAPTER THIRTY-SIX – *Harry Byrd, the Depression and the New Deal*

1. Dabney, Virginius, *Dry Messiah*, 181.
2. Ibid., 195–204.
3. Heinemann, R. L., *Depression and New Deal in Virginia*, unpub. Ph.D. diss., 2, 4, 6. I am indebted to Mr. Heinemann for much material in this chapter.
4. Ibid., 39.
5. *The Negro in Virginia*, ed. and pub. by WPA, 310, 312, 314, 319.
6. Ferrell, Henry C., Jr., *Claude A. Swanson of Virginia*, unpub. Ph.D. diss., 304–6.
7. "News: TVA Aids Private Business," *Business Week*, May 25, 1940.
8. Hatch, Alden, *The Byrds of Virginia*, 295–305.
9. Hathorn, Guy B., *The Political Career of C. Bascom Slemp*, unpub. Ph.D. diss., 171, 179, 181, 187, 190. Horn, Herman L., *The Growth and Development of the Democratic Party in Virginia*, unpub. Ph.D. diss., 192.
10. Hathorn, op. cit., 312.
11. Heinemann, op. cit., 254, 259, 260, 264.

CHAPTER THIRTY-EIGHT – *The Era of "Massive Resistance"*

1. Gates, Robbins L., "*The Making of Massive Resistance*," 30. I am indebted to Mr. Gates for much material in this chapter.
2. Kilpatrick to Tom Waring, December 9, 1955; to Paul D. Hastings, December 28, 1955; to Hugh D. Grant, February 25, 1959; to Harry F. Byrd, January 18, 1960, James J. Kilpatrick Papers, University of Virginia Library, cited by

James W. Ely, Jr., in *The Crisis of Conservative Virginia*, Ph.D. diss. in progress. Kilpatrick to author, November 14, 1970.
3. Gates, op. cit., 148–49.
4. Carl Shires in Richmond *News Leader*, October 6, 1967.

CHAPTER THIRTY-NINE – *Virginia: the New Dominion*

1. Miller, Francis P.: *Man from the Valley*, 199–202.
2. Buni, Andrew, *The Negro in Virginia Politics*, 228–32.
3. Andrews, M. Carl, *No Higher Honor*, 104–7.

BIBLIOGRAPHY

In addition to the materials listed below, I have examined the official messages of all the governors of Virginia since 1800. The Richmond newspapers going well back into the nineteenth century have been highly useful, but I have not listed them individually. The Dictionary of American Biography has been consulted frequently.

BOOKS

ABERNETHY, THOMAS P.: *Three Virginia Frontiers*, Gloucester, Mass., Peter Smith, 1962.

———: *The Burr Conspiracy*, New York, Oxford, 1954.

———: *Western Lands and the American Revolution*, New York, Russell & Russell, 1959.

ADAMS, NEHEMIAH: *A South-Side View of Slavery*, Boston, T. R. Marvin and B. B. Mussey & Co., 1854.

ALDEN, JOHN R.: *The South in the Revolution*, Baton Rouge, L.S.U. Press, 1957.

ALSOP, EM BOWLES, ed.: *The Greatness of Woodrow Wilson*, New York, Rinehart, 1956.

AMBLER, CHARLES H.: *Thomas Ritchie, a Study in Virginia Politics*, Richmond, Bell Book & Stationery Co., 1913.

———: *Sectionalism in Virginia from 1776 to 1861*, Chicago, U. of Chicago Press, 1910.

ANDERSON, DICE R.: *William B. Giles, a Biography*, Menasha, Wis., George Banta, 1915.

ANDREWS, M. CARL: *No Higher Honor: The Story of Mills E. Godwin, Jr.*, Richmond, Dietz, 1970.

ANDREWS, MATTHEW PAGE: *Virginia, the Old Dominion*, Garden City, Doubleday, 1937.

———: *The Soul of a Nation*, New York, Scribner, 1943.

APTHEKER, HERBERT: *Negro Slave Revolts in the U.S., 1526–1860*, New York, International Publications, 1939.

AVARY, MYRTA LOCKETT: *Dixie After the War*, Boston, Houghton Mifflin, 1937.

BAGBY, GEORGE W.: *The Old Virginia Gentleman and Other Sketches*, ed. by Ellen M. Bagby, Richmond, Dietz, 1943.

BANCROFT, FREDERIC: *Slave-Trading in the Old South*, Baltimore, J. H. Furst, 1931.

BARBOUR, PHILIP L.: *The Three Worlds of Captain John Smith*, Boston, Houghton Mifflin, 1964.

———: *Pocahontas and Her World*, Boston, Houghton Mifflin, 1970.

BASSETT, JOHN SPENCER, ed.: *The Writings of Col. William Byrd of Westover*, Garden City, Doubleday, 1901.

BEARD, CHARLES A. and MARY R.: *The Rise of American Civilization*, New York, Macmillan, 1930.

BEMISS, SAMUEL: *Ancient Adventurers*, Richmond, privately printed, 1957.

———: introduction to *The Three Charters of the Virginia Company of London*, Williamsburg, 350th Anniversary Celebration Corp., 1957.

BENÉT, STEPHEN VINCENT: *John Brown's Body*, Garden City, Doubleday, 1928.

BEVERLEY, ROBERT: *The History and Present State of Virginia*, ed. with introduction by Louis B. Wright, Chapel Hill, U.N.C. Press, 1947.

BILL, ALFRED HOYT: *The Beleaguered City, Richmond, 1861–1865*, New York, Knopf, 1946.

BLACKFORD, L. MINOR: *Mine Eyes Have Seen the Glory*, Cambridge, Mass., Harvard U. Press, 1954.

BLACKFORD, W. W.: *My Years with Jeb Stuart*, New York, Scribner, 1945.

BLAKE, NELSON M.: *William Mahone of Virginia*, Richmond, Garrett & Massie, 1935.

BLANTON, WYNDHAM B.: *Medicine in Virginia in the Seventeenth Century, Medicine in Virginia in the Eighteenth Century, Medicine in Virginia in the Nineteenth Century*, Richmond, William Byrd Press, 1930; Garrett & Massie, 1931, 1933.

BODINE, AUBREY A.: *The Face of Virginia*, introduction by Virginius Dabney, Baltimore, Bodine & Associates, 1963.

BOWIE, WALTER R.: *Sunrise in the South, the Life of Mary-Cooke Branch Munford*, Richmond, William Byrd Press, 1942.

BRAWLEY, BENJAMIN: *Dr. Dillard of the Jeanes Fund*, New York, Fleming H. Revell, 1930.

BREWER, JAMES H.: *The Confederate Negro, Virginia's Craftsmen and Military Laborers, 1861–1865*, Durham, Duke U. Press, 1969.

BRIDENBAUGH, CARL: *Seat of Empire—The Political Role of Eighteenth-Century Williamsburg*, Charlottesville, Univ. of Va. Press, 1963.

————: *Myths and Realities*, Baton Rouge, L.S.U. Press, 1952.

————: *The Colonial Craftsman*, New York, N.Y.U. Press, 1950.

BRUCE, PHILIP A.: *Institutional History of Virginia in the Seventeenth Century*, 2 vols., Gloucester, Mass., Peter Smith, 1964.

————: *Economic History of Virginia in the Seventeenth Century*, 2 vols., Gloucester, Mass., Peter Smith, 1935.

————: *Social Life in Virginia in the Seventeenth Century*, Richmond, Whittet & Shepperson, 1907.

————: *The Virginia Plutarch*, 2 vols., Chapel Hill, U.N.C. Press, 1929.

————: *History of the University of Virginia, 1819–1919*, Vol. II, New York, Macmillan, 1920.

BRYDON, GEORGE MACL.: *Virginia's Mother Church*, Vol. I, Richmond, Virginia Historical Society, 1947; Vol. II, Philadelphia, Church History Society, 1952.

BUCK, J. L. BLAIR: *The Development of Public Schools in Virginia, 1607–1952*, Richmond, Virginia State Board of Education, 1952.

BUCK, PAUL H.: *The Road to Reunion, 1865–1900*, Boston, Little Brown, 1937.

BUNI, ANDREW: *The Negro in Virginia Politics, 1902–1965*, Charlottesville, U. Press of Va., 1967.

BUTTERFIELD, ROGER: *The American Past*, New York, Simon & Schuster, 1957.

BYRD, WILLIAM: *A Journey to the Land of Eden and Other Papers*, ed. by Mark Van Doren, New York, Macy-Masius, 1928.

CABELL, JAMES BRANCH: *As I Remember It*, New York, McBride, 1955.

CAMPBELL, CHARLES: *History of the Colony and Ancient Dominion of Virginia*, Spartanburg, S.C., The Reprint Co., 1965.

CARTER, HODDING: *The Angry Scar*, Garden City, Doubleday, 1959.

CARY, WILSON MILES: *Sally Cary: A Long Hidden Romance of Washington's Life*, New York, Devinne Press, 1916.

CATTON, BRUCE: *A Stillness at Appomattox*, Garden City, Doubleday, 1954.

————: *Glory Road*, Garden City, Doubleday, 1954.

CHALMERS, DAVID M.: *Hooded Americanism*, Garden City, Doubleday, 1965.

CHAMBERLAIN, SAMUEL: *Springtime in Virginia*, introduction by Virginius Dabney, New York, Hastings, 1947.

CHAMBERS, LENOIR: *Stonewall Jackson*, 2 vols., New York, Morrow, 1959.

———— and SHANK, JOSEPH E.: *Salt Water and Printer's Ink: Norfolk and Its Newspapers, 1865–1965*, Chapel Hill, U.N.C. Press, 1967.

CHANDLER, J. A. C.: *Representation in Virginia*, Baltimore, John Hopkins U. Press, 1896.

————: *The History of Suffrage in Virginia*, Baltimore, John Hopkins U. Press, 1901.

CHESNUT, MARY BOYKIN: *A Diary from Dixie*, Ben Ames Williams, ed., Boston, Houghton Mifflin, 1949.

CHUTE, MARCHETTE: *Shakespeare of London*, New York, Dutton, 1949.

COLE, ARTHUR C.: *The Whig Party in the South*, Gloucester, Mass., Peter Smith, 1962.

Colonial Medicine, papers by five contributors, Williamsburg, Virginia 350th Anniversary Commission, 1957.

COOKE, JOHN ESTEN: *Virginia, a History of the People*, Boston, Houghton Mifflin, 1911.

CRAVEN, AVERY O.: *Soil Exhaustion as a Factor in the Agricultural History of Virginia and Maryland, 1606–1860*, Gloucester, Mass., Peter Smith, 1965.

————: *Civil War in the Making, 1815–1860*, Baton Rouge, L.S.U. Press, 1965.

————: *Edmund Ruffin, Southerner: A Study in Secession*, Hamden, Conn., Archon Books, 1964.

CRAVEN, WESLEY FRANK: *The Colonies in Transition, 1660–1713*, New York, Harper, 1968.

DABNEY, CHARLES W.: *Universal Education in the South*, 2 vols., Chapel Hill, U.N.C. Press, 1936.

DABNEY, VIRGINIUS: *Dry Messiah: The Life of Bishop Cannon*, New York, Knopf, 1949.

DANIELS, JOSEPHUS: *The Wilson Era*, Chapel Hill, U.N.C. Press, 1944.

DAVIS, DAVID B.: *The Problem of Slavery in Western Culture*, Ithaca, Cornell U. Press, 1967.

DAVIS, RICHARD BEALE: *Intellectual Life in Jefferson's Virginia, 1790–1830*, Chapel Hill, U.N.C. Press, 1964.

DeLEON, THOMAS C.: *Four Years in Rebel Capitals*, New York, Collier, 1962.

DEW, CHARLES B.: *Ironmaker to the Confederacy: Joseph R. Anderson and the Tredegar Iron Works*, New Haven, Yale U. Press, 1966.

DOWDEY, CLIFFORD: *The Land They Fought For*, Garden City, Doubleday, 1955.

————: *Lee*, Boston, Little Brown, 1965.

————: *The Virginia Dynasties*, Boston, Little Brown, 1969.

————: *Experiment in Rebellion*, Garden City, Doubleday, 1946.

————: *Death of a Nation*, New York, Knopf, 1958.

DREWRY, WILLIAM S.: *The Southampton Insurrection*, Washington, D.C., Neale Co., 1900.

DRIMMER, MELVIN, ed.: *Black History: A Reappraisal*, Garden City, Doubleday, 1968.

DRISKO, CAROL F. and TOPPIN, EDGAR A.: *The Unfinished March: The Negro in the U.S., Reconstruction and World War I*, Garden City, Doubleday, 1967.

EATON, CLEMENT: *Freedom of Thought in the Old South*, Gloucester, Mass., Peter Smith, 1951.

———: *The Mind of the Old South*, Baton Rouge, L.S.U. Press, 1967.

———: *The Growth of Southern Civilization, 1790–1860*, New York, Harper, 1961.

EBY, CECIL D., JR.: *"Porte Crayon": The Life of David Hunter Strother*, Chapel Hill, U.N.C. Press, 1960.

ECKENRODE, H. J.: *The Revolution in Virginia*, Boston, Houghton Mifflin, 1916.

———: *The Political History of Virginia During Reconstruction*, Baltimore, Johns Hopkins U. Press, 1904.

FISHWICK, MARSHALL: *Virginia: A New Look at the Old Dominion*, New York, Harper, 1959.

FISKE, JOHN: *Old Virginia and Her Neighbors*, 2 vols., Boston, Houghton Mifflin, 1897.

FITZPATRICK, JOHN C.: *The Writings of George Washington*, Vol. 31, Washington, D.C., U. S. Govt. Printing Office, 1939.

FLEMING, THOMAS J.: *First in Their Hearts*, New York, Norton, 1967.

FOOTE, WILLIAM HENRY: *Sketches of Virginia*, First Series, Richmond, John Knox Press, 1966.

FRANKLIN, JOHN HOPE: *The Militant South, 1800–1861*, Cambridge, Mass., Harvard Press, 1956.

———: *From Slavery to Freedom*, New York, Knopf, 1967.

FREEMAN, DOUGLAS S.: *R. E. Lee*, 4 vols., New York, Scribner, 1934, 1935.

———: *Lee's Lieutenants*, Vol. I, New York, Scribner, 1942.

———: *The South to Posterity*, New York, Scribner, 1939.

———: *George Washington*, Vols. I–VI. Carroll, J. A. and Ashworth, Mary Wells, Vol. VII, New York, Scribner, 1948, 1951, 1952, 1954, 1957.

FRIDDELL, GUY: *What Is It About Virginia?*, Richmond, Dietz, 1966.

GAINES, FRANCIS P.: *The Southern Plantation*, New York, Columbia U. Press, 1924.

GARA, LARRY: *The Liberty Line: The Legend of the Underground Railroad*, Lexington, U. of Ky. Press, 1961.

GATES, ROBBINS L.: *The Making of Massive Resistance*, Chapel Hill, U.N.C. Press, 1964.

GENOVESE, EUGENE D.: *The Political Economy of Slavery*, New York, Random House, 1965.

GEWEHR, WESLEY M.: *The Great Awakening in Virginia, 1740–1790*, Durham, Duke U. Press, 1930.

GORDON, JOHN B.: *Reminiscences of the Civil War*, New York, Scribner, 1903.

GOTTMANN, JEAN: *Virginia in Our Century*, Charlottesville, U. Press of Va., 1969.

GREEN, JOHN RICHARD: *A History of the English People*, Vols. II, III and IV, New York, Philadelphia and Chicago, Nottingham Society, n.d.

GRIGSBY, HUGH BLAIR: *The Virginia Convention of 1776*, Richmond, J. W. Randolph, 1855.

———: *The History of the Federal Convention of 1788*, 2 vols., R. A. Brock, ed., Richmond, Virginia Historical Society, 1858.

———: *The Virginia Convention of 1829–30*, Richmond, Macfarland & Fergusson, 1854.

GUILD, JANE PURCELL: *Black Laws of Virginia*, Richmond, Whittet & Shepperson, 1936.

HARLAN, LOUIS R.: *Separate and Unequal*, Chapel Hill, U.N.C. Press, 1958.

HARRISON, MRS. BURTON: *Recollections Grave and Gay*, New York, Scribner, 1911.

HART, FREEMAN H.: *The Valley of Virginia in the American Revolution*, Chapel Hill, U.N.C. Press, 1942.

HARTWELL, HENRY; BLAIR, JAMES and CHILTON, EDWARD: *The Present State of Virginia and the College*, ed. with intro. by Hunter D. Farish, Charlottesville, U. Press of Va., 1964.

HATCH, ALDEN: *The Byrds of Virginia*, New York, Holt, 1969.

HAVIGHURST, WALTER: *Alexander Spotswood: Portrait of a Governor*, Williamsburg, Colonial Williamsburg, 1967.

HEATWOLE, CORNELIUS J.: *A History of Education in Virginia*, New York, Macmillan, 1916.

HEMPHILL, W. EDWIN; SCHLEGEL, MARVIN W., and ENGELBERG, SADIE E.: *Cavalier Commonwealth*, New York, McGraw-Hill, 1957.

HENDERSON, COL. G. F. R.: *Stonewall Jackson and the American Civil War*, 2 vols., London, Longman's, 1913.

HENRY, ROBERT SELPH: *The Story of the Confederacy*, Indianapolis, Bobbs Merrill, 1931.

———: *The Story of Reconstruction*, Gloucester, Mass., Peter Smith, 1963.

A Hornbook of Virginia History, Richmond, Virginia State Library, 1965.

HORNER, DAVE: *The Blockade-Runners*, New York, Dodd, Mead, 1968.

Howe, Henry: *Historical Collections of Virginia*, Charleston, S.C., Babcock, 1856.

Hubbell, Jay B.: *The South in American Literature*, Durham, Duke U. Press, 1954.

———: *South and Southwest*, Durham, Duke U. Press, 1965.

Hughes, Roscoe D.: and Leidheiser, Henry D., eds., *Exploring Virginia's Human Resources*, Charlottesville, U. Press of Va., 1965.

Hughes, Thomas P.: *Medicine in Virginia, 1607–1699*, Williamsburg, 350th Anniversary Celebration Corp., 1957.

Jackson, Luther P.: *Free Negro Labor and Property Holding in Virginia, 1830–1860*, New York, Appleton, 1942.

———: *Negro Officeholders in Virginia, 1865–1895*, Norfolk, Guide Quality Press, 1945.

James, James A.: *The Life of George Rogers Clark*, Chicago, U. of Chicago Press, 1928.

Jefferson, Thomas: *Notes on the State of Virginia*, Chapel Hill, U.N.C. Press, 1955.

Jenkins, William S.: *Pro-Slavery Thought in the Old South*, Gloucester, Mass., Peter Smith, 1960.

Johnston, Angus J., II: *Virginia Railroads in the Civil War*, Chapel Hill, U.N.C. Press, 1961.

Jones, Howard Mumford: *The Literature of Virginia in the Seventeenth Century*, Charlottesville, U. Press of Va., 1968.

Jones, Hugh: *The Present State of Virginia*, ed. with intro. by Richard L. Morton, Chapel Hill, U.N.C. Press, 1956.

Jones, John B.: *A Rebel War Clerk's Diary*, ed. by Howard Swiggett, 2 vols., New York, Old Hickory Bookshop, 1935.

Jones, Virgil C.: *Ranger Mosby*, Chapel Hill, U.N.C Press, 1944.

Jordan, Winthrop P.: *White over Black*, Chapel Hill, U.N.C. Press, 1968.

Kegley, F. B.: *Kegley's Virginia Frontier*, Roanoke, Southwest Va. Historical Society, 1938.

Kercheval, Samuel: *A History of the Valley of Virginia*. Woodstock, Va. Power Press, 1902.

Key, V. O., Jr.: *Southern Politics in State and Nation*, New York, Knopf, 1949.

Kimball, Marie: *Jefferson—War And Peace, 1776–1784*, New York, Coward-McCann, 1947.

Kincaid, Robert L.: *The Wilderness Road*, Harrogate, Tenn., Lincoln U. Press, 1955.

KIRBY, JACK TEMPLE: *Westmoreland Davis*, Charlottesville, U. Press of Va., 1968.

KLEIN, HERBERT S.: *Slavery in the Americas: A Comparative Study of Virginia and Cuba*, Chicago, U. of Chicago Press, 1967.

LANKFORD, JOHN, ed.: *Captain John Smith's America: Selections from His Writings*, New York, Harper, 1967.

LARSEN, WILLIAM: *Montague of Virginia: The Making of a Southern Progressive*, Baton Rouge, L.S.U. Press, 1965.

LEYBURN, JAMES G.: *The Scotch-Irish, a Social History*, Chapel Hill, U.N.C. Press, 1962.

LINK, ARTHUR S. and PATRICK, REMBERT W.: *Writing Southern History*, Baton Rouge, L.S.U. Press, 1965.

LOCKE, MARY S.: *Anti-Slavery in America*, Boston, Ginn & Co., 1901.

MACRAE, DAVID: *The Americans at Home*, New York, Dutton, 1952.

McCARTHY, AGNES and REDDICK, LAWRENCE: *Worth Fighting For: The History of the Negro in the U.S. During the Civil War and Reconstruction*, Garden City, Doubleday, 1965.

McCOLLEY, ROBERT: *Slavery and Jeffersonian Virginia*, Urbana, U. of Illinois Press, 1964.

McCONNELL, JOHN P.: *Negroes and Their Treatment in Virginia from 1865 to 1867*, Pulaski, Va., B. D. Smith & Bros., 1910.

McDANEL, RALPH C.: *The Virginia Constitutional Convention of 1901–1902*, Baltimore, Johns Hopkins U. Press, 1928.

McGUIRE, JUDITH W.: *Diary of a Southern Refugee*, Richmond, Randolph & English, 1889.

MADDOX, WILLIAM A.: *The Free School Idea in Virginia Before the Civil War*, New York, Columbia U. Teacher's College, 1918.

MALONE, DUMAS: *Jefferson and His Time*, Vols. I, II and III, Boston, Little Brown, 1948, 1951, 1962.

————: *Edwin A. Alderman*, Garden City, Doubleday, 1940.

MANARIN, LOUIS H., ed.: *Richmond at War: The Minutes of the City Council, 1861–1865*, Chapel Hill, U.N.C. Press, 1966.

MAPP, ALF J., JR.: *The Virginia Experiment*, Richmond, Dietz, 1957.

MASSEY, JOHN E.: *Autobiography*, Elizabeth H. Hancock, ed., New York & Washington, Neale, 1909.

MAYO, BERNARD: *Myths and Men*, Athens, Ga., U. of Ga. Press, 1959.

MAYS, DAVID J.: *Edmund Pendleton, 1721–1803*, 2 vols., Cambridge, Mass., Harvard U. Press, 1952.

————: *The Letters and Papers of Edmund Pendleton, 1734–1803*, 2 vols., Charlottesville, U. Press of Va., 1967.

MEADE, ROBERT D.: *Patrick Henry: Patriot in the Making*, Philadelphia, Lippincott, 1957.

————: *Patrick Henry: Practical Revolutionary*, Philadelphia, Lippincott, 1969.

————: *Judah P. Benjamin*, New York, Oxford, 1943.

MEADE, BISHOP WILLIAM: *Old Churches, Ministers and Families of Virginia*, 2 vols., Philadelphia, Lippincott, 1857.

MIDDLETON, ARTHUR P.: *Tobacco Coast*, Newport News, Mariners' Museum, 1953.

MILLER, FRANCIS PICKENS: *Man from the Valley*, Chapel Hill, U.N.C. Press, 1971.

MILLER, HELEN HILL: *George Mason: Constitutionalist*, Cambridge, Mass., Harvard U. Press, 1938.

MOGER, ALLEN W.: *Virginia: Bourbonism to Byrd, 1870–1925*, Charlottesville, U. Press of Va., 1968.

MOORE, GAY MONTAGUE: *Seaport in Virginia: George Washington's Alexandria*, Richmond, Garrett & Massie, 1949.

MOORE, VIRGINIA: *Virginia Is a State of Mind*, New York, Dutton, 1942.

MOREHEAD, JAMES O., ed.: *History of Bland County*, Radford, Va., Commonwealth Press, 1961.

MORISON, SAMUEL ELIOT: *The Oxford History of the American People*, New York, Oxford, 1965.

MORTON, RICHARD L.: *Colonial Virginia*, 2 vols., Chapel Hill, U.N.C. Press, 1960.

————: *The Negro in Virginia Politics, 1865–1902*, Charlottesville, Univ. of Virginia, 1918.

MOTON, ROBERT RUSSA: *Finding a Way Out*, Garden City, Doubleday, 1921.

MUNFORD, BEVERLEY B.: *Virginia's Attitude Toward Slavery and Secession*, Richmond, L. H. Jenkins, 1910.

MUSE, BENJAMIN: *Virginia's Massive Resistance*, Bloomington, Indiana U. Press, 1961.

The Negro in Virginia, compiled by Writers' Program of the Works Progress Administration in the State of Virginia, New York, Hastings, 1940.

NEVINS, ALLAN: *American Press Opinion, Washington to Coolidge*, New York, D. C. Heath, 1928.

————: *The American States During and After the Revolution, 1775–1789*, New York, Macmillan, 1924.

NILES, BLAIR: *The James: From Iron Gate to the Sea*, New York, Farrar & Rinehart, 1945.

OLCOTT, WILLIAM: *The Greenbrier Heritage*, White Sulphur Springs, Arndt, Preston, Lamb & Keen Inc., n.d.

O'NEAL, WILLIAM B.: *Architecture in Virginia*, New York, Walker & Co., 1968.

PAGE, THOMAS NELSON: *The Old South*, New York, Scribner, 1892.

PARRINGTON, VERNON L.: *Main Currents in American Thought*, 3 vols., New York, Harcourt, 1958.

PATRICK, REMBERT W.: *The Reconstruction of the Nation*, New York, Oxford, 1967.

————: *The Fall of Richmond*, Baton Rouge, L.S.U. Press, 1960.

PEARSON, CHARLES C. and HENDRICKS, J. EDWIN: *Liquor and Anti-Liquor in Virginia, 1619–1919*, Durham, Duke U. Press, 1967.

PEARSON, CHARLES C.: *The Readjuster Movement in Virginia*, New Haven, Yale U. Press, 1917.

PENDLETON, WILLIAM C.: *Political History of Appalachian Virginia, 1776–1927*, Dayton, Va., Shenandoah Press, 1927.

PHILLIPS, ULRICH B.: *Life and Labor in the Old South*, Boston, Little Brown, n.d.

————: *American Negro Slavery*, Gloucester, Mass., Peter Smith, 1959.

POWELL, MARY G.: *The History of Old Alexandria, Virginia*, Richmond, William Byrd Press, 1928.

PRYOR, MRS. ROGER: *Reminiscences of Peace and War*, New York, Macmillan, 1904.

PULLEY, RAYMOND H.: *Old Virginia Restored—An Interpretation of the Progressive Impulse, 1870–1930*, Charlottesville, U. Press of Va., 1968.

QUARLES, BENJAMIN: *The Negro in the American Revolution*, Chapel Hill, U.N.C. Press, 1961.

————: *The Negro in the Civil War*, Boston, Little Brown, 1953.

QUINN, ARTHUR HOBSON: *Edgar Allan Poe: A Critical Biography*, New York, Appleton, 1941.

RENIERS, PERCIVAL: *The Springs of Virginia*, Chapel Hill, U.N.C. Press, 1941.

Richmond Portraits: In an Exhibition of Makers of Richmond, 1737–1960, Richmond, Valentine Museum, 1949.

RILEY, FRANKLIN L., ed.: *General Robert E. Lee after Appomattox*, New York, Macmillan, 1922.

ROBERT, JOSEPH C.: *The Road from Monticello*, Durham, Duke U. Press, 1941.

————: *The Story of Tobacco in America*, Chapel Hill, U.N.C. Press, 1967.

ROBERTSON, JAMES I., JR.: *The Stonewall Brigade*, Baton Rouge, L.S.U. Press, 1963.

ROLFE, JOHN: *A True Relation of the State of Virginia*, New Haven, Yale U. Press, 1951.

ROSENBERGER, FRANCIS COLEMAN, ed.: *Virginia Reader: A Treasury of Writings*, New York, Dutton, 1948.

ROUSE, PARKE, JR.: *Virginia and the English Heritage in America*, New York, Hastings, 1966.

——: *Planters and Pioneers, Life in Colonial Virginia*, New York, Hastings, 1968.

ROYALL, WILLIAM L.: *Some Reminiscences*, New York, Neale Publishing Co., 1909.

RUSSELL, JOHN H.: *The Free Negro in Virginia*, Baltimore, Johns Hopkins U. Press, 1913.

RUTLAND, ROBERT ALLEN: *George Mason—Reluctant Statesman*, Charlottesville, U. Press of Va., 1963.

SANBORN, MARGARET: *Robert E. Lee*, 2 vols., Philadelphia, Lippincott, 1966 and 1967.

SCHLESINGER, ARTHUR M.: *Prelude to Independence: The Newspaper War on Britain, 1774–1776*. New York, Knopf, 1966.

SHANKS, HENRY T.: *The Secession Movement in Virginia, 1847–1861*, Richmond, Garrett & Massie, 1934.

SHELDON, WILLIAM DuBOSE: *Populism in the Old Dominion*, Princeton, Princeton U. Press, 1935.

SIMKINS, FRANCIS B.: *A History of the South*, New York, Knopf, 1953.

SIMMS, HENRY H.: *The Rise of the Whigs in Virginia, 1824–1840*, Richmond, William Byrd Press, 1929.

SIMONINI, R. C., JR., ed.: *Virginia in History and Tradition*, Farmville, Va., Longwood College, 1958.

SMEDES, SUSAN D.: *Memorials of a Southern Planter*, intro. by Fletcher M. Green, New York, Knopf, 1965.

SMITH, ABBOT EMERSON: *Colonists in Bondage: White Servitude and Convict Labor in America, 1607–1776*, Chapel Hill, U.N.C. Press, 1947.

SMITH, ALAN, ed.: *Virginia: 1584–1607*, London, Theodore Brun, 1957.

SMITH, BOB: *They Closed Their Schools*, Chapel Hill, U.N.C. Press, 1965.

SMITH, JAMES MORTON, ed.: *Seventeenth-Century America*, Chapel Hill, U.N.C. Press, 1959.

The South in the Building of the Nation, Vol. VII, John B. Henneman, ed. Richmond, Southern Historical Publication Society, 1909.

STAMPP, KENNETH M.: *The Peculiar Institution: Slavery in the Antebellum South*, New York, Knopf, 1956.

——: *The Era of Reconstruction, 1865–1877*, New York, Knopf, 1966.

STANARD, MARY NEWTON: *The Story of Virginia's First Century*, Philadelphia, Lippincott, 1938.

————: *Richmond, Its People and Its Story*, Philadelphia, Lippincott, 1923.

————: *Colonial Virginia, Its People and Its Customs*, Philadelphia, Lippincott, 1917.

STAUDENRAUS, P. J.: *The African Colonization Movement, 1816–1865*, New York, Columbia U. Press, 1961.

STERLING, DOROTHY and QUARLES, BENJAMIN: *Lift Every Voice: The Lives of Booker T. Washington, W. E. B. DuBois and Others*, Garden City, Doubleday, 1965.

STEVENS, WILLIAM O.: *Pistols at Ten Paces*, Boston, Houghton Mifflin, 1940.

STOKES, WILLIAM E., JR., and BERKELEY, FRANCIS L., JR.: *The Papers of Randolph of Roanoke*, Charlottesville, Univ. of Va. Library, 1950.

STONER, ROBERT D.: *A Seed-Bed of the Republic*, Roanoke, Roanoke Historical Society, 1962.

STITH, WILLIAM: *The History of the First Discovery and Settlement of Virginia*, Spartanburg, S.C., The Reprint Co., 1965.

STRACHEY, WILLIAM: *True Reportory*, and JOURDAIN, SILVESTER: *Discovery of the Bermudas*, Wright, Louis B., ed., Charlottesville, U. Press of Va., 1964.

STRAUSS, LEWIS L.: *Men and Decisions*, Garden City, Doubleday, 1962.

STRODE, HUDSON: *Jefferson Davis*, Vols. II and III, New York, Harcourt, 1959, 1964.

SUMMERS, LEWIS P.: *History of Southwest Virginia, 1746–1786; Washington County, 1777–1870*, Baltimore, Genealogical Publishing Co., 1966.

SYDNOR, CHARLES W.: *Gentlemen Freeholders: Political Practices in Washington's Virginia*, Chapel Hill, U.N.C. Press, 1952.

TATE, THAD W.: *The Negro in Eighteenth-Century Williamsburg*, Williamsburg, Colonial Williamsburg, 1965.

TAYLOR, ALRUTHEUS A.: *The Negro in the Reconstruction of Virginia*, Washington, D.C., Assoc. for Study of Negro Life and History, 1926.

TAYLOR, WILLIAM R.: *Cavalier and Yankee*, New York, Braziller, 1961.

THAYNE, ELSWYTH: *Potomac Squire*, New York, Duell, Sloan & Pearce, 1963.

THOMAS, EMORY M.: *The Confederate State of Richmond*, Austin, U. of Texas Press, 1971.

THOMASON, JOHN W., JR.: *Jeb Stuart*, New York, Scribner, 1930.

THOMPSON, EDGAR T., ed.: *Perspectives on the South*, Durham, Duke U. Press, 1967.

TINDALL, GEORGE B.: *The Emergence of the New South, 1913–1945*, Baton Rouge, L.S.U. Press, 1967.

TOYNBEE, ARNOLD J.: *A Study of History*, 1 vol., New York, Oxford, 1947.

TREVELYAN, G. M.: *Illustrated English Social History*, Vol. II, London, Longman's, 1951.

TYLER, LYON G., ed.: *Narratives of Early Virginia, 1606–1625*, New York, Barnes & Noble, 1959.

VANDIVER, FRANK S.: *Their Tattered Flags*, New York, Harper, 1970.

VAN SCHREEVEN, WILLIAM J.: *The Conventions and Constitutions of Virginia, 1776–1966*, Richmond, Virginia State Library, 1967.

VILLARD, OSWALD G.: *John Brown, 1800–1859*, New York, Knopf, 1943.

WADE, RICHARD C.: *Slavery in the Cities: The South, 1820–1860*, New York, Oxford, 1964.

WASHBURN, WILCOMB F.: *The Governor and the Rebel*, Chapel Hill, U.N.C. Press, 1957.

WASHINGTON, BOOKER T.: *Up from Slavery*, Garden City, Doubleday, n.d.

WAYLAND, JOHN W.: *The German Element in the Shenandoah Valley*, Charlottesville, Michie Co., 1907.

WERTENBAKER, THOMAS J.: *The Shaping of Colonial Virginia*, New York, Russell & Russell, 1958.

———: *Torchbearer of the Revolution*, Princeton, Princeton U. Press, 1940.

———: *Norfolk, Historic Southern Port*, Durham, Duke U. Press, 1931; 2nd ed., Marvin W. Schlegel, ed., 1962.

WILEY, BELL I.: *Southern Negroes, 1861–1865*, New Haven, Yale U. Press, 1938.

———: *The Life of Johnny Reb*, Indianapolis, Bobbs Merrill, 1943.

WILKINSON, J. HARVIE III: *Harry Byrd and the Changing Face of Virginia Politics, 1945–1966*, Charlottesville, U. Press of Va., 1968.

WILLISON, GEORGE F.: *Behold Virginia, the Fifth Crown*, New York, Harcourt, 1951.

WILSON, EDMUND: *Patriotic Gore: Studies in the Literature of the Civil War*, New York, Oxford, 1962.

WILSTACH, PAUL: *Potomac Landings*, Garden City, Doubleday, 1921.

WISE, JOHN S.: *The End of an Era*, Curtiss Carroll Davis, ed., New York, Yoseloff, 1965.

WISH, HARVEY: *George Fitzhugh, Propagandist of the Old South*, Baton Rouge, L.S.U. Press, 1943.

WOODSON, CARTER G. AND WESLEY, CHARLES H.: *The Negro In Our History*, Washington, D.C., Associated Publishers, Inc., 1966.

WOODWARD, C. VANN: *Origins of the New South, 1877–1913*, Baton Rouge, L.S.U. Press, 1951.

———: *The Burden of Southern History*, Baton Rouge, L.S.U. Press, 1960.

———: *The Strange Career of Jim Crow*, New York, Oxford, 1966.

———: *Reunion and Reaction*, Boston, Little Brown, 1951.

———: *American Counterpoint, Slavery and Racism in the North-South Dialogue*, Boston, Little Brown, 1971.

WRIGHT, LOUIS B.: *Religion and Empire*, Chapel Hill, U.N.C. Press, 1943.

———: *The First Gentlemen of Virginia*, San Marino, Cal., Huntington Library, 1940.

———, ed.: *The Prose Works of William Byrd of Westover*, Cambridge, Mass., Harvard U. Press, 1966.

———: *The Cultural Life of the American Colonies, 1607–1763*, New York, Harper, 1957.

WUST, KLAUS: *The Virginia Germans*, Charlottesville, U. Press of Va., 1969.

WYNES, CHARLES E., ed.: *Southern Sketches from Virginia, 1881–1901, Orra Langhorne*, Charlottesville, U. of Va. Press, 1964.

———: *Race Relations in Virginia, 1870–1902*, Charlottesville, U. of Va. Press, 1961.

YOUNGER, EDWARD, ed.: *Inside the Confederate Government, the Diary of Robert Garlick Hill Kean*, New York, Oxford, 1957.

PAMPHLETS, MAGAZINES, TRACTS, ETC.

The following abbreviations are used:
Virginia Magazine of History and Biography—VMHB
Virginia Cavalcade—VC
Virginia Quarterly Review—VQR
American Heritage—AH
South Atlantic Quarterly—SAQ

ABBOTT, MARTIN, ed.: "A Southerner Views the South: Letters of Harvey M. Watterson, *VMHB*, October 1960.

ABBOTT, RICHARD H.: "Yankee Farmers in Northern Virginia, 1840–1860," *VMHB*, January 1968.

ABERNETHY, THOMAS P.: "The University—Mr. Jefferson's Academical Village, 1816–1825," *The Jeffersonian*, session 1969–70.

ALDERSON, WILLIAM T.: "The Freedmen's Bureau and Negro Education in Virginia," *N.C. Historical Review*, January 1952.

AMBROSE, STEPHEN E.: "The Bread Riots in Richmond," *VMHB*, April 1963.

AMMON, HARRY: "James Monroe and the Era of Good Feelings," *VMHB*, October, 1958.

ANDERSON, STERLING P., JR.: "Edmund Ruffin, Editor and Publisher," *VC*, Summer 1967.

ARMSTRONG, WILLIAM M.: "Libby Prison: The Civil War Diary of Arthur G. Sedgwick," *VMHB*, October 1963.

"Autobiography of David Meade," *William and Mary Quarterly*, October 1904.

BAILEY, THOMAS A.: "Woodrow Wilson Wouldn't Yield," *AH*, June 1957.

BAILOR, KEITH M.: "John Taylor of Caroline," *VMHB*, July 1967.

BAIN, CHESTER W.: "The Development of Municipal Corporations," *Virginia Municipal Review*, December 1956.

BARBOUR, PHILIP L.: "Captain George Kendall: Mutineer or Intelligencer?" *VMHB*, July 1962.

————: "The First Reconnaissance of the James," *VC*, Autumn 1967.

BERKELEY, EDMUND, JR.: "Prophet Without Honor: Christopher McPherson, Free Person of Color," *VMHB*, April 1969.

BONEY, F. N.: "Virginian, Southerner, American: John Letcher, Virginia's Civil War Governor," *VC*, Summer 1967.

————: "Rivers of Ink and Streams of Blood: The Tragic Career of John Hampden Pleasants," *VC*, Summer 1968.

BOYD, JULIAN P.: Introduction to the *Jeffersonian Cyclopedia*, Russell & Russell, New York, 1967.

BRANDT, IRVING: "Timid President? Futile War?" *AH*, October 1959.

————: "Madison and the War of 1812," *VMHB*, January 1966.

CAMPBELL, NORINE: "Mansion in the Wilderness," *VC*, Summer 1966.

CAPRON, JOHN D.: "Virginia Iron Furnaces in the Confederacy," *VC*, Autumn 1967.

CARDWELL, GUY A.: "The Duel in the Old South," *SAQ*, Winter 1967.

CARPENTER, DELMA R.: "The Route Followed by Governor Spotswood in 1716 Across the Blue Ridge Mountains," *VMHB*, October 1965.

CASTEL, ALBERT: "Zachary Taylor," *American History Illustrated*, June 1970.

CATTON, BRUCE: "Jefferson Davis: The Man Behind the Image," *AH*, June 1967.

CAYWOOD, LOUIS R.: "Excavations at Green Spring Plantation," pub. by Colonial National Historical Park, Yorktown, 1955.

CHAMBERLAIN, GEN. JOSHUA L.: "The Last Salute of the Army of Northern Virginia," *Southern Hist. Soc. Papers*, Vol. XXXII, 1904.

CHAMBERS, LENOIR: "Notes on Life in Occupied Norfolk, 1862–1863," *VMHB*, April 1965.

CLEAVELAND, REV. GEORGE J.: "Henrico's 350th Anniversary," Richmond *Times-Dispatch*, October 23, 1961.

"Conrad Wise Chapman, 1842–1910," booklet pub. by Valentine Museum, Richmond, 1962.

COX, HAROLD E.: "The Jones-Martin Senatorial Campaign of 1911," Univ. of Virginia Dept. of History, Vol. I, Fall 1954.

COX, JOHN AND LAWANDA: "General O. O. Howard and the Misrepresented Bureau," *Journal of Southern History*, November 1953.

CRAVEN, AVERY O.: "Lee's Dilemma," *VMHB*, April 1961.

CRAVEN, WESLEY FRANK: "Twenty Negroes to Jamestown in 1619?" *VQR*, Summer 1971.

CRAWLEY, WILLIAM B.: "Governor William M. Tuck and Virginia's Response to Organized Labor in the Post World War II Era," M.A. thesis, U. Va. Dept. of History, 1968.

CUTHBERT, NANCY B.: "The Norfolk Klan in the '20's," *Virginia Social Science Journal*, November 1967.

DABNEY, RICHARD HEATH: "John Randolph: A Character Sketch," Chicago, the University Association, December 1, 1898.

DABNEY, VIRGINIUS: "From Cuckoo Tavern to Monticello," *Iron Worker*, Summer 1966.

————: "The Pace Is Important," *VQR*, Spring 1965.

————: "Query About the Pilgrim Fathers," *N.Y. Times Magazine*, September 29, 1957.

————: "He Made the Court Supreme," *Saturday Evening Post*, September 24, 1955.

————: "Appomattox, Epic Surrender," *Saturday Review*, March 19, 1955.

————: "Governor Byrd of Virginia," *Nation*, June 6, 1928.

————: "Virginia's Man of the Mid-Century," *Virginia and the Virginia County*, January 1951.

————: "Governor Byrd and the Virginia Assembly," Baltimore *Evening Sun*, March 17, 1926.

————: "Richmond's Quiet Revolution," *Saturday Review*, February 29, 1964.

DANIEL, W. HARRISON: "Virginia Baptists and the Negro, 1865–1902," *VMHB*, July 1968.

DAVIS, CURTIS CARROLL: "Very Well-Rounded Republican: The Several Lives of John S. Wise," *VMHB*, October 1963.

DAVIS, RICHARD BEALE: "The Jeffersonian Expatriates in the Building of the Nation," *VMHB*, January 1962.

————: "The Virginia Novel Before Swallow Barn," *VMHB*, July 1963.

DAVIS, WILLIAM C.: "Confederate Exiles," *American History Illustrated*, June 1970.

DeCoste, Fredrik: "The Point Comfort Affair," *Iron Worker*, Winter 1968.

Dew, Charles B.: "New Approaches to Southern History: Psychology and Quantification," *SAQ*, Summer 1967.

Dos Passos, John: "The Conspiracy and Trial of Aaron Burr," *AH*, February 1966.

Dowdey, Clifford: "Clifford Dowdey's Virginia: A Collection of Editorials and Essays," *Virginia Record*, July 1966.

———: "The Age of 'King' Carter," *Iron Worker*, Spring 1968.

Eby, Cecil D., Jr.: "The 'Old Virginia Gentleman' in New England," *VMHB*, January 1962.

Edmunds, Pocahontas W.: "The Pocahontas-John Smith Story," Richmond, Dietz Press, 1956.

Fahrmer, Alvin H.: "William 'Extra Billy' Smith," *VMHB*, January 1966.

Ferrell, Henry C., Jr.: "The Role of Virginia Democratic Party Factionalism in the Rise of Harry F. Byrd, 1917–1927," *East Carolina Publications in History*, Vol. II, 1965.

Fishwick, Marshall: "Was John Smith a Liar?" *AH*, October 1958.

Fleming, Thomas J.: "The Trial of John Brown," *AH*, August 1967.

Gildersleeve, Basil: "The Creed of the Old South," *Atlantic*, January 1892.

Gipson, Lawrence H.: "Virginia Planter Debts Before the American Revolution," *VMHB*, July 1961.

Godfrey, Michael: "The Commissioners' Report," *VC*, Autumn 1966.

Goode, James M.: "'Old Guff' in Virginia," *VC*, Summer 1966.

Gray, Elizabeth S.: "Donald Robertson and His School in King and Queen County," *Bulletin*, King and Queen Historical Society, January 1963.

Grayson, Admiral Cary T.: "The Colonel's Folly and the President's Distress," *AH*, October 1964.

Greene, Jack P.: "Landon Carter, an Inquiry into the Personal Values and Social Imperatives of Eighteenth-Century Virginia Gentry," Univ. Press of Va., Charlottesville, 1967.

———: "The Opposition to Governor Alexander Spotswood, 1718," *VMHB*, January 1962.

———: "The Attempt to Separate the Offices of Speaker and Treasurer in Virginia, 1758–1776," *VMHB*, January 1963.

Hall, Alvin L.: "Virginia Back in the Fold: The Gubernatorial Campaign and Election of 1929," *VMHB*, July 1965.

Hall, Claude H.: "Abel P. Upshur and the Navy as an Instrument of Foreign Policy," *VMHB*, July 1961.

HALLIDAY, E. M.: "Nature's God and the Founding Fathers," *AH*, October 1963.

HARRISON, J. B.: "Studies in the South," *Atlantic*, April 1882, through January 1883.

HASSLER, WILLIAM W.: "Robert E. Lee: The Educator," *Georgia Review*, Winter 1967.

HATCH, CHARLES E., JR., and GREGORY, THURLOW G.: "The First American Blast Furnace, 1619–1622," *VMHB*, July 1962.

HATCH, CHARLES E., JR.: "Jamestown, Virginia: The Town Site and Its Story," National Park Historic Handbook Series, No. 2, 1955.

HATHORN, GUY B.: "Congressional Campaign in the Fighting Ninth: The Contest Between C. Bascom Slemp and Henry C. Stuart," *VMHB*, July 1958.

HAVIGHURST, WALTER: "A Sword for George Rogers Clark," *AH*, October 1962.

HEITE, EDWARD F.: " 'Extra Billy' Smith," *VC*, Winter 1966.

———: "Painter of the Old Dominion, John Gadsby Chapman," *VC*, Winter 1968.

HENRY, JEANNETTE: "Textbook Distortion of the Indian," *Civil Rights Digest*, Summer 1968.

HERNDON, G. MELVILLE: "Sir Henry Chicheley, Virginia Cavalier," *VC*, Summer 1966.

HICKIN, PATRICIA: "John C. Underwood and the Anti-Slavery Movement in Virginia, 1847–1860," *VMHB*, April 1965.

HOHNER, ROBERT A.: "Prohibition Comes to Virginia; the Referendum of 1914," *VMHB*, October 1967.

———: "Bishop Cannon's Apprenticeship in Temperance Politics, 1901–1918," *Journal of Southern History*, February 1968.

HOLT, WYTHE W., JR.: "The Virginia Constitutional Convention of 1901–'02," *VMHB*, January 1968.

HOUSTON, CHARLES: "Virginians in Congress," 13 articles in Richmond *News Leader*; July 16–August 3, 1965.

HOWARD, A. E. DICK, ed.: "Virginia's Urban Corridor," pub. by Univ. of Va., March 1970.

HUGHES, ROBERT W.: "Editors of the Past," address to Virginia Press Assoc., Richmond, 1897.

HUMELSINE, CARLISLE H.: "Cross and Gown: The President's Report, 1965," Colonial Williamsburg.

———: "Serenity and Growth: The President's Report, 1966," Colonial Williamsburg.

HUNTER, ROBERT F.: "The Turnpike Movement in Virginia, 1816–1860," *VMHB*, July 1961.

————: "Carter Glass, Harry Byrd and the New Deal," *Virginia Social Science Journal*, November 1969.

KAUFMAN, BURTON I.: "Virginia Politics and the Wilson Movement, 1910–1914," *VMHB*, January 1969.

KETCHAM, RALPH L.: "An Unfinished Sketch of James Madison by James K. Paulding," *VMHB*, October 1959.

————, ed.: "Jefferson, Madison and the Doctrines of Interposition and Nullification," *VMHB*, April 1958.

KETCHUM, RICHARD M.: "Faces from the Past"—XIX," *AH*, February 1966.

KIRBY, JACK T.: "Alcohol and Irony: The Campaign of Westmoreland Davis for Governor, 1909–1917," *VMHB*, July 1965.

KNIGHT, EDGAR W.: "Reconstruction and Education in Virginia," *SAQ*, January, April, 1916, Vol. XV, Nos. 1 and 2.

————: "The Academy Movement in the South," reprinted from the *High School Journal*, Vol. II, Nos. 7 and 8, Vol. III, No. 1.

KOENIG, LOUIS W.: "Consensus Politics, 1800–1805," *AH*, February 1967.

LARRABEE, HAROLD A.: "A Near Thing at Yorktown," *AH*, October 1961.

LATIMER, JAMES: "The Night Fitz Lee Had a Ball," Richmond *Times-Dispatch*, January 11, 1970.

LONGAKER, JON: "Strive and Succeed," *Arts in Virginia*, Spring 1970.

McCORMACK, HELEN G.: "William James Hubard," booklet pub. by Valentine Museum and Virginia Mus. of Fine Arts, January 1948.

McDOWELL, CHARLES, JR.: "J. Lindsay Almond, Jr.," *Commonwealth*, January 1958.

MALONE, DUMAS: "Mr. Jefferson and the Traditions of Virginia," *VMHB*, April 1967.

MANCHESTER, WILLIAM: "The Byrd Machine," *Harper's*, November 1952.

MANIERRE, WILLIAM R.: "A Southern Response to Mrs. Stowe: Two Letters of John R. Thompson," *VMHB*, January 1961.

MEADE, ROBERT D.: "Patrick Henry—A Reappraisal," lecture at Emory and Henry College, March 15, 1957, pub. by college.

Medical College of Virginia *Bulletin*, Fall 1963, "The First 125 Years."

MOGER, ALLEN W.: "The Rift in Virginia Democracy in 1896," *Journal of Southern History*, August 1938.

————: Industrial and Urban progress in Virginia from 1880 to 1900," *VMHB*, July 1958.

MOORE, JAMES T.: "The University and the Readjusters," *VMHB*, January 1970.

MORISON, SAMUEL ELIOT: "The Education of John Marshall," *Atlantic*, July 1920.

MORTON, RICHARD L., ed.: " 'Life in Virginia' by a 'Yankee Teacher,' Margaret N. Thorpe," *VMHB*, April 1956.

NASH, HOWARD P., JR.: "The 'Princeton' Explosion," *American History Illustrated*, August 1969.

OLSON, S. DEAN: "Chickahominy Rich in Artifacts," Richmond *Times-Dispatch*, September 13, 1970.

O'NEAL, WILLIAM B.: "Chiselled Lyrics," *Arts in Virginia*, Fall 1966.

ORIANS, G. HARRISON: "Walter Scott, Mark Twain and the Civil War," *SAQ*, October 1941.

PAGE, THOMAS NELSON: "The Old Dominion," *Harper's*, December 1893.

PERCY, GEORGE: "Observations Gathered Out of a Discourse of the Plantation of the Southern Colony in Virginia by the English, 1606," Daniel Quinn, ed., Univ. Press of Virginia.

PHILLIPS, CABELL: "New Rumblings in the Old Dominion," *N.Y. Times Magazine*, June 19, 1949.

PLEASANTS, HUGH R.: "The Constitutional Convention of 1829–1830," *Southern Literary Messenger*, March and May 1851.

POINDEXTER, HARRY E.: "The Virginia Democracy in 1897; Silver-Plated Conservatism," *Essays in History*, U. of Va., Vol. 2, Winter 1955.

POWELL, WILLIAM S.: "Aftermath of the Massacre," *VMHB*, January 1958.

PULLEY, RAYMOND H.: "The May Movement of 1899," *VMHB*, April 1967.

RACHAL, WILLIAM M. E., ed.: "Secession Is Nothing But Revolution: A Letter of R. E. Lee to His Son 'Rooney,' " *VMHB*, January 1961.

————: "A Plague on Us: The Influenza Epidemic of 1918," *VC*, Spring 1952.

RAINBOLT, JOHN C.: "A New Look at Stuart 'Tyranny': The Crown's Attack on the Virginia Assembly, 1676–1689," *VMHB*, October 1967.

REEVES, PASCHAL: "Thomas S. Martin: Committee Statesman," *VMHB*, July 1960.

ROBERT, JOSEPH C.: "A Historian Looks at the Professions in America," *Journal of the American College of Dentists*, April 1966.

ROBERTS, JOHN G.: "Poet, Patriot and Pedagogue," *Arts in Virginia*, Winter 1966.

ROBERTSON, JAMES I., JR.: "Houses of Horror: Danville's Civil War Prisons," *VMHB*, July 1961.

ROSSITER, CLINTON: "Our Two Greatest Presidents," *AH*, February 1959.

ROTTENBERG, SIMON: "The Business of Slave Trading," *SAQ*, Summer 1967.

SEYMOUR, CHARLES: "End of a Friendship," *AH*, August 1963.

SHANKS, HENRY T.: "Disloyalty to the Confederacy in Southwestern Virginia, 1861–1865," *N. C. Historical Review*, January 1952.

SHIRES, CARL: Interviews with former Virginia Governors Darden, Tuck, Battle, Stanley, Almond and Harrison, Richmond *News Leader*, October, 2–7, 1967.

SIMKINS, FRANCIS B.: "New Viewpoints of Southern Reconstruction," *Journal of Southern History*, July 1920.

STEINER, BRUCE E.: "The Catholic Brents of Colonial Virginia: An Instance of Practical Toleration," *VMHB*, October 1962.

STEVENSON, JANET: "A Family Divided: The Great Abolitionist Crusade, 1830–1863," *AH*, April 1967.

STOVALL, FLOYD: "Edgar Poe and the University of Virginia," *VQR*, Spring 1967.

STRODE, HUDSON: "Judah P. Benjamin's Loyalty to Jefferson Davis," *Georgia Review*, Fall 1966.

SUTTON, ROBERT P.: "Nostalgia, Pessimism and Malaise: The Doomed Aristocrat in Late Jeffersonian Virginia," *VMHB*, January 1968.

TAYLOR, DONALD RANSOME: "Virginia's Unknown Benefactors in Education: Benjamin Syms and Thomas Eaton," *Virginia Journal of Education*, January 1963.

TAYLOR, LLOYD C.: "Lila Meade Valentine: The FFV as Reformer," *VMHB*, October 1962.

THOMAS, EMORY M.: "The Richmond Bread Riot of 1863," *VC*, Summer 1968.

THORNTON, J. MILLS III: "The Thrusting Out of Governor Harvey," *VMHB*, January 1968.

TROUBETZKOY, ULRICH: "Acid for an Inkstand," *Iron Worker*, Autumn 1966.

VIPPERMAN, CARL J.: "The Coattail Campaign: James H. Price and the Election of 1937," *Essays in History*, U. of Va., Vol. VIII, 1962–1963.

Virginia Journal of Science, January 1957, "Early Virginia" issue.

VITALE, JOHN C.: "One Hundred Maids for Virginia" and "Virginia vs. Blackbeard," *Iron Worker*, Winter, 1964–1965.

WHITE, WILLIAM S.: "Meet the Honorable Harry (The Rare) Byrd," *Reader's Digest*, April 1963.

WILKINSON, J. HARVIE III: "The Godwin Years," *Commonwealth*, November 1969.

"William Ludwell Sheppard," booklet pub. by Valentine Museum, Richmond, December 1969.

WILSON, JAMES SOUTHALL: "The Personality of Poe," *VMHB*, April 1959.

WRIGHT, LOUIS B., ed.: "Virginia Heritage," Public Affairs Press, Washington, D.C., 1957.

———: "Era of Courage and Hope: Shakespeare's Age and Ours," *VMHB*, April 1962.

WYNES, CHARLES E.: "The Evolution of Jim Crow Laws in Twentieth-Century Virginia," *Phylon*, Atlanta U., Fourth Quarter, 1967.

———: "Lewis Harvie Blair, Virginia Reformer: The Uplift of the Negro and Southern Prosperity," *VMHB*, January 1964.

———: "Charles T. O'Ferrall and the Gubernatorial Election of 1893," *VMHB*, October 1956.

UNPUBLISHED STUDIES

BEAR, JAMES A.: *Thomas Staples Martin—A Study in Virginia Politics, 1883–1896*, M.A. thesis, U.Va., 1952.

CAHILL, AUDREY M.: *Gilbert Carleton Walker, Virginia's Redeemer Governor*, M.A. thesis, U.Va., 1956.

CHEEK, WILLIAM FRANCIS III: *Forgotten Prophet: The Life of John Mercer Langston*, Ph.D. dissertation, U.Va., 1961.

CLARE, CAROL JEAN: *The Woman Suffrage Movement in Virginia. Its Nature, Rationale and Tactics*, M.A. thesis, U.Va., 1968.

DOSS, RICHARD B.: *John Warwick Daniel—a Study in Virginia Democracy*, Ph.D. dissertation, U.Va., 1955.

ELY, JAMES W., JR.: *The Campaign for Massive Resistance: Virginia's Gubernatorial Election of 1957*, M.A. thesis, U.Va., 1968.

———: *The Crisis of Conservative Virginia: The Decline and Fall of Massive Resistance*, Ph.D. diss. in progress, U.Va.

FERRELL, HENRY C., JR.: *Claude Swanson of Virginia*, Ph.D. dissertation, U.Va., 1964.

GAY, THOMAS E., JR.: *The Life and Career of J. Hoge Tyler, Governor of Virginia, 1898–1902*, Ph.D. dissertation, U.Va., 1969.

HALL, ALVIN L.: *James H. Price and Virginia Politics*, Ph.D. dissertation, U.Va., 1970.

HATHORN, GUY B.: *The Political Career of C. Bascom Slemp*, Ph.D. dissertation, Duke U., 1950.

HAWKES, ROBERT T., JR.: *The Political Apprenticeship and Gubernatorial Term of Harry Flood Byrd*, M.A. thesis, U.Va., 1967.

HEINEMANN, RONALD L.: "Depression and New Deal in Virginia, Ph.D. dissertation, U.Va., 1968.

HICKIN, PATRICIA P.: *Antislavery in Virginia, 1831–1861*, 3 vols., Ph.D. dissertation, U.Va., 1968.

HOHNER, ROBERT A.: *Prohibition and Virginia Politics, 1901–1916*, Ph.D. dissertation, Duke U., 1965.

HORN, HERMAN L.: *The Growth and Development of the Democratic Party in Virginia Since 1890*, Ph.D. dissertation, Duke U., 1949.

JONES, ROBERT R.: *Conservative Virginian—The Postwar Career of Governor James Lawson Kemper*, Ph.D. dissertation, U.Va., 1964.

LATIMER, JAMES: *Virginia Politics, 1950–1960*. Notes by the Richmond *Times-Dispatch*'s always well-informed chief political reporter.

LOWE, RICHARD G.: *Republicans, Rebellion and Reconstruction. The Republican Party in Virginia, 1856–1870*, Ph.D. dissertation, U.Va., 1968.

MADDEX, JACK P., JR.: *The Virginia Conservatives: A Study in 'Bourbon' Redemption, 1869–1879*, Ph.D. dissertation, U.N.C., 1966.

MOORE, JAMES T.: *To Carry Africa into the War: The Readjuster Movement and the Negro*, M.A. thesis, U.Va., 1966.

MOORE, JOHN H.: *The Life of James Gaven Field, Virginia Populist (1826–1902)*, M.A. thesis, U.Va., 1953.

POINDEXTER, HARRY E.: *From Copy Desk to Congress: The Pre-Congressional Career of Carter Glass*, 2 vols., Ph.D. dissertation, U.Va., 1966.

POSTON, CHARLES: *Henry Carter Stuart in Virginia Politics*, M.A. thesis, U.Va., 1970.

SHELTON, CHARLOTTE J.: *Woman Suffrage and Virginia Politics, 1909–1920*, M.A. thesis, U.Va., 1969.

SMITH, JAMES DOUGLAS: *Virginia During Reconstruction, 1865–1870*, Ph.D. dissertation, U.Va., 1960.

———: *The Virginia Constitutional Convention of 1867–1868*, M.A. thesis, U.Va., 1956.

UNDERHILL, MARJORIE F.: *The Virginia Phase of the Ogden Movement, A Campaign for Universal Education*, M.A. thesis, U.Va., 1952.

WEATHERS, VICTOR D.: *The Political Career of Allen Caperton Braxton*, M.A. thesis, U.Va., 1956.

WHEATLEY, HAROLD G.: *The Political Career of William Atkinson Jones*, M.A. thesis, U.Va., 1953.

WILLIS, LEE STANLEY: *E. Lee Trinkle and the Virginia Democracy, 1876–1939*, Ph.D. dissertation, U.Va., 1968.

WINTERS, MARVIN E.: *Benjamin Franklin Buchanan, 1859–1932*, M.A. thesis, U.Va., 1969.

INDEX